THE SUPREME COURT OF NOVA SCOTIA, 1754–2004

From Imperial Bastion to Provincial Oracle

Prepared to coincide with the 250th anniversary of the establishment of Nova Scotia's Supreme Court, this volume provides a wide-ranging history of the institution, Canada's oldest common law court. The thirteen essays include an account of the first meeting in 1754 of the court in Michaelmas Term; surveys of jurisprudence covering such topics as the court's early federalism cases, its use of American law, and attitudes to the administrative state; and chapters on the courts of Westminster Hall, on which the Supreme Court was modelled, and the various courthouses it has occupied. Comprehensive introductory chapters on the pre-confederation and modern periods provide a contextual framework for the volume.

Editors Philip Girard, Jim Phillips, and Barry Cahill have put together the first complete history of any Canadian provincial superior court. All of the essays are original, and many offer new interpretations of familiar themes in Canadian legal history. They take the reader through the establishment of the one-judge court to the present day, providing a unique contribution to our understanding of superior courts.

(Osgoode Society for Canadian Legal History)

PHILIP GIRARD is a professor of law, history, and Canadian studies at Dalhousie University.

JIM PHILLIPS is a professor of law and history and is director of the Centre of Criminology at the University of Toronto.

BARRY CAHILL is an independent scholar living in Halifax.

PATRONS OF THE SOCIETY

Aird & Berlis LLP

Blake, Cassels & Graydon LLP

Davies, Ward, Phillips & Vineberg LLP

Gowlings

McCarthy Tétrault LLP

Osler, Hoskin & Harcourt LLP

Torkin Manes Cohen & Arbus LLP

Torys LLP

WeirFoulds LLP

The Osgoode Society is supported by a grant from
The Law Foundation of Ontario.

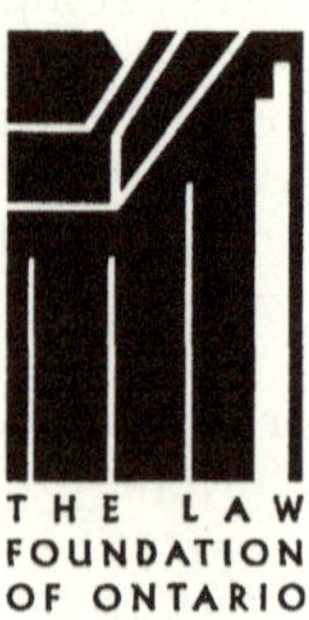

The Society also thanks The Law Society of Upper Canada
for its continuing support.

THE SUPREME COURT OF NOVA SCOTIA, 1754–2004

From Imperial Bastion to Provincial Oracle

Edited by

PHILIP GIRARD, JIM PHILLIPS, AND BARRY CAHILL

Published for The Osgoode Society for Canadian Legal History by

University of Toronto Press

Toronto Buffalo London

Reprinted in paperback 2014

ISBN 978-0-8020-8021-9 (cloth)
ISBN 978-1-4426-2377-4 (paper)

Printed on acid-free paper

Library and Archives Canada Cataloguing in Publication

Supreme Court of Nova Scotia, 1754–2004 : from imperial bastion to provincial oracle / edited by Philip Girard, Jim Phillips, and Barry Cahill.

(Osgoode Society for Canadian legal history)
Includes bibliographical references and index.

ISBN 978-0-8020-8021-9 (bound)
ISBN 978-1-4426-2377-4 (pbk.)

1. Nova Scotia. Supreme Court – History. I. Girard, Philip II. Phillips, Jim III. Cahill, Barry IV. Series.

KEN7935.4.S86 2004 349.716 C2004-903174-0
KF101.9.ZB2S86 2004

University of Toronto Press acknowledges the financial assistance to its publishing program of the Canada Council for the Arts and the Ontario Arts Council.

University of Toronto Press acknowledges the financial support for its publishing activities of the Government of Canada through the Book Publishing Industry Development Program (BPIDP).

This book has been published with the help of a grant from the Canadian Federation for the Humanities and Social Sciences, through the Aid to Scholarly Publications Programme, using funds provided by the Social Sciences and Humanities Research Council of Canada.

Contents

Foreword

The 250th anniversary of the Supreme Court of Nova Scotia is a most auspicious occasion for the Canadian legal community. As the oldest surviving common law court in Canada, it holds an important and distinctive place in Canada's legal tradition.

Not surprisingly, a volume of scholarly essays on the history of the court has been prepared to mark this occasion and The Society thanks the three volume editors, Philip Girard, Jim Phillips, and Barry Cahill, for organizing the volume and seeing it through to publication. The thirteen essays covering most phases of the court's history are of uniformly high quality. Two 'overviews,' dealing respectively with the pre-Confederation and post-Confederation periods, provide a comprehensive narrative history of the Court, while the other eleven deal with various aspects of its fascinating history over two centuries. Altogether this is a unique contribution to our knowledge of the history of Canada's superior courts.

The purpose of The Osgoode Society for Canadian Legal History is to encourage research and writing in the history of Canadian law. The Society, which was incorporated in 1979 and is registered as a charity, was founded at the initiative of the Honourable R. Roy McMurtry, a former attorney general for Ontario, now chief justice of Ontario, and officials of the Law Society of Upper Canada. Its efforts to stimulate the study of legal history in Canada include a research-support program, a graduate student research-assistance program, and work in the fields of oral history and legal archives. The Society publishes volumes of interest to the Society's members that contribute to legal-historical scholarship in Canada, including studies of the courts, the judiciary, and the legal profession, biographies, collections of documents, studies in criminology and penology, accounts of significant trials, and work in the social and economic history of the law.

Current directors of The Osgoode Society for Canadian Legal History are Robert Armstrong, Kenneth Binks, Patrick Brode, Michael Bryant, Brian Bucknall, Archie Campbell, David Chernos, Kirby Chown, J. Douglas Ewart, Martin Friedland, Elizabeth Goldberg, John Honsberger, Horace Krever, Virginia MacLean, Frank Marrocco, Roy McMurtry, Brendan O'Brien, Peter Oliver, Paul Reinhardt, Joel Richler, William Ross, James Spence, and Richard Tinsley.

The annual report and information about membership may be obtained by writing:

The Osgoode Society for Canadian Legal History,
Osgoode Hall, 130 Queen Street West,
Toronto, Ontario, M5H 2N6.
Telephone: 416-947-3321
E-mail: mmacfarl@lsuc.on.ca
Website: Osgoodesociety.ca

R. Roy McMurtry
President

Peter N. Oliver
Editor-in-Chief

Acknowledgments

This project has been in the making for some three years, and we have accumulated a number of debts along the way. First of all, to the contributors, whose enthusiastic response when we initially solicited their participation encouraged us to proceed with this volume. We are grateful too to the members of the committee charged with organizing the events planned to commemorate the two hundred and fiftieth anniversary of the Supreme Court of Nova Scotia. The committee, chaired by George Cooper, Q.C., included a representative of the Court of Appeal (Justice Joel Fichaud) and the Supreme Court (Justice Robert Wright) as well as members of the bar. Its keen interest in the volume was much appreciated, as was its decision to provide us with the fullest editorial freedom. We are deeply saddened that Justice Ted Flinn of the Court of Appeal, who played a vital role on the committee in its early stages, did not live to see the fruits of its labours or this volume.

This volume is historic in more ways than one. When we organized a conference called 'Courts, Communities and Conflict' to be held at Dalhousie Law School in October 2003, at which the contributors would be able to present their papers in draft form, we had no way of knowing that the dates we selected would be only four days after Hurricane Juan unleashed its fury on Halifax on 29 September. Much of the city was still without electricity when the conference participants arrived, but they did not let that intimidate them. We learned much from all those who attended the conference, and are particularly grateful to Australian scholars Andrew Buck, Bruce Kercher and Nancy Wright for sharing their comparative insights on the history of courts and the law in another colonial context. The conference was assisted by a grant from the Social Sciences and Humanities Research Council of Canada under its Aid to Occasional Research Conferences program. Thanks too to Sheila Wile who handled registrations and organized the material side of the conference.

The Foundation for Legal Research provided a grant in aid of publication, and Dean Dawn Russell of Dalhousie Law School and Chief Justice Constance Glube provided support in both material and less tangible but much appreciated ways. We thank the Osgoode Society for agreeing to publish the volume, Marilyn MacFarlane of the Society for her typical cheerfulness and efficiency, the anonymous reviewers who read the manuscript, and all those at the University of Toronto Press who helped produce it, especially Len Husband, Anne Laughlin, and Allyson May. Dianne O'Neill provided invaluable research on the photographs.

PHILIP GIRARD
JIM PHILLIPS
BARRY CAHILL

Contributors

R. BLAKE BROWN is a doctoral candidate in the Department of History, Dalhousie University.

BARRY CAHILL is an independent scholar in Halifax.

BRIAN CUTHBERTSON is Archivist, Anglican Diocese of Nova Scotia and Prince Edward Island. He has written extensively on many aspects of Nova Scotia history.

PHILIP GIRARD is Professor of Law, History and Canadian Studies at Dalhousie University, and Associate Dean Graduate Studies and Research in the Faculty of Law.

JULIAN GWYN is a Professor Emeritus in the Department of History, University of Ottawa.

DOUGLAS HAY is a Professor at Osgoode Hall Law School and the Department of History, York University.

BERNARD J. HIBBITS is a Professor in the School of Law, University of Pittsburgh.

SUSAN S. JONES is an associate with Stewart McKelvey Stirling Scales, Saint John, New Brunswick.

WILLIAM LAHEY is a Professor in the Faculty of Law, Dalhousie University.

JOHN MACLEOD is an archivist, government archives, Nova Scotia Archives and Research Management, Halifax.

ELIZABETH MANCKE is Professor in the Department of History, University of Akron, Ohio.

JAMES MUIR is a doctoral candidate in the Department of History, York University.

JIM PHILLIPS is Professor of Law, History and Criminology at the University of Toronto, and Director of the Centre of Criminology.

Abbreviations

DCB	Dictionary of Canadian Biography
Girard and Phillips, *Essays*	P. Girard and J. Phillips, eds., *Essays in the History of Canadian Law: Volume III – Nova Scotia* (Toronto: University of Toronto Press and Osgoode Society for Canadian Legal History 1991)
MG	Manuscript Group (at NSARM)
NSARM	Nova Scotia Archives and Records Management
N.S.R.	Nova Scotia Reports
NSSC	Nova Scotia Supreme Court
RG	Record Group (at NSARM)
S.N.S.	Statutes of Nova Scotia

Map 1: Nova Scotia Counties, 1851–present. (Antigonish County was Sydney County 1836–63.) Courtesy Nova Scotia Archives and Records Management.

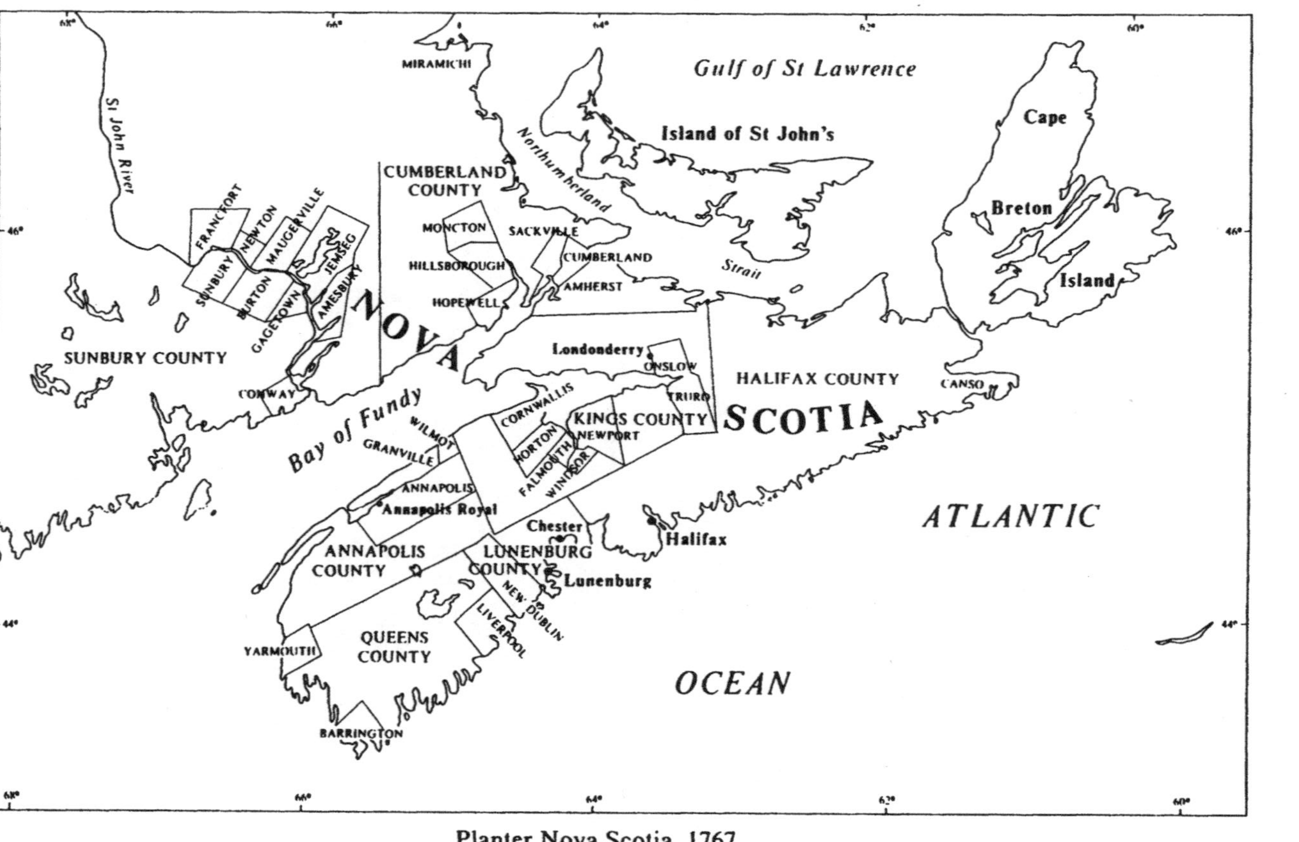

Planter Nova Scotia, 1767

Map 2: Nova Scotia, 1767. From *They Planted Well: New England Planters in Maritime Canada*, edited by M. Conrad (Fredericton: Acadiensis Press 1988). Used with permission.

Jonathan Belcher, 1756

PART I

Introduction

1

Introduction

PHILIP GIRARD AND JIM PHILLIPS

The genesis of this book obviously resides in the fact that in 2004 the Nova Scotia Supreme Court celebrates its 250th anniversary. In anticipation of that event the editors, as three people who have written about the legal history of the province for some years, were asked to compile a volume to coincide with the anniversary. From the outset the organizers of the court's official celebrations made it clear that while they were keen to see a substantial scholarly monograph on the court's history appear in 2004, they had no wish to influence the content of this volume in any way. This book is therefore not intended as a 'celebration' of the court in the sense that that word is usually employed. It does not self-consciously seek to praise its achievements or venerate its judges. But in another sense it might be called a celebration, for it is intended to mark a notable moment. The very fact of the court's longevity, the fact that it has played a major role in provincial life for two and a half centuries, makes it an institution worthy of study, and our task is to use the historian's tools of research and interpretation to highlight many, though by no means all, aspects of the court's long, intricate, and at times controversial history.

This volume has a somewhat unusual format, one that requires some explanation. Choosing a format was, of course, our first task, and debate ensued over the merits of the two standard approaches historians employ – the complete integrated history residing between one set of covers, and the essay collection, in which discrete topics are each given their own treatment and there is little or no attempt to be comprehensive. We rejected the former option, in part for reasons of time, and in part because we wanted to involve a variety of other people who have written, or are writing, about the history of courts and law in Nova Scotia. But we also wanted to provide something of the grand narrative, to trace the broad themes of the court's history across such an expanse of time, and an essay collection *simpliciter* would not achieve that. The result is a hybrid, one that we hope is the better for being neither fish nor fowl. There are eleven chapters dealing with particular issues, about which we will have more to say below. In addition, there are two rather longer overview chapters. These overviews recount the court's history from founding to Confederation (chapter 4), and from Confederation to the present (chapter 5), and provide between them a complete narrative of the history of the court from its founding in 1754 to 2004.

Having decided to adopt this format, important issues remained with regard to the overviews. We opted for Confederation as the dividing line, but not simply because that is a standard way to organize the chronology of any topic in Canadian history. Confederation brought two crucial changes to the NSSC: local appointment of judges gave way to appointment by the federal government in Ottawa, and the court lost much of its autonomy as a provincial lawmaker as it struggled to find its place in a new curial hierarchy below the Supreme Court of Canada (from 1875) and the Judicial Committee of the Privy Council. This apparent diminution in the role of the court was to some extent countered by another 'non-event.' The federal government decided not to create a parallel set of courts, as it might have done pursuant to section. 101 of the British North America Act, for the adjudication of federal and constitutional law matters. Canada retained a unitary court system, as opposed to the dual system used in the United States and later in some European countries. The provincial supreme courts thus retained their roles as the cornerstones of Canadian judicature, even if they were subject to more appellate review after 1867 than before.

A more difficult decision than where to divide the two overview chapters was that of what to include in them. An overview history of the NSSC, or indeed any court, over a long time period might entail any number of things, because there are several ways of looking at the history of courts. One can examine what they say – what has a court contributed to substantive law? One can look at what they do, by studying rates and types of litigation. One can analyse how they are organized – the number of judges, relationships with other courts above and below, curial administration, and so forth. One can try to sort out who the judges were through collective biography. Finally, one might want to know how a court is perceived – how legitimate is it in the eyes of the citizens it serves? Existing court histories are not very helpful because they usually look at only one of these things.[1]

Two features of the NSSC's history determined our choice to include everything but the jurisprudential. First, we felt that a court in a small jurisdiction such as Nova Scotia would not have made major contributions of extra-provincial significance to substantive law. It would not have been able to influence other courts, as Massachusetts might exert a broader influence over other U.S. states, and after Confederation it did not even have the last word on many issues of internal importance. In any event, concentrating on substantive law would have enabled us to say little about the first century or so of the court's life, for the sources for such a study are either non-existent or too diffuse prior to the introduction of law reporting in the 1850s. Second, and more importantly, in a plethora of other ways the NSSC has been a significant institution in provincial life, and we thought it more useful to study and highlight the changing roles and functions of a provincial superior court over time. Perhaps the work closest to what we attempt in this volume is Snell and Vaughan's history of the Supreme Court of Canada, although as largely a trial court the NSSC occupied a rather different place in regional life and law than a national appellate court.[2]

As a result the issues central to the overviews are the institutional, the political, the socio-economic, and the ideological. Courts are unique institutions which affect and are affected by the social, economic, and political context in which they operate. Courts do much more than produce law in the form of written judgments. They provide a venue for the resolution of disputes and the enforcement of obligations that, given traditionally high rates of default judgments and settlements, carries on for the most part without the production of written reasons at all. Courts also play political and ideological roles in any society. A court, especially a provincial superior court such as the NSSC, is a symbol of justice. This symbolic role may be enhanced or diminished by a court's actual decisions, but it is also affected by many other factors such as its organization, its perceived efficiency or inefficiency, the calibre of its personnel and their manner of appointment, and their extra-judicial as well as judicial functions. All of these themes, and others, are canvassed in the overviews, which at the same time provide a basic narrative of the court's history, charting and situating the major events of two and a half centuries.

The overviews have many common themes, despite differences of emphasis dictated by the different histories of the two periods. Both have a lot to say about the judges, although the pre-Confederation account has more on a few individuals, largely because there were fewer judges in the early decades. Both discuss the links among the court, its judges, and provincial politics, although in the eighteenth and nineteenth centuries these were rather more direct than they later became. Both detail crises in the court's history, from an attempted eighteenth-century impeachment of two judges to the Marshall inquiry of the late twentieth century. And both discuss more routine matters such as caseload, court administration, and salaries. Where differences exist in the way various topics are discussed, these reflect the fact that the court's history before and after 1867 was rather different. If judges are discussed as more overt political actors in the pre-Confederation period, for example, especially in the years before responsible government in 1848, that is simply because they were. Jonathan Belcher was for a time the colony's chief administrator; whatever influence Lorne Clarke, chief justice in the 1980s and 1990s, had on provincial life, he was never close to being Nova Scotia's chief executive! In a significant number of ways the court and its judges were at the centre of colonial life before the middle of the nineteenth century to an extent they have not been since.

Distinctions in the sources the two overview chapters employ again reflect what is available and the changing nature of historians' sources between the eighteenth century and the present. The historian of the pre-Confederation period has the luxury of using detailed correspondence with London, individual judges' papers, extensive Assembly reports on courts and the judiciary and the like, as well as statutes, newspapers, proceedings books, and case files. For the later nineteenth and twentieth centuries the prime ministers' papers become an indispensable source, but records generated by the provincial legal system are sparse aside from the court's own records, which are often quite rich. Provincial premiers' papers survived sporadically, while the papers of the provincial attorneys general are disappointing until the 1950s and '60s. Once the power to appoint and the responsibility to pay judges of the Supreme and County Courts moved to Ottawa, the provincial role was limited to supporting the day-to-day administration of justice. The provincial records reflect this reduced role until the new demands of the late twentieth century, when interest in the court revived. Judges' papers are few and far between, with those of Chief Justice Robert Harris being a notable exception. Lawyers' papers have not been systematically canvassed but may reveal more to future researchers.

We have dwelt at some length on the overview chapters because they are intended to anchor the book. But there is much else here, we hope, to engage the reader. The volume begins with two chapters on the background against which the court was established. In chapter 2 Douglas Hay describes the courts of Westminster Hall, on which the Supreme Court was based, as they existed in England in the mid-eighteenth century. He traces themes central to the overview histories of the NSSC – the balance between criminal and civil caseloads, the relationship between court and bar, and the involvement of the judges in politics. His principal message is that this was not an auspicious period for the Westminster Hall courts. The courtrooms were physically dilapidated and the operations of the Courts of King's Bench and Common Pleas were the subject of vociferous critiques. The principal criticisms were of the inordinately expensive and time-consuming procedures in civil litigation, which took decades to reform precisely because they proved so remunerative to judges and court officials. Hay suggests that in this regard at least the Nova Scotia court never replicated, and thus worked much better than, its often revered imperial models.

Chapter 3, by Elizabeth Mancke, sets the origins of the NSSC in the broad sweep of British imperial policy relating to the establishment and role of colonial courts. While it was long believed that British subjects overseas deserved and required English law to govern them, the Empire of the seventeenth and early eighteenth centuries saw a good deal of local variation, especially within chartered and proprietary colonies. By the mid-eighteenth century London was intent on greater uniformity. Nova Scotia's chief justice was one of the first to be directly appointed from London, a practice that later became standard in the Empire, as British authorities began to assert the need for colonial law to mirror that of England.

These introductory chapters are followed by a section we have titled 'Overviews.' Apart from the two long narratives already discussed – chapters 4 and 5 – the section contains two other, more particular, overviews. Blake Brown and Susan Jones provide a collective biography of the court's twentieth-century judges, a complement to one produced a decade or so ago on the judges appointed prior to 1900.[3] Examining a broad range of characteristics – age; tenure; family, religious, ethnic, educational, and geographical backgrounds; practice experience; and political involvements – they identify some important changes in the make-up of the Supreme Court bench, both through the twentieth century and as compared to the preceding 150 years. The former include a broadening of the religious backgrounds of the judiciary and a narrowing of their geographical origins – as time went on judges were more likely to have come from Halifax than elsewhere in the province. The judiciary has also, since the 1960s, become considerably more diverse in terms of gender and ethnicity, having been almost entirely homogeneous before then. Also, merit has come to matter more than connection, and direct involvement in politics is less important than it once was. But some form of political involvement, often back-room activism, still seems to matter. Brown and Jones conclude with an intriguing suggestion that if politics is to count then those who have actually served in government might be more representative of the community than those who played only a supportive background role.

A complete survey of the courthouses in all eighteen Nova Scotia counties is beyond the scope of this volume, but in chapter 7 Brian Cuthbertson takes us into the 'homes' of the Supreme Court in Halifax.[4] Over the past two and a half centuries the court has rarely had its own home, but has invariably shared accommodation with other courts and with the legislature in particular. At times in the late eighteenth and early nineteenth centuries it met in a tavern and a warehouse. Its accommodations were rather more suitable from 1819, when it began to share Province House with the Assembly, and again from the 1860s, when it occupied the courthouse on Spring Garden Road. The latter arrangement lasted for over a century, until the court moved to its present location on the Halifax waterfront.

The remainder of the volume consists of six essays on particular aspects of the NSSC's history. James Muir and Jim Phillips begin this section in chapter 8, with, appropriately, a study of the proceedings at the very first session of the court, held in Michaelmas Term, 1754. They show that attempts were made, even in the somewhat primitive conditions of early Halifax, to reproduce the pomp and pageantry of the English high courts of the period, and discuss in particular Chief Justice Belcher's first grand jury charge, an impassioned invocation to political conformity. The detailed account of the criminal and civil proceedings which follows reveals both a close adherence to English law, especially the English criminal law, and a propensity by juries to act in defiance of Belcher's professed wishes. From its very beginning, therefore, the court has played a broadly political role in colonial administration, with the strictness of law and the partialities of judges tempered by the opinion of the populace.

In chapter 9 Julian Gwyn uses the case files from civil suits litigated in the NSSC prior to 1830 as a window into the roles of women, both as litigants and as social and economic actors more generally. While only 9 per cent of cases involved female litigants, Gwyn's evidence indicates that women nonetheless did participate in the colonial economy separate from their husbands and fathers. Most of the suits filed by or against women were for debt, but women were also involved in a wider range of litigation. Among the few cases examined in some detail are ones in which female slaves sought to use the court to ameliorate their social and legal condition. Gwyn's database is a very full and rich one, and his chapter in this volume is but a preliminary examination of it. Yet here, as elsewhere, we have evidence of women, including those at the bottom of the social ladder, acting independently and assertively in pursuit of legal rights.

The final four chapters are all in various ways studies of the NSSC's approach to the making and interpreting of law. Bernard Hibbitts has previously analysed the reception and use of Canadian law in the nineteenth-century United States.[5] In chapter 10, he looks at the opposite phenomenon, the use of American authority in the Supreme Court of Nova Scotia over seven decades. He finds American law relatively prevalent in the court's decisions prior to *c.* 1875, when the province, although for most of the period a colony of England, had close legal as well as economic ties with its southern neighbours. During the last quarter of the nineteenth century American influence declined significantly, as the province became integrated into a national Canadian and imperial legal structure, paralleling its increasingly closer ties with national and imperial economic and political systems. Hibbitts's essay, which also notes that American influence varied according to the areas of law at issue, is a significant contribution to our still sparse knowledge of Canadian jurisprudence in the nineteenth century.

In chapter 11 James Muir takes on a long-standing debate in Anglo-American legal historiography, over the extent to which nineteenth-century judges were 'instrumentalists,' willing to be innovative and to shape the law in ways they considered desirable, and whether, in their instrumentalism, they favoured economic development over other values. After laying out the broad parameters of that debate Muir examines NSSC decisions in the areas of common carrier liability for damaged goods, negligence generally, and corporate liability and workplace injuries in particular, mostly from the 1860s and 1870s. He finds a complex pattern: the judges were generally beholden to English precedents, yet on occasion they were prepared to criticize the law coming out of Westminster. Whether or not they relied on precedent, they generally approved of the idea of limiting the liability of commercial and industrial enterprises, although suits by seamen for wages and compensation for injuries seem to have struck a sympathetic chord.

Bill Lahey's chapter deals with a topic much discussed in Canadian legal historiography: the ways in which Canadian courts and the Privy Council shaped the federal constitution in the decades immediately following Confederation. The extensive literature, however, has concentrated on the Supreme Court of Canada and the Privy Council, and to some extent on Ontario, with provincial superior courts receiving short shrift.[6] Lahey shows that Nova Scotia's judges brought to the task of constitutional adjudication both great seriousness of purpose and a complex set of values and assumptions about the nature of the federal union, the province's place within it, and the role of judges. He finds continuity in provincial thinking about Confederation, both about the division of powers and the status of the province, despite the fact that local views at times diverged from that of the Privy Council, which had become the orthodox position by century's end. He also draws intriguing links between the court's judgments and the province's difficulties with, and eventual accommodation to, Confederation in the broader political sphere. Lahey reminds us that history, including the history of legal thinking, is not a simple and linear story. The views propounded by the NSSC in the late nineteenth century did not, for the most part, endure. But they are testament to an alternative vision, one marked by what he sees as an enduring commitment to local autonomy.

Finally, in chapter 13 Blake Brown demolishes a long-held view that Canadian courts in the post–Second World War era were invariably hostile to administrative agencies, and to labour boards in particular. In a survey of judicial review of labour board cases from the 1950s and 1960s he reveals that while there was some initial hostility, the court over time came to afford substantial deference to the board. Brown attributes this change generally to a politico-legal culture that increasingly came to accept the legitimacy of the regulatory state, and particularly to the fact that the bench consisted of men with experience within the workings of that state. The province's judges emerge from this study as men more flexible and in keeping with the times than, for example, Ontario High Court Judge J.C. McRuer, who never lost his antipathy to the new order.[7] Interestingly Brown is also able to attribute some of the court's deference to the fact that the board constrained itself and in many ways acted 'judicially.'

While the essays in this volume deal with all periods of the history of the NSSC (albeit with a greater concentration on the years prior to 1900), and with many different subjects, we do not claim to have provided a complete or comprehensive history of the court. That is, perhaps, an impossible task. We have, however, both charted the principal themes and events in its long history and provided a variety of more particular snapshots of that history. Studies of Canadian provincial courts are few and far between, and we see this volume as a significant addition to an important area of inquiry.

NOTES

1 See, for example, the tercentenary history of the Supreme Judicial Court of Massachusetts, which concentrates almost exclusively on that court's contributions to substantive law: R.K. Osgood, *The History of the Law in Massachusetts: The Supreme Judicial Court 1692–1992* (Boston: Supreme Judicial Court Historical Society 1992). For a useful overview of longitudinal studies of courts, see Lawrence Friedman, 'Opening the Time Capsule: A Progress Report on Studies of Courts over Time' 24 (1990) *Law & Society Review*: 229–42.

2 J.G. Snell and F. Vaughan, *The Supreme Court of Canada: History of the Institution* (Toronto: Osgoode Society for Canadian Legal History and University of Toronto Press 1985). Although there is plenty of judicial biography, there are few other Canadian court histories. A volume similar to Snell and Vaughan is I. Bushnell, *The Federal Court of Canada: A History, 1875–1992* (Toronto: Osgoode Society for Canadian Legal History and University of Toronto Press 1997). Also worthy of note is the rather dated J.W. Lawrence, *The Judges of New Brunswick and their Times* (1905–7; rep. Fredericton: Acadiensis Press 1985, with introduction by D.G. Bell). This is much more an account of the judges than the court, however, and contains more on their 'times' than on the men themselves.

3 See C. Greco, 'The Superior Court Judiciary of Nova Scotia, 1754–1900: A Collective Biography,' in Girard and Phillips, *Essays*.

4 See C.A. Hale, *The Early Court Houses of Nova Scotia* (Ottawa: Parks Canada 1977).

5 B. Hibbitts, '"Our Arctic Brethren": Canadian Law and Lawyers as Portrayed in American Legal Periodicals, 1829–1911,' in G.B. Baker and J. Phillips, eds., *Essays in the History of Canadian Law: Volume VIII – In Honour of R.C.B. Risk* (Toronto: Osgoode Society for Canadian Legal History and University of Toronto Press 1999).

6 For a useful review of the literature see R.C.B. Risk, 'Canadian Courts Under the Influence,' *University of Toronto Law Journal* 40 (1990): 687–737; G.B. Baker, 'R.C.B. Risk's Canadian Legal History,' in Baker and Phillips, eds., *Essays in Honour of Risk*; and J. Saywell, *The Lawmakers: Judicial Power and the Shaping of Canadian Federalism* (Toronto: Osgoode Society for Canadian Legal History and University of Toronto Press 2002). For Ontario see in particular R. Vipond, *Liberty and Community: Canadian Federalism and the Failure of the Constitution* (Albany: State University of New York Press 1991). For an exception to the tendency to disregard provincial courts see Lahey's own work on New Brunswick, 'Constitutional Adjudication, Provincial Rights, and the Structure of Legal Thought in late Nineteenth-Century New Brunswick,' *University of New Brunswick Law Journal* 39 (1990): 185–223.

7 See P. Boyer, *A Passion for Justice: The Legacy of James Chalmers McRuer* (Toronto: Osgoode Society for Canadian Legal History and University of Toronto Press 1994).

2

Origins: The Courts of Westminster Hall in the Eighteenth Century

DOUGLAS HAY

The Nova Scotia Supreme Court of 1754 was modelled on the ancient common law courts in Westminster Hall.[1] That great gothic building was the heart of legal London. Originally completed in 1099 and remodelled about 1400, it was the seat of royal justice, and of all the procedural and substantive elements of both the common law and the principles of equity. The common law courts of King's Bench, Common Pleas, and Exchequer coalesced as separate entities out of the early medieval curia regis, the administrative household of the King, or perhaps its exchequer, in a protracted process from the twelfth to fourteenth centuries. The parchment rolls of Common Pleas and King's Bench survive from the end of the twelfth century, are separate by 1232, and exist in continuous runs from the third quarter of the thirteenth century.[2] The Court of Exchequer was the last of the three common law courts to gel, out of the revenue exchequer; each of these courts had only four justices (barons in the case of Exchequer) in the eighteenth century. Chancery emerged out of the royal secretariat into a separate court with its own 'law,' equity, in the fifteenth century. By the mid-eighteenth century, under the influence of Lord Chancellors Nottingham (1674–82) and Hardwicke (1737–56), and of fuller reporting, equity had hardened into almost as fixed a set of remedies as those of the common law, the defects of which it allegedly supplied. This chapter is not, however, about doctrine, although the decisions of their English brethren necessarily concerned the judges of Nova Scotia. The meaning of

English 'high law' in the eighteenth century also resided in its procedure, patterns of litigation, the character of the bar and the benches, and how they were regarded by those outside Westminster Hall.[3]

Half a millenium of Westminster law was a revered inheritance for wealthy and many less propertied English citizens, particularly in its constitutional aspects, but the eighteenth century was also a period of vociferous criticism of the central royal courts for delay, arcane procedures, and the host of fees demanded by counsel, officers, and judges. The Hall itself was badly in need of renovation. In 1734 the courts, divided up by board partitions as they were in earlier centuries, were described as 'slovenly' in appearance; in the winter of 1739–40 tarpaulins were strung up to prevent rain from soaking Chancery and King's Bench. The roof was found to be so weak that timbers were put in place to shore it up. They remained there for eight years, until 1748, when the judges complained to the Board of Works that the props were 'an indecent sight in a Room where all the Courts of Justice sit, and which is the access to both Houses of Parliament.'[4] Meanwhile Chancery and King's Bench were hidden behind a Gothic screen designed by William Kent, and improved in appearance. But the hall was still freezing cold in winter, and Hilary and Michaelmas terms were often misery, until in 1755 the screen was doubled in height and the courts covered over, just below the angels on the magnificent medieval hammerbeam roof.[5]

In 1754 Sir Dudley Ryder became lord chief justice, but the early years of the Nova Scotia court coincided largely with the chief justiceship of the most famous judge of the century, William Murray, Earl of Mansfield. From the time he took his seat in King's Bench in 1756, in the southeast corner of the hall, the growing ascendency of that court over Common Pleas accelerated. King's Bench was the greatest common law court, in any case: appeals ran to it from Common Pleas, and it controlled the process of inferior courts through the prerogative writs, notably those of certiorari and habeas corpus.[6] By the former all proceedings in a lower court could be removed into King's Bench; by the latter, in which the writ had been improved upon by the statute of 1679, all those imprisoned in other jurisdictions (or by private persons) were brought before the judges to have the matter tested. The fact that King's Bench was open to all barristers, whereas Common Pleas was monopolized by the dying breed of serjeants-at-law, increased the popularity of Mansfield's court. His reign there, until the late 1780s, also coincided with the celebration of the genius of the common law in William Blackstone's *Commentaries on the Laws of England* (given as lectures from 1753, first edition 1765–9). Mansfield made suggestions about the text, and Blackstone became briefly a puisne justice of King's Bench in 1770, before moving to Common Pleas later that year. In both the Hall and the law, the third quarter of the eighteenth century was thus a period of some new doctrine, procedural reform, architectural improvement, and a great deal of self-congratulation. The best-known legal innovations were in King's Bench. Mansfield blurred, in the eyes of many lawyers, the boundaries of equity and common law, and he influenced Blackstone's account in a similar way.[7] He also curbed some practices of the clerks, and simplified some process. But these were minor changes in a matrix of rules, forms of process, and daily practices that we now know were being elaborated and complicated in the other courts (notably Chancery), and even in King's Bench, in a manner richly rewarding to judges and lawyers and clerks.[8]

By the later eighteenth century Chancery practice was the most remunerative in the Hall. More lawyers made at least some appearances there, than they did in any other court.[9] Chancery sat in the southwest corner of the Hall, across from King's Bench in the southeast corner, and many suffering litigants sent back and forth between common law and equity in the course of a single lawsuit damned them both. But they did not think (as nineteenth-century reformers did) that putting both remedies in one court was a sure solution. In the one eighteenth-century court with both an equity and common law side, Exchequer, it was not the litigants but the specialized practitioners familiar with its obscure and unique procedures who benefited from this convenience.[10] Such procedures were revered by the profession, and expressions of reverence for the certitude and antiquity of the common law are often inseparable from professional appreciation of the complexity and expense of its process. Many eighteenth-century common lawyers distrusted Mansfield's very minor changes to the law: James Boswell, although a Scot from a different legal tradition, greeted Lord Kenyon, Mansfield's successor, as 'a good fuller's mill to thicken and consolidate the law, which was very necessary after the loose texture which Lord Mansfield had given it.'[11] Particularly during the period of the French and revolutionary wars (1792–1815), which began shortly after Mansfield's retirement, tradition rather than innovation was the dominant value in the highest circles of government and law. Lord Kenyon (CJKB 1788–1802) and other judges made frequent reference to the antiquity and hence wisdom of the common law, and the necessity to maintain it inviolate, fixed, safe from statutory incursions, and distinct from equity.[12] From a layman's point of view, innovation seemed to be limited to an ever-increasing and costly complexity in litigation, growing throughout the century. It was only in the 1830s and 1840s that the judges' patronage positions were finally bought out and they were put entirely on salary, and the prolonged process of simplifying pleadings and unnecessary charges began. Until then both the law and Westminster Hall itself continued to attract much criticism. The young John Beverley Robinson, later chief justice of Upper Canada, visiting the Hall in 1815, thought 'everything about it seems to be tumbling into ruin – the first impression it occasions is melancholy and gloomy ...'[13] This was also the mood of many litigants.

Civil Litigation

Most civil litigation in England took place in borough and a few surviving county and hundred courts dating from the Middle Ages, in statutory courts of request, and in other inferior tribunals with or without juries. The borough courts of record were based on common law process, increasingly so from the early seventeenth century; courts of request, most of them the result of eighteenth-century legislation, were held by lay commissioners using broad equitable powers.[14] Such proceedings were usually fairly quick, inexpensive, and informal: the courts of request in particular were extremely effective venues for enforcing payment of small debts. In contrast, litigation at Westminster was procedurally complex and very expensive, requiring much professional consultation. At common law, the ancient forms of action determined pleadings before simplification began in the 1830s.[15] Each was based on a different writ, and the respective procedure and proofs were distinctive and extremely technical. Actions were real (for land), personal, or mixed. Real actions were displaced by ejectment. Personal actions were on contract or tort. The former comprised assumpsit (on a simple contract), debt (on a deed or on a simple contract), covenant (on deed alone), scire facias (on a judgment), account, and annuity. The actions in tort were trespass (of two sorts, one on real property, one on goods), case (which had become a general category in the absence of a more appropriate form of action), replevin (to recover goods unlawfully taken), trover (to recover the value of such goods), and detinue (to recover the goods, or their value, and damages.)

The crucial importance of choosing the right action to fit the circumstances of the case (a wrong choice was usually fatal), the fact that no two could be joined in one suit, and the costly learning of special pleaders, increasingly employed from mid-century, to winnow the case between the parties down to a limited issue gave the professionals virtually total control of litigation.[16] Once embarked on a suit, plaintiffs found themselves led by attorneys, solicitors, barristers, court officers, and judges, all of whom benefited from a series of procedural tollgates, many of them wholly unnecessary. A plaintiff seeking judgment on a debt could be forced to pay at some forty separate stages, most of them pretrial.[17] Counsel on both sides exploited the fact that the four terms of the judicial year (Hilary, Easter, Trinity, and Michaelmas), within which most motions had to be made, were each of only three to five weeks' duration; in each term, specified return days and other rules required close attention by clerks in court, attorneys, and counsel if an action was to succeed. Given these obstacles, what made a lawsuit worthwhile, particularly in debt collection (which constituted 80 per cent of the work of the common law courts, in both Westminster and Nova Scotia) was the high rate of success for plaintiffs with good evidence, and the payment of costs by the loser. The rolls of the courts were also used extensively to provide security for debts at the time credit was extended, or if doubts arose, through the use of cognovits and warrants of attorney. By agreeing to sign them, the debtor guaranteed the creditor speedy and uncomplicated collection in case of eventual default.

These various advantages accounted for a significant caseload in the central courts of the common law. In the case of King's Bench, the original jurisdiction of the court in Middlesex, extended to out-counties through the fiction of the Bill of Middlesex, was the basis of an increasing dominance over Common Pleas and Exchequer by the eighteenth century. Estimates based on the various entries made by the clerks suggest that over 11,000 suits were begun annually in King's Bench at mid-century; the vast majority of course never proceeded to trial. The distribution of business shifted over time, however. Common Pleas cases dropped from perhaps 16,000 in 1740 to fewer than 6,000 in 1765. Probably something over 1,000 cases began in Exchequer each year. King's Bench was to become by far the dominant court in the later eighteenth century, as Common Pleas had been in the seventeenth.

The Mid-Century Trough

In spite of procedural and substantive innovations, particularly by Mansfield (in the use of special juries; in insurance; in commercial law), the central common law courts dealt with far less litigation than they had a hundred years before or were to see a hundred years later. For centuries the courts had vied among themselves for business, trying to attract litigants with speedier or more convenient process. The Bill of Middlesex and writ of latitat in King's Bench and the elaboration of assumpsit were the two main earlier innovations which led eventually, from about 1750, to the domination of civil suits by King's Bench.[18] But this was a division of a litigation pie that was only a sixth the size of that a century earlier: cases in an advanced stage in the two principal courts, King's Bench and Common Pleas, which numbered about 30,000 in the mid-seventeenth century, amounted to only about 5,000 in 1750, rising to about 10,000 in 1800. Trials, most of which took place outside London at county assizes, in the nisi prius court, had declined by the early eighteenth century to a quarter of their level at the Restoration.[19] This enormous decline in litigation was largely mirrored in the records of other, inferior, and local courts.[20] Only in the nineteenth century did litigation levels again reach those of the early seventeenth.

A number of explanations have been offered for the earlier rise of the litigation wave to its Elizabethan height;[21] they are difficult to disentangle but the results affected all courts. There is a growing consensus in the literature that the subsequent precipitous decline from about the Restoration had fewer and more obvious causes. Stamp duties at the end of the seventeenth century contributed, as did perhaps the growth in the use of penal bonds, but the most important determinant was probably the greatly increased expense of litigation in the hands of the small but entrenched legal fraternity of attorneys, solicitors, barristers, and judges through the seventeenth and into the eighteenth century. Even in inferior local courts, fees increased markedly over the period of the great litigation decline. In Westminster Hall, fees were much higher in the mid-eighteenth century than they had been a century before, and all the lawyers shared in them.[22] Among the greatest beneficiaries were the judges themselves. They controlled immense patronage in the chief clerkships and other important positions in their courts, which they usually granted to their sons and other male dependents; they shared fees from virtually every case and stage of process, directly or indirectly; and they therefore had no incentive at all to attack the cost of law at Westminster.[23]

The profits of the law derived mainly from attracting plaintiffs to Westminster and then milking the defendants. The average cost of the most common kind of proceeding, debt collection, was six or seven times as great as the amount at issue. This could only be attractive to plaintiffs with strong evidence (such as a bond or other sealed instrument), who could be sure of success and who given the rule that the loser paid all costs, were themselves immune from the expense and possibly gratified by the burden on the defendant. Quantitative study of the court records has shown that this was in fact the typical case: for collection of a debt, with a high success rate by plaintiffs, both in pretrial proceedings and in the small proportion of cases that actually went to trial.[24]

Some trials were held 'in banc,' before the judges at Westminster, but the great majority of civil cases were tried by nisi prius juries summoned in the counties in which the action arose. The common law judges on circuit were called justices of assize, after the name of one of the commissions by which they acted. They travelled in pairs, as they generally did in Nova Scotia before 1834, usually twice a year to most counties, throughout the country. Assizes were held in the vacations following Hilary and Trinity terms, and at each assize town one judge held the Crown court for criminal cases, the other the nisi prius court, sometimes relieving each other when one calendar was unusually long. The relative proportions of civil and criminal litigation in the high courts have not been examined in any detail, but an initial distinction is important. At nisi prius were heard not only all civil suits brought to trial, but also a few misdemeanours that had been removed into King's Bench by writ of certiorari from quarter sessions or even an earlier Crown case at assizes, and also criminal informations laid in King's Bench. In one county, Staffordshire, 195 civil cases at Westminster were entered for trial in the county at nisi prius between 1784 and 1791; in the same period, only one criminal proceeding (on an indictment removed by certiorari) – half of 1 per cent – was so entered.[25] Of the 155 of these cases that actually proceeded to trial at nisi prius, 54.8 per cent were case (assumpsit), 18.1 per cent ejectment, 10.3 per cent debt, 7.1 per cent trespass, 5.2 per cent assault, 2.6 per cent covenant, and 0.6 per cent of each of replevin, trover, and criminal on certiorari.[26] After the outcome of the trial was returned to Westminster Hall in a formal statement called a postea, judgment was pronounced there. There could, however, be motions in error (a writ of error in a criminal case) or for arrest of judgment or a new trial, argued at Westminster; if the last was successful, the process began again, with a new trial in the county of origin or (in the rare case of a change of venue) in another county or in Westminster Hall itself.[27]

Assizes brought Westminster to the provinces by means not only of the pomp of javelin men (who met the judges at the county boundary), the opening church service, and the practised rhetoric of death sentences, but also through the charge to grand jurors[28] and a host of informal exchanges between local gentry and officials and the judges and barristers who had arrived in town by coach and on horseback. The judges announced government policy and royal proclamations, denounced sedition, drew attention to new statutes, took advice on pardons, and exhorted magistrates and gave them legal advice in the few days in which they also cleared the gaols, heard important misdemeanour cases, and listened to counsel (including the leaders of the bar, who came with them on circuit) argue their cases before the nisi prius and Crown court juries.[29]

Criminal

Civil suits could be initiated, as we have seen, in any of the three common law courts at Westminster, to be heard by the judge there in term time (in banc), or before the nisi prius judge at assizes.[30] Criminal trials were also heard by all the common law judges, but in two quite different ways. Best known was their role in presiding at the trial of serious criminal offences in the Crown court at assizes in the provinces, and in rough rotation at the Old Bailey in London, where high court judges sat with the recorder and aldermen.[31] In these settings the eighteenth-century judges heard a large proportion of indictable offences. Non-capital cases were in the jurisdiction of magistrates at quarter sessions, but the small number of prosecutions in the eighteenth century allowed the judges to try many lesser felonies and misdemeanours as well, as did the Nova Scotia Supreme Court for decades after its founding. Thus, in the populous midland county of Staffordshire, the judges at assizes heard about 69 per cent of all criminal trials between 1740 and 1800, while the county bench of magistrates at quarter sessions heard only 31 per cent.[32] Quarter sessions was preoccupied with local government; assize judges knew the criminal law.

In term time, apart from occasional service at the Old Bailey, the only judges concerned with criminal cases were the lord chief justice and the three puisne justices who sat with him in King's Bench, the supreme court of criminal law. The criminal proceedings with which they dealt (often making new law in so doing) fell into several categories. They had an original jurisdiction in Middlesex, and therefore heard and determined many misdemeanours, often quite minor ones, prosecuted on indictment in that county.[33] For Middlesex and for the rest of the country, referred to in King's Bench records as the 'out-counties,' the court dealt with indictments removed on certiorari from quarter sessions or assizes; there were also summary convictions before magistrates removed on certiorari; criminal informations filed ex officio by the attorney general; other criminal informations filed by the master of the Crown Office on behalf of private litigants; qui tam proceedings; and proceedings by writ of habeas corpus, which of course were important in civil as well as criminal litigation.[34]

Criminal informations, both ex officio and ordinary ones, were important weapons for both the government and private citizens, making the prosecution of a misdemeanour expensive and speedy and removing the grand jury oversight requisite in prosecutions on indictment. Ex officio informations were exhibited as of right by the attorney general, but 'ordinary' criminal informations required the approbation of the judges before they could be exhibited (that is, become formal charges equivalent to an indictment); the tests that the judges applied changed over time and became an important source of law. A particular version of a criminal information, and the use of certiorari for removing, questioning, and quashing summary convictions, have been celebrated by older histories as the main instruments by which King's Bench supervised, controlled, and punished the misbehaviour of that great mass of inferior magistrates throughout the country, the county justices of the peace and borough justices. Based on an examination of every such case in one county for the second half of the century, my own recent conclusion is that in fact the control exerted by King's Bench was slight, hesitant, and indeed virtually non-existent for much of the country. The simple reason was that if magistrates were punished, even for egregious misbehaviour, it would be difficult to find men willing to take the post.[35] The high court judges were therefore solicitous of magistrates, since most of the work of the criminal law (supervising constables, taking bail, committing for trial, hearing summary cases) was carried out by these unpaid inferior justices.

Attorneys, Solicitors, Barristers, and Clerks

The history of Westminster Hall is also the history of the complex bureaucracies of the courts, and of attorneys and solicitors and the special pleaders who were said to work 'under the bar,' as well as of the barristers, serjeants, King's counsel, law officers of the Crown, and judges who were its most visible performers. There were also other, less noticed men: recent work on King's Bench, particularly the original jurisdiction of the court in Middlesex, shows that 'low attorneys,' many of them men with no formal legal qualifications whatsoever, offered their services on a contingent fee basis to even quite poor people.[36] It is obvious too that perjured witnesses, particularly in criminal trials, were quite freely available for payment. But for most plaintiffs and defendants, the services of qualified legal professionals were absolutely necessary, and their fees an inevitable concomitant of 'moving the court.' Here the clerks of court were as important as the lawyers.

The fullest recent account of the role of the court bureaucracies and the bar in Westminster Hall in the eighteenth century is a damning one. The great litigation decline in England, which reached its nadir at the moment of the founding of the Nova Scotia Supreme Court, seems largely attributable to the increased cost and complexity of going to law in the preceding century. The response of the bar (and of the clerks of court) in the eighteenth was, David Lemmings shows, to serve an increasingly wealthy clientele, largely the London plutocracy, as gentry in the provinces, and lesser citizens, withdrew from litigation. Those able to pay for law were now made to pay much more, and technicalities, unnecessary motions and filings, the employment of multiple counsel, and (a point he does not mention) an increased tendency to argue cases on repeated occasions over a number of terms before judgment all greatly expanded opportunities for making fortunes at the bar. The greatest legal and judicial fortunes were amassed between the 1750s and the early nineteenth century. The winners made spectacular amounts of money and acquired peerages. The losers, including Jonathan Belcher, sought success in lesser places like Dublin and Halifax. The result, argues Lemmings, was a pronounced and deserved erosion of the place of the common law in the life of the community, the constitution, and public esteem. Only the role of a defence bar, in state trials of great constitutional significance, somewhat redeemed the profession and the courts.[37]

Judges and Politics and Law

Blackstone and other contemporary celebrants of the glory of English law contrasted the courts of Westminster Hall with the despotic power of Star Chamber and the other conciliar courts abolished in the 1640s.

They lauded the learned probity of the Hanoverian bench, whose independence from the whims of the Crown, guaranteed by a few words in the Act of Settlement (1701), they argued had ended the corruption and ignorance manifested by the Stuart judges of the later seventeenth century. This achievement was in fact the culmination of a half-century of higher expectations of probity, and constitutional independence, of the judges.[38] Yet the claim of judicial independence in the eighteenth century must be substantially qualified. Of course, the chancellor sat in his court in Westminster Hall, in the House of Lords as principal representative of the government, and in Cabinet; his brother, the Master of the Rolls, could and often did hold a Commons seat, a great convenience to the administration. But several historians have also pointed out that both the notion of independence from political pressure and innocence of other forms of interest were weak because of more general structural characteristics of the bar and bench. Wilfrid Prest argues that gifts and other improper inducements were virtually unknown by the eighteenth century, as judicial salaries and public expectations of probity increased.[39] At the same time, however, judges continued to give advice to private litigants, and, as we have seen, controlled large patronage networks in their courts and profited directly from fees. The attack on legal delay and costs therefore directly implicated them, particularly as the chief justices almost always appointed their immediate family members to the immensely profitable leading clerkships in the courts, the duties of which were all performed by low-paid deputies.

Most important, in the 1760s and 1790s the judges were identified by critics of government as the creatures of the administration, the charge that had been so incendiary under the late Stuarts. From the mid-1760s the Wilkites accused the bench of subverting the rights of jurors in seditious libel cases, and of carrying the malign purposes of the government directly from the council chamber to the seat of justice, notably when Lord Chief Justice Mansfield sat simultaneously in Cabinet and on King's Bench, first from 1757 to 1760 in the administration of Newcastle and Pitt; he remained an active privy counsellor for almost eight years altogether.[40] Judicial independence from royal and ministerial pressure was compromised as well because appointment to the bench, and notably to the chief justiceships, almost always required prior loyal service as a law officer of the Crown in Parliament.[41] Mansfield's stint in Cabinet, briefly as chancellor of the Exchequer from April 1757, then without office until April 1763, when he resigned from Cabinet with Bute's administration, was an unusually open acknowledgment of the well-understood political significance of the chief justices.[42] As a member of the House of Lords, and as an adviser to the King and Cabinet, he defended government policy towards the American colonists and other burning issues. He also drafted legislation and sponsored it in the Lords while chief justice, a practice not challenged until the nineteenth century.[43]

If the chief justices were political (and Mansfield's role at the heart of government is matched by Hardwicke's, even before he was chancellor), they were occasionally on opposite sides of important issues. Perhaps the clearest example is the enmity of Chief Justice Charles Pratt of Common Pleas (later Lord Camden), whose tenure there in 1762–6 overlapped with the early years of Mansfield's reign in King's Bench. In the huge constitutional controversies aroused and sustained by John Wilkes and his supporters, Pratt was heavily engaged on the side of the critics of government and showered with gifts and testimonials for his opposition to the administration and to Mansfield. He was widely believed to have shared in the writing of one of the most vitriolic published attacks on Mansfield.[44] But Camden, who continued to agitate on constitutional issues long after he left the bench, and indeed until the end of his life (in 1792, supporting the Libel Act), was an exception. By the end of the century, in the state trials of Jacobins, popular supporters of the French revolution and advocates of democracy, it was Thomas Erskine and other defence counsel who persuaded jurors to acquit. The judges, in contrast, resisted all arguments that seditious libel was not theirs to define and deplored the lack of convictions. In the early nineteenth century, judges like Simon LeBlanc (JKB 1799–1816) and Alexander Thomson (B 1784–1814, CB 1814–17) were handpicked by government to ensure that large numbers of death sentences were passed and carried out on Luddites; some other members of the bench had been too lenient.[45] The chief justices and lord chancellors remained the staunchest supporters of the death penalty in England until the 1830s.

This fact is one of the many which distinguished the role of the high court judges in England from those in Nova Scotia. The comparisons that arise in the chapters of this book are many, and suggestive, although any overall comparison must be a complex one. In Nova Scotia, legislation had done more than in any other British North American colony to ameliorate the capital code, a source of satisfaction and pride to men like Beamish Murdoch.[46] Although colonial judges were important men, sitting in executive and legislative councils, they arguably never enjoyed the political dominance of their English brethren. Nor, it appears from the immensely interesting research now in progress, was high law in Nova Scotia ever as extortionate, plutocratic, and complacent as it was in the courts of Westminster Hall. Moreover, other British high courts probably substantially influenced that of Nova Scotia, in ways now being explored. The American-born Jonathan Belcher's experience was gained mostly in Dublin, and in spite of the constitutional dominance of the English high courts, and the intimate connections and advice between the English and Irish benches, the nature of justice in Ireland was distinctive in many ways.[47] Scotland's own common law, overlaid and intermixed with civilian influences, was celebrated by its greatest institutional writers in the eighteenth century and had not yet begun to succumb to the English influences increasingly imposed on it by the legislature and the House of Lords in the nineteenth. The literature and the learning of the Court of Session and the High Court of Justiciary came with many Scots to the British colonies. The influences of both Ireland and Scotland, probably less in doctrine than in practice and administration, invite further research. Much more, of course, is now known of the continuing and distinctive influences from other parts of North America on Nova Scotian legislation and practice, and its own indigenous spirit of invention. But like all the colonies that became Canada, eighteenth-century Nova Scotian judges looked, of constitutional necessity, and often filial piety, to the courts of Westminster Hall. They were the font and origin of both common law and equity.

NOTES

1 The restructuring of 1764 emphasized this fact. See Cahill and Phillips, this volume.

2 P. Brand, *The Making of the Common Law* (London: Hambledon Press 1992), 94–6; J.H. Baker, *An Introduction to English Legal History*, 4th ed. (London: Butterworths 2002).

3 On the gulf between the high law of the central courts and the law administered by inferior magistrates, see D. Hay, 'Legislation, Magistrates and Judges: High Law and Low Law in England and the Empire,' in D. Lemmings, ed., *The British and Their Laws in the Eighteenth Century* (London: Boydell and Brewer, forthcoming 2004).

4 H.M. Colvin, J. Mordaunt Crook, K. Downes, J. Newman, *The History of the King's Works* (London: HMSO 1976), 5:388.

5 Ibid., 5:390.

6 W. Blackstone, *Commentaries on the Laws of England*, 12th ed. (London, 1793–5), 3:110, 130–2, 264. The other prerogative or extraordinary writs were mandamus (to compel the performance of a duty), procedendo (from Chancery, to compel an inferior court to proceed to judgment), quo warranto (to inquire by what authority an office was exercised), and prohibition (to restrain an inferior court within its jurisdiction). Prohibition in some cases could be got from the other superior courts or chancery, and statutory habeas corpus under 31 Chas. II c. 2 (1679) was issuable in Common Pleas, although it rarely was: a notable instance, when King's Bench probably would not have done so, occurred in the case of Wilkes (below). It became issuable in all the courts by 56 Geo III c. 100 (1816).

7 J. Oldham, *The Mansfield Manuscripts and the Growth of English Law in the Eighteenth Century* (Chapel Hill and London: University of North Carolina Press 1992), 2:60.

8 Lemmings, *Professors of the Law: Barristers and English Legal Culture in the Eighteenth Century* (Oxford and New York: Oxford University Press 2000), esp. chaps. 3, 5, 8; see also below.

9 Ibid., 183.

10 Ibid., 177.

11 I.S. Lustig and F.A. Pottle, *Boswell: The English Experiment 1785–1789* (New York: McGraw-Hill 1986), 234–5 (12 July 1788).

12 For an instance of subverting statute through recourse to the wisdom of the common law, see D. Hay, 'The State and the Market: Lord Kenyon and Mr Waddington,' *Past & Present* 162 (February 1999): 101–62; for others, see D. Hay, 'Lloyd Kenyon,' *Oxford Dictionary of National Biography*, 60 vols. (Oxford: Oxford University Press 2004).

13 Diary, 5 Nov. 1815, quoted in P. Brode, *Sir John Beverley Robinson: Bone and Sinew of the Compact* (Toronto: Osgoode Society for Canadian Legal History and University of Toronto Press 1984), 29.

14 C. Muldrew, *The Economy of Obligation: The Culture of Credit and Social Relations in Early Modern England* (London: Palgrave 1998), 204ff; on the importance of local courts see also W.A. Champion, 'Recourse to Law and the Meaning of the Great Litigation Decline, 1650–1750: Some Clues from the Shrewsbury Local Courts' and C. Muldrew, 'Rural Credit, Market Areas and Legal Institutions in the Countryside in England, 1550–1700,' both in C. Brooks and M. Lobban, eds., *Communities and Courts in Britain 1150–1900* (London and Rio Grande: Hambleton Press 1997). For a view of the courts of request as they were attacked in the nineteenth century, see H.W. Arthurs, *Without the Law: Administrative Justice and Legal Pluralism in Nineteenth-Century England* (Toronto: University of Toronto Press 1985).

15 Most real and mixed actions were abolished by the Real Property Limitation Act (1833), s. 36; the process was completed by the Judicature Acts of 1873–5. For a summary of the nineteenth-century reforms, see A.H. Manchester, *A Modern Legal History of England and Wales* (London: Butterworths 1980), chaps. 6 and 12.

16 On the growing use of special pleaders in the eighteenth century see Lemmings, *Professors*, 134–5.

17 C.W. Francis, 'Practice, Strategy, and Institution: Debt Collection in the English Common-Law Courts, 1740–1840,' *Northwestern University Law Review* 80 (1986): 859. Francis makes the tollgate comparison and is the source for the statistics in this and the next paragraph (appendix 2 at 910, appendix 5 at 913, rounded percentages for the year 1740). Real actions could only be tried in Common Pleas.

18 C.W. Brooks, 'Litigation and Society in England, 1200–1996,' in *Lawyers, Litigation and English Society Since 1450* (London: Hambleton Press 1998), fig. 4.3, at 68; Francis, 'Practice,' Appendix 1 at 909.

19 J. Cockburn, *A History of English Assizes, 1558–1914* (Cambridge: Cambridge University Press 1972), chap. 7, and tables 3 and 4, at 138–9. Cockburn, at 143, lauds the 'rapidity with which assizes processed civil actions in an age notorious for the slowness of civil litigation,' but this assessment ignores pre- and post-trial proceedings at Westminster, the source of most delay and expense. Actual trials were rare for this reason: see below. 'Nisi prius,' a term originating in the medieval writs of venire for juries to attend by a certain day, referred to the fact that the trial was to be held at Westminster 'unless before' that day it was held before an assize judge on circuit in the county where the suit arose. Such trials were said to be at nisi prius.

20 See the work of Champion and Muldrew, cited above, note 14.

21 The fullest treatment is still Brooks, 'Litigation and Society.'

22 Lemmings, *Professors, passim*, summarizes the literature; his own findings strongly support the primacy of fees as the principal cause. See also C. Churches, 'Business at Law: Retrieving Commercial Disputes from Eighteenth-Century Chancery,' *Historical Journal* 43 (2000): 937–54.

23 D. Duman, *The Judicial Bench in England 1727–1785: The Reshaping of a Professional Elite* (London: Royal Historical Society 1982), provides estimates; Francis, 'Practice,' gives a breakdown of the fee structure as well as diagramming the right of appointment to offices, and summarizing the attack on patronage in the nineteenth century. To take one example at the end of the century: Lord Kenyon, as Chief Justice of King's Bench, received £4,000 a year and appointed to offices in King's Bench worth about £15,000 a year; those appointed were his sons Lloyd (1775–1800) as filazer and George

(1776–1855, second baron) as joint chief clerk. In 1804 Lord Ellenborough appointed Kenyon's youngest son Thomas (1780-) as filazer, and in 1810 shared the post of custos brevium, now in his possession, with George, now second Baron Kenyon. Members of the family still occupied several very remunerative posts in the mid-1830s. Hay, 'Lloyd Kenyon,' *Oxford Dictionary of National Biography*.

24 Francis, 'Practice.'

25 D. Hay, *Crown Side Cases in the Court of King's Bench: Staffordshire, 1740–1800* (Staffordshire Record Society, forthcoming).

26 On certiorari, see below, 'Criminal.'

27 For some instances of misdemeanours on certiorari see Hay, 'The State and the Market.'

28 Georges Lamoine, *Charges to the Grand Jury 1689–1803* (London: Royal Historical Society 1992) (although one reprinted is a satire, not an actual charge).

29 Cockburn, *History of English Assizes*, passim.

30 On nisi prius cases in London see Oldham, *Mansfield Manuscripts*, 1:109, 118.

31 On the judges at the Old Bailey, see J.M. Beattie, *Policing and Punishment in London 1660–1750: Urban Crime and the Limits of Terror* (Oxford: Oxford University Press 2001), 13, 15.

32 Hay, 'Legislation, Magistrates, and Judges.'

33 Ruth Paley deals with this aspect of King's Bench in forthcoming work.

34 Criminal informations allowed prosecutions for serious misdemeanour without indictment; those filed by the attorney general were termed ex officio informations. The first kind was abolished by the Administration of Justice (Miscellaneous Provisions) Act (1938), 1 & 2 Geo. VI, c. 63. Qui tam proceedings, or penal actions, gave a portion of the penalty, usually half, to the 'common informer'; such cases were often heard by magistrates, but could be brought in the high courts. For the use of habeas corpus in marital disputes, see E. Foyster, 'At the Limits of Liberty: Married Women and Confinement in Eighteenth-Century England,' *Continuity and Change* 17 (2002): 39–62. Proceedings in Staffordshire for all these categories are reproduced in Hay, *Crown Side Cases*.

35 D. Hay, 'Dread of the Crown Office: The English Magistracy and King's Bench, 1740–1800,' in N. Landau, ed., *Law, Crime and English Society 1660–1830* (Cambridge: Cambridge University Press 2002), 19–45.

36 Paley, forthcoming work.

37 Duman, *Judicial Bench in England*; Lemmings, *Professors, passim* and especially chap. 8. Lemming's argument that Old Bailey work raised the esteem

of the profession is cast in doubt by the detailed work of Allyson N. May, *The Bar and the Old Bailey* (Chapel Hill: University of North Carolina Press, 2003). Lemming's evidence on fees and complaints is very congruent with the patterns of litigation analyzed by Francis, although he does not cite his work.

38 W. Prest, 'Judicial Corruption in Early Modern England,' *Past & Present* 133 (1991): 81–4.

39 Ibid., 93.

40 J. Brewer, 'The Wilkites and the Law, 1763–1774,' in Brewer and J. Styles, eds., *An Ungovernable People: The English and their Law in the Seventeenth and Eighteenth Centuries* (London: Hutchinson 1980), 157–60; D. Hay, 'Contempt by Scandalizing the Court: A Political History of the First Hundred Years,' *Osgoode Hall Law Journal* 25 (1989): 448–9.

41 D. Lemmings, 'The Independence of the Judiciary in Eighteenth-Century England,' in P. Birks, ed., *The Life of the Law: Proceedings of the Tenth British Legal History Conference Oxford 1991* (London: Hambledon Press 1993); Lemmings, *Professors*, chap. 3; Duman, *Judicial Bench in England*, 87ff.

42 Followed on only one further occasion, by Lord Ellenborough between February 1806 and March 1807, to much criticism: see R.A. Melikan, 'The Judge and the Talents: an Episode in the History of Cabinet Government,' *Parliamentary History* 18 (1999): 131–43. Mansfield also held the seals of the Exchequer again for a few months in 1767, a traditional role of the lord chief justice during transitions between administrations, as he had for three months in 1757: *DNB*.

43 Oldham, *Mansfield Manuscripts*, 1:33.

44 Hay, 'Scandalizing.'

45 Hay, 'Simon LeBlanc,' *New DNB*.

46 P.V. Girard, 'Themes and Variations in Early Canadian Legal Culture: Beamish Murdoch and his *Epitome of the Laws of Nova Scotia*,' *Law and History Review* 11 (1993): 101.

47 On colonial judiciaries, see John McLaren, 'The judicial office ... bowing to no power but the supremacy of the law: judges and the rule of law in colonial Australia and Canada, 1788–1840,' *Australian Journal of Legal History* 7 (2003): 177–92. On Irish-English influences, see W.N. Osborough, 'Letters to Ireland: Professional Enlightenment from the English Bench,' in Osborough, *Studies in Irish Legal History* (Dublin: Four Courts Press 1999). For judges, one mark of Irish difference was the bloody murder of Lord Kilwarden, the Irish lord chief justice, and his nephew, by an enraged street mob during Emmet's insurrection of 1803.

3

Colonial and Imperial Contexts

ELIZABETH MANCKE

In 1748 William Shirley, governor of the Massachusetts Bay Colony, sent the Lords Commissioners for Trade and Plantations, commonly called the Board of Trade, a recommendation for how the government of Nova Scotia should be established after the Ministry and Parliament had decided to build Halifax as the colony's new capital. Many of his suggestions focused on how the legal system should be established.[1] Nearly simultaneously, the Board of Trade was drafting instructions for Edward Cornwallis, the newly appointed governor of Nova Scotia, which also addressed the establishment of a court system.[2]

The attention to the administration of justice in both Shirley's recommendations and the instructions to Cornwallis reflects its general importance in the British world. Each British colony had a legal system, and in territories without colonial governments, the metropolitan government generally provided access to courts for subjects. One of the first acts of civilian government that British military officers provided in Nova Scotia after the 1710 conquest of Acadia was dispute resolution; the governor of Canada did the same after the conquest of that colony in 1760. In 1728, the Board of Trade recommended that year-round magistrates be appointed in Newfoundland, even though the island lacked the other institutions of a colonial government, and one of the reasons for extending the boundaries of Quebec to the Ohio River in the 1774 Quebec Act was to provide access to courts for the French Canadians in the pays d'en haut. For Bengal the 1773 Regulating Act for the reform of the East India Company provided for the establishment of a Supreme Court with royally appointed judges.[3]

These provisions for access to courts in overseas territories reflected the broadly held sensibility that British subjects had a right to English jurisprudence. Nevertheless, the powers and jurisdictions of courts varied widely within the Empire, and thus there was no clear pattern for predicting how Nova Scotia's court system would be established. Shirley assumed that the colony would receive a royal charter similar to the Massachusetts charter, and that the colonial Assembly would create the court system. The Board of Trade, in contrast, had no intention of recommending that Nova Scotia receive a royal charter;[4] instead the instructions issued to Cornwallis gave him, in consultation with the Council, the right to establish what courts were deemed necessary.

Understanding the Nova Scotia legal system within the context of the British Empire requires that we take account of the tension between a broadly held cultural sensibility about a shared system of English liberty and law and the particularities of the legal systems of each overseas jurisdiction. To capture that tension, this essay does two things. First, it positions the institutional development of Nova Scotia's legal system within a structure of imperial administration that was changing rapidly in the eighteenth century. Second, it discusses the nature of the chronologies of law in the British Empire, which were peculiarly expansive and plastic because the past body of law from the British world that might be drawn into a colonial context had no clear limits. Both, I will argue, gave Nova Scotia, and Canada more generally, a legal culture rooted in a dynamic relationship with the past, perhaps more so than either the legal culture of Britain or the United States. In the latter, with its own colonial legacies, a revolution and independence bounded the English legal legacy and replaced the expansive chronologies of colonial law with points of origin and the principle of fundamental law embedded in state and federal constitutions.

Two observations about the history of law in the early modern British Empire offer a basis for understanding the tension between the commonalities and the particularities of the diverse colonial legal systems: first, British subjects were deeply committed to a set of legal rights, including trial by jury, habeas corpus, and legislative representation; and second, laws written in the colonies were not to be repugnant to the laws of England.[5] These two principles were the common reference points for the development of colonial legal systems. Colonists were to be proactive in designing and compiling bodies of law specific to their circumstances. Metropolitan officials served a largely reactive role. They seldom presumed to hand down laws appropriate to discrete colonial circumstances, although they did set legal guidelines in gubernatorial commissions and instructions.[6] They also determined whether any particular colonial law or court decision violated an informed legal sensibility through Crown-in-Council review of colonial legislation (at times leading to its disallowance) and appeals to the Privy Council, respectively.[7] This dialectical process with proactive imperial peripheries and a reactive centre substantiates the observation that authority in all the early modern empires was negotiated jurisdiction by jurisdiction and over an extended period of time, rather than imposed on colonists.[8]

The core principles changed very little between the early seventeenth and early nineteenth centuries, whether one is studying the legal system of Massachusetts, Barbados, Nova Scotia, or Upper Canada, even though how they were institutionalized and administered shifted significantly. As well, they took a sharp turn with the conquest of Canada in 1760. The British faced the quandary in establishing a legal system for the colony when the overwhelming majority of its population was French Canadian, whose myriad civil arrangements from marriages to landholding had been defined by French civil law rather than English common law. The compromise in the 1774 Quebec Act was to introduce English criminal law but continue French civil law, a decision that reflects an awareness of the dangers of too much immediate manipulation of a provincial system of law. The charge that the Quebec Act was a sharp deviation from the principle that colonies were to have laws that were not repugnant to those of England was countered by a conservative, but contrary, observation that French civil law perpetuated customary law in the colony. Honouring regional practices and thereby sanctioning legal diversity in the Empire was normative rather than unusual, and became even more pronounced in the nineteenth century as Britain attempted to accommodate a growing number of non-British peoples, and with them non-English legal systems, within the Empire.

Indeed, there was no normative colonial court system or colonial body of law in the British Empire, whether in the early modern or modern eras, or in the Americas, Africa, Asia, or Australia, New Zealand, and the Pacific.[9] Rather, there were an infinite number of possible combinations of received and locally legislated bodies of laws, as well as myriad variations in the court systems. Nevertheless, at an ideological level, British subjects throughout the Empire believed they shared a common legal culture that could accommodate these variations.[10] At a practical level, the legal culture was sufficiently shared that transactions between and among diverse dependencies could be adjudicated if necessary through a common set of procedures: merchants could send goods throughout the Empire and expect financial transactions to be legally protected; various civil contracts, such as wills, marriages, adoptions, and labour arrangements, were recognized and honoured in diverse jurisdictions; officers of the law could be transferred from one colony to another; officials in Britain could determine whether colonially legislated laws would receive royal approval or be disallowed; and the Privy Council could serve as the last appellate court in the Empire, though not, significantly, within Britain itself.[11]

What changed most over the early modern era were the institutional mechanisms and arrangements that linked the legal systems of overseas dependencies to the metropolitan government in Britain. Four are particularly important: how legal rights and privileges were granted; the Privy Council review of colonial legislation; the process of appeals that led back to the Privy Council; and the royal appointment of law officers, many of whom by the late eighteenth century had experience in more than one British legal system. What emerged by the early nineteenth century was an imperial system that was more carefully articulated, if not integrated, than had been the case in the early modern Empire. A fifth, and hotly debated, shift occurred in the mid-eighteenth century concerning how law was to be used to honour the rights of people who were not English-speaking, Protestant subjects, particularly indigenous peoples and conquered subjects, such as the French Canadians. Nova Scotia's legal system took form during the mid-eighteenth century, when these transitions were especially volatile and fluid. As Canada's oldest British court system and with the oldest high court, its history captures many of those critical changes and their consequences.

During the early modern era there were three primary ways of establishing legal systems overseas and of recognizing the legal rights and privileges of overseas subjects: charters, royal commissions and instructions to governors, and parliamentary legislation.[12] Charters were used primarily in the sixteenth and seventeenth centuries. Parliamentary legislation, such as the 1774 Quebec Act or the 1791 Constitutional Act, were not regularly used until the late eighteenth century. Gubernatorial commissions and instructions generally complemented the other two forms, but in some contexts, such as Nova Scotia, could stand alone to create a legal system. William Shirley's expectation that Nova Scotia would receive a charter harkened back to an older practice of English overseas expansion and reflected his experience in Massachusetts, a colony established by charter in 1628 and rechartered in 1691.

The royal charters granted for overseas expansion, beginning with Elizabeth I's grant to Sir Humphrey Gilbert in 1578 for a colony in Newfoundland, included sections granting companies and proprietors the privilege of adjudicating disputes, and in most cases the privilege of establishing courts and writing laws that were not to be repugnant to the laws of England. Two problems emerged from these charters for the metropolitan government, and they were gradual by abandoned and replaced with other mechanisms to extend legal rights. First, colonists frequently attempted to use charters as bulwarks against future expressions of prerogative power. Second, overseas enterprises, especially colonies, had an autonomy from metropolitan authorities that placed their legal systems outside the English court system. The charters of both the Virginia Company and the Massachusetts Bay Company were revoked by the King's Bench in England in 1624 and 1684, respectively, on the legal premise that each company had a corporate presence in England and hence came within the pale of the English courts. Appeals originating in the colonies, however, went not to one of the English appellate courts but to the Privy Council, because colonial court systems were outside the realm and hence outside the jurisdiction of the realm's courts.[13] Charters, therefore, created weak mechanisms of articulation with England's legal system, and the autonomy they seemed to allow colonists resulted in metropolitan countermeasures to keep colonial governments, and particularly their legal systems, tied to England in some way.

The most extreme seventeenth-century assertion of colonial legal autonomy was in Massachusetts. The colony's government held that its body of laws was distinct from England's. The colony did not receive the body of English law extant at the time of its founding, with colonial statutes added; rather, its laws were only those 'which have heretofore been adopted, used and approved in the Province,' a position that would carry over into the national era.[14] Until the revocation of the charter in 1684, colonists in Massachusetts were prohibited from appealing cases to England, on the grounds that the charter did not allow it.[15] After a difficult and tumultuous three years under the Dominion of New England (1686–9), Massachusetts colonists overthrew the government of Sir Edmund Andros in 1689, on hearing of the abdication of James II. When William and Mary re-chartered the colony in 1691, they explicitly protected the right of Massachusetts colonists to appeal cases to the Crown. The charter allowed the colony's General Court to establish a court system, which it expeditiously did. Significantly, it created a Superior Court through which appeals from all the colony's courts, both civil and criminal, were heard. Ironically, this model of a single high court – rather than multiple high courts such as England had, or having the Governor and Council serve as the highest appellate court in a colony – was quite distinctive in the English world and had first been implemented by Governor Andros in Massachusetts. At the time of the American Revolution, Massachusetts was the only colony in which the Governor and Council did not hear appeals, except in probate cases.[16]

Charters for other colonies posed similar, if not such obvious, problems, and over the seventeenth century the Crown's ministers attempted to limit the rights granted through them. The 1681 charter for Pennsylvania, for example, expressly stipulated that the colonists had the right to appeal cases to the Crown.[17] In a study of charters as law, Christopher Tomlins explores the shifting and often competing ideological and conceptual frameworks that were embedded in charters used for colonization, from the joint-stock charters of the Virginia Company and Massachusetts Bay Company to the proprietary charters of Maryland, Carolina, and Pennsylvania. After the creation of the Massachusetts Bay Company, the Crown ceased granting joint-stock charters for ventures that were predominantly colonial and not commercial, and which would necessitate civil, and not just company, government. Proprietary charters to members of the English aristocracy and elite gentry, who were perceived as agents worthy of creating civilian governments overseas, eclipsed joint-stock charters, but it soon became apparent that these charters gave too much autonomy to proprietors and colonists. By the time William Penn received the charter for Pennsylvania, proprietary interests were more carefully balanced against and circumscribed by imperial interests and the needs of an emergent imperial state.[18]

Despite the gradual imperial shift in the orientation of charters, in the basic structure of power that colonists understood charters as creating, provincial governments were not so much one level in a hierarchy of power reaching from Whitehall and Westminster to the colonies as horizontal barriers against strong vertical linkages of power. Over time, the practice of provincial governments serving as barriers against metropolitan intrusions, both prerogative and parliamentary, assumed institutional and ideological expression. Colonists from New England to the Carolinas, and in the Atlantic and Caribbean island colonies, had no difficulty in mustering both constitutional and ideological arguments to defend this formulation of the function of provincial-level governments in British America.[19]

By the end of the seventeenth century the metropolitan government had largely abandoned the use of charters as the initial mechanism by which colonial governments were established overseas, largely in an attempt to enhance the prerogative, particularly in legal matters. Gubernatorial commissions and instructions, which had long supplemented charters in royal colonies, became the substitute for charters in newly acquired colonies, such as Nova Scotia, and the authority upon which courts were established.[20] Gubernatorial commissions and instructions were part of a larger complex of policies intended to reinforce prerogative powers overseas, such as Crown-in-Council review of colonial legislation and appeals to the Privy Council. At the end of the eighteenth century, the Crown-in-Parliament became important as an expression of sovereign British authority for the creation of overseas governments, as reflected in the Regulating Act of 1773, which created a Supreme Court in Bengal, and the Constitutional Act of 1791, which separated Upper Canada from Lower Canada and established a new colonial government. In these circumstances gubernatorial commissions and instructions from the Crown-in-Council supplemented Crown-in-Parliament authority to create governments, including the authorization to establish courts.[21]

The 1696 establishment of the Lords Commissioners for Trade and Plantations facilitated the emergence of a more integrated imperial legal system.[22] One of the most immediate achievements of the Board of Trade was to oblige the colonies to use common law. Over the course of the seventeenth century, the common law had been gaining ascendancy over other forms of law used in England, such as ecclesiastical law and admiralty law, and colonial manifestations of this development became marked at the century's end. Governor Andros's insistence on the use of the common law in the Dominion of New England invalidated numerous land claims in the northern colonies, and the 1691 Massachusetts charter required the colony's laws to conform to common law. A more uniform and widespread enforcement of common law over other forms, however, occurred because the Board of Trade used the review of colonial legislation as one of its primary instruments of legal oversight and integration. By disallowing legislation that did not conform to common law, the board could reorient the legal cultures of the colonies, which it succeeded in doing by the first decade of the eighteenth century.[23] The consequences of this legal turn are considerable, but for now it is important to note that Nova Scotia was established after it occurred, and thus was firmly within a legal world defined by the primacy of the common law. As discussed below, this development had consequences for questions of reception.

The review of colonial legislation and appeals to the Privy Council were the two primary mechanisms whereby the metropolitan government exercised its powers to intervene in colonial legal systems. Appeals to the Privy Council traced their legacy to the appellate jurisdiction of the Crown-in-Council for royal domains outside the realm; by the early seventeenth century all that remained of these domains were the Channel Islands. All other appellate jurisdiction of the Privy Council had been removed by Parliament in 1641, in 16 Chs. I, c. 10, which required that all legal cases arising within the realm 'be tried and determined in the ordinary courts of justice, and by the ordinary course of law.' During the Restoration Charles II asserted his prerogative power to hear appeals from the colonies, despite resistance from most colonial governments. Legal opinion in England held that it was the Crown's obligation to hear appeals; the prominent jurist, Sir Edward Coke, opined that 'an appeale [to the Crown] is a naturall defence, it cannot be taken away by any prince or power.' The responsibility for hearing appeals was assumed by the Council of Trade and Plantation, a Privy Council committee established in March 1674/5, on the assumption that the overseas colonies were royal domains outside the realm, similar to the Channel Islands. Thus from a nearly moribund royal prerogative exercised over a cluster of small islands off the coast of England developed the Judicial Committee of the Privy Council, a vast expansion of the Crown-in-Council's authority as all the legal systems of the British Empire came within its purview.[24]

In many colonies, both the disallowance of legislation and the right of appeal to the Privy Council met with resistance. Massachusetts enforced the letter of the 1691 charter when it sanctioned only appeals on civil cases of personal actions and not real actions, and established that cases had to have a minimum value of three hundred pounds. The government of Connecticut attempted to block appeals, despite a conciliar order to allow them, and justified its position by noting that the King had not reserved that power when he granted the charter in 1662. The Crown's law officers responded that the right to hear appeals was an inherent right of the Crown (notwithstanding Parliament's removal of that right within the realm in 1641) and did not need to be reserved in charters. Disputes over conciliar appellate jurisdiction in cases arising in the chartered colonies became so contentious that between 1701 and 1706 Parliament considered legislation to revoke all the charters. When colonies tried to limit appeals to the Privy Council with legislation, the Board of Trade recommended disallowance. Among the colonies that had such laws disallowed were New Hampshire, Bermuda, Massachusetts, the Lesser Antilles, Jamaica, Pennsylvania, and the Bahamas.[25]

When the foundations of Nova Scotia's current legal system were first laid in 1749, legal struggles between colonial governments and the Board of Trade were still frequent, with seventeenth-century precedents figuring prominently in the colonists' claims that their rights had been violated through disallowance, appeals to the Privy Council, and prerogative control of the creation of new courts. As Nova Scotia did not have those seventeenth-century precedents, older legal struggles did not have the resonance they had elsewhere in British America.[26] Nova Scotia's struggles revolved around a different set of issues, ones which would come to define legal concerns in the modern British Empire.

Four developments are particularly important. First, colonial high courts staffed with justices trained in the law gradually became normative in the modern Empire. In the older royal colonies, except Massachusetts, the Governor and Council was the highest appellate court, and its members frequently lacked legal training. The appointment of legally trained chief justices reflected Privy Council attempts to gain greater control over colonial legal systems. Second, the appointment of chief justices through either a mandamus or commission direct from the Crown (rather than through a colonial governor), who served on a high court bench on which the governor did not serve, created two increasingly distinct expressions of prerogative power in colonies, one executive, one judicial.[27] In the older colonies the greater blending of executive and judicial functions in the governors tended to create a single focal point for tensions over prerogative control. In the newer colonies, there were more political struggles in which a governor and chief justice took different positions on an issue, and which, in turn, could have significant repercussions for how political struggles were configured within colonies. Third, one of the primary purposes of the greater separation of executive and judicial functions in the colonial courts was to enhance greater legal consistency between a colony and England and among the polities of the Empire. That change shifted the terms of legal controversies from inward-turning and provincial defences of legal practices typical of the older colonies to questions of what greater legal conformity within the Empire entailed and how it might be achieved, given the particular needs of colonies. Finally, the reception of the law in colonies became much more open-ended and the relevant precedents more diverse.

Nova Scotia's court system was established on the basis of the gubernatorial commission to Edward Cornwallis in 1749. The colony had had an earlier 'General Court' composed of the governor and council, which Governor Richard Philipps established in 1721 on the basis of his 1719 commission.[28] The 'General Court' that Cornwallis established in 1749 was composed on the same terms. A committee of the Executive Council subsequently recommended the creation of a lower 'County Court' that would 'hear and determine all causes whatsoever cognizable at Common Law,' except capital crimes and those that involved loss of limb, which would be tried by the General Court, which would also hear appeals in civil cases. That system existed until 1752, when the County Court was split into two courts. The Inferior Court of Common Pleas tried civil cases, a Court of Quarter Sessions of the Peace administered local government and tried crimes of petty larceny and misdemeanours, and the General Court tried felonious crimes, as well as heard appeals on civil cases in which the contested amount of property was over three hundred pounds. New Englanders seem to have instigated this reconfiguration of the courts, given their resemblance to the Massachusetts lower courts. The early system, in contrast, more closely resembled Virginia's County Courts, the model recommended repeatedly in gubernatorial instructions.[29]

In 1754, the Crown-in-Council directly appointed a chief justice for Nova Scotia. Until then, most colonial chief justices had been appointed by colonial governors, though a few chief justices and attorneys general had been appointed out of England. Colonial justices, including chief justices, were frequent objects of criticism: many lacked legal training and others seemed to be too beholden to the governors who appointed them and presided during appeals to General Courts. In 1752, the Board of Trade had revised its standard instructions on judicial appointments and required governors to have the consent of at least three council members to any appointment.[30] Prior to the appointment of Jonathan Belcher, Nova Scotia had a 'first' justice of the Inferior Court of Common Pleas, Charles Morris, who had been appointed to that position by Governor Cornwallis. The initiative for the appointment of a chief justice from outside the colony came from within Nova Scotia. In 1752, an acrimonious dispute arose in the colony over the law that justices of the Inferior Court of Common Pleas used; critics charged that Massachusetts law, not English law, was being used. That dispute, in turn, made Governor Peregrine Thomas Hopson concerned about the legitimacy of legal decisions made in the Nova Scotia courts, and he requested that the Board of Trade appoint a chief justice and an attorney general who were trained in law. The board initially hesitated at honouring this unusual request, but in July 1754 it agreed to one appointment, and in the fall the forty-three-year-old Jonathan Belcher arrived in Nova Scotia with a mandamus from the Crown for the governor to issue a commission for him to be chief justice.[31]

Belcher's appointment created as much as followed colonial precedents.[32] His commission gave him the 'full power and authority to hold the Supreme Courts of Judicature,' thus largely replacing the General Court, on which the governor and council served as judges.[33] The governor could still hold a Court of Chancery and the Governor and Council, including the chief justice, could act as a Court of Errors to hear appeals from the Supreme Court and as a Marriage and Divorce Court. In general, however, the creation of a Supreme Court served to attenuate the blending of executive and judicial functions typical of the older colonies.[34] The subsequent exile from the rebelling colonies of large numbers of Loyalist lawyers, who wanted to remain within the Empire rather than resettle in Britain, must also have helped to reinforce the separation of executive and judicial expressions of prerogative in other post-1783 colonies.[35]

Within months of his arrival in Nova Scotia, Belcher found himself enmeshed in legal controversies. Even an Anglophile lawyer trained at the Inns of Court and with experience practising law in England and Ireland could not have precluded some interventions by the Board of Trade. Three interventions are particularly illustrative of both the problems of colonial law and the challenges of coordinating legal sensibilities regarding colonial rights: the first major one concerned the reception of English criminal law; the second controversy was over Governor Charles Lawrence's resistance to convening an assembly; and the third one occurred in 1760, when the Board of Trade challenged some of the Assembly's first legislation.

A principal reason for appointing a chief justice trained in the law was to ensure that the laws of England, both common and statute, would be applied in Nova Scotia. That task, however, was fraught with great ambiguity, as became apparent in a 1756 criminal case of counterfeiting and circulating Spanish coin. The point of law at issue was what criminal code to apply. A Marian statute defined the crime as 'treason' and Belcher contended it applied in Nova Scotia because the colony had received all English law, statute and common. The defence contended the statute did not apply because it stated that it only applied within the realm. The defendant was found guilty of treason by counterfeiting foreign coin, which normally carried a capital sentence, but the dispute over the applicable law made Belcher delay the sentencing while the case materials were sent to London for the opinion of the attorney and solicitor general. They confirmed the defence lawyer's argument: the Marian statute only applied in the realm. Elaborating the issue further, they stated that Nova Scotia had not received all English law at one time (the date of reception in Nova Scotia has never been resolved), but that the reception of statute law in a colony depended 'upon Circumstances,' including what statutes the colonial assembly reenacted. But in 1757 the colony did not yet have an assembly, and hence that remedy was not available. Without any colonial statutes, the crime, in the opinion of the attorney and solicitor general, 'can be considered only as a High Misdemeanour.'[36]

When the Board of Trade appointed Belcher it had alerted him to the problems posed by the lack of a colonial assembly and expressed its concern about the legality of the Governor and Council legislating for the colony, and before Belcher sailed for Halifax, Thomas Pownall, the board's secretary, had urged him to consult with Governor Lawrence about calling an elected assembly. Lawrence, however, persuaded Belcher that 'Convening an Assembly would at present be not only impolitick but almost impracticable.' Upon receiving this opinion, the board consulted the attorney and solicitor general, who opined 'that the Governor and Council alone are not authorized by His Majesty to make Laws,' and that the governor should follow his instructions and call an assembly. The board instructed Lawrence to have Belcher draw up plans for convening one and Belcher became an advocate for an assembly – along with hundreds of settlers – even though he worked against Lawrence for three years until the first Assembly met in October 1758. Belcher's compliance with the board may have been simply politic, because his commission was at the 'pleasure of the Crown,' but the counterfeiting case demonstrated the critical need for an assembly, and surely confirmed to Belcher the wisdom of calling one. Significantly, Governor Lawrence, as the Crown's direct representative in Nova Scotia, could not remove the chief justice, thus giving Belcher an autonomy of action to oppose Lawrence that he might not have exercised so freely had the governor made his appointment.[37]

The first legislation passed by the Assembly elicited queries from the Board of Trade that it wanted answered before it would 'proceed to advise either the Confirmation or Disallowance of Laws which are intended to be the foundation of the civil Constitution of the Colony.' Although the board acknowledged 'that the Laws are, in general, usefull and proper for the establishing order and Government in a new Colony,' the Assembly had nonetheless taken too many laws 'from Acts of the province of Massachusetts Bay.' The board noted that some Massachusetts legislation had received royal approbation in the years after the Revolution of 1689, 'when the Administration of Government here at home was too well employed in settling those principles upon which the present happy constitution of this Country rests,' and it had not been able 'to attend to the lesser, tho' important, consideration of what might be the principles of Colony Constitution and Government.'[38] In short, the Board of Trade had to tolerate Massachusetts laws from that period, but it would ask for their revision or disallowance if a newer colony tried to reenact them.

Conflicts over Nova Scotia's legal system continued, but they did not polarize between the rights of colonists and the power of the prerogative as so many political controversies in the older colonies had.[39] While Belcher's appointment had technically enhanced prerogative power in Nova Scotia, events also split it, as Belcher's support of and Lawrence's resistance to an assembly showed. The new configuration of political controversies that Nova Scotia exhibited can be seen in its response to the imperial crisis in the 1770s.

In the summer of 1775, the Nova Scotia Assembly drafted an address to the King and both houses of Parliament concerning the escalating imperial crisis and possible resolutions. In the petition, the Assembly acknowledged parliamentary supremacy – which colonists to the south were unwilling to do – and offered to write colonial legislation for a permanent duty on foreign imports into Nova Scotia, excluding 'Bay salt,' the receipts of which would go into parliamentary revenues 'to pay a due proportion of the Expence of this great Empire.' This revenue would not preclude the continued parliamentary appropriations for Nova Scotia, which the Assembly deemed necessary if Halifax was to be 'the Head Quarters of the British Land and Sea Forces in America.'[40] Having positioned themselves within an imperial system, rather than arguing for the autonomy of their province, they offered a series of recommendations for reforming the Empire, most of which tended to enhance prerogative power in principle, while offering numerous critiques for how it should be exercised.

Changes in the appointment of royal officials figured prominently as a way to alleviate the frequency of political battles: neither the governor nor the lieutenant governor should be 'Native of this province'; 'Members of the Legislative Council should be appointed for Life'; Supreme Court judges should be appointed for life and not be natives of the province; the justices of the peace should not be undermined by summary dismissals or suspensions by the governor and executive council. The recommendations that the governor, lieutenant governor, and the chief justice not be natives of the province indicate the extent to which Nova Scotians had come to accept an imperial system (rather than a loosely associated system of British American provinces) with imperial officials who did not have personal ties to a colony and who would be paid out of an imperial purse. In striking contrast, the Declaration of Independence, written a year later, listed the dependence of judges on the Crown for 'payment of their salaries' as a grievance. The Nova Scotia Assembly, however, was in accord with assemblies in other colonies that protested royal commissions for judges and justices of the peace that were 'at the pleasure of the Crown' rather than 'during good behaviour in the same manner as in England.'[41]

Many of the concerns of the Nova Scotia Assembly involved the lack of boundaries between executive and judicial power and excessive power in the hands of a few people. Officials who collected provincial revenues should 'be prohibited from serving as representatives in General Assembly.' Assembly elections should be 'Triennial' and 'fixed by Law,' and government officials should be 'prohibited from interfering in Elections under severe and heavy Penalties.' Too many county-level positions were controlled by a central figure who controlled his own county deputies. Rather than a provost marshal who chose his own deputies, 'and whose power in Elections is absolute,' the Assembly wanted county sheriffs. Similarly, each county should have a registrar of deeds, 'and not a Deputy to a principle residing else where.' The petition recommended that the governor, council, and Supreme Court justices compose the Court of Vice-Admiralty. Rather than the governor presiding over the Court of Equity, two Supreme Court justices and a jury should try equity cases.[42] As these recommendations make clear,

Nova Scotians were not reticently or obsequiously loyal members of the Empire. Rather, they accepted that a more integrated and bureaucratized imperial system would exist, and thus the political debate revolved around the question of how power within it, at both the imperial and provincial levels, should be structured.

The appointment of Belcher as chief justice and a partial separation of executive and judicial functions through the establishment of a Supreme Court on which the governor and council did not sit surely contributed to the imperial turn in provincial sensibilities in Nova Scotia. The imperial turn subsequently shaped the development of the colony's legal system, as well as other polities of the post-1783 British Empire. Increasingly, justices had to assess what law was particular to and necessary for a province, and what law needed to be fitted to the Empire.

A number of mid-eighteenth-century developments in the Empire also broadened the legal discourse and generated expansive chronologies of law. The appointment by Whitehall of chief justices to serve on colonial high courts became commonplace after 1783, rather than exceptional, as was Belcher's appointment. These appointees frequently had experience elsewhere in the British world, and thought of themselves as part of an elite cadre of legal officials who were capable of serving anywhere in the British Empire. In the early nineteenth century, the British North American colonies began to agitate for provincial rather than imperial appointment of judges, a right which Nova Scotia achieved along with responsible government in 1848.[43] But in the meantime, a broad legal discourse had been engendered through the Empire-wide mobility of law officers.

The legal systems of the Empire also became more diverse in the mid-eighteenth century, as Britain absorbed multiple territories in which non-British peoples were the majority population. This ethnic diversification influenced legal discourses in at least three significant ways. First, both the Ministry and Parliament began to recognize the necessity of accommodating non-British legal practices in places such as Grenada, Quebec, and Bengal. In some colonies, law officers recognized that some minority ethnic groups seldom used the courts, relying instead on their own institutions of dispute resolution. In New Brunswick, priests often adjudicated disputes among the Acadians in Madawaska, conflicts that in other communities would have been handled through the county courts. Though the Acadian system was not officially sanctioned, it was accepted as a legitimate deviation to accommodate ethnic differences.[44] For the people who identified themselves as members of an imperial community, if not elites within it, attention to a widening range of legal practices was part of what it meant to belong to the Empire rather than just a colony within it.

Second, in North America, treaties and the Proclamation of 1763 placed many native peoples outside the colonial legal systems. While colonial officials were often charged with negotiating with native nations, as happened in Nova Scotia throughout the eighteenth century, those treaties acknowledged native rights that were not shared with other inhabitants, such as rights to fish and hunt or to cross the border between the United States and the British North American colonies. Throughout late eighteenth- and early nineteenth-century British North America, and indeed throughout the British Empire, imperial officials sanctioned the co-existence of both indigenous and British systems of rights and privileges. In some instances their motivations were expedient, in others they reflected an honest – even if paternal – regard for the customary governmental systems of other societies.

The third legal development influenced by the ethnic diversification of the Empire was the belief among many imperial elites that they could and should use the law to pursue humanitarian goals.[45] In British North America, the high courts of Lower Canada and Nova Scotia 'sought to debilitate slavery without declaring it illegal,' and the Assemblies in both colonies voted against legislation that would have statutorily recognized the legality of slavery. The New Brunswick high court recognized slavery as legal in that colony, even though it was not statutorily established. The first governor of Upper Canada, John Graves Simcoe, convinced the new Assembly to pass legislation to abolish slavery gradually, despite strong opposition to the bill.[46]

Legal activism was prevalent sufficiently among imperial appointees at the end of the eighteenth and the beginning of the nineteenth century that it needs to been seen as imperial legal culture rather than part of a particular colonial legal culture. The distinction between colonial and imperial is significant, because the former could be parochial, inward-turning, and bounded, while the latter was diverse, unbounded, ambiguous, and outward-turning. The response of the Nova Scotia Assembly to Parliament's 1833 Slavery Abolition Act provides a telling illustration of the tension between provincial and imperial legal visions. The Assembly passed and the governor approved An Act to prevent the ... Landing of Liberated Slaves. The Privy Council disallowed it on the grounds that it 'was morally reprehensible and verged on contempt of

Parliament.' The Assembly might have responded that slavery had long since been defunct in Nova Scotia and that the colony's residents should not have to bear the costs of the moral failings of West Indian planters.[47] As the disallowance suggests, using colonial legislation to create provincial bulwarks against the problems of Empire was deemed unacceptable by the metropolitan officials who monitored the imperial legal system. Even though Parliament's abolition of slavery did not directly apply to Nova Scotia and the other British North American colonies where slavery had died out, it had an indirect legal impact.

The post-1783 British Empire offered colonists few legacies of seventeenth-century colonial charters to justify their attempts to check the expansiveness of the chronologies of law that might be operable in any colonial setting. The appointment of Jonathan Belcher and the establishment of the Nova Scotia Supreme Court, only the second colonial high court after Massachusetts in which the governor did not play a significant role, were critical turning points in the development of law in the British world. What remained from the earlier imperial developments were review of colonial legislation and appeals to the Privy Council. To link colonies more closely both to Britain and to each other, the Crown-in-Council appointment of law officers became commonplace in the Empire, and this development engendered a greater separation of executive and judicial functions, as well as a sensibility that law officers worked for imperial interests as well as provincial ones.

NOTES

Jim Phillips, Philip Girard, Barry Cahill, two press reviewers, and Jack Greene made invaluable suggestions for improving this essay. I am grateful to all of them, yet I am responsible for the particular ways in which their comments were integrated into this essay.

1 William Shirley, General Heads of a Plan of a Civil Government proposed for His Majesty's Province of Nova Scotia, 1748, RG 1, vol. 29, 2–14.

2 T.B. Akins, *Selections from the Public Documents of the Province of Nova Scotia* (Halifax: Public Archives of Nova Scotia 1869), 497–562. Excerpts from the commission can also be found in C.J. Townsend, 'Historical Account of the Courts of Judicature in Nova Scotia,' *Canadian Law Times* (1899): 25–37, 58–72, 87–98, 142–57; excerpts from Cornwallis's commission are on 29–30.

3 E. Mancke, 'Imperial Transitions,' in J.G. Reid, et al., *The Conquest of Acadia, 1710: Imperial, Colonial, and Aboriginal Constructions* (Toronto: University of Toronto Press 2003); J.A. Webb, 'Leaving the State of Nature: A Locke-Inspired Political Community in St. John's, Newfoundland, 1723,' *Acadiensis* 20 (1991): 156–65; C. English, 'The Development of the Newfoundland Legal System to 1815,' *Acadiensis* 19 (1990): 89–119; J. Bannister, *The Rule of the Admirals: Law, Custom, and Naval Government in Newfoundland, 1699–1832* (Toronto: Osgoode Society for Canadian Legal History and University of Toronto Press 2003); H. Neatby, *The Quebec Act: Protest and Policy* (Scarborough, ON: Prentice-Hall of Canada 1972); H.V. Bowen, *Revenue and Reform: The Indian Problem in British Politics, 1757–1773* (Cambridge: Cambridge University Press 1991), 93–4, 99–101, 164–5, 179–80; and Clause XIV, 'North's Regulating Act, 1773,' in P.J. Marshall, *Problems of Empire: Britain and India, 1757–1813* (London: Allen and Unwin 1968), 152–3.

4 At various times the Privy Council and Parliament had tried to repeal colonial charters; see P.S. Haffenden, 'The Crown and the Colonial Charters, 1675–1688,' *William and Mary Quarterly* 3rd ser., 15 (1958): 29–311, 452–66; and J.H. Smith, *Appeals to the Privy Council from the American Plantations* (New York: Columbia University Press 1950), 138–9, 147–51.

5 J.P. Greene, 'Empire and Identity from the Glorious Revolution to the American Revolution,' in *The Oxford History of the British Empire*, vol. 2, *The Eighteenth Century*, ed. P.J. Marshall (Oxford: University of Oxford Press 1998), 208, 209.

6 L.W. Labaree, ed., *Royal Instructions to British Colonial Governors, 1670–1776*, 2 vols. (New York: Octagon Books, Inc. 1967), 1:289–343.

7 J.H. Smith, 'Administrative Control of the Courts of the American Plantation,' *Columbia Law Review* 61 (1961): 1210–1253.

8 J.P. Greene, 'Negotiated Authorities: The Problem of Governance in the Extended Polities of the Early Modern Atlantic World,' in Greene, *Negotiated Authorities: Essays on Colonial Political and Constitutional History* (Charlottesville: University Press of Virginia 1994).

9 For a sense of the legal diversity that overseas expansion engendered, see W.M. Offutt, 'The Atlantic Rules: The Legalistic Turn in Colonial British America,' in E. Mancke and C. Shammas, eds., *The Creation of the British Atlantic World* (Baltimore: Johns Hopkins University Press, forthcoming); K. Roberts-Wray, *Commonwealth and Colonial Law* (New York: Frederick A. Praeger, Publishers 1966), 691–913; and L. Benton, *Law and Colonial Cultures: Legal Regimes in World History, 1400–1900* (Cambridge: Cambridge University Press, 2002).

10 One of the important issues that this essay cannot address is the tension

between British law, which people believed could be transplanted anywhere, and the legal systems of indigenous and conquered peoples, whether Bengalis in India or Canadians in North America, which were treated as place-specific.

11 Smith, *Appeals to the Privy Council, passim.*

12 Royal proclamations, such as the Proclamation of 1763, constitute another way to extend rights overseas. In the modern British Empire, orders-in-council were frequently used.

13 The major exception was cases arising in Newfoundland in the seventeenth century, which were tried back in the West Country courts. See R.G. Lounsbury, *The British Fishery at Newfoundland 1634–1763* (New Haven, CT: Yale University Press 1934), 55–91.

14 D.T. Konig, 'The Virgin and the Virgin's Sister: Virginia, Massachusetts, and the Contested Legacy of Colonial Law,' in R.K. Osgood, ed., *The History of the Law in Massachusetts: The Supreme Judicial Court 1692–1992* (Boston: Supreme Judicial Court Historical Society 1992), 83–4, quotation at 84.

15 Smith, *Appeals to the Privy Council*, 45–9, 54–63.

16 J. Goebel, *The History of the Supreme Court of the United States*, vol. 1, *Antecedents and Beginnings to 1801* (New York: Macmillan 1971), 13–15.

17 Smith, *Appeals to the Privy Council*, 51–3.

18 C. Tomlins, 'Law's Empire: Chartering English Colonies on the American Mainland in the Seventeenth Century,' in D. Kirkby and C. Coleborne, eds., *Law, History, Colonialism: The Reach of Empire* (Manchester: Manchester University Press 2001).

19 J.P. Greene, *Peripheries and Center: Constitutional Development in the Extended Polities of the British Empire and the United States, 1607–1788* (Athens: University of Georgia Press 1986).

20 Goebel, *History of the Supreme Court*, 11–15.

21 The elevation of the Crown-in-Parliament probably was a consequence of the redistribution of power between the Ministry and Parliament relative to overseas governance; see E. Mancke, 'Empire and State,' in D. Armitage and M.J. Braddick, eds., *The British Atlantic World* (New York: Palgrave 2002).

22 The Board of Trade was directly under the Secretary of State for the Southern Department, the brief for whom included foreign policy with 'southern' European powers, particularly France and Spain. That chain of command reflects the ambiguity over the status of overseas territories, whether they were 'foreign' or 'domestic.' In 1762 responsibilities for the colonies was delegated to a newly created office of Secretary of State for the Colonies.

23 Offutt, 'The Atlantic Rules.'
24 Smith, *Appeals to the Privy Council*, 3–5, 71–7; and Goebel, *History of the Supreme Court*, quotation on 36–7. After the Union of the Kingdoms in 1707, a few other jurisdictions, such as the Isle of Man, also appealed cases through the Privy Council.
25 Smith, *Appeals to the Privy Council*, 138–77.
26 On the importance of administrative developments in the late seventeenth and early eighteenth century in defining a second pattern of imperial governance in the British world see E. Mancke, 'Another British America: A Canadian Model for the Early Modern British Empire,' *Journal of Imperial and Commonwealth History* 25 (1997): 1–36, and 'Early Modern Imperial Governance and the Origins of Canadian Political Culture,' *Canadian Journal of Political Science/Revue canadienne de science politique* 32 (1999): 3–20.
27 In Nova Scotia the Governor and Council served as the Court of Errors, Chancery Court, and Court of Marriage and Divorce. Until the 1830s, judges served on the Council and hence also served on these courts. See Cahill and Phillips, this volume.
28 T.G. Barnes, '"The Dayly Cry for Justice": The Juridical Failure of the Annapolis Regime, 1713–1749,' in Girard and Phillips, *Essays*.
29 Townsend, 'Historical Account of the Courts of Judicature,' 64–5, quotation at 64; and Cahill and Phillips, this volume.
30 L.W. Labaree, *Royal Government in America: A Study of the British Colonial System Before 1783* (New Haven: Yale University Press 1930), 380–6.
31 See Cahill and Phillips, this volume.
32 See, e.g., D.G. Bell, 'Maritime Legal Institutions under the *Ancien Régime*, 1710–1850,' *Manitoba Law Journal* 23 (1996): 108–9.
33 Mandamus for Ch. J. Belcher, 1 July 1754, in Townsend, 'Historical Account of the Courts of Judicature,' 92–3.
34 J.B. Cahill, 'James Monk's "Observations on the Courts of Law in Nova Scotia", 1775,' *University of New Brunswick Law Journal* 36 (1987): 136–7.
35 On the impact of Loyalist lawyers in Nova Scotia, see Cahill and Phillips, this volume.
36 J. Phillips, '"Securing Obedience to Necessary Laws": The Criminal Law in Eighteenth-Century Nova Scotia,' *Nova Scotia Historical Review* 12 (1992): 98–102, quotation on 102. On reception of the law, see D.G. Bell, 'A Note on the Reception of English Statutes in New Brunswick,' *University of New Brunswick Law Journal* 28 (1979): 195–201; D.G. Bell, 'The Reception Question and the Constitutional Crisis of the 1790's in New Brunswick,' ibid. 29 (1980): 157–72; and B. Cahill, '"How far English laws are in force here":

Nova Scotia's First Century of Reception Law Jurisprudence,' ibid. 42 (1993): 113–53.

37 'Establishment of the House of Assembly of Nova Scotia, 1758,' *Report*, Public Archives of Nova Scotia, 1956 (Halifax, Public Archives of Nova Scotia 1957), 15-71; quotations at 17, 22. The best narrative of the struggle is C.B. Fergusson, *The Origin of Representative Government in Canada* (Halifax: Committee on Bicentenary of Representative Government 1958), 22–47.

38 Board of Trade to Belcher, 12 Dec. 1760, CO 218, vol. 6, 2–4.

39 Greene, *Peripheries and Center*, 47–54, 72–3, 124–8, 142–3.

40 J.B. Brebner, 'Nova Scotia's Remedy for the American Revolution,' *Canadian Historical Review* 15 (1934): 171–82 quotations on 175, 176, and 177.

41 Ibid., quotations at 178.

42 Ibid., quotations at 178, 179, and 180.

43 See Cahill and Phillips, this volume.

44 D.G. Bell, 'A Perspective on Legal Pluralism in 19th-Century New Brunswick,' *University of New Brunswick Law Journal* 37 (1988): 88–9.

45 A. Porter, 'Trusteeship, Anti-Slavery, and Humanitarianism,' in Porter, ed., *The Oxford History of the British Empire*, vol. 3, *The Nineteenth Century* (Oxford: Oxford University Press 1999), 198–221.

46 J.B. Cahill, 'Slavery and the Judges of Loyalist Nova Scotia,' *University of New Brunswick Law Journal* 43 (1994): 73–127, quotation at 76; and D.G. Bell, 'Slavery and the Judges of Loyalist New Brunswick,' ibid. 29 (1980): 9–42.

47 Cahill, 'Slavery and the Judges,' 125–6.

PART II

Overviews

4

The Supreme Court of Nova Scotia: Origins to Confederation

BARRY CAHILL AND JIM PHILLIPS

Introduction

In welcoming the news that London had agreed to establish what would become the Nova Scotia Supreme Court, and pay for an experienced barrister to preside over it, the colony's administrator, and soon to be Lieutenant Governor, Charles Lawrence was confident that the measure would both 'prevent the frivolous litigations that have hitherto subsisted' and 'lay a solid foundation for that concord and tranquillity that is so necessary to the well-being of this infant settlement.'[1] In this succinct appraisal Lawrence recognized that the court would play two major roles in the young colony. It would adjudicate disputes according to English law in a more professional manner than was possible with the non–legally trained judges who had hitherto presided in the colony's courts. At the same time, Lawrence saw an intimate link between the court and the establishment and maintenance of Nova Scotia's place as a loyal colony within the Empire. It was to be a highly visible manifestation, and a crucial bulwark, of royal authority.

The dual roles suggested by Lawrence form the two principal themes of this survey of the history of the court from its establishment in 1754 to Confederation. It includes an account of the institutional history – jurisdiction, personnel, administrative organization, and workload. Here a major theme is professionalization, including attempts to ensure that judges were drawn from the bar and to separate them from other branches of government. At the same time we have written a political history of the court, exploring the various overt and ideological roles it played in provincial politics and government. These two histories, the institutional and the political, are not separate; indeed they are often intimately linked. The attempted impeachment of two of the judges in the early 1790s, for example, was both a professional 'turf war' between sophisticated and experienced barristers from the southern colonies and the indigenous bench and bar, and part of a wider campaign by Loyalist newcomers to establish their place in the colonial power structure.

We have divided our account into three periods. The first takes us from the founding of the court in 1754 to the appointment of Sampson Salter Blowers as chief justice in 1797. It covers the court's establishment as a true provincial, rather than a Halifax, court, and the greatest crisis in its early history, the near removal of two of its judges following charges of incompetence and partiality. The second period takes us to 1848, the year in which Nova Scotia achieved responsible government and, more importantly for our purposes, in which all the Supreme Court judges became formally independent, the chief justice as well as the assistant judges holding their offices thereafter 'on good behaviour.' Here institutional themes – the expansion of the circuit system, the substantial abolition of the inferior courts, increases in the number of judges, and professionalisation of the judiciary – play a larger role than political ones, unlike the first half-century. Political issues were not absent, however, for this period also saw a long and successful campaign to separate the judges entirely from the two other branches of government. Our third period takes us from 1848 to Confederation, and here we are principally concerned with the politics of judicial appointments after responsible government and the transfer of equity jurisdiction to the NSSC.

Founding and Colonial Infancy, 1754–1797

The Establishment of the Supreme Court

For the first five years after the establishment of Halifax in 1749 the colony's highest court was the General Court.[2] Staffed by the governor and his Council, none of whom was legally trained, it had jurisdiction over all criminal matters, including capital cases, and served as an appeal court in civil litigation where the amount in dispute was over three hundred pounds. The appointment of a qualified barrister as chief justice and the concomitant establishment of the Supreme Court separate from the Council was the result of four related concerns.

First, there were complaints in late 1752 about the judges of the Inferior Court of Common Pleas (ICCP), the lower civil court which handled almost all civil cases at first instance. This incident, the 'affair of the justices,' began as a largely personal dispute between Ephraim Cooke, merchant and ship owner, and the ICCP judges but escalated to include accusations that the ICCP bench was applying Massachusetts rather than English law, accusations that revealed and exacerbated the divisions within the colony between settlers from each locale. The dispute was ultimately not about law, or even nationality; it was a vehicle through which merchant groups asserted their power in the young colony. But Governor Peregrine Hopson and his Council, who conducted a long investigation into charges that the ICCP gave 'Countenance and Encouragement' to the use of 'the Laws and Practice of Massachusetts' rather than those of England, were nonetheless persuaded of the need for a court headed by an English-trained professional chief justice.[3]

A second reason for establishment of the NSSC was that by 1753 Hopson seems to have become concerned about the legitimacy of legal decisions made by laymen. Third, Hopson also wanted a source of legal advice on the carrying out of his executive functions. '[W]e much want a lawyer wholly disinterested in the colony to advise in difficult cases,' he told his superiors in asking for the appointments of both a chief justice and an attorney general, people to help 'where our knowledge of law could not be supposed to reach.'[4] Finally, although eighteenth-century Englishmen had a less rigid conception of the separation of powers than later generations, there was some disquiet over having executive and everyday judicial authority vested in the same people.

Each of these concerns was ultimately about the legitimacy and efficacy of government, which required administrative and judicial decision making to be done according to English law, and collectively they are reflected in Charles Lawrence's conviction, quoted above, that a chief justice would augment deference to authority in the new colony. Although initially reluctant because of the expense, the Board of Trade were persuaded by July 1754, and forty-three-year-old Jonathan Belcher Junior was chosen. An expatriate New Englander, he was the son of a governor of Massachusetts who, ironically, had worked to frustrate English settlement in Nova Scotia after Britain had acquired it in the Treaty of Utrecht. Belcher held MAs from both Harvard and Cambridge, had read law at the Middle Temple, and was called to the English and Irish bars. He had practised in both London and Dublin for some twenty years, and although not a great success in court had made a name for himself as a legal scholar by collaborating on an abridgement of the Irish statutes. Though a New Englander by origin, he was an intense Anglophile, a haughty Anglican Tory, and just the man to ensure the supremacy of English law in the nascent settlement.[5]

The new Supreme Court was a creation of the Crown prerogative, not local authority, and in that regard was very much in conformity with the colony's constitution, in which all the major officers of state, from the governor on down, were Crown appointees.[6] Similarly, like all public officials in the colony, and all colonial judges, Belcher held office 'at pleasure,' which meant he was removable for misbehaviour by the local representative of the Crown, unlike English judges who, since the Act of Settlement of 1701, were appointed 'during good behaviour' – not removable except by an address of both houses of Parliament to the Crown. Neither Belcher nor his successors were happy with this, but despite occasional lobbying for change the arrangement persisted until 1848.[7] Belcher's appointment also reflected a common eighteenth-century pattern in which colonial offices were dispensed to the ambitious through a system of patronage; in his case he sought the post, which a friend called 'both Honourable & Profitable,' as much to clear his many debts as for any other reason.[8]

Belcher arrived in Halifax in early October 1754; he was sworn in as a member of the Governor's Council on 14 October, and as chief justice on the 21st, after which he conducted the newly named Supreme Court's first session, Michaelmas Term, 1754.[9] His commission gave the court a limited jurisdiction – 'Supreme Court, Court of Assize, and General Gaol Delivery' – which reflected the fact that it was intended to take over from the General Court as the venue for serious criminal cases.[10] The commission said nothing about civil jurisdiction, but Belcher assumed that as the appeal to Governor and Council was retained for suits worth three hundred pounds or more, his court was to fill the gap between the ICCP and the Governor and Council, constituting an appeal court in civil matters where the amount at stake was less than three hundred pounds, with the ICCP continuing to hear all original civil cases.[11] We will see that this arrangement was altered in 1764, but in its first decade the NSSC's civil jurisdiction was largely limited to oversight of the ICCP; this oversight was accomplished either through the appeal process or by issuing writs of error or of certiorari, by which devices it could ensure the application of English law. In this period the procedure on appeals was that the court would grant a trial de novo with a jury.[12] There were no appeals from the NSSC in criminal cases, although those convicted could petition for a royal pardon.[13]

The court's jurisdiction extended throughout the colony which, after the fall of Louisbourg in 1758, included Cape Breton Island, although the island was a separate colony from 1784 until 1820 with its own Supreme Court. After 1763 it also encompassed what are now Prince Edward Island and New Brunswick; they became separate colonies with their own Supreme Courts in 1769 and 1784 respectively. By local legislation passed from 1758 the NSSC did not have jurisdiction in certain specialised areas – divorce, probate, and escheat.[14] Nor did it exercise jurisdiction in cases traditionally reserved for the Courts of Vice-Admiralty.[15] Most importantly, and as discussed in more detail below, it was a court of common law, with equity jurisdiction residing in a Court of Chancery in which the Governor and Council sat as judges.

The Early Years

The first few years were not easy ones for the NSSC. The first session of the court saw a politically difficult case involving the murder of three naval seamen, one in which Belcher was unable to persuade a jury to come to the result he wanted.[16] Two years later another high-profile and contentious case cast doubt on many of the criminal convictions hitherto recorded in the court. John Young was convicted of treason when Belcher held that a particular English statute was in force in the colony. He did so based on an expansive view of which English laws were received, one no doubt derived in part from his Anglophilia, but was subsequently informed that the Board of Trade's legal advisers disagreed with him. The latter did not, however, make it clear which English statutory penal laws were in force, creating something of a crisis in a colony which had treated almost all such statutes as applicable. The Young case was the likely inspiration for one of the statutes passed by the first Assembly in 1758, which 'ratified and confirmed' all prior 'proceedings, sentences, verdicts and judgments' of the Supreme Court.[17]

There were other problems as well, some personal. Belcher was ever impecunious, the product in part of a spendthrift youth. His salary helped, but the cost of living in Halifax was high and Belcher felt obliged to maintain a certain style as chief justice.[18] During the 1750s Belcher and Lawrence disagreed, at times heatedly, over the issue of an elected Assembly for the colony; Belcher complained that the governor had been unpleasant to him and wanted 'a Chief Justice more subservient to his Measures that I can ever think is consistent with the English Laws & Constitution.'[19] And in the early 1760s Belcher paid little attention to the court because he served as the colony's chief executive for three years, satisfying in some part his long-standing ambition to be appointed governor.[20] While he may have presided over civil appeals during this period, criminal court sessions were held by special commissions of oyer and terminer which usually named judges of the ICCP to preside.[21] Belcher's time as chief executive was not a happy one for the colony, with the result that in 1764 London decreed that the offices of chief justice and head of government should not in future be held by the same man.[22]

The court operated with just one judge until 1764, when two 'assistant' judges, Charles Morris and John Collier, were added. Neither was a lawyer, although both had extensive experience as first justices of the Halifax County ICCP and Collier had been both a judge of the Court of Vice-Admiralty and, as a member of Council from 1752, a judge of the General Court.[23] The new judges were appointed at the behest of the Assembly over Belcher's opposition.[24] The Assembly argued that an increase in personnel would enable the court to sit outside Halifax, and that having more than one judge would make the court 'more conformable to the constitution of the Courts at Westminster.' It also maintained that as the court dealt with 'all matters concerning the life, reputation and ... the property' of inhabitants, a 'trust of so much importance' should not 'depend solely upon the opinion and judgment of any one man, however capable and upright.'[25] Thus institutional demands and broader concerns about political legitimacy played a role in expansion of the bench, and London was happy to accede to the request for more judges, especially as it was not paying for them.[26] But there was likely also a more mundane political consideration; the condescending, intolerant, and politically naive Belcher had made numerous enemies during his years as the colony's chief executive, and many were happy to try to clip his wings by the appointment as assistant judges of two of his Council opponents.[27]

The elevation to the Supreme Court of the current and former first justices of the ICCP brought a major change in the court's jurisdiction. It decided that its commission invested it with the jurisdiction of the three superior courts of common law at Westminster Hall – King's Bench, Common Pleas, and Exchequer – and that as a result it had concurrent jurisdiction in original cases with the ICCP.[28] Even this change had strong political overtones; Belcher's enemies saw it as a way to keep him very busy on the bench and away from politics as much as possible, and thus engineered not just the appointment of assistants but also the expanded jurisdiction. The original civil jurisdiction of the Supreme and Inferior Courts remained unchanged and more or less concurrent until the latter were abolished in 1841.[29] After 1764 the court continued, of course, to act as an appeal court from the ICCPs, but changed the appeal procedure to one more like judicial review, requiring cases to be brought up on a writ of error and 'reversing or affirming ... Judgments upon Matters of Record only.'[30]

Personnel, Status, and Salaries

The assistant judges, like the chief justice, held office 'at pleasure,' which meant that as local appointees they could be removed by the governor, who would then have to justify such a measure to the secretary of state in London.[31] The assistants' status changed in 1789, however, when their appointments became a kind of hybrid – 'at pleasure' and thus removable by the Crown, but also removable on an address of both houses of the local legislature to the lieutenant governor, a parallel but local process to that which was required to remove 'good behaviour' judges in England.[32] In other respects the assistants had an inferior status to their chief justice. Belcher may not have been able to prevent their appointment, but at his behest their commissions prevented them from sitting without him, and according to one contemporary observer he generally treated them and their opinions with contempt.[33] The limitation on the assistants' power was lifted in 1773, when Belcher's declining health made it necessary to hold court without him.[34]

In addition, the assistants were paid much less than the chief justice. The chief's salary was £500 sterling for most of this period, raised to £850 in 1792.[35] The assistants' salaries fluctuated but were never as high as that of the chief, and Governor Parr, for one, thought them too low.[36] Although London initially recommended that the assistants be paid £300 a year, which would 'enable His Majesty to appoint persons properly qualified for such trusts,' they were consistently below that sum before the 1780s. The initial salary was £100, although revenue shortfalls meant that in some years in the 1760s they were paid only £50, and raised to £150 in the 1770s – all figures in local currency. They were raised again to £400 local currency, c. £320 sterling, in 1789, but there is evidence that this was not enough to tempt the best of the local lawyers to take the job.[37] The chief justice also received fees for every suit in addition to his salary, for both Halifax and circuit cases, a substantial augmentation to his salary; the assistants got a much smaller sum in fees.[38]

In addition, unlike the chief justice, the assistants were not paid from the civil list but from annual Assembly appropriations, which meant that before the 1789 statute both set the salary and guaranteed payment salaries fluctuated and were on occasion not paid on time.[39] Although salaries were never actually withheld, perhaps because long-serving judges Deschamps and Brenton had seats in the Assembly while on the bench, it was a concern in some quarters that the judges could be 'dependent upon the smiles of the populous, or the Clamors of a Junto in a turbulent House of Assembly.'[40]

The court's membership stayed at three throughout this period, with a number of the judges serving long terms.[41] Collier sat only until his death in 1769, and was briefly replaced by John Duport, the latter leaving the Court in 1770 when appointed chief justice of the new colony of St John's Island (now Prince Edward Island). Duport was not a lawyer, but he had collaborated on a revision of the Nova Scotia statutes and was probably a justice of the peace (JP) in England. His replacement, Isaac Deschamps, was entirely uneducated in the law, although he had experience as an ICCP judge for King's County and (very briefly) had been first justice of the St John's Island ICCP. When Belcher died in March 1776 after nearly twenty-two years as chief justice, his replacement, Irish barrrister Bryan Finucane, although appointed in 1776 did not arrive until 1778, and thus for two years the only two judges in situ, Deschamps and acting Chief Justice Morris, were men without legal training. Finucane served until his death in 1785, without great distinction as a jurist for he was more interested in courtiership and high living. After he died it took three years to get a replacement – another British import, Jeremy Pemberton, one of the Loyalist Claims Commissioners. Pemberton arrived in July 1788, officiated at the Michaelmas Term that year, and left in December.[42]

During the later 1780s therefore Deschamps and former attorney general James Brenton, appointed in 1781 after the death of Morris, carried the load, and became embroiled in a bitter dispute with a coterie of new Loyalist lawyers from the former colonies to the south, a dispute that resulted in attempts to impeach both judges. This episode is discussed in more detail below, and was perhaps the lowest period in the court's early history. It ended only when thirty-four-year-old Thomas (later Sir Thomas) A.L. Strange, of Lincoln's Inn, arrived in 1790 to take the chief justice's position. Strange had hardly any experience, and like others before him he obtained the post through patronage and connections; his father was England's best-known engraver and his mother probably a mistress of Lord Chief Justice Mansfield.[43]

Strange was the NSSC's fourth chief justice, and all four were outsiders, reflecting a preference for men without local connections and biases and, probably, a sense that the local bar could not produce men of sufficient stature. As late as the 1790s it was the general view in London that the chief justice should be an English or Irish lawyer.[44] Lieutenant Governor John Parr, struggling in 1787 with the deteriorating relations between bench and bar, thought the colony 'disagreeably circumstanced ... from not having a Chief Justice appointed,' and pleaded for one. He would have been happy with Attorney General Sampson Salter Blowers, but was equally adamant that Stephen DeLancey, a Loyalist New York lawyer, was a 'provincial Lt. Col.' who had 'not one of the ... requisites' for the 'important office.'[45] The pattern of appointments also meant that Nova Scotia's eighteenth-century chief justices were relatively young – Belcher was forty-three and Finucane thirty-nine on appointment.

While all assistant judges were local men, the first 'local' chief justice was Blowers, elevated from the attorney generalship in 1797; he had been in the colony since the Loyalist exodus of 1783. Serving under Blowers initially were Deschamps, who stayed on the court a total of thirty-one years until his death in 1801, and Brenton, who served twenty-five years until his death in 1806. With just three judges throughout this period the court was probably consistently understaffed; as we shall see, there were constant difficulties in manning the circuits. In comparison, the New Brunswick Supreme Court had four judges from its founding in 1784, while that of the much less populous Prince Edward Island had three from the late eighteenth century.[46]

Deschamps was the last man appointed without legal training, although when a possible fourth judge was discussed in the mid-1790s Loyalist clergyman Isaac Wilkins, first justice of the Shelburne County ICCP, was a serious candidate.[47] The idea that a fully professional bench was necessary was slow to take root in both London and Halifax. The committee of the Privy Council that found for judges Deschamps and Brenton in the impeachment crisis of the early 1790s opined that while it was 'always to be wished that the Office of Judge should be conferred on Men of sufficient Learning in the Law,' and while the chief justice should always be a lawyer, there was nothing wrong with lay assistant judges provided they were 'Men of Understanding.'[48]

The Supreme Court and Politics

To the extent that there was a judicial qualification for much of this period, reflecting a Baconian conception of judges as loyal servants to their political masters, it resided in the judges' political suitability. Solicitor General Richard John Uniacke was considered unsuitable for judicial appointment in the 1790s because he had been arrested on suspicion of treason in 1776 and his mentor Finucane was long dead.[49] The links between judges and government were close and constant, as they were in eighteenth-century England where two occupied Cabinet positions. All chief justices were automatically members and presidents of the Council, taking precedence next to the lieutenant governor, and four of the assistants were also councillors – Collier (1752–1769), Morris (from 1755 until his death in 1781), Brenton (from 1799), and Deschamps (from 1783). Blowers was elevated to that body in 1788, nine years before he became chief justice. Brenton and Deschamps were also at various times members of the House of Assembly (MHAs) while sitting on the bench, the former representing Halifax County until 1785 and the latter being the member for Newport Township for thirteen years after his appointment to the bench; he also served as clerk of the Assembly during that same period, and was closely tied to the powerful Mauger interest in Nova Scotia politics. Blowers had been an MHA and Speaker of the House until his appointment to Council in 1788. For many of the judges a place on the bench was but one post in a long line of office-holding: Morris was also the colony's first surveyor-general, Deschamps had been overseer of Indian Affairs, Duport had been secretary of the Council, and Brenton and Blowers were both attorney general. The lay judges – Morris, Duport, and Deschamps – were senior ICCP justices at a time when appointment to that court was reserved for senior bureaucrats and others with the right political connections and attitudes.

The judges were at the centre of politics; as elsewhere, they 'were viewed by London as key players in colonial governance and administration.'[50] Although only Belcher served as chief executive, others' presence on the Council made them key advisers. Judges were used for commissions of inquiry and as government emissaries.[51] They were drafters and revisers of legislation as well as its interpreters, and the principal legal advisers to government, playing the role that we more usually associate with Crown law officers.[52] And in this period few objections were made to this lack of separation. A 1782 attempt by Assemblyman Dr. John Phillips to have judges barred from sitting as members of the House was the only one of its kind, and it failed.[53] Belcher's disputes with other local leaders, and the judges' affair, discussed below, aside, none of the judges, in this period or later, precipitated serious conflict with the colony's power elite, as occasionally happened elsewhere in the Empire.[54] It was perhaps a desire to avoid such open conflict that led them to undermine, but never seek to judicially abolish, the institution of slavery in the colony. In both this period and the early nineteenth century the judges were 'emancipationist rather than abolitionist,' consistently preventing owners asserting their property rights in litigation over individual alleged slaves but never denying the institution itself.[55]

More generally, but no less importantly, the Supreme Court and its judges had a crucial ideological role to play, as the symbol and the representatives of both the law and royal authority in a world where the prevailing Tory ideology conflated the two. In England the majesty, as Douglas Hay has termed it, of the court's formalities played an important role in persuading people of the power of the law and the concomitant need to defer to authority. Events such as the assize sermon and the public procession at the opening of the term, and symbols like the scarlet robes, the wigs, and black cap expressed the power of the law. The grand jury address and the awe-inspiring sentencing speech for capital convicts provided more overt opportunities for lectures on deference to authority.[56] Much of this was replicated in the colony, and court meetings were also used for the reading of proclamations, such as the declaration of martial law in 1775.[57] The need for the 'force and terrors of the laws' as necessary bulwarks of royal authority were acknowledged in a 1768 statute increasing the number of court sittings; to similar effect, special sessions were held to deal in exemplary fashion with notorious crimes.[58]

No area of the criminal law so obviously manifested the power of the law, and the court that enforced it, as the capital sentence, available for murder, rape, treason, and a variety of property crimes in this period.[59] Belcher's first one was handed down two years into his tenure, at the Michaelmas Term of the court in 1756, although both of the two men sentenced that term were pardoned. While a little more than half of those similarly sentenced by the NSSC in this period likewise escaped the gallows, forty or so men and women were hanged.[60] The custom was to have the execution take place as near as possible to the site of the crime, as the execution was to serve as a grisly warning to others. Hence Cornelius Driscoll and David Lawlor were dispatched at Dartmouth in 1765, their bodies left hanging on the gibbet for some time after death, and Peter Manning was hanged at Horton on a specially constructed gallows, the executioner travelling there from Halifax.[61] But most executions took place in Halifax, and the few reports we have of these events often stressed the warnings they represented. When John Cox and Nathaniel Crew were executed in Halifax in 1779, for rape and burglary respectively, they were apparently 'sensible of the Justice of their Sentences,' acknowledged their guilt, blamed their crimes on 'Spirituous Liquor and bad company,' and 'earnestly exhorted the Spectators' to eschew both.[62]

Despite the close ties between court and government there were few occasions on which the latter appear to have tried to influence decisions. One was the 1775 trial of Jonathan Binney for money owed to government from Binney's position as a collector of customs revenue; Governor Legge not only played the leading role in hand-picking a special jury, he also attended the trial. His actions caused a furore, contributed to his already considerable unpopularity, and may well have been the impetus for an Assembly demand that judges be Englishmen appointed in England and that they enjoy tenure during good behaviour.[63] But concerns about a governor's influence on the judicial process were unusual; generally, as David Bell has pointed out, the judges were free from direct government interference, perhaps precisely because they were so intimate a part of the colonial administration.[64] Nonetheless, if government rarely tried to influence particular cases, the links between law and politics were a feature of the court's early history. No two aspects of that history exemplify those complicated links better than the decision to introduce a circuit system and the impeachment crisis of the late 1780s and early 1790s.

Law and Authority in the Hinterland: The Circuit System

Before the passage of the 1774 Supreme Court Circuit Act,[65] the court sat only in the capital, venturing outside very occasionally for serious criminal cases on special commissions of oyer and terminer. While the lack of circuits caused little problem in the very early years of the colony, the only other substantial settlements being Lunenburg, Annapolis Royal (the old capital), and Windsor, the influx of settlers after 1759 to occupy the vacated Acadian lands and other areas created an increasing need for the court to travel. On the civil side, although the creation of new townships, districts, or counties was always followed by the establishment of ICCPs, some litigants preferred to sue in the Supreme Court, and that meant substantial expense and delay in getting the case heard in Halifax. In addition, appeals were only heard in the capital. On the criminal side county Courts of Sessions, in which non–legally trained JPs presided, were simply inappropriate venues for trying capital cases. The problem was dealt with for criminal cases on an ad hoc basis, occasionally by adjourning the court to the locality, more often by issuing special commissions of oyer and terminer and general delivery naming either one of the assistant judges or the attorney general to preside.[66] A third expedient was to bring defendants and witnesses to Halifax, thus trying them outside the community in which the offence had been committed. This departure from principle was permitted by a 1768 statute, although only for crimes committed in places not reachable from Halifax other than by a sea passage. London accepted the statute as one 'suited to the present condition of the province,' but did not consider it a particularly desirable measure.[67]

The introduction of a circuit system was thus in part an administrative solution to a problem of colonial governance. The 1774 Act referred to the expense of individuals litigating in the capital, and to the costs to government of conveying all those involved in a criminal case to Halifax. But the circuits were brought in for more broadly political reasons as well. In England the assizes 'were a formidable spectacle in a country town, the most visible and elaborate manifestation of state power to be seen in the countryside,'[68] and the NSSC on circuit was intended to replicate them. James Monk, solicitor general in 1774 and an impassioned advocate of the circuit system, saw the county ICCPs as fora in which popular orators could declaim about 'Equity, Liberty and Constitutional Justice' at a time when agitation in more southerly colonies was building towards the momentous events of 1775–6. The NSSC would provide a counterweight, with the judges – men of 'knowledge, Wisdom and *attachment to the Crown*' – evoking 'a degree of dignity and Authority that would overawe, punish and prevent any tumultary meetings'; court sittings in the scattered out-settlements would 'keep the Clamorous and disaffected in quietude, duty and subordination.'[69]

The circuit system introduced in the mid-1770s was limited initially to the three most populous counties – Annapolis, Kings, and Cumberland. Hants was added in 1781 when it became a separate county from Kings, but the rest of the colony was not included in the circuit until the nineteenth century.[70] In 1794, however, ad hoc arrangements were made for the South Shore (Lunenburg, Queens, and Shelburne counties) and for Sydney County to the east, when courts of nisi prius were established, to consist of one NSSC judge and one or more local JPs. For civil business only, they were a response to population increases in areas where 'there are not roads practicable to the Supreme Court' and they were intended as a limited term measure of three–four years' duration.[71]

Replicating the English assizes, circuits were bi-annual (becoming annual for Cumberland only in 1783), the court travelling outside Halifax between terms, and each involved two judges – again a mirroring of English practice – although the chief justice was not required to go. The time taken to expand the circuits was the product of both the general inadequacy of the road system and a shortage of judges.[72] Not only was it at times difficult, with no more than three judges, to staff the circuits, there were often only two in situ and, more seriously, the chief justices prior to Strange – Belcher, Finucane, and Pemberton – refused to travel. One result was that special commissions continued to be used regularly for the trial of serious crimes outside Halifax, with some naming persons other than a Supreme Court judge to preside.[73]

The absence of the chief justice prior to the 1790s must have reduced the effectiveness of the circuit as a political device, but the idea that an itinerant royal court served an important political end continued to have much currency. At century's end Lieutenant Governor Sir John Wentworth, pushing for an expanded circuit, asserted that '[i]t is of great importance that the Supreme Court should sit in the remote districts, as it makes great impression on the minds of the people.' A few years later, commenting favourably on an Act to expand the circuit, he repeated his belief that it 'impresses the minds of the people with deference to the laws.'[74] We cannot, of course, know the extent to which the court fulfilled this role in practice, especially when circuit travel was often far from pleasant or dignified and hardly exemplified ceremonial majesty. One lawyer who travelled the circuit in the early nineteenth century recalled having to 'rough it,' and court parties would at times arrive exhausted, bedraggled, and late.[75] But it is nonetheless significant that throughout this period the colony's elite continued to see the circuit not only as an administrative device for settling disputes in local communities, but also as a potent force for political orthodoxy.

The Judges' Affair

Personal, political, and professional disputes lay behind the most traumatic episode of the NSSC's first forty years, the near impeachment of two of its judges.[76] The roots of the crisis can be found in the northeastward migration from 1776 of a coterie of experienced and able Loyalist lawyers. It included men like Sampson Salter Blowers, who became attorney general in 1785 and chief justice in 1797, and Foster Hutchinson, brother of the last royal governor of Massachusetts, a Harvard graduate, former Superior Court judge, and father and namesake of a future NSSC judge. Of greatest importance to this story were Jonathan Sterns and William Taylor. Sterns was a Harvard graduate who had fought on the Loyalist side and spent much of the war in New York as judge advocate to the British forces; Taylor was a New Jersey lawyer and 'a man of reputation in his profession.'[77]

Men like these probably outnumbered the small Nova Scotia bar of the early 1780s, and they certainly had more experience and better qualifications than the indigenous lawyers. They competed for the limited amount of legal work available and sought official preferment, but some met with more success than others. Sterns quickly became one of the busiest lawyers in Halifax, specializing in Vice-Admiralty cases; from 1783 he appears as counsel for the claimant in every case but one that was tried in that court, and he also had a civil and criminal practice in the Supreme Court.[78] But he failed in a bid to become clerk of the House of Assembly and was defeated when he stood to become the Halifax County representative in 1788. Unlike Blowers, he did not have influential patrons like Sir William Pepperrell, the Massachusetts baronet domiciled in London. Taylor was admitted to the Nova Scotia bar in 1785, and practised both in Halifax and on the circuit, but, perhaps because he was a relative latecomer among the Loyalists, much less successfully than Sterns. In 1787 he petitioned the Loyalist Claims Commission for a continuation of his allowance, noting that he had not been able 'to advance himself in the practice of the Law' because 'the little Law business of a New Country' was 'crowded with Gentlemen of the Bar, most of whom are among their friends and connections, and are established in business.'[79]

Tensions between the Loyalist lawyers and the assistant judges of the Supreme Court were quickly manifested, exacerbated by Finucane's absences in Ireland and on the Saint John river, where he had been sent by Governor Parr to mediate disputes among the Loyalists newly settled there. Those tensions increased after Finucane's death in 1785; for the next five years, with the exception of the one term in which Pemberton sat, Deschamps was acting chief justice. Sterns and others, who thought themselves better educated and more knowledgeable than the judges, were quick to criticize Deschamps, by now not only a lay judge but also an elderly one. Brenton, though an experienced lawyer and a former law officer of the Crown, also came in for his share of adverse comment. Criticisms of rulings and judgments were made in court and out of it, and were joined by suggestions that the judges were not only ignorant of law and practice but also partial to litigants depending on their connections. In particular, it was increasingly alleged that Loyalists represented by Loyalist lawyers stood little chance against old inhabitants.

The judges reacted with an asperity heightened by their sense that juries were showing them increasingly less deference as well. The gathering crisis is captured well in the judges' later comment on the Easter 1787 term of the court: 'the Conduct and behaviour of Mr Sterns during this Term towards the Court had been so glaringly indecent in address and language that they were frequently tempted to proceed to measures of severity with him, that the Order and Dignity of the Court might be preserved ... [T]he Stile and manner of his controverting the Opinion of the Ch. Justice as so rude and disrespectfull that the Ch. Justice [Deschamps] was under the necessity of ordering him to set down and be Silent. The bold Attacks this practitioner had repeatedly made upon the Authority of the Court would have justified us in the Eyes of an Astonished Public, if we had Suspended him from all further practice.'[80] It was in this context that Parr pleaded with London for a replacement for Finucane, an 'able impartial Chief Justice' who would 'keep up the dignity of the Bench,' a man of sufficient status 'to protect him from the abuse and Browbeating of a Tribe of Lawyers from the United States.'[81]

Matters became worse as other lawyers also began to complain about decisions rendered against the law and the evidence, and jurors lent their voices to the tide of criticism. Unsuccessful litigants were emboldened to complain to their MHAs and this, plus the fact that some of the complaining lawyers were also Assembly members, led to the judges' conduct being discussed in the Assembly. Brenton and Deschamps were, by late 1787, under siege, not just as allegedly incompetent and partial jurists but also as symbols of the indigenous office-holding class which the Loyalists wanted to supplant. There is not space here to analyse the extent to which the complaints were well-founded, although in at least one case the judges' decision is difficult to account for by anything but partiality and/or incompetence.[82] What matters is that by November 1787 concern was widespread, and the result was a resolution, moved by Thomas Millidge, Loyalist MHA for Digby Township, that 'Dissatisfactions having prevailed in the Province relative to the Administration of Justice in the Supreme Court' the House should conduct an investigation.[83] The motion passed unanimously.

The Assembly investigation resulted in an address to Lieutenant Governor Parr asking that he inquire into the conduct of the judges. Parr was reluctant, for he supported the judges and was generally hostile to the new Loyalist interest in the colony, but he did submit the matter to his Council (of which Deschamps was a member), although not before getting a reply from the judges and appointing Attorney General Blowers to the Council. A private critic of the judges, Blowers had no intention of spoiling his own chances for preferment by acting against established authority. In February 1788 the Council 'cleared' the judges of charges of both incompetence and partiality and labelled the Assembly's allegations 'groundless & Scandalous.'[84]

The matter did not end there, however, and Parr's attempt to dismiss, and label as close to seditious, the complaints against the judges exacerbated existing tensions between Council and Assembly and between the old establishment and the Loyalists. A war of words erupted in the press, Sterns and Taylor published a long account of their complaints with supporting documents, and Parr's response to his increasingly bellicose opposition was not to recall the Assembly, prorogued just after it had submitted its address against the judges in December 1787, until March 1789. The judges hit back also, disbarring Sterns and Taylor for contempt of court on account of letters published in the newspapers. Disbarment from the NSSC was followed shortly afterwards by a similar prohibition from appearing before the Council, which cut them off from appeal and Chancery work as well. This was a tactical error, for it left the two lawyers with nothing to do but rouse public support, and gave them a cause with which to do so. Petitions on their behalf were sent to Parr from Halifax and other localities. When this effort failed, they took their case for reinstatement to London, where it was rejected.

The Loyalist opposition in the Assembly, however, maintained their agitation against the judges in 1789 and early 1790. Opinion swung in the opponents' direction following two high-profile criminal cases in mid-1789 in which the judges appeared to act with partiality,[85] and with Sterns back in the colony in 1790 to organize a campaign events moved rapidly when the Assembly met in February 1790. Thirteen draft 'articles of impeachment' accusing Deschamps and Brenton of 'high crimes and misdemeanours' were passed by the House in March, with many non-Loyalist members joining the newcomers. Between them the articles cited sixteen cases in which it was alleged that the judges acted either in ignorance of the law or with partiality, or both. After many days of hearing witnesses, in April the House formally passed seven articles of impeachment, consolidating some of the original thirteen but also eliminating three in which the evidence was not considered sufficient. The articles not only concerned cases; they also flatly accused the judges of lying when they had replied to the Council in answer to the Assembly's original request for an investigation in December 1787.

The charges were sent to London with a request that the judges be dismissed; locally the Assembly also asked that they be suspended pending that dismissal, but this Parr refused to do. The Privy Council heard the case for four days early in 1792, and in a report issued five months later cleared the judges of all charges and excoriated their detractors. Long before the Committee of the Privy Council rendered its decision Thomas Strange had arrived and taken measures to reduce local tension. He treated his fellow judges with respect, but also effected Sterns's readmission to practice. He conducted an informal inquiry of his own into the affair, and was in England on leave when the Privy Council met to consider the case; he likely threw his weight behind his colleagues.

While the judges' affair was ultimately a victory for Brenton and Deschamps, and while part of the motivation for the impeachment lay in the power struggles between old and new settlers and Assembly and Council, it was a landmark event in the court's history. Dissatisfaction with the judges was widespread in the late 1780s, voiced not only by Loyalist lawyers but also by many in the Assembly and out of it who had no connection to them. There were serious questions about the competence of Deschamps in particular, and although he remained on the bench until his death in 1801 he had lost much of his authority and all of his hitherto considerable prestige. The Loyalist lawyers had forced themselves to the forefront of Nova Scotian politics and law. Sterns returned to his practice, became an MHA for Halifax County in

1793, and in 1797 was named solicitor general. Thomas Barclay, the Annapolis lawyer who had led the fight for the impeachment in the House, became speaker in 1793. And when the chief justiceship became vacant a few years later, it was Attorney General Blowers, a Loyalist, albeit one who had supported the judges, who succeeded to it.

Jurisdiction, Institutional Organization, and Caseload

Before the introduction of circuits in the mid-1770s the court met in regular term only in Halifax. From 1754 until 1768 it met for only two terms, Easter (April-May) and Michaelmas (October-November); the Hilary (January-February) and Trinity (July) terms were added in the latter year, as a response to the increased caseload which followed the assumption of original civil jurisdiction four years earlier.[86] Hilary Term was eliminated in 1780, ostensibly because grand and petit jurors found it very inconvenient to attend so often, but in truth because it interfered with Finucane's social life and, perhaps, because the chief justice did not care for the cold weather.[87] In Nova Scotia grand jurors were called for a year, and thus had to attend all four sessions.[88] Hilary Term was reinstated in 1796, with the injunction that jurors were not required to attend unless specially ordered. It seems likely, therefore, that the term was intended to be used for appeal cases only, although since criminal trials with juries were held in most Hilary Terms after 1798 this intention was not always carried out.[89] In the 1760s Halifax terms lasted thirteen to fifteen days, although they could be as long as twenty-one, but they dropped to nine to eleven after the move to four annual terms, although again there was quite a broad range, from five to as many as twenty-eight days. The tewnty-eight-day term in Michaelmas 1772, and a twenty-three-day session in Hilary Term 1773, may have been the cause for a 1774 statute which limited sitting days to fourteen; in no term thereafter in this period did the court sit for more than twelve days, despite the fourteen-day restriction being removed in 1793.[90] When the court went on circuit sitting days in the out-settlements were strictly limited.

The administrative business of the court was organized by the prothonotary and clerk of the Crown, the name given to the chief clerk of the Courts of King's Bench and Common Pleas in England. Holders of the office in this period included lawyers John Kerr in the 1750s and James Monk Junior from the mid-1760s until he secured the post of solicitor general in 1772. From 1787 until 1834 the post was held by

William Thomson, who was largely absent from the colony, the work being done by deputies. The prothonotary of the court in Halifax held the same office for the entire colony, with the duties performed for each county by deputies; the deputies were appointed by the prothonotary and paid one-third of their fees to him. The prothonotary was paid a salary for his Halifax work in criminal cases, and remunerated by fees for civil ones.[91] In addition to performing all the necessary administrative tasks, the prothonotary acted as clerk of the Crown in criminal cases, impanelling and swearing juries, swearing witnesses, arraigning prisoners, recording verdicts, and so forth.[92]

Discussion of the court's caseload requires a brief review of its relationship to the colony's inferior courts, whose jurisdiction was limited to the county, district, or township. The lower criminal court was the Sessions of the Peace, with JPs as judges. The sessions, with its grand jury, was also the local administrative body. In Halifax it met quarterly, like its English counterpart, in other counties less often, usually semi-annually. On the civil side a short-lived County Court gave way in 1752 to the ICCP, also staffed by JPs, and meeting at the same times as the sessions. All JPs 'of the quorum' were entitled to sit as judges when the sessions court met, but the county ICCPs were constituted by commissions which named just five of the JPs. As new counties, townships, and districts were created through the second half of the eighteenth century new courts and sessions and common pleas were established; some large counties, such as Halifax, were divided into districts and district courts created.[93]

In criminal cases the jurisdiction of the NSSC and the sessions was theoretically almost coterminous, but for a couple of centuries the practice in most of England had been for all serious cases, certainly all capital cases, to be heard by the royal judges, and the same demarcation was followed in Nova Scotia. Trials for capital offences – principally murder, rape, burglary, robbery, and capital larceny – were conducted in the Supreme Court before juries, as were trials for a number of other offences, principally assaults and non-capital larcenies.[94] For these less serious offences jurisdiction was shared with the sessions. By the late eighteenth century petty larcenies were mostly heard in the sessions, not the Supreme Court, and an effective if informal line seems to have been drawn in assault cases, with those considered more serious because of the severity of the injury or because they involved attacks on peace officers tried in the Supreme Court, and the remainder tried in sessions. Prosecution rates fluctuated in this period, at times quite dramatically, but on average the Supreme Court heard fourteen to fifteen serious criminal cases a year in Halifax. Most – some 62 per cent – were for property offences, but the court also conducted some sixty-eight murder trials prior to 1805, a few of which involved killings outside Halifax County.[95] The court also heard the same range of cases when it went on circuit after 1774, but we have no consistent statistics on criminal trials outside of Halifax.[96] Trials were, by modern standards, short and relatively informal, rarely lasting more than a day and often taking just an hour or so, even in a capital case.[97]

Criminal cases were a small part of the court's workload; most of its sitting time from the mid-1760s was occupied with civil disputes. Limits on the jurisdiction of both the NSSC and the ICCPs were provided by a variety of measures which, over time, hived off petty civil causes into what we would now term small claims courts – giving such disputes to the jurisdiction of JPs. This process had begun in the early 1750s, and the small claims jurisdiction was gradually expanded, with the major statute being a 1774 enactment which gave two JPs exclusive jurisdiction in small debts up to three pounds in value.[98] Other measures sought to reduce the costs of petty litigation, in all areas, not just debts, by providing for summary proceedings in both the ICCP and the Supreme Court. Initially summary trials were permitted, though not required, for suits of no more than ten pounds in value; this figure was raised to twenty pounds in the 1770s.[99]

Practically no research on the NSSC's civil litigation caseload has been undertaken, making it difficult to say much about it here. We do know that in its first decade the court only heard appeals, and even though there were over 100 of these before 1764 that still represented only a fraction of the colony's civil litigation, with some 3,500 suits being launched in the Halifax County ICCP before 1766.[100] After the court assumed original civil jurisdiction its caseload expanded rapidly. The evidence of knowledgeable observers like Gibbons and Monk indicates that in addition to Halifax-based litigants the court heard numerous cases brought from the out-settlements by litigants who preferred to use the NSSC rather than their local ICCP. Gibbons attributed the choice of forum to a desire to avoid 'the Danger apprehended from the Partiality, Prejudice and Ignorance' of ICCP judges.[101] Lawyers preferred to sue before a professional barrister, and litigants were happy to risk the extra expense and engage those lawyers. The court also heard appeals from the ICCPs brought on writs of error, and a rather larger number of certiorari cases.

Any estimate of the numbers of cases sued must be tentative.[102] As few as 26 suits were disposed of at the four Halifax sittings in 1775, but the volume of litigation rose steadily in subsequent years, to an average of around 52 in the early 1780s. There was a substantial jump in the mid-1780s – 116 in 1784 and 214 in 1785 – as a result of the Loyalist influx and post-war economic difficulties, but volume decreased again from 1789. In the 1790s the court resolved about 87 cases a year in Halifax, with fluctuations between a low of 45 in 1790 and a high of 151 in 1791. Relatively few cases – about a third – went to jury trials. Throughout this period a substantial majority of the cases, around 80 per cent, were suits for debts, with the vast majority of those uncontested. While there were a rich variety of other kinds of actions, including trover, assault, trespass, ejectment, and slander, the court therefore largely functioned on the civil side as a debt collection agency. Much about the social history of early Nova Scotia could be learned from an intensive study of civil litigation, but regrettably, to this point the civil case files are a greatly underutilized source.[103]

A discussion of the court's civil jurisdiction would not be complete without a brief analysis of Chancery; equity jurisdiction was given to the court in 1855, and thus it forms an integral part of its history.[104] From 1749 the colony's chancellor was the governor, and in the early years the General Court, over which he presided, exercised equity jurisdiction. After 1754 the governor remained as chancellor, sitting with his councillors.[105] After 1764 Chancery consisted only of the governor, with the help of the assistant judges of the NSSC as masters in Chancery until 1782 when the position of Master of the Rolls (M.R.) was also created and the first lawyer appointed as a master in Chancery. No governor and few masters were lawyers, nor was the first M.R., Provincial Secretary Richard Bulkeley, who held the post for ten years. In effect decisions were often made by the NSSC judges in their capacity as informal advisers.[106] Chancery, which likely adopted the Irish Exchequer rules of practice as a result of the influence of Irish Exchequer attorney Richard John Uniacke, who served as both solicitor general and attorney-general, probably heard only a small number of cases in this period. There are only 132 extant case files from 1751 until 1797, an average of three a year, although there may have been rather more cases. Fire likely consumed some records and in any event the court's early files may not have been well maintained. Some 70 per cent of the cases were mortgage foreclosures, but Chancery also dealt with lunacy cases, trusts, partnerships, and the administration of estates.[107] In addition it is clear that Chancery effectively operated at times as a kind of court of appeal from Supreme Court decisions, through the device of applying for an injunction to prevent an order of the common law court being carried out or a proceeding being allowed to continue.[108]

The Supreme Court and the Bar

The 'gentlemen of the bar attending in their gowns' must have been conspicuous in the procession from governor's house to courthouse on the first opening of the Supreme Court, 22 October 1754.[109] A small but not undistinguished group, they were led by Attorney General William Nesbitt, and included his law partner, George Suckling, clerk of the Crown, and a future attorney general of Quebec and chief justice of the Virgin Islands. With the establishment of the NSSC control of the bar devolved to it from the General Court. Professional regulation – pupillage, admission, and discipline – lay entirely in the hands of the court, which exercised its hegemony through the rules of practice which prescribed the terms and conditions of bar admission.[110] As in England and America, lawyer training was by apprenticeship – although there does not appear to have been a set number of years until 1799, when the court mandated four – followed by the court examining and admitting a candidate. The oath was then subscribed and the attorney entered into practice. Not until the impeachment crisis was discipline an issue, and then the court did not hesitate to disbar for contempt the two attorneys at the heart of the controversy.

In writing of the Nova Scotia legal system as a whole in this period, David Bell has argued that it was 'beset ... by the scrambling precariousness characteristic of colonial infancies,'[111] and this seems an apt judgment on the Supreme Court's first four decades, especially on the crisis of the judges' affair. Yet the same author has also stressed that this period was one in which the authorities faced numerous difficulties, notably the challenges of internal dissent in an age of revolution and imperial warfare and of administering colonies with few resources and rudimentary institutions. The Supreme Court played an important role in both maintaining order and fostering loyalty. It was a visible and tangible manifestation, in Halifax and elsewhere, of sovereign authority, from which it also derived its power and prestige, and brought to the colony all the benefits, as its supporters saw them, of

English law and English justice. There were growing pains aplenty, but the American challenges of revolution and impeachment were rebuffed, the Tory constitution was sustained and with the appointment of Blowers in 1797 the court had both survived its most turbulent period and was demonstrating a new maturity.

Stability in an Era of Change: The Supreme Court, 1797–1848

The first half of the nineteenth century saw a number of important developments. Membership of the NSSC grew from three to five judges, the circuit system was expanded in stages until it served the whole of the colony, and a series of measures largely eliminated the formal role in politics that the judges had previously played. The 1830s and 1840s saw much contentious debate about judicial remuneration, and the latter decade also witnessed two very important institutional changes. In 1841 the ICCPs were abolished and the sessions greatly restricted in jurisdiction, so that the NSSC became in effect the sole court exercising civil and criminal common law jurisdiction. In 1848 responsible government brought with it changes in judicial tenure; from then on all judges were local appointments and all held office during good behaviour rather than at pleasure. Amid these various, often far-reaching, changes, the NSSC enjoyed an era of considerable stability. In over fifty years there were only two chief justices – Blowers from 1797 to 1833 and Brenton Halliburton thereafter until his death in 1860. More importantly, the court was for the most part staffed by able and effective lawyers, and there were no crises either of absenteeism or incompetence. Thus the various administrative and constitutional changes of the period took place against a background of considerable stability in personnel and public confidence.

Judicial Appointments in the Blowers and Halliburton Eras: Expansion and Legitimacy

The court's membership increased by two during Blowers's thirty-six-year term as chief justice. Deschamps died in 1801 after thirty-two years on the bench, and was replaced by George Henry Monk.[112] Five years after Monk was appointed the long-serving (twenty-five years) James Brenton died, replaced by his nephew Brenton Halliburton. In 1810 the court acquired a fourth judge in Foster Hutchinson Junior, largely a response to the reinstatement of the requirement that all circuits were to consist of two judges.[113] Hutchinson served only five years before his death in 1815, and Solicitor General James Stewart took his place. Eighteen-sixteen saw two new judges appointed and the court grow to five members in total. Monk resigned that year and was replaced by Lewis M. Wilkins Senior. At the same time, an expansion of the circuit system led to the creation of the post of 'associate circuit judge,' filled by Peleg Wiswall, an Annapolis-based lawyer. Thereafter the court remained at five during Blowers's tenure as chief justice – with Wiswall restricted to the circuit – although Stewart died in 1830, replaced by Richard Uniacke Junior. Wiswall was twice passed over for a full judgeship; he lobbied for the seats given to Uniacke and Stewart.[114]

The resignation of Blowers in 1833, at the age of ninety-one, represented a major landmark of the pre-Confederation period. He was succeeded as chief justice by his protégé Brenton Halliburton, who for some ten years had done much of the work as Blowers's powers faded. Halliburton won the job in a fierce contest with Attorney General Samuel G.W. Archibald. The vacancy on the bench as assistant judge was filled by Solicitor General William Hill. The following year Uniacke died and was replaced by William Blowers Bliss. When Wiswall died in 1836 he was not replaced as associate circuit judge, and in 1841 the post itself was abolished, but the court acquired a fifth full judge that year when the ICCPs were abolished. The new appointee was Thomas Chandler Haliburton, the province's most famous author. Although by then an arch-Tory, Haliburton was not especially loved by the establishment, whom he had satirized more than a decade before, an attack which brought an anonymous rebuke authored by his new chief justice, Halliburton.[115] Eighteen-forty-eight, the year of responsible government, saw a flurry of changes in personnel, with both Wilkins and Hill dying and being replaced by Edmund Murray Dodd and William Frederick DesBarres, successive solicitors general.

The court did not simply grow in numbers during these years; there were also marked differences in the nature of judicial appointments from the eighteenth century. None of the new men were imports from England, although only Richard Uniacke Junior was born in the colony – the first NSSC judge to be so. Monk was a Boston-born pre-revolutionary immigrant, while the other five were all of Loyalist background and had emigrated to Nova Scotia as children or young men. As importantly, none lacked legal training, and all were experienced lawyers. Indeed 1809 saw the first formal qualification for judicial office, Supreme Court judges henceforth being required to have been called to the bar for ten years and to have practised law for the five years immediately preceding their appointment. The qualification was still extant at Confederation, meaning that all subsequent appointees were lawyers of some experience.[116]

More importantly, the Blowers and Halliburton eras were generally very good ones for the NSSC, in marked contrast to so much of the eighteenth century. Blowers was widely viewed as a man of substantial intellect and immense knowledge of the law and legal process, and he 'led the bench into an era of comparative respectability.'[117] He stayed too long, resigning when he was more than ninety years old and not having been very effective or diligent for some time before, and his motive for lingering may not have been the most creditable.[118] But he was, for the most part, a formidable figurehead for the early nineteenth-century court.

While often less able than Blowers, other appointees were generally men of substance in the profession. His successor Halliburton was astute, quick-witted, and 'highly respected in publick & private life.'[119] Stewart was an Edinburgh University graduate, a protégé of Blowers, and solicitor general. He 'possessed a good degree of mental power, and of legal and other attainments.'[120] Hutchinson – dubbed 'The Honest Lawyer' – was the son and namesake of a former Massachusetts Superior Court judge and the man who effectively ran Nova Scotia's Court of Chancery, as well as being an accomplished Oriental scholar and a highly regarded lawyer in his own right. The son of Jonathan Bliss, Loyalist attorney general and then chief justice of New Brunswick, William Blowers Bliss received his legal training in England and was one of the leaders of the Halifax bar before his appointment and a partner with Alexander Stewart, a future Master of the Rolls, and James W. Johnston, a future attorney general, premier, and NSSC judge. Haliburton, in addition to being the colony's most famous author, had served as chief justice of the ICCP and president of the Court of Sessions for the middle division from 1829 to 1841, taking over that job on the death of his father William H.O. Haliburton. Hill had over twenty years' experience at the bar when appointed and was the only King's Counsel (KC) in the colony. DesBarres was a long-time Guysborough MLA and a reformer who was serving as solicitor general when appointed. Dodd was also the solicitor general at the time of his appointment, a Queen's Counsel (QC), and the son of Archibald Charles Dodd, former chief justice of Cape Breton.

Perhaps the only exception to this rosy picture was Monk, who had a varied pre-judicial career as, among other things, deputy surveyor-general of the King's woods, superintendent of Indian affairs, prothonothary and clerk of the Crown, deputy registrar of Chancery, and a member of the Assembly. He owed his appointment more to his family relationship to Lieutenant Governor Sir John Wentworth than to any legal abilities, and indeed was disappointed to get it rather than a collector's place. Constantly in debt, his overriding concern, before and after his appointment, seems to have been financial advancement; shortly after appointment he asked for an increase in salary and told his brother that he would continue to lobby for the more remunerative collectorship. Monk had a very poor reputation as a judge, and in 1816 retired and moved to Montreal, where his rather more talented brother Sir James was chief justice of the Court of King's Bench of Lower Canada. He was the only assistant judge in the period to wangle himself a retirement pension, worth four hundred Halifax pounds, or 80 per cent of his salary.[121]

None of this is to say that neither family connection nor political soundness counted in the appointment process; indeed judgeships were often given as 'rewards for public service.'[122] But although some of the colony's best legal minds, especially S.G.W. Archibald, declined a seat on the bench,[123] those who were appointed were generally very able. In marked contrast to the eighteenth century, there were few complaints about the competence or abilities of the judges in this period. In one author's words, 'the legitimacy of the judges was not seriously in doubt.'[124] Judges were no longer imports on the make or untrained place-seekers and, in the absence of a true party system, appointments were not yet spoils of office with which to reward partisans. That would change with responsible government in 1848, and the first sign of the new politics of patronage was perhaps DesBarres's elevation that year. But the first half of the nineteenth century was in this respect perhaps the golden age of judicial appointments in the province, free from the very different problems of both the earlier and later periods.

The Completion and Operation of the Circuit System

This era saw the completion of the circuit system and a number of changes in circuit practice. Colchester district of Halifax County was added in 1802, the court sitting at Truro, and Pictou district of Halifax and Lunenburg County in 1805, meetings held at Pictou and Lunenburg respectively. The addition of Liverpool (Queen's County), Shelburne (Shelburne County), and Antigonish (Sydney County) in 1816 meant that the circuit now covered the whole of the mainland. As mentioned above, it also resulted in the appointment of a fifth NSSC judge, an 'associate circuit judge,' who was required to have the same qualifications as the other judges but who would act only on the circuit. When Cape Breton Island was re-annexed to Nova Scotia in 1820 as Cape Breton County the circuit was extended there also, meeting at Sydney, Arichat, and Port Hood, and the new Digby County was put on the circuit in 1838. With the formation of new counties in the late 1830s and the substantial abolition of the lower courts in 1841, discussed in detail below, more locations were brought onto the circuit – Yarmouth County (Tusket Village), and Guysborough County (formerly part of Sydney County, Guysborough).[125] The circuit was almost complete – the only remaining future addition was a sitting at Baddeck inaugurated in 1851 with the creation of Victoria County.

There were also alterations in the frequency of the judges' visits and in staffing requirements. In 1799 the Hants, Kings, and Annapolis circuits were reduced from semi-annual to annual, apparently because of a lack of business, and the new circuits added in the first decade of the new century were also annual. But in 1816, when the mainland circuit was completed and the associate circuit judge position established, these three counties were restored to semi-annual status, and the same was done for the Pictou and Colchester districts. The court continued to visit Cumberland and Lunenburg counties just once a year, with the same itinerary for the new counties added in 1816: Sydney, Queens, and Shelburne. The Cape Breton circuit introduced in 1821 was also an annual one. These arrangements remained in place until 1834, when all circuits were made semi-annual, although the districts of Sydney County were quickly reduced to annual visits. When the lower courts were substantially abolished in 1841 semi-annual circuits were maintained.[126]

The Act of 1774 had specified two judges for each circuit, although as we have seen this made staffing difficult on many occasions in the eighteenth century. When Truro was added in 1802, it and the Amherst circuit were allowed to be staffed by one Supreme Court judge and one or more others – either local ICCP judges or lawyers, appointed ad hoc – and this provision was extended to all the circuits in 1805.[127] This permissive legislation was intended to lighten the burden on the judges; it seems likely that one-NSSC judge circuit courts became standard practice, with ICCP judges usually joining the itinerant judge on the bench.[128] But it was a short-lived practice. After 1809 the circuits had again to consist of two judges, and only in the event of illness or some other unavoidable problem could a judge do the circuit alone. This change led to the 1810 appointment of the fourth judge, Foster Hutchinson Junior. A quarter of century later, however, in 1834, single-judge circuits were restored, the dual requirement having apparently been found 'difficult and inconvenient in practice,' presumably by the judges. As discussed below, by the mid-1830s some of the circuits were indeed lengthy and arduous, and the judges resented the work. Wilkins lobbied for some years to have the system changed so that he could do less circuit work, and he and others may well simply have evaded the law by pretending sickness part way through a circuit and by taking a liberal view of what constituted an unavoidable absence.[129] An immediate advantage of the new system was that more circuits could be held concurrently; new itineraries were established in 1834 whereby the court could sit in three places at the same time. As discussed later, by the mid-to-late 1830s the court's caseload on circuit was rather light, and two judges must have seemed unnecessary, as well as something of a burden for the judges themselves. The reduction to one judge meant that when Wiswall died the Assembly barred the appointment of a successor. The single-judge rule was retained with the major court reforms of 1841.

The first three decades of the nineteenth century thus saw the expansion of the circuit system throughout the colony, as increases in population and economic activity brought demands for the court to visit more and more localities. There were numerous instances of lobbying by communities either to be placed on the circuit or to change the meeting times or place. The fluctuations in rules about the frequency and staffing of the itinerant court were, to some extent, caused simply by the administrative difficulties of manning circuits with so few judges. But in this period, as earlier, circuit arrangements were also political. Some local communities pushed for more frequent circuits, others for the county or district courthouses to be moved to their towns, because they wanted speedier access to the NSSC and concomitantly less reliance on the adjudication of ICCP judges, local laymen with local ties and interests. For its part the central government, while it already had de facto representatives in each county in the principal JP or *custos rotulorum*, nonetheless also had an interest in pushing for more frequent visits to more communities by other men imbued with royal power as well as legal training.[130]

For much of this period all the judges did their share of circuit work, including Blowers before he became too old; Halliburton seems to have stopped travelling by the early 1850s, probably for similar reasons.[131] This is not to say that the judges enjoyed going on circuit. Wilkins was never keen on it, and when his lobbying helped to eliminate the two-judge requirement in 1834 he 'rejoiced' in the fact that the younger judges would henceforth do the majority of the work.[132] The circuits often remained hard toil, with many routes still rudimentary and journeys long.[133] In the early 1830s, for example, the court would sit in Halifax for the Easter and Hilary terms, and in the last week of May the judges would go out on circuit.[134] The 'western spring circuit,' considered the easiest, made a circle, taking in Windsor, Kentville, Annapolis, Lunenburg, Liverpool, and Shelburne, with court sessions in each locality starting a week apart and the circuit not being complete until mid-July. At the same time two other judges went out on the 'eastern spring circuit,' a much shorter one involving sessions at Pictou, Truro, and Amherst and which was over by mid-June. By that time Blowers was too old to travel and the three assistants and the associate judge did all the work. Trinity Term began in Halifax on the second Tuesday of July, meaning that there was a small overlap between it and the sitting at Shelburne, the final stop on the western circuit. In early September two judges were out again, conducting the western fall circuit, a shorter one than in the spring and taking in only Annapolis, Kentville, and Windsor – the reverse order of the spring circuit. These judges were back in Halifax by late September or early October. Two others had a much more arduous journey, one that included both the Cape Breton circuit and the eastern fall circuit. It started at Sydney in late August and went through Arichat, Dorchester [now Guysborough], Pictou, and Truro, but was completed at about the same time as the western circuit. Some two to three weeks later the full court could conduct Michaelmas Term in Halifax, which began on the 3rd Tuesday of October.

The circuits were no easier after 1834 and the change to one judge, for at the same time all circuits were made semi-annual. And in 1841 more ports of call were added. Throughout the period the court's itinerant business had to be squeezed into the May-October period because of the difficulties of winter travelling. But even with that complaints were frequent; T.C. Haliburton called the duty 'severe labour.' Cape Breton was the hardest route, with no roads that could accommodate wheeled transport. Bliss said the circuit was 'in the highest degree arduous and severe,' while Halliburton 'by no means wish[ed] to repeat [his] visit to that Island' after doing so three times, and wished 'with all [his] heart' that 'the malcontents had their own Island again.'[135] Statutory provision was made for travel by water to some of the island's locations, but the government provided only a revenue cutter with no special accommodations, leading to a journey replete with 'miseries and privations.' The judges pleaded for something more: "Our request ... is not an extravagant one, we require no luxuries nor superfluities, but only the indispensable necessaries of life, and those common decent comforts absolutely requisite for any gentleman on such a voyage."[136] In contrast, the western route along the good roads and relatively short distances that connected Windsor and the Annapolis Valley was 'the easy circuit' and everybody's favourite.

Local lawyers appeared before the court when it called, and Halifax-based lawyers also travelled the circuit. Lewis Wilkins Senior, for example, had an extensive practice on the eastern circuit. Prior to 1817 the Crown law officers also travelled with the court at times to conduct serious criminal prosecutions, although local lawyers often prosecuted ad hoc. An 1812 proposal to appoint a circuit prosecutor went nowhere, but in 1817 the colony's first KCs were appointed to do the prosecution work on circuit formerly undertaken by the law officers. The arrival of the court was a major event in the life of the community, as it brought not only the power and majesty of the law but a flock of lawyers, litigants, and witnesses.[137]

Despite the extension of the circuit special commissions of oyer and terminer continued to be issued for the trial of serious criminal offences outside of regular circuit times. A special commission court sat at Guysborough in June 1812, for example, for the trial of Walter Lee on a charge of murder, with Judge Monk presiding.[138] Issuing a special commission 'where the Supreme Court would not sit in the county for a considerable period' was a practice that continued throughout the nineteenth century and indeed into the twentieth.[139] Special commissions relieved rural communities from having to harbour a suspected serious offender among them, and from the expense of doing so. After 1824 and the appointment of lower court divisional chief justices, discussed below, they were frequently used for this service.[140]

Modernization and Reform: Judges and Politics

That there were no major crises in the first half of the nineteenth century does not mean that the NSSC escaped controversy; indeed significant developments, some contentious, occurred in three areas. All of these developments can be linked to major themes in the cultural and political history of the province, especially to the emergence of a reform movement in the 1830s, itself an indication that colonial society was becoming more mature, self-aware, and confident, which brought change to a variety of areas of social, economic, and political life. Reformers looked variously to reduce the cost, and to improve the efficiency, of local administration, while also bringing about a series of changes that led eventually to responsible government in 1848.[141]

One manifestation of reform sentiment was an increasing sense that the close links between the court's judges and politics should be lessened, and by the late 1830s judges were excluded from all formal political involvements. From 1809 NSSC judges were barred from holding any government office other than master in Chancery or councillor. Consistent with the idea that offices were a form of property, the Judicial Qualifications Act was prospective only – it did not prevent any sitting judges 'from holding any Office they may have been in possession of' before its passage. This statute did not explicitly exclude the judges from sitting in the Assembly, probably because none did so at the time the Act was drafted, although the Assembly decided that that was its intention, and it seems to have been assumed from then on that judges could not sit as MHAs.[142] This sentiment was reflected in the 1816 Act which established the post of associate circuit Judge; it contained the same strictures as the 1809 Act plus an additional provision excluding the appointee from the Assembly.[143] Similarly in 1824, when the lower courts of the mainland were organized into three divisions, each with its own full-time and salaried 'first justice' (a matter discussed in detail below), those appointees were made subject to the same restrictions as the associate circuit judge.[144] But as late as 1835 a scandal was created by M.R. Fairbanks, who refused to vacate his Assembly seat on the grounds that the 1809 Act did not apply to him, and after much heated debate another statute was passed specifically to exclude him.[145]

The struggle over judges in the Assembly reflected evolving ideas about professionalism and the separation of powers, as did changes to qualifications for legal practice, discussed below. The underlying ethos was aptly summarized by the colony's leading legal author, Beamish Murdoch, in commenting on the prohibitions on office holding for the first justices of the lower courts. They were, he asserted, sound policy, 'intended to place the office beyond the suspicion of improper influence.' He insisted that it was 'desirable' that 'all judges should be removed (as far as possible) from the hopes and fears of political life, and the strife of business' so that 'their minds may be undisturbed by any passions that would bias their judgment.' It was also 'a fair principle of constitutional governments, to require a thorough separation of the judicial, the legislative, and the executive powers.'[146]

The various measures excluding the judges from offices extant when Murdoch wrote in the early 1830s exempted membership on the Council. In the Tory world-view, of course, sitting on the Council was not so much involvement in 'politics' as the judges taking their natural and rightful place among the leaders of the community. The chief justice remained president of the Council until its re-formation in 1837, and in addition to Blowers and Halliburton, Hutchinson and Stewart also served on the Council – the former was appointed after joining the bench, the latter was a councillor on appointment. The high Tory Halliburton was a member from 1815, well before his elevation to chief justice, and he was very active on that body, working to manage joint conferences with the Assembly and sitting on various committees. He authored a Council memorandum in the late 1820s which insisted that that body had the right to reject money bills passed by the Assembly, travelled to London as the lieutenant governor's emissary in 1831, and generally was 'the very heart and soul of Nova Scotia's reactionary government of the 1830s.'[147] However, by the time Murdoch wrote it was also increasingly believed, as it was in Upper Canada, that judges should ideally not be on the Council either.

As Joseph Howe put it, 'the presence of the Chief Justice at the Council Board is unwise and injurious, having a tendency to lessen the respect which the people ought to feel for the Court over which he presides.' Indeed for Howe more than appearances were involved; Halliburton had always taken a 'warm interest ... in public questions,' and had 'frequently been brought into violent conflict with a People imbued with the truly British idea that Judges ought not to mingle in the heats and contentions of Politics.[148] In 1830 London told Lieutenant Governor Maitland not to appoint any other assistant judges to the Council, and in 1837, when the Council was split into a legislative and an executive council, all judges were excluded from both in the future. 'The principle to be steadily borne in mind,' insisted the colonial secretary, was that 'all the Judges should be entirely withdrawn from all political discussions.'[149] Halliburton stayed on as President of the Legislative Council, and in addition to his formal involvement in the political process he continued to take a keen interest in a variety of issues, and whatever reticence he displayed in public he frequently expressed strong views in private.[150]

As in the eighteenth century the judges' formal political involvements were only part of the many ways in which they were embroiled in local administration. They continued to play the role of legal advisers to government. They were, said Attorney General Archibald in 1830, 'the constitutional expounders of the statute law,' and their out-of-court opinion on the meaning of local statutes was to be considered 'binding.'[151] They also provided advice on a variety of matters. Halliburton, for example, gave an opinion about the terms of a treaty with the United States over fishing rights,[152] and they all used their circuit experience to report on local conditions.[153] They also became embroiled in various cause célèbres: in the early 1830s, for instance, Halliburton, a High Churchman, was heavily involved in the dispute over state support for the Seceder Presbyterian Pictou Academy.[154]

Judicial Salaries and Fees

A second product of the reform movement was a long-running battle over judicial remuneration, one which had a number of facets involving how much the judges should get, how they should be remunerated, and who should pay. None of these issues caused problems between 1789, when the Assembly had voted permanent salaries for the assistant judges, and the early 1830s. The chief justice's salary stayed at its 1792 level, £850 sterling plus fees, until 1838, while the assistants' increased gradually, from £400 local currency at the start of this period to £500 in 1809, probably the result of lobbying by Monk and Halliburton which cited inflation as the reason, and to £600 in 1822, as a result of increased duties following the annexation of Cape Breton. The associate circuit judge received less than his colleagues – just £400 local currency.[155] The conversion rate for local currency by the 1830s was £1 sterling to £1 5s local, meaning that the assistants' £600 local was the equivalent of £480 sterling, little more than half the chief justice salary.[156] From the statutory entrenchment of the position of M.R. in 1826, a matter discussed below, its incumbent also received £600 local currency.[157] While remuneration was relatively handsome, it was also the cause of frequent complaint by the assistants. Wilkins lobbied continually to have his augmented and Colonial Secretary Lord Goderich thought the pay too low to attract the very best lawyers from private practice. The assistants' frequent complaints about their salaries acquired some force from the fact that they were the lowest paid among the various British North American colonies.[158]

The chief justice also received much larger amounts in fees than his colleagues – they fluctuated but probably averaged between £400 and £500 local currency in the 1820s and 1830s. The assistants did rather better in this regard than in the eighteenth century, for under Blowers the practice grew up of the chief justice relinquishing his circuit fees to the judges who actually heard the cases, and of sharing them with his colleague when he was one of the two presiding. Hill and Bliss acquired £112 and £140 sterling from fees respectively in 1838, and estimates of the assistants' additional income put it at between £125 and £175 a year in the 1830s, although this may be a little low, for Hill and Bliss claimed in the 1840s to have received 'fees to a large amount,' and as we shall shortly see the assistants agreed in 1838 to commute the fees for a salary increase in excess of £200 currency.[159]

The first major issue concerning judicial remuneration arose in the mid-1830s, when reforming Assemblymen took on, not for the first time, the issue of fees.[160] The problem for many was the price of litigation for ordinary inhabitants, and fees also served as a proxy for a broader critique of both the cost of the justice system generally and the privileged position of the Tory elite. An Assembly motion of 1836 condemned fees as 'unconstitutional and repugnant,' and Halliburton was asked to justify them. He vigorously defended the practice as allowed by the chief justice's commission and in line with English practice. Moreover, he saw them as a grant from the Crown, and not capable of being interfered with by the local legislature. Yet for all his impassioned constitutional defence of the arrangement he was largely concerned about the money, seeing any potential abolition as a 'sacrifice of income without which I could not maintain the respectable station which my predecessors have always held in this community.'[161] And under pressure from Colonial Secretary Glenelg he and the assistants agreed in 1838 to a commutation of fees in return for salary increases; Halliburton's salary was raised to £1,000 sterling, an increase of £150 sterling, and the assistants' to £650 sterling, or £812 10s local currency, an increase of £212 10s local currency. Halliburton claimed that he would not have agreed if only he had been involved, for the arrangement was disadvantageous to him; however, it benefitted his colleagues and he accepted the deal for their sake. This was just an informal commutation, but it marked the end of judicial fees; they were formally abolished in the Civil List Act of 1849.

Salary levels, not fees, were the contentious issue of the 1840s, although resentment of judicial salaries had a long history. When the assistants had petitioned for an increase in 1830 the Assembly turned them down, motivated by a belief that '[t]he judges were wallowing in wealth' and that the legal profession was 'the best paid in the community, and the least entitled to an augmentation of profit.'[162] A decade later reformers were intent on reducing the cost of the judicial establishment. A large aspect of this campaign was the abolition of the ICCPs, discussed below, but salaries were also implicated. Hence when the fifth judgeship was established in 1841 his salary was set lower than his colleagues, at £560 sterling.[163] The man appointed, T.C. Haliburton, was never happy about this, and claimed later to have been promised the higher salary when a judge senior to him died or resigned, but his entreaties fell on deaf ears.[164]

More importantly, through the 1840s the Assembly sought to reduce salaries, in part because reformers never accepted the legality of fees and thus never saw the 1838 compromize commutting fees for a higher salary as legitimate. The judicial salary question was linked to the readjustment of relations between Colonial Office, local executive, and the Assembly that led up to responsible government, in two principal ways.[165] London had long been keen to end its responsibility for paying official salaries in Nova Scotia, including that of the chief justice. In the 1830s they removed the salaries from the parliamentary grant and paid them from the 'casual and territorial revenues' of the Crown, generated locally. Ultimately London wished to see the Assembly vote a permanent civil list for the salaries, but the Assembly, while it was willing in principle, wanted reductions and control of the local revenues. London was happy to concede that revenue, but it would not agree to salary reductions for the incumbent judges or other principal officers of government. The result was some sixteen years of haggling over a civil list before the issue was resolved. Civil List Acts were passed by the Assembly in 1844 and 1848 but refused royal assent because they involved judicial salary reductions for the incumbents – for the chief justice to £880 sterling and for the assistants to £560 sterling. London also insisted that all salary arrears, discussed below, be fully paid.

The matter was finally resolved by the Assembly's capitulation, embodied in the Civil List Act of 1849, which retained the chief's justice's salary at £1,000 sterling and kept Bliss at £650 sterling. The other three judges – Haliburton, DesBarres, and Dodd – all received £560 sterling, as did the MR, for whom it represented an increase over the £600 local currency set in 1826.[166] This was not a reduction for Haliburton, who had been paid £560 sterling since his 1841 appointment, and

London found it acceptable to pay DesBarres and Dodd less because they had taken the job in 1848 knowing that the Assembly had set £560 as the level in both 1844 and 1848. Thus the Assembly got its wish to reduce salaries in the long term, while London successfully defended the 'vested rights' of incumbents.

There was one additional problem with judicial salaries – the fact that they were not paid in full because the casual and territorial revenues, which principally meant the rents and royalty payments from the Cape Breton and Pictou coal mines, were inadequate to meet them.[167] Not only was the chief's justice's salary paid from this account, but when assistants' salaries were increased as part of the 1838 commutation agreement all of the increases were supposed to be met from it as well. (The assistants' pre-1838 salaries were still paid by the Assembly, as guaranteed in the 1789 statute.) Halliburton was owed over £1,000 sterling by the mid-to-late 1840s, out of total arrears to all public officers of £7,800. He lobbied continuously for redress, for a person 'filling the High Office' that he did 'should possess the means of supporting himself with decency'; I am 'your servant,' not the coal operator's, he told the crown, expressing certainty that it would not allow him to be 'reduced, in ... old age to the humiliating condition of being compelled to announce to ... creditors that he is unable to fulfill his ... obligations to them.' Hill, Bliss, and Haliburton also had salary arrears. These arrears were another impediment in the negotiations for a local civil list and its quid pro quo, the surrender to the colony of the casual revenues, for London insisted that some arrangement be made to satisfy them. They were eventually paid off in instalments.

The Supreme Court Ascendant: The Abolition of the ICCP and Tenure During Good Behaviour

Economics had much to do with one of two large institutional changes of this period, the abolition of the ICCPs. The cost of the judicial establishment in general, not just fees and salaries, was a contentious issue in the 1830s, and the result was the substantial abolition of the inferior courts and a consequent redefinition of the NSSC's role. The other major change came a few years later; the winning of responsible government in 1848 led to changes in the judicial appointment process and reform of judicial tenure.

Two related critiques of the judicial system arose in the 1830s, both of which animated reformers' concern for economy and greater efficiency in government. First, there was simply not enough work for two levels of court. Only 189 civil trials were conducted in 15 county and district ICCPs in the five years from 1835 and 1839, for example, an average of just 2–3 a year per court. During the same period the NSSC on circuit heard 257 civil trials, and it adjudicated a further 102 in Halifax. While many other claims were disposed of without trials, the overall civil trial caseload of all courts was very light, and some 65 per cent of all trials were being conducted in the NSSC. The criminal caseload was even smaller: 60 trials were conducted in the NSSC in the same five-year period, 10 in Halifax and 50 in 16 other counties and districts, and approximately 220 trials with juries took place in the county and district sessions courts, just 44 a year in the entire colony, excluding Halifax. There must have seemed little point indeed in maintaining such an extensive judicial establishment in these circumstances.[168] As the Pictou *Bee* put it, not only was the ICCP 'utterly useless' given the preference for the NSSC, it was also 'positively injurious' because it took people away from useful pursuits for its meetings.[169]

Second, and as importantly, the reforms of 1841 were the product of concerns about the cost of the judiciary, and understanding that issue requires a brief look at the restructuring of the inferior court system in the early 1820s. In 1823 and 1824 the various county and district ICCPs and Courts of Sessions had, with the exception of Halifax district, been organized into four divisions, with all the courts within each division to be presided over by one man, styled the president of the Court of Session and the first justice of the ICCP.[170] The first justice of the Cape Breton division was required to be an attorney of five years in practice, those for the other divisions had to have the same qualifications as NSSC judges – ten years' practice. The eighteenth-century jurisdictional divisions between the Supreme Court and County and District inferior courts continued, with the NSSC and the ICCPs having concurrent original civil jurisdiction while the NSSC and the sessions split the criminal work according to seriousness of offence.

Although the pretext for these arrangements was to ensure greater legal competence on local courts and lessen the demands on the NSSC, the new judgeships were seen from the start by many as an unnecessary waste of scarce resources, and as jobbery on the part of lawyer-politicians, the creation of more places for 'government men.' The 1824 Act passed by just one vote in the Assembly,[171] with three of those who voted in favour subsequently receiving divisional judgeships, and over time the same reform advocates who sought to separate the judiciary from politics and to abolish fees also looked to rationalize a system that was increasingly regarded as too expensive and inefficient. Through the 1830s complaints about the cost of the judicial establishment were voiced with increasing frequency, and took in the salaries, fees, and travelling expenses of the five NSSC judges and the four divisional first justices.[172] John Young pointed out as early as 1830 that Nova Scotia had nine judges for a population of 124,000, whereas England had twelve high court judges for a population of 12 million.[173] Financial concerns dominated debates over the 1841 Act and over prior reform bills which failed, and the preamble to the 1841 statute itself referred to the 'great saving of the expense of the Judiciary' that would be achieved.[174]

When some reformers were given seats on the newly formed executive council in 1838, and when the reformers followed this up with a decisive victory in the 1840 Assembly elections, court reform was high on the legislative agenda. There was some disagreement about whether savings should be achieved by cutting back on both the NSSC and the inferior court establishments or by abolishing the lower courts, which delayed the reform package. The issue was resolved in favour of abolition. By the Courts Act of 1841 all ICCPs were abolished, leaving the NSSC as the colony's sole court of civil jurisdiction above that exercised summarily by JPs. Sessions courts lost all their criminal jurisdiction, although JPs retained some in petty criminal matters. Other than in Halifax the sessions remained in place as county and district administrative bodies. Halifax was incorporated and its elected council structure included a new Mayor's Court with both civil and criminal jurisdiction.[175] These various small exceptions aside, the NSSC after 1841 was effectively the colony's only court for the vast majority of civil and criminal causes, at least outside of Halifax, which also retained its commissioners' court (see below).

As we have seen, the 1841 Act also created a fourth assistant judge position on the NSSC. The job went to Thomas Chandler Haliburton, satirical novelist, rather than to the legal author and first justice of the Cape Breton Inferior Courts, John George Marshall, who had lobbied for a place on the NSSC bench a year earlier.[176] It was not really necessary to add a judgeship at all, given the light load of the ICCPs, as perhaps evidenced by the concomitant abolition of the post of associate circuit judge, unfilled since 1836, and Haliburton's success reflected his superior influence with Lieutenant Governor Falkland rather than legal abilities. In the short term the savings were minimal since, in line with the idea that such posts were vested entitlements, although not without opposition, the four sitting first justices were each granted a pension of three hundred pounds a year.[177] But this fact perhaps also explains why, if some positions were to be abolished, the inferior courts were the losers. That is, the NSSC won out in part because the idea that judicial office was an entitlement was still strong,[178] and thus it was accepted that individual office holders would have to be pensioned off. If pensions were to be paid, better to provide them for the less well paid lower court first justices and have the NSSC judges actually work for the money.

While the cost of the judicial system to the public was the principal cause of the 1841 reforms, civil suitors' preference for the NSSC was a clear endorsement of professionalism. The 1841 Act stated explicitly that 'a more uniform and improved administration of the law' could be expected from the NSSC than from the inferior courts, and it also lamented the fact that the presence of the ICCPs meant the NSSC visited infrequently.[179] Thus while there is some contemporary evidence that the first justices elevated adjudicative standards in the inferior courts,[180] the fact remained that the ICCPs and sessions were still largely the preserve of local amateur judges, with all the accompanying vices of incompetence and partiality.[181] It was no coincidence that the 1841 reforms included, as we have seen, confirmation of semi-annual circuits.

The other major developments of the 1840s were two important changes to the constitution of the court, both embodied in the Judges Act of 1848, one of the first acts of the first responsible government ministry.[182] The chief justice like the assistants, was made a local appointment. And the tenure of all judges, including the M.R., was changed from 'at pleasure' to 'during good behaviour.' This, announced the preamble of the statute, was to 'render the judges of the Supreme Court ... independent of the Crown.' Henceforth judges could only be removed on a joint address of the Legislative Assembly and the Legislative Council. Even if removed in this way a judge had six months to appeal to the Privy Council in London and could remain in office pending London's determination. Dodd, the former Tory solicitor general, was the last judge appointed under the ancien regime, in March 1848.

The Judges Act was opposed by Conservative leader J.W. Johnston, who likely objected to local appointment of the chief justice rather than independence. Master of the Rolls Alexander Stewart and chief justice Halliburton also objected; the latter was happy to see the assistant judges given greater security of tenure than under the 1789 statute, but did not care for the chief justice being placed on the same footing. The result of such opposition was that the bill only passed the legislative council by a vote of ten to nine, and the president of that body, the former M.R. Simon Bradstreet Robie, resigned in protest.[183] But the 1848 changes were an inevitable consequence of the new political arrangements; indeed the 1848 Act was 'the first step designed to introduce the new order.'[184] Local control of all aspects of internal government surely required local appointment of the chief justice, and the change in tenure was an aspect of the separation of powers discussed above, as well as the beginning of the transition to a more political process of judicial selection.

Jurisdiction, Institutional Organization, and Caseload

The NSSC had original civil jurisdiction with the ICCPs until 1841, and was the sole court of civil jurisdiction thereafter. Before 1841 it also heard appeals from the ICCPs.[185] Appeals from the NSSC continued to go to the Council until that body was split into executive and legislative branches in 1837; the new Executive Council did not take on the appeal jurisdiction, and thus there was no automatic appeal for a quarter century, until the Judicial Committee of the Privy Council was designated as the colony's appeal court in 1863.[186]

The court's effective civil jurisdiction was limited by the continuation of the eighteenth-century statutes giving small claims jurisdiction to JPs. Magistrates' authority in this area was expanded in 1807 from suits of three pounds to ones of five pounds, and outside of the capital JPs retained this largely exclusive jurisdiction down to the abolition of the ICCPs, with an appeal to the ICCP or the NSSC.[187] After the abolition of the ICCPs new small claims legislation raised the limit before two JPs to ten pounds and provided for trial by three-person jury in claims over five pounds; this seems likely to have been an attempt to provide some alternative to the ICCPs. In 1817 the JPs' jurisdiction was briefly enlarged, with permissive legislation allowing for the establishment of three-person commissioners' courts to meet monthly and adjudicate most civil claims of less than ten pounds.[188] The commissioners' courts legislation was given effect to in a variety of counties, but not renewed when it expired in the early 1820s except for Halifax, where it continued in force until the large changes of 1841, albeit with the ten pounds jurisdiction only in debt actions, and five pounds the limit otherwise in place.[189] Separate commissioners' courts were established on Cape Breton Island in 1837.[190] In Halifax itself the commissioners' court as the cheaper and quicker substantially supplanted the ICCP alternative to the NSSC.[191]

Along with small claims courts the Assembly looked to reduce the cost of litigation by continuing and expanding the summary jurisdiction of the NSSC and ICCPs, to twenty pounds in 1807 and, for a brief period, to fifty pounds in 1832.[192] The purpose of this summary trial legislation was 'to combine cheapness with despatch,' and to that end summary cases were heard in the NSSC at Halifax on the last two days of each term set aside for that purpose; on circuit the court would not allow such cases to be continued from term to term.[193]

The NSSC's caseload in the first half of the nineteenth century was dominated as before by debt actions, most of them uncontested. The numbers of cases that went to judgment in Halifax rose steadily over time, although with fluctuations, from an average of about 110 in the early years of the century to roughly 170 in the 1820s to well over 300 by the mid-1830s.[194] The dominance of debt collection continued, at about the same 80 per cent level as in the eighteenth century, with most cases uncontested.[195] Jury trials became rarer over time; just 13–15 per cent of cases were resolved this way in the 1810s, and the proportion dropped to less than 10 per cent in the 1830s. In the five years between 1835 and 1839 the Supreme Court in Halifax conducted just 102 civil trials, or 20 a year.[196] Litigants were by no means only members of the city's elite; one study of a law practice in the 1820s shows that the court was used by small merchants, artisans, farmers, shopkeepers, and widows.[197]

The same general patterns of litigation held true for the court on circuit. Not surprisingly, given the population differences, the volume of litigation varied widely from location to location, with the Pictou and Kings circuits providing the itinerant judges with the most work, and places like Cumberland, Annapolis, and Queens the least. About 100 cases a year were resolved on the Pictou circuit in the 1820s and early 1830s, 50–60 at Horton, Kings County, although both circuits saw many more suits filed. While almost 900 actions were entered for Pictou in the years between 1832 and 1836, the numbers for Lunenburg, Annapolis, and Queens were 309, 146, and 141 respectively. As in Halifax, debt cases predominated and jury trials were rare; on average just 17 civil jury trials per county took place in the five years between 1835 and 1839, fewer than 4 a year.[198] Overall the colony's inhabitants were not averse to going to law, a fact noted, although not always approved of, by a variety of commentators.[199] When they did so, they seem to have been equally willing to use the more expensive NSSC on circuit as the local ICCP, although on this issue there was substantial regional variation, with the more far flung counties seeing more litigation in the lower court.[200]

On the criminal side the same demarcation between the NSSC and the sessions and/or JPs as had evolved in the eighteenth century was carried into the nineteenth, with the latter hearing regulatory offences as well as minor thefts and, for the most part, assaults.[201] As one newspaper put it, '[l]arcenies and petty misdemeanours are generally tried ... at the Sessions.'[202] The Supreme Court, in Halifax and on circuit, heard both capital offences like murder and burglary as well as a number of larcenies and a few assaults; it retained effective jurisdiction over all felonies and a smattering of minor offences.[203] There is, however, some suggestion that the appointment of experienced lawyers as presidents of the Sessions Courts led some to take on a larger jurisdiction, trying more serious offences as the commission of the peace theoretically allowed but which in practice had always been reserved for the NSSC.[204] After 1841 some cases that had formerly gone to sessions in the counties were probably now dealt with in the Supreme Court, although in the capital the new Mayor's Court largely replaced the sessions. The only other substantial change after the reforms of 1841 came with the appointment of stipendiary magistrates in 1864 to take over the petty civil and criminal jurisdiction of JPs.[205]

Criminal cases were but a small part of the NSSC's work; indeed prosecution rates seem to have been considerably lower in the nineteenth than they had been in the eighteenth century. In Halifax they held steady at roughly sixteen people a year until 1815, and then rose substantially in the immediate post-war period. But by about 1823 they were down to just ten a year, despite increases in population, and continued very low through the 1830s – there were only ten criminal trials in the NSSC in Halifax between 1835 and 1839, involving thirteen people. Although much more research is needed before we can be confident about the data, serious crime does not seem to have been considered a problem by contemporaries in the first half of the nineteenth century, in terms of either absolute numbers or the kinds of cases involved – larceny was by far the principal offence prosecuted. Of course, the occasional high-profile murder case made for lurid headlines, but such cases contributed little to the court's workload. As a result executions were also rare; not only were capital convictions few, no more than a dozen in Halifax between 1820 and 1840, the royal power of pardon saved most of those convicted, and in that twenty-year period only Lawrence Griffin (1821) and John Lee (1834) were executed in Halifax.[206] The court had even less in the way of criminal work on circuit; between 1835 and 1839 it heard just fifty criminal trials, an average of ten a year for all the circuits,[207] although this figure needs to be supplemented by special commission cases. As in Halifax, such trials occasionally resulted in capital convictions and executions. Walter Lee, tried on special commission at Guysborough in 1812, was hanged despite locals' pleas for mercy, as were John Gregory at Annapolis in 1833 and Morris Doyle at Amherst in 1838. But such executions were rare; Gregory and Doyle were two of just four capital convicts executed outside of Halifax between 1817 and 1840, out of some twenty-eight capitally convicted.[208] While very few doubted the legitimacy of capital punishment, reform sentiment in the 1830s believed that it should be used very sparingly and resulted in a significant reduction of the number of capital crimes on the books in the early 1840s.[209]

Although the NSSC did not take on any of the jurisdiction of the colony's specialized courts in this period, its judges effectively did. Courts for the trial of piracy and other criminal offences committed at sea – Admiralty Sessions – were presided over largely by the NSSC judges.[210] In 1841 the lieutenant governor was excluded from membership in the Court of Marriage and Divorce, and the position of vice-president of the court was created and given to the chief justice.[211]

Throughout this period the NSSC remained a court of common law only, the Court of Chancery established with the founding of Halifax continuing as a separate institution until 1855.[212] The lieutenant governor remained as chancellor, aided by the M.R. as 'responsible adviser and judge of the Court'; he also took the advice of the NSSC judges on a variety of matters.[213] In 1825 the post of M.R. was formally re-established, like the NSSC judges with a salary of six hundred pounds local currency a year and until 1848 with tenure 'at pleasure,' to hear all Chancery suits at first instance.[214] There had been an M.R. since 1782, but the holder of that office was not a lawyer and depended on the Masters in Chancery, who generally were. The creation of the MR position was recognition of the incongruity of having the lieutenant governor/chancellor presiding in a court, but it also attracted criticism as yet another expensive addition to the judicial system.[215] Its second incumbent, Charles Rufus Fairbanks, also seems to have seen himself as superior to the common law judges, and on more than one occasion precipitated disputes with them by his attitude.[216] Although Chancery had a distinct jurisdiction, the NSSC judges were not afraid to discuss equitable approaches to problems when it was necessary for their decision.[217]

Chancery was attacked by reformers in ways very familiar to students of nineteenth-century English and American history, for its delays and 'unnecessary prolixity of pleadings,' as well as for the fact that it stood for privilege and inaccessibility. But perhaps surprisingly given the 1841 changes, it survived until 1855, despite suggestions that it be abolished and its jurisdiction given to the NSSC.[218] The reason may have been, in part at least, that, unlike its English equivalent, it was not so very inefficient, given the caseload and its small staff. The caseload increased substantially after the end of the Napoleonic Wars; from the turn of the century to 1815 the court had an average of just half a dozen cases or so a year, but the annual average for the 1820s was fifty-three cases, and it fluctuated between twenty-six and fifty-five thereafter. As before its principal workload was the foreclosure of mortgages, which accounted for 79 per cent of its cases after about 1820, 10 per cent more than during the eighteenth century.[219]

Little change was made to the NSSC's institutional organization for much of this period. In Halifax it continued to sit the standard four terms, although the precise term dates varied from time to time. From 1825 the Trinity term was largely turned over to non-jury proceedings, and in 1841 the number of terms was reduced to three with the abolition of Hilary Term.[220] While a series of statutes continued the eighteenth-century practice of limiting the number of days per term, it is clear that the judges had the power, and often exercised it, of extending the periods.[221] Eighteen-forty-seven saw a major change, with the separation of the trial of original cases from appeals. Henceforth the court would sit in Halifax at what were termed 'sittings' for the trial of all cases, civil and criminal, jury and summary. Three 'sittings' were designated, each to commence approximately two weeks after the start of the regular 'terms' of Easter, Trinity, and Michaelmas, which were in turn limited to a maximum of fourteen days. The 'sittings' could run for sixteen days, with any one or more of the judges presiding.[222] It is not clear why this change was made but the likely reason was the convenience of jurors. Under the old system jurors were called to attend a court term and could be forced to wait around for weeks if the fourteen-day limit was extended to allow for the hearing of all appeals and original causes. Segregating appeals and trials meant that no jurors would need to be called for the 'term' period, and thus they would not have to attend court with nothing to do while legal argument took place. Sittings appear to have been largely single-judge affairs, while the full bench could be present for appeals and motions.

Throughout this period the court's administrative organization in Halifax was in the hands of just two men: William Thomson, prothonotary and clerk of the Crown from 1787 until 1834, and James W. Nutting, who succeeded Thomson. Nutting, as Thomson's deputy for Halifax County, actually did all the work from 1811, when Thomson left the colony but retained the post despite a requirement that the holder of the office be a resident. Deputies were appointed in each county, initially by Thomson but, from 1819, by the chief justice as a result of Thomson's absence.[223] County deputies organized the circuit dockets, acting as both clerk of the Crown and prothonotary, and paying the Halifax prothonotary one-third of all fees received, fees being set by local statute. Although they received a salary for Crown clerk work, many struggled to make much of a living from the post.[224] The prothonotary was responsible for a wide range of tasks from providing fuel for the courthouse to calling jurors to attend court to preparing documents like indictments, swearing witnesses, and keeping minutes of proceedings.[225]

The Supreme Court and the Bar

During this period the relationship between the Supreme Court and the bar began to undergo a profound change, a transition from judicial to statutory regulation of the legal profession. In 1797 the chief justice, not the attorney general, was the head of the bar. The 1811 Attorneys' Act, modelled substantially on a 1729 English statute, marked the beginning of legislative involvement in the regulation of the profession. The Act required candidates for attorney of the NSSC to be twenty-one, and to have served a five-year clerkship – an increase of a year from that previously mandated by NSSC-made rules. (The new rules did not apply to those who had already embarked on their apprenticeship.) It also retained the NSSC judges as the ultimate gatekeepers, for after apprenticeship it was necessary to prove fitness and capacity to act as an attorney in an oral examination conducted by a judge. Once admitted as an attorney a candidate still had to wait a year before being allowed to appear in Chancery, the NSSC, or the Vice-Admiralty Court, and during that year was required to attend at three terms of the NSSC. Only then could a new attorney also be a barrister, be permitted to appear at the bar of the court. The Act exempted lawyers who had qualified in Britain or the American colonies, who had only to show admission elsewhere, practise for a year after admission, and good character. The NSSC judges were asked to decide whether the applicant had qualified in a jurisdiction whose rules 'would afford a reasonable opportunity to such person to have acquired a competent knowledge' of the law. Neither barristers who had qualified elsewhere, nor local attorneys with a BA from King's College, Windsor, had to wait the extra year before admission as a barrister.[226] Although a few men remained attorneys only, most went on to qualify to practise at the bar.[227]

The 1811 Act was renewed but expired in the 1820s, and it was replaced in 1836 by a new consolidation in which the status quo remained largely unchanged. One amendment presaged future control by the bar rather than the court; henceforth the examination as to 'fitness, capacity, and qualification' was to take place before a judge and 'two of the Senior Barristers of the Court.' But it was still the judge alone who decided whether the candidate passed, and thus even as the bar increased in numbers and influence the judiciary continued to exercise hegemony over it.[228] Given that the 1811 and 1836 Acts served to entrench and confirm, rather than abridge, the judges' responsibility for, and authority over, the bar, it might not be thought of as representing much change. But the mere existence of a lawyers' Act was an implied limitation on, if not diminution of, judicial authority. That was certainly how its supporters saw it, even if its principal advocate was not primarily motivated by a wish to undermine the judges. The father of the Attorneys Act was Simon Bradstreet Robie, an American Loyalist refugee who articled with his brother-in-law Jonathan Sterns, of impeachment fame. In those early days of his long political career Robie was a Whig and his lawyers' bill was considered a radical measure aimed at undermining the authority of the judiciary. But for Robie it was more of an ad hominem response to a situation which had arisen when a Bermudan, John Harvey Tucker, a member of the English bar admitted in Nova Scotia in 1807, claimed (and was denied) precedence over all the other members of the Nova Scotia bar.[229]

Other changes in the relationship between court and bar lay on the horizon, many of them spurred by the considerable growth in the profession which took place in the second quarter of the nineteenth century.[230] The lawyers' collective consciousness would soon articulate itself in the establishment of a professional association that was less a licensing agency than a club. Shortly after the English Law Society was founded the Society of Nova Scotia Barristers (now the Nova Scotia Barristers' Society) came into existence in March 1825, which makes it the second oldest in British North America.[231] The lieutenant governor (ex officio chancellor) and the chief justice were patrons, while the other judges of the NSSC were honorary members. All barristers were regular members of the society, and all attorneys candidate members. The Barristers' Society served no real purpose other than looking after the law library and was to play no part in professional regulation for another fifty years. Yet it marked the beginning, at least symbolically, of the bar's emancipation from the bench, and 'exercised a certain moral authority, or informal peer control, which can be glimpsed periodically.'[232]

The society's very existence brought to the bar a sense of collective solidarity, corporate identity, and unified purpose. Lawyers were no longer purely place-seekers, judges in waiting. Henceforth the sole aim of a legal career would not necessarily be the procuring of a superior court judgeship. Careerism began to be complemented by professional self-determination and individualism by collectivism. When in 1837 Fairbanks, M.R., judge in Vice-Admiralty, imprisoned and suspended from practice an advocate of eight years' standing, the bar on its own initiative struck a committee to investigate. The chief justice, in whose court admission to practice in all the other courts had to be granted, sided with the beleaguered barrister, whose suspension was lifted.[233] In 1844, however, an attempt to incorporate the society floundered on the rock of partisan politics, because Reformers such as James Boyle Uniacke were prominent in its affairs.[234]

The Supreme Court in the Age of Responsible Government

The two decades before Confederation saw little change in many aspects of the court's operation. Jurisdiction over civil and criminal matters remained essentially the same, with no new courts created between the NSSC and JPs/stipendiary magistrates; that would come seven years after Confederation with the establishment of County Courts. The circuit system was not materially altered, for by 1841 it had covered the entire province, although there were, as before, numerous small changes to circuit times and session length.[235] Judicial salaries conformed to the arrangements made in 1849, with no further problem of accumulating arrears. Halliburton received his £1,000 sterling until his death in 1860, and his successor, as contemplated in 1849, got £650 or, as of the adoption of the dollar system in 1864, $3,200. The assistants, other than Bliss, and the M.R., received £560 sterling, $2,800 as of 1864; Bliss got £650, or $3,200 as of 1864.[236]

There were nonetheless some major developments in the two decades prior to Confederation. Principal among them was the abolition of the separate Court of Chancery and, a decade later, its partial re-establishment with the creation of a senior assistant judgeship, the judge in Equity, giving the court six judges. This period also saw judicial appointments become largely subjected to the dictates of patronage politics. Law reporting began in the 1850s, presumably leading to greater stability in adjudication. Finally, in 1863 the NSSC got a court of appeal (the Judicial Committee of the Privy Council) to replace the old pre-1837 Council, ending a twenty-six-year hiatus in which no regular appeal lay from its decisions.

Jurisdiction, Institutional Organization, and Caseload

There were also some less dramatic changes as the NSSC sought to modernize its procedures. In 1866 the involvement of executive councillors in the Divorce Court was ended, leaving that jurisdiction solely in the hands of an NSSC judge. The court was renamed the Court for Divorce and Matrimonial Causes, the same name given to the equivalent court in England, and the newly created judge in equity made its sole judge.[237] The 1850s also saw significant change in civil procedure, the NSSC picking up the modernizing and simplifying trends of many other jurisdictions. The issue had been in the air for some time as part of the pre–responsible government reform agenda, and its first manifestation had been the establishment in 1832 of a commission to recommend changes in substantive law and to 'render the practice of the Courts of Law and Equity more simple and less expensive.' The commissioners proved a grave disappointment and were disbanded five years later, having accomplished little or nothing.[238] But demands for simpler and less costly procedures continued, and part of the 1841 reforms had involved requiring the NSSC judges to amend their rules to those ends.[239] It is not clear what, if anything, was done in response, but substantial change came in 1848 and 1853. In the former year all NSSC rules were voided and the judges told to make new ones 'suited to our own Legislation, and to the circumstances of the country'; if they failed to do so then, somewhat contradictorily, English ones would apply, for the English court rules had been reformed in recent decades.[240] The latter year saw legislation reducing reliance on strict adherence to the forms of action, modelled on, and in many sections an exact reproduction of, the English Common Law Procedure Act of 1852; abolition of the forms of action would come in 1884.[241] The year before the Assembly had also reduced the technicality of criminal procedure, abolishing common law rules about the strict forms of indictments by making it possible to amend them.[242] The 1853 reforms followed a report of another blue ribbon law reform commission, one that examined both the possibility of Chancery abolition and simplification of common law and equitable procedures.[243]

Finally, the prothonotary system was significantly reformed in 1853, when the county deputy system was abolished in favour of a separate prothonotary for each county. Nutting lost his job as prothonotary for the province but retained the post for Halifax county. Other county prothonotaries were no longer required to remit one-third of their fees to him; they were, however, still made to pay them away, the money now going to the provincial treasury. The accumulated fees comprised a fund which guaranteed Nutting's income at five hundred pounds a year.[244] Like a judgeship, the post of prothonotary was thus seen as an entitlement that could not be taken away without compensation. Nutting drew on the fund in 1854 and 1855, but not thereafter, and the system of collecting one-third of the fees from the county men was suspended by the Assembly in 1860. If Nutting's income guarantee kicked in again, the collection of one-third of fees from the counties was to resume. Nutting obviously did well from the job, but many local prothonotaries were remunerated much less handsomely.[245]

Reforms in procedure and institutional organization were in part driven by the fact that for perhaps the first time in its history the court struggled in this period to clear its docket, both in Halifax and on circuit. The evidence about caseload in this period is somewhat contradictory. The judgment books suggest that the Halifax caseload did not increase with the abolition of either the ICCPs in 1841 or Chancery in 1855. They show roughly the same numbers for the mid-1840s as a decade earlier, and a significant decline by the early-to-mid-1850s. They also suggest that the number of uncontested debt cases remained large – at over 85 per cent of the total.[246] Yet other evidence indicates that the NSSC was increasingly burdened by its caseload. Bliss claimed in the 1860s that during his time on the bench the abolition of other courts had doubled the NSSC's work,[247] and while he might be said to be indulging in special pleading, the case burden may have been heavier, especially in the 1850s.[248] More research is needed to resolve this apparent contradiction. But it seems most likely that litigation may have decreased in absolute numbers but increased in complexity, with more detailed legal arguments absorbing more and more of the court's time.[249] What little evidence exists suggests that the court encountered similar problems on circuit.[250]

By the mid-1850s the system was clearly under strain, and procedural reforms resulted. Statutes sought to deal with the criminal caseload in the counties by holding additional circuit sessions, and, in more minor cases, to shift them to JPs.[251] It seems likely that the same problem lay behind the passage of enabling legislation in 1864 which permitted counties to appoint stipendiary magistrates, although none did until Halifax in 1867.[252] On the civil side, because the court was unable to clear its docket in many locations before having to move on, provision was made in the 1860s for additional terms in the places where the problem was most acute, although only to deal with jury trials.[253]

The workload problem is less evident in criminal law. The limited evidence we have for the 1850s suggests that levels of serious crime remained low, certainly in the capital. Between 1850 and 1852 only thirty-two people were indicted in the NSSC in Halifax, with only one indictment for murder and another for manslaughter.[254] Unofficial reports of the NSSC's criminal proceedings for other years suggest similarly low criminal dockets; seven cases were prosecuted in Michaelmas term 1855, five in Michaelmas 1857, and four in Easter Term, 1862.[255] The same was likely true for the counties as far as the most severe crimes were concerned. Occasional high-profile murder cases attracted public attention, such as that of William Sims in Halifax in 1854 or of James Heislin, a Pubnico stonemason convicted before chief justice Young at Yarmouth in 1861, who had his sentence commuted to life imprisonment,[256] but the NSSC's work was generally much more mundane.

Judicial Appointments and Provincial Politics, 1848–1867

The five-person court in 1848 – Halliburton, CJ, Bliss, Haliburton, Dodd, and DesBarres – remained a relatively stable bench through the 1850s, with the only change being the replacement of Haliburton, who resigned in 1856, by Lewis Morris Wilkins Junior. Haliburton had offered to retire two years earlier if the Assembly would allow him the pension of three hundred pounds a year that had been given to the former ICCP first justices in 1841 and for which he had not been eligible because he obtained the NSSC post. The offer was but one in a long string of attempts to improve his terms of office, but was not accepted.[257] The 1860s saw two further changes, the most important of which was Halliburton's replacement as chief justice in 1860, after twenty-seven years as the colony's principal jurist and fifty-three years on the bench, by Liberal premier William Young. Halliburton, whom age prevented going on circuit in the 1850s and despite attempts to persuade him to resign, was still presiding in 1859 at the age of eighty-four, even though increasingly blind, and he steadfastly maintained that he would remain until death. He did, although he did not sit during the last year of his life because of illness. In 1864 the court got its sixth judge, Conservative premier James W. Johnston, who at seventy-two was the oldest judge at date of appointment in the court's history.[258]

This simple narrative does not convey the profound change that occurred in the nature of judicial appointments after 1848. Wilkins had hoped to get the seat on the bench vacated when his father died in 1848, but it had gone to Dodd instead, and his 1856 elevation was clearly a reward for a late-in-life conversion to the Liberal cause. He had been an undistinguished lawyer and a not very successful politician, and proved to be no more than a capable judge. The first post–responsible government appointment was therefore very much a patronage one; the next two were even more so, and highly controversial. Bliss wanted the job of chief justice when Halliburton died in 1860, and as an able and experienced jurist, and the senior assistant judge, he might reasonably have been expected to get it. But politics intervened. Young became premier in February 1860 and when Halliburton died a few months later Young took his job, one that he had long coveted. The appointment precipitated numerous protests and appeals to London, but it stood, and in the tradition of his two immediate predecessors Young had a long tenure, twenty-one years in his case.

Young was and remains a controversial figure. He had been a very successful lawyer in the 1830s, but for most of the quarter-century prior to his elevation his principal involvement was in politics, although he did serve as attorney general and took an active interest in law reform. Although he is not usually credited with being a great jurist, he had an extensive law library and supported university legal education.[259] The circumstances of his appointment were obviously tainted, but much research remains to be done on the value of his contribution to the court and Nova Scotia law.

The appointment of Premier James W. Johnston as judge in equity in 1864 also met with much protest and was arguably another example of gross patronage – although, as discussed below, there may be a better explanation. The Conservatives had returned to power under Johnston's leadership in 1863, but a year later Johnston retired from politics and took a place on the bench. The creation of a new senior assistant judgeship, while ostensibly a response to problems created by the fusion of law and equity a decade earlier (see below), was seen by many as intended in effect to pay back the Liberals for Young's appointment – an irony given that Johnston had fulminated both against party government in general and the resulting patronage in particular. Like Young, Johnston had been principally a politician in the three decades prior to 1864, as well as solicitor general and attorney general. Some viewed him as a more deserving appointee, however, for he had had an extensive practice in the old Court of Chancery and, as we argue below, his appointment may well have been a response to problems created by the abolition of that court.

The personal attributes of these two lawyer-politicians who so dominated the province's history at mid-century aside, the real significance of the post–responsible government appointments is that they confirmed the entrenchment of a more blatantly party political judicial selection process than had pertained before. After 1848 and the vesting of appointments locally, Girard argues, 'the conclusive influence of partisan politics was laid bare for all to see.'[260]

Law, Equity, and the Supreme Court

The 1855 abolition of the Court of Chancery and the concomitant institutional fusion of law and equity in the Supreme Court was a notable landmark in the campaign to reform various aspects of the substantive law and the judicial system in nineteenth-century Nova Scotia.[261] Anti-Chancery feeling went back a long way, at least to the late 1820s, and by mid-century it was joined to a desire to see the common law practice of the NSSC simplified. The main themes of Chancery's critics were high costs, inefficiency, and inaccessibility. Those critiques were especially sharp because they were for the most part valid, even if proceedings were not always as slow as critics charged.

The anti-Chancery campaign also gained momentum from the fact that reforms had been effected in the mother country. In addition, local critics had easy targets in judges (the M.R.s) who drew large salaries while performing no circuit work and dealing with a relatively modest workload. Two of those judges in particular – the first, Simon Bradstreet Robie, and the last, Alexander Stewart – were high and haughty Tories, contemptuous of their critics and apparently unwilling to reform the institution to any great extent. Perhaps most importantly, because Chancery dealt largely with foreclosures it seemed to be a judicial tool for the use of the wealthy and privileged. The plaintiffs were mostly large merchants or others from the provincial elite, the defendants farmers, artisans, and small traders who could not repay their mortgages. Thus reformers could paint the court as costly to the public purse while inaccessible to all but the wealthy few and much more available to those in the capital than others.

The reform campaign was aimed as much at the M.R.s – all of them except for the universally respected S.G.W. Archibald came in for some invective – as at the institution itself. Its first fruit was the commission of 1832, which effected some modest reforms,[262] while more thoroughgoing changes proposed in the late 1830s were defeated. Chancery reform was a moribund issue in the 1840s, partly because reformer Archibald was the M.R., but also because the struggle for responsible government and hard economic times pushed it into the background. But it was those same economic difficulties – and the foreclosures they brought – that revived the critiques of Chancery when the reformers came to power at the end of the decade. The court was almost abolished in 1851, saved at the last minute by the Legislative Council deferring a bill to effect it; they did so following a vigorous campaign by Stewart and some NSSC judges and likely at the behest of Lieutenant Governor Sir John Harvey, who seems to have thought abolition an ill-advised aping of American precedent.[263]

But despite the opposition of Halliburton and other Tories, despite Stewart's defence of his own record of reform, and despite Dodd's plaintive assertion that he was completely ignorant about equity and unlikely to do much of a job as judge,[264] Chancery reform could not long be stayed. A commission, the same one that advised on the reform of Supreme Court practice, reported initially in 1852. But its members were split – the judges favouring the status quo and reformers like Young insisting on abolition – and in the end it said only that Nova Scotia should wait to see what the English did. The commission's final report, in 1853, similarly showed a lack of agreement, with three individual members offering an opinion; Young was pro-abolition and Halliburton and Bliss were against it.[265] But it was the politicians' views that mattered, and the Assembly responded with a commission to prepare a bill for abolition. In the end much of the debate was not about abolition as such, but rather about whether the incumbent M.R. Alexander Stewart should receive a pension or be transferred to the

Supreme Court, as was done in New Brunswick. By late in 1853 Stewart had seen the clear writing on the wall, and confined his lobbying to securing the best possible pension for himself.[266] In the event the bill passed twenty-eight to twenty in the Assembly in March 1855, and as of 1 August 1855 equity jurisdiction was transferred to the NSSC.[267] Among many procedural changes suits were to be commenced by summons, not the lengthy bills in equity, and the taking of evidence in writing was abolished. Nova Scotia charted a middle ground between completely revolutionizing practice, as some American states had done, and merely transferring the jurisdiction to an equity judge, as in New Brunswick, which constituted reform in form but not substance.

We know little about how fusion worked in the decade or so after 1855, a subject which deserves much more study. There is some evidence that the NSSC judges' lack of experience with equity caused problems, and that delays in suits based on equitable causes of action actually became longer than before.[268] However, while, as we have seen, Dodd at least knew little of the subject, elite lawyers like Bliss had had plenty of Chancery practice before their elevation. Indeed if the reported cases are any guide Bliss seems to have become the de facto equity judge. Of the sixteen cases which were principally equity suits reported between 1856 and 1864 and on which he sat, he wrote a judgment, usually the principal judgment, in twelve, and probably authored the 'judgment of the court' in another. Halliburton also wrote, on four occasions, two in addition to Bliss and two on his own. Wilkins and DesBarres occasionally offered an opinion, as did Young after 1860 – one of Young's opinions drew a rare dissent from Bliss. Largely true to his word, Dodd had nothing to say until 1863 when, with Young, he dissented from a Bliss judgment.[269] It should perhaps not be a surprise that Bliss assumed the role he did; he was not only the senior assistant, but also the best-educated lawyer on the bench and a member of the Inner Temple, and he had practised with Alexander Stewart before the latter became M.R. in 1846.

The fact that Bliss was effectively the equity judge after 1855 may have contributed to a further change in 1864, the creation of the judge in equity position given to Johnston. As judge in equity he was principally to hear equity cases, although he could also sit when the court sat en banc and do chambers work. He was not to preside over trials of original causes at common law or, in the normal run of things, to go on circuit.[270]

The creation of the judge in equity position has been seen as both a result of problems caused by abolition, and thus as a vindication of

Stewart and other contemporary critics of abolition,[271] and, as discussed above, as the provision of a job for Johnston and the conservatives' payback for Young's hubris in making himself chief justice in 1860.[272] The principal cause, however, was the need to replace Bliss as an equity expert. As the man expected and entitled to succeed Halliburton in 1860 he had no desire to serve under Young, but delayed resigning until his Conservative Party returned to office, which occurred in 1863. Early in 1864 Bliss submitted his resignation, on condition that he receive the same pension as the former M.R. – four hundred pounds.[273] The government would not oblige, for it was already carrying Stewart's and Haliburton's pensions. Nonetheless, the very day that Provincial Secretary Charles Tupper replied to Bliss's offer the correspondence between them was tabled in the Assembly and the judge in equity bill introduced. The context suggests that its purpose was not so much to provide for the septuagenarian premier's retirement from active political life, but for continuity in the concurrent administration of law and equity in the NSSC when it looked like Bliss was about to depart. Moreover, Johnston, an elite lawyer-politician who had never been interested in a judicial appointment, did not want the job but agreed to take it on as a favour to Tupper. The years since 1855 had suggested that the only way law and equity could be concurrently administered in practice was by assigning the latter to an equity lawyer. Such were Bliss and his 'successor' Johnston – perhaps the most experienced and successful equity lawyer of his generation. This argument gains some additional support from the fact that the legislation which created Johnston's post also provided that the vacancy that would be created when Bliss left the bench was not to be filled.[274]

The Introduction of Law Reporting

A significant landmark of the court's history was the beginning of official reporting of its decisions in the mid-1850s. It is perhaps surprising that it took so long for this to happen. Case reports for the Canadas and New Brunswick had been around for some time, and reports from the colony's Admiralty Court had appeared in the early nineteenth century.[275] Moreover, the Nova Scotia Reports appeared more than a half-century after the first major compilation of the provincial statutes, some twenty years after Beamish Murdoch's encyclopaedic account of the law, and a decade after the other major piece of legal literature for the colony, John George Marshall's JP manual.[276] In the late 1820s T.C. Haliburton had lamented the fact that 'the decisions of the court are not easily known for want of reports' as there were 'a great variety of questions constantly arising upon our provincial statutes.' He advocated 'correct reports' so as to produce 'a uniformity of decision.'[277]

Haliburton may also have provided much of the explanation for why there were no reports before the mid-1850s; very few people other than lawyers would be interested in buying them and publication would not therefore be commercially viable. Haliburton argued that this was a service which 'most unquestionably deserves to be borne by the public purse,' and urged the Assembly to provide the money for it. Its failure to do so delayed law reporting for a decade even after somebody was eager and able to undertake it. Alexander James, then a young lawyer and later, from 1877, an NSSC judge himself, was appointed official law reporter to the NSSC, Chancery, and Vice-Admiralty in 1845, but the lack of a salary or publication subsidy meant, as he explained in his preface to volume 2 of the NSRs, that no reports issued.[278] James's persistent lobbying for government support got him only a grant of fifty pounds on condition that he provide about one hundred free copies to town clerks throughout the colony, which would, he reasonably argued, have left him as badly off as if he had published without assistance.[279] Although James claimed to have many decisions ready to go to press, the first volume of reports were produced not by him but by James Thomson, who in 1853 petitioned for a subsidy to publish a collection of 'the more important decisions of our Supreme Court.'[280] He acquired a grant without the condition, and in 1855 brought out volume 1, a retrospective of cases from 1834 to 1851.

It is unclear why the unencumbered money eventually went to Thomson, but James seems not to have resented it and when the Assembly finally voted a salary for the official law reporter in 1855 it went to James, allowing him to produce volume 2, covering 1853 to 1855 – although there was no further subsidy until 1856. James resigned his post in 1856,[281] but Thomson continued the work and volume 3, 1856–9, is his. Four further volumes appeared before Confederation, although the process continued to be bedevilled by uncertainty about the payment of the subsidy. Fitzgerald Cochran, who succeeded James as official reporter in 1859, had to petition for payment, and this was still an issue in the mid-1860s.[282] Eventually both the salary and a subsidy became regular charges, and when Henry Oldright became official reporter in 1865 printing was taken over by the government printer.

The first seven volumes of the NSRs reported some 400-plus cases from the 1834–67 period. Case reports often included counsels' arguments, and sometimes exchanges between counsel and bench. More than half of the reported cases, about 250, dealt with debt collection, procedural matters, and real property (adverse possession, trespass, rights of way, improper conveyances). The overwhelming preponderance of suits for debt was thus to some extent reflected in the court's rulings on points of law. Other areas covered include shipping insurance, seamen's wages and injuries, contracts, wills, and municipal tax/poor rate disputes, and there were a few criminal cases. It is beyond the scope of this chapter to analyse the court's jurisprudence, a subject which merits substantial research if we are to more fully understand the role the NSSC played in the social and economic development of nineteenth-century Nova Scotia.[283]

The Haliburton Pension Case and the Establishment of an Appeal to the Privy Council

T.C. Haliburton's ultimately successful fight for his pension had an ironic by-product – the establishment of the Judicial Committee of the Privy Council as the Court of Appeal for Nova Scotia. Six months before he retired in August 1856, Haliburton formally sought the restoration of the pension for ICCP first justices which he had forfeited fifteen years earlier by accepting appointment as an assistant judge of the NSSC.[284] He received a flat refusal from the Reform-Liberal government of Attorney General William Young and, after retirement, turned to the courts, by which time the Conservatives were back in power.

The case was twice before the NSSC. In 1859 Haliburton sued for a mandamus to compel the receiver general to pay him the pension. Wilkins did not sit because he had previously given an extra-judicial opinion on the claim, and the other four judges (Halliburton, Bliss, Dodd, and Desbarres) all held that a mandamus could not be brought to compel the receiver general to pay money, whatever the merits of the case – he could only do so pursuant to a warrant issued by the lieutenant governor. Three of the judges nonetheless went on to rule that Haliburton's claim was valid, with Bliss not offering an opinion on that issue. Then Attorney General Johnston agreed to a full rehearing on the merits; it appears that the government was prepared to order the receiver general to pay if they lost the case on the merits. By the time what was effectively a reference was argued Young had become chief justice. He ruled against Haliburton, but all three assistants supported their former colleague.

Though Haliburton had in effect twice been successful, the Liberal government of Joseph Howe was unmoved and decided in 1862 to petition for special leave to appeal to the Judicial Committee. It was necessary to get leave because an appeal should ordinarily have gone first to the Executive Council, which was in effect the defendant in the case. Despite the best efforts of Sir Roundell Palmer QC, solicitor general and afterwards attorney general and lord chancellor, *In re petition of John Hawkins Anderson, Receiver General of Nova Scotia*, was denied in 1863, on the ground that the government had delayed too long in filing its motion for leave. Haliburton, who by this time was not only resident in England but MP for Launceston, was awarded costs.

Special leave to appeal was needed in the Haliburton case because the Judicial Committee was not constituted as an appeal court from Nova Scotia decisions. The 1844 Imperial Act amending the Privy Council's appellate jurisdiction provided that Whitehall could designate the Judicial Committee as the court of civil appeal for any colonial superior court.[285] This was done for New Brunswick in 1852, but not for Nova Scotia. It took the Supreme Court's decision in the Haliburton pension case to force the issue. It made Attorney General Adams George Archibald sensitive to a lacuna in the administration of justice, and barely two months after the petition was disposed of – in March 1863 – an imperial order-in-council was passed designating the Judicial Committee of the Privy Council the court of civil appeal for Nova Scotia. The principal effect of the 1863 order-in-council was to turn the Supreme Court in banco into an intermediate court of civil appeal. Although the order allowed for appeals from judgments at trial, in practice this did not take place. This system, in which the judges who had not presided at trial were collectively acting as a court of appeal from decisions of the one who had, endured until 1966.

NOTES

We thank Blake Brown, Philip Girard, Balfour Halevy, Douglas Hay, Peter Oliver, Barry Wright, and two anonymous reviewers for comments on earlier drafts. Joseph Berkovits and Petra Fisher provided invaluable research assistance.

1 Lawrence to Board of Trade, 1 Aug. 1754, Colonial Office Correspondence [CO] 217, vol. 15, 76. See also similar comments in same to same, 14 Oct. 1754, CO 217, vol. 15, 133.

2 There are a number of accounts of the early court system and the establishment of the Supreme Court which we have drawn on for this section, and supplemented from our own research: see C.J. Townshend, 'Historical Account of the Courts of Judicature in Nova Scotia,' *Canadian Law Times* 19 (1899): 25–37, 58–72, 87–98, and 142–57; C. Greco, 'The Superior Court Judiciary of Nova Scotia, 1754–1900: A Collective Biography,' in Girard and Phillips, *Essays*; D.G. Bell, 'Maritime Legal Institutions under L'Ancien Regime,' *Manitoba Law Journal* 23 (1995): 103–31. Also very useful are two contemporary critiques of the court system: 'James Monk's "Observations on the Courts of Law in Nova Scotia", 1775,' and 'Richard Gibbons' "Review of the Administration of Justice",' both published with introductions and annotations by J.B. Cahill in the *University of New Brunswick Law Journal* 36 (1987): 131–45 [Monk] and 37 (1988): 34–58 [Gibbons]. The former also includes a shorter but also useful commentary by Monk, 'Observations on the Present Practice of the Circuit Courts.'

3 The affair can be followed in Council Minutes, RG 1, vol. 186, 291–8, 303–18, and 329–44. The best account of it is in J. Muir, 'Civil Law and the Colonial Economy in Halifax, 1749–1766' (PhD thesis, York University 2004), chap. 2.

4 Hopson to Board of Trade, 1 Oct. 1753, CO 217, vol. 14, 297. See also Board of Trade to Hopson, 9 July 1753, CO 218, vol. 4, 463–7.

5 For Belcher see R.G. Lounsbury, 'Jonathan Belcher, Junior, Chief Justice and Lieutenant Governor of Nova Scotia,' in *Essays in Colonial History* (New Haven: Yale University Press 1931); C.J. Townshend, 'Jonathan Belcher, First Chief Justice of Nova Scotia,' *Collections of the Nova Scotia Historical Society* 18 (1914–18): 25–57; and S. Buggey, 'Jonathan Belcher,' *DCB*, vol. 4, 50–3. We have also drawn on Belcher's letters and papers, in MG 1, vol. 1738, and at the University of British Columbia Library. The abridgment is J. Belcher and E. Bullingbroke, *An Abridgement of the Statutes of Ireland ....* (Dublin: Grierson 1754). For Belcher Senior's role, see J.G. Reid, et al., *The 'Conquest' of Acadia, 1710: Imperial, Colonial and Aboriginal Constructions* (Toronto: University of Toronto Press 2004)

6 For this point, and an excellent general discussion of the colonial constitution, see Bell, 'Maritime Legal Institutions,' 108.

7 For the reforms of 1848 see below; for a useful review of the status of colonial judges see J.P.S. McLaren, 'The Challenges to Judicial Independence and the Price of Judicial "Misbehaviour" in Settler Colonies of the British Empire, 1760–1870,' paper presented to the conference on Courts, Communities and Conflict, Dalhousie University, 2003. For Belcher's complaints see Belcher to William Belchier, 1 Apr. 1757, MG 1, vol. 1738, no. 30. The

Assembly petitioned for good behaviour appointments in 1775 and tried to legislate the principle in 1782–3, but the Act was disallowed in London: see Assembly Address to the Crown, 24 June 1775, CO 217, vol. 51, 214, and, for 1782–3, the correspondence in CO 217, vol. 56, 263, and CO 218, vol. 25, 196–207.

8 Quotation from Mrs Sarah Lyde to Belcher, 30 Dec. 1754, MG 1, vol. 1738, no. 65. Belcher's finances are discussed below. For his obsession with patronage and preferment generally see his letters in ibid., and for the influence of the Earl of Halifax in getting him the job see Earl of Halifax to Belcher, 26 Jan. 1754, ibid., no. 80.

9 For Belcher's arrival and the first session see Muir and Phillips, this volume.

10 For the criminal jurisdiction of the English high courts see the chapter by Hay, this volume.

11 The commission, dated 1 July 1754, is at Commissions Etc Series, RG 1, vol. 164 [B], 36. Belcher was given a second commission in 1761, following the death of George II and the ascendancy of George III: see Townshend, 'Historical Account,' 93–4. For civil appeals from the NSSC see Instructions to Hopson, 7 May 1752, in ibid., 66, and Wilmot to Board of Trade, 17 Dec. 1764, CO 217, vol. 21, 133. Appeals could also be had for amounts less than three hundred pounds if the matter concerned the rights of the Crown to duties, fees, or rents: see T.C. Haliburton, *An Historical and Statistical Account of Nova Scotia*, 2 vols. (Halifax: Howe 1832), 2:328. On original jurisdiction see also Belcher's 'A Description of Nova Scotia, January 1755,' MG 1, vol. 1738, no. 123. The early civil case files of the court therefore always refer to the parties as 'appellant' and 'appellee': see Supreme Court Records, RG 39, Series C, vols. 1 et seq. For the court's jurisdiction see also Courts Act, S.N.S. 1758, c. 29.

12 For the appeal process see Gibbons, 'Review,' 50. The NSSC had the power to grant certiorari because it had the powers of the Court of King's Bench and Common Pleas in England. The power was confirmed by local statute in 1774, probably to remove any doubts about its authority when on circuit: see generally B. Murdoch, *Epitome of the Laws of Nova Scotia*, 4 vols. (Halifax: Howe 1832–4), 4:22, and Certiorari Act, S.N.S. 1774, c. 8.

13 For the pardon system see J. Phillips, 'The Operation of the Royal Pardon in Nova Scotia, 1749-1815,' *University of Toronto Law Journal* 42 (1992): 401–49.

14 Divorce jurisdiction was given to the Governor and Council: see Marriage and Divorce Act, S.N.S. 1758, c. 17, s. 6, and K. Smith-Maynard, 'Divorce in Nova Scotia, 1750–1890,' in Girard and Phillips, *Essays*. The governor was judge of probate for the colony, with surrogates in each county, and president of a Court of Escheats and Forfeitures: see Wills Act, S.N.S. 1758, c. 11,

and Bell, 'Maritime Legal Institutions,' 112. For nineteenth-century changes to these arrangements, by which Supreme Court judges replaced the governor in many instances, see below.

15 For the Nova Scotia Court of Vice-Admiralty see A.J. Stone, 'The Admiralty Court in Colonial Nova Scotia,' *Dalhousie Law Journal* 17 (1994): 363–429.

16 See Muir and Phillips, this volume.

17 See Courts of Judicature Act, S.N.S. 1758, c. 27, s. 2. Section 37 of the Treasons and Felonies Act, S.N.S. 1758, c. 13, similarly provided that 'all convictions, attainders, judgments, and executions for any felonies ... before the making of this Act' were 'good and valid in law' and 'ratified and confirmed.' For a full discussion of this case see J. Phillips, '"Securing Obedience to Necessary Laws": The Criminal Law in Eighteenth-Century Nova Scotia,' *Nova Scotia Historical Review* 12 (1992): 87–124.

18 See a letter from his father, 9 Sept. 1756, in MG 1, vol. 1738, no. 14, advising him to act frugally until he had paid off his many debts, so that he would never 'become again as distresst and wretched as you were for a Number of Years.' See also to the same effect letters of 1 Dec. 1756 and 18 May 1757, ibid., nos. 15 and 21, and Governor Belcher to William Story, 7 Dec 1756, ibid., no. 84, referring to Belcher's 'foolish Difficulties' and 'profuse way of life.' His English debts in 1757 were some £230.

19 Belcher to William Belchier, 1 Apr. 1757, ibid., no. 30. See also Belcher's reference to his 'disagreeable Residence under Military Government': Belcher to Revd. Burr, 5 Nov. 1756, ibid., no. 83.

20 Belcher served as chief executive in two different ways. When Governor Lawrence died in October 1760, and with Lieutenant Governor Robert Monckton absent, he became administrator and commander-in-chief by virtue of being ex officio president of the Council. In March 1761 London appointed Henry Ellis, governor of Georgia, to succeed Lawrence, and Belcher to succeed Monckton. Ellis never went north to Nova Scotia, and Belcher was in control as lieutenant governor until September 1763, when London appointed Montagu Wilmot to replace him: see J.M. Beck, *The Politics of Nova Scotia*, 2 vols. (Tantallon, NS: Four East Publications 1985), 1:28–9 and 289. For Belcher's ambition see Belcher to William Belchier, 10 Nov. 1757, MG 1, vol. 1738, no. 35.

21 Some of these commissions are at RG 1, vol. 164, 25, 132–3, 165, and 219, and RG 39, Series C, vol. 4, no. 1. The Supreme Court Proceedings Book listing criminal cases, RG 39, Series J, vol. 117, as a result contains no entries for this period.

22 For Belcher's period as administrator see principally J.B. Brebner, *The Neutral Yankees of Nova Scotia* (New York: Columbia University Press 1937).

23 Collier was a former first justice of the Halifax County ICCP, and Morris was the current one in 1764. Collier was a retired army officer who had come to Halifax with the first fleet in 1749: see W.B. Hamilton, 'John Collier,' *DCB*, 3: 130–1. Morris was surveyor-general of Nova Scotia and a former soldier: see J.A. Chisholm, 'Hon Charles Morris: A Lay Chief Justice,' *Collections of the Nova Scotia Historical Society* 28 (1949): 48–158. 'Puisne' judges is the common term for superior court judges other than the chief justice, but we use the official term employed in the colony – 'assistant judges.' It derived from the Massachusetts majority in the Assembly.

24 For Belcher's opposition see Belcher to Pownall, 14 Dec. 1763, MG 1, vol. 1738, no. 195. The Assembly Address on this issue is at *Journals of the Nova Scotia House of Assembly* [hereafter *JHA*] 25 Nov. 1763, and is reproduced in CO 217, vol. 21, 9. For the Assembly campaign see also Wilmot to Board of Trade, 10 Dec. 1763 and 24 June 1764, CO 217, vol. 20, 357, and vol. 21, 201.

25 A decade later Richard Gibbons Junior, one of the colony's leading lawyers, made much of this reason in his review of the Supreme Court's history, arguing that the Assembly had been responding to 'frequent Complaints of Suitors and other Inhabitants of the Province, that the People were aggrieved ... by having all Causes ... determined by the Opinion of a Single Judge': Gibbons, 'Review,' 48.

26 Board of Trade to Wilmot, 13 July 1764, CO 218, vol. 6, 226.

27 See Brebner, *Neutral Yankees*, 75, arguing that the appointments were the product of Belcher's 'implacable enemies.'

28 Gibbons, 'Review,' 50–1. See also Governor Wilmot's summary of the effect of the change, that the court's 'power and jurisdictions extend as far as the hearing and determining all causes civil or criminal after the manner of the courts of common pleas, King's Bench or Exchequer in England': Wilmot to Board of Trade, 17 Dec. 1764, CO 217, vol. 21, 133. There is some uncertainty about whether the court had Exchequer jurisdiction before 1775, for which see J.B. Cahill, 'The Court of Exchequer (1775): The Stillbirth or Short Life of a Prerogative Court in Eighteenth-Century Nova Scotia,' in R.G. Bonnel, ed., *Facets of the Eighteenth Century* (North York: Captus 1991).

29 See, inter alia, Supreme Court Circuit Act, S.N.S. 1774, c. 6, preamble; Courts of Justice Act, S.N.S. 1841, c. 3, preamble; Murdoch, *Epitome*, 3: 57 and 64.

30 Gibbons, 'Review,' 50.

31 See in this regard the Colonial Leave of Absence Act, 22 Geo. III, c. 75 (1782), which gave colonial governors the power to dismiss officers who held office under royal warrant for misconduct, dereliction of duty, or absenteeism, subject to a power of review by the Privy Council.

32 Assistant Judges Act, S.N.S. 1789, c. 12, s. 2.

33 The commissions are at RG 1, vol. 164 [B], 302. For Belcher's role and for his treatment of his colleagues see Gibbons, 'Review,' 48–9.

34 Bulkeley to Morris and Deschamps, 17 Dec. 1773, RG 1, vol. 168, 346–7.

35 For the chief justice's salary see variously Wilmot to Board of Trade, 17 Dec. 1764, CO 217, vol. 21, 133; J.B. Cahill, 'Henry Dundas' Plan for Reforming the Judicature of British North America, 1792,' *University of New Brunswick Law Journal* 39 (1990): 160 and 167. Chief Justice Finucane, discussed below, was able to use his influence with the Protestant Ascendancy in Ireland to get his salary raised as high as nine hundred pounds in 1782, but the salary for his successor dropped again to five hundred pounds.

36 Parr to Council, 29 June 1784, RG 1, vol. 298, no. 86.

37 Salary figures are from Board of Trade to Wilmot, 13 July 1764, CO 218, vol. 6, 226; Gibbons, 'Review,' 48–9; Assistant Judges Act, S.N.S. 1789, c. 12. For the currency conversion see below. Sampson Salter Blowers apparently told Chief Justice Strange in the early 1790s that he would not give up the attorney generalship, which gave him an income of some eight hundred pounds a year, for a seat on the bench worth half that amount: Strange's Memorandum on the Bar of Nova Scotia, 10 Mar. 1792, CO 217, vol. 63, 353.

38 The payment of fees to the chief justice was based on the practice in the English courts in the eighteenth century; for the English fee system see the chapter by Hay, this volume. The practice continued throughout this period, although Chief Justice Pemberton accepted a commutation of fees – an annual grant of two hundred pounds in lieu – during his brief tenure, which gives us some sense of how much they were worth. The assistants did collect fees for issuing recognizances, taking affidavits, etc., out of court. For all of this see the full discussion of the history in Halliburton to James, 23 Mar. 1836, RG 1, vol. 278, no. 47, and, for the regulation of fees, Council Minutes, 1 Sept. 1785, RG 1, vol. 278, no. 23; Fees Act, S.N.S. 1766, c. 11; Fees Act, S.N.S. 1787, c. 15. For the abolition of the fee system, see below.

39 For late payments see Thomas Strange's Memorandum on the Bar of Nova Scotia, 10 Mar. 1792, CO 217, vol. 63, 353. Attempts were made to establish a permanent fund in the 1770s and 1782, but foundered because the Assembly also wanted to change the judges' tenure to 'good behaviour.' The Assembly partly got its wish in 1789 – see above. For all of this see Monk, 'Observations on the Courts of Law,' 139, note 38; House of Assembly to Legge, Nov. 1774, CO 217, vol. 51, 41–2, and Legge to Assembly, 6 July 1775, RG 1, vol. 286, no. 109; Memoranda and Correspondence in 1783 in CO 217, vol. 35, 365–6, and vol. 56, 263, and CO 218, vol. 25, 196, and 206–7.

40 Monk, 'Observations,' 139.

41 The various judicial appointments discussed in this and the next paragraph can be followed in Greco, 'Superior Court Judiciary,' *passim*, which also discusses the individual judges. See also J.B. Cahill, 'Fide et fortitudine vivo: The Career of Chief Justice Bryan Finucane,' *Collections of the Royal Nova Scotia History Society* 42 (1986): 153–69; J. MacLeod, 'A Forgotten Chief Justice of Nova Scotia [Strange],' *Dalhousie Review* 1 (1921): 308–23; D.F. Chard, 'Sir Thomas Strange,' *DCB*, 7:831–2; J.A. Chisholm, 'Three Chief Justices of Nova Scotia [Morris, Pemberton, Blowers],' *Collections of the Nova Scotia Historical Society* 28 (1949): 148–58, 'Sir Thomas Strange, C.J.,' *Canadian Bar Review* 24 (1946): 600–3, and 'Hon. Sampson Salter Blowers, C.J.,' *Canadian Bar Review* 27 (1949): 575–9; *A Directory of the Members of the Legislative Assembly of Nova Scotia, 1758–1958* (Halifax: Public Archives of Nova Scotia 1958).

42 For his one term presiding see *Gazette*, 21 Oct. 1788.

43 The relationship is not certain, but is hinted at in Strange's entry in the *Dictionary of National Biography* [*DNB*] (London: Oxford University Press 1882–1900), 55:27. Were it not for such a connection it is otherwise difficult to see why Strange would have received the post after just four years at the bar and very little practice experience.

44 See Cahill, 'Henry Dundas' Plan,' 160.

45 Parr to Nepean, 7 June 1787, CO 217, vol. 60, 21. On DeLancey's lobbying see Fanning to Sydney, 26 June 1785, CO 217, vol. 57, 207–8, and his 'State of the Bench of the Supreme Court of Nova Scotia, 1786,' in ibid., vol. 58, 281, also reproduced in J.B. Cahill, 'A Loyalist Attorney's Critique of the Supreme Court of Nova Scotia, 1786,' *Nova Scotia Historical Review* 11 (1991): 151–5. See also Parr to Nepean, 30 Jan. 1788, CO 217, vol. 60, 148. Parr's letters recommending Blowers arrived in London too late to be effective, Strange having already been given the appointment.

46 Bell, 'Maritime Legal Institutions,' 109, note 13.

47 See generally Cahill, 'Henry Dundas' Plan,' 167. See also Wentworth to Dundas, 6 Dec. 1793, CO 217, vol. 65, 8, and Dundas to Wentworth, 14 Feb. 1794, CO 217, vol. 65, 101–2.

48 Cited in Cahill, 'Henry Dundas' Plan,' 163.

49 For Uniacke's role in the rebellion and his release see E.A. Clarke and J. Phillips, 'Rebellion and Repression in Nova Scotia in the Era of the American Revolution,' in F.M. Greenwood and J.B. Wright, eds., *Canadian State Trials: Volume I – Law, Politics, and Security Measures, 1608–1837* (Toronto: University of Toronto Press and Osgoode Society for Canadian Legal History 1997), 180 and 198. See also B. Cuthbertson, *The Old Attorney-General: A*

Biography of Richard John Uniacke, 1754–1830 (Halifax: Nimbus 1980), 7–10. A 'Baconian' judge was one who followed the imprecation of Sir Francis Bacon, James I's attorney general, to be deferential to the sovereign, to see his first duty as supporting government. For a fuller discussion of this, and competing conceptions, see F.M. Greenwood, *Legacies of Fear: Law and Politics in Quebec in the Era of the French Revolution* (Toronto: Osgoode Society for Canadian Legal History and University of Toronto Press 1993).

50 McLaren, 'The Challenges to Judicial Independence,' 2. For judges as political advisers in other Canadian colonies see generally P. Oliver, 'Power, Politics, and the Law: The Place of the Judiciary in the Historiography of Upper Canada,' in G.B. Baker and J. Phillips, eds., *Essays in the History of Canadian Law: Volume VIII – In Honour of R.C.B. Risk* (Toronto: University of Toronto Press and Osgoode Society for Canadian Legal History 1999).

51 For the former see the commission of inquiry into the disputes between former Loyalists and patriots in Cumberland County in the 1780s: E.A. Clarke and J. Phillips, '"The Course of Law Cannot be Stopped": The Aftermath of the Cumberland Rebellion in the Civil Courts of Nova Scotia,' *Dalhousie Law Journal* 21 (1998): 460 et seq. For the latter see Governor John Parr's use of Chief Justice Finucane to try to settle disagreements among the newly arrived Loyalists on the Saint John River: Parr to Nepean, 12 May 1784, CO 2127, vol. 59, 116, and D.G. Bell, *Early Loyalist Saint John* (Fredericton: Acadiensis Press 1984).

52 Belcher drafted most of the first Assembly's statutes: see Phillips, 'Criminal Law,' 115, and MG 1, vol. 1738, nos. 106 and 109. See generally Gibbons, 'Review,' 57, supporting his idea of more judges in part because government would then have 'a set of Honorable and able Law Counsellors to advise in points of Law and Constitutional Measures, and to revise and correct Proposed Acts of Legislature.'

53 *JHA*, 19 and 20 June 1782.

54 For examples see McLaren, 'The Challenges to Judicial Independence.'

55 See generally J.B. Cahill, 'Slavery and the Judges of Loyalist Nova Scotia,' *University of New Brunswick Law Journal* 43 (1994): 73–135; quotation at 89. For two of these slavery cases see the chapter by Gwyn, this volume.

56 See generally D. Hay, 'Property, Authority and the Criminal Law,' in Hay et al, *Albion's Fatal Tree: Crime and Society in Eighteenth Century England* (London: Allen 1975), and J.M. Beattie, *Crime and the Courts in England, 1660–1800* (Princeton: Princeton University Press 1986), chap. 7. See also the chapters by Hay and Muir and Phillips, this volume.

57 See Muir and Phillips, this volume; Phillips, 'Royal Pardon,' 401–3, and 'Criminal Law,' 109 et seq.

58 Supreme Court Act, S.N.S. 1768, 2nd Session, c. 5; Commission for the Trial of Goff et al., 1776, RG 1, vol. 168, 462, stating that a trial before the Easter Term had started would 'prevent as far as may be the commission of such horrid offences.'
59 For the content of the criminal law see Phillips, 'Criminal Law.'
60 See RG 39, Series J, vol. 117, and Phillips, 'Royal Pardon.'
61 For Driscoll and Lawlor see *Boston Weekly Newsletter*, 6 June 1765. For Manning see Execution Accounts, in Chipman Papers, MG 1, vol. 183, no. 18.
62 *Gazette*, 10 Aug. 1779.
63 For this incident see Beck, *Politics*, vol. 1, 35–8 and Cahill, 'Court of Exchequer.' For the Assembly's 'Petition of Right' which included these proposals on the judiciary see J.B. Brebner, 'Nova Scotia's Remedy for the American Revolution,' *Canadian Historical Review* 15 (1934): 171–80.
64 Bell, 'Maritime Legal Institutions,' 119.
65 S.N.S. 1774, c. 6. For a more extended discussion of the origins and operations of the circuit system see J. Phillips, 'The Majesty of the Law: The Early Nova Scotia Supreme Court Circuit in Theory and Practice,' unpublished paper, 2002.
66 For two of more than a dozen surviving examples see Council Minutes, 30 Jan. 1762, RG 1, vol. 188, 293–4, naming Duport, Deschamps, and Attorney General Nesbitt to sit in King's County, and 17 Oct. 1767, ibid., 79, a commission for Annapolis.
67 Supreme Court Act, S.N.S. 1768, 2nd Session, c. 9. In 1777 the Halifax Supreme Court was also given jurisdiction to try any political crime wherever committed in the colony: see Crimes Against His Majesty Act, S.N.S. 1777, c. 13, at RG 5, Series S, vol 5.
68 Hay, 'Property, Authority and the Criminal Law,' 27.
69 Monk, 'Observations on the Courts of Law,' 138 and 140, and 'Observations on the Circuit Courts,' 142–3; emphasis in original.
70 Supreme Court Circuit Act, S.N.S. 1774, c. 6; Courts Act, S.N.S. 1781, c. 6.
71 Quotation from Wentworth to Duke of Portland, 18 May 1795, RG 1, vol. 51. For the creation of these courts see Nisi Prius Act, S.N.S. 1794, c. 10, and for the jurisdiction of such courts see J. Cockburn, *A History of English Assizes, 1558–1714* (Cambridge: Cambridge University Press 1972), 17, and the chapter by Hay, this volume. The Act was to stay in force for just three years, or until all cases begun under it had been completed.
72 See in particular Wentworth to Dundas, 6 Dec. 1793, CO 217, vol. 65, 8, and State of the Bench of the Supreme Court of Nova Scotia, 1786, by Lt. Col. DeLancey, CO 217, vol. 58, 281.
73 Numerous examples of special commissions could be given. See, for Shel-

burne, Court of Sessions Records, RG 60, Shelburne, vol. 2, no. 2.1, and Richard Bulkeley to Shelburne JPs, 24 Sept. 1784, RG 1, vol. 136, 345, and for Lunenburg, *The Trials of George Frederick Boutelier and John Boutelier, for the Murder of Frederick Eminaud ... Held At Lunenberg ... At the Court House in the Town of Lunenberg, 4 May 1791* (Halifax: Stewart 1791).

74 Wentworth to John King, 15 Sept. 1800, RG 1, vol. 53, 134–5, and to Windham, 14 Nov. 1806, RG 1, vol. 54, 135.

75 J.G. Marshall, *Personal Narratives; with Reflections and Remarks* (Halifax: Chamberlain 1866), 72. See also J.G. Marshall, *A Brief History of Public Proceedings and Events ... During the Earliest Years of the Present Century* (Halifax: Wesleyan n.d.), 5.

76 The most complete account of this episode is unpublished: J.B. Cahill, 'The "Judges Affair": An Eighteenth-Century Nova Scotian Cause Célèbre,' unpublished ms, 1986, on file with the authors. What follows is largely taken from this source. Other accounts are contained in M. Ells, 'Nova Scotian "Sparks of Liberty",' *Dalhousie Review* 16 (1937): 475–92; Beck, *Politics*, 1:47–50, and Murdoch, *A History of Nova Scotia, or Acadie*, 3 vols. (Halifax: Barnes 1867), 3:56–7, 66–72, 87–92, and 101. There is a wealth of published documentary material on the judges' affair, in *Collection of the Publications Relating to the Impeachment of the Judges of His Majesty's Supreme Court of the Province of Nova Scotia* (Halifax: Howe 1788), and *The Reply of Messrs Sterns & Taylor to the Answers Given by the Judges of the Supreme Court of Nova Scotia ...* (London: Stockdale 1789). See also 'The Answer of the Judges of the Supreme Court to the Allegations Annexed to the Address of the House of Assembly ... Containing Complaints against them for Improper and Irregular Proceedings,' 10 Dec. 1782, CO 217, vol. 60. For the only comparable incident in Canadian history see E. Kolish and J. Lambert, 'The Attempted Impeachment of the Lower Canadian Chief Justices, 1814–1815,' in Greenwood and Wrights, eds., *Canadian State Trials, Volume I.*

77 E.A. Jones, *The Loyalists of New Jersey* (Newark: New Jersey Historical Society 1927), 215–216. For Sterns see C.K. Shipton, comp., *Sibley's Harvard Graduates: Volume XVII, 1768-1771* (Boston: Massachusetts Historical Society 1975), 434–5.

78 For his Vice-Admiralty work see Vice-Admiralty Court Records, RG 1, vols. 496–7. For his appearances in the Supreme Court see RG 39, Series J, vol. 2, *passim* (criminal work), and vols. 3–11, *passim* (civil cases). He also represented many clients prosecuted in Halifax Quarter Sessions: see Sessions Court Records, RG 34-312, Series P, vol. 1.

79 Taylor's Loyalist Claim, Public Record Office, London, Audit Office Records, 13/112, 311–37; his Memorial is at ibid., 319–20 (mfm at NSARM).

80 'Answer of the Judges,' 162.
81 Parr to Nepean, 5 Dec. 1787, CO 217, vol. 60, 75.
82 This is *Bent v. Watson*, discussed in Clarke and Phillips, 'The Course of Law,' 464 et seq.
83 *JHA*, 28 Nov. 1787.
84 Council Minutes, 28 Feb. 1788, RG 1, vol. 189, 139.
85 These were *R. v. Bartling* and *R. v. Small*. They can be located at RG 39, Series J, vol. 2, 81 and 86, and Series C, vol. 56, nos. 65 and 74.
86 Courts of Judicature Act, S.N.S. 1758, c. 29, in Assembly Records, RG 5, Series S, vol. 1, 1758, c. 29; Wilmot to Board of Trade, 17 Dec. 1764, CO 217, vol. 21, 133; Supreme Court Act, S.N.S. 1768, c. 5; Gibbons, 'Review,' 52.
87 Supreme Court Act, S.N.S. 1780, c. 1, s. 1.
88 See J. Phillips, "Halifax Juries in the Eighteenth Century,' in G. Smith, A. May, and S. Devereaux, eds., *Criminal Justice in the Old World and the New: Essays in Honour of J.M. Beattie* (Toronto: Centre of Criminology 1998).
89 Courts of Justice Act, S.N.S. 1796, c. 3, ss. 1 and 2. For trials in Hilary Term 1798–1804 see RG 39, Series J, vol. 2, 182, 194–5, 202–6, 219–20, 227–30, 242–4, and 255–6.
90 The 1774 statute is the Supreme Court Circuit Act, S.N.S. 1774, c. 6, s. 2. For the 1793 repeal of this limitation see Courts of Justice Act, S.N.S. 1793, c. 17, s. 1. The calculations of sitting days are from the proceedings books at RG 39, Series J, vols. 1 and 2.
91 See variously Townshend, 'Historical Account,' 59; William Thompson's Mandamus, RG 1, vol. 347, no. 44; *Boston Weekly Newsletter*, 24 Mar. 1757; Monk, 'Observations on the Circuit Courts,' 143; Affidavit of William Nesbitt, 8 Sept. 1770, in Monk Papers, microfilm at NSARM; Haliburton, *Historical Account*, 2:339; Gibbons, 'Review,' 55.
92 See the list of tasks given in J.W. Nutting to Assembly, 24 Feb. 1829, RG 5, Series P, vol. 41, no. 102.
93 There is some useful information on the lower courts in S. Oxner, 'The Evolution of the Lower Court of Nova Scotia,' in P.B. Waite, et al., eds., *Law in a Colonial Society: The Nova Scotia Experience* (Toronto: Carswell 1984), 59–79. Gibbons, 'Review,' 44 is also informative. For the sessions as local government see D.C. Harvey, 'The Struggle for the New England Form of Township Government in Nova Scotia,' *Report of the Canadian Historical Association*, 1933, 15–22, and Trespass Act, S.N.S. 1758, c. 14. The creation of County and District Courts can be followed through the statutes.
94 The English court system is described in Beattie, *Crime and the Courts*, 4–6 and 283–8; for the criminal law in Nova Scotia in this period see Phillips, 'Criminal Law.'

95 The general figures are from a database compiled by Jim Phillips from the Supreme Court records, and within that for the 1754–97 period. For a discussion of that database and for other prosecution statistics see J. Phillips and A.N. May, 'Female Criminality in 18th Century Halifax,' *Acadiensis* 31 (2002): 71-96. For homicide cases see the same authors' 'Homicide in Nova Scotia, 1749–1815,' *Canadian Historical Review* 82 (2001): 625–61. More details on the effective jurisdictional breakdown between the courts are available in J. Phillips, 'Crime and Criminal Justice in Early Canada: Nova Scotia, 1749–1841,' monograph in progress, chap. 6.

96 Some accounts of circuit cases are in the bench books of Brenton and Deschamps, respectively at Acadia University Archives (microfilm at NSARM), and RG 39, Series C, Box A. We also have accounts of circuit and special commission trials from judges' reports to Governor and Council following capital convictions. The only published trial account for this period is a Lunenburg case, *The Trials of [the] Boutiliers*.

97 See J. Phillips, 'The Criminal Trial in Nova Scotia, 1749–1815,' in Baker and Phillips, eds., *Essays in Honour of Risk*.

98 Summary Trial Act, S.N.S. 1774, c. 15. For other legislation in this area, some of which was temporary albeit frequently renewed, see Murdoch, *History of Nova Scotia*, 2:198; Courts of Judicature Act, S.N.S. 1758, c. 36, in RG 5, Series S, vol. 1; Wilmot to Board of Trade, 17 Dec. 1764, CO 217, vol. 21, 132; Summary Trial of Actions Act, S.N.S. 1765, c. 11; Summary Trial Act, S.N.S. 1771, c. 21. The first 'small claims court,' a three-JP court, was introduced in Halifax in 1792: Summary Trial of Actions in Halifax Act, S.N.S. 1792, c. 14.

99 Courts of Judicature Act, S.N.S. 1758, c. 36, in RG 5, Series S, vol. 1; Courts of Judicature Act, S.N.S. 1763, 2nd Session, c. 6, in RG 5, Series S, vol. 2; Summary Trial of Actions Act, S.N.S. 1765, c. 11; Summary Trial of Actions Act, S.N.S. 1773, c. 9.

100 These figures are from Muir, 'Civil Law and the Colonial Economy in Halifax.'

101 Gibbons, 'Review,' 52.

102 What follows is very tentative and, unless otherwise stated, based on sampling of the Judgment Books in RG 39, Series J, Halifax, vols. 3 et seq. The figures given are thus for cases concluded, not suits filed. There are no available figures for the circuit courts in this period.

103 A notable exception is the work of Julian Gwyn, including his chapter in this volume, which also provides a useful summary of the types of cases litigated in the NSSC in this period.

104 What follows is based on principally on J. Cruikshank, 'The Chancery

Court of Nova Scotia: Jurisdiction and Procedure 1751–1855,' *Dalhousie Journal of Legal Studies* 1 (1992): 27–48; C.J. Townshend, *History of the Court of Chancery in Nova Scotia* (Toronto: Carswell 1900), 63–98; and two articles by J.B. Cahill: 'Bleak House Revisited: The Records and Papers of the Court of Chancery of Nova Scotia, 1751–1855,' *Archivaria* 29 (1989): 149–67 and 'From Imperium to Colony: Reinventing a Metropolitan Legal Institution in late Eighteenth-Century Nova Scotia,' in D.W. Nichol et al., eds., *Transatlantic Crossings: Eighteenth-Century Explorations* (St John's: Memorial University 1995). The best account of a Chancery case is P.V. Girard, 'Taking Litigation Seriously: The Market Wharf Controversy at Halifax, 1785–1820,' in Baker and Phillips, eds., *Essays in Honour of Risk*. See the sections below for nineteenth-century developments.

105 See Lawrence's request for precedents and proceedings books, Lawrence to Board of Trade, 15 Jan. 1754, CO 217, vol. 15, 3. For the kinds of cases heard in the years before 1764 see Chancery Records, RG 36, vol. 72.

106 This seems to have been the received wisdom about how the court worked in the eighteenth and early nineteenth centuries: see Undated Memorandum, c. 1852, in William Young Papers, MG 2, vol. 733, no. 324.

107 The figures are from Cruikshank, 'Chancery Court,' 31 and 33; the figure for mortgage foreclosures is for the 1751–1821 period.

108 For examples see Clarke and Phillips, ' The Course of Law,' at 464 et seq., and Gibbons, 'Review,' 51 and note 56.

109 The 'directions ... given by the Chief Justice for the conduct of practitioners' on that occasion have not survived; T.B. Akins, *History of Halifax City* (1895; repr. Halifax: Brook House Press 2002), 45.

110 The history of the first century of the bar of Nova Scotia has not been comprehensively studied, but for useful work see Bell, 'Maritime Legal Institutions,' and J.B. Cahill, 'The Origin and Evolution of the Attorney and Solicitor in the Legal Profession of Nova Scotia,' *Dalhousie Law Journal* 38 (1991): 277–95. See also, for colonial practitioners in Quebec and the southern colonies, D. Lemmings, *Professors of the Law: Barristers and English Legal Culture in the Eighteenth Century* (Oxford: Oxford University Press 2000), 225–74.

111 Bell, 'Maritime Legal Institutions,' 15.

112 Basic appointment and biographical information on the judges in this period is taken from the same sources as for the earlier discussion of the eighteenth-century appointees. In addition see also P. Blakeley, 'Sir Brenton Halliburton,' *DCB*, 8:354–7; B. Cuthbertson, 'Richard John Uniacke,' *DCB*, 6:792 and *The Old Attorney-General;* C.J. Townshend, 'Hon William Blowers Bliss,' *Collections of the Nova Scotia Historical Society* 17 (1913): 23–

46; P. Blakeley, 'William Blowers Bliss,' *DCB*, 10:72–3; D.G. Bell, 'Paths to the Law in the Maritimes, 1810–1825: The Bliss Brothers and their Circle,' *Nova Scotia Historical Review* 8 (1988): 6–39; P. Blakeley, 'Lewis Morris Wilkins,' *DCB*, 7:910–11; F. Cogswell, 'Thomas Chandler Haliburton,' *DCB*, 9:348–57; V.L.O. Chittick, *Thomas Chandler Haliburton: A Study in Provincial Toryism* (New York: Columbia University Press 1924); and A.A. Mackenzie, 'Edmund Murray Dodd,' *DCB*, 10:232–3.

113 For the establishment of the position see Supreme Court Act, S.N.S. 1809, c. 15, s. 6. Changes to circuit practice are discussed below.

114 See Blowers to Wiswall, 21 Jan. 1815, and Halliburton to Wiswall, 3 May 1830, Wiswall Papers, MG 1, vol. 979, folder 3, no. 6, and folder 5, no. 7.

115 Blakeley, 'Brenton Halliburton,' 355.

116 Supreme Court Act, S.N.S. 1809, c. 15, s. 7; Judicial Qualifications Act, R.S.N.S. 1864, c. 37.

117 Bell, 'Maritime Legal Institutions,' 122. On Blowers see also Girard's assessment that he was 'extremely competent and authoritative' and viewed by contemporaries as 'administering justice fairly according to law': 'Taking Litigation Seriously,' 226.

118 In part he wished to ensure that the job did not go to Attorney General R.J. Uniacke, Senior, a long-time rival; their enmity almost led to a duel in 1796. In part also he wanted to advance the claims of his protégé, Brenton Halliburton, who did get the post: see G. Patterson, 'Three Famous Duels,' in Patterson, ed., *Studies in Nova Scotian History* (Halifax: Imperial Publishing Co. 1941), and Cuthbertson, *The Old Attorney-General*, 118.

119 As described by Lieutenant Governor Dalhousie and cited in Blakeley, 'Brenton Halliburton,' 354.

120 Marshall, *A Brief History*, 3.

121 In addition to the general sources cited above, this paragraph is from B. Cuthbertson, *The Loyalist Governor: Biography of Sir John Wentworth* (Halifax: Nimbus 1983), 44 and 116; G.H. Monk to Sir James Monk, 23 Aug. 1801, Monk Papers, NSARM, Reel 1; Biographical notes on G.H. Monk, Monk Papers. For the pension see Monk Pension Act, S.N.S. 1816, c. 16.

122 P.V. Girard, 'The Supreme Court of Nova Scotia, Responsible Government, and the Quest for Legitimacy, 1850–1920,' *Dalhousie Law Journal* 17 (1994): 433.

123 Archibald turned down the offer in 1830 because he was waiting to inherit Blowers's job as Chief: see Cuthbertson, 'Richard John Uniacke,' 792, and Blowers to Wiswall, 6 Feb. 1830, MG 1, vol. 979, folder 3, no. 14.

124 See Girard, 'The Supreme Court of Nova Scotia,' 434.

125 For all of this see variously Colchester District Circuit Act, S.N.S. 1802, c. 1;

Pictou and Lunenburg Circuit Act, S.N.S. 1805, c. 13; Supreme Court Circuit Act, S.N.S. 1816, c. 2; Cape Breton Laws Act, S.N.S. 1820–1, c. 5, s. 2; Circuit Court Act, S.N.S. 1838, c. 6; Courts Act, S.N.S. 1841, c. 3, s. 22. The 1794 Nisi Prius Act, which had covered the South Shore and Sydney County and had expired some years earlier, was briefly renewed in 1804, but lasted only a year: see Nisi Prius Act, S.N.S. 1804, c. 3.

126 See Circuit Courts Act, S.N.S. 1799, c. 5, s. 1; Supreme Court Circuit Act, S.N.S. 1816, c. 2; Cape Breton Laws Act, S.N.S. 1820–1, c. 5, s. 2; Supreme Court Circuit Act, S.N.S. 1834, c. 4, s. 3; Sydney County Circuit Act, S.N.S. 1834–5, c. 52, s. 1; Courts Act, S.N.S. 1841, c. 3, s. 22.

127 The legislation discussed in this paragraph is Colchester District Circuit Act, S.N.S. 1802, c. 1, s. 2; Pictou and Lunenburg Circuit Act, 1805, c. 13, s. 5; Judicial Qualifications Act, S.N.S. 1809, c. 15, ss. 3–4; Supreme Court Circuit Act, S.N.S. 1834, c. 4 (quotation from preamble); Supreme Court Circuit Act, S.N.S. 1837, c. 54; Courts Act, S.N.S. 1841, c. 3, ss. 9 and 34.

128 See the various commissions issued to ICCP judges and others to sit at Truro, Pictou, and Amherst, in Council Minutes, 15 Apr. 1802, 21 May 1809, and 3 Aug. 1809, RG 1, vol. 191, 94, 330, and 346; Commissions, RG 1, vol. 172, 211; vol. 173, 46; and vol. 251, 153. For one-judge courts being the common, if not invariable practice, see G. Patterson, 'Old Court Records of Pictou County,' in Patterson, *Studies in Nova Scotia History*, 47, which shows Monk present at every session between 1806 and 1809, usually with no other NSSC judge present.

129 Blakeley, 'Lewis Morris Wilkins,' 911; Blowers to Wiswall, 28 Apr. 1831, MG 1, vol. 979, folder 3, no. 20, and Wilkins to Wiswall, 14 Mar. 1831, ibid., folder 6, no. 17; Halliburton to Wiswall, 12 May 1828, ibid., folder 5, no. 5.

130 Numerous examples of lobbying could be cited; the petitions series at NSARM is replete with them. For changing demographics see Lieutenant Governor Wentworth's comment on the 1805 statute which extended the circuit to Lunenburg County and Pictou district, that 'the increased population, property and commerce of those districts renders it necessary to provide for the more immediate administration of justice and laws, in them. It was very burdensome for the people to come to Halifax in pursuit of their business in the supreme court, and always attended with expense and frequently with insuperable difficulties in bringing evidence from such distance': Wentworth to Windham, 14 Nov. 1806, RG 1, vol. 54, 134–5.

131 Blowers did not go on circuit for 'many years' prior to 1833, except for the short trip to Windsor: Halliburton to Administrator of the Government, 15 Feb. 1833, in *JHA*, 1838, Appendix 2. For the widespread taking on of cir-

cuit duty see the public accounts in the Assembly Journals, which list payments for circuit expenses and from which one can calculate the days travelled by each, and the Judgment Books in the NSSC records for the various counties. See also, inter alia, A. Rizzatto and K. Peterson, 'The Supreme Court in Pictou, 1805–1867,' unpublished paper, 2003; Peleg Wiswall papers, MG 1, vol. 979; Supreme Court Judges to Lieutenant Governor, 21 Jan. 1842, RG 1, vol. 254, no. 72.

132 Blakeley, 'Lewis Morris Wilkins,' 911.

133 For an interesting overview of roads in the period see R. Mackinnon, 'Roads, Cart Tracks, and Bridle Paths: Land Transportation and the Domestic Economy of Nineteenth-Century Eastern British North America,' *Canadian Historical Review* 84 (2003): 147–216.

134 What follows is based on the various statutes already cited and on Beamish Murdoch's account of the circuit system, in *Epitome*, 3:55. See also for a similar general description set in the late 1820s Haliburton, *Historical and Statistical Account*, 2:332.

135 Bliss to Lieutenant Governor, 30 Jan. 1836, RG 1, vol. 241, no. 15; Blakeley, 'Brenton Halliburton,' 354; Halliburton to Wiswall, 13 July 1825, MG 1, vol. 979, folder 5, no. 3.

136 Halliburton, Bliss, Wilkins, Hill, and Haliburton to Lieutenant Governor Falkland, 29 Apr. 1842, *JHA*, 1842, Appendix 63. See also Haliburton to Howe, 21 July 1848, RG 1, vol. 257, no. 132; Haliburton to Stanley, 21 Aug. 1843, RG 1, vol. 255, no. 60; Courts Act, S.N.S. 1841, c. 3, s. 44.

137 See variously, inter alia, Marshall, *A Brief History*, 5; P. Girard, 'Patriot Jurist: Beamish Murdoch of Halifax, 1800–1876,' 132–53; Rizzatto and Peterson, 'The Supreme Court in Pictou,' 19; Blowers to Wiswall, 12 Nov. 1812, MG 1, vol. 979, folder 3, no. 3; T.C. Haliburton, *The Old Judge; or, Life in a Colony* (1849; Ottawa: Tecumseh Press Reprint 1978), 8.

138 Discussed in Phillips, 'The Criminal Trial,' 472–4.

139 Quotation from Murdoch, *Epitome*, 4:166. Numerous examples of the use of special commissions have survived: evidence can be found of them in various collections, especially the Council Minutes.

140 For examples see Report of J.G. Marshall, 1837, RG 1, vol. 252, no. 120; Haliburton to Hill, 15 Nov. 1830, RG 1, vol. 236, no. 91; Appropriations Act, S.N.S. 1834, c. 11, s. 1.

141 The best account of the movement is P.A. Buckner, *The Transition to Responsible Government: British Policy in British North America, 1815–1850* (Westport, CT: Greenwood Press 1985). Also useful is J.M. Beck, *Joseph Howe: Volume I – Conservative Reformer, 1804–1848* (Montreal and Kingston: McGill-Queen's University Press 1982). For general reviews of the

decade of the 1830s in particular see Beck, *Politics*, 1:101 et seq., and R. Ommer, 'The 1830s: Adapting Their Institutions to Their Desires,' in P.A. Buckner and J. Reid, eds., *The Atlantic Region to Confederation: A History* (Fredericton: Acadiensis Press 1994), chap. 13.

142 Judicial Qualifications Act, S.N.S. 1809, c. 15, ss. 8 and 9. When Foster Hutchinson Junior was appointed in 1810 he was the sitting member for Halifax Township. The Assembly's Committee on Privileges reported that the intention of the 1809 Act was to debar judges from membership, and the Assembly adopted that report and declared Hutchinson's seat vacant. When L.M. Wilkins Senior was appointed in 1816 he resigned his Assembly seat about a year later: see Cahill, 'The "Judges' Affair",' 200 and 203.

143 Supreme Court Circuit Act, S.N.S. 1816, c. 2, s. 3.

144 Equal Administration of Justice Act, S.N.S. 1824, c. 38, ss. 5 and 6. A similar measure had been put in place for Cape Breton Island the previous year, but there were no such restrictions on the person appointed: see Cape Breton Justice Act, S.N.S. 1823, c. 36.

145 See Girard, 'Supreme Court of Nova Scotia,' 433; *Master of the Rolls Act*, S.N.S. 1834–1835, c. 26; *JHA*, 1834–35, *passim*.

146 Murdoch, *Epitome*, 3:61.

147 Blakeley, 'Brenton Halliburton,' 355. For his conservative views see, inter alia, Halliburton to Wiswall, 3 May 1830 and 8 May 1835, MG 1, vol. 979, folder 5, nos. 9 and 13.

148 JHA, 1837, 1 March 1837, 85–6.

149 Glenelg to Campbell, 30 Apr. 1837, in *JHA*, 1838, Appendix 2. See also generally Bell, 'Maritime Legal Institutions,' 121, and Girard, 'The Supreme Court of Nova Scotia,' 433–4. Councillors could, however, be appointed to the bench, as was the case with Simon B. Robie, made M.R. in 1826. For the exclusion of the judges in the Canadas from formal political posts see Oliver, 'Power, Politics, and the Law,' esp. at 456–7, and many of the essays in Greenwood and Wright, eds., *Canadian State Trials: Volume I*.

150 Halliburton to Sir Howard ?, 14 Nov. 1844, MG 1, vol. 334, no. 104.

151 Archibald to William Hill, 10 Dec. 1830, RG 1, vol. 282, no. 25.

152 Halliburton to Admiral Sir Charles Ogle, 23 Mar. 1837, RG 1, vol. 282, no. 13.

153 See, for example, Halliburton and Stewart to Provincial Secretary, 5 Nov. 1822, RG 1, vol. 230, no. 199, answering the government's question about whether more JPs were needed in the 'eastern districts' and making recommendations. See also Wilkins recommending the removal of a JP and Blowers offering names of who might be added to the commission of the peace: Wilkins to Kempt, 5 Aug. 1828, RG 1, vol. 235, no. 43 and Blowers to Kempt, 10 Aug. 1828, ibid., no. 50.

154 Halliburton's Observations, July 1831, RG 1, vol. 282, no. 132. For Halliburton's involvement with this issue see Blakeley, 'Brenton Halliburton,' 355.

155 See generally Murdoch, *Epitome*, 3:53–4; Judicial Qualifications Act, S.N.S. 1809, c. 15, s. 9; Supreme Court Act, S.N.S. 1816, c. 2, s. 5; Judicial Qualifications Amendment Act, S.N.S. 1822, c. 33; Memorial of Monk and Halliburton to Governor, 16 Dec. 1808, RG 1, vol. 287, no. 176. In fact the assistants often received six hundred pounds before 1822, by means of ad hoc appropriations: see Appropriations Act, S.N.S. 1815, c. 1, and 1816, c. 1, giving them an extra one hundred pounds. The 1822 statute referred to the one hundred pounds as 'hitherto voted annually' and now being made 'a permanent provision.'

156 Currency Act, S.N.S. 1834, c. 61, s. 1.

157 Master of the Rolls Act, S.N.S. 1826, c. 11, s. 1.

158 Blakeley, 'Lewis Morris Wilkins,' 911; Goderich to Officer Administering the Government, 4 Dec. 1832, *JHA*, 1832, Appendix 2. For the comparison see Halliburton to Assembly Committee on the Judiciary, 21 Feb. 1838, in *JHA*, 1838, Appendix 39, showing that Nova Scotia's £480 sterling compared unfavourably with New Brunswick (£650), Newfoundland (£700), and Upper and Lower Canada (each £900).

159 For this information on fees see, inter alia, Campbell to Glenelg, 26 Aug. 1837, Halliburton to Administrator of the Government, 15 Feb. 1833, and Halliburton to George, 18 Jan. 1838, all in *JHA*, 1838, Appendix 2; Halliburton to George, 20 Feb. 1834, ibid. 1834, Appendix 20.

160 Sources for the fees issue are scattered throughout the Assembly Journals of the 1830s. See particularly Halliburton to Administrator of the Government, 15 Feb. 1833, Glenelg to Campbell, 31 Oct. 1837, and Halliburton to George, 18 Jan. 1838, all in *JHA*, 1838, Appendix 2; Halliburton to James, 23 Mar. 1836, ibid., 1836, Appendix 76.

161 Halliburton to James, 23 Mar. 1836, *JHA* 1836, Appendix 76. For the Assembly resolution see JHA 1836, 26 Mar. 1836, 1003. The Assembly twice passed bills, in 1835 and 1836, to abolish fees, but each was rejected by council.

162 Blowers to Wiswall, 18 Mar. 1830, MG 1, vol. 979, folder 3, no. 16.

163 Courts Act, S.N.S. 1841, c. 3, s. 33.

164 Haliburton to Howe, 21 July 1848, RG 1, vol. 257, no. 132.

165 For what follows see principally P. Burroughs, 'The Search for Economy: Imperial Administration of Nova Scotia in the 1830s,' *Canadian Historical Review* 49 (1968): 24–43; D.C. Harvey, 'The Civil List and Responsible Government in Nova Scotia,' *Canadian Historical Review* 28 (1947): 365–82; and

J. Phillips, 'Reformers, Judges, and Coal Miners: The Politics of Judicial Reform in Nova Scotia, 1824–1848,' unpublished paper, 2004. There is also a wealth of material on the judicial salary issue in the Assembly Journals for the 1830s and 1840s.

166 Civil List Act, S.N.S. 1844, c. 63, s. 2; Civil List Act, S.N.S. 1848, c. 24, s. 2; Civil List Act, S.N.S. 1849, c. 1, s. 2. The M.R.'s salary was also set at £560 sterling in the 1844 and 1848 Acts.

167 This section on arrears is from a variety of sources, principally Burroughs, 'Search for Economy,' and Halliburton to Lieutenant Governor, 14 Aug. 1843, Halliburton Papers, MG 1, vol. 334, no. 46, from which the quotations are drawn. See also the correspondence and other documents in *JHA*, 1838, Appendices 80 and 83; 1839, Appendix 21; 1846, Appendix 14; 1849, Appendix 10.

168 These figures are from a report presented to the Assembly in early 1841, and reproduced in *JHA*, 1841, Appendix 22. There were similarly low figures in the early 1830s: see *JHA*, 1838, Appendices 12 and 39. The figure for sessions court trials is approximate because there were no returns from three counties and the committee assigned them an average of the others.

169 Pictou *Bee*, 21 Sept. 1836, cited in Rizzatto and Peterson, 'The Supreme Court in Pictou,' 23.

170 This was done in 1823 for Cape Breton and 1824 for the rest of the colony: see Cape Breton Justice Act, S.N.S. 1823, c. 36, and Equal Administration of Justice Act, S.N.S. 1824, c. 38. The mainland divisions were designated as eastern (Sydney, Cumberland, Pictou, and Colchester), middle (Hants, Kings, Lunenburg, and Queens), and western (Annapolis, Shelburne, Yarmouth, and Argyle). First justices of the middle division were father and son William Hersey Otis Haliburton (1824–9) and Thomas Chandler Haliburton (1829–41); for the eastern division they were Jared Ingersoll Chipman (1824–32) and William Sawers (1832–41); for the western division Thomas Ritchie served from 1824 until abolition in 1841; and John George Marshall was first justice for Cape Breton 1823–41.

171 *JHA*, 1824, 395. See generally J.M. Beck, *Government of Nova Scotia* (Toronto: University of Toronto Press 1957), 67, and Murdoch's comment that '[o]pinion was much divided as to the propriety' of the division system: *Epitome*, vol. 3, 60. Critics' concerns were to some extent borne out by the case of William Sawers, a Halifax lawyer. The original Act had required first justices to live in the division, but he was able to get an amendment allowing him to live 'in any part of the district of Halifax': Equal Administration of Justice Amendment Act, S.N.S. 1833, c. 64.

172 Each had a salary of four hundred pounds local currency; the first justice

for Cape Breton had a maximum travel allowance of one hundred pounds, the others one of fifty pounds.

173 Speech to Assembly, *Acadian Recorder*, 20 Mar. 1830, cited in Beck, *Government of Nova Scotia*, 128.

174 For previous reform bills see *Novascotian*, 23 Jan. 1840; RG 5, Series U, vol. 14, 1838; *JHA*, 1840, 659 and 792. For brief accounts of the court reforms see Beck, *Government of Nova Scotia*, 128, and *Joseph Howe*, 174, 207, and 227. For the dominance of financial concerns in the debates see the reports in, inter alia, *Novascotian*, 11 Feb. and 4 and 18 Mar. 1841, and *Acadian Recorder*, 20 Mar. 1841.

175 Courts Act, S.N.S. 1841, c. 3. There is not space here to discuss the Halifax courts. For more on the new arrangements for the capital, and on subsequent changes, see P. Girard, 'The Maritime Provinces, 1850–1939: Lawyers and Legal Institutions,' *Manitoba Law Journal* 23 (1996): 383, and 'The Rise and Fall of Urban Justice in Halifax, 1815–1886,' *Nova Scotia Historical Review* 8 (1988): 57–71.

176 Marshall to Sir Rupert George, 11 Mar. 1840, RG 1, vol. 253, no. 75; Lieutenant Governor Falkland to Marshall, 30 Mar. 1841, and Marshall to Falkland, 30 Mar. 1841, J.G. Marshall Papers, MG 1, vol. 1282, nos. 7 and 9.

177 The pensions were to cease if the payees took a government post of at least equal value. Ritchie died in 1852 but Marshall and Sawers were still receiving their pensions in 1864: see Civil List Act, R.S.N.S. 1864, c. 36. Marshall lobbied for a larger pension than the others, on the grounds that his salary had been greater and his service longer: see Marshall to Lord Stanley, 3 Jan. 1842, and enclosures, MG 1, vol. 1282, no. 10. For Haliburton's pension, see below.

178 In January 1840, for example, John Morton, MHA for Cornwallis Township, brought in a bill to reduce the costs of the judiciary by eliminating one of the NSSC assistant posts. Although Joseph Howe insisted that the Assembly had every right to either reduce judicial salaries or abolish positions, Morton himself acknowledged that 'the present officers should be provided for, that the House could not touch them': *Novascotian*, 23 Jan. 1840.

179 Courts Act, S.N.S. 1841, c. 3, preamble.

180 Murdoch wrote very favourably about the experiment: see *Epitome*, 3:60–1. But he also thought there was generally something 'incongruous' in the fact that 'private gentlemen, not lawyers' acted as assistant judges in the ICCPs deciding 'questions of a legal character': ibid., 60.

181 See here William Young's complaint during an Assembly debate over the 1841 Courts bill that some sessions presidents had taken on a larger crimi-

nal jurisdiction for their courts than had been the practice, and his assertion that 'it would never do to leave trials by Jury to the Courts of Quarter Sessions unless they had legal minds to preside over them': *Acadian Recorder*, 6 Mar. 1841.

182 Judges Act, S.N.S. 1848, c. 21.

183 The various observations and protests of the objectors can be found in *Legislative Council Journals*, 1848, Appendix 29, and *JHA*, 1848, Appendix 7. See also Halliburton to Provincial Secretary, 18 Mar. 1848, RG 1, vol. 257, no. 67. For a brief account of the controversy see Townshend, 'Historical Account,' 94.

184 Beck, *Politics*, 1:132.

185 A full discussion of appeals can be found in Murdoch, *Epitome*, 4:22–7.

186 This issue is discussed in detail in Part III, below.

187 Summary Trial Act, S.N.S. 1807, c. 12. It is very difficult to chart whether this regime was in force in every single year after 1807, for the statutes all expired after short intervals. There were, however, numerous, although not annual, renewing statutes, and the 1807 regime is the one described in Haliburton, *Historical Account*, 2:332–7, J. McGregor, *Historical and Descriptive Sketches of the Maritime Colonies of British America* (London: Longman 1828), 128, and Murdoch, *Epitome*, 4:19.

188 Summary Trial Act, 1817, c. 11.

189 Halifax Court of Commissioners Act, S.N.S. 1824, c. 36. Again, it is very difficult to follow the precise progress of the various Acts which revived and continued expired legislation in this area, but the 1817 legislation does seem to have expired before 1822, when it was revived (Summary Trial Act, S.N.S. 1822, c. 35), and from 1825 there are almost annual statutes continuing the commissioners' court in Halifax.

190 Cape Breton Summary Trial Act, S.N.S. 1837, c. 59.

191 Girard, 'Patriot Jurist,' 161–2.

192 Summary Trial of Actions Act, S.N.S. 1807, c. 12, s. 1; Expenses of Suits Act, S.N.S. 1832, c. 53, located at RG 5, Series S, vol. 19, 1832. The latter expired after two years and was not revived.

193 Murdoch, *Epitome*, 4:22.

194 As before, caseload information is from sampling of the Judgement Books in RG 39, Halifax, Series J, vols. 12 et seq.

195 For other evidence about the profile of litigation see the chapter by Gwyn, this volume; D. Darling, 'Nova Scotia Supreme Court Records, 1830–1832,' unpublished paper, 1993; Girard, 'Patriot Jurist,' esp. at 161 et seq.

196 In addition to the judgment books, jury trial figures are from *JHA*, 1841, Appendix 22. See also for the early 1830s *JHA*, 1838, Appendices 12 and 39.

197 See Girard, 'Patriot Jurist,' esp. at 160 and 176.
198 The information summarized here is from RG 39, Kings County, Series J, vol. 1; Rizzatto and Peterson, 'The Supreme Court in Pictou,' 14 and 19; *JHA*, 1838, Appendices 12 and 39, and 1841, Appendix 22.
199 See the comment by Nathaniel White, writing from Annapolis Royal in 1815, cited in Girard, 'Patriot Jurist,' 81: 'There is ... scarcely an individual who is not in the course of the year either a Plaintiff or Defendant.' See also one traveller's complaint that 'the people fly to litigation on the most trivial occasion': McGregor, *Historical and Descriptive Sketches*, 128.
200 Between 1832 and 1836 there were 3,790 actions entered in the NSSC in all counties, and 4,064 in the ICCP. There were, however, considerably more trials in the former: see *JHA*, 1838, Appendices 12 and 39, and 1841, Appendix 22. See the county breakdowns in these sources for regional variations.
201 The figures collected by the Assembly for the 1835–9 period show that 137 of 185 (74 per cent) trials held with juries in the sessions courts outside Halifax were for assault. Larceny accounted for a further 27 (15 per cent). See *JHA*, 1841, Appendix 22. For the prevalence of assault cases see also the various reports sent to Halifax by the divisional chief justices. An example is W.H.O. Haliburton to Sir James Kempt, 9 Feb. 1828, RG 1, vol. 235, no. 4, reporting that at Lunenburg there had been 'several trials on Indictments for assault and Battery,' but no other criminal cases, while the Horton sessions similarly saw 'several trials for assault and battery.' In the same year Jared Chipman reported for his division, the eastern, that there were 'occasional convictions for Petit Larcenies & misdemeanours & some for ... Assaults and Batteries': Chipman to Sir James Kempt, 16 Feb. 1828, ibid., no. 8.
202 *Novascotian*, 9 Nov. 1825.
203 See *JHA*, 1838, Appendix 75, and 1841, Appendix 22.
204 This suggestion comes from a speech by William Young, later Nova Scotia chief justice, in an 1841 Assembly debate: see *Acadian Recorder*, 6 Mar. 1841.
205 Stipendiary Magistrates Act, S.N.S. 1864, c. 15.
206 This discussion of criminal cases in the NSSC at Halifax, and of commutations and executions, is from *JHA*, 1841, Appendix 22, for which the detailed breakdowns are at RG 1, vol. 245, no. 98; Phillips, 'Royal Pardon'; Deputy-Prothonotary Nutting's list of cases prosecuted in the Supreme Court, RG 5, Series P, vol. 41, no. 102; Council Minutes, RG 1, vols. 193–8, *passim*.
207 *JHA*, 1841, Appendix 22. The same report shows some 220 trials at county and district sessions in the same period, for petty larcenies and assaults.
208 For these cases see Phillips, 'Criminal Trial,' 472–4; Council Minutes,

1817–40, RG 1, vols. 193–8, *passim.* Walter Lee's execution warrant is reproduced in the illustrations section.

209 For criminal law reform see J. Phillips, 'The Reform of Nova Scotia's Criminal Law, 1830–1844,' unpublished paper, presented to the Canadian Law in History Conference, Ottawa, 1988.

210 For Admiralty Sessions see the essay by Muir and Phillips, this volume. For examples see *R. v. Lovegrove*, 1793, in RG 1, vol. 342, and the 'Court of Piracy and Murder' convened for the trial of the crew of the *Saladin* in 1844, for which the five judges were Vice-Admiral Sir Charles Adam, and Halliburton, Hill, Bliss, and Haliburton: RG 1, vol. 255, no. 126.

211 Girard, 'The Maritime Provinces,' 380; Divorce Court Act, S.N.S. 1841, c. 13, s. 1. See generally Smith-Maynard, 'Divorce in Nova Scotia.'

212 This section on Chancery is drawn principally from the sources listed for the earlier discussion of it in this chapter.

213 See Halliburton, Bliss, and Hill to N.W. White, Registrar of Chancery, 19 May 1835, RG 1, vol. 252, no. 32; Undated Memorandum, c. 1852, William Young Papers, MG 2, vol. 733, no. 324.

214 Master of the Rolls Act, S.N.S. 1826, c. 11. The first holder of the post was Simon Bradstreet Robie, former solicitor general. He replaced Blowers, who had been M.R. since 1818. Robie was succeeded by Charles Rufus Fairbanks (1834–41), S.G.W. Archibald (1841–46), and Alexander Stewart (1846 until the abolition of the court in 1855).

215 See William Young's complaint about the cost and his suggestion that the position be a temporary one, cited in Murdoch, *History of Nova Scotia*, 3:547. See to similar effect Joseph Howe's objections, to this and the division system for the lower courts, both of which he viewed as the unnecessary creation of judgeships to be parcelled out to government supporters: Beck, *Joseph Howe*, 111.

216 See Halliburton, Bliss, and Hill to N.W. White, Registrar of Chancery, 19 May 1835, RG 1, vol. 252, no. 32, and Glenelg to Campbell, 29 May 1838, RG 1, vol. 252, no. 142.

217 See *Mason v. Chamberlain* (1834), 1 N.S.R. 7; *Metzler v. Harvie* (1836), 1 N.S.R. 64; *Miller v. Lanty* (1840), 1 N.S.R. 161, per Hill J.; *Ells v. Ells* (1841), 1 N.S.R. 173. The court would not, however, deal with a case that was squarely one for Chancery: see *Etter v. Copp* (1855), 2 N.S. R. 344.

218 Quotation from Haliburton, *Historical Account*, 2:328. For critiques of Chancery see also Girard, 'The Maritime Provinces,' 382 and 'Married Women's Property, Chancery Abolition, and Insolvency Law: Law Reform in Nova Scotia, 1820–1867,' in Girard and Phillips, eds., *Essays*, and Beck, *Government of Nova Scotia*, 130.

219 These figures are from Cruickshank, 'The Chancery Court of Nova Scotia,'

31 and 33. See also the listing of all causes commenced in the court in the period 1826–36, in *JHA*, 1838, Appendix 12.

220 Supreme Court Act, S.N.S. 1825, c. 23, and Murdoch, *Epitome*, 3:55; Courts Act, S.N.S. 1841, c. 3, s. 32.

221 See, for example, Supreme Court Terms Act, S.N.S. 1833, c. 59, and Murdoch, *Epitome*, 3:55.

222 Administration of the Law Act, S.N.S. 1847, c. 2.

223 Appointment of County Clerks Act, S.N.S. 1819, c. 10.

224 See, inter alia, Haliburton, *Historical Account*, 2:339; Nutting Papers, MG 1, vol. 1126; Attorneys Act, S.N.S. 1811, c. 3, s. 15; Supreme Court Clerks Act, S.N.S. 1819, c. 10, s. 1; Nutting's Report, 10 Mar. 1841, RG 1, vol. 254, no. 16. Cape Breton was the exception to this system. It had its own Supreme Court and prothonotary (Charles Leonard) as an independent colony until 1820. After annexation Leonard was appointed prothonotary for the Island by Blowers and the lieutenant governor. In the early 1840s there was some question about whether this arrangement was compatible with Nutting's patent appointment as prothonotary for the whole colony, but Leonard's status, and the validity of all acts performed by him, were confirmed by statute. For the Cape Breton system see Nutting's Report, 10 Mar. 1841, RG 1, vol. 254, no. 16, and Cape Breton Prothonotary Act, S.N.S. 1841, c. 45.

225 See Nutting's Petition to Assembly, 24 Feb. 1829, RG 5, Series P, vol. 41, no. 102.

226 Attorneys Act, S.N.S. 1811, c. 3. See also the useful discussion in Girard, 'Patriot Jurist,' 118 et seq.

227 See the examples in Girard, 'Patriot Jurist,' 129.

228 Barristers and Attorneys Act, S.N.S. 1818, c. 19; Barristers and Attorneys Act, S.N.S. 1836, c. 89. There were other small changes, such as the introduction of a minimum period of practice for lawyers who qualified elsewhere, and the removal of the need to attend the terms of the Supreme Court before call, but the 1836 regime was not materially different from its predecessor. It was continued by Barristers and Attorneys Act, S.N.S. 1846, c. 42.

229 For this incident see Cahill, 'Origin and Evolution,' 285 and note 35.

230 The best account of the profession in this period is Girard, 'Patriot Jurist,' chap. 4.

231 Only the Law Society of Upper Canada (1797) is older: see C. Moore, *The Law Society of Upper Canada and Ontario's Lawyers, 1797–1997* (Toronto: University of Toronto Press 1997). For brief accounts of the Barristers' Society see Girard, 'Patriot Jurist,' 146 et seq., and the same author's 'The

Roots of a Professional Renaissance: Lawyers in Nova Scotia, 1850–1910,' *Manitoba Law Journal* 20 (1991): 53–155.

232 Girard, 'Patriot Jurist,' 148.

233 For this case see Stone, 'Admiralty Court,' 407–9. The lawyer concerned, William Sutherland, afterwards became recorder of Halifax.

234 RG 5, Series P, vol. 8A, no. 80 (27 Feb. 1844); *JHA*, 1844, Petition No 40, Bill no. 81. The incorporation bill was deferred until the next session and not reintroduced. Incorporation was achieved in 1858.

235 The various administrative changes in circuit operation can be traced through the statutes; examples include Supreme Court Act, R.S.N.S. 1851, c. 126, s. 3; Supreme Court Amendment Act, S.N.S. 1855, c. 20; Supreme Court Amendment Act, S.N.S. 1859, c. 33; Supreme Court Act, R.S.N.S. 1864, c. 123, s. 4; Supreme Court (Cape Breton Circuit) Act, S.N.S. 1866, c. 39.

236 See the various Civil List Acts at S.N.S. 1849, c. 1, s. 2; R.S.N.S. 1851, c. 34, s. 1; R.S.N.S. 1859, c. 34, s. 1; R.S.N.S. 1864, c. 36, s. 1. See also Salaries and Pensions for 1857, RG 1, vol. 267, no. 135, and List of Officers and Salaries, 1858, RG 1, vol. 268, no. 111.

237 Divorce and Matrimonial Causes Amendment Act, S.N.S. 1866, c. 13; Smith-Maynard, 'Divorce in Nova Scotia,' 241. For the judge in equity, see below.

238 Law and Equity Commission Act, S.N.S. 1832, c. 42; Law and Equity Commission Repeal Act, S.N.S. 1837, c. 50.

239 Courts Act, S.N.S. 1841, c. 3, s. 43.

240 Supreme Court Practice Act, S.N.S. 1848, c. 41.

241 See Supreme Court Practice Act, S.N.S. 1853, c. 4. For the English reforms, which began in the early 1830s see J.H. Baker, *An Introduction to English Legal History*, (4th ed. (London: Butterworths 2002), 83–4. For the abolition of the forms of action see the chapter by Girard, this volume.

242 Administration of Criminal Justice Act, S.N.S. 1852, c. 1.

243 See Report of the Law Reform Commissioners, 29 Mar. 1852, in *JHA*, 1852, Appendix 73. See also an earlier report in ibid., Appendix 16. The commission members were Haliburton, Bliss, Howe, J.B. Uniacke, J.W. Johnston, William Young, and W.A. Henry. For the commission's reliance on recent English changes see Halliburton to Harvey, 5 June 1853, MG 1, vol. 334, no. 57.

244 Prothonotaries and Clerks of the Crown Act, S.N.S. 1853, c. 13.

245 See variously *JHA*, 1860, 183–4, and Appendices at 225–6; Prothonotaries and Clerks of the Crown Act, R.S.N.S. 1864, c. 43; J. Rowley, Yarmouth, to Tupper, 12 Feb. and 17 Dec. 1863, RG 1, vol. 273, nos. 20 and 69; R. Thom-

son, Shelburne, to Wilkins, 15 June 1854, RG 1, vol. 264, no. 57. It seems probable that Nutting did not need to draw on the fund after 1855 because of the transfer of equity cases to the NSSC from that year, discussed below, which increased the NSSC's caseload, and in consequence, his fees.

246 In three terms in 1845 the court recorded 303 judgments, compared to 344 in four terms of 1835. In 1853 only 193 judgments were recorded. These figures are from RG 39, Halifax, Series J, vols. 47–8 and 54.

247 See Bliss to Administrator of the Government, 4 Apr. 1864, RG 1, vol. 274, no. 37.

248 See the commentary in *Acadian Recorder*, 8 Dec. 1855, suggesting that not only had Chancery abolition caused an expansion of the docket, but also that the 'ordinary business' of the court had 'increased very much within the last few years.' See also *JHA*, 1856, Appendix 83, and the evidence of the fund to guarantee the salary of the Halifax prothonotary, discussed in note 245 above.

249 See RG 39, Series C, Box A, no. 11, a list of arguments in the NSSC at Halifax from 1850 to 1854, compiled by prothonotary Nutting and also published in *JHA*, 1854–5, Appendix 61. It shows the court regularly engaged on motions and other argument on nine to twelve days a term. See also the court reports in *Acadian Recorder*, 21 Nov. and 26 Dec. 1857, which imply that cases were taking a good deal of time.

250 For an increase in the Pictou caseload in the 1840s and 1850s, after the abolition of the ICCP, see Rizzato and Peterson, 'The Supreme Court at Pictou,' 30.

251 For the former see the Supreme Court Special Sittings Acts: S.N.S. 1854, c. 20; S.N.S. 1857, c. 17. For the latter see Summary Proceedings Act, S.N.S. 1858, c. 16.

252 See Stipendiary Magistrates Act, S.N.S. 1864, c. 15. The magistrates were to be appointed by JPs in sessions from among their number. Halifax chose Henry Pryor, QC and MHA: see Stipendiary Magistrates Act, S.N.S. 1867, c. 82.

253 Supreme Court Act, S.N.S. 1862, c. 5, s. 1. On the uncleared docket, see one local newspaper's comment that '[t]here still remains a large amount of business on the docket which will not be reached this term' and its assertion that 'something must be done to relieve the Court of the large amount of business that accumulates from term to term': *Colonial Standard* (Pictou), 28 Oct. 1862, cited in Rizzatto and Peterson, 'The Supreme Court at Pictou,' 35.

254 Record of Criminal Trials Conducted in Halifax, 1850–1852, RG 39, Series C, Box A, no. 12.

255 *Acadian Recorder*, 8 Dec. 1855, 5 Dec. 1857, and 26 Apr. 1862.

256 See Haliburton's Trial Report, RG 1, vol. 264, no. 140; Pardon of James Heislin, OS Series, no. 426.

257 See Memorial from Judge Haliburton to Howe, Provincial Secretary, 21 July 1848, RG 1, vol. 257, no. 132, re an addition to his salary, and Haliburton to Lord Stanley, 21 Aug. 1843, RG 1, vol. 255, no. 60, re an exemption from the rule that judges on leave of absence received only half-pay. Halliburton won the latter argument, but lost a later attempt to receive full pay while on leave: see Haliburton to Howe, 29 Oct. 1853, Howe to Haliburton, and Opinion of Attorney General J.B. Uniacke, 10 and 15 Nov. 1853, RG 1, vol. 263, nos. 85, 88, and 94.

258 For all of this, and for much of what follows, see the sources on the judges cited above, and J.M. Beck, 'Sir William Young,' *DCB*, 11:943–9; D.A. Sutherland, 'James William Johnston,' *DCB*, 10:383–8; J.Y. Payzant, 'James William Johnston, First Premier of Nova Scotia Under Responsible Government,' *Collections of the Nova Scotia Historical Society* 16 (1912): 61–92; L. Kernaghan, 'Lewis Morris Wilkins,' *DCB*, 11:925–6.

259 See W. Laurence, 'Acquiring the Law: The Private Law Library of William Young,' *Dalhousie Law Journal* 21 (1998): 490–515.

260 Girard, 'The Supreme Court of Nova Scotia,' 434.

261 This section is largely based on Girard, 'Chancery Abolition,' 106 et seq., the most comprehensive account of the reform process. It has been supplemented by the other sources on the history of Chancery in Nova Scotia, cited above, and by a useful account of the court through the practice of one Halifax lawyer, Beamish Murdoch, in Girard, 'Patriot Jurist,' 205 et seq.

262 They were enacted in Chancery Practice Act, S.N.S. 1833, c. 52.

263 See, inter alia, Stewart to Harvey, 28 Mar. 1851, and to Keating, 4 Apr. 1851, and Harvey to Earl Grey, 30 Apr. 1851, at RG 1, vol. 260, nos. 23, 29, and 52.

264 'I am unacquainted with the principles and proceedings of Equity jurisdiction,' he told Provincial Secretary Howe, adding that while he would do his best he feared that 'the fusion of the courts of law and equity ... will tend to embarrass the proceedings of the Supreme Court': Dodd to Howe, 17 Mar. 1853, RG 1, vol. 263, no. 24. Halliburton argued that if the court was abolished it would later have to be reconstituted: Blakeley, 'Brenton Halliburton,' 357. For his objections see Observations on Proposed Changes to Courts and Law, 31 Dec. 1854, RG 1, vol. 282, no. 126; Halliburton to Harvey, 28 June 1853, MG 1, vol. 334, no. 57; and Halliburton's Notes on Chancery, n.d., MG 1, vol. 334, no. 57A.

265 Report of the Law Reform Commissioners, 1853, in *JHA*, 1853, Appendix 16.

266 Stewart to Lieutenant Governor, 21 Oct. 1853, RG 1, vol. 263, no. 82; Stewart to Wilkins, 2 Mar. 1855, RG 1, vol. 265, no. 22. He consistently argued that he was entitled to his full salary, that the Legislature could abolish the court, but not his office.

267 Chancery Abolition Act, S.N.S. 1855, c. 23.

268 Bliss apparently said that 'we would have to feel our way' when dealing with formerly Chancery cases. For this and for other evidence of difficulties see Girard, 'Chancery Abolition,' 113.

269 This analysis is from volumes 3–6 of the Nova Scotia Reports.

270 Judge in Equity Act, S.N.S. 1864, c. 10; Bliss to Provincial Secretary, 4 July 1864, RG 1, vol. 274, no. 71.

271 See Townshend, 'Historical Account,' esp. at 96–7. Although an NSSC judge himself, Townshend was also Stewart's grandson and his account of the abolition of Chancery and the creation of the judge in equity is very much a defence of Stewart.

272 Girard, 'The Maritime Provinces,' 382.

273 For this and what follows see Judicial Resignation, in *JHA*, 1864, Appendix 30.

274 Judge in Equity Act, S.N.S. 1864, c. 10, s. 1. In fact it was filled and another judgeship created, but by then Confederation had intervened.

275 The New Brunswick Reports date from 1835, those for Upper Canada from the same decade. These admiralty 'reports' consisted of five pamphlets about particular decisions of Vice-Admiralty Judge Alexander Croke and a one-volume compilation of Croke's decisions by then Solicitor General James Stewart: see Bell, 'Maritime Legal Institutions,' 125; J. Stewart, *Reports of Cases, Argued and Determined in the Court of Vice-Admiralty, at Halifax* (London, 1814).

276 See variously R.J. Uniacke, comp., *The Statutes at Large Passed in the Several General Assemblies Held in His Majesty's Province of Nova Scotia* (Halifax: King's Printer 1805); Murdoch, *Epitome*; and J.G. Marshall, *The Justice of the Peace and County and Township Officer* (Halifax: Gossip and Coade 1837). For the significance of Murdoch's *Epitome* see Girard, 'Patriot Jurist,' chap. 8 and 'Themes and Variations in Early Canadian Legal Culture: Beamish Murdoch and his Epitome of the Laws of Nova Scotia,' *Law and History Review* 11 (1993) 101–44. For a general discussion of legal publishing in the Maritimes before c. 1850 see Bell, 'Maritime Legal Institutions,' 123–5.

277 Haliburton, *Historical Account*, 2:333; quotation below at 334.

278 A succinct account of the early history of law reporting can be found in J.

Nedelsky and J. Long, *Law Reporting in the Maritime Provinces: History and Development* (Ottawa: Canadian Law Information Council 1981). For James's petition to be appointed law reporter see James to Falkland, 31 Dec. 1844, RG 1, vol. 255, no. 138.

279 For this and a long account of his efforts see James to Howe, 5 Apr. 1853, RG 1, vol. 263, no. 33. See also James to Attorney General, 30 Jan. 1852, RG 1, vol. 261, no. 37.

280 *JHA*, 1853, 28 Jan. and Appendix 64. See also Thomson to Howe, 27 Oct. 1852, RG 1, vol. 262, no. 72, indicating that he had Halliburton's support for the venture.

281 See RG 1, vol. 266, no. 11.5 (from catalogue, document not extant).

282 See Cochran to Lieutenant Governor Mulgrave, 4 Mar. 1862, RG 1, vol. 272, no. 24, and Memorial of Nova Scotia Barristers' Society, 8 Feb. 1865, RG 1, vol. 276, no. 24.5.

283 Some work has been done. See the essays by Hibbitts and Muir, this volume. See also P. Karsten, *Between Law and Custom: 'High' and 'Low' Legal Cultures in the Lands of the British Diaspora – The United States, Canada, Australia, and New Zealand, 1600–1900* (Cambridge: Cambridge University Press 2002), *passim*.

284 This account of the pension case is principally based on 'Mr. Haliburton's Pension: Copies of the Opinions of the Justices of the Supreme Court on the Question Raised by the Application of J. [sic] C. Haliburton, Esq., for a Pension as one of the Judges of the Court of Common Pleas, abolished in 1841,' in *JHA*, 1862, Appendix 15. See also 'Mr. Haliburton's Pension' and 'Appeals to Privy Council,' in ibid., 1863, Appendices 24 and 48.

285 Privy Council Appellate Jurisdiction Act, 7 & 8 Vict., c. 69 (1844).

5

The Supreme Court of Nova Scotia: Confederation to the Twenty-First Century

PHILIP GIRARD

Introduction

In its purely institutional aspect the first century of the Nova Scotia Supreme Court's post-Confederation history is easily related. After an initial decade which saw numerous structural changes – the increase of the bench by two, the establishment of the County Courts, the insertion of the NSSC into an expanded curial hierarchy below the newly created Supreme Court of Canada and the Judicial Committee of the Privy Council, the migration of the appointing power to Ottawa, and the provision of more secure conditions of employment for judges – no further alterations occurred for nearly a century. In spite of a number of proposals for institutional reform (especially prior to 1925), centring mainly on merger of the County and Supreme Courts and the creation of separate trial and appeal divisions, no alteration to the section 96 courts in Nova Scotia was made until 1966.[1] Given the near doubling of the Nova Scotia population between 1875 and 1965, from 400,000 to 750,000, the maintenance of the same number of section 96 judges over this period suggests political inertia, a complacent bar, the development of a highly efficient judiciary – or perhaps all of these. In fact, the significant decline in caseload from about 1880 to the end of the Second World War meant that judicial efficiency was not generally an issue. Attention centred rather on the failings of the lower court bench, which was slowly professionalized until legislation in 1938 and

1942 created a provincewide court staffed exclusively by legally trained judges whose tenure was secure after an initial probationary year.[2]

Changes in staffing arrangements for the court were painfully slow, and illustrated the two fundamental aspects of continuity in the justice system from 1867 until nearly the end of the twentieth century: the reluctance of the provincial government to surrender control over positions that might be useful in the calculus of patronage; and the key rôle played by counties rather than the province in funding many justice services. The judges did not get their own 'stenographer' until 1916 (one for the entire court) and even that was a Cabinet appointment. The sheriff was given tenure during good behaviour in 1883, the prothonotary not until 1958. Both offices, along with that of registrar of deeds, remained remunerated by fees, although the prothonotary at Halifax enjoyed a salary for part of the period. Other clerks were hired as necessary by these officers and paid directly out of their own fees. These officers were obliged to pay one-third of their fees over to the provincial government as of 1921, but in other respects the proprietorial notion of office enjoyed remarkable longevity. The absorption of court officials and staff into the civil service was an extremely gradual process, and not until the 1996 Court and Administrative Reform Act was it fully achieved. The counties were obliged to build and maintain courthouses, and to provide space and supplies for court officials, and most expenses of criminal prosecution long remained their responsibility. This localism was probably defensible until the post-war period, but was increasingly condemned as a relic of the horse-and-buggy days by the 1960s.

If formal institutional reform was slow during the first century after Confederation, in other respects neither the court, nor public perceptions of it, remained static. A changing legal profession, different patterns of judicial appointment in successive federal administrations, a changing economy resulting in significant fluctuations in caseload, a long-term decline in lay participation in the administration of justice, and altered expectations of judges and judicial behaviour by the public all helped to shape the history of the NSSC. The professional renaissance of the Nova Scotia bar, which began soon after Confederation, contributed powerfully to the emergence of a climate hostile to lay participation in judicial matters. The Dominion Speedy Trials Act of 1889 diverted trials for all but the more serious crimes to the County Court, where they were heard without juries. And if the grand jury lingered on for criminal matters in Nova Scotia until 1984, juries in civil matters had largely disappeared by 1914.

Higher expectations of the judiciary led to a number of strong appointments in the later Macdonald and early Laurier years. The imperial connections of many of these – through lifestyle, knighthoods, travel, appearances as counsel before the Judicial Committee of the Privy Council and so on – helped to enhance the legitimacy and reputation of the court at the height of Empire in the decades before the Great War. The death of Chief Justice Sir Wallace Graham, arguably the most talented of this cohort, in 1917, and the appointment of a number of prominent corporate lawyers to the bench, ushered in a new and much more difficult period for the court. It could not avoid the class struggle of the interwar years and tended to favour capital unduly over labour, so noticeably that accusations of pro-capital bias on the part of the judges were made in Parliament by CCF spokesman J.S. Woodsworth in 1924. The dismissal of one County Court judge and resignation of another in the 1930s, both resulting from official malfeasance, did nothing to alleviate the cynicism hovering over the Nova Scotia judiciary during this period.

Mackenzie King's appointments were generally unremarkable but at the very end of his long reign and in the early St-Laurent years the NSSC bench was almost totally transformed. The eminence grise behind this transformation was probably J.L. Ilsley, Canada's minister of finance during the war and minister of justice thereafter. He retired from politics in 1948, accepted an appointment to the NSSC in 1949, and was elevated to chief justice in 1950. He was joined by four men whose collective experience of academe, private practice, and government service during the war years was highly impressive, while two Bennett appointees provided some continuity with the past. Perhaps most indicative of the new ethos in the court was the 1949 appointment of Lauchlin Currie, who had been a bricklayer and coal miner, and later a solicitor for one of Cape Breton's most militant unions. All these men were in sympathy with the post-war shift to public law and the administrative state, as illustrated by Blake Brown's paper later in this volume. The marked increase in divorces and motor vehicle accidents, accompanied by economic recovery, sparked a dramatic rise in litigation, first visible in the County Courts and later in the Supreme Court. A long-standing irritant was at last removed in 1966 when two judges were added to the NSSC so that it could be split into separate trial and appellate divisions.

From the mid-1960s onwards, the principal theme in the history of the court is simply 'more': more judges, more lawyers, more litigation, more staff, more money, more space, more documents, more information, more administration, more computers, and more publicity. In 1964 the salaries of all fourteen section 96 judges in Nova Scotia totalled $193,000 per year. In 2000 the salary of one Supreme Court judge was approximately $200,000 (figure 1). The number of section 96 judges, stable at fourteen for nearly a century after 1876, is now forty after the merger of the County and Supreme Courts (both regularly enlarged through the 1970s and 80s) in 1993 and the appointment of eleven judges to a newly created Family Division of the Supreme Court in 1999 (figure 2). After a long period of relatively modest change and stable understandings of the court's role, the last forty years have seen a dizzying variety of material changes and altered expectations. While many of these may be attributed to post-war prosperity and the changing social attitudes that accompanied it, several other factors are also identified in what follows: the 'nationalization' of the provincial judiciaries with the development of numerous organizations in which they interact; an emerging rights consciousness across Canada, evident in but not limited to the adoption of the Canadian Charter of Rights and Freedoms; the expectation that courts will function in a recognizably 'modern' way, usually articulated as a demand about the legal or judicial 'system,' which in turn gives rise to judicial administration as a discrete field of study and practice; and finally, the late twentieth-century turn to alternative forms of dispute resolution designed to avoid courts altogether or to invoke their aid in new ways.

The higher expectations of courts and of judicial ethics in the later twentieth century were not accompanied by the devotion of more provincial resources to the administration of justice. A federal study in the late 1970s showed that Nova Scotia's spending on justice services was one-third to one-half of that in most other provinces outside the Atlantic region. The salaries of section 96 judges may be comparable across the country but the conditions under which they work are not. (Not all improvements in the justice field require money, of course, but many do.) The clash of higher expectations and underfunding became painfully evident in the saga of Donald Marshall, a Mi'kmaq wrongfully convicted of murder at seventeen and released after eleven years. While the royal commission charged with inquiring into this miscarriage of justice rightly focused on the role of racism throughout the provincial legal system, it also made clear that poorly trained and underfunded

Figure 1. Salaries for Supreme and County Court judges, Nova Scotia, 1867–2001

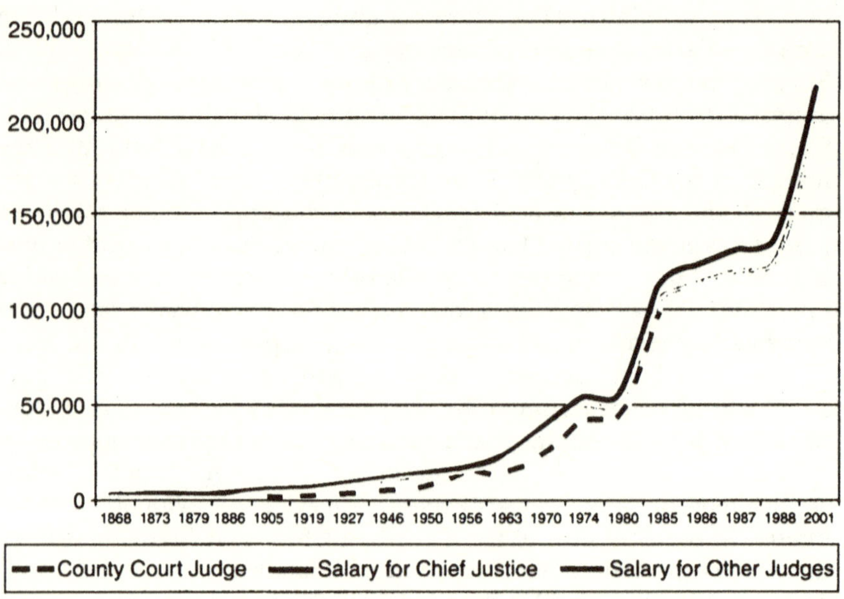

Figure 2. Number of federally appointed judges, Nova Scotia, 1867–2001

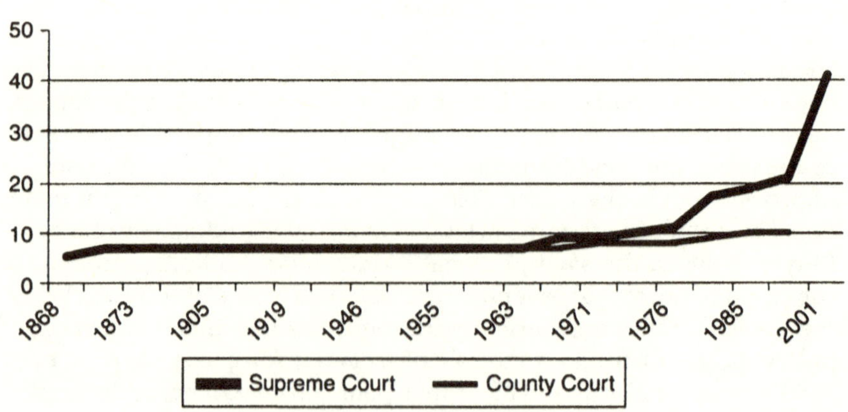

police and prosecutorial officials made the key decisions putting Marshall in jeopardy in the first place. The decision of the Appeal Division releasing Marshall but appearing to blame him for the course of events was harshly criticized, and in this respect the inquiry represented the biggest challenge to the NSSC's legitimacy since the judges' affair of the late eighteenth century. In retrospect, the Marshall inquiry can be seen as the first of a series of indictments of provincial justice systems made in the context of inquiries into race-related issues (such as the 1995 report of the Commission on Systemic Racism in the Ontario Criminal Justice System) or particular miscarriages of justice. Disheartening as these inquiries are in one sense, in another they are to be welcomed. They demonstrate that the citizen has the right to expect equality before the law from all legal actors, from the lowest official to the chief justice of the province, and that legal actors can and must be held to account for their actions. With the Marshall inquiry, Nova Scotia was for once in the vanguard. In pointing to the need for law and the legal order to respond to Canada's changing demography by taking racism seriously, it recommended many changes which will redound to the benefit of all citizens.

Confederation and its Aftermath

For several decades after 1867 there was much debate over the status of the provinces and their legislatures within the new federation. Were they sovereign or quasi-sovereign entities, or mere statutory creations of the British North America Act? New bodies or continuations of old ones? No such uncertainty afflicted the superior courts of the four confederating provinces, Ontario, Quebec, Nova Scotia, and New Brunswick. As Chief Justice of Canada W.J. Ritchie declared in 1879, '[t]hey are not mere local courts for the administration of the local laws passed by the Local Legislatures of the Provinces in which they are organized. They are the courts which were the established courts of the respective Provinces before confederation, and were continued with all laws in force, as if the Union had not been made.'[3] The courts presented a reassuring touchstone of continuity after the second major constitutional realignment in less than a generation. Nor were they soon to be overshadowed by new federal courts, as happened in the United States after the American Revolution. Ottawa would only hesitantly exercise its power under section 101 of the British North America Act to create a national Supreme Court and a rather marginal Exchequer Court (mainly for claims against the federal Crown and, after 1890, maritime law disputes) in 1875. The provincial superior courts would interpret and apply both federal and provincial laws.[4]

Nonetheless, Confederation did bring some changes, both in the court's jurisdiction and in relation to conditions of appointment and salaries. The new federal constitution clothed the court with an authority never before seen in the annals of British jurisprudence: the power to annul a statute duly passed by a competent legislature. The NSSC was soon compelled to play a role in the federal-provincial battles of the fin-de-siècle, one analysed by William Lahey in this volume. With regard to appointments, future elevations to the provincial superior courts would be made by the new government at Ottawa. Thus ended two decades of pure local control over judicial appointments, which had led to the startling spectacle of a Nova Scotian premier naming himself chief justice, as William Young had done in 1860. Whatever the benefits of responsible government in the political sphere, in the judicial arena it had helped to diminish the legitimacy of candidates for the bench. Transferring the appointment power to Ottawa removed some of the worst features of local patronage but did not fundamentally alter the nature of the exercise. As Charles Townshend confessed to John Thompson in 1882, 'My tastes and ambition have been to excel in the profession [;] outside of it – for politics I care nothing and only went into them with a view to the Bench.'[5] His game plan succeeded: after a decade in provincial and federal politics he was duly appointed to the court in 1887. Judicial nominations would henceforth involve a complex mix of provincial and federal politics and personalities, where Ottawa definitely held the upper hand. After 1867 judicial salaries were drawn from the pockets of all Canadian taxpayers rather than purely provincial ones, and in 1868 a pension plan was established for superior court judges allowing them to retire after fifteen years' service.[6] This measure removed a frequent source of conflict between judges and colonial legislators and represented a significant enhancement of judicial independence. It also helped reduce the numbers of the truly elderly on the bench; unlike their predecessors, judges appointed after Confederation rarely remained in office after the age of seventy-five. The average age of the bench in 1870, just before the two new appointees joined it, was seventy-two; by 1905, after Chief Justice McDonald's resignation, it was fifty-nine.[7]

The federal power to make appointments also entailed an effective veto over the size of the court. The province might try to enlarge it pursuant to its authority over the administration of justice, but such mea-

Figure 3. Civil cases commenced in the NSSC and the Halifax County Court, 1865–1975, excluding bankruptcy and divorce

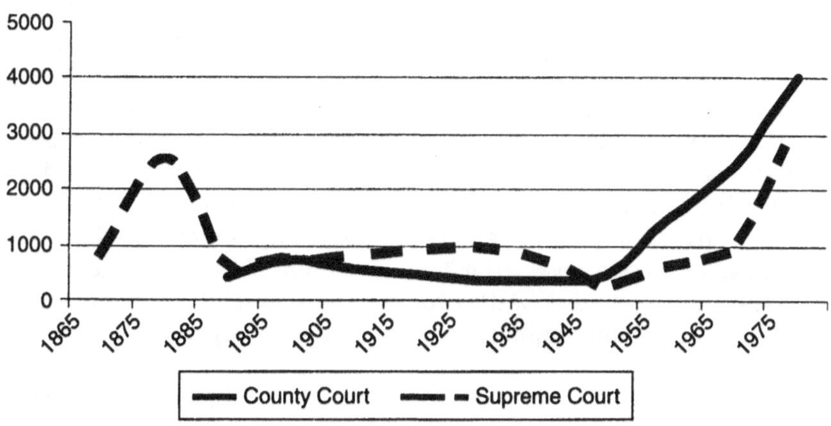

sures availed nothing unless Ottawa could be persuaded to fund additional salaries and make the appointments. In the case of the NSSC, two additional appointments were procured in 1870, augmenting the court to seven judges, and then none for nearly a century. Contemporary observations about a sudden increase in the court's caseload in the late 1860s and early 1870s are borne out by empirical research (see figure 3), but it was the age and ill health of most of the sitting judges that converted this increase in business into a mountain of arrears. J.W. Johnston's arrears as judge in equity 'had so multiplied,' according to one dismayed observer, that 'they could never be overtaken by [his successor].'[8] In spite of this state of affairs, the anti-Confederate provincial government of the day was not keen to give Sir John A. Macdonald the chance to appoint his political friends to plum judicial posts. Eventually it was obliged to relent and two fathers of Confederation, Jonathan McCully and John W. Ritchie, were duly translated from the Senate to the court on 28 September 1870.[9]

Confederation soon produced significant structural changes to the provincial judicial system. As discussed in the preceding chapter, the pre-Confederation trend was towards rationalizing the plethora of colonial courts by abolishing them (the Inferior Court of Common Pleas, Chancery) and/or transferring their jurisdiction to the Supreme Court (the Court of Marriage and Divorce). The latter was supreme in function as well as in name, since Nova Scotian appeals to the Privy Council were extremely rare prior to 1867; there were probably no more than a half-dozen between 1800 and 1867.[10] There still remained a rather confusing tangle of first instance courts for minor disputes, with justices of the peace, municipal courts, and stipendiary magistrates possessing overlapping jurisdictions, but at the level of the superior courts at least some progress had been made. After Confederation complexity reasserted itself, and the Supreme Court of Nova Scotia soon found itself an intermediate court, subject to appeals to the new Supreme Court of Canada after 1875, and increasingly to the Privy Council after an imperial order-in-council of 1863 constituted that body a regular court of appeal from NSSC decisions. The court's new position thus mimicked that of the province itself, as it left behind a period as a functionally autonomous unit and entered a larger and more complex entity.

Nova Scotians lost no time in availing themselves of their new opportunity to challenge decisions of the province's highest court. Halifax lawyer Thomas J. Wallace, disbarred by the Supreme Court after writing an insulting letter to Chief Justice Young regarding his experiences as a litigant, had his disbarment reversed by the Privy Council in 1866 on the ground that the offence was punishable as contempt only because Wallace had not made the remarks in his professional capacity. In 1873 the Privy Council restored the decision of the judge in equity, J.W. Johnston, in a case involving the interpretation of a deed of land in New Glasgow. The defendant had appealed to the NSSC in banco, who would have split evenly–thus affirming the trial decision–but for the fact that Johnston sat with them and changed his mind. The plaintiff then appealed to London, where Sir Montague Smith expressed the board's 'regret that the learned Judge should have found occasion to change the opinion to which he had originally come, for, after full discussion of the case, [they] are of the opinion that his first judgment was right in its reasoning and sound in its conclusion.'[11]

At the same time, a functional equivalent to the Inferior Court of Common Pleas was re-created in the form of the County Courts in 1874, which were staffed by federally appointed judges as of 1876 and began hearing cases in 1877. A true County Court would have seen a judge in each of Nova Scotia's eighteen counties, but Minister of Justice Edward Blake was prepared to pay for no more than seven new judges. The province was thus divided into seven districts containing, except for Districts One (Halifax County) and Five (Pictou and Cumberland), three counties each.[12] In fact, each of the Ontario counties had two to three times the population of most Nova Scotian counties, so a rough equality of the workload per judge was maintained. Each of the county judges held in effect a mini-circuit among his three counties, in a manner similar to the old Inferior Court of Common Pleas after 1824, and even the County Court judge for Halifax held court at Middle Musquodoboit as well as the capital. Provision was made for clerks to each of the County Courts (paid by fees and serving at pleasure, of course), but in practice the prothonotary resident in the county town usually held both offices. The accent in the County Court was on speed and accessibility, best illustrated in the jury provisions. Trials were to be non-jury, but the judge had the power to order a jury for the trial of any controverted fact in any case where over eighty dollars was at stake. Five men were to constitute a jury, 'four of whom, in case they cannot agree after two hours absence, may render a verdict.'[13] With jurisdiction over contracts to the amount of four hundred dollars and torts to two hundred dollars, and appellate jurisdiction over the magistrates' courts in their counties, the County Courts took a considerable burden off the Supreme Court – presumably the same burden the two extra judges appointed to the court in 1870 were also supposed to bear. In addition, any cause in the Supreme Court could be tried in the County Court with the consent of both parties.

Relations between the Supreme Court and the new County Courts were strictly hierarchical. The judges were to be barristers of at least seven years' standing – ten was the minimum for the Supreme Court – and while a quorum of four could make rules for the new court, these were subject to a power of revision and disallowance by a majority of the Supreme Court. Stare decisis was also engraved in a statutory prescription: 'the Judges of [the] County Courts shall be governed by decisions of the Supreme Court.'[14] A clear badge of inferiority was inscribed in the County Court's virtual exclusion from land law matters; it could not pronounce on any matter involving the title to land or the interpretation of wills, and could not at first order foreclosure and sale of mortgaged properties.[15] Supreme Court judges were appointed for life, while County Court judges faced (after 1903) compulsory retirement at eighty. A strict separation between the courts was also maintained by the federal government's policy of never promoting County Court judges to the Supreme Court; the first instance in Nova Scotia would occur nearly a century after the court's creation.

Seen from the apex of the provincial court hierarchy the County

Court judges lacked prestige, but on their own turf they represented the pinnacle of the local legal order. Resident in their districts, they were much more visible in local society than the occasional Supreme Court judge on circuit. For many a provincial lawyer, an appointment as County Court judge in one's home town was a long-cherished prize after a quarter-century of practice. Where the NSSC represented a force for uniformity in the provincial legal order, the County Courts epitomized localism. They existed only in the plural, with no chief justice, central office, or coordinating body. Not until the 1940s would they form an association to advance their common interests and to share information on matters of mutual concern. Aside from an occasional appeal of his decision to the NSSC in banco, the County Court judge thus possessed a peculiar kind of independence.

Chief Justice William Young and his colleagues were no doubt gladdened at the prospect of the County Courts relieving them of some of their work, but they were less happy with their treatment at the hands of the Supreme Court of Canada. NSSC decisions had a fairly high reversal rate in Ottawa during the first few decades after the creation of the new Supreme Court, in the region of 38–40 per cent, but it is only fair to observe that every province outside Ontario had a somewhat comparable rate. Such a reversal rate could only inspire Nova Scotian lawyers to take their chances with an appeal, and indeed they went to the Supreme Court of Canada in higher numbers proportionate to population than any other province. The voting patterns of Nova Scotian politicians on legislation affecting the Supreme Court of Canada also reveal very strong support for the institution. These trends suggest a certain dissatisfaction with the NSSC in the post-Confederation years, reflecting in part its continuing malaise after the achievement of responsible government.[16]

If parties were dissatisfied, however, they certainly did not show it by boycotting the court. The Supreme Court at Halifax at least was a very busy court in the years after Confederation. Some 2,500 civil cases were filed there in 1875, of which just under half (1,251) proceeded to judgment. The subject-matter breakdown reveals an essential continuity with the pre-Confederation period in the overwhelming predominance of commercial causes: some 88 per cent of the pleadings involve accounts payable for goods and services, promissory notes, mortgages, bills of exchange, or actions on bonds. A sample of some 10 per cent of the case files revealed only three tort actions, one each for trespass to land, battery, and libel. Only two divorce petitions were filed in 1875 and no other cases in the sample dealt with family law in any way. A few suits by labourers for unpaid wages were probably unrepresentative; several people hired by Cameron's Oriental Circus and Egyptian Caravan sued – unsuccessfully – when the company's agent left the jurisdiction without paying them. Suits for unpaid wages would seldom justify the expense of starting them in the Supreme Court and would usually be heard by magistrates.[17]

The judges of the Supreme Court were richly rewarded for their vocal support of Confederation in a province where the new national project remained controversial for some time. Less than a decade after 1867, the admittedly overburdened Supreme Court had been enlarged by two members and had seen a significant portion of its more tedious work taken up by the newly created County Courts. Its judges enjoyed an increase in salary and, more importantly, secure pension entitlements. The federal appointment power meant that the judges were also insulated from the nastier aspects of provincial politics, such as the abolition of Alexander Stewart's court out from under him in 1855.[18] In this respect, Confederation provided considerably more safeguards for judicial independence than had existed during the more turbulent colonial era.

The New Professionalism and the New Imperialism, 1880–1918

With the Maritimes' own National Policy-driven industrial revolution, a new confidence and energy emerged in the region which soon inspired various progressive reform movements. The professional reform movement which led to the creation of Dalhousie Law School and the transformation of the Barristers' Society from an old boys' club into a modern professional organization has been treated elsewhere and need not be re-examined here.[19] Such trends affected the judiciary itself only after a considerable time lag, but they certainly marked the environment in which courts operated. The Simon Holmes-John Thompson provincial administration enacted a number of measures which together constituted a new point of departure for the legal profession, the court, and the entire legal order. The judges' disciplinary power over the bar, the subject of numerous contretemps earlier in the century, was removed from them and vested in the Barristers' Society itself, as was the judicial role in entry to the legal profession.[20] The bar became a fully autonomous branch of the legal profession, its powers over entry, education, and discipline formalized in legislation, rather than a quasi-stepchild of the bench. To symbolize this transfer of power, from 1880 the certificates of admission of barristers and attorneys (soon to be solicitors) were to be given by the secretary of the Barristers' Society, 'not by the prothonotary at Halifax, who shall charge no fee for admission of barristers, except .50 for signing and filing the certificate of admission.'[21]

John Thompson also addressed the backlog of cases still haunting the court by a rudimentary form of imposed case management. In 1879 the existing sittings of the court were statutorily declared to be for civil causes only, and if they were not sufficient, another was to be held in January 1880; there were to be in addition two sittings for criminal causes. In 1882 An Act to Facilitate the Disposal of Arrears in the Docket of the Supreme Court of Nova Scotia allowed the court to sit simultaneously in panels of three for in banco matters (four was the normal quorum). Attention focused next on the officers of the court. The legal status of the office of sheriff, in many ways the linchpin of the entire legal system, was upgraded to tenure during good behaviour, a significant concession at a time when most legal office-holders were appointed at pleasure.[22] Thompson also had the courage to take on the forms of action, the highly technical style of pleadings which had shaped the common law for centuries. The Judicature Act 1884 abolished the old forms of action, introduced a new more informal style of pleadings and completed the fusion of law and equity initiated in 1855 with the abolition of the Court of Chancery. It also mandated the maintenance of cause books in which cases were to be numbered consecutively, a modest but significant first step in the creation of curial information systems. Substantive legal reforms accompanied these important changes in procedure: 1884 also saw the enactment of the Married Women's Property Act, allowing married women to hold property and commence legal actions in their own names, without the interposition of husbands or trustees. Imprisonment for debt went in 1890, removing one of the last barriers to the emergence of a consumer society.[23]

The circuit work of the post-Confederation judge was considerably eased by the completion of the provincial railway network, and the amount of time each judge was required to devote to the circuit fell considerably, to roughly one month per year. As in the 1850s, complaints were still voiced about the tendency for criminal trials to occupy the whole of the regular sitting, with civil business thus postponed for six months until the next regular sitting, or the county put to the expense of an extra one.[24] The fall 1880 sitting at Annapolis was insufficient to finish even the criminal business much less the civil. An extra sitting had to be arranged to deal with the sensational trial of Joseph Thibault, found guilty of murdering a female pauper entrusted to his care by the overseers of the poor. (Hangings were supposed to be held in private after 1869, but a crowd of county folk pulled down the prison wall so as to be able to witness the dispatch of this criminal.) In the fall sitting at Lunenburg that year, five of the seven days were occupied with criminal trials and only two civil trials were conducted, each occupying one day. Nor was this exceptional; the previous two years had likewise seen only two civil causes per sitting, while fifteen to eighteen criminal trials took place. About half of these were said to be assaults, 'most of which should have been disposed of by magistrates by summary trial.' The remedy advocated for this state of affairs was transfer of some criminal jurisdiction to the County Courts as had been done in New Brunswick, where since 1867 all non-capital crimes could be tried. The Nova Scotia County Courts were already admitted to 'relieve the Supreme Court of a large amount of civil business, and enable suitors to get many cases ... disposed of with comparatively little delay,' so it was natural to think an extension of their criminal jurisdiction would prove similarly beneficial.[25]

The desired reform ensued in 1889 when the Dominion Speedy Trials Act was extended to Nova Scotia, but it came at the expense of the traditional jury trial. The Act allowed those accused of all but a few crimes to elect a non-jury trial before a County Court judge.[26] In some rural areas the Speedy Trials Act meant that the Supreme Court had virtually no criminal business while on circuit. Consider the experience of Victoria County, a long thin wedge of the eastern Cape Breton Highlands stretching from Baddeck, the county seat on Lake Bras d'Or, to the very northern tip of the island. The least populous Nova Scotian county from 1901 on, it was home to barely 10,000 persons. The returns of the prothonotary show only thirteen criminal trials before the Supreme Court at Baddeck between 1891 and 1924, or one every 2.5 years. Even then, only five of these involved serious crimes: three charges of manslaughter, one of rape, and one of perjury. The rest involved assaults or charges of burglary which might just as well have been dealt with by the County Court. In Colchester County, with a population of nearly 25,000 in 1901, the Supreme Court presided over three criminal cases per year on average between 1886 and 1919, usually more serious property crimes or occasionally rape, indecent assault, or murder.[27] Civil matters dominated after 1889 however, with 6.5 trials on average per year between 1890 and 1919, and a considerable amount of chambers business, especially relating to foreclosure of mortgages and partition of land among co-owners. Over the same period there were only three years, 1901, 1911, and 1916, in which there were more criminal trials than civil on the Colchester circuit. These changes show that the goal of keeping the Supreme Court's docket free of all but the most serious crimes in order to prioritize economically related disputes was finally achieved in the late nineteenth century.

The prothonotary's minute books for the Colchester circuit have survived in unbroken sequence from 1886 to 1952, providing a unique window on the court's circuit duties. In 1901 Colchester's population of 24,900 made it the province's fourth largest county after Halifax, Cape Breton, and Pictou. Its 900,000 acres form a rough square, bounded by the Northumberland Strait, the Minas Basin, and Cumberland and Halifax counties, with Truro, the county seat, near the centre. A wealth of natural resources including rich soil, extensive tracts of good forest, quarries, iron deposits, and fish provided the basis for a diversified economy. Colchester was home to a number of manufacturing concerns such as industrial dairy processing, textiles (Truro Knitting Mills was taken over by the Stanfield family in 1906), and furniture production. Until 1920, the number of days per year a judge might sit at Truro varied wildly around a mean of ten days, from only two or three days (1886, 1914), to thirty-one days in 1897, when the eight-day trial of seventeen-year-old Lyman Dart for murdering Armenian pedlar Ashard Deron added an extra session to an already busy year. The ritual of the circuit changed little. The session always began with the grand jurors being sworn, twenty-four of them until legislation reduced the required number to twelve in 1898, of whom seven were required to find a true bill. The sheriff might then offer some remarks of welcome on a judge's first visit to the circuit in question, as he did on Justice Townshend's inaugural visit to Colchester on 2 October 1888. The judge 'eloquently replied' on that occasion but then 'addressed the grand jury animadverting very severely on the Clerk of the Crown for not handing him the criminal papers last night.' Four years later, Townshend used his grand jury address to complain about the state of the courthouse as 'totally unfit for the business and a discredit to the county.' The grand jury remonstrated, correctly, that paying for a new courthouse was no longer their responsibility; their administrative functions had been taken away by an 1879 statute mandating elected county councils. A decade later Townshend was still complaining but in 1904 Justice Nicholas Meagher was at last able to congratulate the county on the construction of a new courthouse, financed by a provincial statute authorizing the council to borrow $30,000 for the purpose. The grand jury address might also serve as a vehicle for patriotic sentiments: on 5 June 1900 Chief Justice McDonald informed the grand jury that the British army had occupied Pretoria, and two years later Justice Townshend congratulated them on the end of the war in South Africa.[28]

After the introductory remarks it was time to call the petit jurors. Obtaining the requisite twenty-four, or forty-eight for a 'long' session (more than one week), was sometimes a problem, as it was elsewhere in British North America.[29] If fewer than twenty showed up, those summoned but not present were routinely fined at a rate of two dollars per day.[30] The judge usually heard motions first, then went through the indictments with the grand jury and sent them to deliberate. Once they were gone he began the civil business and with any luck would get through all the evidence and argument in a case before the grand jury came back with their findings. True bills were virtually always found; on the rare occasion when no indictments were brought forward, as at the fall 1890 session, the sheriff 'presented the Judge with a pair of white gloves,' an echo of a custom followed at the English assizes. The criminal and civil trials were mixed, with the goal of having one petit jury deliberating on a verdict while another was hearing a case. Civil cases were heard with nine jurors, criminal juries with twelve, though after 1856 jurors on a civil case could bring in a verdict concurred in by seven of their number after four hours. Even the four-hour requirement could be waived on consent of both parties; a case called *Creelman v. Tupper* only went to the jury at 6:00 pm on 13 June 1892, but seven jurors returned a verdict of five hundred dollars damages for the plaintiff at 7:40 pm.[31]

Although the pattern of the circuit remained the same on the surface, the roles of the parties were changing quite dramatically, with lay participation on the wane over this period and professionals on the ascendant. The halving of the grand jury was one sign. Civil non-jury trials, rare before 1895, were more and more conspicuous thereafter. The Judicature Act 1884 had provided for such trials on consent of both parties, but also gave presiding judge a discretion to order one even where the parties did not request it. In 1897 the first 'special term for non-jury causes' was held at Truro. In 1911 and 1915 the prothonotary saw fit to record two instances where a case started with a jury but 'an arrangement was consummated by which the case was taken from the jury and [left] for the decision of the judge.' The decline of the civil jury was swift. The period 1886–1919 divides neatly into two seventeen-year halves: in the first, five civil jury cases and three civil cases without a jury were heard annually. During the second, the non-jury cases remained more or less constant at 3.5 per year on average, but the jury trials dropped to only one per year. Circuit business declined noticeably during the war, but the drop in civil jury trials had begun over a decade earlier. In absolute numbers, only nineteen civil jury trials were held at Truro between 1903 and 1919, where that many had been held there in only three years in the early 1890s. It is not clear exactly what caused this decline, but the new type of 'expert' professionalism accompanying the shift to university-based legal education must have played a role.

The relatively low number of criminal trials conducted by the Supreme Court on circuit, whether at Baddeck or Truro, has already been noted, but evidence from the County Court is needed to round out the picture. Evidence from the County Court at Colchester is lacking, but fortunately the prothonotary for Victoria County was also clerk of the County Court and his returns show activity in both courts. These records mirror the same story of declining lay participation and also bear witness to relatively low rates of serious crime. The County Court at Baddeck did not do much more criminal business than the Supreme Court, just over a trial per year between 1891 and 1924. Every accused chose to be tried by judge alone under the Speedy Trials Act, even when, as not infrequently happened, a Gaelic interpreter was required (as late as 1941 Victoria County's population comprised 13 per cent native Gaelic speakers). The record of both the Supreme Court and the County Court over this period appears remarkably lenient where crimes against the person were concerned. Seven of the thirteen Supreme Court trials resulted in acquittals, including those on rape and perjury charges. While convictions were recorded in all three cases of manslaughter the sentences were light: a year in the county jail in one case, two years at Dorchester Penitentiary in a case of 'unlawful shooting with intent to murder.' In the third case, the court seemed more concerned about defraying the costs of the prosecution than punishing the offender. When fisherman Firman McDougall was convicted of manslaughter on 29 May 1906 he was sentenced to a month in the county jail and ordered to pay fifty dollars to the county treasurer 'to be devoted towards discharging the county's portion of the costs of prosecution,' and in default of payment 'to be further confined for the term required by law.'[32] A young woman appearing before the County Court on a charge of concealment of birth in 1899 received one month in the county jail.

Sentencing for property crimes, whether by the Supreme Court or the County Court, and whether in Colchester or Victoria, tended to be harsher than for crimes against the person. Property crimes were more frequent in Colchester, and breaking into a shop frequently netted the offender two to seven years in Dorchester Penitentiary. A conviction on a charge of cattle stealing in 1897 put one Eagles in Dorchester for six years, while assaulting a police officer put Henry Parris in the county jail for only three months. In the County Court at Baddeck, a verdict of theft of firearms resulted in a five-year sentence at Dorchester in 1899, while an incest perpetrator received only three years in 1920, albeit with hard labour.

In towns such as Baddeck, where the Supreme Court showed up only two weeks per year, it could easily share facilities with the County Court. In Halifax, where both courts sat frequently, competition over the two suitably outfitted courtrooms in the Spring Garden Road courthouse was inevitable. When the County Court judge, supported by the attorney general, requested that he be allowed to use them, the Supreme Court firmly refused. The 'room in which the County Court is now held is very objectionable,' admitted Sir William Young in 1881, but the east courtroom was always required for Supreme Court business while the west courtroom was needed for the equity court, chambers business, the admiralty court, and occasionally the Court of Marriage and Divorce. The only alternative, according to Young, was to convert existing space within the building into two new courtrooms.[33] In fact, an addition to the courthouse in 1882 relieved the congestion.

After the huge increase in business in the Supreme Court in the first decade after Confederation, the 1880s saw a rapid return to a more manageable caseload. About five hundred cases were commenced at Halifax in 1885, and this figure would not quite double over the next forty years. The profile in the Halifax County Court began somewhat similarly, with some four hundred civil cases commenced in 1885, followed by a slow rise to 1905, then tapering back to four hundred again by 1925. The nature of both courts' civil business stayed largely the same over the period, with the principal subject of litigation being the enforcement of debt obligations of one kind or another. Sampling was done at twenty-year rather than decadal intervals (1885, 1905, 1925) because the subjects of litigation change more slowly than the amount of it in any given period. Enforcing mortgage security, and suits based on debts, promissory notes, and bills of exchange made up three-quarters of the Supreme Court's business at Halifax in 1885, but almost 90 per cent of the county court's business in 1885 and 1905. By 1905 the proportion of the Supreme Court's business comprising these matters had slipped slightly, and some modest signs of the province's industrial and commercial expansion were evident: the enforcement of foreign judgments and the dissolution of companies made up 8 per cent of the court's business in 1905.

The overall pattern of rise and fall in the last quarter of the nineteenth century is consistent with studies of Gloucester County, New Brunswick, and major urban centres in the United States. These three areas had very different economies, but the courts functioned largely as debt-collection agencies in all of them. The Nova Scotia evidence appears to confirm Jacques Paul Couturier's view that 'common-law courts [were] the scene of routine activity, quasi-administrative in nature.' The spread of credit-reporting agencies across North America reduced the risk of incurring bad debt, generating what U.S. scholar Robert Kagan calls a 'systemic stabilization' by the early twentieth century, which in turn rendered debt litigation less necessary.[34]

What was excluded from the business of the courts is more striking than what was included. Tort law and family law in particular are notable by their absence. In 1885, aside from two divorce petitions for the whole province, there was nothing at all in the sample that might be termed family law for example;[35] in 1905 there were a few petitions for guardianship and a few divorce petitions but nothing else. One has to look ahead to 1925 to see divorce securely on the legal radar screen, with thirty petitions in the province in that year.[36] Tort law comprised only 2 per cent of claims in the 1885 sample, rising to nearly 7 per cent in 1925, half of those being personal injury actions related mainly to motor vehicle accidents. The civil side of the courts' business up until after the First World War is almost exclusively about contracts, credit relations, and to a much lesser extent, land.

These fluctuations in caseload had significant repercussions for office-holders whose remuneration flowed wholly or partly from fees. In some cases incumbent prothonotaries functioned as clerks for the new County Courts, but this was not always as profitable as might be assumed. The irrepressible Martin I. Wilkins, named prothonotary of the Supreme Court at Halifax in 1871 after a somewhat chequered political career that included service as attorney general, laid out his woes in a long memorial to the chief justice in 1880. When he took the office, said Wilkins, all the court's business was conducted in one courtroom; when he was required to be present in court, he hired a clerk to attend at the court office. (Clerks were employed directly by the prothonotary, and had to be paid out of his fees.) Recently he had been compelled to hire three clerks, one for the County Court and two for the Supreme Court. Moreover, the business of the County Court consisted 'principally of causes formerly disposed of in the Upper Court and ... it has not increased the profits of my office to anything near the amount of the expense of a Clerk to attend on that Court.'[37] Wilkins died in office in 1881 and was replaced by former premier Simon Holmes, who remained in office until his death in 1919. In spite of Wilkins's protestations, the Assembly found the prothonotary to enjoy an unconscionably high income, and imposed a ceiling of three thousand dollars on his office. Even after payment of his expenses, it was observed, he would still be left with a higher income than a Cabinet minister. Holmes was prone to absenting himself without leave but his wife conscientiously filled in for him on such occasions, providing an unusual female face in the all-male world of the court.[38]

With the remarkable decline in litigation in the 1880s – and there is no reason to believe it was any less noticeable outside Halifax – the issue of the day soon became salary floors rather than ceilings. In 1895 the province redeployed a device first used for the prothonotary at Halifax in the 1850s. While leaving the fee system in place, the government guaranteed to make up any deficit in years when a prothonotary's gross fees fell below $250 if he served as clerk of the County Court, or $125 if he did not; the floor for County Court clerks was likewise set at $125. The next year the plan was extended to sheriffs, with an annual guarantee of $600.[39] In return, the position of inspector of legal and registry offices was created in 1901 to provide at least the appearance of supervision for officials who might now draw on public funds in lean years. In 1903, probably at the request of the bar, the attorney general was authorized to hire 'court stenographers' to act as official reporters.[40]

On the surface a Supreme Court which remained the same size for nearly a century, dealt with a constantly declining amount of civil litigation for two-thirds of that period, and was the last in Canada to develop a separate Court of Appeal may look like a stagnant institution, one contemporaries did not value enough to change. Yet this impression is somewhat misleading for the period before about 1920. A number of reform suggestions were made, mostly centred on the vexed question of the in banco appeal. In 1890 the judges themselves passed a rule stating that the trial judge should not sit with his colleagues on an appeal unless a majority of them requested him to do so. Even had trial judges stopped sitting on appeals this would not have remedied the problem of appearances. The constant mingling of the judges would naturally give rise to a perception of reluctance to overturn their colleagues' decisions while on circuit, however inaccurate that may have been in fact. Yet the judges continued at least occasionally to sit on appeals from their own decisions – and sometimes changed their minds in the process, as Justice J.W. Longley did in a 1907 decision.[41]

In 1897, while attorney general, Longley had proposed a merger of the County and Supreme Courts and the creation of a separate Court of Appeal out of the enlarged body. He had the power to engineer this provincially and his fellow Liberals were in power under Laurier; former premier W.S. Fielding was a powerful voice for Nova Scotia in the federal Cabinet as minister of finance. The proposal could have been implemented with little overall increase for salaries, but it was not acted upon for reasons that remain unclear. Probably the lack of strong financial incentive explains the long inaction on this front. With the judicial salaries of these courts paid by Ottawa, local courthouses maintained by the counties, and court officials remunerated principally by the litigants' fees, merger of the courts presented no strong financial incentive to the provincial government. As J. Murray Beck observed wryly, 'one thing that may be safely inferred is that Nova Scotia will not set a precedent by reducing the number of judges who are paid by another authority.'[42]

The most ambitious plan for securing a 'complete and modern administration of justice in [Nova Scotia]' came from the Barristers' Society in 1913. In content and rhetorical fervour it bore the hallmarks of many progressive reform proposals that pulsed through the Edwardian Maritimes. After passing a resolution designed to render its own governance more democratic by mandating the election of the bar council by all Society members across the province, council was moved to advocate what the *Herald* called 'radical reform in our law courts.' Once again the in banco appeal process was castigated as 'generat[ing] mistrust' and 'not in keeping with the dignity of a proper appeal court' while the county courts, with the exception of Halifax, were condemned as sinecures.[43] The Society called for a royal commission 'to investigate and report on the constitution, maintenance and organization of the various courts in Nova Scotia,' hoping it would recommend a separate appeal court along the lines of that being created in New Brunswick, as well as a transfer of the civil jurisdiction of justices of the peace and other lower courts to the County Courts, and a transfer of the criminal jurisdiction of the justices to stipendiary magistrates in urban areas.[44] The Society did its own bit for modernity by resolving to admit 'lady barristers,' the first of whom was Frances Fish, admitted in 1918. A trickle of women followed her but the presence of a female litigator in court would remain exceedingly rare for decades.

Attorney General O'Hearn took up most of the Society's ideas in 1923, and joined to them a proposal to abolish appeals from Nova Scotia to the Privy Council. Curiously, however, he presented them to the House of Assembly for debate as a private member's resolution, not a government bill. In that form they predictably generated more rhetoric than action.[45] As in 1897, there was a congruence of Liberal governments in both Nova Scotia and Ottawa, but once again no change was forthcoming. The long delay in institutional reform seems to be attributable to a lack of political leadership rather than any principled defence of the status quo.

If legislative reforms remained on the back burner, the judges themselves, and to some extent the appointing authorities in Ottawa, moved rather aggressively to try to rehabilitate the image of their court, sullied as it was by the practice of overt patronage appointments. The appointment of federal minister of justice James McDonald as chief justice in 1881, rewarded for his role in defending John A. Macdonald's government during the Pacific Scandal, appeared to follow the usual conventions, but it was during his tenure that the image of the court underwent a definite amelioration. This process involved three main strategies: a greater insistence on the professional attainments of aspirant judges and a slow suppression of the more obvious manifestations of patronage; the creation of an 'official' history for the court and its judges; and an emphasis on imperial linkages in the form of knighthoods, lifestyle, and imagery.

Laurier's appointment of Benjamin Russell, second in command at the Dalhousie Law School, to the NSSC was greeted by those of all political stripes as a welcome move to improve the calibre of the bench.[46] Joseph Chisholm was the first Dalhousie law graduate appointed to the bench (1916) and all but one judge appointed after him would also hold a university law degree; that degree would invariably be from Dalhousie until much later in the twentieth century.[47] After McDonald's retirement in 1904 the next three chief justices were appointed with reference to their seniority rather than their party affiliation, though Sir Robert Borden returned to the old pattern in 1918 when he promoted Conservative Robert Harris to the post after only three years on the bench. Unlike the responsible government period, when nine out of ten appointees had served in the local legislature, many men were appointed to the bench after 1880 without having held political office. Through service on the Nova Scotia Historical Society and their own writing of history – Chief Justice Townshend's *History of the Court of Chancery in Nova Scotia* (1900) being the most prominent example – the judges catered to the appetite for history in the industrializing fin-de-siècle and helped to secure their own place in it.[48] But it was probably through their efforts to create and emphasize imperial linkages that the judges did the most to enhance their position in provincial society. Through invented genealogies, participation in imperial extravaganzas such as the dedication of the Halifax Memorial Tower in 1912, and the successful launching of their children on imperial careers, the chief justices who followed James McDonald succeeded in creating a kind of imperial aura around the NSSC that did wonders for its reputation. The new legitimacy of the court was confirmed in 1913 when Justice Wallace Graham was named to chair a provincial royal commission into some questionable land dealings of the attorney general. Judges had not been appointed to such a role since 1848, but they would soon be almost indispensable to royal commissions; in 1918, Justice J.A. Chisholm could be appointed to chair a federal royal commission to inquire into a subject as sensitive as unrest in the mining and steel industries. To some extent this period was a new golden age for the court, as it overcame many of the problems it had experienced in the years after 1848.[49]

It was also a golden age for law reporting. After a somewhat hesitant start in the 1850s and '60s, described in the previous chapter, the Nova Scotia Reports began to flourish in the 1870s. Beautifully produced, carefully indexed, and elaborately digested on a periodic basis, the production of the pre-1929 reports set a standard that would never again be matched. A shift from publication in Halifax to Toronto in 1886 reflected a more general problem, however: out-migration of some of the province's best and brightest, attracted by opportunities in central and western Canada and the United States that Nova Scotia could not provide, even at the Edwardian height of its prosperity. Even senior lawyers such as William Bruce Almon Ritchie, president of the Barristers' Society in 1905–6, followed the siren call of the west when he emigrated to Vancouver in 1911 in search of greener professional pastures.[50] Fortunes were still to be made in early twentieth century Halifax, but primarily by a small coterie of lawyers who serviced banks and large corporations.[51] The financial success (or otherwise) of non-metropolitan lawyers has yet to be studied.

The cross-currents of optimism and despair in this period are well symbolized by the too-short life of James Robinson Johnston, Nova Scotia's first black lawyer. A graduate of Dalhousie Law School in 1898, Johnston articled with Nova Scotia's first labour lawyer, the socialist and anti-racist activist John Thomas Bulmer, and with Frank Russell, son of Justice Benjamin Russell, and was called to the bar in 1900. Johnston had many influential patrons in the white community and as he prospered his career was a symbol of hope for Nova Scotians of all races. When he was murdered by his brother-in-law in 1915 in the course of a domestic dispute, his ignominious death cast a long shadow. Someone who just might have become the first black judge in Canada was dead, and this loss was only the first of a number of problems that would plague the legal order in Nova Scotia at the close of the Great War.[52]

The most notable of these was the litigation following the Halifax Explosion of 6 December 1917. Justice Arthur Drysdale of the NSSC was immediately appointed by the Dominion minister of marine and fisheries as a commissioner under Part X of the Canada Shipping Act to conduct a formal investigation into the disaster.[53] The inquiry convened only a week after the event in the gloom of the Spring Garden Road courthouse, where the blown-out windows had been boarded up and the loss of electricity forced the inquiry to rely on oil lamps. Prejudice ran high against Captain Le Médec of the French ship *Mont Blanc*, who had managed to escape with his crew before his munitions-laden vessel exploded after colliding with the Norwegian ship *Imo*. Drysdale would not restrain the *Imo*'s counsel C.J. Burchell, who repeatedly 'browbeat and misled witnesses ... and on a number of occasions violated the standards of legal ethics.' In a vituperative one-page decision Drysdale found the pilot and captain of the *Mont Blanc* solely responsible for the disaster. Within days manslaughter charges were laid against Le Médec, the Halifax pilot Mackey, and Commander Wyatt of the Dockyard. The charges were ultimately dismissed but not before Drysdale had sat on appeals from habeas corpus applications made on behalf of the accused men (and dissented from his brethren).[54] And when both parties launched civil actions against each other for $2 million, the trial judge was none other than Arthur Drysdale, sitting in his capacity as District Admiralty Judge of the Exchequer Court of Canada.[55] Once again he issued a one-page decision holding the *Mont Blanc* liable, but failed to set out any factual findings. For this he was criticized both in the Supreme Court of Canada and at the Privy Council, and his possible anti-French bias was also noted with adverse comment in the Supreme Court. The courts in Ottawa and London agreed that both ships were equally responsible for the accident. In allowing local prejudice to overwhelm his own sense of propriety, Justice Drysdale's professionalism was found wanting in higher tribunals, if not (at least not publicly) on the home front.[56] It was not a good omen for the post-war years.

The Long Day Wanes, 1918–1950

The economic distress of the 1920s and '30s led to increased social tensions in the province, and as usual Nova Scotia's steel and coal industry offered a flashpoint of class conflict. Compared to previous periods of economic stringency, this time industry and the provincial state were inclined to try to use the courts to restore order and to suppress dissent. The situation in Cape Breton was particularly dire and the court's role highly controversial. In 1923 union leader J.B. McLachlan was tried for seditious libel, though in Halifax rather than Sydney, as will be seen below. Glace Bay saw food riots in January 1926, when a thousand people raged through the streets of the town. The event generated the largest criminal docket before the Supreme Court in the history of the island, with eighty-four defendants set to stand trial, most on charges of break and enter arising from the riots.[57] Yet when labour tried to invoke the law's protection, it was not forthcoming for reasons that often seemed illegitimate. After a New Waterford mine disaster in 1917 in which sixty men died, the Dominion Coal Company and some of its officials were charged with manslaughter. The trial was held before Humphrey Mellish, who had served as solicitor to the company and helped to prepare its defence before his appointment to the NSSC intervened on 11 February 1918; he heard his former law partner plead for the defence, and a directed verdict of not guilty ensued. It was Mellish again to the rescue of his former client in 1922 when he wrote a decision rejecting union arguments for a stay of large wage reductions in the Cape Breton coal mines until a board appointed under the federal

Industrial Disputes Investigation Act could report on the situation. Such a stay seemed clearly mandated by the legislation and had been granted by Benjamin Russell at first instance, but two colleagues joined Mellish in overturning the decision.[58] Mellish's actions appear to have violated contemporary standards of judicial ethics as some of his colleagues did recuse themselves when former clients came before them.[59]

The appointment of several prominent corporate lawyers to the Supreme Court bench, beginning with Robert Harris in 1915, severely tested its reputation for impartiality in the interwar years. When future CCF leader J.S. Woodsworth toured Nova Scotia in January 1924, he was told that 'corporation influence on the [Supreme Court] bench was so strong that the court is looked upon by labour as a company department.'[60] He was advised that Chief Justice Harris, a former president of Nova Scotia Steel and Coal, had 'the mind of a slave owner [and] appear[ed] incapable of seeing any merit in Labor's contentions.' Mellish's connections to Dominion Coal have been noted, and Daniel D. McKenzie, appointed in 1923, was local solicitor for the Nova Scotia Steel Co. and 'very closely in touch with BESCO [British Empire Steel Company, the holding company one of whose operating companies was Dominion Coal].' Tecumseh Sherman Rogers, appointed in 1921, had been a member of the Halifax firm which acted as solicitor to Nova Scotia Steel, but Woodsworth's informant considered him 'the most honest and fearless [member] of the Court.' Justice Chisholm was 'honest and gentlemanly and ha[d] a desire to be fair, but [was] not very aggressive in his views, nor very firm in his convictions,' while Benjamin Russell was not anti-labour but 'very old and deaf' (he would retire later that year).[61] J.J. Ritchie had also litigated for Dominion Coal before his appointment in 1912.

Those concerned about the possible impact of such corporate connections would not have had their suspicions allayed by the trial and conviction of union leader J.B. McLachlan on a charge of seditious libel in December 1923. *The King v. McLachlan* well deserves the label 'gross miscarriage of justice' conferred on it by Barry Cahill in his study of the case. The case arose out of a recognition strike by Sydney steelworkers, during which BESCO called for the aid of Nova Scotia's short-lived provincial police force to maintain order. In response, a cohort of mounted police officers charged a crowd of strikers and onlookers, causing many injuries. As secretary of District 26 of the United Mine Workers of America, J.B. McLachlan wrote to all local union officers, accusing the provincial government of being 'the guilty and responsible party for this crime' and calling on them 'to spread the fight against [premier] Armstrong to every mine in Nova Scotia.' As a mere private letter this communication was probably privileged but the company caused it to be published both in Sydney and in Halifax. The publication in Halifax was crucial to the government's attempt to crush McLachlan, as it was highly doubtful whether a jury in Sydney would convict. The trial was duly held in Halifax, presided over by none other than Humphrey Mellish. McLachlan's lawyers applied for a change of venue but Mellish refused and the accused was convicted by the jury. On appeal, the Supreme Court noted a journalist's evidence to the effect that he had transmitted the letter to the *Morning Chronicle* at the behest of the company, and set aside the conviction as to the Halifax publication. Severing the connection with Halifax arguably should have led to a new trial at Sydney, but the court unanimously affirmed McLachlan's conviction.[62]

In spite of the court's apparent lack of sympathy for labour, its authority does not seem to have been overtly challenged even in Cape Breton. When Justice W.F. Carroll travelled to Sydney in February 1926 to deal with the aftermath of the food riots, he was obliged to stay for five weeks to conduct over fifty trials. Contrary to the usual pattern, most of the offenders requested jury trials in the Supreme Court rather than opting for the County Court, no doubt hoping for leniency from fellow community members. The jurors were not exactly peers of the offenders, however. A property qualification ensured that they were drawn from small-holders and small businessmen, the very groups which had suffered losses in the riots. In the result the juries were no more lenient than usual, even though Carroll criticized police practices, deprecating 'un-British third degree methods [which] may be considered proper in the United States as a means of extracting confessions and evidence from accused persons.' About half of the offenders were acquitted, and a number of charges were thrown out because of problems with the evidence. Sentences were meted out at a marathon session on the last day of the term. Carroll's remarks were reported at some length and the demeanour of those convicted seems to have been respectful and devoid of bravado for the most part. He handed out mostly sentences of two years at Dorchester, except for the three women found guilty, to whom he gave a stern lecture and ten days in the county jail. At the end of the term the jurors and court officials gave Carroll 'a handsome meerschaum pipe and tobacco pouch as a memento of his first criminal term in the county where he had practised so long.'[63]

In other conflicts too the court maintained its independence and did not capitulate to the needs of capital or government. At a crucial moment in the 1933 Acadia Coal Strike, for example, the court refused to allow the company to abandon certain mines, which would have greatly strengthened the company's bargaining position.[64] And in the summer of 1933, with a provincial election looming, the Court intervened decisively to rectify egregious governmental misconduct in the creation of the voters' lists. Taking advantage of an ambiguity in the relevant legislation, the Conservative government announced that only one registrar would be appointed for each of three Halifax constituencies. With only a few days allotted for registration, there was a real prospect of hundreds of citizens losing their votes. The Liberal Party applied for a mandamus requiring the appointment of forty registrars, one for each polling station, and the matter was heard by Justice W.F. Carroll at a special evening sitting on 19 July. Just before midnight, the Liberal *Chronicle* reported, 'tumultuous cheers echoed through the Court House as Angus L. Macdonald, leader of the Liberal Party, climaxed the most sensational and unprecedented court hearing since the days of Joseph Howe by reading aloud the text of [the] decision.'[65] A week later some registrars were still refusing to make voters' lists public, or posting them in obscure places for brief periods of time. Long waits to register provoked hundreds to demonstrate at Province House, and another mandamus had to be issued by Justice R.H. Graham forcing the registrars to make the lists public. The controversy provided the relatively unknown Macdonald with the issue upon which he swept into power on 22 August.[66]

Commentators have treated the Franchise Scandal as just another example of the questionable tactics employed in Nova Scotia's partisan rivalries, but this interpretation understates its significance. Rather, we should stress the key role played by an independent judiciary in challenging a bald manipulation of the electoral process, and the widespread acts of resistance by citizens to a widely resented abuse of state authority. An inquiry conducted by Justice Hugh Ross found that the registrars had not carried out their duties, and had simply used preliminary lists prepared by campaign organizers for the Conservative candidates in Halifax, Pictou, and Kings; the lists had omitted up to half the electors, most of the omissions being Liberals. At a time when economic dislocation helped fuel fascism in Europe and in Britain itself, Nova Scotian courts and citizens made clear their adherence to democratic values. While both judges involved in granting a remedy against a Conservative government were Liberals, the widespread dissatisfaction even among senior Conservatives with the government's course of action suggests partisan bias did not play an appreciable role in the decisions.

Macdonald's election cry was 'the restoration of responsible government' and the court had occasion to make known its views on the nature of responsible government in 1926 when Premier E.N. Rhodes referred to it the question of the legality of his plans to abolish the province's upper chamber, the Legislative Council. The court sat with only four judges, who divided evenly. The judgments of Chief Justice Harris and Justice Chisholm, both validating Rhodes's plan and essentially upholding responsible government values, were affirmed on every point in the Privy Council.[67]

Attorney General O'Hearn's reform proposals in 1923 were the last to surface in the province until the 1960s (he presented a bill for the abolition of grand juries in 1924 but it did not pass). The dramatic contraction of the provincial economy after 1920, the Depression of the 1930s, and the upheaval of the war years meant that Nova Scotians had more pressing things to worry about. The caseload of both the Supreme Court and the County Court was either stable or in decline during these years, so that overworked judges were not likely to be lobbying for reform. In spite of the social upheaval around them, there was an aura of complacency, conservatism, and nostalgia among the judges, traits which were widespread among the provincial elite in the interwar years.

The careers of the two chief justices who spanned this entire period, Robert Harris (chief justice 1918–31) and Joseph Chisholm (1931–50), provide some evidence in this direction. Harris was one of the leaders of a dynamic generation of corporate lawyers who presided over a period of industrial growth and corporate concentration in the decades prior to the First World War. Prime Minister Robert Borden named him to the bench in 1915, then elevated him to the chief justiceship three years later ahead of several senior members of the court who all, with one exception, happened to be Liberals. Harris is remembered as an efficient chief justice and as the instigator of an addition to the courthouse at Halifax, but his final gift to his native province was a piece of imperial flummery. A year before his death in office in 1931, Harris presented to the province a ceremonial mace. This symbol of the speaker's authority, manufactured in England, was to be carried by the sergeant at arms of the House of Assembly in accordance with parliamentary procedure. The House had resolved as long ago as 1819 to acquire a mace but for some reason none was obtained and Harris's was the first to be used. Harris chose to focus on a symbol which for contemporaries evoked only the memory of 'dim and ancient things, the ghosts of a vanished past.'[68]

Harris's successor Joseph Chisholm actively pursued a cult of nostalgia through his many historical notes on Nova Scotian judicial figures, most of whom belonged to the eighteenth century. He was also the last Nova Scotian chief justice to be knighted, benefitting from the brief window of opportunity under R.B. Bennett when the honour was permitted to Canadians. When Bennett wrote to ask him if he would like a knighthood, he could not signify his assent fast enough.[69] Aside from that, Chisholm's main aim in life seemed to be outlasting some of his nineteenth century predecessors; he remained in office until his death at the age of eighty-seven in 1950. His judicial longevity is also an implicit confirmation of the relatively undemanding nature of the office in the first half of the twentieth century.

By 1925 civil litigation at Halifax was running at about nine hundred cases filed per year, but their composition was changing fairly significantly. Debt-related litigation was still the single most important category, but its proportion of total business dropped from 75 per cent in 1885 to about 65 per cent in 1925; promissory notes became significantly rarer as more modern forms of credit emerged. The difference was taken up by tort cases in particular, with a sample mean of 6 per cent intentional torts and 6 per cent negligence claims for personal injuries. About half of the latter related to motor vehicle accidents. The total number of cases filed at Halifax dropped steadily after the early 1920s, reaching a historic low of 269 in 1945. The general pattern is similar to that in the Winnipeg Court of Queen's Bench between 1909 and 1939, outlined by Dale Brawn in one of the very few quantitative studies of Canadian courts.[70]

As the civil docket declined, the criminal law took on more significance, at least where capital crime was concerned. The 1930s was the most punitive decade in Canadian history, with 80 per cent of 208 capitally convicted persons hanged, as against a historic norm of about 50 per cent.[71] Nova Scotia's execution rate had always been considerably lower than the rest of Canada, roughly one-third except for the 1910s, when it approached 50 per cent (seven out of sixteen hanged). In the 1930s it reached its historic peak, with half of the dozen men sentenced actually executed. Three of the sentenced men were black, and two of them were hanged. If one reaches back to 1928 to include the hanging of black Louis Jones of Halifax for murdering his wife, the racial imbalance in the statistics becomes even more shocking given the small proportion of Afro-Nova Scotians (about 3 per cent) in the province's population.[72] The only positive outcome of the high execution rate in the 1930s was that it seems to have operated as a kind of catharsis: Everett Farmer, a black man hanged on 11 December 1937 in the Shelburne jail for murdering his half-brother, was the last man executed in Nova Scotia for a capital crime, a quarter-century before the last hanging in Canada.[73]

If blacks did not fare well at the hands of the courts, juries, or those charged with administering the system of executive clemency, the Mi'kmaq also experienced a serious defeat in this period. In 1928 the grand chief of the Mi'kmaq, Gabriel Syliboy, was charged with hunting muskrats out of season in Cape Breton, contrary to provincial legislation. His defence rested on a provision of a 1752 treaty granting 'free liberty of hunting and fishing as usual,' based on the oral understanding of the treaty passed down from his ancestors. County Court Judge George Patterson rejected the defence on the basis that the treaty covered only a small group of mainland Indians. Even if it did purport to extend to Cape Breton, he decided, the treaty was 'not made between competent contracting parties,' as the attorney general would paraphrase him in 1974. According to Judge Patterson the Mi'kmaq of 1752 were not an independent people capable of entering into a treaty. This decision, together with the establishment of the residential school at Shubenacadie in the next year, marked a significant disjunction in the life of the Mi'kmaq. It would be forty years before the ensuing pattern of cultural loss and disorientation began to reverse itself, and a reclaiming of the eighteenth century treaties was initiated.[74]

If litigation was down so significantly at Halifax, there was even less for County Court judges to do in the interwar years. In Hants County, for example, a total of 484 civil cases were filed between 1930 and 1938, or about 60 per year, while in Kings County 1,000 suits were filed during the same period, or about 130 per year.[75] Most of these were routine proceedings not resulting in trials, and the criminal business of the County Courts was relatively light. Holding a sinecure did not prevent two County Court judges from coming to grief during these years, however. Lewis Martell, appointed to the County Court at Windsor by the Liberals in 1925 after a term in the House of Commons, seems to have had no conception of his role. Within a few short years he had managed to break every conceivable canon of judicial ethics and etiquette. When Martell did not respond to an invitation to resign, Chief

Justice Chisholm was appointed to conduct an inquiry under the Judges Act. He found ample evidence of official misconduct and Martell was removed from office on 19 August 1932, the only County Court judge in Nova Scotia to experience this fate. A near contemporary, however, Bennett appointee William Angus Livingstone, County Court judge for District No. 3, resigned in 1938 'in advance of being tried, convicted and sentenced to two years in Dorchester Penitentiary for theft and perjury.'[76] These disasters illustrated the perennial difficulty of using judgeships as patronage rewards. While in opposition R.B. Bennett pledged to appoint only on the basis of merit, but two years later, as prime minister, he was obliged to eat his words. Acknowledging the criticism of judicial appointments made on grounds other than merit, he observed: 'To get away from that in a new democracy is not an easy thing. No one knows the difficulty better than I.'[77]

Bennett at least seems to have worried about the questionable merit of some of his appointees to the bench. Mackenzie King, by contrast, was content to regard judgeships as part of the cold calculus of patronage and nothing more. When King had to consider the claim to a Cabinet post of long-serving Cape Breton MP Daniel D. McKenzie, he mused to his diary, 'I thought of [a] judgeship for him – am not keen on him [for the Cabinet].' In the end he did appoint McKenzie to be solicitor general, but only for a year until a vacancy opened up on the NSSC. Other judges seem to have made more of an impression on King's fertile subconscious. In 1945 he recorded a dream about the long-deceased judge Benjamin Russell:

> [S]omeone told me that Benjamin Russell ... a great student of Matthew Arnold, wanted to see me. I said that I was too busy and could not see him. A little later, I seemed to suddenly come into a party of ladies and one of them came over to speak to me and said that she was Mrs. Benjamin Russell and had been looking for me ... I had never seen [her] before. Judge Russell has been dead some years. I have known nothing about Mrs. Russell. She looked very cheerful, bright and pleasant. There were a number of ladies with her. All rather elderly. The sort of group one sees at a woman's afternoon tea though they were out of doors ...
>
> When I came to make a note of the vision, after breakfast, I was so tired that I could not think of Judge Russell's name. I could think of Matthew Arnold but for the life of me could not think of the association. This rather alarmed me ...

Even at this late date, the clothing of Nova Scotia judges with imperial associations seems to have been engraved on King's mind.[78]

As economic conditions deteriorated, the bar became so traumatized that many lawyers could not afford to continue their subscriptions to the Nova Scotia Reports, leading to a long hiatus in its publication as a stand-alone series. In 1929 Carswell was obliged to consolidate the reports from Nova Scotia, New Brunswick, and Prince Edward Island into a new series, the Maritime Provinces Reports. It would be four decades before the NSRs re-emerged as an autonomous case reporter. The Depression also led to an increase in lawyerly malfeasance, but throughout the period the bar maintained an easy-going attitude towards professional misconduct. In spite of dozens of formal written complaints against barristers during the 1930s, only two members were struck from the rolls and one was censured. Only in 1932 did the Barristers' Society create a standing committee on discipline, rather than appointing an ad hoc committee to investigate each complaint, and express legislative provision for such a committee did not come until 1941.[79]

The position of court staff changed little over the period except for the initiation of a modest pension scheme for court officials. With the first steps towards the welfare state taken after the First World War, senior court officials (sheriffs, prothonotaries, registrars of deeds) were in 1918 granted a pension after forty years of service based on two-thirds of the annual average of their gross fees earned in the last five years. In 1916 the judges of the Supreme Court at last got a 'stenographer' of their own, one Robert Eccles, though the appointment was to be made by Cabinet. All court officers (including registrars of deeds) were required to turn over one-third of their fees to the provincial treasury in 1921; this may well have functioned as a type of equalization tax from the wealthier counties to fund the income floor which had been set for such officers in the nineteenth century. In 1939 the Cabinet was authorized to direct any court officer remunerated by fees to pay all costs and fees received by him to the provincial treasury in return for a yearly salary, but this provision seems to have been little used.[80] A provincial civil service was slowly being established but the senior court-related offices remained a patronage preserve until late in the twentieth century.

Sheriffs had security of tenure, but as of 1928 sheriffs reaching the age of seventy-five might have their commissions revoked by the Cabinet.[81] The office of prothonotary was statutorily defined as held at pleasure until 1958, making its holders vulnerable to removal after a change of government. When the Conservatives won the 1925 provincial election after forty years out of power, there was no wholesale firing of the incumbents but the prothonotaries of both Cumberland and Kings counties were replaced for political reasons in 1926. In Halifax, A.G. Cummings, KC, was dismissed immediately in November 1927 on being charged with defalcation of funds paid into court. Some three thousand dollars was admitted to be missing, but two juries acquitted him of any criminal act. Cummings was of course replaced by a Conservative, who turned out to be Reginald Vanderbilt Harris, nephew of the chief justice.[82]

There were few notable improvements in the administration of justice during the interwar years. One change worthy of note is the official appearance of women in the courts, both as lawyers and as staff. Provincial enfranchisement in 1918 probably helped legitimate their entry into a field of work previously closed to them. Women began to be hired in the 1920s by the prothonotaries, who were still responsible for obtaining and paying their staff out of their own fees. One Marjorie Leck began working as a 'stenographer' for the disgraced prothonotary A.G. Cummings at Halifax in the 1920s, for example. Grace Wamboldt was the fifth woman to be admitted to the Nova Scotia bar when she was called in 1925, but collected a plethora of 'firsts': she was apparently the first woman to appear in the Supreme Court in the 1930s; to practise law in her own name when she took over her principal's firm after his death in 1940; to be elected to the council of the Nova Scotia Barristers' Society in 1945; and to receive a KC (1950). Wambolt was also a tireless advocate of the right of women to serve on juries, a right not granted until 1960.[83]

The Challenge of Post-War Affluence, 1950–1982

It is not surprising that the enormous changes in Canadian society after 1945 would be reflected in the life of a provincial superior court. The affluence of the post-war decades led to a marked increase in the NSSC's caseload, and to significant changes in its composition. Tort law and family law emerged more prominently, while administrative law and public law in general also occupied more of the court's attention. Divorce and motor vehicle accidents came to preoccupy the court in the post-war period, with divorce making up one-third of its caseload and motor vehicle accident litigation some 15 per cent. Debt-related matters declined dramatically to about 30 per cent of the court's caseload and a miscellany of other matters made up the rest. Prosperity and shifting social mores also led to changes in the caseload of the county court. Although it could not hear divorces until 1962, adoption applications surged in the 1950s and '60s to form 10 to 20 per cent of its docket. Eight to ten per cent of its workload comprised motor vehicle accidents during this period, and the restoration of suspended motor vehicle licences also occupied a good deal of its time. The Supreme Court's criminal docket almost vanished, and the County Court took up the slack. Death sentences were ordered much less frequently, with only twelve recorded between 1940 and 1966, when the carrying out of the final penalty was suspended pending abolition a decade later. All of these were either overturned on appeal or commuted to life imprisonment.

The County Court at Halifax experienced the litigation boom more quickly and acutely than the Supreme Court. Its caseload had been stable at 350 to 450 cases per year from at least 1915 to 1945 but then tripled in the decade 1945–55 (from 485 cases to 1,484) and continued to rise steadily to 2,430 (1965) and 4,032 (1975). The Supreme Court's non-divorce caseload doubled between 1945 and 1955, but the increase is somewhat deceptive, given the extremely low figure for 1945: a mere 269 cases, a historic low caused by unusual wartime conditions. The 631 cases filed in 1955 were still on the low side by historical standards and even in 1965 only 957 cases were filed (other than divorces), equivalent to the 910 filed in 1925 if population increase is taken into account. After 1965 the rate of litigation in the Supreme Court increased very substantially, as will be seen. The real challenge to the Supreme Court in the immediate post-war period was keeping up with the divorce petitions, of which there were on average 250 per year between 1945 and 1960. In only one year were there fewer than 200 (145 in 1948), while in 1953 they spiked to nearly 500 and in 1960 to 580. This was the most dramatic transformation in its work that the Supreme Court would experience in its entire history. Within a few years it had become, in effect, a divorce court, with the dissolution of marriages no longer a marginal and slightly distasteful part of its work but at least one-third of its caseload. Under pre-confederation legislation one judge of the Supreme Court was named the judge ordinary in the Court of Divorce and Matrimonial Causes but the incumbent in 1945, seventy-five-year-old Justice Robert Graham, was almost overwhelmed by the avalanche of petitions; one wonders whether they drove him into retirement four years later. In 1948 all the judges were empowered to

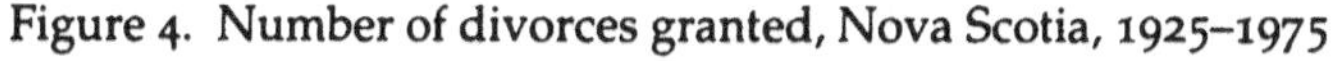
Figure 4. Number of divorces granted, Nova Scotia, 1925–1975

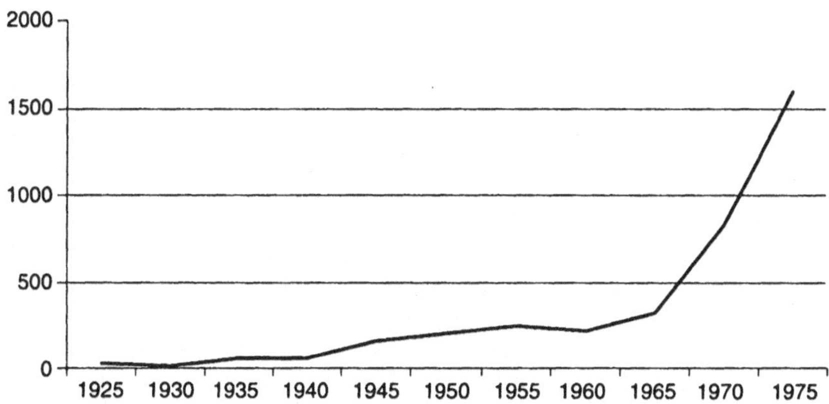

grant divorces, and divorce petitions could be heard for the first time on circuit. When the avalanche showed no sign of slowing down, even the County Court judges (outside Halifax) were harnessed to the cause in 1962.[84]

This revolution in caseload might have caused some to question both the appointments process and the preparation of judges for dealing with this new and significant part of their work. The experience of lawyers appointed to the court in this period tended to be in commercial and corporate law, labour relations, and political life – not particularly good training for adjudicating family law issues. The very small numbers of women lawyers made appointment of one to the bench unlikely, but it is not clear if the possibility was ever considered or advocated. How women reacted as direct participants in the divorce process or as members of the public remains a mystery, but when considering the 'legitimacy' of the court in the post-war period, the possibility of differing reactions based on gender should be kept in mind. In a general sense, however, a combination of social and institutional change helped to overcome the legitimacy problems of the interwar period. The revolution in labour relations during the war, reviewed in Blake Brown's paper in this volume, provided a much more stable framework for relations between capital and labour. With recognition strikes a thing of the past, and most industrial relations matters now within the purview of the provincial labour relations board, the NSSC's role was limited to the less directly political function of judicial review; even there, as Brown shows, the court largely deferred to the labour board after some initial hesitation.

Just as important in this rehabilitation process was the character of the post-war appointments. Within a few years the seven-man bench was almost completely replaced. From 1950 on, only John Doull and W.L. Hall, both former Conservative attorneys general, remained from an earlier era. Josiah MacQuarrie (1947), Eugene Troop Parker (1948), J.L. Ilsley (1949), Lauchlin Currie (1949), and Vincent MacDonald (1950) were all well known for their sympathy towards labour. Unlike some of their predecessors who were closely identified with the corporate bar, these men came from a variety of backgrounds: public service, academe, and, in Currie's case, a labour-oriented practice before his political career, which included long service as minister of mines and labour (1940–7) and attorney general (1947–9). Currie was particularly notable as he had been a bricklayer and coal miner before studying law and had even been solicitor to District 26 of the United Mine Workers of America, J.B. McLachlan's old local. All were of course Liberals, indeed three had been in Liberal Cabinets, but their talents and experience forestalled criticism on this ground. MacQuarrie had been attorney general in Angus L. Macdonald's first Cabinet, called the strongest in Nova Scotia history by J. Murray Beck. Ilsley had recommended Parker to the Minister of Justice Louis St-Laurent; he was 'not as brilliant a man as [a competitor] but has had a great deal of experience in all kinds of practice in several parts of N.S. and is noted for good judgment and good character.'[85] In Ilsley's own case, a brief stint in corporate law practice in Montreal after he left the federal Cabinet in 1948 was a convenient haven until a judicial position opened up in his native province. Macdonald had been federal assistant deputy minister of labour during the war, then chaired the N.S. Wartime Labour Relations Board and its successor while serving as dean of Dalhousie Law School. The Ilsley court was undoubtedly the strongest bench that had emerged since Confederation, and the most in harmony, ideologically speaking, with the population it served. Such harmony was admittedly much easier to achieve in the consensus-oriented society of the 1950s and early 1960s than it had been during the strife-ridden inter-war years, or would be after the upheavals of the later 1960s.

The succession to W.F. Carroll, who retired on 14 May 1949, reveals some key features of the appointments process in the post-war period. It appears that the seventy-two-year-old Carroll was under some pressure to retire to make way for the new broom Ilsley.[86] Rather than retreat into semi-seclusion Carroll surprised everyone by re-entering the political arena after a quarter-century's absence. He wrote to Prime Minister St-Laurent that he 'had intended all along to retire this summer and did want to have something to do for the next three or four years, hence my entry into politics.' Only a few weeks after his retirement Carroll sought and won the nomination in the riding of Inverness-Richmond (the incumbent Liberal had conveniently died after the election was called), and went on to win the election and serve out his term as an MP. Nova Scotia judges had occasionally returned to politics after leaving the bench but Carroll was the last member of the NSSC, and quite possibly the last superior court judge in Canada, to do so. By the post-war period the conventions around the separation of politics and judging had hardened to the point where political careers for retired judges were viewed as unseemly. Prime Minister St-Laurent congratulated Carroll on winning the nomination in 1949, but he may well have gritted his teeth in doing so.[87]

Carroll, a Catholic, had definite ideas about his successor. It was high time 'the French Acadians in this Province were given at least the same opportunities of getting prominent positions in the judiciary and elsewhere as others.' In Carroll's view the ideal candidate was County Court judge Vincent Pottier, 'a tremendously good lawyer [with] a keen sense of justice and fair play.' The first Nova Scotian Acadian to serve as an MP, Pottier had represented Shelburne-Yarmouth-Clare in the House of Commons from 1935 to 1945, and his appointment to District No. 1 (Halifax) in 1947 illustrated an initial nod to the idea that a provincial judiciary should broadly reflect the ethnic and racial make-up of its population. In the event, Carroll's successor was the Catholic Lauchlin Currie, in spite of some strong lobbying by Robert Winters, Nova Scotia's representative in the federal Cabinet, for a Protestant lawyer from his home constituency of Lunenburg.[88] Carroll's hopes for Pottier would eventually be realized, but only in the twilight of his career. In the meantime he became the provincial government's man of all work, chairing key commissions of inquiry into public school financing, mental hospitals, and municipal taxation in Halifax. Pottier became the first judge in Nova Scotia promoted from the County Court to the NSSC in 1965 but he served only five years, leaving close to the mandatory retirement age. With his unquenchable thirst for public service, he then served as a much-valued volunteer mentor at the new Dalhousie Legal Aid Service until his death.[89]

When Chief Justice Chisholm died in office on 22 January 1950, Ilsley was appointed to the post with almost unseemly haste three days later. The symbolism of the shift could not have been more fitting. Chisholm, born before Confederation and middle-aged by Queen Victoria's death, was one of a group Christopher Moore has labelled (in the Ontario context) the 'last patricians,' a fragment of the legal elite who remained fixated on British justice, imperial ties, and an idealized common law.[90] His death came just months after appeals to the Judicial Committee were abolished, an event which led to a certain attenuation of legal ties between Britain and Canada. Ilsley had lived in a very different world from Chisholm's; he virtually ran the country during the war as minister of finance, helped create Canada's version of the welfare state, and sympathized with the shift to public law and administrative justice. Running the NSSC was pretty small potatoes after his previous career, but his skills as an administrator were nonetheless required as the 'divorce crisis' struck the court with full force during his tenure. He must have been appalled to find that the judges still shared only the one secretary authorized in 1916; he ensured that the province would provide more, hired through the Civil Service Commission rather than by Cabinet.[91] Ilsley was likely behind a rationalization of the County Courts in 1949 which allowed the judges to be appointed as 'additional judges' in each other's districts, thus enabling them to preside in case of the absence or incapacity of the judge of a given district.[92] The one puzzle about Ilsley's long tenure is why the long-sought separation of the trial and appeal divisions did not occur until the very end of it. When he took over as chief justice one former Cabinet colleague was prime minister (St-Laurent) and another premier of Nova Scotia (Angus L. Macdonald), and the coincidence of Liberal regimes continued until the provincial victory of the Stanfield Conservatives in 1956. If Ilsley had made a priority of getting the necessary complementary legislation passed, he could surely have done so in those six years.

Coincidentally, when the time came for Bennett appointees W.L. Hall and John Doull to be replaced in 1958 and 1961 respectively, the Conservatives were back in power in Ottawa as well as Halifax. After such a long period out of office, partisan considerations played a major role in the Diefenbaker government's judicial appointments, in spite of Diefenbaker's own pious pronouncements on the subject while in opposition. When Justice Hall died in the summer of 1958, Attorney General Richard Donahoe wrote to his federal counterpart Davie Fulton indicating a preference for Frederick Bissett to fill the vacancy. 'Mr. Bissett was twice a candidate for our party, served for a long period as

President of the party organization for this federal constituency and is a past President of the Nova Scotia Bar Society,' Donahoe reported. His nomination was 'on the understanding that neither Mr. Nowlan [Nova Scotia's representative in the federal Cabinet] nor Mr. G.I. Smith, Provincial Secretary of Nova Scotia is seriously seeking this appointment.' For Nova Scotia Senator Felix Quinn, too, Bissett's party loyalty was a paramount consideration: 'he ran two elections for us – not successfully, of course – and he has taken part in every general election that I can recall in the last thirty years.'[93] In spite of this impressive support Frank Harris Patterson received the appointment, but Bissett duly got his judgeship at the next opportunity, when John Doull retired in 1961. The Conservatives also appointed Thomas Coffin as successor to Eugene Troop Parker when he retired in the same year. (Both Doull (eighty-two) and Parker (seventy-five) were compulsorily retired with the coming into force of the constitutional amendment mandating retirement of federally appointed judges at seventy-five.) Patterson was Premier Robert Stanfield's law partner in Truro, and Coffin was a Halifax lawyer and treasurer of the federal Conservative Party who had promoted Stanfield back in the days when the Conservatives were in the political wilderness.[94]

By 1960 Richard Donahoe was tired of recommending others and began to lobby for a position for himself on the NSSC bench. Knowing that Doull and Parker's forced retirements would create two vacancies in 1961, he wrote directly to Prime Minister Diefenbaker to plead his case. Donahoe pointed to over thirty years of party service, 'having been an active platform speaker even before I had the vote' and having run in six elections, one federal and five provincial. After his long detour into politics he did not relish returning to the practice of law if the Stanfield government were defeated. As a Catholic he acknowledged the two vacancies as Protestant but argued the balance could be adjusted later. When he missed his chance in 1961 there was not to be another with the Conservatives' long absence from power in Ottawa. Compared to the claims of those who were appointed in 1961, Donahoe's appear stronger; to the end of his life he felt his religion had been used to deny him a post that was rightfully his.[95]

On 10 December 1962 Donahoe reported that 'the amendments to the *Judges Act* required to permit establishment of Appellate and Trial Divisions in Nova Scotia appear to be making leisurely progress through the House of Commons, but passed and implemented will, I suspect, cause a grave problem of accommodation in the existing Court House.

I believe the municipal bodies concerned are endeavouring to reach agreement upon the establishment and location of a new Court House.'[96] It may indeed have been the space problem that caused the long-delayed separation of the appellate and trial divisions of the court to be postponed even further. Or it may have been the lack of political congruence between Ottawa and Halifax, with the Liberals back in power federally as of April 1963 while the Stanfield Conservatives ruled Nova Scotia. The federal legislation authorizing the appointment of two extra judges was duly passed in July 1963, but proclamation of both the federal and provincial acts was delayed for a full three years until 1 August 1966.

In the meantime, the bar and the public were getting restless. On 15 July 1964 the *Chronicle-Herald* called for a 'comprehensive study of the administration of justice with a view to effecting a reorganization of the province's court system,' to be carried out by the attorney general's department in conjunction with the Barristers' Society. The cry for reform did not seem to be motivated by any specific grievances in the justice system – delay was not overtly mentioned, for example – but simply by a sense that 'the administration of justice in Nova Scotia is archaic, a legacy of horse-and-buggy days.' The eleven demands made by the newspaper called for more accountability, better access to justice, and a more professional system, in contrast to the middle-class demands for speed and efficiency that had fuelled critiques of the courts in earlier times. Legal aid for indigent defendants was advocated, as was more ready access to the facilities of the Supreme Court for those living outside Halifax, preferably by merging the County and Supreme Courts and providing for some resident Supreme Court judges outside the capital. Increasing the salaries and benefits of provincial magistrates, and thus raising the character of the lower court bench, was also a priority, as was providing for security of tenure for Crown prosecutors, who were liable to dismissal for partisan reasons. Critics also called for creation of a family court, better ways of dealing with the growing numbers of divorce petitions, and abolition of the grand jury. (A provincially appointed family court was created in 1963 but not brought into operation until early 1965.) There is no doubt that much of Nova Scotia's legislation was shockingly out of date. Outside those cities and towns with stipendiary magistrates, many civil matters were still supposed to be brought before justices of the peace. The 1864 provision allowing for three-person juries in such cases at the suit of either party remained in force until 1980, when the small claims courts were created.[97]

When added to the growing human rights consciousness emerging in the province, these demands represented a new and quite different kind of public interest in the courts and the justice system. While citizens wanted a professionalized and well-run system, they wanted more than a technocratic machine for dispensing justice. Rather, they urged the main actors in the legal system to recall their purpose: they were there not simply to perpetuate the system or to serve the interests of the legal profession and the state, but to provide justice-related services to the public. The call for relevance, for substantive rather than formal justice, for a justice system that reflected contemporary values, would be heard with increasing frequency and insistence in the years ahead, not just in Nova Scotia but across Canada. By the mid-1960s, the complacent post-war consensus had evaporated, never to return. The Ilsley court's golden glow would not be recreated in the foreseeable future, as the courts, the justice system, and indeed the entire legal order came under increasing critical scrutiny.

At least one of the *Herald*'s demands was soon satisfied. On 1 August 1966 two new positions were created as the separation of the trial and appeal divisions was finally implemented. One went to Alexander McKinnon, promoted from the County Court of Antigonish directly to the new Appeal Division, and the other to Gordon Cowan, a senior lawyer at Stewart McKeen & Covert in Halifax named to the Trial Division. Cowan was a Rhodes Scholar who had begun his career as a law professor at Dalhousie and in Manitoba; more recently he was narrowly defeated for the leadership of the provincial Liberals in 1962. McKinnon would finish his judicial career as chief justice of Nova Scotia (1968–73), an unthinkable occurrence for a County Court judge in any previous decade. Within Ottawa circles at least, the old status divisions were at last breaking down, however powerful they might remain locally. Lauchlin Currie was promoted to chief justice of the new Trial Division in 1966, then only seven months later became chief justice of Nova Scotia after the death of Chief Justice Ilsley in January 1967; Gordon Cowan replaced him in the Trial Division.

The extra positions came just in time, as the rate of non-divorce litigation increased spectacularly from the mid-1960s, from 957 cases filed at Halifax in 1965 to 3,214 in 1975 (an increase of 335 per cent), the population of the city and county having increased only 16 per cent during that period. The increase in the Halifax County Court was not quite as large, from 2,430 to 4,032 (166 per cent), but there was only one judge in that court until 1971, when a second was added. County Court judges were made local judges of the Supreme Court in 1972, a major step forward in coordinating the business of the two courts, and the grand jury was abolished in 1979.[98] The new judges and the explosion of paper led to a need for new premises, which was satisfied when the new Law Courts opened in 1971.[99] If the building's architectural style spoke of impersonal bureaucracy, the location on a Halifax waterfront in the process of a complete physical rehabilitation suggested at least a metaphorical reply to contemporary concerns about access to justice and a more responsive legal order. The appointment of the court's first Acadian judge in 1965 and its first Jewish judge, J. Louis Dubinsky, in 1967, also hinted at a new inclusiveness.

The increased caseload in all Nova Scotia courts also revealed the inadequacy of the voluntarist model of legal aid provision. In 1951 the Nova Scotia Barristers' Society had provided for a weekly two-hour 'clinic,' staffed by two junior lawyers, to be held in Halifax. A clinic in Sydney was short-lived and the concept was resisted by local bar associations elsewhere in the province. The demand for family law advice after the expansion of divorce in 1968 overwhelmed the modest supply of pro bono legal services the bar was prepared to provide. Using primarily federal funding, students and faculty at Dalhousie Law School started their own stand-alone clinic in the north end of Halifax in 1970, where they served some 1,400 clients in their first year of operation. In 1971 the provincial government provided funds to the Barristers' Society to open and operate a network of legal aid offices around Nova Scotia. By 1973 ten such offices were in operation, using a staff lawyer model with two or more lawyers plus support staff at each location. The partnership with the Barristers' Society ended in 1977 when the Nova Scotia Legal Aid Commission was created as an independent body at arm's length from government, with sole responsibility for administering legal aid in the province. By the early 1980s, N.S. Legal Aid served some 11,500 'full service' clients, as well as providing summary advice to many more.[100]

The prosperity of the post-war decades allowed the Barristers' Society to reconsider its Depression-era decision to get out of the law reporting business. In the late 1960s the Society responded favourably to a proposal by the upstart Maritime Law Book Company in Fredericton to re-institute the Nova Scotia Reports (the New Brunswick bar was about to make a similar deal). Not only would the new reports be more directly under the supervision of the bar, they would be published in the Maritimes again for the first time since 1886. Five volumes of cases covering the period 1965–9 were issued in 1969, and in 1970 the Nova Scotia Reports (2nd series) resumed publication. Carswell's Maritime Provinces Reports ceased to exist, and a new series covering only Prince Edward Island and Newfoundland was created.

Just as citizens began to think in terms of a provincial 'justice system' comprising courts, police, probation officers, Crown counsel, and the attorney general's office, so Ottawa began to think of a national justice system. As federal expenditures on courts, corrections, and legal aid increased dramatically in the 1960s and '70s, the Department of Justice began to collect information on the administration of justice by the provinces (criminal justice in particular), as a prelude to rationalizing its outlay. This research revealed that in many areas Nova Scotia's spending on justice services was the lowest per capita in the country, or barely ahead of Prince Edward Island and Newfoundland. For example, the department estimated that all levels of government in Canada spent $110 per person on justice services in 1977–8. Nova Scotia spent only $65.69 (a figure which included $24.73 from federal coffers), 35 per cent below the national average. This deficit ranged from a low of 52 per cent below the national average for legal aid, to only 22 per cent below the national average for corrections, with the courts coming in at 36 per cent below the national average. The diffusion of authority within the province reflected long traditions of downloading fiscal responsibilities to municipal units. Among other provinces, only in New Brunswick was the provincial contribution to justice services approximately equal to the municipal contribution (in Nova Scotia, $20.88 and $20.08 respectively). Municipal responsibility meant considerable variation in the level and quality of particular services, a situation suitable for an earlier age when local differences loomed larger. As people began to think in more systemic terms, however, such variety was less defensible.[101]

Similar thinking also led to the first steps towards the integration of provincial superior court judges into a national judicial network. A conference on criminal law held at the new Centre of Criminology at the University of Toronto in 1964 marked the inaugural meeting of the National Conference of Chief Justices, and it was followed by the annual Canadian Judicial Conference for puisne judges, first held in 1969. Both eventually became informal continuing education exercises covering both criminal and civil law topics. These were the first occasions on which judges from all provinces were able to meet in a professional context to discuss matters of mutual interest. In 1971 the

Canadian Judicial Council was created and charged with investigating complaints against federally appointed judges. Its membership comprised all provincial chief justices, and their regular meetings helped to draw the various provincial superior courts closer together. Within these bodies, judges from smaller provinces such as Nova Scotia could sometimes exercise national leadership.

The larger expectations around Trudeau's 1968 election promises of a 'Just Society' were disappointed fairly quickly, but a heightened focus on law reform, justice issues, and judicial appointments remained a continuing preoccupation of his government. The Divorce Act, 1968 led to a dramatic spike in the number of divorces granted across the country; in Nova Scotia they increased fivefold, from 323 in 1965 to 1,597 in 1975. A 1973 federal-provincial cost-sharing agreement led to a major infusion of funds into recent provicial legal aid systems, to be used for criminal defence work. Federal funding for civil legal aid under the Canada Assistance Plan followed in the early 1980s. A major change in the federal court system, with a new itinerant Federal Court of Canada replacing the old Exchequer Court, meant that Nova Scotia judges no longer needed to serve as local judges in Admiralty, though they did agree to share their quarters in the new waterfront courthouse with the Federal Court judges (as they still do).

Trudeau and his early ministers of justice, John Turner and Otto Lang, regarded judicial appointments as more than just government patronage, though this is not to say that candidates' political affiliations suddenly became irrelevant. When minister of justice, Trudeau began a process of consultation with the Canadian Bar Association and provincial law societies, while Otto Lang created the post of special adviser on judicial appointments in 1973. The adviser was to provide more objective information on informally nominated candidates, to seek out the opinion of relevant constituencies, and to try to interest talented persons whose names might not have been put forward. Information is power, and the minister wished to acquire more to avoid being so dependent on the recommendations of regional ministers. The result was a shake-up in the cosy conventions of judicial appointments, fuelled also by the demands of the youth revolution. For some time a certain inertia had crept into the appointment of chief justices in particular, with promotion of the senior judge being accepted as a matter of course. Otto Lang denounced this practice as 'an irresponsible abdication of our duties,' and in 1974 declared proudly that of the last ten chief justice appointments, only one had gone to the senior judge on his court. The most spectacular of these had been the unexpected elevation of Bora Laskin, the second most junior judge on the Supreme Court of Canada, to the chief justiceship on 27 December 1973.[102]

Nova Scotia's top judicial job opened up with the death in office of Chief Justice McKinnon on 14 June 1973. Trudeau, on Lang's recommendation, decided to appoint Ian MacKeigan directly from the profession to the post in September, the first time this had been done in Nova Scotia since James McDonald's appointment in 1881. The Chief Justice of the Trial Division, Gordon Cowan, had very good qualifications for the job and six years' experience, but his unpopular jailing of forty-five fishermen in 1970 for illegal picketing in their attempts to form a union may have tarnished his image. He was also viewed as something of an autocrat, overly concerned with efficient administration and lacking in people skills. In spite of the small size of the Trial Division at the time, Cowan never held meetings of the full court and simply administered by memo without ever consulting his colleagues. MacKeigan had significant Ottawa and Liberal connections, having been president of the Atlantic Development Board and a member of the Economic Council of Canada, and he was also well known in the corporate world through the directorships he held in some of Canada's largest companies.[103]

Chief Justice MacKeigan was effective in getting more resources for his court and the County Court at a time when they were sorely needed. A fourth judge was added to the Appeal Division in 1973, two more judges to the Trial Division in 1976 and 1977, another four in 1983, and two more county court judges in 1985, the year he retired as chief justice. The seven-person bench of 1965 had become fourteen by 1983. The difficulties in securing complementary legislation when changes to the court were required seem to have diminished in the 1970s and 1980s. Recognizing the higher profile of the justice system that emerged in the 1960s, federal and provincial politicians tried to set aside partisan differences where reforms to the courts were required.

The increase in caseload created needs for more support personnel and more effective systems for managing information and documents, forcing a kind of managerial revolution on Canadian courts in the 1960s and 70s. It is one that has continued ever since, even after the peak of the caseload crisis passed in the 1980s. Rapidly changing forms of information and communications technology, the proliferation of experts in court administration, changing paradigms of dispute resolution in the field of civil justice, constitutionalized requirements of criminal trials within a reasonable time, the necessity of communicating effectively with the public, and the fiscal demands of 1990s retrenchment have all forced judges to become ever more involved in the administrative side of the curial mission. The publication of Carl Baar and Perry Millar's *Judicial Administration in Canada* in 1981, the first comprehensive study of the subject in this country, conveniently marks the coming of age of the phenomenon.

Even before the advent of computers and the trend to alternative dispute resolution, the NSSC pioneered case management techniques. Historically, litigation was understood to be in the hands of the parties and their solicitors, and it was not for the judges to try and speed it up or alter its course in any way. With the spectacular growth of the docket in the 1960s, this laissez-faire approach could no longer be sustained. After his appointment as chief justice of the Trial Division in 1967, Gordon Cowan took a more active approach to case management by overhauling the rules of court, redrafting the Judicature Act in 1972, and introducing new administrative practices. A new rule of court forced parties to apply for a hearing date once six months had elapsed after the filing of a statement of defence; otherwise the registrar of the court would do so. When on circuit, all cases in which statements of defence were filed more than six months earlier had to be disposed of before the judge could leave town. Cases were assigned to a single judge, who was allowed to adjourn for reasonable cause only to a day certain when he or she would try it, instilling a sense of individual responsibility for seeing cases through to conclusion. And Cowan did not shrink from instituting some shaming techniques. He caused a reserve list to be prepared each month showing every case started and not finished, with the names of the judges assigned to those cases. As of 31 January 1976 he was able to report that the seven-man Trial Division had only nine cases on its reserves list, represented by two judges, and six of these had been heard in January. Cowan circulated this list to his colleagues each month, and noted 'the judges try to keep their names off that list!'[104]

In the same year Nova Scotia appointed an Administrator of the Provincial Courts and Inspector of Legal and Registry Offices.[105] The judicial establishment was now fairly sizeable, with 21 section 96 judges (plus one supernumerary), 34 provincially appointed judges, and 243 support staff for both courts, for a total of 299 persons. (By comparison, there are currently some 450 full-time support staff, in addition to 100 casual part-time staff.) Centralized purchasing and standardized personnel policies made sense in this context. Conjoining the administrator and inspector roles was significant. The province's goal of providing a wide range of legal services in every county was laudable in the nineteenth century, given the difficulties of transportation. By the mid-twentieth, with much easier transportation and declining rural populations, the survival of such a multiplicity of registry offices and circuit stops seemed unjustifiable. Yet, as with rural hospitals and post offices, the attachment of citizens to their local services runs deep and attempts to modify them are often met with determined community and political resistance. Chief Justice Cowan publicly advocated 'fewer and larger judicial districts with more and better courtroom facilities in the larger centres of each judicial district,' though he was told it was 'politically unwise' to say so. Aside from some minor tinkering, the status quo remained until the major reforms of the early 1990s.

On the surface it appeared that the 'horse-and-buggy' approach to the justice system decried by the *Herald* in 1964 was being rapidly abandoned a decade later. Yet there was cause for concern on at least two fronts. Nova Scotia's low spending on justice services has already been noted. Rather than a laudable efficiency, such economy likely indicated both an absence of services provided elsewhere in Canada and low salary levels making it difficult to attract well-trained people. The presence of ill-trained police and prosecutorial personnel would come back to haunt the Nova Scotia justice system in later years as various miscarriages of justice came to light. Aside from the question of resources, there was also concern about the quality of justice being meted out to the province's minorities, especially the black and Mi'kmaq communities. The late 1960s saw a rejuvenation of the Nova Scotia black community, partly motivated by the Black Pride movement sweeping North America, while the destruction of the peri-urban Halifax community of Africville galvanized Afro-Nova Scotians around issues of racism. The creation of the Nova Scotia Human Rights Commission in 1967 was in large measure a response to demands by Afro-Nova Scotians and their supporters in the white community. The Mi'kmaq too shared in the rebirth of aboriginal consciousness and activism that swept Canada in the late 1960s and early 1970s. The Union of Nova Scotia Indians was founded in 1969 in response to the federal government White Paper proposing the abolition of the Indian Act and the assimilation of native peoples into Canadian society. A 1978 Dalhousie study revealed a disquieting disparity in the treatment of first offenders charged with summary offence convictions. Among whites, 23 per cent were discharged while 77 per cent received a sentence; among blacks, none was discharged and all were sentenced.[106] The study looked only at practices by magistrates and justices of the peace, but observers could not have failed to wonder whether such inequalities were present in the section 96 courts as well.

Heightened Expectations, 1982–2004

The adoption of the Canadian Charter of Rights and Freedoms on 15 April 1982 had important ramifications for all branches of government and for Canadian society as a whole. Unlike the very modest power granted to Canadian courts under the 1960 Canadian Bill of Rights to review legislation for consistency with fundamental constitutional rights, the Charter provided a full-blown power of judicial review of legislation and a remedial power limited only by judicial creativity. It brought an unprecedented addition to judicial responsibilities, and with it an entirely new level of public scrutiny. The Trudeau government hoped to signal the beginning of the 'Charter era' with some symbolic judicial appointments: that of Bertha Wilson on 4 March 1982 as the first woman on the Supreme Court of Canada, and in Nova Scotia that of Constance Glube as chief justice of the Trial Division, and the first female chief justice of a section 96 court in Canada, a week later.

On 29 March 1982 occurred another event rich with symbolic resonance for both the Charter era and the NSSC. Inmate 1997 at Dorchester Penitentiary in New Brunswick, Donald Marshall, Jr, cleaned out his cell for the last time. He was being released on parole, but hoped the imminent reopening of his case would free him permanently. Marshall, son of the grand chief of the Mi'kmaq Nation, had been found guilty in 1971 of the murder of a black acquaintance, Sandy Seale, at the age of seventeen. The young man steadfastly maintained his innocence and in 1981 information came to light pointing conclusively to the identity of the real killer. On 16 June Justice Minister Jean Chrétien referred Marshall's case to the Appeal Division of the NSSC under section 617(b) of the Criminal Code, which requires it to hear the case 'as if it were an appeal by the convicted person.' The Appeal Division duly acquitted Marshall in May 1983 but in the course of its decision blamed him for being the author of his own misfortune and stated that any miscarriage of justice was 'more apparent than real.' The judges blamed Marshall for concealing from police that he and his friend had badgered the murderer and his companion for money in the lead-up to the murder. They were not aware of the extensive police and Crown counsel misconduct which led to Marshall being charged, and then to a failure to follow up on credible allegations as to the identity of the real murderer.

Finally, under pressure from the public (principally the national rather than local media) and federal authorities, the provincial government reluctantly agreed to an inquiry by three out-of-province judges. The commission itself strayed into controversy in carrying out its mandate. Perhaps disoriented by descending into deeper waters than any comparable Canadian inquiry, it violated the most fundamental tenet of judicial immunity by attempting to force the judges on the 1982 Marshall appeal to testify before it, an attempt rebuffed by the Supreme Court of Canada.[107] When released on 26 January 1990, the Report of the Royal Commission on the Donald Marshall, Jr, Prosecution, had harsh words for the entire justice system, including its judicial component. The commission declared flatly that Justice Leonard Pace, who was attorney general at the time of Marshall's initial conviction, should not have sat on the 1982 appeal and placed some responsibility on Chief Justice MacKeigan for assigning him to the case. Attorney General Thomas McInnis subsequently requested the Canadian Judicial Council to inquire into the conduct of the five judges in order to ascertain if there were grounds for their removal. Former Chief Justice MacKeigan and Justice Pace both retired before the inquiry began, so that only the conduct of the three remaining judges was investigated. The inquiry committee said it could not 'condone or excuse the severity of the Reference Court's condemnation of Donald Marshall, Jr., and in particular its extraordinary observation that any miscarriage of justice was "more apparent than real",' but found that neither these comments nor other impugned statements involving either legal errors or findings on credibility constituted grounds for removal.[108]

In the wake of the Marshall inquiry, morale at the NSSC was probably at an all-time low. Lorne Clarke, chief justice since 1985, proved to be the right person to take on the task of rehabilitation and received the full support of Chief Justice Glube of the Trial Division in this task. They faced an enormous burden through the 1990s: responding to the concerns raised by the Marshall commission, repairing the judges' own sense of self-esteem, coordinating a major expansion of the court consequent upon its absorption of the County Courts, and dealing with an unprecedented shake-up of court facilities and registries around the province. Chief Justice Clarke embarked on an ambitious campaign designed to make the Nova Scotia courts national leaders in judicial education, public accessibility, and accountability. He aimed constantly to reach out to others – to other courts, to the bar, to academe, to the public at large – with the goal of making the courts more transparent and learning where they could improve. One of his first acts as chief justice was to organize a judicial education conference for all Nova Scotian judges, whether section 96 or provincially appointed, and this practice has continued ever since. (The status divisions between provincially and federally appointed judges run very deep in Canada, and most judicial programs still envisage only one or the other of these groups and not both.) Chief Justice Clarke promoted continuing education for judges on substantive law issues and was an early leader in the field of social context education, initially resisted by many judges across the country. He arranged for the televising of proceedings before the Court of Appeal, for a 'stand-alone' Court of Appeal, and for a pilot project for the evaluation of judicial performance by lawyers.[109] Most importantly, Lorne Clarke's humanity, empathy, and common touch had a therapeutic effect on his court and helped begin the process of restoring Nova Scotians' confidence in their judiciary. The title of a symposium arranged in honour of his 1998 retirement spoke to his principal preoccupations: 'Law, Justice and Community.'

This is not to say that the NSSC did not face further challenges in the post-Marshall era. The Westray mine disaster of 9 May 1992, which killed twenty-six miners, revealed a legal apparatus seemingly incapable of bringing to justice the corporate agents alleged to be responsible for the deaths. The constitutionalization of criminal procedure in the wake of the Charter demanded a heightened level of expertise and professionalism from police and prosecutorial authorities, one they found difficult to attain while labouring under at times severe resource constraints. Negotiating the co-existence of a public inquiry with the laying of criminal charges proved to be a legal nightmare, as other provinces were finding out at the same time. The NSSC itself was not the main problem in the Westray prosecutions, but a mistrial on the criminal charges occurred when it was revealed that the trial judge, Justice Robert Anderson, had secretly telephoned the head of the prosecution service in an attempt to get the lead Crown prosecutor on the case removed. The problem this time was not, as in the past, excessive deference to corporate capital, but an excess of zeal on the part of a judge who believed the Crown prosecutor was not up to the job. The Court of Appeal found that there were grounds for an appearance of bias against the Crown, and ordered a new trial, but one was never held.[110] On the positive side, Justice Peter Richard conducted a probing public inquiry into the disaster which 'made solid findings of blame and far-reaching recommendations for change.'[111] One of these was for amendments to the Criminal Code making corporate officials criminally responsible for knowingly maintaining unsafe workplaces, legislation which finally passed in the fall of 2003.[112]

Issues of race and aboriginal rights came to national attention again in the later 1990s as two important cases worked their way through the Nova Scotia courts to the Supreme Court of Canada. In *R. v. R.D.S.* an Afro-Nova Scotian Youth Court judge made a credibility finding against a white police officer in a case involving his handling of a black youth, in the course of which she made a generalization about interactions of this kind. The Crown appealed the acquittal on the basis that the judge's remarks revealed an appearance of anti-white racial bias, an argument accepted in the Court of Appeal. The Supreme Court of Canada restored the acquittal and in doing so issued a landmark decision on the meaning of judicial impartiality.[113] In *R. v. Marshall* the same Donald Marshall who had spent eleven years in jail as a result of legal error decided to try and vindicate what the Mi'kmaq had always understood as their right to fish as their ancestors had done, based on a 1761 treaty. He deliberately courted a conviction for catching eels out of season, but his treaty defence was unsuccessful in the Nova Scotia courts. The Supreme Court of Canada allowed it in a 5–2 decision which revived the long-dormant treaties of Jonathan Belcher's day. The Supreme Court attempted to draw a line between a permissible 'modest living' and an impermissible commercial exploitation, which caused considerable confusion in the short term and resulted in a virtually unprecedented 'clarification' of the ruling two months later.[114]

The Marshall inquiry unleashed a spate of law reform and court restructuring initiatives. The very month that the commission submitted its report, the Nova Scotia Court Structure Task Force began its work. Chaired by former Dalhousie law dean William Charles, the final report of the task force made a number of important recommendations.[115] The difference with previous studies lay in the almost immediate implementation of the recommendations through complementary provincial and federal legislation.[116] As a result of the task force recommendations, the County Courts were abolished and their judges and personnel merged with the Supreme Court of Nova Scotia (the last jurisdiction in Canada to do so). The latter was recreated as a trial court with twenty-five judges, including a chief justice and an associate chief justice, and a stand-alone Court of Appeal was created with eight judges including the chief justice of Nova Scotia. The province was divided into four judicial districts – Cape Breton, Halifax, the Southwestern District, and the Central District (the northern and eastern mainland counties) – with at least two Supreme Court judges resident in each. The long-mooted idea of Supreme Court judges resident in the counties at last came to pass, though of course in the short term the judges in question were the former County Court judges with their new hats on. The Supreme Court still goes on circuit, but the judges resident in the counties also sit in Halifax from time to time so as to ensure their continued exposure to the full range of judicial business. The recommendation for a new Unified Family Court to be created as a division of the NSSC took longer to implement, but finally became a reality in 1999.

The merger of the courts and the fiscal crisis of the early 1990s provided the final impetus to reform the support staff of all courts within the province. The 1996 Court and Administrative Reform Act finally abolished the separate acts and peculiarities of the offices of prothonotary and sheriff and did away with distinctions between section 96 and provincial courts.[117] It states simply: 'there shall be appointed, in accordance with the Civil Service Act, court administrators and such other officers and employees as are considered necessary for the administration of the courts in the Province.' The duties of these employees may include the duties formerly assigned to court reporters, sheriffs, and prothonotaries. The Marshall inquiry had deplored the continuing appointment of prothonotaries outside the civil service, a practice that would appear to be precluded by the new legislation. A new Court Services Division of the provincial Department of Justice has tried to rationalize support services to the courts, while emphasizing client satisfaction. Its most recent business plan states, 'we strive for superior quality in service delivery, and to meet the unique needs of our diverse client and stakeholder groups while ensuring consistency and quality.'[118]

Post-Marshall the enlarged NSSC has been preoccupied with re-establishing its morale and its legitimacy in the eyes of the citizens it serves. It has initiated a wide range of measures from ambitious judicial education programs to the evaluation of judges by lawyers with a view to improving the quality of justice throughout the province. After the huge increase in caseload of the 1960s through the 1980s, the numbers have levelled off. In 1975 the actual number of County and Supreme Court civil files opened at Halifax, excluding divorce petitions, was some 7200. In 2002–3, including about divorce applications, the number

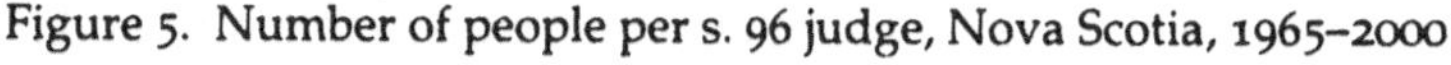
Figure 5. Number of people per s. 96 judge, Nova Scotia, 1965–2000

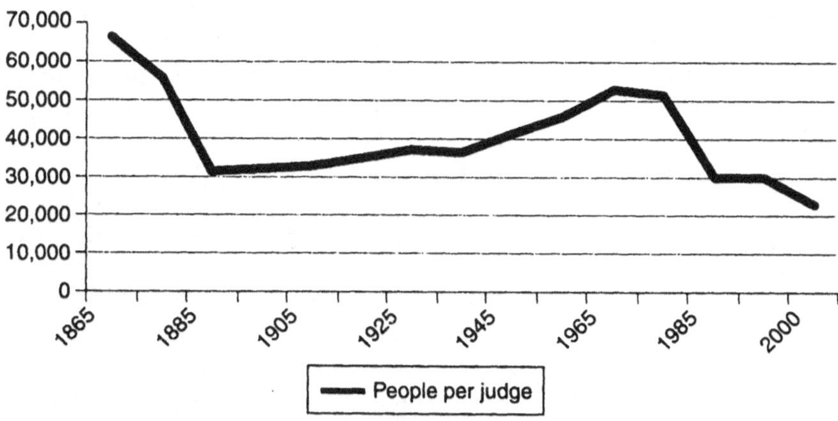

was 7047, a substantial decline once the capital's 50% increase in population over that period is taken into account. In fact the court is probably larger now than it needs to be (see figure 5). The trend in the sphere of civil justice is towards alternatives to court action, including resort to 'collaborative law' – arrangements where opposing parties agree not to go to court at all. In criminal law there is a parallel movement towards restorative justice, where the victim, the offender, and community representatives are all involved in trying to repair the damage caused to human relationships by criminal acts; Nova Scotia is now regarded as having one of the most comprehensive restorative justice programs in the world.[119] These developments should decrease pressures on the Supreme Court, though this may be offset by the increasing length and complexity of those trials that do occur, especially criminal trials. Shortly after her appointment as a trial judge, Justice Constance Glube conducted two consecutive murder trials, each of a week's duration. Now, she estimates, each would take three to six months. A different kind of challenge arises from the increasing number of self-represented litigants; as many as one-third of litigants now appear in the Supreme Court (Family Division) without counsel. The court's principal role will continue to be dispute resolution, but it will function increasingly as one alternative among others. It will likely be called upon to play a coordinating role in a situation of growing legal pluralism, in which one important component is a carefully modulated return to the community of its role in the administration of justice.

This overview has included many references to Nova Scotia being the last province in Canada to adopt various kinds of court reforms. Let us conclude, then, with some 'firsts.' In 1982 Justice Constance Glube was appointed the first female chief justice of a superior court in Canada, and her 1998 appointment as chief justice of the province (in succession to Chief Justice Lorne Clarke) made her only the second female chief justice in Canada, well ahead of the appointment of Justice Beverley McLachlin as chief justice of Canada on 7 January 2000.[120] Although the last province to merge its County and Supreme Courts, Nova Scotia has now become a leader in merging the administration of the section 96 and the provincial courts; in 2002 an executive officer to the chief justices of all courts in the province was created. In the wake of the Marshall inquiry the court has embraced innovation and become a national leader in a number of areas such as social context education and judicial performance evaluation. It has adopted a service orientation and reached out to the bar and the public in order to make its role better understood. It has understood that judicial independence has to be made compatible with judicial accountability, and that the judges themselves have to lead the way in this regard. As it enters the twenty-first century, the court appears to have dealt with the challenges of the last two decades with due seriousness, but also with imagination and 'grace under fire.' Such responsiveness stands as an example of true judicial accountability that other courts would do well to emulate.

NOTES

1 S. 96 of the British North America Act, 1867 (BNA Act) provided for federal appointment of 'the Judges of the Superior, District, and County Courts in each Province.' The term 's. 96 court' is thus a shorthand way of referring to both the county and Supreme courts in a given province, and 's. 96 judge' has a corresponding meaning. All judges not coming within the purview of s. 96 are provincially appointed. Only sources not footnoted in the body of the paper are referenced in this introduction. I would like to thank two former students: Andrea Rizzato, for her excellent research assistance, and Matthew Moir, whose paper on litigation trends in the Halifax Supreme Court helped stimulate my thinking on the topic.

2 S.N.S. 1938, c. 1, 1942, c. 19; R. Kimball, *The Bench: The History of Nova Scotia's Provincial Courts* (Halifax: Province of Nova Scotia 1989). Aside from the work of Murray Beck, cited below, the only attempt to provide a

historical survey of the post-confederation NSSC is found in an unpublished manuscript by the dean of Dalhousie Law School (as he than was). Horace Read, and John Barker, 'The Judicial Systems of the Common Law Provinces and Federal Courts of Canada' (n.p., c. 1963), Dalhousie University Archives, Horace Read Papers, MS-2-322.

3 *Valin v. Langlois* (1879), 3 S.C.R. 1 at 19–20. The concluding words of the quotation repeat the wording of s. 129 of the BNA Act in relation to 'all Courts of Civil and Criminal Jurisdiction.'

4 On the Exchequer Court, renamed the Federal Court of Canada in 1971, see I. Bushnell, *The Federal Court of Canada: A History, 1875–1992* (Toronto: Osgoode Society for Canadian Legal History and University of Toronto Press 1997).

5 National Archives of Canada (NA), J.S.D. Thompson Papers, no. 2867, Townshend to J.S.D. Thompson, 11 July 1882, as cited in P. Girard, 'The Supreme Court of Nova Scotia, Responsible Government, and the Quest for Legitimacy,' *Dalhousie Law Journal* 17 (1994): 440; see also Girard, 'Townshend, Sir Charles,' *DCB*, vol. 15, forthcoming.

6 S.C. 1868, c. 33.

7 C. Greco, 'The Superior Court Judiciary of Nova Scotia, 1754–1900,' in Girard and Phillips, *Essays*, 45–7; see R. Blake Brown and Susan Jones's paper, this volume, for the twentieth-century experience.

8 Cited in G. Patterson, 'The Establishment of the County Court in Nova Scotia,' *Canadian Bar Review* 21 (1943): 405.

9 On the enlargement of the court, see J.M. Beck, *The Government of Nova Scotia* (Toronto: University of Toronto Press 1957), 287–8.

10 I thank Bruce Kercher of Macquarie University for sharing his research on colonial appeals to the Privy Council. No firm figure can be given because there are some gaps in the Privy Council's own records.

11 *In re Wallace* (1865), 5 N.S.R. 654, (1866), 1 L.R.P.C. 283; *McLean v. McKay* (1873), 5 L.R.P.C. 327.

12 Patterson, 'Establishment,' 404.

13 An Act to Establish County Courts, S.N.S. 1874, c. 18, s. 32.

14 S.N.S. 1874, c. 18, s. 13.

15 This power was granted later, by S.N.S. 1890, c. 11, s. 1.

16 J.G. Snell, 'Relations between the Maritimes and the Supreme Court of Canada: The Patterns of the Early Years,' in J. Yogis, ed., *Law in a Colonial Society: The Nova Scotia Experience* (Toronto: Carswell 1984). For similar trends in New Brunswick, see D.G. Bell, 'Judicial Crisis in Post-Confederation New Brunswick,' in D. Gibson and W.W. Pue, eds., *Glimpses of Canadian Legal History* (Winnipeg: Legal Research Institute 1991).

17 M. Moir, 'A Litigation Community: A Social Comparison of Lawyers, Clients and The Nova Scotia Supreme Court in Halifax, 1875 and 1925' (unpublished paper, Dalhousie University 2000). The divorce petitions represent the total for the province, not just Halifax County, as all such petitions had to be filed there.
18 See Cahill and Phillips, this volume.
19 Girard, 'Professional Renaissance.'
20 As to the latter see S.N.S. 1880, c. 11; the removal of the judges' disciplinary powers, except for contempt, begins with S.N.S. 1885, c. 20 and continues in stages over the next two decades.
21 S.N.S. 1880, c. 11.
22 S.N.S. 1882, c. 2; 1883, c. 9. The non-renewal of a sheriff's appointment for political reasons was not unknown. George Craigie Laurence, high sheriff of Inverness County from 1837 to 1868, was not reappointed by the anti-Confederate provincial government after his pro-Confederate sympathies became public knowledge, in spite of a protest from the NSSC judges that it was improper to displace him without any evidence of public complaints: W.H. Laurence, 'Process and Particulars: The Informational Needs and Sources of a Nineteenth-Century Nova Scotian Sheriff,' *Épilogue* 12(1) (1997): 2.
23 R.S.N.S. 1884, c. 109; c. 94; S.N.S. 1890, c. 17.
24 See Cahill and Phillips, this volume.
25 *Lunenburg Progress*, 7 Dec. 1880.
26 See N. Parker, 'Reaching a Verdict: The Changing Structure of Decision-Making in the Canadian Criminal Courts, 1867–1905' (PhD dissertation, York University, 1999).
27 In addition, the court decided on sentence after guilty pleas, but these were infrequent. Given a relatively high acquittal rate, the accused had little incentive to plead guilty.
28 RG 39, Series J (CO), vol. 15 (minute book 1886–1921). On the construction of the courthouse, where the Nova Scotia Supreme Court still sits on circuit, see N. Hamilton and P. Sexton, *History of Municipal Government in Colchester County 1879–1979* (Truro: Colchester County Council 1979), 20. The grand jury legislation is S.N.S. 1898, c. 38.
29 D. Murray, 'Just Excuses: Jury Culture in Barrington Township, Nova Scotia, 1795–1837,' in M. Conrad and B. Moody, eds., *Planter Links: Community and Culture in Colonial Nova Scotia* (Fredericton: Acadiensis Press 2001); and his *Colonial Justice: Justice, Morality and Crime in the Niagara District, 1791–1849* (Toronto: Osgoode Society for Canadian Legal History and University of Toronto Press 2002).

30 The two dollar fine was still being imposed in 1952. Exemptions in the records were granted on the basis of occupation (fireman, dentist), 'age' (over sixty), and inability to follow the proceedings through mental defect or deafness.

31 This amendment to the Juries Act did not expressly mention the possibility of waiver on consent; R.S.N.S. 1856, c. 7, s. 1. S. 2 stated 'the practice of keeping a jury without meat, drink or any other comfort until they have reached a verdict is abolished,' suggesting such a practice had existed earlier. Both these changes to the law were frequently sought, but not achieved, in nineteenth-century England; see Michael Lobban, 'The Strange Life of the English Civil Jury, 1837–1914' in John W. Cairns, ed. *'The Dearest Birth Right of the People of England': the jury in the history of the common law* (Oxford: Hart 2002).

32 NSARM, County of Victoria Court House minutes, 1877–1950, reel 13488.

33 NSARM, Sir William Young Papers, MG 1, vol. 3362, no. 46, Young to Attorney General, 6 Jan. 1881.

34 J.P. Couturier, 'Courts and Business Activity in Late 19th Century New Brunswick: A view from the Case Files' *Acadiensis* 26 (1997): 77–95; R.A. Kagan, 'The Routinization of Debt Collection: An Essay on Social Change and Conflict in the Courts,' *Law & Society Review* 18 (1984): 323–71.

35 This is not to say that family law itself did not exist, but rather that it took a different form and was dealt with in the lower courts rather than the Supreme Court. See J. Fingard, *The Dark Side of Life in Victorian Halifax* (Halifax: Pottersfield Press 1989), especially chapter 8 on the work of the Society for the Prevention of Cruelty in dealing with domestic violence and family conflict.

36 J. G. Snell, *In the Shadow of the Law: Divorce in Canada 1900–1939* (Toronto: University of Toronto Press 1991), 10–11, provides annual figures on divorce petitions by province. The highest number in any previous year in Nova Scotia was forty-five in 1920.

37 William Young Papers, MG 2, vol. 3363, no. 38.

38 J.M. Beck, *The Politics of Nova Scotia*, II (Tantallon: Four East Publications 1988), 217–18. A.C. Dunlop, 'Holmes, Simon,' *D.C.B.*, vol. 14: 502–4.

39 S.N.S. 1895, c. 31; S.N.S. 1896, c. 7; raised to $700, S.N.S. 1923, c. 31; and to $1,000, S.N.S. 1928, c. 45. The deficit was payable out of the consolidated revenue of the province, not county funds.

40 S.N.S. 1901, c. 5; S.N.S. 1903, c. 21. The stenographers were hired on a piece-work basis, but at the generous rate of ten dollars per day plus expenses.

41 *Chisholm v. Chisholm* (1907), 45 N.S.R. 288; *NS Debates*, 1897, 141–2. Perhaps Longley's action was rare, because Robert Borden's impression in 1907 was

that 'the judge from whose decision an appeal is taken, or who sat with the jury to try the action in respect to which any motion is made for a new trial, is disqualified from sitting in banco': *Hansard* (28 Feb. 1907) at 3917. The 'double sitting' problem arose in a number of contexts in late twentieth-century Canada: see G. Bale, *Chief Justice William Johnstone Ritchie: Responsible Government and Judicial Review* (Ottawa: Carleton University Press 1991), chap. 15.

42 Beck, *Government of Nova Scotia*, 297.

43 The Victoria County records, above note 32, tend to confirm the bar's assertion. The judge for District No. 7, Duncan Finlayson, arrived at Baddeck for a day's business on 21 May 1912. The court was supposed to meet again in November, but 'owing to the non-arrival and absence of the Judge the Court [was] adjourned until 3rd December.' On that date the clerk recorded with barely concealed irritation, 'the Judge not having arrived, and in the absence of any communication from him, the Court was adjourned sine die.' On 20 May and 25 November 1913 the judge was present but the court was adjourned sine die for lack of business. Not until 15 January 1914 did Judge Finlayson have any business again at Baddeck – a contested election petition. Victoria was one of three counties making up District No. 7, but if its experience is at all representative, the lot of a county court judge was not a difficult one.

44 *Halifax Herald*, 26 Mar. 1913.

45 *Morning Chronicle*, 19 Apr. 1923.

46 *Canada Law Journal* 40 (1904): 89, 441, 724–6; *Canadian Law Times* 24 (1904): 187, 418; *Canadian Law Review* 3 (1904): 600–2.

47 See Blake Brown and Susan Jones's paper in this volume.

48 Townshend's book was mistitled by the publisher; in fact, it included a history of the Supreme Court as well as the Court of Chancery.

49 Girard, 'The Supreme Court and the Quest for Legitimacy.'

50 P. Girard, 'Ritchie, William Bruce Almon,' *DCB*, 14: 872–3.

51 See, for example, Barry Cahill, *The Thousandth Man: A Biography of James McGregor Stewart* (Toronto: Osgoode Society for Canadian Legal History and University of Toronto Press 2000).

52 Barry Cahill, '"The Colored Barrister": The Short Life and Tragic Death of James Robinson Johnston, 1876–1915,' *Dalhousie Law Journal* 15 (1992): 336–79; J. Fingard, 'Johnston, James Robinson,' *DCB*, 14: 543–4. Although some Caribbean blacks attended Dalhousie Law School in the interwar years, a second native Afro-Nova Scotian would not graduate from there until George W. Davis did so in 1952.

53 R.S.C. 1906, c. 113.

54 *In re Frank Mackey* (1918), 52 N.S.R. 165 (in banco). Benjamin Russell decided that there was insufficient evidence to support the magistrate's committal, and released the men on a habeas corpus application. On appeal, the Supreme Court in banco decided it had no jurisdiction to review Russell's decision. Russell expresses a dim view of Drysdale's legal talents in his *Autobiography of Benjamin Russell* (Halifax: Royal Print & Litho 1932), 268–72.

55 In view of the judge's previous involvements it may seem strange that counsel for the *Mont Blanc* did not request Drysdale's recusal; nor did he try to attack Drysdale's decision on the ground of bias when he appealed. Probably counsel did not wish to risk alienating a judge before whom he would have to appear many times in the future.

56 D.A. Kerr, 'Another Calamity: The Litigation,' in A. Ruffman and C.D. Howell, eds., *Ground Zero: A Reassessment of the 1917 Explosion in Halifax Harbour* (Halifax: Nimbus 1994), 365–76.

57 *Halifax Herald*, 13 Feb. 1926.

58 *District 26, U.M.W. et al. v. Dominion Coal Co.* (1922), 55 N.S.R. 121 (in banco).

59 In 1928 Justice Stuart Jenks declined to try a case at Sydney in which his law firm had been involved; *Halifax Chronicle*, 10 Apr. 1928.

60 House of Commons *Debates* (4 Mar. 1924) at 64, as cited in J.B. Cahill, '*Howe* (1835), *Dixon* (1920) and *McLachlan* (1923): Comparative Perspectives on the Legal History of Sedition,' *University of New Brunswick Law Journal* 45 (1996): 288. See also D. Frank, *J.B. McLachlan: A Biography* (Toronto: Lorimer 1999), 321.

61 I would like to thank David Frank for providing me with a copy of this letter in the Woodsworth Papers, from an unknown Sydney correspondent (possibly lawyer A.D. Gunn) to J.S. Woodsworth, 9 Feb. 1924. The signature portion of the letter is torn off.

62 (1924), 56 N.S.R. 413.

63 *Sydney Record*, 5, 24, 25 Mar. 1926.

64 M. McCallum, 'The Acadia Coal Strike, 1934: Thinking About Law and the State,' *University of New Brunswick Law Journal* 41 (1992): 179–96.

65 *Halifax Chronicle*, 20 July 1933.

66 Ibid., 25–8 July 1933; *Halifax Herald*, 20 and 25 July 1933; Beck, *Politics of Nova Scotia II*, 147–51; S. Henderson, 'A Provincial Liberal: Angus L. Macdonald, 1890–1954' (PhD dissertation, York University 2003), 103–6; M. Conrad, *George Nowlan: Maritime Conservative in National Politics* (Toronto: University of Toronto Press 1986), 52–4.

67 *Re Legislative Council of Nova Scotia No. 1* (1926), 59 N.S.R. 1; [1928] A.C. 107.

68 *Halifax Daily Star*, n.d., cited in Beck, *Politics of Nova Scotia II*, 135.
69 Personal comunication from P.B. Waite, who is currently writing Bennett's biography.
70 Moir, 'A Litigation Community.' Dale Brown, 'Manitoba Litigants and their Lawsuits, 1909–1939; Quantitative Patterns and Results' (LLM thesis, University of Manitoba 1995).
71 See generally C. Strange, 'The Lottery of Death: Capital Punishment, 1867–1976,' in D. Guth and W.W. Pue, eds., *Canada's Legal Inheritances* (Winnipeg: Legal Research Institute 2001).
72 See M. Boudreau, 'Crime in a City of Order: Halifax, 1918–1935' (Phd dissertation, Queen's University 1996), 440–6. The jury recommended commutation of the sentence to life imprisonment but the minister of justice allowed the law to take its course.
73 Information on capital cases derived from NA, RG 13, F.A. 13-39, pt. 1 (capital case file summaries). On the Farmer case, see D. Jobb, *The Novascotian*, 6 Oct. 1984. Two women were sentenced to death for murder after 1867; Carmella Marablito was convicted of murdering her husband in 1917 but died in the Pictou jail before it was clear whether her sentence would be commuted. Mary Hope Young was convicted at Digby of murdering a seven-year-old girl in 1905, but the conviction was quashed on appeal and a new trial ordered: *R. v. Hope Young* (1905), 38 N.S.R. 427.
74 *R. v. Syliboy* (1928), 50 C.C.C. 889. W.C. Wicken, '"Heard it from our Grandfathers": Mi'kmaq Treaty Tradition and the *Syliboy* case of 1928,' *University of New Brunswick Law Journal* 44 (1995): 145–61.
75 NSARM, RG 38, Series C.
76 J.B. Cahill, 'Removing a "Section 96 Judge": An Historical Case Study,' *Dalhousie Law Journal* 23 (2000): 247. While judges of provincial Supreme Courts were removable only after a joint address to both Houses of Parliament, a simpler inquiry process existed for County Court judges.
77 (1932) *Hansard* 2997–3002 at 2999, cited in W.H. Angus, 'Judicial Selection in Canada – the Historical Perspective,' *Canadian Legal Studies* 4 (1967): 241.
78 William Lyon Mackenzie King Diaries, online version at NA, www.archives.ca, 10 Dec. 1921 and 25 Sept. 1945.
79 K. Semple, 'The Evolution of Professional Ethics: The Nova Scotia Experience' (unpublished paper, Dalhousie Law School 1994).
80 S.N.S. 1916, c. 7; S.N.S. 1921, c. 1; S.N.S. 1939, c. 12.
81 S.N.S. 1928, c. 21.
82 Figures derived from comparison of the lists of prothonotaries in *Belcher's Farmer's Almanac*, 1924–9. On Cummings's trials, see NSARM, Halifax

Supreme Court Criminal Cases, RG 39, Series C, vol. 710, no. 416; *Halifax Chronicle* 7 and 9 Nov. 1927, 10, 13, and 14 Apr., and 20 Oct. 1928. R.V. Harris compiled the first *Catalogue of Portraits of the Judges of the Supreme Court of Nova Scotia*, published by the court itself in 1929.

83 J. Servinis, 'The Exclusiveness of the Legal Profession in Canada and how one Nova Scotian Woman Rose to the Challenge: M. Grace Wambolt Q.C.' (unpublished paper, Dalhousie Law School 1998).

84 S.N.S. 1962, c. 17. This power was taken away from them, perhaps inadvertently, by the federal Divorce Act, 1968, which authorized only judges of the Trial Division to hear divorces. Note that the number of divorces actually granted (see figure 4) was considerably lower than the number of divorce petitions filed.

85 NA, St-Laurent Papers, MG 26L/58/J-22, Ilsley to St-Laurent, 17 Sept. 1948.

86 I thank Barry Cahill for suggesting this interpretation of events to me, which I find plausible even though there is no clear documentary evidence for it.

87 NA, St-Laurent Papers, MG 26L/58/J-22, Carroll to St-Laurent, 9 June 1949, replying to the latter's congratulatory letter.

88 Ibid., Winters to St-Laurent, 17 June 1949. Winters's favoured candidate, W. Pitt Potter, was named to the Exchequer Court in 1953 but died in office in 1955.

89 Pottier's career is reviewed in the Halifax *Mail-Star*, 1 May 1970.

90 C. Moore, *The Law Society of Upper Canada and Ontario's Lawyers, 1797–1997* (Toronto: University of Toronto Press 1997).

91 S.N.S. 1953, c. 3.

92 S.N.S. 1949, c. 57.

93 NSARM, RG 10/A/20/4-15, Quinn to Donahoe, 27 June 1958; Donahoe to Fulton, 7 July 1958. Bissett was strongly criticized in Justice Ross's inquiry into the franchise scandal in 1934.

94 On the partisan nature of Diefenbaker's judicial appointments, see S. Hughes, *Steering the Course: A Memoir* (Montreal: McGill-Queen's University Press 2000). Patterson was the nephew of County Court judge George Patterson.

95 NA, Diefenbaker Papers, MG 26 N, no. 246891, Donahoe to Diefenbaker, 29 Nov. 1960; communication from Barry Cahill regarding interview with Senator Donahoe.

96 Ibid., Donahoe to Justice L. McC. Ritchie, 10 Dec. 1962.

97 Small Claims Court Act, S.N.S. 1980, c. 193.

98 Judicature Act Amendment Act, S.N.S. 1972, c. 2; S.N.S. 1978–9, c. 41, proclaimed in force 1 Aug. 1984.

99 See the chapter by Cuthbertson, this volume.

100 Legal Aid Planning Act, S.N.S. 1970–71, c. 14; Legal Aid Act, S.N.S. 1977, c. 11. Dale Poel, *The Nova Scotia Legal Aid Evaluation Report: Entering the Third 'Generation'* (Halifax: N.S. Legal Aid Commission and Department of Justice Canada 1983). Roland Penner, 'Evolution of Parkdale Community Legal Services, Point St. Charles and Dalhousie Legal Aid Service' (n.p., n.d. [c. 1977]).

101 National Task Force on the Administration of Justice, *Justice Services in Canada 1977–78* (Ottawa, 1979).

102 O. Lang, 'Address to Vancouver Bar Association,' [B.C.] *Law Society Gazette* 8 (1974): 121.

103 E. Ratushny, 'Judicial Appointments: The Lang Legacy,' in A.M. Linden, ed., *The Canadian Judiciary* (Toronto: York University 1976). R. Chodos, 'The First Strike,' *The Last Post* 1(5) (1970): 35–47. The fishermen were on strike against fish-packing companies that allegedly forced them to work under inhuman conditions for very low wages; the provincial Trade Union Act excluded them from the collective bargaining regime enjoyed by other workers.

104 G. Cowan, 'Comment,' in Linden, ed., *The Canadian Judiciary*, 196.

105 Baar and Millar, *Judicial Administration*, 110.

106 A. Warner and K.E. Renner, 'Research on the Halifax Criminal Courts: A Technical and Conceptual Report,' (Unpublished paper, Dalhousie University 1978).

107 *MacKeigan v. Hickman*, [1989] 2 S.C.R. 796.

108 *Report to the Canadian Judicial Council of the Inquiry Committee established pursuant to subsection 63(1) of the Judges Act at the request of the Attorney General of Nova Scotia* (August 1990). Chief Justice MacKeigan had stepped down in 1985, but remained a member of the court on a supernumerary basis until 1990.

109 On the latter, see D. Poel, *The Nova Scotia Judicial Development Project: A Final Report and Evaluation* (Halifax: Dalhousie University 1997).

110 *R. v. Curragh Inc. et al.* (1995), 146 N.S.R. (2d) 161.

111 D. Jobb, 'Legal Disaster: Westray and the Justice System,' in C. McCormick, ed., *The Westray Chronicles: A Case Study in Corporate Crime* (Halifax: Fernwood 2000).

112 An Act to amend the Criminal Code (Criminal Liability of Organizations), S.C. 2003, c. 21.

113 [1997] 3 S.C.R. 484 and see (1995) 18 *Dalhousie Law Journal* for a thematic issue on the case.

114 [1999] 3 S.C.R. 456 and 533; see (2000) 23 *Dalhousie Law Journal* for a thematic issue on the case.

115 *Report of the Nova Scotia Court Structure Task Force* (March 1991).
116 An Act to Reform the Courts of the Province, S.N.S. 1992, c. 16; Nova Scotia Courts Amendment Act, 1992, S.C. 1992, c. 51.
117 S.N.S. 1996, c. 23.
118 Court Services Division Business Plan 2002–03 at 3, www.gov.ns.ca/just/busplan_2002_03, accessed 27 Apr. 2004.
119 B. Archibald, 'Citizen Participation in Canadian Criminal Justice: The Emergence of "Inclusionary Adversarial" and "Restorative" Models,' in S. Coughlan and D. Russell, eds., *Citizenship and Citizen Participation in the Administration of Justice* (Montreal: Thémis 2001), 149–92; and see *Restorative Justice: A Program for Nova Scotia* (Halifax Department of Justice 1998).
120 Catherine Fraser was the first female chief justice in Canada, becoming chief justice of Alberta in 1992.

6

A Collective Biography of the Supreme Court Judiciary of Nova Scotia, 1900–2000

R. BLAKE BROWN AND SUSAN S. JONES

Introduction

There has been no dearth of judicial biographies in the United States over the past several years, and Melvin I. Urofsky, author of 'Beyond the Bottom Line: The Value of Judicial Biography,' gives three reasons why this should be so. One is simply the popularity of this form of writing. There seems to be an audience for works about the distinguished and powerful members of society. A second reason, according to Urofsky, is the greater awareness by the public of the impact of judicial rulings in their lives. The final reason for the numerous biographies is the availability of collections of judges' papers.[1] Judicial biography has not only become popular in the United States; a number of publications have filled bookshelves in Canada over recent years.[2]

This substantial body of work has done much to improve legal historians' knowledge of the legal profession and the personal factors that have shaped legal decisions. However, a concentration on a few major judicial figures tells us little about the composition and background of any particular bench, which is often made up of many less noteworthy figures. In Canada, few scholars have undertaken collective biographies. Louis Knafla and Richard Klumpenhouwer have recently lamented this fact, though they do laud one of the few existing prosopographical studies in Canada: Clara Greco's 'The Superior Court Judiciary of Nova Scotia, 1754–1900.'[3] Greco offered a descriptive collective biography, noting the trends and patterns of age and tenure, political careers, and other factors about the judges of the Nova Scotia Supreme Court up to the beginning of the twentieth century.

Our article continues Greco's work, and employs a similar methodology in studying the ninety women and men appointed to the NSSC between 1900 and 2000.[4] Part I examines the age and tenure of the judges, while Part II considers the general background of each of the appointees, including birthplace, social status, religion, education, gender, and ethnicity. Part III examines the legal practices of the judicial appointees. In Part IV, we analyse their judicial experiences prior to their appointment to the NSSC. Finally, Part V studies the political careers of the NSSC judges.

Some initial comment is necessary regarding two changes in the structure of the NSSC that affect the statistical aspects of this article. First, while the court remained relatively unchanged from the late nineteenth century to the mid-1960s, on 1 August 1966 it was divided into a Trial Division and an Appeal Division. Originally, the Trial Division consisted of a chief justice and five other judges, and the Appeal Division consisted of a chief justice and two additional judges.[5] This division thus brought with it the creation of separate chief justice positions. When discussing issues concerning the province's chief justices, such as calculations of tenure and age at appointment, we consider only the highest judicial office in Nova Scotia: the chief justice of Nova Scotia (who also serves as the chief justice of the Court of Appeal). Second, the courts of Nova Scotia were amalgamated in January 1993 when the County Court of Nova Scotia became part of the Supreme Court. Our study includes the County Court judges who joined the Supreme Court. However, we will not provide information on the Family Court judges who became members of the NSSC when, in 1999, that body became the Supreme Court of Nova Scotia (Family Division).

Our examination offers a number of interesting comparisons to the patterns reported by Greco in her earlier study. The decline in the legitimacy of the Supreme Court of Nova Scotia in the latter half of the nineteenth century prompted a number of strategies to repair its image.[6] One such strategy was the insistence upon professional qualifications and credentials. Related to this was the modernization of the legal profession, or what has been called a 'professional renaissance' during the last quarter of the nineteenth century.[7] This renaissance brought about a number of significant changes to the legal profession, including transformations to legal education and to the role of the Barristers' Society. Increasingly, judicial appointees were required to possess at least a minimum of educational and professional attainments. These strategies of legitimation, however, allowed for the continued recourse to political patronage. In the twentieth century, criticism grew of the long-standing role of patronage in judicial selection, eventually leading to a reduction in political favouritism, at least patronage that was obvious to the public. Like other judiciaries across Canada, the NSSC also slowly became more representative – the appointees included women, Jews, a visible-minority, and a disabled justice.

Judges' Age and Tenure

Before 1900, the average age on appointment for the judges was 48.1 years, while the average age for chief justices was slightly higher, at 52.1 years; the lack of a significant difference between the ages on appointment of chief justices and the puisne judges suggests that considerations other than age and experience determined appointment to the highest office.[8] In the twentieth century, the mean age on appointment for all the judges rose to 53.6 years; the average age of the eleven chief justices of Nova Scotia was 63.7 years, an increase of over eleven and a half years.[9] This increase reflects the break with the nineteenth-century practice of making appointments directly to the chief justice position.[10]

The twentieth-century increase in the age at appointment masks a larger trend in which the mean age of appointees to the Supreme Court rose during the first two-thirds of the twentieth century, then declined. From 1900 to 1966, the average age on appointment was 57.2 years. Beginning in the late 1960s, there was a reversion to selecting younger judges. The fifty-eight judges appointed from 1967 to 2000 were, on average, 51.6 years of age; this figure decreases even further if the County Court judges, several of whom were near retirement when they joined the NSSC in 1993, are removed from the calculation. The twelve judges who joined the NSSC between 1995 and 2000 also demonstrate the trend towards younger appointees. While J. Edward Flinn was 58, the other eleven appointees ranged from 40 to 52, with the average age at 48.1.[11]

The age at which people became judges varied greatly before 1900. The youngest to be appointed to the bench was Thomas Strange, who became chief justice at the age of thirty-three. The oldest was seventy-two-year-old James W. Johnston.[12] The present study reveals a similar variation in age, at least if one includes the County Court judges who

Table 6.1 Tenure on NSSC (years)

	All justices	Puisne justices
1754–1900	17.4	16.0
1900–1970	15.2	15.6

joined the NSSC. J. Edward Scanlan was only thirty-seven when he joined the Trial Division of the NSSC in 1993. The oldest judge was Murray James Ryan, a County Court judge just days shy of his seventy-fourth birthday when the courts amalgamated in 1993. The oldest judge to join the court directly was Frank Harris Patterson, who was sixty-eight years of age when appointed in 1958.

Calculating the tenure of the twentieth-century judges is complicated by the fact that many judges appointed during the 1970s, 1980s, and 1990s remain on the court. As Malachi Jones, appointed in March 1970, still sits on the bench, the present study will calculate the mean tenure of the judges only up to the time of his appointment. As can be seen in table 6.1, the judges appointed before 1970 each served 15.2 years as members of the NSSC. Those who never became chief justice held office an average of 15.6 years. These figures are slightly lower than those presented by Greco. Before 1900, each judge spent an average of 17.4 years on the bench, while those who never became chief justice remained on the court for an average of 16.0 years.[13]

When he died in office at the age of eighty-seven, Joseph Chisholm, just one month shy of his thirty-fourth anniversary on the bench, became the longest serving judge appointed in the twentieth century. Malachi Jones will surpass Chisholm's tenure if he remains on the bench until his seventy-fifth birthday in September 2004, when he will have been a member of the NSSC for just over thirty-four years. While these are impressively long careers, the imposition of compulsory retirement has put an end to the lengthy tenures of the pre-1900 period. Chisholm's thirty-three-year tenancy seems relatively short in comparison to Brenton Halliburton's remarkable fifty-three years on the bench.[14]

The shortest tenure of any twentieth-century judge was that of Murray James Ryan. A County Court judge for ten years, he joined the NSSC on 30 January 1993 and retired on 31 January 1994, one day before his seventy-fifth birthday. Duncan Cameron Fraser had the shortest tenure of the non-County Court judges. Appointed on 10 February 1904, he resigned on 27 March 1906 to take up the position of lieutenant governor of Nova Scotia. It seems that the preparation and study required of a judge did not suit Fraser, and there were complaints about his performance.[15]

Of the fifty-three twentieth-century judges who have left the NSSC,[16] 58.5 per cent retired, while 41.5 per cent died in office. The percentage of judges who died in their posts is thus lower than the 51.1 per cent of judges appointed before 1900 who died in office. A reluctance to resign was typical of judges appointed early in the 1754–1900 period. Of those appointed prior to 1834, only 31.5 per cent resigned from the office, while 54.1 per cent of those appointed after that date did so.[17] The trend towards retirement has increased since 1970. Between 1900 and 1970, 50 per cent of the judges retired. However, of the seventeen judges appointed since 1970 who have left their judicial posts, thirteen, or 72.2 per cent, retired.

A combination of factors explains the twentieth-century decline in length of tenures and the increase in the percentage of the judges who retired. The reluctance to resign during the eighteenth century and much of the nineteenth stemmed from the lack of pensions. Retirement was not an option for the many judges who did not possess substantial financial resources outside of their judicial salaries. However, the federal government began to provide pensions to its judges in 1869.[18] The increasing rate of retirements in the late twentieth century can be attributed, in part, to a 1960 amendment to the BNA Act that set the retirement age of provincial superior court judges at seventy-five.[19] Also, the 1971 Judges Act allowed judges with fifteen years of service to retire with a full pension at sixty-five, and permitted federal judges with ten years' experience to become 'supernumerary,' meaning that they could become 'part-time' judges with reduced workloads at age seventy.[20] Finally, the slight twentieth-century decline in tenure may have resulted from the fact that judges were generally older on their appointment in the first two-thirds of the twentieth century.

General Background

Birthplace

Between 1900 and 2000 all of the NSSC judges were born in Canada. This represents the culmination of a trend towards a Canadian-born judiciary. During the period 1754–1849, eleven of the judges appointed to the Supreme Court were from New England, seven from Nova Scotia, and five from the United Kingdom. Between 1849 and 1890,

Table 6.2 Birthplace

Region	Judges (%)	County (# of judges)
Cape Breton	17 (23.6)	Inverness (5) Victoria (0) Cape Breton (11) Richmond (1)
Annapolis Valley	11 (15.3)	Digby (2) Annapolis (4) Kings (4) Hants (1)
Northern Nova Scotia	17 (23.6)	Cumberland (3) Colchester (3) Pictou (8) Antigonish (3)
Halifax and Guysborough	23 (31.9)	Halifax (21) Guysborough (2)
South Shore	4 (5.6)	Lunenburg (1) Queens (1) Shelburne (1) Yarmouth (1)

however, none of the judges were from New England, thirteen were Nova Scotians, and only one came from the United Kingdom.[21]

Seventy-two of the ninety twentieth-century judges were born in Nova Scotia; a further ten hailed from other parts of Atlantic Canada.[22] The seventy-two native-born judges represent all but one of the counties that make up Nova Scotia, though the distribution of the appointees indicates that some areas of the province have received greater representation than others. As table 6.2 demonstrates, Nova Scotia's judiciary was drawn primarily from counties with major urban centres, such as Halifax, Cape Breton, and Pictou. These three counties were the birthplace of 56.9 per cent of the appointees. The low number of judges from the South Shore could stem from a lack of emphasis on higher education in the area, deeply embedded cultural assumptions about the legal profession, a dearth of good candidates with the appropriate social status, or the region's lack of political influence. Closer inspection also shows that as the population of Halifax grew, so too did the proportion of the NSSC occupied by Halifax-born lawyers. Between 1900 and 1967 only 14.8 per cent of the NSSC appointees came from Halifax County; however, after 1967 42.2 per cent of appointees did so.[23]

Social Status

Greco examined the social status of each person appointed to the bench using fathers' occupations as an indicator. She reveals that many of the judges appointed before 1900 had fathers in the elite professions, namely, judges, lawyers, merchants, physicians, politicians, government officials, and clergy. Seventy per cent had fathers in these elite professions, with 28 per cent having fathers who were themselves judges or lawyers. While this figure might indicate the advantage of legal roots in the family tree, Greco notes that the trend declined in importance over the years as a new tendency towards non-elite recruitment began to appear.[24]

We also employ fathers' occupations as an indicator of social status. However, information about the parents of twentieth-century judges was not as frequently reported as it was during the first 150 years of the court, especially for the judges appointed towards the end of the twentieth century. A further complication is that, while the occupation of the father is important, by the mid-twentieth century an increasing number of women were entering the workforce. Given these complications, we have only traced social status in a systematic way for the 1900–1967 period. For the period before 1967 parental occupation was found for twenty of the thirty-two judges. Although social status was still an important factor during this period, perhaps the importance of making one's social status known was not.

The fathers of the judges appointed between 1900 and 1967 reflect a variety of occupations, in both the professional and non-professional spheres, as well as in the business world. Three of the judges had fathers with professional backgrounds – one was a lawyer and two were clergy. Two more were involved in the administration of justice: one as a sheriff, another as a justice of the peace. Five of the men appointed to the court between 1900 and 1967 had fathers with a business or mercantile background, including one sea captain, and one shipbuilder and owner. The remaining ten judges had fathers with non-professional backgrounds, mostly in farming, which is not surprising since many came from small agricultural communities across Nova Scotia.

While the lack of data makes an analysis of the post-1967 period extremely difficult, the same trend appears to continue. A substantial percentage of NSSC appointments came from privileged backgrounds, though having parents in a lower social class did not preclude many judges from achieving their position. Thus, there were several judicial appointments that suggest the benefit of established parents in receiving an appointment to the bench, such as Angus Lewis Macdonald (the son of Premier Angus L. Macdonald), R. MacLeod Rogers (son of former federal Liberal Cabinet minister Norman McLeod Rogers), and David R. Chipman (who belonged to a long line of 'Ritchie' family lawyers).[25] However, for many other members of the NSSC it is impossible to identify any obvious family connection that enhanced their chances of appointment.

Recruitment in the twentieth century thus depended less on a privileged background or a prominent family. The percentage of judges with fathers in the elite professions had dropped significantly. The recruitment of men and women with more humble origins indicates that less emphasis was placed on social status and family background, and more on educational qualifications and professional credentials. However, this is not to say that the membership of the NSSC was wholly determined by merit. As will be shown later in this article, political connections remained important in judicial selection. What had perhaps changed was that individuals with more humble social backgrounds could, through hard work, the creation of a particular type of resumé, and the careful development of political connections, receive an appointment to the NSSC.

Religion

In Greco's study, religion was used as a further indication of social status. As can be seen in table 6.3, from 1754 to 1900, Anglicanism dominated the judiciary.[26] As with family background, judges were increasingly unlikely to report their religious beliefs as the twentieth century progressed. This results in a somewhat incomplete statistical picture of the NSSC and religion, although some broad trends do emerge. Of the fifty-six judges whose religion could be positively determined, the numbers reflect something quite different than that found by Greco.

There are at least three striking aspects to table 6.3. The first, and most obvious, is the decline in the central place of Anglicanism in judicial appointments. The second is the substantial number of Roman

Table 6.3 Religion

Religion	1754–1900 (%)	1900–2000 (%)
Anglican	28 (65.1)	8 (8.9)
Other Protestants	10 (23.3)	
United Church		15 (16.7)
Presbyterian		10 (11.1)
Baptist		5 (5.6)
Methodist		1 (1.1)
Catholic	3 (7.0)	14 (15.6)
Jewish		3 (3.3)
Unknown	2 (4.7)	34 (37.8)

Catholics appointed to the bench. A closer inspection, however, shows that there were limits placed on the number of Catholics on the NSSC, as there were 'Catholic seats' for the first two-thirds of the twentieth century.[27] Hugh McDonald, appointed in 1873, was the first Catholic in the history of the court. Another Catholic, Nicholas Hogan Meagher, joined the court in 1890, three years before McDonald resigned. When Meagher resigned in January 1916, another Catholic, Joseph Chisholm, filled his seat one month later. When Chisholm died in January 1950, Catholic Vincent Christopher MacDonald replaced him. The pattern continued when the government appointed Vincent Joseph Pottier in 1965 to replace MacDonald, who had died several months previously. William Francis Carroll held a second Catholic seat on the court from 1925 to 1949; when he retired, the government appointed another Catholic, Lauchlin Currie. A third Catholic seat appears to have been 'created' in 1966, when Alexander Hugh McKinnon became a member. Despite these appointments, the percentage of Catholic appointees was not representative of the Catholic population in Nova Scotia between 1900 and 1967 (a period during which we can identify the religious affiliation of all the judges appointed). From 1901 to 1971, approximately 33 per cent of the province's population was Catholic, yet the number of Catholic appointments amounted to just 18.8 per cent. By the late 1960s, however, the strict adherence to 'Catholic seats' seems to have waned. The Catholic appointments after about 1967 do not neatly follow one another.

A third striking feature of the religious breakdown of the twentieth-century court is the appointment of Jewish judges. Discrimination against Jewish Canadians in the legal profession had deep roots. Bora

Laskin became the first Jewish justice of the Supreme Court of Canada when Pierre Trudeau appointed him in 1970;[28] the NSSC received its first Jewish member, Justin Louis Dubinksy, when Prime Minister Pearson appointed him to the Trial Division in 1967. Born and raised in Glace Bay, Dubinsky had graduated from Dalhousie with BA and LL.B degrees and articled with future Nova Scotia Chief Justice Lauchlin Currie. He then entered his own practice in Glace Bay, became highly involved in community activities, and ran unsuccessfully as a Liberal Party candidate in the 1958 federal election.[29] Trudeau subsequently appointed two additional Jewish judges to the NSSC during his time as prime minister: Constance Glube in 1977 and Hilroy Selig Nathanson in 1982.[30] These three judges represent 3.3 per cent of the twentieth-century appointments, higher than the Jewish percentage of the Nova Scotian population, which fluctuated between approximately 0.2 and 0.4 per cent during the century.

Gender, Disability, and Race

For much of Canada's history, women also faced substantial barriers to entering legal practice and the judiciary. In the first half of the twentieth century, only a handful of women entered Canada's law schools, and they often had difficulty securing articling positions. Women's enrolment in law schools began to increase around 1970, but did not equal male enrolments until the late 1980s.[31] The Canadian judiciary also remained a predominantly male preserve throughout the twentieth century, though the percentage of women gradually increased. In 1993, 12 per cent of the federally appointed judiciary was female; by 1999 this figure had risen to 22 per cent.[32]

Constance Glube became the first woman on the NSSC when Trudeau appointed her in 1977.[33] After completing her BA at McGill in 1952 and LL.B at Dalhousie in 1955, Glube worked in private practice in Halifax, then for the City of Halifax, first in its legal department, then as city manager. She combined her legal work with active involvement in the Jewish community, serving, for example, as president of the Shaar Shalom Synagogue Women's League. 'Truly a woman of firsts,'[34] Glube became the first woman to act as a chief justice of a federally appointed court when she became chief justice of the Trial Division in March 1982, just a few days after Trudeau made Bertha Wilson the first woman on the Supreme Court of Canada.[35]

Despite Glube's groundbreaking appointments to the court and to a chief justice position, the number of women on the NSSC did not rapidly increase. In 1993 only four of the NSSC's thirty-seven judges were women, or about 11 per cent.[36] It was twelve years after Glube's appointment before another woman joined the NSSC. Elizabeth Roscoe had been appointed the first female Family Court judge in Nova Scotia in 1984, and in 1989 the federal government elevated her first to the Trial Division of the NSSC and then, in 1992, to the appeal division. Another member of the Family Court, Margaret Stewart, went to the NSSC in 1992. The federal government had appointed Nancy Bateman as the first female Nova Scotia County Court judge in 1990. She joined the Supreme Court in 1993 as part of the County Court–NSSC amalgamation, and received a promotion to the Court of Appeal in 1995. Two more women, Marlene Jill Hamilton and Suzanne Hood, joined the Trial Division in 1995.[37] Despite recent appointments, the percentage of women on the NSSC in February 2002 was 21.4 per cent of the court and just 8.9 per cent of all the NSSC judges appointed in the twentieth century.[38]

Glube's appointment is perhaps most remarkable for the fact that she had to overcome two traditional barriers to joining the judiciary in Nova Scotia: her Judaism and her gender. The appointment of Linda Oland and M. Heather Robertson broke down other barriers. A first-generation Chinese Canadian, Oland was a partner in the prominent Halifax law firm McInnes Cooper and Robertson, where she specialized in corporate, commercial, estate, and immigration law. With her 1998 appointment she became the only visible-minority member of the NSSC during the twentieth century – no African or Aboriginal Canadians received appointments despite the substantial populations of both minority groups in Nova Scotia, and the controversy resulting from the failure to elevate the sole black Nova Scotia Family Court judge, Corrine Sparks, to the new Family Court Division of the NSSC in 1999.[39] Robertson, confined to a wheelchair in the mid-1990s after a skiing accident, became the first disabled justice on the NSSC with her 1998 appointment.[40]

Education

Of the judges appointed before 1900, the vast majority received their training as apprentices to practitioners; only six attained a university legal education, and three had no legal training at all.[41] In comparison, from 1900 to 2000, only seven judges received their training as apprentices to practitioners, while eighty-three had a university legal education.

The late nineteenth century was a time of great change in legal education in Nova Scotia, and throughout most of the common law world.[42] Until 1883, legal education in Nova Scotia consisted of apprenticeship in a law office, followed by examinations administered by the judges of the Supreme Court, and later, by the Nova Scotia Barristers' Society. This method of bar qualification, however, was gradually phased out, and in its place developed a formal system of university legal education followed by a bar admissions exam. Instrumental in this shift was the founding of Dalhousie Law School in 1883, where almost all the university-educated judges in this study received their degrees.[43] Students entering the school in 1883 were required to have either the equivalent of a grade eleven education, or a passing mark on the Barristers' Society's apprenticeship qualification examination or the Law School's own matriculation examination. The Law School introduced new admission standards in 1914. By 1924, all entering law students were required to have two years of university education.

The establishment of Dalhousie Law School, and its requirement of two years of university study before admission, increased the number of judges who had attended university. Of the twentieth-century judges, at least eighty-six, or 95.6 per cent, pursued university study at the undergraduate, graduate, or law school level. This is substantially higher than the roughly 50 per cent of judges with post-secondary educations appointed during the first one hundred and fifty years of the NSSC.[44] All four of the judges who did not attend university rose to the bench during the early twentieth century. The last person appointed who did not have any university education was Daniel Duncan McKenzie in 1923.[45]

Undergraduate study at a Nova Scotia university soon became the norm. At least sixty-two of the twentieth-century judges had Bachelor of Arts degrees (68.9 per cent), eight received Bachelor degrees in business (8.9 per cent), two had education degrees, and one completed a Bachelor of Music. As can be seen in table 6.4, a substantial majority of the judges who received undergraduate degrees acquired them from Nova Scotian universities.

Eighty-three judges, or 92.2 per cent, received Bachelor degrees in law. Eighty of these (96.4 per cent) received their LL.Bs from Dalhousie. The exceptions were James Johnston Ritchie, who earned his LL.B at Harvard in 1877; Edward Scanlan, who received his law degree from the University of New Brunswick; and Arthur Gordon Cooper, whose sole law degree was a BCL from Oxford. Stuart Dixon Jenks

Table 6.4 Undergraduate education

University	Graduates
Dalhousie / King's	24
St Francis Xavier	14
Acadia	11
Mount Allison	6
Saint Mary's	5
Oxford	2
Queen's	2
Mount Saint Vincent	1
Prince Edward Island	1
McGill	1
Western Ontario	1
Bishop's	1
Montreal	1

received two law degrees, one from Cornell Law School and one from Dalhousie, as did Gerald Freeman, who attained a BCL from McGill in 1960 and an LL.B from Dalhousie the following year.

There is a distinct lack of graduate study among the judges of the NSSC. Only three of the judges received LL.Ms.[46] Two others pursued advanced legal studies at Oxford, and received BCLs as second law degrees.[47] The percentage of judges who pursued graduate study does not substantially increase if non-legal study is considered. Six judges possessed MAs, and one a Master of Library Studies. In total, just 13.3 per cent received a graduate degree. There are likely several reasons for this, including the dearth of graduate schools in the Maritimes for most of this period, a lack of financial resources for some students, and, perhaps most importantly, a belief that other professional and political opportunities were more likely to further one's legal career.

Legal Practice

In comparison to the pre-1900 period, in the twentieth century judicial appointees often spent more time at the bar before their rise to the bench (see table 6.5). Prior to 1900, three (7.9 per cent) of the judges did not spend any time at the bar, and incidentally, had no legal training, but these were also early appointees.[48] In the twentieth century, the range between judges' call to the bar and their first judicial appointment was in part due to the fact that several members of the NSSC had, at quite

Table 6.5 Time at bar before first judicial appointment

Time at bar	Pre-1900 (%)	Post 1900 (%)
0 Years	3 (7.9)	0 (0)
1–10	4 (11.0)	5 (5.6)
11–20	12 (31.6)	21 (23.3)
21–30	13 (34.2)	33 (36.7)
31+	6 (15.8)	31 (34.4)

early ages, been Provincial or Family Court judges. Of the five judges who practised for ten years or less when appointed, two (Elizabeth Roscoe and Margaret Stewart) began as Family Court judges, and two (Hiram Carver and Joseph Kennedy) started at the Provincial Court.

Recall the decline in the average age on appointment of the judges towards the end of the twentieth century. Not surprisingly, this meant shorter periods at the bar for judges selected after about 1967. For example, only one judge appointed between 1900 and 1967 had fewer than twenty-one years at the bar. After 1967, twenty-four lawyers with this level of experience became judges. The judges appointed before 1967 had spent an average of approximately thirty-one years as members of the bar; from 1967 new members of the NSSC had spent only twenty-three years at the bar on average. The reasons for this shift include the aforementioned movement of judges from other courts to the NSSC, and, perhaps, a decline in the appointment of elected politicians. Rather than seek a judicial appointment after an extensive period in elected office (during which their time at the bar continued to tick even though they did not practise), many of the judges in the last three decades of the twentieth century did not serve in an elected office.

The shortest time in practice spent by any of the judges was Margaret Stewart. She was thirty-five years of age when she became a Family Court judge in November 1985 and she had been a member of the bar for just six years (though she was thirteen years removed from her call to the bar when she became a member of the NSSC in 1992). Kenneth Peter Richard, appointed in 1978, had the shortest time at the bar of anyone sent directly to the NSSC, at ten years and six months. Forty-six years old at his appointment, Richard had completed a commerce degree at St Francis Xavier and been involved in business before entering law school and then joining the bar in December 1967.[49]

Some of the longest-serving members of the bar combined their legal practice with other interests. For example, some worked within the business community. Robert MacDonald was a director of Maritime Steel and Foundries, and Ian Malcolm MacKeigan was a director of John Labatt and Gulf Oil Canada.[50] Perhaps the most prominent lawyer/businessperson to join the NSSC was Robert Edward Harris. Harris was not only a successful corporate and finance lawyer, first practising in Yarmouth (1882–92) and then in Halifax (1892–1915), he was also associated with many leading enterprises in Nova Scotia. He served as a director of a number of major corporations, including Eastern Trust, Eastern Car, Bank of Nova Scotia, Maritime Telegraph and Telephone, Acadia Sugar Refinery, and Robb Engineering Company, in addition to holding the presidency of Nova Scotia Steel, Eastern Trust, Demerara Electric, and Trinidad Electric.[51]

While some Nova Scotian lawyers worked in corporate circles, a large number also combined their legal practice with part-time or full-time government service. At least fifteen (16.7 per cent) of the appointees acted as town, city, or municipal solicitors; sixteen (17.8 per cent) worked as Crown prosecutors on either a full-time or part-time basis; and seventeen (18.9 per cent) served on administrative boards such as the Workers' Compensation Board, the Nova Scotia Labour Relations Board, the Nova Scotia Civil Service Administration Board, or the Expropriation Compensation Appeal Board. Two future judges worked as legal aid lawyers: Felix A. Cacchione and Douglas L. MacLennan. Jamie S.W. Saunders acted for the Nova Scotia attorney general for three years during the Marshall inquiry; C. Denne Burchell practised in the federal Department of Justice, while N. Robert Anderson was the director of criminal law in the provincial attorney general's office.

Legal education was also an interest for many of the twentieth-century judges, though there were few full-time law professors. Benjamin Russell was instrumental in the establishment of Dalhousie Law School, where he taught for several decades.[52] Vincent C. MacDonald ended ten years of practising law in 1930 when Dalhousie Law School hired him full time. He became dean after only four years, a position he held until his elevation to the bench in 1950. Lorne Clarke received an LL.M from Harvard in 1955 and taught full-time at Dalhousie Law School between 1952 and 1959, while D. Merlin Nunn served as an assistant professor for one year immediately after receiving his LL.M from Harvard in 1958. With an LL.B from Dalhousie and three degrees from Oxford, Gordon Stewart Cowan was a professor at Dalhousie from 1937 to 1939 and at the law school in Manitoba from 1939 to 1941 before returning to private practice in Halifax. Most recently, Thomas Albert Cromwell was a law professor at Dalhousie from 1982 to 1997.[53]

While full-time law teachers did not rapidly populate the Nova Scotia bench, a substantial number of the appointees taught part-time in universities, bar admissions courses, or continuing legal education programs. The number who became involved suggests that an interest in legal education was beneficial to securing a judicial appointment. At least twenty-two NSSC judges lectured at Dalhousie Law School before their appointment. Allan Boudreau lectured part-time in commercial law at St Mary's and in the commerce department at the Université Sainte-Anne; Kenneth Peter Richard lectured in business law at St Francis Xavier; Robert William Wright taught commercial law at Mount Saint Vincent; and M. Heather Robertson was a lecturer in the commerce department at Saint Mary's. Others lectured in the Nova Scotia Bar Admissions Course, and/or were involved in the Continuing Legal Education Society of Nova Scotia. Still others took part in the Public Legal Education Society of Nova Scotia. In all, at least 46.7 per cent of the NSSC judges were involved with some facet of legal education, either full or part time, before their appointment.

A substantial majority of the judges appointed between 1900 and 2000 had been very involved in the Nova Scotia Barristers' Society. This trend reflects the 'professional renaissance' of last quarter of the nineteenth century, during which the Barristers' Society switched from being a gentlemen's club to an important regulatory body that determined admission to the profession and maintained disciplinary control over its members.[54] The correlation between Society leadership and the Nova Scotia bench also mirrored patterns in other provinces. William Klein's work on judicial selection in Manitoba, Ontario, and Quebec between 1900 and 1970 demonstrates the increased importance of holding an executive office in a professional association. For example, he notes that in the 1960s, 78 per cent of the Canadian Bar Association's executive members from these three provinces became judges.[55] Peter Russell and Jacob Ziegel, furthermore, claim that during Brian Mulroney's first term as prime minister, active participation in the Canadian Bar Association and/or provincial bar associations 'frequently served as an entrée into the networks that lead to federal judicial appointments.'[56] No fewer than eighteen of the twentieth-century NSSC appointees served as president of the Barristers' Society.[57] Vincent Joseph Pottier, Gordon L.S. Hart, and Hilroy S. Nathanson also served as vice-presidents of the Society, though none went on to serve as president because they were appointed to the bench. Membership on the Barristers' Society's Bar Council – the elected body responsible for the governance of the Nova Scotia Barristers' Society – was also a common feature among the NSSC justices. In all, at least sixty-seven of the judges, or 74.4 per cent, served as president, vice-president, or as a Council member.[58]

While active membership in the Barristers' Society was important, many future judges were also involved in local and national professional organizations. For example, at least six members of the NSSC had been presidents of the Cape Breton Barristers' Society.[59] In addition, William Johnston Grant acted as president of the Colchester County Bar Association in the 1960s, while Hugh MacDonnell was president of the Pictou County Bar Society. An increasing number of appointees also involved themselves in the Canadian Bar Association towards the end of the twentieth century, including Arthur Gordon Cooper, who was president of the CBA in 1967–8.

Halifax-based lawyers dominated the court appointments between 1754 and 1900, when approximately 59 per cent of the judges practised law in Halifax at some point in their career.[60] This figure did not substantially change in the twentieth century, when at least 54.4 per cent practised in Halifax/Dartmouth.

It was not unusual for judges to have worked together in a professional capacity before rising to the bench. Just as many of the judges were classmates at Dalhousie Law School,[61] so were they members of the same law practices.[62] For example, all three founding members of the New Glasgow firm of MacIntosh, MacDonnell & MacDonald became members of the NSSC. The government appointed Alexander Murdoch MacIntosh in 1973, Hugh MacDonnell became a County Court judge in 1982 and joined the NSSC upon amalgamation in 1993, and Robert B. MacDonald briefly served as a Provincial Court judge before his elevation to the NSSC in 1985. It also appears that in the last decades of the century a substantial number of judges came from the handful of large Nova Scotian law firms and their predecessors.[63]

Prior Judicial Experience

For most of the twentieth century, the federal government was reticent to appoint judges to the NSSC who had first acted as judges in other courts. For example, between 1900 and 1967 only four members of the

Supreme Court had prior judicial experience. Frederick Andrew Laurence was a justice of the peace from 1879 to 1905. Daniel Duncan McKenzie became a judge of the County Court in 1906 after six years in provincial and federal politics. He resigned two years later to return to politics and take a seat in the House of Commons, which he held until his appointment to the NSSC in 1923. Vincent Joseph Pottier and Alexander Hugh McKinnon were County Court judges until their respective elevations to the Supreme Court in 1965 and 1966. Pottier was not only the first County Court judge to be elevated to a higher bench, but also the first Acadian appointed to the NSSC.[64]

In the last third of the twentieth century an increasing number of the NSSC's judges first served on other courts. At least four judges acted as adjudicators of small claims' courts.[65] Gerald B. Freeman served briefly on the County Court before joining the NSSC in 1990. In 1993, twelve County Court judges joined the NSSC on the amalgamation of the two courts.[66] The federal government also appointed three NSSC justices from the Nova Scotia Family Court.[67] Furthermore, the government broke with past practice by selecting members of the Supreme Court from the ranks of the Provincial Court. The federal government's slowness to appoint members of the Provincial Court to the NSSC was perhaps due to long-held assumptions about the lower standards applied by provinces in selecting their judiciaries.[68] In 1985, however, the Mulroney government elevated Robert B. MacDonald to the NSSC after a short time at the Provincial Court. In the 1990s two more Provincial Court judges became members of the NSSC. Hiram Carver joined the Provincial Court in 1963 at the age of thirty-three. Twenty-seven years later he became a County Court judge, and in the 1993 amalgamation he became a NSSC justice. Joseph Phillip Kennedy was also just thirty-three years of age when appointed to the Provincial Court in 1978. After rising to the position of chief judge of the Provincial Court in 1996, the federal government elevated him to the NSSC in April 1997.[69]

Political Activities

The last third of the twentieth century also saw a shift in the nature and extent of the political involvement of the judges prior to their appointment. A political career was an important stepping-stone to the judiciary before 1900, when 58 per cent of the NSSC judges held a seat in provincial and/or federal levels of government.[70] Political activity remained an important factor in attaining a judicial appointment during the twentieth century, although politicians gradually received fewer appointments while the number of unelected political supporters who became judges increased.

Of the thirty-two judges appointed between 1900 and 1966, at least twenty-six (81.2 percent) ran in federal, provincial, or municipal elections. Eight judges (25 per cent) held the position of attorney general or solicitor general,[71] and eighteen (56.2 per cent) were members of the Legislative Assembly and/or House of Commons at some point during their careers.[72] Some of the appointees had significant political careers. For example, James Lorimer Ilsley represented King's-Hants in the House of Commons from 1926 to 1948. In that time, he acted as minister of national revenue (1935–1940), minister of finance (1940–6), and minister of justice and attorney general of Canada (1946–8). For his efforts, Ilsley became a member of the Imperial Privy Council in 1946, only the fifth Canadian so honoured. The political career of Duncan Cameron Fraser overshadowed the short time he spent at the Supreme Court. Involved in provincial politics from 1875 to 1891, he then moved into the federal realm until his appointment to the bench in 1904. He practised law when politics permitted. After just two years on the bench, he resigned and became lieutenant governor of Nova Scotia, a position he held until his death in 1910.[73] Others with prominent political careers included James Wilberforce Longley, Josiah H. MacQuarrie, and Ronald Manning Fielding.[74]

A political career for those appointed before 1967 was thus more the rule than the exception. This was not lost on Nova Scotians who knew about the workings of the appointment process. In 1960 Richard Donahoe wrote to Prime Minister Diefenbaker to request an appointment to the NSSC. He noted that he had run in five provincial elections, twice federally, and been mayor of Halifax. He had served the Conservative Party for more than thirty years, and had been 'an active platform speaker even before I had the vote.'[75] The continuing role of politics at mid-century can be summed up in a story told by Dalhousie law professor Moffatt Hancock, who recalled that after Dean Vincent MacDonald 'had regaled us with a fascinating account of some complex litigation he had once been involved in, Jim Milner spoke up and said "Vincent, you really ought to be a judge," to which Vince replied, "Oh, no, that's impossible. You see, I haven't lost enough elections."'[76]

After about 1967, however, the percentage of ex-politicians appointed to the bench substantially declined. During the 1967 to 2000 period, approximately 22.4 per cent of the fifty-eight appointments had run for some form of elected office, a marked decline from 81.2 per cent between 1900 and 1966. Just four (6.9 per cent) had sat in either the House of the Commons or the Nova Scotia Legislative Assembly. While a few high-profile politicians received judicial appointments, such as former Nova Scotia Cabinet minister and Attorney General Leonard Pace,[77] the blatant practice of rewarding electoral participation declined.

This change likely resulted from two factors. First, in the nineteenth century it was easier to combine legal and political careers. Serving as a member of the Legislative Assembly, for example, was not a full-time job. As well, lawyers typically had sole practices or worked in very small partnerships.[78] Lawyers could thus combine legal and political careers without, as late twentieth-century lawyers in large firms had to do, needing to demonstrate the value of their substantial periods away from practice.

Second, important changes occurred in what was considered an appropriate level of public political involvement for judicial candidates. Towards the end of the twentieth century it appears that Canadians' attitude towards 'patronage' often dictated increased caution and attempts on the part of government to limit, or hide, the political nature of judicial appointments.[79] Despite its long and deeply entrenched tradition of political patronage, Nova Scotia became a centre of this elevated sensitivity, in part because of the wrongful murder conviction of Donald Marshall Jr. A royal commission appointed in 1986 concluded that his conviction was the result of a legal system rife with racism, incompetence, and overt political favouritism.[80] The Nova Scotia judiciary came under special scrutiny. The attorney general of Nova Scotia requested that the Canadian Judicial Council investigate the actions of the Appeal Court, which had overturned Marshall's conviction but de-emphasized the biased treatment he had received. Adding to the sense of judicial wrongdoing was the refusal of the appeal judges to testify before the Judicial Council inquiry, a refusal that ultimately led to legal arguments before the Supreme Court of Canada.[81]

The developments in Nova Scotia strengthened an emerging sense in Canada, especially since the entrenchment of the Charter of Rights and Freedoms, that political considerations had to be removed from judicial selection. The Marshall affair suggested a need for better-qualified jurists, and for limiting close relationships between the government and the judiciary. Appointing judges on the basis of party loyalty and legislative service seemed to undermine the achievement of both goals. The federal government responded to this growing perception. Since 1988 the commissioner for federal judicial affairs has solicited applications from people interested in a judicial appointment. This new system requires assessment committees with representatives from government, the judiciary, and bar societies to evaluate judicial candidates. The assessment committees can decide to 'not recommend,' 'recommend,' or 'highly recommend' applicants, though the final selection of judges still rests with the prime minister and the Cabinet. According to federal guidelines, public service should be a prime motivation for seeking judicial office, and the primary qualification for the bench is 'merit,' the evaluation of which is based upon proficiency in the law, a well-rounded legal experience, maturity and objectivity in judgment, and an appreciation of social issues that could arise in litigation.[82]

The decline in the percentage of politicians on the bench, however, did not mean that politics had disappeared as a relevant factor in judicial appointments. It seems that the route to the judiciary had changed such that active political involvement behind the scenes became more important. In several instances, the federal government rewarded lawyers with judicial appointments who had been involved in party apparatuses and fundraising, though these party men and women had never run for political offices themselves. This practice, which had the benefit of hiding the political nature of judicial selection from most of the public, was not completely new. Several judges appointed before 1967, although not holding seats in Ottawa or Halifax, were involved in politics to some degree at the provincial or federal level.[83] However, towards the end of the twentieth century a significant number of judicial appointments are notable for their substantial behind-the-scenes work for the Liberals or Progressive Conservatives, rather than their service as elected politicians.[84] This type of political involvement was more flexible and less time consuming than serving as a legislator. Lawyers at law firms could continue to bill substantial numbers of hours while involving themselves in political activities when time allowed. Several appointments illustrate the trend away from elected politicians. R. MacLeod Rogers was president of the Nova Scotia Liberal association and helped rejuvenate the provincial party in the 1960s.[85] M. Heather Robertson acted as chief of staff for Liberal Premier John Savage and was a top fundraiser in Savage's leadership campaign. David R. Chipman was active in the Nova Scotia Progressive Conservative Association, a top party fundraiser, and a long-time friend of Premier John Buchanan. The *Halifax Chronicle-Herald* commented on the 1995 appointment of Edward 'Ted' Flinn that 'another well-known

Halifax Liberal lawyer, Ted Flinn, was appointed to Nova Scotia's Appeal Court.'[86] Ian Palmeter had 'an extensive political background' prior to his 1985 appointment, including his work as president of the Halifax Young PC's, president of the Halifax Federal PC Association, and campaign manager for a variety of candidates, including Robert Stanfield's bid for a seat in the House of Commons.[87] Walter R.E. Goodfellow acted as president of the Nova Scotia PC Party Association. Edward Scanlan was president of the Central Nova Progressive Conservative Association and, before his appointment to the NSSC at the age of thirty-seven, acted as campaign manager for federal Public Works Minister Elmer MacKay. The Liberal justice critic suggested in response to Scanlan's appointment that the Tories had 'not learned a thing from the Marshall Inquiry.'[88]

That judicial appointments were biased towards candidates who had supported the party in power is apparent in the connection between the stated political affiliation of the judges and the appointing governments between 1900 and 2000. The Laurier government appointed five Liberals to the bench during the first eleven years of the twentieth century. Robert Borden, a Conservative, named three Conservatives to the bench, but also one Unionist-Liberal, Humphrey Mellish, during the period of Unionist government. William Lyon Mackenzie King appointed Liberals throughout his time as prime minister, although the political affiliation of two of his appointees is unknown. Arthur Meighen, Richard B. Bennett, Louis St Laurent, John Diefenbaker, and Lester Pearson appointed only men who had supported the party in power.

The appointments of Pierre Trudeau are particularly interesting because, early in his federal career, he attempted to temper the use of patronage. For example, Trudeau became the first minister of justice to seek an opinion of the CBA's National Council on the Judiciary before making appointments.[89] However, as Peter Russell concludes, by the end of his time in office Trudeau had returned 'to blatant patronage appointments.'[90] Of the twenty-three judges Trudeau appointed directly to the NSSC or to the County Court who became members of the NSSC, political affiliations have been identified for eleven, all of whom were Liberals.[91] These appointments thus suggest that Trudeau did not completely remove himself from considering party loyalty. Brian Mulroney appointed twenty-three judges to the NSSC, or to the County Court who joined the NSSC. We have identified political connections for eight, all of whom were Progressive Conservatives. Jean Chrétien appointed eleven NSSC judges between 1993 and 2000; we have identified the political connections of five, all of whom were Liberals. The substantial difficulty we have encountered in determining the political affiliations of the judges since Trudeau may reflect the increasing tendency to select judges from party faithful who stay out of the electoral limelight, a growing belief on the part of judges that their allegiances to particular political parties is part of their 'private' not their public life and thus need not be divulged, or, most optimistically, it may indicate that fewer of the judges were politically partisan prior to their appointment.

Conclusion

This prosopography of the judicial appointments to the Nova Scotia Supreme Court during the twentieth century reveals both expected and unexpected trends, and, perhaps more importantly, raises questions about the representativeness of the modern judiciary. The trends can best be captured through two characterizations, one for the NSSC judges appointed before 1967, and another for those who joined the court between 1967 and 2000.

Until about 1967, the 'average' judge had certain characteristics: *he* might have been born anywhere in the province, his parents were white, and probably middle class, English-speaking, and Protestant. Educated in Nova Scotia and a graduate of Dalhousie Law School, he was a member of the bar for two or three decades before his appointment, practised in a small firm, and was active in the Nova Scotia Barristers' Society. He was involved in electoral politics as a candidate, whether at the municipal, provincial, or federal level, for either the Liberal or Conservative parties. An appointment to the bench came while he was in his mid-to late fifties.

In the last third of the twentieth century, our 'typical' judge changes in some important ways. There is a chance that *he* might be a *she*. He was more likely to have been born in Halifax to middle-class, white parents who were probably Protestant, though he might have been Catholic or even Jewish. After receiving a law degree from Dalhousie, he practised for twenty or so years, perhaps combining his work at a respectable sized law firm with fundraising and other behind-the-scenes service to the Liberals or Progressive Conservatives, as well as work on the executive of the NS Barristers' Society or the CBA. He accepted a judicial appointment in his mid-to late forties.

Historians are often uncomfortable evaluating the meaning of modern developments, and we cannot determine with certainly the long-term implications of recent changes in judicial appointment practices. Nevertheless, we would like to conclude by making three comments, one regarding the possibility that alterations in judicial selection might reflect the development of a system of 'meritocracy,' and two concerning the role and value of patronage and politics in the appointment of judges.

It seems quite clear that the Nova Scotia judiciary is no longer just a placement opportunity for the sons of leading families. The emphasis on academic and professional qualifications of appointees that began in the late nineteenth century continued in the twentieth, and lawyers with careers demonstrating 'merit' constituted the majority of appointments made between 1900 and 2000. However, this does raise issues of what constitutes merit. Some of the ways lawyers have improved their chances for judicial appointment include teaching a course at Dalhousie Law School, working at a larger firm, or taking an active role in the Barristers' Society. Unfortunately, given that these activities are more difficult for lawyers to undertake in rural areas of the province, one might ask: how many NSSC judges in the future will have practised in Yarmouth, New Ross, or Antigonish?

Perhaps the most striking change in judicial selection in the twentieth century was the decline in the appointment of former politicians. In the last third of the twentieth century, the federal government was quite careful to make judicial appointments in Nova Scotia that, at least to the majority of the voting public, did not *appear* to have a political motivation. There has been a decline in the appointment of party politicians as judges, but the selection of party fundraisers and political organizers continues. Political appointments thus frequently fly below the radar of the press and the public, a problem made worse by the creation of administrative 'systems' for judicial selection that evaluate potential candidates and smooth over criticisms of an appointment system still dominated by the prime minister and the federal Cabinet.

Finally, we wonder whether criticism of the appointment of former politicians might have a perverse effect on the quality of courts in Nova Scotia (and Canada for that matter). Whatever the defects of politicians as judges, life in elected office does have certain advantages for the creation of good judges. For example, serving as a member of the House of Commons or Legislative Assembly provides ample opportunity to consider policy questions, parse the wording of legislation, and gain knowledge of government administrative structures. When combined with a lengthy legal practice before or after political office, this knowledge is undoubtedly beneficial to judges. Spending considerable amounts of time as a party fundraiser or campaign organizer would not seem to offer the same educational benefits for potential judges and in combination with the substantially fewer years at the bar, one may ask whether judicial candidates who appear non-political to most of a province's citizens may in fact be less prepared for the bench.

APPENDIXES

Appendix A: The Chief Justices of Nova Scotia, 1900–2000

Name	*Tenure*
James McDonald	1881–1905
Robert Linton Weatherbe	1905–1907
Charles James Townshend	1907–1915
Wallace Graham	1915–1917
Robert Edward Harris	1918–1931
Joseph Chisholm	1931–1950
James Lorimer Ilsley	1950–1967
Lauchlin Daniel Currie	1967–1968
Alexander Hugh McKinnon	1968–1973
Ian Malcolm MacKeigan	1973–1985
Lorne Otis Clarke	1985–1998
Constance Rachelle Glube	1998–

Appendix B: Justices of the NSSC (Appeal Division) and Nova Scotia Court of Appeal

Name	*Tenure at Appeal Court*
James Lorimer Ilsley	1966–1967
Josiah H. MacQuarrie	1966–1968
Alexander Hugh McKinnon	1966–1973
Lauchlin Daniel Currie	1967–1968
Thomas Herbert Coffin	1968–1982
Arthur Gordon Cooper	1968–1983
Ian Malcolm MacKeigan	1973–1990
Angus Lewis Macdonald	1973–1992
Gordon Leavitt Shaw Hart	1978–1999

Leonard Lawson Pace	1978–1990
Malachi Cornelius Hubert Jones	1979–
Vincent Alan James Morrison	1982–1987
Kennth McNeill Matthews	1985–1997
Lorne Otis Clarke	1985–1998
David Ritchie Chipman	1987–
James Doane Hallett	1990–
Gerald B. Freeman	1990–
Elizabeth Ann MacKinnon Roscoe	1992–
Ronald Newton Pugsley	1993–2000
Nancy Jean Bateman	1995–
John Edward Flinn	1995–2002
Thomas Albert Cromwell	1997–
Constance Rachelle Glube	1998–
Jamie William Sutherland Saunders	2000–
Linda Lee Oland	2000–

Appendix C: Justices of the Nova Scotia Supreme Court, 1900-2000

(* Joined NSSC in 1993 County Court–NSSC amalgamation)

Name	*Tenure*
Duncan Cameron Fraser	1904–1906
Benjamin Russell	1904–1924
James Wilberforce Longley	1905–1922
Frederick Andrew Laurence	1907–1912
Arthur Drysdale	1907–1921
James Johnston Ritchie	1912–1925
Robert Edward Harris	1915–1931
Joseph Chisholm	1916–1950
Humphrey Mellish	1918–1937
Tecumseh Sherman Rogers	1921–1928
Daniel Duncan McKenzie	1923–1927
William Francis Carroll	1925–1949
Robert Henry Graham	1925–1949
Stuart Dixon Jenks	1927–1932
Vincent John Paton	1928–1932
Hugh Ross	1929–1939
William Lorimer Hall	1931–1958
John Doull	1933–1961
Maynard Brown Archibald	1937–1948

John Stanley Smiley	1938–1945
Josiah H. MacQuarrie	1947–1968
Eugene Troop Parker	1948–1961
James Lorimer Ilsley	1949–1967
Lauchlin Daniel Currie	1949–1968
Vincent Christopher MacDonald	1950–1964
Frank Harris Patterson	1958–1965
Frederick William Bissett	1961–1977
Thomas Herbert Coffin	1961–1981
Vincent Joseph Pottier	1965–1970
Ronald Manning Fielding	1965–1972
Gordon Stewart Cowan	1966–1981
Alexander Hugh McKinnon	1966–1973
Justin Louis Dubisky	1967–1976
Arthur Gordon Cooper	1968–1983
Donald Joseph Gillis	1968–1973
Gordon Leavitt Shaw Hart	1968–1999
Malachi Cornelius Hubert Jones	1970–
Vincent Alan James Morrison	1973–1987
Ian Malcolm MacKeigan	1973–1990
Alexander Murdoch MacIntosh	1973–1991
Angus Lewis Macdonald	1973–1992
William Johnston Grant	1977–1995
James Doane Hallett	1977–
Constance Rachelle Glube	1977–
Leonard Lawson Pace	1978–1990
Kenneth Peter Richard	1978–
Charles Denne Burchell	1979–1989
Roderick MacLeod Rogers	1981–1990
Lorne Otis Clarke	1981–1998
Daniel Merlin Nunn	1982–
Hilroy Selig Nathanson	1982–
Robert Buckley MacDonald	1985–1995
Kenneth McNeill Matthews	1985–1997
Francis Bernard William Kelly	1985–
Gordon Alfred Tidman	1985–
John McNab Davison	1987–
David Ritchie Chipman	1987–
Elizabeth Ann MacKinnon Roscoe	1989–
Gerald B. Freeman	1990–

Allan Paul Boudreau	1990–
Walter Robert Evans Goodfellow	1990–
David William Gruchy	1990–
Jamie William Sutherland Saunders	1990–
Angus David MacAdam	1992–
Margaret Jane Stewart	1992–
Ronald Newton Pugsley	1993–2000
*Murray James Ryan	1993–1994
*John Hugh MacDonnell	1993–1995
*Norman Robert Anderson	1993–1998
*Frank Campbell Edwards	1993–
*Douglas Lawrence MacLennan	1993–
*Donald MacKinnon Hall	1993–
*Simon James MacDonald	1993–
*Ian Harold Morton Palmeter	1993–1997
*Charles Edward Haliburton	1993–
*Felix Antonio Cacchione	1993–
*Nancy Jean Bateman	1993–
*Hiram Joseph Carver	1993–
J. Edward Scanlon	1993–
John Edward Flinn	1995–2002
Marlene Jill Hamilton	1995–
Joseph Michael MacDonald	1995–
Suzanne Margaret Hood	1995–
Gerald Reid Paul Moir	1997–
Joseph Phillip Kennedy	1997–
Thomas Albert Cromwell	1997–
Arthur Joseph LeBlanc	1998–
Linda Lee Oland	1998–
Robert William Wright	1998–
Mary Heather Robertson	1998–

NOTES

R. Blake Brown would like to gratefully acknowledge the financial support of the Social Science and Humanities Research Council of Canada and the Izaak Walton Killam Trust. The authors wish to express their sincere thanks to Justice Charles E. Haliburton for sharing his research notes on the justices of the NSSC.

1 M.I. Urofsky, 'Beyond the Bottom Line: The Value of Judicial Biography,' *Journal of Supreme Court History* 2 (1998): 143–4. Judicial biography has become so popular that the value of this form of writing was the theme of a major conference at New York University Law School. See 'National Conference on Judicial Biography: Symposium,' *New York University Law Review* 70 (1995): 485–809.

2 See, e.g., R. Sharpe and K. Roach, *Brian Dickson: A Judge's Journey* (Toronto: Osgoode Society and University of Toronto Press 2003); E. Anderson, *Judging Bertha Wilson: Law as Large as Life* (Toronto: University of Toronto Press and the Osgoode Society 2001); W.H. McConnell, *William R. McIntyre: Paladin of the Common Law* (Montreal: McGill-Queen's University Press 2000); R.W. Pound, *Chief Justice W.R. Jackett: By the Law of the Land* (Montreal: McGill-Queen's University Press 1999); D. Vaneck, *Fulfillment: Memoirs of a Criminal Court Judge* (Toronto: Dundurn Press for the Osgoode Society 1999); W.G. Morrow, *Northern Justice: The Memoirs of Mr. Justice William G. Morrow* (Toronto: Osgoode Society and the Legal Archives Society of Alberta 1995); G. Bale, *Chief Justice William Johnstone Ritchie: Responsible Government and Judicial Review* (Ottawa: Carleton University Press 1991); J.A. Arnup, *Middleton: The Beloved Judge* (Toronto: University of Toronto Press and the Osgoode Society 1988); and D.R. Williams, *Duff: A Life in the Law* (Toronto: UBC Press and the Osgoode Society 1984). For a discussion of the Canadian (and British and Australian) historiography, see P. Girard, 'Judging Lives: Judicial Biography from Hale to Holmes,' *Australian Journal of Legal History* 7 (2003): 87–106.

3 L. Knafla and R. Klumpenhouwer, *Lords of the Western Bench: A Biographical History of the Supreme and District Courts of Alberta, 1876–1990* (Calgary: Legal Archives Society of Alberta 1997), 7; C. Greco, 'The Superior Court Judiciary of Nova Scotia, 1754–1900: A Collective Biography,' in Girard and Phillips, eds., *Essays*.

4 See Appendix C for a list of the names and tenure of the judges included in this article.

5 Changes would be made to the number of judges in each of the divisions in the following years. Judicature Amendment Act, S.N.S. 1962, c. 18; *Report of the Nova Scotia Court Structure Task Force* (Halifax: The Task Force 1991), xvii.

6 P. Girard, 'The Supreme Court of Nova Scotia, Responsible Government, and the Quest for Legitimacy, 1850–1920,' *Dalhousie Law Journal* 17 (1994): 430–57.

7 P. Girard, 'The Roots of a Professional Renaissance: Lawyers in Nova Scotia 1850–1910,' *Manitoba Law Journal* 20 (1991): 148–80.

8 Greco, 'The Superior Court Judiciary of Nova Scotia,' 45.

9 The various summaries and calculations that appear in this paper are based on a large number of primary and secondary sources. A full bibliography of these sources is on file with the authors. Justice Charles E. Haliburton, who has distributed a questionnaire to current and former judges requesting biographical information, kindly allowed us to examine his research. The NSSC had twelve chief justices between 1900 and 2000. James McDonald (1881–1905) was appointed directly to the position of chief justice in 1881 from his post as federal minister of justice. The next three chief justices, Robert Linton Weatherbe (1905–7), Charles James Townshend (1907–15), and Wallace Graham (1915–17), were appointed puisne judges prior to 1900, but were elevated to the senior position on the court during the first fifteen years of the twentieth century. The remaining eight judges, Robert Edward Harris (1918–31), Joseph Chisholm (1931–50), James Lorimer Ilsley (1950–67), Lauchlin Currie (1967–8), Alexander Hugh McKinnon (1968–73), Ian Malcolm MacKeigan (1973–85), Lorne O. Clarke (1985–98), and Constance Glube (1998–), served their entire judicial careers during the twentieth century. Note that McDonald has not been included in this article's statistical analyses as his appointment to the chief justice position occurred before 1900. Weatherbe, Townshend, and Graham were appointed to the NSSC before 1900 but became chief justices after 1900; we have thus only included them in our discussions of chief justices.

10 Six of the eleven chief justices appointed before 1900 assumed the position directly, with no prior experience at the NSSC. Greco, 'The Superior Court Judiciary of Nova Scotia,' 66–8. In contrast, all but one of the chief justices appointed between 1900 and 2000 served first as puisne judge. Ian Malcolm MacKeigan is the exception; the federal government appointed him directly to the position in September 1973.

11 This trend towards younger judicial appointments has been reported for other jurisdictions. See P.H. Russell, *The Judiciary in Canada: The Third Branch of Government* (Toronto: McGraw-Hill Ryerson 1987), 162–3. There was little difference in the mean age of the chief justices before and after 1967. While the average age of the seven judges elevated to the position of chief justice of Nova Scotia was 65 years before 1967, after that the average age of the next five chief justices was 63.9.

12 Greco, 'The Superior Court Judiciary of Nova Scotia,' 45.

13 Ibid.

14 Ibid.

15 A.C. Dunlop, 'Fraser, Duncan Cameron,' *DCB*, 13: 357.

16 As of April 2003.

17 Greco, 'The Superior Court Judiciary of Nova Scotia,' 46.
18 Ibid.
19 Constitution Act, 1982, s. 99, being Schedule B to the Canada Act 1982 (U.K.), 1982, c. 11; 9–20 Elizabeth, S.C., c. 56, s. 7, 20; Russell, *The Judiciary in Canada*, 173–5. For the purpose of this article, retirement dates for judges were calculated using the 'full' retirement of judges, not the shift to supernumerary status.
20 Russell, *The Judiciary in Canada*, 173–5.
21 Note that during the period 1749–1849, two judges came from parts classified as 'other,' and the birthplace of one judge could not be determined. During the period 1849–90, three judges came from parts classified as 'other.' Greco, 'The Superior Court Judiciary of Nova Scotia,' 47.
22 Humphrey Mellish and F.B. William Kelly were from Prince Edward Island; John Stanley Smiley, Arthur Gordon Cooper, Ian Malcolm MacKeigan, Kenneth M. Matthews, and Nancy Bateman were from New Brunswick; and Frederick William Bissett, Gordon Stewart Cowan, and David W. Gruchy were from Newfoundland. The judges born outside Atlantic Canada include Vincent John Paton, Constance Glube, Walter R.E. Goodfellow, Margaret Stewart, Ronald Pugsley, and Thomas Albert Cromwell from Ontario, Jamie W.S. Saunders from Saskatchewan, and Quebec's Felix A. Cacchione.
23 Metro Halifax's percentage of the Nova Scotia population grew from 12.9 per cent in 1921 to 36.6 per cent in 1996. See J. Fingard, J. Guildford, and D. Sutherland, *Halifax: The First 250 Years* (Halifax: Formac Publishing 1999), 7.
24 Greco, 'The Superior Court Judiciary of Nova Scotia,' 49–51. For a similar approach see J.R. Schmidhauser, 'The Justices of the Supreme Court: A Collective Portrait,' *Midwest Journal of Political Science* 3 (1959): 1–57. On the class composition of Canadian judges also see G. Adams and P.J. Cavaluzzo, 'The Supreme Court of Canada: A Biographical Study,' *Osgoode Hall Law Journal* 7 (1969): 61–86.
25 'Angus L. MacDonald Appointed to N.S. Supreme Court,' *Halifax Chronicle Herald*, 29 Dec. 1973, 1; 'Rogers, Hon. Roderick MacLeod,' in K. Simpson, ed., *Canadian Who's Who*, vol. 23 (1988) (Toronto: University of Toronto Press 1988), 725.
26 Greco, 'The Superior Court Judiciary of Nova Scotia,' 51.
27 Richard Donahoe, a Conservative who had served in the Nova Scotia Assembly and run in two federal elections, acknowledged this fact in a letter he wrote to Prime Minister Diefenbaker asking for an appointment to the NSSC. NAC, John Diefenbaker Papers, MG 26 N, 246891-2.
28 I. Bushnell, *The Captive Court: A Study of the Supreme Court of Canada* (Mont-

real: McGill-Queen's University Press 1992), 343–4; J.G. Snell and F. Vaughan, *The Supreme Court of Canada: History of the Institution* (Toronto: University of Toronto Press and the Osgoode Society 1985), 217–18; C. Moore, *The Law Society of Upper Canada and Ontario's Lawyers* (Toronto: University of Toronto Press 1997), 199–201.

29 'J.L. Dubinsky Dies,' *Halifax Chronicle Herald*, 5 Sept. 1989, 4; 'L.D. Currie Chief Justice; Dubinsky Elevated to Bench,' *Cape Breton Post*, 22 Feb. 1967, 1; 'Colorful Career is Recognized,' *Cape Breton Post*, 22 Feb. 1967, 3.

30 E. McCluskey, 'Supreme Court Justices Named,' *Halifax Chronicle Herald*, 21 Sept. 1977, 1; 'Justice Hilroy S. Nathanson – Distinguished Appointment,' *Shalom* 8(1) (1982): 6.

31 C. Backhouse, *Petticoats and Prejudice: Women and the Law in Nineteenth-Century Canada* (Toronto: University of Toronto and the Osgoode Society 1991); Moore, *The Law Society of Upper Canada*, 180–4, 202–3, 268–9, 306–7; M. Kinnear, *In Subordination: Professional Women, 1870–1970* (Montreal: McGill-Queen's University Press 1995).

32 Canadian Bar Association Task Force on Gender Equality in the Legal Profession, *Touchstones for Change: Equality, Diversity and Accountability* (Ottawa: Canadian Bar Association 1993), 50; C. L'Heureux-Dubé, 'Outsiders on the Bench: The Continuing Struggle for Equality,' *Wisconsin Women's Law Journal* 16 (2001): 15–30. Also see I. Grant and L. Smith, 'Gender Representation in the Canadian Judiciary,' in Ontario Law Reform Commission, *Appointing Judges: Philosophy, Politics and Practice* (Ontario: Ontario Law Reform Commission 1991); E.P. Mendes, '"Promoting Heterogeneity of the Judicial Mind": Minority and Gender Representation in the Canadian Judiciary,' in *Appointing Judges*; C. L'Heureux-Dubé, 'Conversations on Equality,' *Manitoba Law Journal* 26 (1999): 273–98.

33 She was not, however, the first woman to receive a judicial appointment in Nova Scotia. Sandra Oxner joined the Provincial Court in 1971. R.E. Kimball, *The Bench: The History of Nova Scotia's Provincial Courts* (Halifax: Province of Nova Scotia 1989), 87.

34 'Chief Justice Constance Glube,' *Shalom* 7(4) (1982): 8.

35 'PM Appoints Woman to Head of N.S. Court,' *Globe and Mail*, 10 Mar. 1982, A10. On Wilson's appointment, see Anderson, *Judging Bertha Wilson*, 124–9.

36 *Touchstones for Change*, 50.

37 'Roscoe Becomes First Woman Appointed Family Court Judge,' *Halifax Chronicle Herald*, 2 Feb. 1984, 4; D. MacDonald, 'Elizabeth Roscoe Elevated to Supreme Court,' *Halifax Chronicle Herald*, 7 Oct. 1989, A1; D. Madill, 'Province's Top Court Gets Female Justice,' *Halifax Chronicle Herald*, 25 July 1992, A3; 'Supreme Court Judge Sworn In,' *Halifax Chronicle Herald*, 5 Dec.

1992, A4; 'Campbell Makes 10 Judicial Appointments,' *Globe and Mail*, 30 Nov. 1992, A4; Kimball, *The Bench*, 185, 191; 'Hamilton, M. Jill' and 'Hood, Hon. Suzanne' in *Who's Who of Canadian Women, 1997*, 7th ed. (Toronto: Who's Who Publications 1997), 433, 475; R. Jones, 'Hood Appointed to Supreme Court,' *Halifax Chronicle Herald*, 22 Dec. 1995, A5.

38 Again, this figure excludes Family Court judges, three of whom were women in February 2002. The current Nova Scotia percentage of women trails the percentage of women on the courts of Ontario and Quebec, though it is higher than the federally appointed courts in Prince Edward Island, New Brunswick, and Newfoundland. For statistics on the gender balance of federally appointed courts see Government of Canada, Office of the Commissioner of Federal Judicial Affairs website, <http://www.fja.gc.ca/map_inter/index_e.html> (date accessed: 1 May 2003).

39 S. Borden, 'McLellan Ignores Sparks Protesters: Group Says Racism Reason Judge Passed Over for Appointment,' *Halifax Chronicle Herald*, 25 Sept. 1999, A4; A.P. Fraser, 'Exclusion "Smacks of Racism": Feds Wrong Not to Appoint Black Judge – Race Watchdog,' *Halifax Chronicle Herald*, 9 Apr. 1999.

40 F. Armstrong, 'Changing the Face of Justice: First Disabled Supreme Court Judge Promises To Help System,' *Halifax Chronicle Herald*, 1 Aug. 1998, A6; F. Armstrong, 'Justices Bring Diversity, Experience To Bench,' *Halifax Chronicle Herald*, 25 Feb. 1998, A3.

41 Greco, 'The Superior Court Judiciary of Nova Scotia,' 52.

42 J. Willis, *A History of Dalhousie Law School* (Toronto: University of Toronto Press 1979), 19; G.B. Baker, 'Legal Education in Upper Canada, 1785–1889: The Law Society as Educator,' in D.H. Flaherty, ed., *Essays in the History of Canadian Law: Volume II* (Toronto: University of Toronto Press 1983); J.P.S. McLaren, 'The History of Legal Education in Common Law Canada,' in R. Matas and D.J. McCawley, eds., *Legal Education in Canada* (Montreal: Federation of Law Societies of Canada 1987); D. Bell, *Legal Education in New Brunswick: A History* (Fredericton: University of New Brunswick 1992); Girard, 'Roots of a Professional Renaissance,' 174–5; W.P. LaPiana, *Logic and Experience: The Origin of Modern American Legal Education* (New York: Oxford University Press 1994); B.A. Kimball, 'Young Christopher Langdell: The Formation of an Educational Reformer 1826–1854,' *Journal of Legal Education* 52 (2002): 189–237; B.A. Kimball and R.B. Brown, 'The Highest Legal Ability in the Nation: Christopher Columbus Langdell on Wall Street, 1855–1870,' forthcoming in *Law & Social Inquiry*.

43 Willis, *History of Dalhousie Law School*, 6, 10, 22–3.

44 Greco, 'The Suprerior Court Judiciary of Nova Scotia,' 52.

45 The other three who did not attend university were Robert Edward Harris, Arthur Drysdale, and Frederick Andrew Laurence. There is reference to Laurence having attended Dalhousie University, but the University Archives reveals no record of his having graduated or attended the school.

46 Lorne Otis Clarke and D. Merlin Nunn from Harvard, and Marlene Jill Hamilton from the University of London.

47 Gordon Stewart Cowan and Thomas Albert Cromwell.

48 Greco, 'The Superior Court Judiciary of Nova Scotia,' 54–5.

49 'Supreme Court Judge Sworn In,' *Halifax Chronicle Herald*, 5 Dec. 1992, A4; 'Campbell Makes 10 Judicial Appointments,' *Globe and Mail*, 30 Nov. 1992, A4; Kimball, *The Bench*, 191; 'New Justice to be Sworn in Monday,' *Halifax Chronicle Herald*, 24 June 1978, 1; 'Richard, Hon. Kenneth Peter,' in Simpson, ed., *Canadian Who's Who*, vol. 23, 709.

50 'MacDonald, The Hon. Mr. Justice Robert,' in Simpson, ed., *Canadian Who's Who*, vol. 27 (1992) (Toronto: University of Toronto 1992), 653; 'MacKeigan, Hon. Ian Malcolm,' in Simpson, ed., *Canadian Who's Who*, vol. 27, 659.

51 R.E. Inglis, 'Sketches of Two Chief Justices of Nova Scotia,' *Collections of the Nova Scotia Historical Society* 39 (1977): 113; NSARM, MG 1 357 #4; 'Harris, Robert Edward,' in H.J. Morgan, ed., *The Canadian Men and Women of the Time: A Handbook of Canadian Biography of Living Characters*, 2nd ed. (Toronto: William Briggs 1912); T.W. Acheson, 'The National Policy and the Industrialization of the Maritimes, 1880–1910,' *Acadiensis* 1(2) (1972): 25.

52 B. Russell, *Autobiography of Benjamin Russell* (Halifax, N.S.: Royal Print & Litho 1932), 118; Willis, *History of Dalhousie Law School*, 29.

53 Willis, *History of Dalhousie Law School*, 104–5, 121, 168; DUA, MS 2 171 C2; 'McLellan Announces Six Judicial Appointments,' *Globe and Mail*, 29 Aug. 1997, A7; 'Nunn, The Hon. Mr. Justice D. Merlin,' in Simpson, ed., *Canadian Who's Who*, vol. 23 (1988): 635; H. MacDonnell, 'Jurists Eulogize Retired Chief Justice G.S. Cowan,' *Halifax Chronicle Herald*, 13 June 1988, 10; 'Retired Chief Justice Cowan Dies,' *Halifax Chronicle Herald*, 13 June 1988, A1.

54 Girard, 'Roots of a Professional Renaissance,' 150–5, 174.

55 W.J. Klein, *Judicial Recruitment in Manitoba, Ontario, and Quebec* (PhD thesis, Department of Sociology, University of Toronto 1975), 152.

56 P.H. Russell and J.S. Ziegel, 'Federal Judicial Appointments: An Appraisal of the First Mulroney Government's Appointments and the New Judicial Advisory Committees,' *University of Toronto Law Journal* 41 (1991): 16.

57 Arthur Drysdale (1904–5), Robert Edward Harris (1907–8; 1908–9), James Johnston Ritchie (1910–11; 1911–12), Humphrey Mellish (1912–13; 1913–14), Stuart Dixon Jenks (1923–24; 1924–5), Ronald Manning Fielding (1946–7),

Eugene Troop Parker (1948–9), Frederick William Bissett (1950–1), Thomas Herbert Coffin (1953–4), Arthur Gordon Cooper (1956–7), Gordon Stewart Cowan (1957–8), Ian Malcolm MacKeigan (1959–60), David R. Chipman (1982–3), Kenneth M. Matthews (1983–4), Edward J. Flinn (1984–5), Walter R.E. Goodfellow (June 1990), Ronald N. Pugsley (1991–2), and Jill Marlene Hamilton (1993–4).

58 Nova Scotia Barristers' Society, *Annual Report* (1899/1900–2000/2001). Also see Nova Scotia Barristers' Society, Minutes of Meetings of the Barristers' Society (1896–1970), which can be found at the Barristers' Library in Halifax.

59 Hilroy S. Nathanson, Jamie W.S. Saunders, C. Denne Burchell, Murray J. Ryan, Simon J. MacDonald, and J. Michael MacDonald.

60 Greco, 'The Supreme Court Judiciary of Nova Scotia,' 55. This figure excludes judges appointed directly from England, those without legal training, and those for whom there is inadequate information.

61 For example, Frank Harris Patterson (1916) and James Lorimer Ilsley (1916); Hugh Ross (1896) and Stuart Dixon Jenks (1896); Vincent Joseph Pottier (1920) and Vincent Christopher MacDonald (1920); Ronald Manning Fielding (1922) and Lauchlin Currie (1922); Donald Joseph Gillis (1948), Gordon L.S. Hart (1948), Vincent Morrison (1948), Hugh MacDonnell (1948), and Murray J. Ryan (1948).

62 The various partnerships included James Lorimer Ilsley and Maynard Brown Archibald; Duncan Cameron Fraser and Robert Henry Graham; Arthur Drysdale and Joseph Chisholm, and later Arthur Drysdale and Humphrey Mellish; Donald Joseph Gillis and K. Peter Richard; Tecumseh Sherman Rogers and Stuart Dixon Jenks, and later Tecumseh Sherman Rogers and Robert Edward Harris; and Hilroy S. Nathanson and C. Denne Burchell.

63 For example, the Maritime law firm of Patterson Palmer is an amalgam of several firms from which the government has selected several NSSC judges, including William Johnston Grant, Lorne O. Clarke, Kenneth M. Matthews, Jamie W.S. Saunders, Nancy Bateman, Marlene Jill Hamilton, and Robert W. Wright.

64 'Laurence, Frederick Andrew,' in *A Directory of the Members of the Legislative Assembly of Nova Scotia: 1758–1958* (Halifax: Public Archives of Nova Scotia 1958), 184; NSARM, MG 100 v.183 #10; 'Mr. Justice Pottier 1st County Court Judge Given Higher N.S. Bench,' *Halifax Chronicle Herald*, 5 Jan. 1965, 1.

65 F.B. William Kelly, Gerald B. Freeman, J. Edward Scanlan, and Charles E. Haliburton.

66 Frank C. Edwards, Douglas L. MacLennan, N. Robert Anderson, Donald

M. Hall, Hugh MacDonnell, Murray J. Ryan, Simon J. MacDonald, Ian Palmeter, Charles E. Haliburton, Felix E. Cacchione, Nancy Bateman, and Hiram Carver.

67 Margaret Stewart, F.B. William Kelly, and Elizabeth Roscoe.

68 Russell and Ziegel, 'Federal Judicial Appointments,' 10.

69 Kennedy was named chief justice of the Supreme Court in 1998. Kimball, *The Bench*, 73, 111; M. Doyle, 'Judge Carver Takes County Court Oath,' *Halifax Chronicle Herald*, 8 Dec. 1990, C1; 'Nova Scotia Judicial Appointments Announced' Department of Justice Website <http://canada.justice.gc.ca/en/news/ja/1997/ns4.html>; D. Madill, 'Provincial Court Has New Chief Judge,' *Halifax Chronicle Herald*, 27 June 1996, A9; A.P. Fraser, 'Chief Provincial Judge Moving On,' *Halifax Chronicle Herald*, 22 Apr. 1997, A5.

70 Greco, 'The Superior Court Judiciary of Nova Scotia,' 57.

71 James Wilberforce Longley, Arthur Drysdale, William Lorimer Hall, John Doull, Josiah H. MacQuarrie, and Lauchlin Currie were provincial attorneys general. James Lorimer Ilsley was federal attorney general. Daniel Duncan McKenzie was federal solicitor general.

72 Members of Legislative Assembly include Duncan Cameron Fraser, James Wilberforce Longley, Arthur Drysdale, Frederick Andrew Laurence, Daniel Duncan McKenzie, Robert Henry Graham, William Lorimer Hall, John Doull, John Stanley Smiley, Josiah H. MacQuarrie, Ronald Manning Fielding, Lauchlin Currie, Gordon Stewart Cowan, and Alexander Hugh McKinnon. Members of Parliament include James Lorimer Ilsley, Duncan Cameron Fraser, Benjamin Russell, Frederick Andrew Laurence, Daniel Duncan McKenzie, William Francis Carroll, and Vincent Joseph Pottier.

73 NSARM, MG 100 v.251 #30; L.J. Hayes, 'Final Tribute Paid – Chief Justice J.L. Ilsley,' *Canadian Bar Journal* 10 (1967): 141; J.M. Cameron, *Political Pictonians: The Men in the Legislative Council, Senate, House of Commons, House of Assembly, 1767–1967* (Ottawa: The Author 1966), 200; Dunlop, 'Duncan Cameron Fraser,' 356–7.

74 James Wilberforce Longley's legal career was secondary to his political one. Apart from a short period of time when he unsuccessfully pursued a federal seat, he represented Annapolis County in the House of Assembly from 1882 until his appointment to the bench in 1905. He was a member of the Executive Council without portfolio from 1884 to 1886, attorney general from 1886 to 1896, and commissioner of Crown lands from 1896 to 1905. Josiah H. MacQuarrie spent fourteen years representing Pictou in the House of Assembly during which time he was attorney general (1933–47) and minister of lands and forests (1938–47). In 1936, he organized the province's Department of Municipal Affairs and became its first minister, hold-

ing the position until 1947. Ronald Manning Fielding had a political career that spanned close to twenty years. A member of the Legislative Assembly for Halifax ridings from 1941 to 1960, he acted as minister of municipal affairs (1949–55), provincial treasurer (1954–56), and minister of education (1955–6). P. Girard and B. Cahill, 'Longley, James Wilberforce,' *DCB*, 15 (forthcoming); 'Longley, James Wilberforce,' in *A Directory of the Members of the Legislative Assembly*, 193; 'MacQuarrie, Josiah H.,' in *A Directory of the Members of the Legislative Assembly*, 238; 'University to Honor Jurist, Cleric,' *Halifax Chronicle Herald*, 13 Aug. 1959, 13; 'Fielding, Ronald Manning,' in *The Canadian Who's Who*, vol. 13 (1973–5) (Toronto: Who's Who Canadian Publications 1975), 334.

75 NAC, John Diefenbaker Papers, MG 26 N, 246891-2. Donahoe believed that his Roman Catholicism kept him off the bench.

76 M. Hancock, 'My Memories of Vincent MacDonald,' 8, in Vincent MacDonald Paper, DUA, MS-2-171, Box 1. On the traditional role of patronage in the selection of judges in Canada see Russell, *The Judiciary in Canada*, 113–16; J. Simpson, *Spoils of Power: The Politics of Patronage* (Toronto: Collins 1988), 305; W.H. Angus, 'Judicial Selection in Canada – The Historical Perspective,' *Canadian Legal Studies* 1 (1967): 220–51; G.T. Stewart, 'Political Patronage Under Macdonald and Laurier, 1878–1911,' *American Review of Canadian Studies* 10 (1980): 8–9; S. Hughes, *Steering the Course: A Memoir* (Montreal: McGill-Queen's University Press 2000), 166–9.

77 'Leonard Pace Dies in Halifax at 62,' *Halifax Chronicle Herald*, 25 Mar. 1991, A1; 'Pace, Hon. Leonard,' in Simpson, ed., *Canadian Who's Who*, vol. 23 (1988), 648.

78 C. Wilton, 'Introduction: Inside the Law – Canadian Law Firms in Historical Perspective,' in C. Wilton, ed., *Essays in the History of Canadian Law: Volume VII – Inside the Law: Canadian Law Firms in Historical Perspectives* (Toronto: University of Toronto Press 1996).

79 Although a few very high profile patronage appointments continue to be made, such as the selection to the judiciary of former premiers Joseph Ghiz and Clyde Wells in Prince Edward Island and Newfoundland, respectively.

80 Nova Scotia, *Royal Commission on the Donald Marshall, Jr. Prosecution* (1989); M. Harris, *Justice Denied: The Law Versus Donald Marshall* (Toronto: HarperCollins 1990).

81 For a discussion of these events see Girard, this volume. Also see *MacKeigan v. Hickman*, [1989] 2 S.C.R. 796; *Report to the Canadian Judicial Council of the Inquiry Committee established pursuant to subsection 63(1) of the Judges Act at the request of the Attorney General of Nova Scotia* (August 1990); *R. v. Marshall* (1983), 57 N.S.R. (2d) 286; C. Baar, 'Judicial Independence and Impar-

tiality in the Aftermath of the Marshall Case,' *University of New Brunswick Law Journal* 40 (1991): 253–61; M. Crawford, 'Canadian Judicial Council v. Nova Scotia Court of Appeal: A Judicial Review More Apparent than Real,' *University of New Brunswick Law Journal* 40 (1991): 262–7; '2 Marshall Case Judges Quit Bench After Probe,' *Montreal Gazette*, 10 Apr. 1990, B1.

82 R. Devlin, A.W. MacKay, and N. Kim, 'Reducing the Democratic Deficit: Representation, Diversity and the Canadian Judiciary, or Towards a "Triple P" Judiciary,' *Alberta Law Review* 38 (2000): 734–866; Russell and Ziegel, 'Federal Judicial Appointments,' 26–33; Canada, Department of Justice, *A New Appointments Process* (Ottawa 1988); *Touchstones for Change*, 185–6. The NSSC also undertook reforms to repair its image and discourage claims of racism. Girard: see in this volume. Other Canadian courts have experienced similar image crises. For a discussion of how the Supreme Court of Canada's reputation was improved during the 1930s see R.B Brown, 'The Supreme Court of Canada and Judicial Legitimacy: The Rise and Fall of Chief Justice Lyman Poore Duff,' *McGill Law Journal* 47 (2002): 559–91.

83 Stuart Dixon Jenks was deputy attorney general from 1909 to 1917. Vincent C. MacDonald was the secretary to William Lyon Mackenzie King in 1927, and assistant deputy minister of labour of Canada from 1942 to 1944, while Thomas Herbert Coffin was the national treasurer of the Progressive Conservative Association of Canada before his appointment to the bench. MacDonald was also a close personal friend of Angus L. Macdonald. Moffat Hancock recalled that Angus L. MacDonald was 'a close friend of Vince's and a frequent visitor to the house on Jubilee Road.' Hancock, 'My Memories of Vincent MacDonald,' 11, in DUA, MS-2-171, Box 1; 'Retired Supreme Court Judge Dies at VG,' *Halifax Chronicle Herald*, 3 July 1992, A7.

84 Russell, *The Judiciary in Canada*, 115. On the declining percentage of judges who held political office also see G. Bouthillier, 'Matériaux Pour une Analyse Politique des Juges de la Cour d'Appel,' *Revue Juridique Thémis* 6 (1971): 563–94; G. Bouthilleur, 'Profil du Juge de la Cour Supérieure du Québec,' *Canadian Bar Review* 55 (1977): 436–91; Klein, *Judicial Recruitment in Manitoba, Ontario, and Quebec*; Canadian Bar Association, *Report of the Canadian Bar Association Committee on the Appointment of Judges in Canada* (Ottawa: Canadian Bar Foundation 1985), 55–6.

85 'Mr. Justice Rogers Retires,' *Halifax Chronicle Herald*, 28 Aug. 1990, A6; J.M. Beck, *Politics of Nova Scotia, Volume Two: Murray-Buchanan, 1896–1988* (Tantallon, NS: Four East Publications 1988), 284.

86 'Grits Accused of Patronage in Judicial Appointments,' *Halifax Chronicle Herald*, 6 Apr. 1995, A6; C. Doucet, 'Robertson Named to Judiciary,' *Halifax*

Chronicle Herald, 2 July 1998, A1; J. Meek, 'Justice Heather Robertson: "Not Recommended"' *Halifax Chronicle Herald*, 14 July 1998, B1; D. MacDonald, 'Chipman Appointed Appeal Court Judge,' *Halifax Chronicle Herald*, 17 Sept. 1987, 1; 'Chipman Sworn in as Appellate Judge,' *Halifax Chronicle Herald*, 10 Oct. 1987, 37.

87 T. O'Blenis, 'Matthews, Palmeter Get Judicial Posts,' *Halifax Chronicle Herald*, 14 Feb. 1985, 16; 'Palmeter, The Hon. Ian Harold Morton,' in Simpson, ed., *Canadian Who's Who*, vol. 23, 651.

88 W. Taylor, 'Tory Lawyer's Appointment Sparks Furore,' *Halifax Chronicle Herald*, 1 June 1993, A1; A. Harder, 'Scanlan Sworn In; Pictou Lawyer Among the Youngest N.S. Supreme Court Judges,' *Halifax Chronicle Herald*, 23 June 1993, A5.

89 Canadian Bar Association, *Report of the Canadian Bar Association Committee on the Appointment of Judges in Canada* (Ottawa: Canadian Bar Foundation 1985), 29.

90 Russell, *The Judiciary in Canada*, 113.

91 Former Sydney steelworker Vincent Allan James Morrison (appointed in 1973) had contested two provincial elections as a CCF candidate, but in the 1968 federal election ran as a Liberal.

7

Halifax Homes of the Nova Scotia Supreme Court

BRIAN CUTHBERTSON

The First Courthouse

When Jonathan Belcher presided over the first session of the newly created Supreme Court he did so in the Buckingham Street courthouse, located at the north-east corner of the Grand Parade, at Buckingham and Argyle.[1] In the initial town plan laid out by Lieutenant John Brewse in 1749 a courthouse was to have been built on the south side of the Parade, but, for reasons unknown, St Paul's Church was placed there instead. We do not know when the Buckingham Street courthouse was finished, although some form of construction was going on in the summer of 1750.[2] It was reasonably commodious, a two-and-a-half storey building standing on a lot ninety-four by forty-three feet. It had to be, for the Supreme Court shared the building with the Halifax County lower courts – quarter sessions and Inferior Court of Common Pleas – and, from October 1758, with the newly created General Assembly. This chapter charts the history of the Supreme Court's home in Halifax. The court, of course, had many homes; it began to go on circuit in 1775, and as the circuits expanded each county was obliged to provide accommodation for it. Most of these county courthouses were multipurpose buildings, housing the local registry of deeds, probate court, sheriff's office, jail, and some municipal offices. Some of the county courthouses remain among the best examples of the province's architectural heritage, such as the courthouse in Annapolis Royal, which dates from 1837 and is still used, and that in Antigonish, built in 1855. Space constraints, unfortunately, do not permit any extended account of the development of county courthouses across Nova Scotia.

Dissatisfaction with the Buckingham Street courthouse developed in the 1780s, particularly after the Loyalist influx. There was not even an appropriate jury room until the Assembly passed a resolution to combine two small rooms into one for that purpose.[3] By 1787 the courthouse and other public buildings had apparently become 'incommodious and greatly out of repair,' and given the increase in the city's population as a result of the Loyalist influx the Assembly legislated the construction of a new building to hold the courts, Assembly, and Council.[4] This structure, to be built of brick or stone, was described as 'Public Hall' or 'Province House' and was to be built on the Lower Parade, the present site of Halifax City Hall. The cost of settling the Loyalists, however, had plunged Nova Scotia so far into debt, with government often unable to pay its bills, that nothing came of these grand plans.

The Buckingham Street courthouse survived legislative action, but not fire. Early Halifax was built almost entirely with wood and fire was always a fearsome threat. Ironically, concern about fire had led the Assembly to pass a resolution in 1780 for a 'press' to be made to hold the records in the Buckingham Street courthouse, so that in case of fire they could be quickly and easily removed.[5] On the evening of 27 July 1789 a fire broke out in Mr Kerby's Soap House. An alarm was instantly given and the bells ordered rung, a great number of people collected, soldiers from the garrison arrived, and boats from the Navy filled with seamen hastened to fight the fire. Yet 'the flames raged with irresistible impetuosity,' and the courthouse and several other buildings were entirely consumed.[6] We do not know if the 'press' for the records was ever made; certainly some were destroyed while others, though preserved, still bore 'the marks of the flames' in the 1830s.[7]

Temporary Quarters, 1789–1819

After the fire the various courts used the 'long room' of the Golden Ball Tavern, located at the southwest corner of Sackville and Hollis Streets.[8] The province's financial situation made it impossible to consider any new public buildings so the legislators sold off the courthouse lot and seized on the idea of renting space in one being constructed by Thomas, James, and William Cochran, who were among Halifax's wealthiest merchants. Their previous building had been destroyed by fire.[9] The new building was located opposite the then Government House on the site where the Art Gallery of Nova Scotia stands today. For an annual rent of two hundred pounds and the expenditure of one hundred pounds in furniture the Assembly obtained for its sittings, and for the King's Courts, the use of a low, dark, upstairs room. The Cochran Building was little more than a large warehouse, although perhaps it was not much less majestic than the delapidated Westminster Hall of the period.[10] After the war with revolutionary France began in 1793, it stored prize goods awaiting judgments of the Vice-Admiralty Court.

This temporary courthouse nearly suffered the same fate as its predecessor when, on an early February morning in 1793, the Cochran buildings caught fire. Initially, it looked as though the town faced destruction, but the combined efforts of the soldiers, seamen and the volunteer fire companies with their different engines preserved much of the Cochran structure from destruction. With its move to the Cochran Building (usually called 'the Court-House'), the court became the site for the sedan chair stand. You could be carried 'by sober, able men' from 'the Court-House Northward, to that street leading to Dutch-Town by the Haunted House, and up Cornwallis Street to Brunswick Street, Dutch-Town' for one shilling three pence.[11] The courthouse was also used for elections. Although the usual practice was to conduct polling at courthouses, the first reference to this happening in Halifax was for the 1793 Assembly election.[12] Hustings were erected consisting of a raised platform with two passageways, one for electors to mount and declare their vote, the other for them to leave. On the platform stood the sheriff, his assistants, and the candidates with their inspectors. Candidates were officially nominated from the hustings and could then address the assembled freeholders. Voting involved freeholders climbing up the passageway to the platform where they declared their vote. The sheriff recorded the elector's vote by placing a check mark opposite his name in the column of the candidate or candidates named by him. Voting took two days, and on this occasion the *Royal Gazette* noted approvingly that the contest had not been 'obstructed by the least tumult or irregularity.'[13]

War with revolutionary France brought not only Prince Edward, Duke of Kent, and his mistress Madame Julie St Laurent to Halifax, but also a new prosperity. By 1797 the provincial finances were sufficiently in order that the Assembly created courthouse commissioners to plan for a new building for the Supreme Court, Court of Chancery, and Vice-Admiralty Court.[14] By that time Vice-Admiralty and the Court of

Escheats were meeting in the dining room of Provincial Secretary Richard Bulkeley's mansion, which could seat fifty, in preference to the Cochran Building, because the Court of Quarter Sessions occupied the courthouse too much of the time.[15] The commissioners included Attorney General (and soon to be Chief Justice) Sampson Salter Blowers, Richard J. Uniacke, solicitor general and shortly afterwards to be attorney general, and Jonathan Sterns of judges' impeachment fame, who succeeded Uniacke as solicitor general.[16] They were to select a site and purchase lots of ground for a range of public buildings of brick or stone to house the Assembly, the courts, and public offices. The various buildings were not to exceed 129 feet in length, 50 feet in depth 50 feet, and 41 feet in height. This Act repealed the 1788 Act and with it the idea of siting the buildings on the Lower Parade, opposite St Paul's Church, likely because more space was desired for the projected range of buildings than was available on the Grand Parade.

The commissioners purchased a lot of ground with houses and improvements at the south end of Hollis Street for £1,000. They also bought 120,000 feet of the best pine and boards for finishing the wooden work of the buildings from the Miramichi at a cost of £450. A tender call for materials provides a picture of what the commissioners had in mind: it called for 26,000 cubic feet of free stone, of the best and most durable quality, and 80,000 bricks.[17] But these grand plans were soon abandoned, the result of a compromise brought on by a common Nova Scotian political issue, demands to spend money on roads rather than other schemes. Lieutenant Governor Sir John Wentworth had long complained of the poor condition of old Government House and had gone back year after year with requests for hundreds of pounds for repairs. He claimed it had been built of green wood and was so cold and damp that he and his imperious wife Frances's health were being affected. His perhaps somewhat exaggerated complaints, even when added to the cost of repairs, were not in themselves sufficient for the Assembly to abandon its original plan of a range of buildings to be erected south of Hollis Street. But there was also much pressure from country members to spend the increasing provincial revenues on roads. An arrangement was eventually reached whereby Wentworth would get his new Government House and the country members more money for roads. It was also agreed that the new residence would be built on the lands purchased by the commissioners for public buildings. The agreement, given legislative form in 1799, included a provision that when the new Government House was completed, old Government House was to be used for the Assembly and courts.[18]

In the meantime, with the ten-year lease for the Cochran Building coming to an end, and plans abandoned for any public buildings except Government House, there was pressing need to find suitable accommodation for the courts and the Assembly. An Assembly committee viewed a house on the public grounds where Government House was to be erected, but concluded that three hundred pounds was needed to repair the house for Assembly use and it would be necessary to build a convenient room for the Supreme Court to sit. But such alterations would so weaken the structure that gusts of wind could cause the house to fall down. Instead, the committee recommended the extension of the lease to the Cochran Building for a further three years, by which time it was expected the old Government House would become vacant. The Cochran brothers left it up to the Assembly to decide how much rental it would pay and the sum settled upon was three hundred pounds. The committee also recommended that one-fourth of the annual rental should be paid either by the Township of Halifax or by Halifax County. This recommendation likely was a factor in decision of the Court of Quarter Sessions to consider pulling down the Market House on the waterfront and erecting a County Courthouse on the site. Although the suggestion was made time and again, not until 1806 did the Sessions move to build a County Courthouse, a two-storey brick building where the old Market House stood. It took until 1810 for the building to be completed, and although much criticized, it then served as city hall, police station, and magistrates' and sessions courts until the opening of new city hall in 1890.[19]

Province House and the Supreme Court

The three-year lease for the Cochran Building allowed for an extension of up to ten more years. The Assembly and all the courts remained in that building at least until 1805, when the old Government House became vacant. Whether the courts moved into old Government House is uncertain; it is possible they remained in the Cochran Building until 1810, when the new County Courthouse was finished. Both old Government House and the Cochran Building were in a dilapidated state and unsuitable and perhaps as a result of this, or perhaps spurred by the completion of the County Courthouse, government revived the idea of new quarters for the Court. Lieutenant Governor Sir George Prevost's speech from the throne at the opening of 1811 Assembly session made specific reference to the necessity of a government building, considering the 'prosperous state of the Province.'[20]

The moment had arrived when the political will was present to proceed with the construction of a Province House, suitable to the needs of a prospering and growing province nearing 80,000 in population.

In response an Assembly committee reported in detail on its considerations for erecting a province building. It argued that 'the province is bound to provide suitable accommodation for the sitting of his Majesty's Superior Court,' and that there would be enough room in a new Province House for the Assembly, government offices, and the Supreme Court.[21] The committee thus abandoned the notion of a range of public buildings on the then outskirts of Halifax. The plan was now for a single building, accommodating the legislative bodies, the courts, and public offices; moreover, it would be located in the town's centre axis from the Grand Parade down to the waterfront and on the old Government House site. The plan was largely the work of John Merrick, the resulting legislation stating specifically that the proposed Province House was to be built to the plan and elevation made by Merrick.[22] The resulting structure, with its symmetry, regularity and uniformity, followed the British Palladian tradition in creating one of the finest, if not the finest, examples of that style in the nation.

The new Province House was completed in 1818, and the Assembly met there for the first time on 11 February 1819. Lieutenant Governor Dalhousie's speech from the throne captured the pride and confidence that it engendered: 'The circumstances of meeting you for the first time in this place, leads me to congratulate you on now occupying this splendid Building erected for the reception of the Legislature, the Courts of Justice, and all the Public Officers. It stands and will stand, I hope, to the latest posterity, a proud record of the public spirit, at this period of your history. And I do consider this magnificent work equally honorable and useful to the Province, I recommend it to your continued protection.'[23] Province House had cost £55,000 and had been built entirely at the expense of the province, but Halifax County grand juries used the building. The first grand jury to sit there echoed Dalhousie's approval of the new arrangements: 'As the Grand Inquest of this County we would do injustice to the liberality of the Legislature, did we not express our Gratitude to the General Assembly for providing so Substantial, Spacious and elegant a Building for the accommodation of the several branches of the Legislature, the Courts of Justice and all the public officers of the Province.'[24]

Of particular interest are the interior arrangements for the Supreme Court. It is clear from the exterior that the second floor, with its tall stately windows, was to be the building's chief focus. In Palladian buildings the central hall plan determined the layout of principal rooms. In Province House, these rooms on the second floor were laid out around the transverse axis of the building and centred on the grand staircase leading to the second floor. As one reached the second floor the front opened to view the Supreme Court room, while to right and left were the Council and Assembly chambers. As it was originally constructed, all these three principal rooms had high ceilings, but at some point, probably in 1824, the ceiling of the Supreme Court room was lowered to allow for a law library. When, in the last quarter of the nineteenth century, the room was converted into the Legislative Library, alcoves, shelving, and the mezzanine balcony were added. In the change to a library the room lost much of its original classical appearance and became Victorian in its decorative character.

In appearance, then, the Supreme Court room would have been more similar to the Council or Red Chamber, when the first criminal trial took place in the court's new surroundings on 28 July 1819. On trial for murder was Richard John Uniacke Jr, who had killed one William Bowie in a duel. In the first exchange both had missed, but Uniacke's second had insisted that the duelists fire again and Bowie had fallen mortally wounded. The duel and death shocked Halifax; the flags of all the vessels in the harbour were hung at half mast, and 'a general gloom seemed to pervade all ranks of the society.'[25] The attorney general should have prosecuted for the Crown, but as that individual was the father of the accused he could not do so. S.B. Robie, the solicitor general, refused because of his friendship with Bowie. The task fell to S.G.W. Archibald, a King's Counsel and a leading light of the bar. The drama of young Uniacke's trial for murder was captured by the *Acadian Recorder*: 'about 20 minutes past 11 o'clock, the Hon. Richard J. Uniacke entered the Court, supporting his son on his right arm ... He advanced to the Bench and stated to the Court, under feeling which evidently almost overpowered him, that he had an important and melancholy duty to perform that whatever his feelings might be upon the occasion, they must be subservient to the laws of the land, which he did no doubt would be administered with justice and mercy.'[26] No one apparently thought it odd that Norman Uniacke, another son and a Lower Canadian judge, sat at the table throughout the trial with Archibald, who was prosecuting his brother for murder. Another son, Crofton, sat with his accused brother. Young Uniacke's only defence was that his and his family's honour were at stake. The jury took half an hour to find him not guilty.[27]

A New Courthouse

By mid-century there was considerable unhappiness over the use of rooms in Province House by Halifax County. Although the province had paid the full cost of the building, the county registry of deeds had an office in it, and the Supreme Court room, the adjacent robing rooms, the prothonotary's office, and the law library were occupied for both provincial and county purposes. It was felt that Halifax County, 'as a county, have [sic] no just right in the building over any other county in the province.'[28] Most importantly, perhaps, it was becoming necessary for the conduct of legislative business to convert the Supreme Court room into a legislative library with committee rooms. The result was a plan for the erection of a separate courthouse to house both the Halifax County Courts and the Supreme Court, put into legislation in 1851.[29] The courthouse was to contain two rooms for the Supreme Court, with such robing and jury rooms as would be necessary. There would also be space for a law library and offices for the prothonotary and the registrar of chancery. The Courts of Chancery and Vice-Admiralty were to have the use of the courtrooms, as might be required, but were not to interfere with their use by the Supreme Court. Costs were to be shared two-thirds by Halifax County and one-third by the province. A symbol of increasing civic and provincial pride, the courthouse was just one of a series of public and commercial buildings erected and civic improvements made in Halifax between 1850 and 1870. Rockhead prison (1857) and the County Jail (1863) date from this period, as do many commercial buildings which replaced those destroyed in three major fires between 1857 and 1861. Construction in brick and stone became virtually mandatory for all new major buildings.[30]

In 1854 commissioners for the construction of the new courthouse procured plans from Henry Hill, a Halifax carpenter who had developed a successful architectural practice using wood. When tenders were called, however, none were received because the projected cost exceeded what the county and province had allocated for funding.[31] Hill was told to produce a much less expensive design, again in wood, which he did. The first of the major fires, in 1857, resulted in all thought of wood being abandoned. William Thomas & Son won the architectural competition for a new design in stone or brick. A prestigious Toronto firm, it had come to Halifax to rebuild St Matthew's Church in stone after the previous wooden church had burned down. The new site chosen was at the bottom of Spring Garden Road, a district then attracting considerable residential construction.

A vigorous debate immediately broke out in the press, not over the design, but the site. Originally the commissioners had chosen the Poor House Burying Ground, where today stands the Halifax Memorial Library. Then Messrs. Doull & Miller, who wanted to build a store on Hollis Street, convinced the commissioners that courthouse and store should be built together. A few of the legal profession with offices around Province House supported the idea. Perhaps reflecting a broader anti-lawyer sentiment then current, the *Acadian Recorder* remarked: 'A Court House is to be brought to them; not they to the Court House: such is the fiat of these gentlemen.' The newspaper vehemently opposed the notion that the court should 'engage rooms' among drapers, grocers, and druggists' shops in a crowded block on one of the noisiest streets in Halifax. Except in Halifax, 'A man would be laughed out of countenance who would propose such a thing.'[32] It favoured the Poor House site, but in the end the commissioners chose the Governor's Field, across Spring Garden from the Burying Ground and adjacent to St Paul's Cemetery, which had been closed in 1844. George Laing, who had carved the stone lion atop the Sevastopol arch at the entrance to the cemetery, received the contract to construct the new courthouse.

The laying of the cornerstone on 13 June 1859 attracted little attention; few beyond the commissioners, architect, and workmen knew about it.[33] Nor does it seem that there was any official opening; the closest to that was a speech by the chief justice to the first grand jury to meet there commenting on the 'handsome building.' The courthouse was first used in October 1860, when the Supreme Court sat there for Michaelmas Term, and by February 1861 the new courthouse was fully open for business, with the prothonotary and sheriff's office the first occupants. It was apparently not a popular location with the lawyers, who 'complain that the building is too far away from the business parts of the city.'[34] Nor was it considered an improvement; for some its 'inconvenience and discomfort' made it 'worse than the old Court Room, in the Province Building.'[35] But beyond the profession it was more warmly regarded. Built of sandstone from Wallace, Cumberland County, the new courthouse would, in the words of the *Halifax Business Directory* for 1863, 'do honour to any city in Europe, and cannot be surpassed for architectural beauty by any city of the same size on the continent of America.'[36] It was originally topped by a cupola, but that leaked and was removed in 1867.

In the allocation of space the Supreme Court received two courtrooms on the eastern and western sides of the building, on the second floor. A problem that arose immediately was the need for a room for the sessions. The Supreme Court judges 'cheerfully concurred' in the use of the western courtroom by the sessions, although at the same time they insisted that their 'independant [sic] control over their own apartments which is necessary for the convenient and comfortable discharge of their public duties while in session' should not be 'interfered with.'[37] The judges also used this opportunity to complain that 'the plan of warming the Court rooms by heating air had proved a complete failure,' arguing that it would be necessary to place stoves in the hall and courtrooms to be heated by wood. In the end, accommodation on the second floor consisted of two courtrooms, with rooms for judges' robing, witnesses, law library, barristers, and a water closet. Space on the first and third floors was entirely devoted to county offices.

In succeeding years there would be alterations and additions, including an addition at the rear of the building in 1881–2, which added the County Court room,[38] and the construction of a west wing in 1908 and a complementary east wing in 1930 as space needs grew. The 1917 Halifax explosion caused some $19,000 worth of damage to the courthouse. After the Second World War, criticism of the working arrangements and general deterioration resulted in calls for a new courthouse along with a new jail. A damning report by a grand jury in 1960 listed the problems, including poor acoustics, no separate toilet facilities for each sex, inadequate facilities for records storage, concerns that the courtrooms were so old that the ceiling might collapse, the excessive cost of heating, a lack of elevators and so on.[39] Because the cost of repairs would be so high, the grand jury recommended the construction of a new courthouse.

At the time Halifax was undergoing, as in the 1860s, a period of redevelopment, which saw the demolition of slums and the construction of such developments as Scotia Square. A century earlier the *Acadian Recorder* had sarcastically commented: 'we should not have been surprised if the Court House had been located on the Market Wharf.'[40] This, however, became the site favoured by the Court House Commissioners and Halifax City Council in 1969 for an eight-storeyed building designed by Fowler, Bauld & Mitchell. A new courthouse, it was asserted, should epitomize the revitalization of an area that had once been the busy heart of Halifax. The location of the new Law Courts was clearly intended to give impetus to civic renewal, focusing on the waterfront. By constructing a pedestrian footbridge from the downtown to an urban park or plaza surrounding the new building, Haligonians were given an opportunity to see and enjoy their harbour in pleasant surroundings, which had not been the case for decades. A central feature of this plaza is the granite fountain, a gift of the Nova Scotia bar. The city, province, and Halifax Courthouse Commission anticipated that a new Halifax-Dartmouth Ferry Terminus would be built nearby and there would be a redevelopment of the historic buildings to the north. Both these have happened, dramatically transforming the waterfront into a enviable model of its kind.

By contrast perhaps, the new seven-story courthouse was pre-eminently functional, with an exterior of precast concrete panels with virtually no decorative detailing. Functionality of purpose, not majesty, was the overriding theme. The courtrooms' interior panelling, however, involved a wide variety of fascinating materials, including 'colonial mahogany brick,' 'flat cut black cherry wood,' African mahogany, Burma teak, American black walnut and red oak. These were all chosen in part for their acoustic qualities, as the architects gave special attention to acoustics.

Reflecting the federal contribution to the new structure John Turner, minister of justice and attorney general of Canada, was the chief speaker at the formal opening ceremonies. The newspaper record of his remarks suggests he confined them to the theme that the law must reflect change in society in search of new values and defining Trudeau's 'just society.' As Turner looked ahead, some were nostalgic about the past. Just before the Supreme Court moved to its new premises in 1971, a hundred or so members of the judiciary and the Nova Scotia Barristers' Society gathered in the Supreme Court Chambers to honour the late Henry Poole Mackeen, QC and former lieutenant governor of Nova Scotia. Donald McInnes in his eulogy noted that: 'our courts will soon be moved to the new Court House. Perhaps some of the qualities and personalities of the older lawyers will be lost with this move. This very court room, and the adjoining room, can still echo the great advocacy of Henry P. MacKeen over a long period of time. Perhaps he would not have been entirely happy with new and modern facilities, but this old and revered building was his forum, and its very atmosphere was virtually part of him.'[41]

With the move to the new courthouse on the Halifax waterfront, the Supreme Court had its own building after over two centuries of sharing with other government bodies. From its inception in 1754 it had shared accommodation with the quarter sessions and the Inferior Court of Common Pleas. After the opening of Province House in 1819, the Supreme Court continued to share space, as it had from 1758, with the

Assembly. From what evidence exists it seems that this accommodation generally satisfied the court's needs, but eventually those of the Assembly necessitated the building of the Spring Garden Road Court House. While in Province House, if the splendid classical grandeur of the adjoining Council Room is any model, that of the Supreme Court room would have given an Augustan aura to judicial proceedings.

NOTES

1 For the first meeting of the Supreme Court see Muir and Phillips, this volume. In the research and writing of this paper I am much indebted to an article by the late provincial archivist, Bruce Fergusson, 'The Court Houses Built in Halifax City,' *Chronicle-Herald*, 9 July 1971. His notes can be found in NSARM, MG 1, vol. 1855, F2. Information in this paper not specifically cited is from this source and from C.A. Hale, *The Early Court Houses of Nova Scotia*, 2 vols. (Ottawa: Parks Canada Manuscript Report No. 293 1977). Jeannie Peterson undertook much of the newspaper research for this paper for which I am most grateful. Dianne O'Neill provided some useful commentary on an earlier version.

2 Cornwallis to Board of Trade, 10 July 1750, CO 217, vol. 10, 5.

3 Assembly Resolution, 31 Oct. 1780, Assembly Papers, RG 5, Series A, vol. 1b, no. 29.

4 Public Buildings Act, S.N.S. 1787, c. 10; for the text see RG5, Series S, vol. 7. Quotation from preamble.

5 Assembly Resolution, 31 Oct. 1780, RG 5, Series A, vol. 1b, no. 29.

6 *Gazette*, 28 July 1789.

7 Brenton Halliburton to Thomas James, 23 Mar. 1836, RG 1, vol. 278, no. 47.

8 *Gazette*, 22 Dec. 1789 and 16 Feb. 1790. For the Supreme Court meeting that year on a special commission of oyer and terminer see the venire issued by the judges to Sheriff James Clarke to bring twenty-four grand jurors and thirty-six trial jurors to the Golden Ball tavern at 11 a.m. on 19 February, 1790: Sessions Records, RG 34-312, Series J, vol. 4.

9 *Gazette*, 6 July 1790; Assembly and Courts Building Act, S.N.S. 1790, c. 10 – text at RG 5, Series S, vol. 7. See also T.B. Akins, *History of Halifax* (1895; Halifax: Brook House Press 2002), 100.

10 See the essay by Hay, this volume.

11 *Gazette*, 26 Mar. 1793.

12 See *Gazette*, 7 Feb. 1793, announcing that 'in obedience of the King's Writs to me directed [the High Sheriff], a Poll will open and continue agreeably to Law at the Court-House in Halifax.'

13 Ibid.
14 Court House Commissioners Act, S.N.S. 1797, c. 1.
15 Bulkeley's mansion had been reputedly built of stone carried from Fortress Louisbourg after its 1758 capture and demolition. Foundations of the mansion were incorporated into the Carleton Hotel (still standing and restored), on the corner of Prince and Argyle Streets. As the war brought more prizes to Halifax, naval captains became vociferous in their criticism of Bulkeley's use of his dining room because of the crowded atmosphere. He responded that it was a 'spacious Hall' and that the doors were always open for those who wished to attend: see Council Minutes, 19 June 1798, RG 1, vol. 213.
16 For Blowers, and for Sterns's role in the attempted impeachment of two Supreme Court judges, see the chapter by Cahill and Phillips, this volume. The other commissioners were councillors Charles Morris Junior and Thomas Cochran, and MHAs Michael Wallace and Lawrence Hartshorne.
17 Commissioners Report, 4 July 1798, RG 5, Series A, vol. 6; *Gazette*, 19 Mar. 1799.
18 Court House Commissioners Amendment Act, S.N.S. 1799, c. 9. For Wentworth's role see B. Cuthbertson, *The Loyalist Governor: A Biography of Sir John Wentworth* (Halifax: Petheric Press 1983), 109.
19 See generally B. Cuthbertson, *Halifax City Hall* (Halifax: Regional Municipality of Halifax 2000). In 1872 the *Acadian Recorder* described it as an 'uncomfortable, dirty hole,' giving off 'the rankest compound of villainous smell that e'er offended [the] nostril': *Acadian Recorder*, 15 Feb. 1872.
20 *Journals of the House of Assembly* [hereafter *JHA*], 14 Feb. 1814
21 RG5, Series A, vol. 17.
22 Merrick (1756–1829) trained in his father's Halifax painting and glazing business, and during the first decade of the nineteenth century was involved in such varied architectural projects as St George's Church, the Halifax County Court House, and the renovation of St Matthew's Church. In addition to being responsible for the plan of Province House, he was one of three commissioners who supervised its construction. See Cuthbertson, *The Loyalist Governor*, 110 and Akins, *History*, 129; E. Christian, 'John Merrick Esq, 1756–1829: Architect of Province House,' unpublished ms, 1983, at NSARM.
23 *Acadian Recorder*, 13 Feb. 1819.
24 Grand Jury Book, 12 Apr. 1819, RG34-312, vol. 13.
25 *Acadian Recorder*, 24 July 1819.
26 Ibid., 31 July 1819.
27 For this trial see B. Cuthbertson, *The Old Attorney-General: A Biography of Richard John Uniacke* (Halifax: Nimbus 1980), 76–7.

28 Committee Report, Apr. 1856, *JHA*, 1856, Appendix 83.
29 Court House Act, S.N.S. 1851, c. 3. See also Committee Report, 18 Mar. 1851, *JHA* 1851, Appendix 56. The protracted debates over the new courthouse are well summarized in Hale, *Early Court Houses*, vol. 2 171–4.
30 See S. Buggey, 'Building Halifax 1841–1871,' *Acadiensis* 10 (1980): 90–8.
31 *JHA*, 1854-55, Appendix 15 and 93.
32 *Acadian Recorder*, 22 May 1858. For anti-lawyers sentiment in the period see P. Girard, 'The Roots of a Professional Renaissance: Lawyers in Nova Scotia, 1850–1910,' in D. Gibson and W. Pue, eds., *Glimpses of Canadian Legal History* (Winnipeg: Legal Research Institute 1991).
33 *Novascotian*, 20 June 1859.
34 *Evening Express*, 11 Feb. 1861.
35 *Acadian Recorder*, 27 Apr. 1861.
36 As quoted in S. Oxner, *The Restored 1860 Halifax Court House March 1, 1985* (Halifax: n.p. 1985).
37 Clerk of the Peace to W.H. Keating, Deputy Provincial Secretary, 27 Jan. 1862, and Supreme Court Judges to Keating, 9 Jan. 1862, RG 1, vol. 271, no. 124.
38 For the dispute over space which likely precipitated this expansion see Hale, *Early Court Houses*, vol. 2, 176–7, and the chapter by Girard, this volume.
39 *Mail Star*, 28 June 1960.
40 *Acadian Recorder*, 21 Aug. 1858.
41 *Chronicle-Herald*, 24 Apr. 1971.

PART III

Case Studies

8

Michaelmas Term 1754: The Supreme Court's First Session

JAMES MUIR AND JIM PHILLIPS

Introduction

The first meeting of the Nova Scotia Supreme Court, a session of five weeks, took place shortly after Chief Justice Jonathan Belcher's arrival in Halifax on 11 October 1754. On Monday, 14 October Belcher took his seat in Lieutenant Governor Charles Lawrence's Council, and a week later, on 21 October, he was sworn in as chief justice. Though a New Englander by origin, Belcher was very much a conservative Anglophile, seeking fortune and advancement through a sojourn in a recently established colony. He doubtless liked the fact that his commission gave him all the powers of the superior common law courts at Westminster (King's Bench, Common Pleas, and Exchequer).[1] He did not proceed to exercise them for a week or so after his swearing in, but in the meantime, equally to his liking, we suspect, he took the lead role in an elaborate opening ceremony that demonstrated the majesty of the common law and the royal power that supported it.

The opening of the Supreme Court on 22 October mirrored the pageantry that attended such occasions in the English courts.[2] It began not in court at all, but at the governor's residence, from which Belcher, Lawrence, and the other members of the Governor's Council walked in stately procession through streets that the chief justice declared to be 'of a very convenient Breadth' even though 'not yet levell'd or paved.'[3] With Belcher dressed in the scarlet robes of the English High Court judiciary, they were preceded by the Provost Marshal William Foye (Nova Scotia's equivalent of the English sheriff)[4] and a man carrying the chief justice's tipstaff, as well as the constables of the town. Following on were other dignitaries and 'the gentlemen of the Bar attending in their gowns.' There would not have been many lawyers. At this time the Halifax bar had no more than seven members, including 'King's Attorney' (later attorney general) William Nesbitt, who was among those in attendance.[5] Surely Alexander Winniett, not a lawyer but the clerk of the Supreme Court, was also present; as the son of William Winniett of the Annapolis Royal Council he represented continuity with the court of the pre-Halifax regime.[6]

The party stopped first at Pontac's Inn, at the corner of Duke and Water Streets, the principal hostelry and assembly room of the new settlement, for 'an elegant breakfast' shared with other leading citizens and Army officers. Sustenance for the body was followed by food for the soul, in the form of a service of thanksgiving at St Paul's, the town's Church of England establishment on the Grand Parade. There the Rev. John Breynton, SPG missionary, preached an 'assize sermon,' one that no doubt consciously linked the earthly power of the law with the higher power of God.[7] Following the service the congregation went in solemn procession along Argyle Street to the court house at the corner of Buckingham and Argyle, which for the occasion had been 'very handsomely fitted up.'[8] Belcher took his place on the bench with Lawrence beside him, and was presented with his commission by the clerk of the Crown. The commission was then read, and the court was officially in session. Belcher was not sworn in as chief justice; that act had been completed privately, in a Council meeting the day before.[9]

The elaborate opening ceremonies – the procession through the streets, the assize sermon, the public meal – were very much a reflection of the pomp and pageantry that accompanied the meetings of the English assizes in county towns. There the full power of the law and the King's authority were paraded before the inhabitants with 'deliberate theatricality.' It was a theatricality designed to achieve multiple purposes; to demonstrate the legality of the proceedings through reading the commission, to impress upon onlookers the solemnity of an occasion that might end in one or more sentences of death, and, perhaps most importantly, to link the power of the law with two other sources of immense authority – the Crown and God. The pageantry enhanced both what has been termed the 'majesty' of the law, impressing onlookers with its mystical power, as well as its 'terror,' the very real authority of life and death over those subject to its processes.[10] The spectacle must have been rather less impressive in the still small settlement with its dirt streets and hastily built wooden houses, and perhaps had less impact on a transient and diverse population than it did in the settled communities of rural England. But it nonetheless represented an assertion of the power of the King's law and an attempt to transplant its ideology to a northern outpost of empire.

No cases were heard that day, and another week would pass before any trials took place. But the day was far from over. Although we have no record of what he said, Belcher used the occasion to give 'directions ... for the conduct of the practitioners,' and, more importantly, to swear in and address the grand jury. The twenty-three grand jurors had been chosen by lot by court clerk Winniett shortly before the court session, from a list drawn up by the provost marshal. As in England there was no formal qualification for grand jury service at this time, beyond the requirement that they be 'honest and legal men,' although a property qualification would be introduced in 1760 by local statute.[11] Despite the lack of a qualification, it was understood that grand jury service was reserved for the more eminent and wealthy members of the community; being put on the list by the provost marshal was a reflection of status and concomitantly conferred authority and influence on those chosen. The twenty-three citizens who were sworn in this day included Charles Morris, the foreman, surveyor-general of the colony, custos rotulorum (chief justice of the peace, JP) of the county, first justice of the lower civil court, the Inferior Court of Common Pleas, and a man who would later become a councillor (1755) and an assistant judge of the Supreme Court (1764). It also included Malachy Salter, one of the 'three great merchants during the first ten years of Halifax,'[12] and other leading commercial figures such as Robert Sanderson, who was later the first speaker of the Assembly, as well as JP and future councillor Benjamin Gerrish. To the extent that Halifax had an elite in 1754, many of the grand jurors belonged to it, and those that did not were lesser merchants and officials.[13] This approximately mirrored English practice, where grand jurors were always from the top rungs of town or country society, and continued to be a feature of Halifax grand juries for the next half-century at least.[14]

With the grand jury sworn Belcher 'charged' them, an event discussed in detail in the following section. The charge completed the business of the ceremonial first day, and the court adjourned. It met again for business a week later, but in the interim all its officers –

Belcher, the grand jurors, the lawyers, officials – presented a congratulatory address to Lawrence, who had just been confirmed as lieutenant governor, and he responded in kind.

Charge to the Grand Jury

The charge to the grand jury was an integral aspect of English criminal procedure. A typical address 'consisted of a ... preamble in which the virtues of the constitution and the common law, the benefits of living under the present monarch, and the mutual dependence of liberty and property were the chief themes, followed by an outline of the laws that the grand jury were particularly charged to uphold.'[15] Many English grand jury charges were published,[16] but colonial Nova Scotia does not seem to have provided much of a market for this particular literary genre; a few published in newspapers have survived, but none appear to have been printed and distributed in pamphlet form. Fortunately one of the few grand jury addresses we have from archival sources is the one Belcher delivered on 22 October 1754. It was part political sermon, part constitutional lecture, and part instruction in the content of the criminal law and the role of the grand jury in its administration.[17]

Belcher spent relatively little time on the grand jurors' role in deciding on indictments. Coming as it did in the early years of the colony and at the first meeting of the court, his address consciously linked the authority of the courts and the law to political issues. After having heaped praise on the King, and having noted that the establishment of the court over which he presided was in itself a clear example of 'Royal ... Concern for the Rights and Liberties of his Loyal Subjects,' he adjured the jurors and other listeners to be satisfied with their 'respective Spheres in Society.' This was particularly important 'in the infancy of this Colony,' one that 'has been founded and is yearly continued at a vast Emission of the British Treasure.' Belcher issued a clear warning against political dissent: 'No considerate Person will suffer himself to conceive, that any loyal Subject of His Majesty residing in this Province, *and especially any subsisting on Bread from the Crown*, can be so weak and infatuated, as to disturb and interrupt our Peace and happiness, by introducing distinction and Parties against the Government of this Province ... If this spirit should ever arise in this Province ..., we may boldly conclude that as such persons are not with us they are against us, and enemies to our Peace and Order [emphasis in original].' This was not political conformity for its own sake. Security of lives and property depended on obedience to government, for 'it will be in vain to the Execution of Laws, if any persons should be suffer'd in their Attempts to sap the very foundations of Government.'

Belcher was no doubt influenced in his remarks by two incidents which could indeed potentially sap the 'very foundations of Government.' One was the recent Lunenburg insurrection, quelled by troops early in 1754. Its leader was imprisoned in the Halifax jail.[18] The other was a case pending in the court that term, which involved the murder of two naval sailors. The priggish Belcher's address also expressed sentiments common in eighteenth-century England; he devoted some of the time to urging the jurors to go after sabbath breakers, drinkers, idlers, and gamblers because he believed that such practices led inexorably to more serious forms of criminality.

The address also discussed the grand jurors' criminal law duties, but not until he had reminded them of the links between political subordination and the criminal law. Belcher outlined the different classes of crimes and urged the jurymen to indict only on good evidence. They should weigh the 'Credit and Character of Witnesses in their Country,' and be wary of malicious prosecution. They should also decide doubtful cases in favour of the accused, for 'it is for the public Interest that the Guilty should rather escape than the Innocent should be punished.' Yet he also warned that the guilty should 'find no refuge' in the jury room. In this he returned to a theme with which he had begun. The 'Sword of Justice' was given them, he had said, and 'it highly imports you for the sake of your Country to wield it for the safeguard and protection of the innocent, and to the terror of the noxious and guilty.'

On other occasions Belcher probably spent more time on the substantive criminal law. Among his papers are a set of notes on charges to grand juries, which shows him to have relied on a published English standard charge. There is a good deal in these notes about the different roles of grand and trial juries and the definitions of offences.[19] But this was his first address, and he tailored it to fit the occasion. He ended with a clarion call to arms: 'The expectation of your Country, Gentlemen, is attentively fix'd upon your proceedings,' because 'their Prosperity and happiness are so deeply involved, in a vigorous Execution of the Laws, for the Defence and Practice of Religion and Morality upon which must depend the being and quiet of this and every other Community.'

Similar sentiments, and a similar sense of the link between the law and loyalty, were expressed in the addresses which the court and

Lawrence presented to each other a few days after the ceremonial opening. Lawrence was promised the court's 'most vigilant endeavors for the ease and success of your administration,' and he in turn assured the court that 'the authority of Government shall be ready to support the law.' The law, said the lieutenant governor, 'is the form and solid basis of civil society, the guardian of liberty, the protection of the innocent, the terror of the guilty, and the scourge of the wicked.'[20]

The Court at Work: The Criminal Calendar

The criminal calendar of the NSSC's first session was extensive compared to most of the previous sittings of the General Court, which had last met in late April. Belcher had to deal with all the cases which had occurred since then – ten incidents involving some twenty-one defendants. The cases provide a rich source for examining many aspects of mid-eighteenth-century criminal law and procedure.

The first stage in the process was the presentation of those accused of an offence to the grand jury, which took place in the grand jury room, in the absence of the judge and the public, when the court reconvened on Tuesday, 29 October.[21] The prisoners charged with serious property and violent crimes had been languishing in jail because bail was very rarely granted, and were now brought in by the provost marshal and the indictments, prepared by the court clerk from depositions taken by JPs , were read to the accused and the grand jurors.[22] The grand jury heard only the prosecution evidence, given on oath, a proceeding justified in English law by the fact that their role was only to decide whether a case should go to trial, not to deliberate on guilt or innocence.[23] The grand jurors heard only the oral evidence of usually two or three witnesses, and did not consider the depositions taken by JPs in investigating complaints. As Belcher himself had put it in his address to the grand jury, this supposedly permitted them to 'discern the Countenance when it gives the Lye to the Tongue.'[24] It took a simple majority, and a total of twelve jurymen, to find that there was a case to answer, and in that instance they returned the indictment a 'true bill.' If not, the foreman wrote 'ignoramus' on the back and the prisoner was discharged.

Perhaps because this was the first meeting of the court absenteeism was not an issue among the grand jurors; all twenty-three ruled on one of the indictments, twenty-two on the others.[25] The grand jury found all but one of the indictments presented to it, involving twenty-one individuals, to be 'true bills,' a high but not unusually large ratio;[26] John Hovey avoided indictment only because he had escaped from jail and was not present in court.[27] Belcher ordered that outlawry proceedings be begun against him; we have no evidence that this was done, but if it had been Hovey would have effectively been convicted and liable to have his property forfeited to the Crown.[28] There were a number of reasons why grand jurors indicted most defendants, and did so quickly, usually disposing of all the cases in one day. In part it can be attributed to the fact that the standard of evidence required was not high. But indictment was also likely because grand jurors were very much the kind of men with substantial property to lose and thus inclined to be concerned to prosecute crime vigorously. Seven of the twenty-three men who were grand jurors at the Michaelmas Term are known to have prosecuted at least once in the Halifax courts in the 1750s and 1760s. In addition, grand jurors were experienced at the process. Over 60 per cent of the grand jurors who served in the Halifax General and Supreme Courts in the 1749–65 period did so in more than one session, and on multiple cases within sessions.[29] Nineteen of the twenty-three had served previously on a General Court grand jury, and one other on a General Court trial jury. One of the three who had not served was Morris, the foreman and Inferior Court judge.

As it turned out there were no Supreme Court trials for twelve of the people indicted, for Belcher ordered their cases to be sent to Quarter Sessions for trial. By the mid-eighteenth century the English assizes were trying only the more serious cases, and for the most part the Supreme Court adopted the same jurisdictional demarcation between it and the sessions. Thus four people charged with assault, three accused of 'riotously & forcibly entering the house of Thomas Youngson and abusing the wife of the said Youngson,' and five indicted for keeping a disorderly house were all sent to the Quarter Sessions. That left seven men and women indicted by the grand jury on 29 October to be tried for more serious offences. Belcher's arrival thus represented an immediate change in practice for the colony's highest court. In the previous five years the General Court had tried many less serious offences, but Belcher saw his court as one in which only 'Criminal Matters of an higher nature are cognizable.'[30]

The criminal law applied in Belcher's court was that of England. It was universally accepted that the common law was in force in the new colony, and Belcher believed that all of the English statute law on crimes and punishments was also in force – although he was to be disabused of this notion a few years later.[31] Briefly, that meant that offences were divided into felonies and misdemeanours. The former included all the serious offences against the person, such as murder, manslaughter, and rape, as well as all property offences. The history of punishments in this period is complicated, but two general features are important. First, all felonies were capital at common law, although that same common law allowed a first-time offender to escape punishment by pleading benefit of clergy. Although benefit of clergy was at various times restricted – to men, to the clergy, to the literate – by the mid-eighteenth century it was available to everyone. However, and this is the second key feature of the law of punishments, a series of statutes from the Tudor period on had removed clergy from particular offences, so that by the 1750s a wide range of offences were automatically capital ones, including murder, rape, burglary, robbery, and dozens of thefts carried out in particular circumstances and involving goods of a particular value. After 1691 it was a capital offence, for example, to break into a house during the day if nobody was at home and steal goods worth five shillings.[32] Had the offence occurred at night, it would have been burglary and capital even if no goods were taken.

All serious criminal trials in this period were jury trials. Sometime before the session the provost marshal had selected a group of about thirty to thirty-five men to attend the court for jury service, and when the court convened on the 29th those present were assigned to cases as they came up. English law required trial jurors to meet a property qualification of ten pounds a year in freehold, copyhold, tenements, or rents, or a long leasehold of twenty pounds a year, although the first Nova Scotia Assembly reduced this qualification substantially in 1759. The English rules were probably thought applicable in Halifax before 1759, and likely introduced by Council ordinance, for the trial jurors of this and other court sessions in the first decade and a half of Halifax's existence were not markedly different in socio-economic status from the grand jurors. There were fewer members of the elite, and more artisans, on trial juries than on grand, but the status gap between the juries was nowhere near as great as it was in England nor as great as it became in Halifax. More than half of those who served on grand juries in the 1749–65 period also did trial jury service.[33] Like the grand jurors, trial jurors were experienced at the process. At least eleven of the twenty-four men who sat this term had been on trial juries before, and a further three had been on a grand jury. Repeat service continued to be a feature of the trial process throughout the eighteenth century.

Four general features of the trials that took place this term are noteworthy. First, although more men had likely been called for jury service, only twenty-four of them served for the five cases of the session, involving eight defendants, that were actually tried. Three men served on all five juries, six on four of them, and a further three on three. This was an unusually high degree of turnover between cases, the result probably of the fact that one trial was very long and that the trials were quite widely spaced through the session, as discussed below. Other sessions in the 1750s saw most trial jurors chosen to adjudicate sit on most if not all of the cases. Second, trials were generally short affairs, involving limited evidence, mostly that of the victim/prosecutor, and a short, sharp confrontation between accuser and accused. This first session of the court, however, saw an unusually long, ten-hour trial. Third, in this period the prosecution of most crime was the preserve of the victim or victim's family. It was the victim who was expected to carry the case, first to the JP and then, when the offender got to the court, he or she was expected to turn up and provide the principal evidence. If there were other witnesses, it was again the victim, not a police agency, who was responsible for getting them to court. Most of the questioning would be done by the judge. However, once in court, Nova Scotian procedure differed from England in that the attorney general prosecuted many cases. Belcher spoke warmly of the 'services and diligence' of Nesbitt on this occasion, referring to his 'great usefulness and assistance to me in the court,' and he probably prosecuted all the cases.[34]

Fourth, and finally, defence lawyers played a very limited role. Although they seem to have been permitted in all cases by the rules of the General Court, English law, which Belcher insisted on, left it entirely to the discretion of the judge whether to permit them. Only about a quarter of the defendants in the Supreme Court had counsel in the second half of the eighteenth century, about the same ratio as in England. Of course many defendants could not afford a lawyer in any event, and others would have found one of little use, for lawyers' roles were greatly circumscribed. They could argue points of law, and some judges allowed the questioning and cross-examination of witnesses. But defence counsel could not address the jury. Although over time more and more defendants, especially those accused of capital crimes, were permitted counsel, it did not become a right until 1840, four years after English law made it one, and at that time the restrictions on what lawyers' could do were lifted.[35]

When it came time to try the various defendants each was brought in by the provost-marshal and arraigned by the clerk of the court. The records do not allow us to know exactly the order in which the court's criminal business was conducted, but it seems likely that the five cases were dealt with in three blocks. First came three trials, probably conducted on 29 October, the same day that the grand jury found their indictments. In one Samuel Chip, a private soldier, and his wife Elizabeth Chip, described as alias Elizabeth Burt, had been indicted for robbery and assault on one John Folliard. The crime had taken place on one of the main streets of the town on 1 June, and the couple had therefore spent almost five months in jail awaiting trial. The offence of highway robbery was capital under English law, having been removed from clergy in 1531.[36] The Chips, as was invariably the case, pleaded not guilty, and escaped conviction because the prosecutor failed to appear. They therefore benefited from the system's substantial reliance on the initiative of the victim, and from the fact that it was rare for a case to be held over from one term to another; it may have been that, in any event, the victim had left Halifax. Elizabeth was discharged but Samuel Chip did not go free, although the proceedings book and Belcher's report on the session state that he was found not guilty. His case is noted in another source as 'continued,' and the same source also says that he was 'put on board a Man of War.'[37] The legal basis for this is unclear but it was likely an exercise of the royal prerogative of mercy. Unusually, since he had not been convicted, he was given a pardon and relieved from possible future prosecution by 'agreeing' to serve in the navy.[38] Elizabeth Chip stayed in Halifax for a few more years, eking out a living on the margins of society, and she reappears in the court records of Michaelmas Term, 1757, convicted of petit larceny with one Mary Penfold for stealing two shirts. Each was sentenced to be publicly whipped with twenty strokes on their bare backs.[39]

The second of the cases probably disposed of on 29 October involved one George Lease (an anglicized version of Leau), a mason from Montbeliard who was tried for petit larceny.[40] The indictment recounted that he had stolen goods worth ten pence from the house of his master Charles Morris, on or about 15 October. In what would seem to us a remarkable conflict of interest Lease was therefore prosecuted by the foreman of the grand jury that had indicted him. Yet Lease may have benefited from this; had the grand jury set the value of the goods stolen at a shilling or more he would have been charged with the more serious offence of grand larceny. Grand larceny was one of two felonies capital at common law but to which benefit of clergy still applied (the other was manslaughter). A person convicted of grand larceny could plead clergy and escape with the thumb being branded (to show that they had 'had their clergy'). The penalty for petit larceny, as we have just seen, was perhaps worse – a public whipping – but it did not risk a capital sentence on a second offence. The list of goods stolen in the indictment suggests that Lease actually took more than a shillings' worth, and the value given in the indictment demonstrates another feature of the period's criminal law – prosecutors and/or grand or trial juries had the power to 'down charge' an offence if they chose.[41] Lease pleaded not guilty, and after hearing the evidence the jury – the same twelve men who had sat for the Chips's trial – retired for 'a short time' and returned with a verdict of not guilty.

The third case was unusual in involving as defendant a woman alone; only some 15 per cent of prosecutions were brought against women in eighteenth-century Halifax.[42] Anne Westman was accused of grand larceny, the indictment alleging that she had broken into the house of one Ann Davis, widow, and stolen pewter dishes and linen cloth. The indictment made it clear that nobody had been at home when she entered; had there been somebody the theft would have been a felony without benefit of clergy, a capital crime. Had the goods taken been valued at five shillings, whether or not someone was present, it would again have been a capital offence.[43] This seems another and even clearer case of down-charging, for the grand jury valued the pewter at three shillings but left the value of the cloth unstated. The evidence, whatever it was, did not convince the jury, and after retiring for a few minutes they also found her not guilty. For the jury to return not guilty verdicts in three cases was unusual for eighteenth-century Halifax. In non-capital offences the conviction as charged rate was 59 per cent, with a further 9 per cent of defendants convicted for a lesser offence.[44] The numbers are too small, however, for this session to have been significant, and in any event the Chips were only acquitted for lack of evidence.

The fourth case, the trial of John Moor, must have taken place well after the start of the session, for it was on 7 November that Moor was alleged to have stolen twelve fowls worth a total of nine shillings from the warehouse of Calvin Gay. Moor's case shows us that the grand jury stayed constituted throughout the session, and that offences which were detected while the court sat could be brought forward immediately. On apprehension Moor was taken before the same grand jurors as the other defendants, and indicted. He was on trial for his life, for stealing goods worth at least five shillings from a warehouse was capital by the 1691 English statute that removed clergy from housebreaking in the same circumstances. His indictment referred to the offence as 'against the form of the statute in that case made and provided,' a term used when the offence or punishment was statutory rather than common law in origin (in which case the phrase was 'against the peace of our said Lord the King his crown and dignity'). No prosecutor took pity on him, nor did the grand jury. But the trial jurors did. They found him guilty after retiring for a little while, and must have known about and discussed the sentence for stealing goods worth nine shillings, for they valued the stolen property at only 4*s* 10*d*. This took the case out of the statute and made Moor guilty of grand larceny only. He was still sentenced to death, but was able to plead his clergy and received a brand of the letter 'T,' for thief, on his thumb.

By far the major case of the session was the trial of three merchant seamen, Benjamin Street, Samuel Thornton and John Pastree, for the murders of two naval sailors, John McDermott and Isaac Jolly.[45] The incident took place in the Bay of Fundy on 27 July. Captain Kinsey of *H.M.S. Vulture* suspected, correctly, that a Boston-based sloop, the *Nancy and Sally*, was trading with the French at Fort Beausejour. *Vulture* chased the *Nancy and Sally* around the Bay of Fundy for a day, firing at her to get her to stop and be searched, but she ignored the command and took refuge in Musquash Cove. Kinsey considered the anchorage too dangerous to take his ship into, so he sent a boat. As the sailors neared the merchant ship shots were fired at them, which the ship's pinnace returned, and once alongside a volley of small arms fire was emptied into the boat, killing Jolly instantly and mortally wounding McDermott – he died at Annapolis four days later. Kinsey took all the crew prisoner and brought them to Halifax. The case was a politically charged affair. In September and October the Council passed regulations prohibiting the export of grain without the governor's permission, largely because it was believed that ships like the *Nancy and Sally* were providing provisions to the French.[46]

The four presented to the grand jury included three who had fired at the *Vulture's* boat – Street, Thornton, Pastree – and John Hovey, captain, who had apparently given the orders to resist and to fire, although he was in his cabin when the crucial events took place. As noted above, however, Hovey had broken out of Halifax jail in late September, and no indictment was returned in his case. True bills were found, but the

The First Courthouse, 1754–89. Richard Short came to Halifax in 1758 as a purser with the Royal Navy prior to the Siege of Louisbourg, and over-wintered before going with Wolfe to Quebec in 1759. His drawings of Halifax were worked up as paintings by Dominic Serres and issued as a suite of six engravings in 1764. Together, his *View down George Street* and *View down Prince Street* provide a panorama of early Halifax. A building running 94 feet along Buckingham Street and 43 feet along Argyle served as the first courthouse in the province. This can be seen at the extreme left of the detail picture, just above the Printing House, the small building with a steeple. On 22 October 1754, Chief Justice Belcher in his scarlet robes led a procession from the Governor's House to the Pontac Inn (the large four-gabled building in the centre of the detail photo) for a ceremonial breakfast, thence to St Paul's Church for a sermon, and finally to the courthouse for the first session of the Supreme Court in the province. After a fire in July 1789 destroyed the building, the court met for a few months in the long room of the Golden Ball, a tavern at the corner of Sackville and Hollis.

The Second Courthouse, 1790–ca. 1819. Between 1790 and 1819, the court met in rooms rented from the Cochran brothers, who had just erected a building on the site now occupied by the Art Gallery of Nova Scotia. The building also housed the Legislative Assembly. The earliest depiction of the Cochran Building, in John Elliott Woolford's 1817 view of Halifax from the Citadel, dates almost to the end of its tenure as the Supreme Court. In the detail picture, this two-and-a-half-storey building can be seen to the left of the not-yet-completed Province House, the building with the pillared portico just beyond the tall steeple of St Paul's Church and the Town Clock.

The Court at Province House, 1819–61. The Supreme Court and Legislative Assembly continued to share space in Province House, completed after eight years of construction in 1819. The first purpose-built quarters for the court lay at the head of the staircase on the second floor, where the Legislative Library is today. Almost immediately the space became too small, so the ceiling was lowered about 1824 to create a law library on an upper level. Inspired by the Crystal Palace exposition of 1851 in London, Nova Scotia turned Province House into the venue for its own Agricultural and Industrial Exhibition in 1854. The enthusiasm of the Victorian period for all things progressive is captured in Robert Wilkie's depiction of Province House in its Exhibition guise, when the Supreme Court briefly became home to a display of labour-saving devices.

Spring Garden Road Courthouse, 1860–1971. Jurisdictional disputes among the province, city, and county delayed the erection of a new building, which was needed long before one was actually achieved in 1860. After Halifax's disastrous fire of 1857, the original plans for a wooden structure were abandoned in favour of one built of brown stone from Mary's Point, N.B., to an elegant design submitted by William Thomas & Sons of Toronto and executed by George Laing (or Lang) of Halifax. With the creation of the County Court in 1876 competition over space became acute, and a new courtroom was added to the rear of the building in 1882. West and east wings constructed of sandstone from Wallace, N.S., were added in 1908 and 1931.

The most elaborately decorated courthouse in the province, the new building aroused great civic pride among the citizenry. In 1878, after the Marquis of Lorne took his oath of office as Canada's governor general in Halifax, he and Princess Louise were brought in a celebratory procession to the courthouse through a triumphal arch erected on Spring Garden Road. The steeple is that of St Matthew's Church, also newly erected after the fire of 1857.

Spring Garden Road Courthouse in oils. Artist Anthony Law based his painting on the 1872 photo, but added more street life in contrast to the serene, almost laconic photographic rendering by Rogers. After briefly serving as the provincial library when the Supreme Court vacated in 1971, the Spring Garden Road Courthouse became the home of the Provincial Court in Halifax, in which capacity it still serves.

Spring Garden Road Courthouse. The Supreme Court sat in the East Court Room on the second floor, where impressive Eastlake panelling imparted a sense of stability, solidity, and awe.

Lady Justice, stained glass window, Spring Garden, by Robert McCausland, 1883. With a wreath of mayflowers (the provincial emblem) in her hair, the Crown of St Edward at her feet, and a border of maple leaves around her, Lady Justice symbolizes Nova Scotia's ties to English common law and the federal law of a new Canada. The window was designed for the County Court Room addition to the courthouse in 1883. This Justice wears no blindfold, perhaps so she can see the splendid surroundings the province has afforded her in what has been described as one of the most flamboyantly decorated courthouses in the country.

The Law Courts, 1971–. By 1960, the courtrooms at Spring Garden Road were obsolete and acoustically inefficient, the jail deplorable, witness rooms non-existent, and the library floor in danger of collapse. Although the market wharf north and east of Province House had been deemed an inappropriate site in the 1850s, with the opening of the new seven-storey Law Courts Building in 1971 near the site of the earlier market, the Supreme Court returned to the heart of the city. Designed by C.A. Fowler, its concrete and glass exterior reflects the modernist ideals established by Mies van der Rohe for material honesty and structural integrity. The same minimalism obtains inside, where acoustic concerns dictated the various woods chosen for panelling each courtroom.

The Law Courts in oils. Seen from across the harbour, the law courts appear to float on the water in this painting by Anthony Law. Their prime waterfront location may make them vulnerable to relocation: in early 2004 the use of the site for a much-expanded ferry terminal was being discussed.

General Trollope's Arch. A triumphal arch erected for the visit of the Prince of Wales to Halifax in 1860 provides a frame for the newly constructed courthouse (right). The original cupola seen here was later removed because of leaking.

Argyle Township Courthouse in Tusket. The oldest standing courthouse in Nova Scotia, and in Canada, hosted its first court session on 29 October 1805. The Court of General Sessions was held here at least once a year until 1836, and thereafter the Supreme Court visited Tusket annually on circuit until 1925. Gordon Hatfield's photograph of voters gathering outside the courthouse in 1901 suggests the central role the building played in the community. Hatfield, who abandoned a successful career as a professional photographer in 1915, served as stipendiary magistrate in the courthouse until his death in 1944.

Liverpool Courthouse. Considered one of the finest American Greek Revival buildings in the province, the Queen's County Court House was built in 1854 by George W. Boehner to plans drawn by William G. Hammond, a local carpenter. The grand jury had accepted Boehner's gift of the land on which the courthouse sits, but when Boehner submitted his construction bill for four hundred pounds, the local magistrates refused to pay it because they would have preferred a different site. Finally, Mr Justice Haliburton settled the matter in favour of Mr Boehner at a sitting of the Supreme Court in the new 'comfortable and commodious' courthouse in 1855.

Annapolis Courthouse. Built in 1836–7 by Francis Lecain to replace a 1793 structure destroyed by fire, the courthouse at Annapolis Royal is the oldest operating courthouse in the country. The judge's bench is backed by rich panelling in a Palladian design. In 1994 the municipality designated this courtroom as the Grand Chief Membertou Room, in honour of the Mi'kmaq chief who welcomed Champlain and Des Monts to the region in 1604.

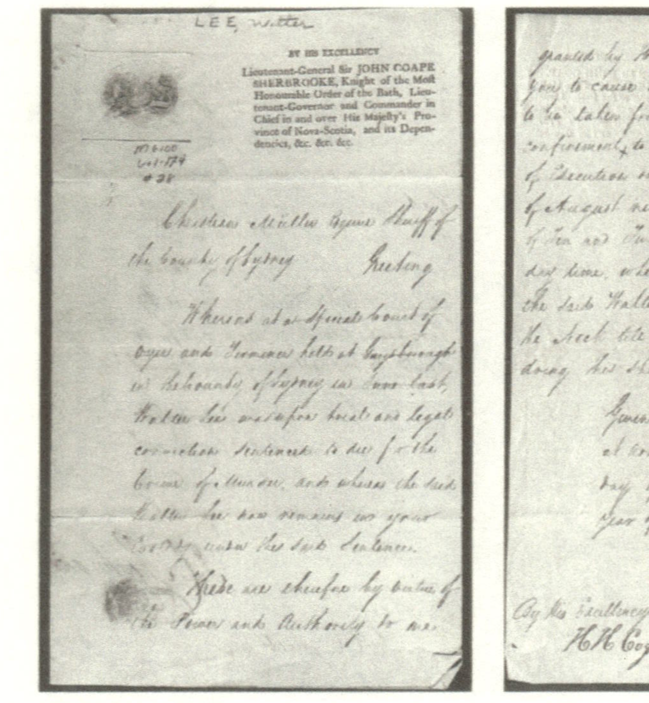

LEE, Walter

BY HIS EXCELLENCY

Lieutenant-General Sir JOHN COAPE SHERBROOKE, Knight of the Most Honourable Order of the Bath, Lieutenant-Governor and Commander in Chief in and over His Majesty's Province of Nova-Scotia, and its Dependencies, &c. &c. &c.

Christopher Miller Esquire Sheriff of the County of Sydney Greeting

Whereas at a Special Court of Oyer and Terminer held at Guysborough in the County of Sydney in June last, Walter Lee was after trial and legal conviction sentenced to die for the Crime of Murder, and whereas the said Walter Lee now remains in your Custody under the said Sentence.

These are therefore by virtue of the Power and Authority to me

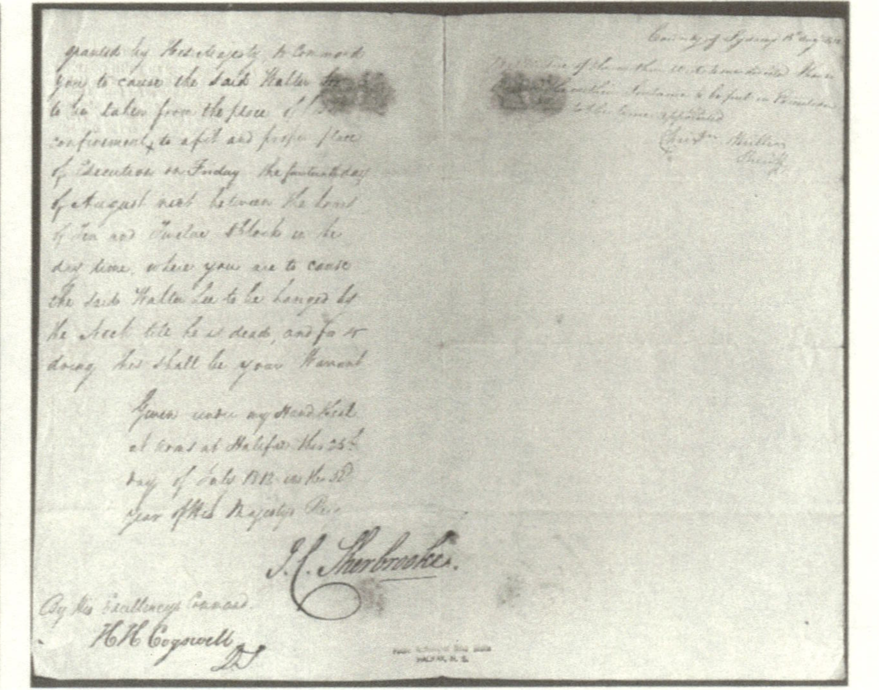

granted by His Majesty to Command you to cause the said Walter Lee to be taken from the place of his confinement, to a fit and proper place of Execution on Friday the fourteenth day of August next between the hours of Ten and Twelve o'Clock in the day time, where you are to cause the said Walter Lee to be hanged by the Neck till he is dead, and for so doing this shall be your Warrant

Given under my Hand and Seal at Arms at Halifax this 25th day of July 1812 in the 52d year of His Majesty's Reign

J. C. Sherbrooke.

By His Excellency's Command

H H Cogswell

Warrant for the execution of Walter Lee, 1812. Lee was convicted of murder at Guysborough in June 1812 and hanged on 14 August. He was tried by a special commission of oyer and terminer naming Supreme Court Judge George Henry Monk to preside.

Bas-relief of Joseph Howe's trial for libel, 1835. To commemorate the centenary of Joseph Howe's birth in 1904, the Nova Scotia government commissioned a statue of Joseph Howe to be erected on the grounds of Province House. To execute it they chose Quebec artist Louis-Philippe Hébert, the most skilled Canadian sculptor of his generation. On the pedestal of the statue Hébert added this bas-relief of the 1835 trial.

Following the verdict of acquittal, Howe was met with a terrific ovation outside the Province Building, where a vast crowd had gathered to await the historic decision of the jury.

pal government anywhere in the province and the affairs of the city and county were managed by the magistrates, appointees of the Crown. Grievances abounded on every side, for which redress was sought in vain. Excessive assessments were

shook their heads and advised Howe

returning with a verdict of "n guilty."

It was then that pandemonium broke loose in the streets and Halifax went wild with joy, the Freedom of the Press was once and for all decided, and Howe, exhausted but happy, was the idol of the hour. What had been done was realised at once as

Joseph Howe victory cartoon, *Daily Star* (Halifax), 4 March 1935. The centenary of the trial evoked some self-congratulation, and a commemorative ceremony organized by Chief Justice Joseph Chisholm, who also published in the *Canadian Bar Review* that year the first, and for a long time the only, scholarly account of the trial.

Gallows, Halifax, 1935. The makeshift appearance of the structure belies its sombre purpose. On 7 March 1935 Daniel Sampson was the last person to be executed in Halifax, for the murder of two boys, Edward and Bramwell Heffernan. When Everett Farmer was hanged in Shelburne County Jail on 11 December 1937 for the murder of his half-brother Zachariah, he became the last person to be hanged in Nova Scotia. Both Sampson and Farmer were Afro-Nova Scotians.

'The Nova Scotia Justice System,' *Chronicle Herald*, 30 January 1990. This reaction to the revelations of the Royal Commission on the Donald Marshall, Jr, Prosecution illustrates how the Supreme Court had come to be seen as one part of a larger apparatus understood in systemic terms.

Media coverage of the Donald Marshall case and the inquiry was extensive. 'Anything on the Hook' unconsciously predicts Marshall's second round of litigation before the Nova Scotia courts, where he sought recognition of aboriginal fishing rights granted under a treaty of 1760–1 and succeeded in the Supreme Court of Canada.

'Anything on the Hook?' *Chronicle Herald*, 2 February 1990

'Nova Scotia Five Donald Marshall,' June 1990.

Sampson Salter Blowers (1742–1842), chief justice of Nova Scotia 1797–1833. A Boston-born Loyalist, Blowers had achieved professional distinction and high office before the American Revolution, having been appointed solicitor general of New York in 1781. He served as attorney general of Nova Scotia from 1784 before being named chief justice in 1797. His long tenure marked the end of a somewhat insecure colonial infancy for the court, and saw its status and reputation secured as a respected provincial institution.

Sir Brenton Halliburton (1775–1860), assistant justice, 1807–33, chief justice of Nova Scotia, 1833–60. Born in Rhode Island, Halliburton came to Halifax with his Loyalist parents as a child. His marriage to the daughter of Bishop Charles Inglis cemented his status within the Nova Scotian elite, and he was named to the court as an assistant justice in 1807 at the age of thirty-one. Like Blowers, Halliburton imparted an aura of authority and respectability to the court.

Thomas Chandler Haliburton (1796–1865), a justice of the Nova Scotia Supreme Court 1841–56. Haliburton served as chief justice of the Middle Division of the Inferior Court of Common Pleas from 1829 to 1841 before his appointment to the Supreme Court. He was the court's best-known nineteenth-century judge, albeit more for his literary reputation as author of the 'Sam Slick' stories than for his legal acumen. Upon his resignation from the court he moved to England, became MP for Launceston, and received an honorary DCL degree from Oxford in 1858.

Sir William Young (1799–1887), chief justice of Nova Scotia 1860–81. Nova Scotians never quite got over Premier Young's decision to appoint himself chief justice in 1860. In the public mind his egotism always overshadowed his positive qualities. Young could be an astute if occasionally temperamental jurist; he was a strong supporter of the establishment of Dalhousie Law School in 1883; and his philanthropy aided libraries, education, and helped to embellish the Halifax Public Gardens with statuary.

Sir Charles Townshend (1844–1924), puisne judge 1887–1907, chief justice of Nova Scotia 1907–15. Townshend had been a member of both the provincial Assembly and Parliament before his appointment, but hated politics and only put in time in that capacity in order to secure a judicial position. He served the court with distinction and became its first historian, publishing a book-length history of the Supreme Court and the Court of Chancery (of which his grandfather Alexander Stewart had been the last Master of the Rolls) in 1900. His imperial affinities were matched by his imperious demeanour, caught here by Sir Edmund Wyly Grier, one of Canada's prominent portraitists of the first half of the twentieth century. Grier lived in Halifax from 1940 to 1945 and painted portraits of several Nova Scotian judges and politicians.

James Lorimer Ilsley (1894–1967), puisne judge 1949–50, chief justice of Nova Scotia 1950–67. A brilliant politician, Ilsley served as MP for King's-Hants 1926–48 and held three Cabinet portfolios under Mackenzie King: national revenue (1935–40), finance (1940–6), and justice (1946–8). His tenure was marked by a surge of divorce petitions which transformed the court into a family law court almost overnight. The photographer's presentation of Ilsley suggests efficiency and earnestness, lightened by his slight smile, in contrast to the feelings of awe evoked in portraits of earlier chief justices.

Vincent-Joseph Pottier (1897–1980), puisne judge 1965–70. The first Acadian appointed to the Nova Scotia Supreme Court, Pottier had strong advocates as far back as 1949 but had to settle for a place on the County Court instead. He was named to the County Court at Halifax in 1947 and served there until his promotion to the Supreme Court. While a judge he conducted a number of important royal commissions on the financing of the public education system, municipal taxation, and conditions in mental hospitals. The strong, weathered hands in this heroic Karsh portrait have an elemental quality suggesting firmness, solidity, and humanity.

Lorne Otis Clarke, puisne judge 1981–5, chief justice of Nova Scotia 1985–98. Lorne Clarke taught at Dalhousie Law School from 1952 to 1959 before entering private practice. He dealt with the aftermath of the Marshall inquiry and inaugurated sweeping changes in the relationship between the court, the bar, the media, and the public during the 1990s. This portrait and the next suggest both professionalism and accessibility; the subjects are portrayed as human beings who happen to be judges, rather than icons of law, order, or justice.

Constance Rachelle Glube, puisne judge 1977–82, chief justice of the Trial Division 1982–98, chief justice of Nova Scotia 1998–. Born in Ottawa, Constance Glube was one of very few married women with children to attend law school in the 1950s. Chief Justice of the Trial Division Gordon Cowan was initially highly sceptical of his female colleague but came to respect her to such an extent that he probably recommended her as his successor. She became the first female chief justice in Canada with her appointment as chief justice of the Trial Division in 1982, just days after Bertha Wilson was appointed as the first woman on the Supreme Court of Canada.

trial did not take place until 25 November. The delay was the product of doubts about whether the Supreme Court had jurisdiction in the case or whether the killings had been committed on the high seas, which would have made it a matter for the Admiralty. Although the Admiralty Court proper had once had jurisdiction over capital crimes committed at sea, the inadequacies of the civilian procedures used there had led in the sixteenth century to a shifting of jurisdiction to something called Admiralty sessions. A commission would be issued to the Admiral or his deputy, and three or four other persons, to try the case by common law procedures and with a grand and trial jury drawn from whatever county the commission designated. Trial by Admiralty sessions was thus not unlike trial on a special commission of oyer and terminer, especially given that at least one common law judge was invariably included in the commission. The principal differences were that special commissions had to sit in the county they were named for and try the case with a jury from that county; Admiralty sessions could sit anywhere, as designated by the commission, and draw a jury from anywhere.[47]

The geographical distinctions between Admiralty sessions' and common law courts' jurisdiction evolved over time, and were on occasion the subject of contention, for the Admiralty and the common law courts engaged in a centuries-long battle for jurisdiction in a variety of areas of law. Space does not permit a detailed account of the law and its application to this case, but there were 'several arguments' during November 1754 about whether bodies of water within county boundaries meant it was an Admiralty sessions case, and about the fact that one person had been wounded at sea and died on land. Both issues were canvassed in an opinion written for Belcher, probably by Nesbitt. The law on the problem of two locations, the author said, was 'not certainly fixed at this day,' although Belcher himself seems to have had no doubt that '[i]f Part of the Matter be done upon the Sea, and part in a County, the Common Law shall have all the Jurisdiction.'[48] Concern about whether the *Nancy and Sally* had been within the headlands of Musquash Cove, making it within the county, was manifested before and during the trial; lawyers on both sides asked questions determined to elicit exactly where the merchantman was when the attack occurred.[49]

Belcher thought the jurisdictional issue one 'of some difficulty,'[50] and has left us with inconsistent evidence of his opinion. On the one hand he ruled that the Supreme Court did have jurisdiction. On the other hand, when sentencing the convicted defendants, he noted that 'as the stroak appears by the evidence to have been given to Jolly and McDermott at full tide in the cove, that it then appeared to the court that the cognizance of the facts belonged more properly to the admiralty.' He may have changed his mind after hearing the trial evidence. Given that he would have had access to the depositions and the full facts of the case before trial, however, the inconsistency is more likely explainable in part by the fact that the form of trial would be the same in any event: 'As the Law now Stands the Tryal before the Admiralty must be by Jury the same as by Oyer & Terminer or before this Court.' Another part of the explanation may simply be that he was dissatisfied with the result – conviction for manslaughter, not murder – for after expressing his doubts he went on to say that 'the proceedings of this court on these facts should by no means be looked upon as determinative if they should hereafter be considered as not within the jurisdiction of the court, and that the verdict of the jury should be subject to this reserve.' In any event he was anxious to know London's opinion of his decision to proceed, and concerned when he still had not had an answer at the end of 1755.[51]

When the case finally came on it proved to be an unusual one, both for its length – it lasted some ten hours – and for its complexity, for it saw extensive legal argument and a substantial role played by lawyers for both prosecution and defence. 'King's Attorney' William Nesbitt presented the crown's case, as he likely had done in most, if not all, of the other cases. But unusually there were defence counsel present as well, in the persons of Otis Little, the second man to become a member of the Nova Scotia bar and formerly the King's attorney, and his Harvard classmate Joseph Kent. Little's chequered legal career in Massachusetts and Nova Scotia included being dismissed from the post of Nova Scotia's King's attorney in 1753 for extorting a bribe. Although he was also forbidden to practise at the General Court, he was able to make a living in private practice for a brief while before leaving the colony, and his 'disbarment' was either unknown to Belcher or ignored by him, or perhaps not applicable to criminal proceedings. Kent was the leading criminal defence counsel of the period as well as having an extensive practice in the Inferior Court of Common Pleas, and he had defended John Hoffman earlier in the year on his trial for instigating the Lunenburg uprising.[52] Little and Kent were allowed to participate by Belcher, a decision he would later regret.[53]

Before the jury was chosen the defence lawyers introduced a legal issue, arguing that the *Vulture* had had no right to stop, board, and search the *Nancy and Sally*. If it did not, the lawyers argued, the accused were within their rights in repelling an armed invasion of their property. We assume, although it is not stated in the trial report, that the purpose of introducing this argument at this stage was to have the murder indictment quashed. The principal argument was based on the Navigation Acts, the foundation of the old colonial system which sought to exclude foreigners from the imperial trading network. The law required all colonial trade to be carried out in British owned and manned ships, which included colonial ships. In addition, all goods going to the colonies, whatever their point of origin, had to go through a British port, and specifically enumerated articles of colonial produce had first to be exported to a British port. To help enforce these laws Courts of Vice-Admiralty were established in the colonies and the British commissioners of customs appointed colonial agents – Captain Kinsey was one, although naval ships had the power in any event to seize any merchantman that imported or exported goods into or from a colony in any other ship.[54]

While the trade laws were wide-ranging, Little argued that the *Nancy and Sally* had not breached any of the regulations. Thus it did not matter that the *Nancy and Sally* was trading livestock and provisions with the French; there were no laws against doing so if the countries were not at war. Having asserted the lack of any statutory power, Little also insisted, citing Hawkins's *Pleas of the Crown*,[55] that the general powers given to sheriffs and other peace officers to break in doors and arrest persons required that a prior demand be made, and that even with a demand either a warrant or clear evidence that a felony had been committed was required. By analogy a ship at sea was the same as a man's house on land, and given that the first attack had come from the *Vulture* the merchantmen were entitled to defend themselves. The defence also argued that the captain of a naval ship had no powers once on land, which was effectively where the events had taken place for the purpose of giving the Supreme Court jurisdiction.

Little and Kent were perhaps encouraged to make these arguments by the fact that in early October, when it legislated to prohibit the export of grain from Nova Scotia, the Council had also conferred search and seizure powers on the navy to enforce the new regulations.[56] The Council's actions suggested that such powers had previously been lacking. But Belcher clearly found the defence arguments unpersuasive, though it is not known why. He did manage to force Little to a concession that a naval captain had the power to stop a vessel on the high seas to check whether it was a pirate ship, and we would surmise that Belcher saw the action in the cove as a continuation of a legitimate stop and search exercise, one that the crew of the *Nancy and Sally* had no right to resist. But it is also worth noting that the *Nancy and Sally* was found to have traded illegally by the Court of Vice-Admiralty, and designated as a prize as a result.[57]

The defence arguments against the validity of the indictment having been rejected, the trial proceeded. As usual the defendants pleaded not guilty. The twelve jurors comprised seven of the men who had sat a few weeks earlier for the Chip and Lease cases, one man who had been on Westman's trial, and four others who had not served on any previous cases that term. But the final jury was constituted only after Nesbitt had challenged two jurors for cause and the defence had exercised nine peremptory challenges. At common law, and by local statute after 1758, the accused had a right to challenge as many as twenty peremptorily and others for cause, and the Crown had a right of challenge as well. But neither in England nor Nova Scotia were juror challenges common in this period; unfortunately we do not know the basis of any of the objections, nor indeed who the challenged men were.[58]

The prosecution called five witnesses, officers and sailors from the *Vulture*, who gave what must have been in some cases extensive testimony. The principal points which Nesbitt seemed to wish to draw out, in addition to the easy and uncontested fact that the sailors had been killed by shots fired from the *Nancy and Sally*, were fourfold. First, that Captain Kinsey had reliable information that the merchant ship had traded with Fort Beausejour, had sold the French garrison provisions and livestock. Second, that the *Nancy and Sally* had initially entered the Bay of Fundy flying the English flag, then had put up French colours, and then, on her last voyage when she was overhauled, had flown no flags at all. Both of these first two points presumably went to the validity of the decision to stop and search the merchantman, as did the third – that Kinsey believed he had the right to stop the ship if it was trading with the French, both by virtue of his status as a naval Captain and because he had a customs officer commission. Fourth, that while both parties had engaged in warning shots from a distance, the first shots fired when the two boats were close together had come from the *Nancy and Sally*, and had followed a clear statement that she was to be boarded in the name of the king. Here the prosecution wished to undercut any argument that Street et al. were engaging their right to self-defence. All of the Crown witnesses were cross-examined by Kent and/or Little, who mostly seem to have tried to cast doubt on whether the merchantmen had been warned that it was a naval boarding party, whether they could have been sure of that fact.

When the defence turn came, Kent's opening statement indicated that he would seek to establish that the men who had fired did not know that the *Vulture's* crew claimed to be conducting a lawful search; rather, they were concerned about being press-ganged. While impressment was legal, there was strong authority for the need for it to be carried out with due process – the proper warrants, reasonable force, and the like – and many lawyers considered resistance to it reasonable in the absence of such proper authority.[59] But the evidence of the defence witnesses, three men who had been on board the *Nancy and Sally* but who were not charged, went not only to the issue of the crew's belief that they were being pressed but also cast doubt on who had fired first. One witness also suggested that the merchant seamen were concerned that they were to be boarded by Indians.

With the evidence completed Little again argued, this time in front of the jury, his points about the validity of the search, as part of his claim that it was not murder but justifiable homicide. He did not address the jury, for lawyers could not do that, but rather made his arguments to Belcher. Little does not seem to have pressed the impressment point, but made two other arguments. He cleverly suggested that if it was done by virtue of Kinsey's status as the commander of a naval ship it was illegal because it was not carried out on the high seas: it must have been carried out within the bounds of land, 'otherwise this court could not proceed in the trial.' He also claimed that a search based on Kinsey's customs commission was invalid because Kinsey himself was required to be present. Belcher rejected both arguments. Kinsey was allowed to continue his pursuit which had started on the high seas, and he needed to remain in command of the ship and was fully justified in deputing the actual search to those under his command. Little also argued the more general point, that the navy had been the aggressors and that if Street et al. believed they were being unlawfully attacked they had a right to defend themselves. Kent made the same argument.

Obviously none of this impressed Belcher. And, as was often the case with English judges, he made his views on guilt plain. In his summation to the jury he made it clear that in his opinion '[t]he evidence appeared plain and sufficient to support the indictment for murder.'[60]

He also told the jurors that the jurisdictional question was still unresolved, and that if some higher authority deemed that it was an Admiralty matter the present proceedings might be a nullity.

Belcher clearly believed in the defendants' guilt, but he was not the man making the ultimate decision. The lawyers' arguments impressed the trial jurors enough that after the usual 'short time' retiring and deliberating they acquitted on the murder indictment and found the three men guilty only of the lesser offence of manslaughter. Belcher was furious. He could do nothing to stop the defendants pleading benefit of clergy when sentenced to death, but he did tell them in his sentencing speech that he thought them guilty, that they were lucky to have had lawyers who had likely allowed them to 'escape the just sentence of death,' and that the branding they were to receive would mean that they 'were publicly marked out as offenders and criminals in blood' so that 'on any future verdict you may be known and excluded from this benefit [of clergy], and receive death as your immediate portion.' They had spilled blood 'in the cause of treachery to your sovereign,' resisting when called to account for 'supporting the enemies of the King' who were intent on 'the destruction of the province.' He warned them that they might yet be prosecuted for high treason, although this proved an empty threat. All that he ultimately could do was impose an additional punishment of nine months' imprisonment, allowed by an Elizabethan statute. This was done, Belcher fulminated, because 'your Crimes are attended with such circumstance of indignity to the Crown, of treachery and ruin to His Majesty's faithful subjects of this province.'[61] In similar vein he told London that he had imposed the additional sentence of imprisonment because '[t]he circumstances in the course of the evidence was so apparently full of insult and indignity to the Crown, and of dangerous consequences to this province, that it was thought highly incumbent on the court to manifest its resentment against their crimes.'[62] Like Samuel Chip earlier, the three were 'put on Board a Man of War' in July 1755, an act which appears to have had no legal basis, unless it was seen as a form of impressment.[63]

We cannot know why the jury decided that the defendants' offence did not merit capital punishment. They may genuinely have believed that the men were defending themselves against an over-zealous navy, although in that case an acquittal might have been more in order. As many were merchants, some may have harboured a more general dislike of navy captains who enforced the trade rules too vigorously. Given the extensive trading and other relationships between Halifax and Boston some among the jurors might have had ties with Bostonians who lobbied on behalf of the accused; we know that this went on, at least in the case of Street, and we know also that Hovey was well-connected to Boston merchant circles.[64] Any of these reasons might suffice to lead the jury to find the men guilty of the lesser, effectively non-capital offence, or it may simply have been that this jury, like many others in eighteenth-century Halifax and England, shrank from a finding of guilt because they did not wish to see men hang in the particular circumstances of the crime.[65] Discretion has been a consistent presence throughout this account of the criminal cases decided in Michaelmas Term, 1754. The discretion of victims, prosecutors, grand jurors, and trial jurors all worked to defendants' advantage; that was never so obvious as here, where the jury, with the power of life and death, manipulated a result to spare three men the gallows.

The Court at Work: The Civil Calendar

When the 1754 Michaelmas session started seven civil trials were scheduled. Like the General Court before it, the Supreme Court's civil jurisdiction was essentially limited to appeals. Although actions involving members of the General Court (councillors) could begin at the Supreme Court, all other civil actions had to go first to the quarterly Inferior Court of Common Pleas.[66] As in older British North American colonies, however, it was relatively easy to appeal. English common law allowed dissatisfied litigants to appeal judgments only through the use of a variety of narrowly defined writs, including those of false judgment, attaint, and error, each of which required the appellant to prove specific faults with judge, jury, or the writs and pleas in the original trial. The hearing would be on the contention of the writ. If the appellant succeeded, a new trial or hearings would be held in the original court. An appeal doctrine did develop in the English civilian courts (ecclesiastical, Chancery, and Admiralty) that allowed for retrying disputes in a different, higher, court, but there was no analogue at common law.

In contrast Virginia, Massachusetts, and other North American colonies had created a hierarchical court structure in the seventeenth century, with summary jurisdiction, lower courts, higher courts, and the Governor and Council at the local peak. Colonial lawmakers established new rules for appeals at common law based to some degree on the civilian appeal doctrine, whereby litigants who felt the result of a trial was unjust could appeal to the next court up the hierarchy.[67] Nova Scotia followed these North American practices. Appellants could request an appeal on decisions they felt were unjust without having to use the English common law writs. At the appeal the action would be tried again, without requiring the appellant to prove any specific legal failings or errors at the first trial. All seven of the civil actions scheduled for the Michaelmas Supreme Court term of 1754 were appeals from the Halifax Inferior Court's June and September sessions. As things turned out Belcher had a significantly smaller role to play in the civil proceedings at this early court than he did in the criminal cases, because none of the seven actions actually went to trial before judge and jury.

Two of the cases ended in arbitration. In the first, William Russell, a trader, had sued John Young, described by Russell as a 'gentleman or trader,' for thirty pounds at the June 1754 Inferior Court session.[68] Russell accused Young of failing to pay an outstanding account debt of £24 15*s* for the rent of a longboat for fishing expeditions. David Lloyd represented Russell at trial and Joseph Kent represented John Young.[69] Civil defendants, unlike those involved in criminal trials, had the right to an attorney, and often the attorney would represent an absent defendant at all stages of the trial. The dispute was tried before a jury, which found for Russell but awarded him only 11*s* 3*d* in damages. Russell was not prepared to accept such a small damage award, and Lloyd immediately announced his intention to appeal. Merchant John Webb put up a bond of twenty pounds, and two other merchants, Nepthali Hart and Joseph Jones, each put up sureties of ten pounds, guaranteeing that Russell would follow through with his appeal and appear to try the action again. A bond and sureties were required of all appellants before their appeal could go ahead so as to prevent frivolous appeals.

Sometime prior to the start of the trial Russell, the appellant, and Young, styled the 'appellee' in this period rather than 'respondent,' agreed to avoid a second trial by going to arbitration, and thus on the day scheduled for their trial the two litigants and their attorneys appeared before Belcher and moved for arbitration by rule of court. The motion was granted. Russell appointed Thomas Hardwell, a merchant and shipwright, as his arbitrator and Young appointed Napthali Hart, merchant and one of Russell's sureties. The parties nominated their third arbitrator as well – Francis Coburn, a tavern keeper and trader.

Private arbitration had a long history in England, Europe, and the Americas. By the 1690s the English courts of Common Pleas and King's Bench were willing both to allow arbitration by rule of court as a substitute for litigation and to enforce awards through writs of attachment for contempt of court. The 1698 Arbitration Act codified the practice of ensuring that agreements to arbitrate could be made rules of court and confirmed enforcement through contempt proceedings. Similar practices of allowing rule of court arbitration and of enforcement marked the work of North American colonial courts before and after the 1698 statute.[70]

Arbitrators appointed under a rule of court would meet away from the court, hear whatever evidence the parties wished, and then make an award; a majority, not unanimity, was all that was needed. Having decided, the arbitrators would report back to the court. In Russell's case the arbitrators reported back to Belcher on 6 December 1754, awarding Russell damages of £9 18*s* 6*d* and costs. Belcher confirmed it as his judgment in the case, and as a result it could be enforced in the same manner as any other judgment of the court, by writ of execution allowing Russell to have the provost marshal imprison Young or take and auction Young's property to cover the outstanding debt. We assume that Young paid up, for there is no record of an execution. There are, ironically, records of the later fates of two of the men involved in this case. Young was convicted in 1756 of the offence of counterfeiting and uttering foreign coin and sentenced to death; he escaped the gallows when London told Belcher that the English statute making his offence a capital one was not in force in Nova Scotia.[71] Coburn was similarly fortunate; he too was sentenced to the gallows by Belcher following a 1768 burglary conviction, but he was pardoned on condition that he leave the colony.[72]

The second case not to be tried at the Michaelmas session because it went to arbitration was *Balitho* v. *Catherwood*.[73] Halifax merchant Richard Catherwood had been sued at the September 1752 meeting of the Inferior Court by John Balitho, a mariner who identified himself as being from 'Halifax alias Philadelphia,' which probably meant he was usually resident in Philadelphia. He made no other court appearances in Halifax. Balitho's suit was on a debt owed for casks of wine valued at £11 5*s*. To prove his case at the Inferior Court Balitho presented a copy of his accounts, showing Catherwood's debt. Catherwood provided an alternative account, showing payments of £12, suggesting, in fact, that Balitho owed him 15*s*. The jury did not accept Catherwood's counter-account, and they entered a verdict for £11 5s as Balitho claimed. Catherwood also tried to counter Balitho's suit with one of his own at the same Inferior Court session, claiming a debt of £12 10s. The action was dismissed by the justices without going to a jury.[74]

Catherwood appealed his loss in Balitho's action to the Supreme Court. Like Russell, each litigant appointed his own arbitrator: Catherwood appointed William Magee; Balitho appointed Jonathan Prescott. In this case, and in most arbitrations, the court appointed the third arbitrator; Belcher selected Charles Hay. There is no record of the arbitrators' award in this action.

The resort to arbitration in these two cases was by no means unusual. In the Supreme Court's first decade at least twelve actions ended in arbitration, with thirty-three going to jury trials.[75] Like the jurors discussed above, arbitrators often developed a great deal of experience. Arbitration was available in Halifax at both the Inferior and Supreme Courts, and there seems to have been no difference in the arbitration practice of the two. Of the arbitrators selected in *Russell v. Young*, Francis Coburn was acting as one for the first time in Halifax, Napthali Hart had already arbitrated one other civil action in 1754, and Thomas Hardwell had arbitrated four others between 1751 and 1754. Charles Hay, the court's chosen arbitrator in *Catherwood* v. *Balitho*, had never before arbitrated, but Jonathan Prescott had been on four arbitration panels since 1752 and William Magee had been on twenty-one panels since 1750. Prior experience allowed arbitrators to better evaluate the evidence presented and to determine fair awards. 'Fairness' here was a different sort of fairness from that expected of a jury trial. Arbitrators were selected because of their experience not just as arbitrators, but as men (at this time in Halifax they always were men) experienced with the workings of business. It is no coincidence that among the arbitrators selected for both of these disputes were several merchants or traders. These were men who could understand the documents put before them. They also shared with the merchant and trader litigants a common sense of justice, especially as it related to credit and good business practice. For litigants involved in trade it must have seemed sensible to rely on the opinions of three men involved in a similar occupation and invested in the same sorts of credit relations as those disputed in the action – more sensible than relying on a jury composed not just of fellow traders, but also yeomen and craftspeople.

The other five cases scheduled for the Michaelmas 1754 session demonstrate other aspects of civil litigation in this period. For example, the ease with which appeals could be pursued allowed litigants to utilize them as delaying tactics. William Piggot, a tavern keeper and trader, was sued at both the June and September Inferior Courts in 1754. In June, Piggot was called to answer the suit of William Frobisher, a Boston chandler. Frobisher accused Piggot of being in debt to him for £35 16*s* on a promissory note. Piggot denied the debt, but the jury found for Frobisher for all he claimed. In September Piggot was sued by John Anderson, a Halifax merchant, for £52 17*s* 6*d* on an account debt. Again Piggot fought, and again the Inferior Court jury found for the plaintiff to the full value of his claim.[76]

Piggot appealed both actions to the Supreme Court, even though his chances in either case were slim. The promissory note alone was sufficient evidence in court to prove Piggot's debt to Frobisher. Only if he could successfully challenge the note as a forgery or prove that he had paid back the debt, in full or in part, could he beat Frobisher. His failure at the Inferior Court suggests he had no such evidence. Account debts were easier to contest in court because defendants, like Catherwood when Balitho sued him, could present alternative accounts showing different debts. Juries or arbitrators would then evaluate the two accounts and any additional evidence that either litigant presented to decide the true value of the debt. When Anderson sued Piggot in September, Piggot appears not to have presented any alternative account. If he did, the jury remained unconvinced.

Piggot's appeals would therefore have been unlikely to succeed, and he realized this himself. When the two cases were called to be tried at the Supreme Court, Piggot's attorney appeared and withdrew the actions. Piggot, the attorney said, could not deny that he owed Anderson £52 17*s* 6*d*. Similarly, Piggot acknowledged his debt to Frobisher and withdrew. The Inferior Court judgments now stood unchallenged and Anderson and Frobisher could return to that court to seek executions. In the circumstances the appeals to the Supreme Court were likely for the purpose of delaying payment. Faced with two sizeable debts, and without the cash or goods on hand with which to pay them, Piggot had few options to avoid imprisonment or sale of his property by public auction. Appealing both actions would postpone his creditors' ability to collect on the debts and allow him time to acquire what he needed to pay them. Defendants used a variety of delaying tactics – seeking continuances, bargaining with the plaintiff, concealing assets – to postpone having to pay the judgment, hoping any extra time would help. Going to appeal entailed accumulating greater court costs and finding a bond and sureties, but people resorted to it nonetheless.

The only records that remain of the other three civil cases scheduled for the Michaelmas 1754 term are notes prepared for trial by George Suckling, perhaps Halifax's leading attorney.[77] One of Suckling's cases, *Winston v. Grant*, involved a female appellant, Catherine Winston.[78] At the Inferior Court Winston had been sued by John Grant, a local surgeon, for £25 6s, most of which was for medicines and medical care Grant had administered to her now deceased husband. Winston's presence was an unusual event; between 1754 and 1764, in cases where we know the gender of the parties, only 7 of 114 appellants or plaintiffs were women, and only 6 of 108 appellees or defendants. Several of the women who appeared in the court were widows like Catherine Winston, sued for their husbands' debts or suing his debtors. The most frequent female litigant in the Supreme Court in its first ten years was Anne Webb, who took over her husband John Webb's trade after his death, and appeared in the court four times.

Another of Suckling's cases, *Binney v. Lowell*, was an appeal by local merchant Jonathon Binney, who lost in the Inferior Court, against Ebenezer Lowell of Boston. Like Frobisher and Balitho, Lowell was from the older North American colonies to the south, and in this respect an uncommon sight in the Supreme Court. Between 1754 and 1764, most of the 219 litigants at the court whose homes can be identified were from Halifax and the surrounding area; only four were from the rest of British North America, eight from other parts of Nova Scotia, and seven from other parts of the world.

The third of Suckling's cases, *Schuchard v. Young*, involved John Young, the same 'gentleman and trader' sued by William Russell. Young and Piggot thus both made multiple appearances in the Supreme Court. This was common. Between 1754 and 1764, 134 different people appeared as litigants in the court, 81 appearing in only one action. Thirty-five people appeared twice as litigants and 18 between three and eight times. The 53 people who appeared in the court two or more times account for more litigant appearances than those who appear only once. Moreover, as an appellate court, all the litigants in the Supreme Court had already appeared in lower courts prior to coming to this court. That Young and Piggot were each involved in two appeals at one time was exceptional, but their experience at litigation was not. All Supreme Court litigants had some experience in courtrooms before coming to the court, and several acquired a great deal of experience in the Supreme

Court itself. This experience allowed them to better predict outcomes for actions and strategize about their courtroom appearances and decisions to appeal, to go to trial, and to arbitrate.

Two more points can be made about the civil docket for the court's opening term. First, litigants used attorneys much more frequently in civil actions than they did in criminal trials. Records from the supreme court between 1754 and 1764 show appellants using attorneys in twenty-eight (27 per cent) of 105 cases, appellees using thirty-nine (37 per cent). Attorneys were more prominent in civil than criminal proceedings because there were few restrictions on their use and because the litigants involved were on the whole probably better able to afford legal counsel. Over time, the presence of attorneys could change the shape of the trial. Bruce Mann has argued that in the first half of the eighteenth century, as attorney use grew in the Connecticut civil courts, the attorneys changed from pleading to the issue and going to trial to pleading in bar of the action or demurrer.[79] Both of these pleas turned on issues of law or the conjunction of law and facts; attorneys would present arguments and the judge or judges would decide without juries.[80] This was not the case in Halifax in the early years, although things would change with the exercise of original civil jurisdiction by the Supreme Court after 1764.[81] Despite the use of defence attorneys, most defendants before the mid-1760s chose either trial by judge and jury or arbitration. There is little evidence of attempts to plead either demurrer or in bar of an action in Halifax. Sucklings's notes in the three cases in which he was involved seem to be in preparation for trials by jury, although whether they got that far is unknown.

Second, the evidence presented here shows that civil litigants were often from particular groups within Halifax society. Jonathan Binney, Richard Catherwood, and John Anderson were all identified in court documents as 'merchants'; William Piggot, William Russell, John Schuchard, and John Young were all identified as 'traders' of one sort or another. This dominance of traders and merchants was a general facet of the court's work in the early years. Of sixty-one appellants identified by occupation between 1754 and 1764, twenty-two were called 'merchants' and four 'traders'; of 58 appellees, eighteen were 'merchants' and five 'traders.' No other occupations were as well represented; artisans and craftsmen (butchers, carpenters, masons, tailors, and others) only account for nine plaintiffs and nine defendants. Overall, therefore, the litigants in the civil actions at this first session were representative of Supreme court litigants during the Court's first decade. Most litigants were male, local, and merchants, traders, or of similar background. Nonetheless, some women and some people from away did come to the court, and while those involved in commercial careers predominated among litigants, people from other occupations and backgrounds appeared as well, including chandlers and other craftsmen.

Conclusion

From the beginning the Nova Scotia Supreme Court, with its criminal and civil jurisdiction, touched upon the lives of a wide range of the colony's populace as litigants, jurors, and others. As historians of eighteenth-century England have argued, the courts were frequently the arm of the state with the most direct and regular contact with the populace.[82] In Halifax this most certainly was true. But while the courts and law touched the lives of a wide variety of Halifax residents, their dealings with the law were often mediated through others. Attorneys for both plaintiffs and defendants were common in civil suits; they appeared regularly even without their clients being present. On the criminal side many prosecutions were conducted by the attorney general, a departure from English practice. If attorneys mediated litigants' place in the courtroom, the frequent service of members from a variety of classes as jurors and arbitrators ensured that locals played a direct role in deciding cases and determining punishments and awards. And however much their appearances as litigants were shaped by their attorneys' advice, as jurors and arbitrators, as these cases show, they were willing to take positions different from those of Chief Justice Belcher.

Belcher's own involvement in the activities of the Supreme Court changed depending on the matters before him. In the opening ceremonies and in his charge to the grand jury Belcher was the centre of attention. During the proceedings that followed, he remained ultimately in charge and made rulings on the law. Yet he could not tightly control the juries in criminal trials, and his role was even more reduced in civil actions; litigants either dropped actions or removed them from the purview of the court to be decided by arbitrators. Although in the end Belcher would confirm the arbitrators' awards as his judgments, he had no control over the evidence presented to them, the arguments made, or their methods of decision making.

As first chief justice of the colony and sole judge of the Supreme Court, Belcher was an exemplar of the law he enforced. Born in Massachusetts and a member of the English and Irish bars, his life spanned the eighteenth-century Atlantic world. The law in Halifax was likewise Atlantic in its origins. The criminal law and the criminal procedures were derived entirely from England. Yet the very idea of a supreme court, superior to other courts in the colony, and the appellate jurisdiction it had in civil actions, were American innovations. The grand and petit juries were similar in make-up, and in the decisions they made, to those of England, yet while arbitration existed in England, its practice in Nova Scotia was closer to that of other parts of British North America. The Nova Scotia Supreme Court, like its chief justice, was an Atlantic institution.

The first session of the Supreme Court was not very different from those that followed. Other essays in this volume trace the history of the court, its litigants, its juries, and its decisions over time. A close investigation of this single session complements those studies by offering a sense of how the court worked on a day-to-day basis. The opening ceremonies and the address to the grand jury exemplified the majesty of colonial governance, while the proceedings themselves show us how ideas of justice shifted between people of different ranks in the society and in different roles in the courts: prosecutors, defendants, jurors, and judge all probably shared a belief in justice, yet the justice each championed was different. In the course of indicting, trying, reaching verdicts, and proclaiming judgments these understandings of justice could come into conflict; the final results were essentially compromises, sometimes between judge and jury, on other occasions between peers sorting out the fairest resolution of their problems.

NOTES

We thank Petra Fisher for research assistance, and Blake Brown, Barry Cahill, Philip Girard, and anonymous reviewers for their comments on an earlier draft.

1 For Belcher's arrival see the announcement in *Halifax Gazette*, 12 Oct. 1754, and Belcher to Pownall, 16 Jan. 1755, CO 217, vol. 15, 187. Belcher's accession to the Council, but not the meeting of the court, was reported in *Boston Weekly Newsletter*, 7 Nov. 1754. For Belcher's commission, dated 1 July 1754, see RG 1, vol. 164 [2], 36; for his swearing in as councillor see Council Minutes, 14 Oct. 1754, RG 1, vol. 187, 149. An account of the background to the

establishment of the court, and a more extended survey of Belcher's previous career and character than can be given here, may be found in the chapter by Cahill and Phillips, this volume.

2 This account of the ceremonies that attended the opening of the court is principally from B. Murdoch, *A History of Nova Scotia, or Acadie*, 3 vols. (Halifax: James Barnes 1865–7), 2:250–1; all quotations not otherwise referenced are from this source. Murdoch's account appears with some additions in T.B. Akins, *History of Halifax City* (1894; Halifax: Brook House Press 2002), 44–6, and is reproduced verbatim in C.J. Townshend, 'Historical Account of the Courts of Judicature in Nova Scotia,' *Canadian Law Times* 19 (1899): 142–3.

3 Belcher, 'A Description of Nova Scotia, January 1755,' Belcher Papers, MG 1, vol. 1738, no. 123.

4 Sheriffs were not introduced until 1782. Until then the provost marshal in Halifax (in Foye's term invariably via a deputy), and his deputies elsewhere in the colony, carried out all court orders, empanelled juries, served processes, etc. For Foye's appointment see commission of 21 July 1749, RG 1, vol. 164, 86. For descriptions of the provost marshal system see B. Murdoch, 'An Essay on the Origins and Sources of the Laws of Nova Scotia,' 1863, in T.G. Barnes et al., eds., *Law in a Colonial Society: The Nova Scotia Experience* (Toronto: Carswell 1986), 194, and Wilmot to Board of Trade, 17 Dec. 1764, CO 217, vol. 21, 134. For the move to sheriffs see Sheriffs Act, S.N.S. 1778, c. 2, assented to in 1780.

5 The other six were Joseph Kent, John Kerr, Otis Little, David Lloyd, George Suckling, and Daniel Wood. One of Governor Cornwallis's clerks, Nesbitt was an original settler of Halifax and served as clerk of the General Court in 1749 and 1750. He became King's attorney in 1753 and held the post of attorney general until 1779. He was also variously an MHA and Speaker of the Assembly for twenty-five years. See L. Kernaghan, 'William Nesbitt,' *DCB*, 4:581–2; T.B. Akins, ed., *Selections from the Public Documents of Nova Scotia* (Halifax: Annand 1869), 558; RG 39, Series J, vol. 117; Hopson to Board of Trade, 22 Oct. 1753, CO 217, vol. 14, 280. For the early bar generally see Cahill and Phillips, this volume, and J.B. Cahill, 'The Origin and Evolution of the Attorney and Solicitor in the Legal Profession of Nova Scotia,' *Dalhousie Law Journal* 38 (1991): 277–95.

6 For William Winniett see C.B. Fergusson, 'William Winniett,' *DCB*, 3:665. Alexander Winniett also served as French interpreter when needed: see 'The King v. Street and Others: Arguments and Evidence Upon the Trial for Murder,' enclosed in Belcher to Pownall, 16 Jan. 1755, CO 217, vol. 15, 323. He presumably learned the language from his Acadian mother.

7 For Breynton see C.E. Thomas, 'John Breynton,' *DCB*, 4: 93–4. The text of the sermon was the words: 'I am one of them that are peaceable and faithful in Israel': Murdoch, *History of Nova Scotia*, 250. The text is from 2 Samuel 20:19, and is part of what is spoken by 'a wise woman' of a city besieged by an army under Joab. She persuaded him to lift the siege in return for the head of one Sheba, who had 'lifted up his hand against the King' who Joab served. Most likely the sermon was against disloyalty; treason, the passage says, is punishable by death, and, per verse 22, the 'wisdom' of the woman was evident in her persuading the other besieged citizens to cut off Sheba's head and throw it out to Joab.

8 For the courthouse see the chapter by Cuthbertson, this volume.

9 Council Minutes, 21 Oct. 1754, RG 1, vol. 187, 153.

10 Quotation from J.M. Beattie, *Crime and the Courts in England, 1660-1800* (Princeton: Princeton University Press 1986), 316. For the concepts of 'majesty' and 'terror,' and for the ways that displays like these contributed to the effectiveness of the ideology of the law, see D. Hay, 'Property, Authority and the Criminal Law,' in Hay et al., eds., *Albion's Fatal Tree: Crime and Society in Eighteenth Century-England* (London: Allen 1975). See also the brief description in the chapter by Hay, this volume.

11 For the process of grand jury selection see J. Phillips, 'Halifax Juries in the Eighteenth Century,' in G. Smith, A.N. May, and S. Devereaux, eds., *Criminal Justice in the Old World and the New: Essays in Honour of J.M. Beattie* (Toronto: Centre of Criminology 1998), 138–9.

12 J.B. Brebner, *The Neutral Yankees of Nova Scotia* (New York: Columbia University Press 1926), 15.

13 The other members were Matthew Barnard, Richard Catherwood, John Codman, Henry Ferguson, James Fillis, James Hall, Giles Harris, Charles Hay, Jonathan Hoar, Jacob Hurd, Bartholomew Kneeland, Samuel McClure, Alexander McKeown, William McGee (or Magee), William Pitman, Aaron Porter, Jonathon Prescott, Charles Proctor, and George Saul. We do not have a list of those who attended on opening day, but it is reasonable to assume that all chosen to serve did so, and these names are from the trial reports for the session in Belcher to Pownall, 16 Jan. 1755, CO 217, vol. 15, 194–6. Note that some of these names appear again later in this essay, as litigants or arbitrators in the court's civil proceedings.

14 For English grand juries see Beattie, *Crime and the Courts*, 320–7. For the socio-economic composition of Halifax grand juries generally, and for a more nuanced comparison with England than is possible here, see Phillips, 'Halifax Juries,' 140–56.

15 Beattie, *Crime and the Courts*, 331.

16 See G. Lamoine, *Charges to the Grand Jury 1689–1803* (London: Royal Historical Society 1992).

17 The original of Belcher's charge is in the Belcher Manuscripts at the University of British Columbia Library. It is reproduced in T.B. Vincent, ed., 'Jonathan Belcher: Charge to the Grand Jury, Michaelmas Term, 1754,' *Acadiensis* 7 (1977): 103–9.

18 The best account of this incident and the consequent legal proceedings is J.B. Cahill, 'The 'Hoffman Rebellion' (1753) and Hoffman's Trial (1754): Constructive High Treason and Seditious Conspiracy in Nova Scotia under the Stratocracy,' in F.M. Greenwood and J.B. Wright, eds., *Canadian State Trials: Volume I – Law, Politics, and Security Measures, 1608–1837* (Toronto: University of Toronto Press and Osgoode Society 1996).

19 MG 1, vol. 1738, no. 110. The English address was Sir James Astry, *A General Charge to All Grand Juries, With Advice to those of Life and Death* ... This was first published in London in 1703; a second edition came out in 1725.

20 Cited in Akins, *History of Halifax*, 45–6.

21 The following account of the criminal cases is based on four principal sources, and all information is from these unless otherwise stated. The Supreme Court proceedings book, RG 39, Halifax, Series J, vol. 117, contains brief summaries of each case. Belcher sent a more extensive report on the session to London: 'Abstract of the Proceedings of the Supreme Court, Michaelmas Term, 1754,' in Belcher to Thomas Pownall, 16 Jan. 1755, CO 217, vol. 15, 194–210. There are brief summaries of each case in 'A General Return of Prisoners Tryed at His Majesty's Supreme Court,' RG 1, vol. 342, no. 50. Finally, Belcher also sent a much longer account of one case, the murder trial of Street et al. discussed in detail below, in Belcher to Pownall, 15 May 1755, CO 217, vol. 15, 310–29.

22 The general observations on the nature of the criminal trial in this period which follow are principally from J. Phillips, 'The Criminal Trial in Nova Scotia, 1749–1815,' in G.B. Baker and J. Phillips, eds., *Essays in the History of Canadian Law Volume VIII – In Honour of R.C.B. Risk* (Toronto: University of Toronto Press and Osgoode Society 1999). The best short account of the English criminal trial in this period remains Beattie, *Crime and the Courts*, chap. 7. For the prisoners being brought from the jail see 'Return of the Halifax Gaol, October 29, 1754,' RG 1, vol. 342, no. 43.

23 Beattie, *Crime and the Courts*, 319; Belcher's Notes on Grand Jury Charges, MG 1, vol. 1738, no. 110.

24 Vincent, 'Jonathan Belcher,' 107.

25 In future years the size of grand juries was generally smaller, ranging from fifteen to twenty men.

26 Halifax grand juries returned an indictment rate of 90 per cent in the first half-century of the city's existence: see Phillips, 'Halifax Juries,' 168.
27 *Halifax Gazette*, 28 Sept. 1754.
28 For outlawry generally, and another instance of its use in Nova Scotia, see E.A. Clarke and J. Phillips, 'Rebellion and Repression in Nova Scotia in the Era of the American Revolution,' in Greenwood and Wright, eds., *Canadian State Trials: Volume I*, 192–5.
29 Phillips, 'Halifax Juries,' 157. The figures for prior service given here, and those for prosecuting below, are likely lower than the true numbers, because we do not have complete information on the grand juries for the 1749–54 period.
30 Belcher, 'A Description of Nova Scotia, January 1755,' MG 1, vol. 1738, no. 123. For the General Court's work see RG 39, Halifax, Series J, vol. 117.
31 For Belcher's views, and for London's disagreement with them following the trial and conviction of John Young in 1756, see J. Phillips, '"Securing Obedience to Necessary Laws": The Criminal Law in Eighteenth-Century Nova Scotia,' *Nova Scotia Historical Review* 12 (1992): 87–124. For the structure of the English law of crimes and punishments see ibid. and Beattie, *Crime and the Courts*, 141–8.
32 Beattie, *Crime and the Courts*, 144.
33 For this information on the trial jurors see Phillips, 'Halifax Juries,' 139–40 and 145-7. As with grand jurors, the figures given for repeat service are probably too low, because trial jury information is not complete for the 1749–54 period.
34 Belcher to Pownall, 16 Jan 1755, CO 217, vol. 15, 187–8.
35 Defence Counsel Act, S.N.S. 1840, c. 9. This stayed in force until 1842, but was revived and made perpetual in Defence Counsel Act, S.N.S. 1844, c. 41. For the continuing limitations on lawyers in the 1830s see Beamish Murdoch's statement that 'counsel can only examine witnesses, or address the court on questions of law ..., the prisoner being only allowed to state his defence himself to the jury': *Epitome of the Laws of Nova Scotia*, 4 vols. (Halifax: Howe 1832–3), 4:190. It is unclear why the colony lagged behind England in enacting this reform; like other legislation, it may have been delayed by the constitutional struggles between Assembly and Council in the late 1830s.
36 Beattie, *Crime and the Courts*, 148.
37 'A General Return of Prisoners Tryed,' RG 1, vol. 342, no. 50.
38 For the royal pardon in Nova Scotia, including the use of the condition of serving in the forces, see J. Phillips, 'The Operation of the Royal Pardon in Nova Scotia, 1749-1815,' *University of Toronto Law Journal* 42 (1992): 401–49.

39 RG 39, Halifax, Series J, vol. 117.

40 This account of Lease's case is from the sources listed above. For Leau/ Lease see E.C. Wright, *Planters and Pioneers*, 2nd ed. (Wolfville, NS: Lancelot Press 1982), 174.

41 The goods stolen were given as 'one brown coat, one ... bottle, one powder horn, and the head of a hammer': Abstract of the Proceedings, CO 217, vol. 15, 207.

42 See J. Phillips and A.N. May, 'Female Criminality in 18th-Century Halifax,' *Acadiensis* 31 (2002): 71–96.

43 Statutes of 1547 and 1691 respectively removed both offences from clergy: Beattie, *Crime and the Courts*, 143–4.

44 Phillips, 'Halifax Juries,' 171. The conviction rate for the main offence was considerably lower for capital offences – 39 per cent – although when convictions for lesser included offences are added the overall conviction rate for those individuals rises to 61 per cent.

45 In addition to the sources cited above for all cases in the session, this case is also briefly recounted in Akins, *History of Halifax*, 43–4; Vincent, 'Jonathan Belcher,' 103–4; *Gazette*, 30 Nov. 1754; and Phillips, 'Securing Obedience to Necessary Laws,' 87–90. The depositions taken before Halifax County JP John Duport in August 1754 are at RG 1, vol. 342, no. 44; draft of the trial account sent by Belcher to London in 1755 is at RG 1, vol. 342, no. 45.

46 See Council Minutes, 17 Sept. and 5 Oct. 1754, RG 1, vol. 187, 104–5 and 137–44.

47 For an excellent description of the history and form of Admiralty sessions see M.J. Prichard, 'Crime at Sea: Admiralty Sessions and the Background to Later Colonial Jurisdiction,' in Barnes et al., eds., *Law in a Colonial Society*. See also W. Holdsworth, *A History of English Law*, 16 vols. (London: Methuen 1966), 1:546–51. The earliest known use of admiralty sessions in Halifax was the Shearer and Butler case of 1777: see Record of the Trial of Thomas Shearer and Timothy Butler, in Arbuthnot to Germain, 16 Jan. 1778, CO 217, vol. 51, 21–9. See also the William Corram case, July 1794, at RG 1, vol. 343.

48 Quotations from Belcher to Pownall, 16 Jan. 1755, CO 217, vol. 15, 187; Opinion of ?, MG 1, vol. 1738, no. 113; Belcher's Notes on Jurisdiction, ibid., no. 107.

49 Joseph Marriott, for example, Master of the *Vulture* and a prosecution witness, stated in direct examination '[t]hat when they fired from the sloop they were within the points of the cove': The King v. Street and Others,' enclosed in Belcher to Pownall, 15 May 1755, CO 217, vol. 15, 316.

50 Belcher to his Father, 14 Nov. 1754, MG 1, vol. 1738, no. 4.
51 Belcher to Pownall, 24 Dec. 1755, CO 217, vol. 16, 22. Other quotations in this paragraph from 'The King v. Street and Others,' enclosed in Belcher to Pownall, 15 May 1755, CO 217, vol. 15, 329, and Belcher's Notes on Jurisdiction, MG 1, vol. 1738, no. 107.
52 For Little see J.M. Bumsted, 'Otis Little,' *DCB*, 3:403–5; J. Doull, 'The First Five Attorney-Generals of Nova Scotia,' *Collections of the Nova Scotia Historical Society* 26 (1945): 35–6; and Cahill, 'Origin and Evolution,' 278. For Kent see Cahill, 'Hoffman's Rebellion,' 80. Kent died in the small pox epidemic of 1757.
53 Belcher to Pownall, 15 May 1755, CO 217, vol. 15, 330.
54 For useful summaries of the mercantilist system see D.K. Fieldhouse, *The Colonial Empires: A Comparative Survey from the Eighteenth Century* (New York: Delacorte 1965), 66–7, and T.A. Lloyd, *The British Empire, 1558–1983* (Oxford: Oxford University Press 1984), esp. at 32 and 48–9. Some of the legislation was cited by Little, especially 12 Chas. II, c. 18, and 13 & 14 Chas. II, c. 11. Also noted were 10 & 11 Will. III, c. 10; 11 & 12 Will. III, c. 13; 5 Geo. II, c. 21; and 12 Geo. II, c. 21.
55 W. Hawkins, *A Treatise of the Pleas of the Crown* (1724–6; repr. New York: Arno Press 1972), 2, chap. 14.
56 Council Minutes, 5 Oct. 1754, RG 1, vol. 187, 137–44.
57 Lawrence to Board of Trade, 1 Aug. 1754, CO 217, vol. 15, 76.
58 See Beattie, *Crime and the Courts*, 340; Treasons and Felonies Act, S.N.S. 1758, c. 13, s. 31.
59 The leading case was *R. v. Broadfoot*, 2 Salk. 31, 168 E.R. 78. For an excellent general discussion see N. Rogers, 'Impressment and the Law in Eighteenth-Century Britain,' in N. Landau, ed., *Law, Crime and English Society, 1660–1830* (Cambridge: Cambridge University Press 2002), 71–94.
60 Belcher to Pownall, 16 Jan. 1755, CO 217, vol. 15, 187. For the practice of English judges on occasion telling juries what their verdict should be see Beattie, *Crime and the Courts*, 406–10.
61 Belcher's Sentencing Speech, enclosed in Belcher to Pownall, 15 May 1755, CO 217, vol. 15, 330–1.
62 Belcher to Pownall, 16 Jan. 1755, CO 217, vol. 15, 188.
63 See RG 1, vol. 342, no. 50.
64 For Street see Governor Lawrence to Thomas Gunter, 6 Nov. 1754, RG 1, vol. 134, 267–8. John Hovey's brother Joseph had tried to give evidence at the trial, but Belcher had not allowed it because it was apparently irrelevant to the issues.
65 For the tendency of jurors to convict less when a capital sentence would be

the result, see Beattie, *Crime and the Courts*, 410-30, and Phillips, 'Halifax Juries,' 170–4.

66 See General Court Rules, in Council Minutes, 14 Jan. 1751, RG 1, vol. 186, 102–9. The exception was 'where the suit is upon a specialty for payment of money,' that is, actions arising to enforce a previous decision of the Supreme Court.

67 For both English civil appeal procedure and the colonial innovations discussed here see M.S. Bilder, 'The Origin of Appeal in America,' *Hastings Law Journal* 48 (1996–7), esp. at 924–7, 930–40, and 945–9.

68 All information on *Russell v. Young* is from Inferior Court of Common Pleas Records, RG 37, vol. 3, no. 44.

69 Lloyd was one of the handful of men admitted to the Nova Scotia bar in the early 1750s (see note 5 above). He was clerk to the County Court (the predecessor to the ICCP) and the sessions until the affair of the justices (for which see Cahill and Phillips, this volume), and thereafter went into private civil and criminal practice. His civil practice was quite extensive, involving some 72 cases in 1754, although not as great as the other members of the bar, who ranged from 85 cases (Daniel Wood) to 177 (Nesbitt). See RG 39, Halifax, Series C, vol. 2, no. 2; J. Muir, 'Civil Law and the Colonial Economy in Halifax, 1749–1765' (PhD thesis, York University 2004).

70 See An Act for Determining Differences By Arbitration, 9 & 10 W & M, c. 15. On the origins of the Act and arbitration at common law prior to it see H. Horwitz and J. Oldham, 'John Locke, Lord Mansfield, and Arbitration During the Eighteenth Century,' *Historical Journal* 36 (1993): 138–44. On North American practices see S. Ames, ed., *County Court Records of Accomack-Northampton, Virginia, 1632–1640* (Washington: American Historical Association 1954), lvi–lviii, and B. Mann, *Neighbors and Strangers: Law and Community in Early Connecticut* (Chapel Hill: University of North Carolina Press 1987), 128–9.

71 For an extensive analysis of Young's case see Phillips, 'Securing Obedience to Necessary Laws,' 98–106.

72 For Coburn's case see RG 39, Halifax, Series J, vol. 1, 56; *Gazette*, 21 Apr. 1768; *Boston Weekly Newsletter*, 5 and 26 May 1768; Belcher's Notes, Sentencing Speech, 18 Apr. 1768, MG 1, vol. 1738, no. 111; Proclamation, 27 Apr. 1768, RG 1, vol. 166, 52–3; Pardon for Francis Coburn, 31 Oct, 1768, RG 1, vol. 170, 1–2.

73 The following account of this case is from RG 37, vol. 3, no. 44, and RG 37, vol. B, 65–8.

74 *Catherwood v. Balitho*, RG 37, vol. B, 69–71.

75 These figures are derived from Muir, 'Civil Law and the Colonial Econ-

omy,' chap. 5. Over the same period six actions were withdrawn by the appellant, and one was defaulted when the appellee did not appear.

76 For the two cases involving Piggot as defendant see RG 37, vol. 3, no. 44, and vol. B, 44–8 and 65–8.

77 Known as 'the English attorney' because he was admitted to practise at Westminster Hall, Suckling had been clerk to the General Court and was later attorney general of Quebec (1764–6) and chief justice of the Virgin Islands. In the mid-1750s, in partnership with Nesbitt, he had the most extensive practice among the small Halifax bar, but his reputation suffered when he was accused of sharp practice; Governor Lawrence called him 'a rascally Attorney' and 'a Newgate sollicitor.' See J. L'Heureux, 'George Suckling,' *DCB*, 4: 724–6; RG 39, Halifax, Series J, vol. 117; Lawrence to Halifax, 3 Feb. 1759, cited in J.B. Brebner, *New England's Outpost: Acadia Before the Conquest of Canada* (New York: Columbia University Press 1927), 269.

78 This and the following two cases are at RG 37, vol. 3, no. 44.

79 A demurrer occurred when a defendant agreed with the plaintiff's facts but denied they gave rise, in modern parlance, to a cause of action. A plea in bar occurred when the defendant offered his or her own version of the facts which, if true, would avoid liability. It might be said, for example, that the condition on a conditional bond had been performed. See Mann, *Neighbors and Strangers*, 81.

80 Ibid., 81–3.

81 For this development see Cahill and Phillips, this volume.

82 See, for example, A.W. Gunn, 'Eighteenth-Century Britain: In Search of the State and Finding the Quarter Sessions,' in J. Brewer and E. Hellmuth, eds., *Rethinking Leviathan: The Eighteenth-Century State in Britain and Germany* (London: German Historical Institute and Oxford: Oxford University Press 1999).

9

Women as Litigants before the Supreme Court of Nova Scotia, 1754–1830

JULIAN GWYN

In the seventy-seven years covered by this study, there are more than one thousand case files involving female litigants either as plaintiffs or defendants before the Supreme Court. As women were involved in an estimated 9 per cent of the estimated 11,300 extant cases filed in the Supreme Court of Nova Scotia at Halifax to the end of 1830, this amounted on average to only thirteen annually.[1] It should be remembered that until 1764 the Supreme Court did not have original jurisdiction, but only heard appeals in such cases. The records, housed in some 175 boxes at Nova Scotia's provincial archives, deserve the close scrutiny of historians. Combined with documents from other courts, they tell us more about the social history of women in colonial Nova Scotia than perhaps any other body of surviving manuscripts.[2] This is important as few young historians have any interest in the women of pre-Confederation Nova Scotia, while progress by an older generation remains either almost invisible or 'lamentably slow.'[3]

The extensive concern for gender history that has characterized much recent historical writing has focused new attention on women's involvement in litigation. In colonial American legal historiography, of which this study forms a part, a 'bustling academic cottage industry' has emerged in the last few years.'[4] Mann, for instance, notes that civil procedure, not criminal, was the form of law that 'touched most people.'[5] Calling for more research on the court actions of women, Snyder deplores the lack of research on litigants and litigation. 'The county court was a central institution in the colonial South,' she writes, 'but we know little about its caseload.' Dayton complains that evidence from civil suits has rarely touched 'the issue of women and gender.' A rare example is Norton's interest in women litigants from late seventeenth-century Maryland. Useful scholarship on women and property in the colonial era was pioneered by Salmon, who studied the period 1750–1830, and by Briggs Biemer.[6]

Within the socio-legal historiography of British North America to 1867, concern for women and civil procedure provides a welcome balance to the focus on criminal activity among women.[7] If women were to appear before the courts, they were more likely to do so as a result of civil litigation, rather than through criminal process. Scholars who study nineteenth-century Ontario and pre-1825 Quebec understand this.[8] Among them, Kolish explicitly advocates the use of court records in the form of civil action case files for the social history of women. Nova Scotia's historiography, while in part reflecting a particular focus on deviant or victimized women,[9] is enriched by the work of Girard and Veinott on women's property.[10] As well, there are studies of rare civil matters like divorce and child custody.[11] Civil actions in the courts particularize disputes not on such matters, but principally on debt and credit, defamation, and dower rights. In the Court of Chancery, installed in Nova Scotia from 1751, and which Salmon believes instituted a set of rules and precedents favouring 'greater independence for women,' the business of three-quarters of the cases was mortgage foreclosure, while much of the rest was for injunctions against proceedings simultaneously being carried on in other courts.[12] Widows frequently found themselves, from the 1750s, enmeshed in civil actions as administrators of the estates of their late husbands. If they remarried, they were named as co-plaintiffs or co-defendants with their new husbands. The study of such civil actions provides evidence of women in the economic sphere, hitherto obscure, at least in the historiography of early Nova Scotia.

Litigation Profile

More than eight out of ten cases dealt with matters of debt, while about one in ten dealt with the three next most important cases combined: trespass or ejectment, assault, and dower rights. Table 9.1 provides broad details. In the 1,019 cases under study, some 565 different women appeared as either plaintiffs or defendants.

Table 9.1 Case Types: Supreme Court, 1754–1830

Case type		n	%
Debt		830	81.4
Trespass & ejectment		74	7.3
Assault		22	2.2
Dower rights		16	1.6
Miscellaneous		37	3.6
Detained chattels & goods	7		
Defamation	7		
Breach of covenant	7		
Breach of promise	4		
Partition of land	2		
Writ of error	2		
Other	8		
Unspecified causes		40	3.9
Total		1,019	100

Source: RG39C/1-175

Space constraints prevent a detailed analysis of debt, the largest category; a fuller treatment of debt in all the civil courts of Nova Scotia to the end of 1801 is found elsewhere.[13] The present study provides instead a taste of the various types of litigation in which women found themselves involved before the Supreme Court.

Debt

Let us first consider the cases of debt.[14] Such suits provide the most detailed evidence of women's participation in the colonial economy, and they supplement comments on women in the economy from account books such as those for Horton township studied by Mancke.[15] The court evidence describes the integral part that women played within the business world of eighteenth-century Nova Scotia. That world was built upon an elaborate system of credit flowing first from Great Britain. In the absence of banks, credit was extended by those with even the smallest amounts to advance, such as impoverished widows to their lodgers. Elsewhere credit, underpinning the Atlantic economy, was the sinew of intercolonial trade, and after 1783, the trade between Nova Scotia and the United States. A few women were drawn into this form of external commerce. Most generated their debts and extended

Table 9.2 Debts

Years	Median	Number	Cumulative
1754–63	22.56	8	
1764–75	16.99	46	54
1776–83	12.08	52	106
1784–92	15.9	124	230
1793–1815	31.13	210	440
1816–30	44.64	268	708
Unknown amounts		122	830

their credit within the confines of Nova Scotia's internal economy; the principal instruments of this system were the ledgers maintained by retailers and wholesalers, mortgages on real property, promissory notes, and bills of exchange. Almost all such creditors, whether London merchant banker or Halifax widow, were themselves simultaneously also debtors, an important point usually overlooked by economic and business historians.

Most cases went undefended. Yet in cases that were defended, a system of arbitration, sanctioned by colonial statute in 1768, was open to the disputants. Arbitration, of course, might occur before the matter was brought to court, or the Supreme Court itself could order, with the consent of all parties, binding arbitration. The panel of three to five freeholders was usually composed of those thought to be familiar with financial accounts and matters relating to real property. Of the 830 suits, only 16 were submitted to arbitration. None was of sufficient interest to cite here.

The Supreme Court acted as a court of appeal in few of these debt cases, especially after 1768. For instance, of the first dozen Supreme Court debt cases involving women, eleven were appeals from the Halifax Inferior Court of Appeals. Thereafter only a handful of such cases followed that route.

Through war-induced inflation the median value of these debts tended to rise, particularly from the outset of the French wars beginning in 1793.[16] The details are found in table 9.2. Severe recession can partly explain the steep rise in the median debt in 1816–30, as many failed to adjust from wartime prosperity accompanied by high prices to greatly reduced rents and commodities prices in the post-war era. Median measurements, however, mask the fact that the Supreme

Court dealt with several cases for the recovery of very large debts. One of H£8,248.34 occurred in 1759; others of £5,600 and £5,750 in 1786; and another of H£4,000 in 1817. In three of the cases alleged mercantile debts were at issue, widows being the defendants, while the fourth involved the unpaid balance for the purchase of £10,000 of 3 per cent consols.[17] Evidence from such debt cases, taken together, reveal the active role of women in the colonial economy.

These cases involved every imaginable sort of debt: promissory notes, bonds, unsecured large unpaid accounts with wholesalers and smaller sums owing retailers, and unpaid rent either for daily board and lodging or for farms on long leases. As many such women acted either as the administrators of estates or as executors of wills, the cases indicate their familiarity with financial and business matters, as well as the confidence placed in them by their husbands and others whom they represented. Some 44 per cent of the debt case files involved women acting either as administrators or as executors.

The experience of the most litigious woman, Phoebe Moody, will serve as a sufficient example of both creditor and debtor. She was partner of her merchant husband, James Moody, in a Halifax wholesale-retail business, based on their Hollis Street shop. Upon her husband's death at age thirty-three in 1796, widow Moody not only maintained the business but set about, with the other co-administrators of his estate, suing both her husband's debtors and her own. Employing a variety of lawyers, by 1811 she had been involved in forty-nine suits at the Supreme Court and six at the Inferior Court of Common Pleas for Halifax County.[18] Furthermore, upon her marriage to William O. Parker in 1814 she, with her new husband, brought four more suits before the Supreme Court, for debts outstanding before her new marriage, and one foreclosure cause before the Court of Chancery. If Akins could describe James Moody as among the 'chief merchants' of Halifax in the 1790s, we could make the same claim for his widow, who from 1801 to 1806 advertised in Halifax's *Royal Gazette* her latest imports from London.[19]

The debts there could be either commercial or personal. Given the range of the goods she carried in her store, many of her debtors were from the elite: merchants, gentlemen, and garrison officers from Windsor, Halifax, and Dartmouth. These included those from whom Moody had accepted promissory notes. At the other end of the social scale were farmers and yeomen from Boydville on the Windsor Road, Truro, and Lunenburg, who had failed to make timely payment of their annual rent. Others of her debtors included a St Margaret's Bay fisherman, a Cornwallis township sailor, a Truro saddler, a Dartmouth boatbuilder, and from Halifax a tailor, an upholsterer, a trader, and a labourer. Those without adequate chattels to be attached to cover the size of the debt were arrested and imprisoned. One of these was Hannah Grant, a widow, arrested for a debt of H£6.50.[20] Employing her clerks to submit the initial depositions, Moody perhaps never had to appear herself before the court.[21] In total the debts amounted to H£4,141 or an average of H£231.75 for each of the eighteen years in which her name appeared as a litigant.

It should be remembered that Phoebe Moody was also a defendant in several debt cases. Her co-administrator, the Halifax merchant Robert Lyon, was the plaintiff in two of the suits. The jury's verdict went against her in the first and she was required to pay £114.10.[22] On a second occasion, in July 1807, she was arrested and then discharged, but the matter came to trial only four years later, when she had to repay H£323.54.[23] The same Phoebe Moody became involved in civil cases of trespass and ejectment, which were rather common; slander, which was less common; and for harbouring a slave, which was extremely rare.

Enslavement

Let us first consider the case involving the slave. Black slavery was widespread in late eighteenth-century Nova Scotia.[24] Well established by the French in Louisbourg, slaves were frequently listed among the chattels of early Halifax settlers. When some 8,000 New Englander planters immigrated to Nova Scotia in the 1760s, the slave population swelled. Twenty years later, an estimated 1,200 slaves accompanied loyalist refugees to Nova Scotia. When freed blacks from Shelburne and Halifax Counties departed Nova Scotia in 1792 for Sierra Leone, the blacks left behind were principally slaves, and concentrated in Annapolis County, which then included Digby Township. Yet slavery never acquired a statutory basis in the colony. Rather, it was 'presumed implicitly to be lawful until adjudged or legislated to be explicitly illegal.' Attempts thereafter by blacks to assert their rights to freedom had the widespread freedom and assistance of the 'Supreme Court bench and most of the bar.'

The case against Phoebe Moody involved Rachel Fair (alias Bross) and was brought by Fair's putative owner, Frederick William Hecht,

Esq., an Annapolis County JP. Five years after Rachel married, Hecht ordered her arrested and jailed in Annapolis, actions that greatly exceeded his authority. His intention was to offer her for sale at public auction. Before this occurred, word of the proposed sale reached Halifax, and Rachel was escorted to appear before Chief Justice Blowers, who promptly discharged the prisoner. Moody thereupon hired Rachel in her shop, whereupon Hecht sought H£100 damages from Moody for employing her. Thus came about, as Barry Cahill has noted, 'the first case in which compensatory damages in trespass were sought by a slaveholder against someone who allegedly by fraud and deception had procured the personal services of a fugitive slave as a wage labourer.'[25] When Blowers determined that Hecht's proof of purchase did not afford the slaveholder a 'marketable title,'[26] the jury found in Moody's favour and awarded her costs.[27]

Had the case been heard twenty years earlier and under a different chief justice – Bryan Finucane – an altogether different verdict probably would have obtained, as one Elizabeth Watson experienced. In March 1778, the Halifax Inferior Court of Common Pleas declared Watson a free black woman, in an action brought against her by John Woodin Sr.[28] This decision hung largely on the evidence of Elizabeth Reed, another free woman of colour, who had lived in Boston from her childhood, and for thirteen years knew Watson to be free, as her parents, both of whom had died by 1778, had been. Reed further identified Watson as having been a servant of Agnes Lobdell in Boston before coming to Halifax and working for Woodin. This case, unique in Nova Scotia's court records and hitherto unreported, arose because Watson had petitioned the court claiming that she had been brought to Halifax and unknown to herself had been sold there to Elias Marshall.[29] Her declaration deserves close attention as it is the earliest such example by a black woman in Nova Scotia. It is also a remarkable testimony to the brutality to which servants, of whatever race, could then be subject. When she was heavily pregnant, Watson was stripped and repeatedly beaten by Marshall some eight days after she joined the household. This brought on her labour. When she appealed to her master for help with the delivery, Marshall put her in the cellar, after again beating her. Watson gave birth without assistance in a stable on the property. Unable to work the next day, she complained to Marshall of the cold, it being early March. Marshall, in response, ordered another servant to pour throw buckets of icy water over her, and she fled. Watson said that when she was brought back the next morning, Mr Marshall took up a flat iron and split my skull almost open. After that he carried me into the cellar, tied me down to a beam hands and legs and beat me for one hour. He continued the same at dinner. The same in the afternoon and the same at night, being so beat the skin almost every part of the body so that I was neither able to go or lie in bed, but upon my hands and knees. He was obliged at last, my life being in danger to apply to Dr. Phillips.[30] When that gentleman came in to see me, seeing such a miserable sight as I was, he fainted. After having recovered himself, went away. He applied to Dr. Fletcher,[31] who in cutting me was obliged to cut the skin & flesh as broad as my hand over my whole body. After I was recovered a little he would give me nothing to eat but peas, or what I could get out of the hog's trough to keep in my life.[32]

A month and a day after the Inferior Court rendered its decision, Elizabeth Watson was seized by the Halifax butcher, William Proud, who insisted she was his runaway slave, known as Phyllis. A special sessions of the peace, beginning on 1 August 1778, sat for the trial. This court consisted of the same three justices who had heard the original suit, with a fourth now added. Described in the proceedings not as Phyllis, but as Elizabeth Watson, her sworn deposition marked with her 'X' reported that, on a mid-July night about 3:30 a.m. 'being warm, and much fatigued by cooking &ca in the house of Mr. William Proud, she went out to the necessary.'[33] She was followed there by Proud carrying a candle, who demanded to know who she had with her in the outhouse. Alone she emerged and went into the house, where there was a Mr Barn 'much in liquor,' upon which Elizabeth unwisely commented: 'Mrs. Proud, the wife, immediately struck the deponent in the face with her hand, after which the deponent went upstairs, and Mr. Proud and his wife both followed. Proud flogged her or beat her violently with a horse whip he had brought up with him until he broke it & after got another, and continued to repeat the same for a long time and then kicked her with his feet down the stairs or some part thereof.'

The Supreme Court became involved when Watson sued Proud for H£100 by way of damages for illegal confinement and assault. With Chief Justice Finucane presiding, the case was heard in mid-September. Elizabeth Watson was represented by George Thomson, then the most junior member of the bar, while Proud retained Richard Gibbons, Jr, the solicitor general and the senior member of the bar and its most prominent practitioner.

At the October 1779 trial the key witness for the defence was Stephen

Laka, who in mid-September had responded to a series of questions before Chief Justice Finucane. Laka swore that he had purchased the slave, whom Proud called Phyllis, from Agnes Lobdell in Boston, though he produced no bill of sale. He then claimed to have brought her to Halifax and sold her to Mrs Elias Marshall, the bill of sale for which he exhibited. He denied that he had ever heard of her as a free woman; rather, he knew of her for about the last six months of her time with Mrs Lobdell, whom he believed had formerly bought her from one Ebenezer Gorham. Watson's attorney was present but never opened his mouth to protest any part of Laka's sworn testimony. His performance was far removed from Thomas Jefferson's characterization of the lawyer's trade as 'to question everything, to yield nothing, and to talk by the hour.' If Elizabeth Reed was still available to testify on Watson's behalf, she was not summoned to appear. When the trial took place on 20 October, the cause was entitled 'Elizabeth Watson alias Phillis a Negro Woman, Plaintiff vs Wm. Proud, Defendant.' The evidence considered by the court was presented by Gibbons alone. Without hearing any evidence on behalf of the plaintiff the jury found for Proud, and declared that 'the said Elizabeth Watson is his property and slave.'[34]

Another case, both less pathetic and less tragic, equally underscored the fragility of the personal freedom of blacks in wartime Nova Scotia at the hands of New England immigrants. In April 1780 Thomas Ball, of Windsor, applied to the Halifax Supreme Court for the relief of his wife, Priscilla Ball, treated as a slave and taken into custody for bail as part of, in the words of Deputy Provost Marshal William Simpson, 'an attachment & property of Joseph Haines impleaded at the suit of John McMonagle.'[35] When the court ordered her immediately released, Simpson refused to comply, noting a fortnight later, 'No security being offered by the within said Thomas Ball, the said Priscilla Ball is still in custody of the Provost Marshall as assets on behalf of John McMonagle.' Although the issues were illegal confinement and false imprisonment, these were the first known cases in Nova Scotia to test the legality of slavehold tenure. That during the War of Independence 'free-born or freed Blacks in Nova Scotia could seek judicial redress against the presumption of slavery ... is significant for the legal history of slavery during the post-bellum, loyalist period, when it became a question more of perpetuating the status of Black slaves who had been introduced into Nova Scotia by loyalists, than of pressing free-born Blacks into slavery.'[36]

Trespass and Ejectment

In each year covered by this study, the Supreme Court on average dealt with no more than a single case of trespass or ejectment involving women. Trespass was frequently associated with theft or destruction of property, while ejectment dealt with the attempt to remove a tenant who overstayed a lease. More commonly, it could be used to try title to land where it was disputed, with the 'lease' being a pure legal fiction. It is probable that the bulk of the cases cited here were of this latter sort.

The earliest case involving a female litigant with which the Supreme Court dealt occurred in 1755 on appeal from the Inferior Court of Common Pleas for Halifax County. Catherine, widow and executor of John Winston, bellman, was a tenant in a house owned by John Grant, surgeon. Their home had been sold at public auction to meet debts owed the doctor. As widow Winston refused to vacate the property, Grant sued her successfully with his costs. She lost her appeal with further costs of H£2.40.[37]

In 1781, Catherine O'Brien, tenant since 1777 in the Lighthouse tavern, successfully sued her landlord, James Creighton, who had evicted her from her establishment. It was one of her few successes in court. Catherine O'Brien, a spinster, had returned to Nova Scotia from Ireland upon learning of the death of her brother, James Quin, a Halifax tavern-keeper. She had earlier hitched her fortune to that of Montagu Wilmot, governor of Nova Scotia, her companion since 1752, and had been left stranded when death overtook him in 1766.[38] Her decision to return to Nova Scotia must have been borne of a serious misunderstanding of the extent of her late brother's estate. It consisted of two small houses near Quin's wharf and a third small house near the barracks. Quin had died intestate in June 1768; his then companion, Jane Tracey, was named administrator, but O'Brien obtained an order revoking these letters of administration and substituting herself in this role. Almost at once she found herself defending a suit for H£223, the unpaid wages now claimed by Tracey 'as a manual and domestick servant or housekeeper.'[39] By 1770 O'Brien felt obliged to apply for an injunction against Tracey, her daughter Mary Sherlock, and Tracey's son-in-law, Foster Sherlock. For not only had Tracey, as initial administrator, refused to provide O'Brien with an accounting of her stewardship, she successfully sued O'Brien for 'a pretended bond debt' of Quin's for H£100, in the Supreme Court. To execute the judgment, Quin's real estate was due to be auctioned; O'Brien sought an injunction from the Court of Chancery to stay the proceedings, a process she was still pursuing unsuccessfully as late as 1780.[40] Without her consent, O'Brien's lawyer had withdrawn her complaint, behaviour so outrageous that it was commented upon by the leading lawyer, Richard Gibbons, Jr.[41]

Many poor widows, probably ignorant of the law, refused to vacate their leased premises when, at the end of their leases, they were required to comply. In 1802, as an example, William Ryan wanted to recover possession of his house on Prince Street in Halifax from his tenant, widow Catherine Sullivan. When she refused he sued her, and though she was defended by Attorney General Richard John Uniacke, the jury's verdict went against her and she was taxed for H£12.40 in costs. Sullivan was jailed until she paid the debt.[42]

In 1812 Ann Phelan, a Halifax spinster, desired possession of a lot she had recently inherited and that was occupied on a seven years' lease by the Halifax printer, William Minns. On account of her extreme poverty the court granted her request to be admitted *in forma pauperis*, and assigned her Simon Bradstreet Robie as counsel. A year later the Supreme Court found the defendant guilty of trespass.[43]

Examples of trespass where damage had occurred include the suit initiated by Margaret, widow of Jacob Hurd, the long-time clerk to the storekeeper at the careening yard, against the Halifax cooper, William Newman. In 1815 'with force of arms' he broke into a close of hers, stole five loads of earth, sand, gravel, and rocks, and erected wooden fences and subdivided the field without her knowledge or permission. She sought damages of H£500.[44] In 1816 widow Elizabeth Embley of Point Sandwich successfully sued William Baisley, a Halifax fisherman, for breaking into her field near York Redoubt and removing a stone wall, for which the Supreme Court awarded her H£5 and her costs.[45] The following year Baisley sued her and two yeomen, also of Point Sandwich, for cutting five acres of trees to the value of H£100 and hauling away the wood by cart.[46] In 1818 he and his wife, Barbara, secured Embley's eviction at the end of her seven years' lease. Embley's costs came to H£16.75.[47]

Of more importance was the suit brought in 1821 by Elizabeth and William Letson, tanners on the North West Arm, against two Halifax butchers, George Thompson and John Parker. They were accused of having often broken into two North West Arm fields, where they trampled and soiled the grass, of having broken into three bark mills, twenty tan pits, three shops, and three outhouses, and of having removed some

50 cords of hemlock bark, 500 sides of sole leather, 350 sides of harness and bridle leather, 140 sides of bridle and neat's leather, 6 horse hides, 400 calfskins, 370 sealskins, 700 sheepskins 920 sides of other leather, some 6 other sides, and 1,470 other skins, valued at H£2,500, all of which they had converted to their own use.[48] In all these cases, where the verdicts are known, the Supreme Court acted in a manner no different than they habitually behaved when hearing disputes between men.

Dower Rights

Some Supreme Court cases related to dower rights. Owing to a wife's dower rights, purchasers needed her consent before they would buy land from her husband. The widow enjoyed a one-third dower right to whatever freehold property her husband owned in his lifetime. In Nova Scotia, by a 1768 Act for the Convenient and Speedy Assignment of Dower, a widow had to be granted her dower within a month of her husband's death, or she gained the right to sue freeholders, with rights to damages. By a further Act in 1771 To Secure the Title of Purchasers Against Claims of Dower, in order to ensure that consent to any sale was freely given by the wife, she had to acknowledge before a JP that she had done so 'freely, voluntarily, and without compulsion from her husband,' which undertaking the justice had to certify on the deed of conveyance.[49] She had a life interest only and could not herself convey such real property nor undermine its value by waste. If she died childless, the property went to her husband's heirs, not hers. If her husband died insolvent, her dower rights preceded the demands of his creditors. All remaining land, which at the time of her husband's death she had brought into the marriage, she recovered as a widow, as well as all land they had jointly acquired during the marriage. A widow also had a one-third claim to her husband's personal effects, if he died intestate.

The sixteen cases surviving in the Supreme Court records indicate that a widow's dower rights went largely unchallenged. There were exceptions. In 1774, Rebecca, widow of Benjamin Gerrish – one of the New England merchants who had come to Halifax at its first settlement – sued Robert Walker, a Falmouth husbandman, Richard Jacobs, a Halifax baker; and John Breynton, rector of St Paul's, for one-third of the H£73 in annual rents. Walker occupied the 1,200-acre Gerrish farm near Windsor, Jacobs a house in the north suburbs of Halifax, and Breynton the Gerrish Halifax house.[50] In another case Ann, widow of Leonard Dunn, sued John Lawlor, a Fort Sackville innkeeper. Dunn, twice widowed, claimed that Lawlor occupied land upon which she held dower rights. The matter had earlier been submitted to arbitration, and the five prominent Halifax merchants had awarded her a dower of H£10 annually for her lifetime to begin in 1802. For twenty-one years Lawlor faithfully paid the amount; Ann Dunn sued him for the stopped payments, and the matter came before the Supreme Court in 1825.[51]

While the Supreme Court in Nova Scotia invariably upheld the widow's dower rights, dower law ensured that a widow's standard of living would fall dramatically, when compared to the one she had enjoyed when married. Even when she needed her late husband's property, the courts denied it her. Thus widows without families tended to become a burden on public charity.

Assault

Alleged victims of assault pursued civil actions in an attempt to secure damages. It is not clear that such actions followed jury acquittals in criminal actions. Let a few typical cases provide the contemporary flavour. The court awarded Jane Bateman five shillings in 1794 when the jury found James Jennings, a Herring Cove fisherman, guilty of beating her such that 'her life then and there was greatly despaired of.'[52] In 1802, Catherine Clyne, a minor represented by her guardian, Valentine Clyne, brought suit for H£300 damages against Clements Horton, Esq. of Halifax, who had 'with force and arms' injured her on the head, shoulder, and breast, resulting in 'a great spitting of blood.' Though Richard John Uniacke represented Horton and he denied any wrongdoing, the jury awarded Clyne H£100 and taxed her costs at H£18.25.[53] A third case involved Mary Cantley, who through her lawyer, Simon Bradstreet Robie, sought H£200 damages from the Halifax cooper, William Allardice, for assault. Cantley was hurt, especially in one leg, and was now lame. In his defence Allardice's lawyer explained that at the time of the alleged assault, Cantley had entered his shop without his leave, and 'greatly disturbed him and his servant.' When asked to leave, she had instead assaulted him with stones. The jury awarded Cantley H£25 and her costs.[54] A fourth case saw Hannah Ward seek, in 1810, H£300 in damages from her lodger, William Lindop, a Halifax merchant. Around midnight, when the defendant, 'in liquor,' came into her kitchen and began abusing his black servant, she told him to find a better time and place to discipline his servant, whereupon Lindop struck her in the face with his fist, knocking her down. Ward claimed to have laid out some H£50 in medical costs arising from the attack. The jury awarded her H£50 exclusive of her doctor's fees.[55]

An 1816 action brought by two couples of Duncan's Cove was of a somewhat different nature. William Smith and Thomas Hackett, both fishermen, with their wives Margaret and Elizabeth sued Simon Crabb, also a fisherman of the same place, for assault. They claimed that Crabb 'often and at different times threatened to beat, wound, maim, kill, or do some bodily harm to them.'[56] Though Crabb was bound over to keep the peace, he continued his threats 'in a most violent manner.' A warrant had been issued for Crabb's arrest, yet all were too afraid of him to carry out the arrest. The outcome is unknown.

Men were not the defendants in all cases. In September 1815 Charles Jones claimed that Halifax widow Sarah Polette had twice assaulted him. In the first instance she spat in his face, held him by the nose, tore out 'divers large quantities' of his hair from his head, then struck him both with her fists and a stick, from which attack he fell to the ground, where he was then violently kicked, and suffered when boiling water was thrown on his face, neck, and breast. His clothes – coat, waistcoat, breeches, stockings, cravat, shirt, and hat – were torn and otherwise damaged. The thorough beating left him 'sick, sore, lame and disordered and so remained ... for the space of ten weeks.' He claimed to have spent H£30 'endeavouring to be cured of the bruises, wounds, and sickness,' and sought damages of H£100.[57] Again the court appears to have acted in a gender-neutral way, whether the plaintiff was a man or a woman.

Slander

The common law protects persons from harm to their reputation by false and derogatory remarks about their person. Civil actions for damages arising from slander date from thirteenth-century England. Known as defamation, it imputes the commission of a crime, the unchaste status of a woman, or an affliction with a loathsome disease. In Nova Scotia, defamation suits were much more commonly heard by the Inferior Court of Common Pleas than by the Supreme Court. The only suits involving women were for slander.

As a light cast on what contemporary society thought was improper public language, such suits are of particular interest to historians.[58] Unsupported accusations, such as 'rogue,' 'villain,' 'scoundrel,' 'thief,' 'you cannot pay your debts,' 'whore,' 'you sold your daughter into whoredom,' 'you had a bastard child,' 'you murdered your bastard child,' 'you threw your bastard mulatto child into the swamp' were among the most common. For the matter to be brought before the court, the offending words had always to be uttered in the hearing of diverse subjects of the king. As reputation and moral standing mattered, and slander stuck, plaintiffs used the law in an attempt to gain redress, both from the publicity the case aroused and through the damages the jury awarded.

Female litigants could become either the object of defamation or its agent, while men defamed other men differently than they defamed women.[59] In July 1792 Lovat Thorogood, a settler of Ship Harbour, was abused by Mary, the wife of John Wolfe of the same place, 'using language unbecoming any Christian, in calling his wife, her sister and mother, whores and every bad expression she could make use of and concluded by threatening his life if ever she got an opportunity.'[60] A petition signed by thirty inhabitants complained both of the lack of a justice of the peace in Ship Harbour and of Mary Wolfe, who as 'a common practice disturbed the settlement.' When in 1796 Tamison, the wife of John Moody, a Halifax barber and tenant of John Johnston, was accused by her landlord of stealing a shirt, 'in the presence and hearing of divers faithful and liege subjects of the King' the couple sought H£500 in damages. Moody declared that his wife was 'a true, faithful, pious, honest and sincere subject of the Lord ... and was of good name, reputation, conversation and condition, and was reputed as such among her neighbours and other faithful subjects of the Lord, the King.'[61] They were awarded their costs, amounting to sixteen shillings.

It was also upon an accusation of stealing that Phoebe Moody felt obliged in 1798 to defend her reputation by initiating a suit against her accuser, Ann Brown. Phoebe had entered Ann Brown's shop, asked to see some black lace, and was accused by the shopkeeper of secreting it under her cloak with the intention of stealing it. Ann put her hand under Phoebe's cloak, found a piece of lace, and accused her of stealing. She thereupon repeated the story to many of her customers. When the case was heard, Ann Brown was in custody, presumably because she and her husband possessed too little property to attach to meet the damages sought. Phoebe Moody recovered judgment for H£50 and costs of H£22.65, which were fully satisfied in May 1799.[62]

Phoebe Moody launched a second defamation suit, this time in 1805 against Lieutenant James Schoedde, of the 60th Foot Regiment, and sought damages of H£5,000. His offence was to have presented her with what he believed was an unpaid debt of hers, amounting to H£175, owing to his late father's estate. When presented with the document, Phoebe Moody 'coloured up and appeared confused,' and then tore it to pieces, stating 'I should have convinced you that the business was settled before I tore the paper.'[63] She then showed the lieutenant her books. Her suit, the outcome of which is unknown, was presumably designed to secure her reputation as an honest retailer.

The last defamation case to be considered here was brought in 1829 by Adam Moschell against Anna Marcia Spindler, both of Lunenburg. Moschell was a minister of the German Reformed Church. In July 1827 Anna Marcia accused him of adultery and of teaching 'false, unChristian and diabolical doctrines' that, he claimed, led his congregation and neighbours to begin to suspect that he had been guilty of adultery, drunkenness, intemperance, and diffusing false doctrines. Speaking in German she stated in Lunenburg, 'he has taught me whoring was no sin ... He has done it to me at Moser's Head. He has done to me on the road from our house to Moser's. He has bespoken to me to come in the garden to fuck me; he wanted to have to do with me in the church.'[64] Moschell won his case, but when the jury awarded him but one shilling in damages, the moral victory was hers, though she had to pay his costs of H£26.75. Thus, in those cases where we know the outcome, the Supreme Court appears to have dealt slightly more harshly with men who slandered women than with women who slandered each other.

Breach of Promise

Breach of promise was another civil matter occasionally dealt with by the Supreme Court. The common law courts in sixteenth-century England had begun to offer a remedy of an action for breach of promise of marriage, which enabled the plaintiff, if successful, to recover damages. The law was not particularly complicated, despite the best efforts of lawyers. There could be no breach of promise unless a contract had been made. The contract needed not have been in writing, however; mutual promises to marry might be implied from the conduct of the parties. Promises to marry might be sued by a minor, but a minor could not be sued. Some corroborating material evidence in support of such promise might help a plaintiff, but it became a statutory requirement only later in the nineteenth century. A defendant could invoke a variety of approaches. For instance, the bad character of the plaintiff excused the defendant from the performance of the contract, unless the defendant was aware of the bad character before making the contract.

The matter could be sued before either the Inferior Court of Common Pleas or the Supreme Court. The earliest known case before the Supreme Court in Nova Scotia dates from 1785, when Elizabeth, a servant of the Halifax merchant Samuel Ferrand Waddington, sued her master, whom she claimed had discussed the prospects of their marriage on every one of the first twenty days of October 1784. The marriage was to have occurred within the following week, as she stated in her deposition in March 1785.[65] The matter did not proceed to trial.

It was almost thirty years before another case was brought before the Supreme Court, in 1814. Then Ann Catherine Mason sued John Dauphine, a St Margaret's Bay farmer, for H£1,000 in damages for having failed to carry through with his New Year's Day promise of marriage. Her plea, filed six months later, stated that Dauphine was 'contriving and fraudulently intending craftily and subtly to deceive and defraud.' When she had incurred costs of H£4.70, the prosecution was discontinued, and substituted by a suit brought by her father against Dauphine for 'contriving and wrongfully and unjustly intending to injure' him and 'to deprive him of the service and assistance' of his daughter. For John 'debauched and carnally knew' Ann 'then and there and from thence for a long space of time' until she became pregnant and was delivered of a child in October 1814.[66]

Though the outcomes of these and other Supreme Court proceedings remain unknown, it seems clear from proceedings undertaken elsewhere that suits alleging breach of promise were taken very seriously. In three surviving cases in 1830, 1832, and 1833 the Inferior Court of Common Pleas for Lunenburg County awarded damages of H£40, H£60, and H£80 respectively and with costs. In the first instance, Mary Smith, aged nineteen and represented by her 'next friend' David Wight, claimed in March 1830 that Henry Feener, a Lunenburg blacksmith, had promised to marry her the previous December. She had become pregnant and Feener claimed to be unsure that the child was his. His letter to her in mid-December is a rare document. 'I received a letter from you this morning asking me to come up and see you and let you know if I intended marrying you. I answer I have to inform you that I cannot go up to your house nor need you depend on my marrying you. If the child is mine I must put up with what has happened to others. It never shall want. I trust that this will put an end of your sending me letters or troubling me in any other way. If you had not said about me what you have and sent the messages to my father you did, you would perhaps not be in the situation you are. You must blame yourself and not me. Your well wisher, Henry Feener.'[67] In the second, Elizabeth Arenburg successfully sued Garret Wile of Upper LaHave for having breached his promise of marriage first made in September 1831 and repeated on four further occasions.[68] Two years later Wile's brother Andrew, apparently having learned nothing from his brother's experience, was sued by Elizabeth Randall. Owing to her extreme poverty, Randall was permitted by the court to prosecute her action *in forma pauperis*. Andrew Wile wrote to the court that he feared great injury, as, in order to defend the suit, he needed as a material witness, John Arenburg, long absent from Nova Scotia and thus unable to be served with a subpoena to appear.[69] Nevertheless, the case went ahead, and Wile did not appeal its verdict to the Supreme Court, while the lower court's execution remained unsatisfied. Thus we see a consistent record, when the matter came to trial, of the Supreme Court upholding the claims filed by women, invariably the plaintiffs in such cases.

Conclusion

Alongside the need to study women in the past, one of the compelling reasons for having undertaken this research was the manageable number of cases. However large the sample the thousand cases studied here might seem, it is dwarfed by the more than ten thousand unreported cases exclusively involving men that are estimated to form the rest of the Supreme Court files to the end of 1830. Only with a substantial research grant can the full study of the early work of the Supreme Court be attempted.[70]

Historians are deeply divided about the condition of women in this era. Some believe they can chart a deterioration in status in the eighteenth and early nineteenth century, when compared to the seventeenth. The working of common law, especially its impact on married women's rights, is often now found to be odious.[71] Others see an amelioration of women's legal status, especially through the equity courts, which in British North America was the Court of Chancery.[72] Through the use of trusts set up before marriage, a woman's real property, owned by her before her marriage, could be kept at arm's length from an improvident husband so long as the marriage endured. Even in this instance, however, there is evidence in other jurisdictions of such trusts acting against the interests of married women.

The evidence thrown up in this study, covering the first couple of generations following the resettlement of Nova Scotia, does not support an interpretation of a deterioration in the condition of women. The Supreme Court's behaviour appears almost gender-neutral. This seems particularly the case in matters of debt and of trespass and ejectment, where the Supreme Court's treatment of female litigants was no different than that observed in cases involving men exclusively. Elsewhere, Nova Scotia's Supreme Court upheld the widow's dower right and supported female litigants as plaintiffs in breach of promise suits. If the damages awarded to plaintiffs in breach of promise suits seem high, the awards made for civil actions arising from assault seem on occasion inadequate. This doubtless reflected the biases of the all-male juries which made the awards. In matters of slander the court dealt somewhat more harshly with men who slandered women than women who slandered each other. Even in the cases involving re-enslaved black women, we know from the behaviour of Supreme Court trials from the late-1790s onwards that the condition of such women improved, as the status of slave in Nova Scotia was judicially abolished by about 1810.

This study also offers important evidence about widows, a subject to which many historians, at some point in their careers, seem drawn, if not directly, as here, then obliquely in some other context. Some 40 per cent of the female litigants in this study were widows. They ranged from the almost impecunious – many of whom were illiterate – through several social layers to the few among the social elite. Most of them were involved in debt cases, as some sixty-five functioned as executors of their late husbands' wills and another eighty as administrators of their estates. In these capacities many appeared both as plaintiffs seeking payment and as defendants being sued for non-payment. In addition, three-quarters of the suits to establish dower were launched by widows, and the balance by widows already remarried.[73] If the women were assertive in claiming their rights in this way, the Supreme Court appears to have ensured them the full support of the law.

Much remains to be accomplished before the social history of women in the colonial era of Nova Scotia's history can be written, but this study of civil litigation in early Nova Scotia, together with the research already being published on criminality, allows us to begin to understand their socio-legal position before the era of marriage law reform. At the very least, the research exposes the condition of a considerable group of women – spinsters and wives, as well as widows – hitherto obscure or unknown.

NOTES

1 The data also include 622 cases from the Inferior Court of Common Pleas and 344 causes in the Court of Chancery. In addition are data on all surviving wills by women, and, by way of comparison, a large sample of men's wills.

2 Professor Phillips, having studied criminal cases in Nova Scotia to 1815, concluded that 'perhaps the best evidence about the social roles of women in 18th-century Halifax can be derived from the criminal justice records themselves.' J. Phillips and A.N. May, 'Female Criminality in 18th-Century Halifax,' *Acadiensis* 31 (2) (2002): 83.

3 G.G. Campbell, 'Canadian Women's History: A View from the Atlantic,' *Acadiensis* 20 (1) (Autumn, 1990): 185. Dr Phillips, of course, is an exception, with his series of path-breaking studies of criminal justice. See J. Phillips, 'Women, Crime and Criminal Justice in Early Halifax, 1750–1800,' in Phillips, T. Loo, and S. Lewthwaite, eds., *Essays in the History of Canadian Law: Volume V – Crime and Criminal Justice* (Toronto: Osgoode Society for Canadian Legal History and University of Toronto Press 1994), and 'Halifax Juries in the Eighteenth Century,' in G.T. Smith, S. Devereaux, and A.N. May, eds., *Criminal Justice in the Old World and the New: Essays in Honour of J.M. Beattie* (Toronto: Centre of Criminology 1998); A.N. May and J. Phillips, 'Homicide in Nova Scotia, 1749–1815,' *Canadian Historical Review* 82 (2001): 625–61.

4 R.J. Ross, 'The Legal Past of Early New England: Notes for the Study of Law, Legal Culture, and Intellectual History,' *William and Mary Quarterly* 50 (January, 1993): 30, n. 9.

5 B.H. Mann, *Neighbors and Strangers: Law and Community in Early Connecticut* (Chapel Hill: University of North Carolina Press 1987), 6. Lack of concern for the social history of the civil law and the civil courts in Great Britain was noted by G.R. Rubin, 'The County Courts and the Tally Trade, 1846–1914,' in Rubin and D. Sugarman, eds., *Law, Economy and Society, 1750–1914: Essays in the History of English Law* (Abingdon: Professional Books 1984), 321. See also Rubin 'Law, Poverty and Imprisonment for Debt, 1868–1914,' in ibid., i–xv, 241–99, 322, noting that the law as applied to those who were 'simply too poor to pay off their consumer debts ... imprisonment for debt struck at those unable to pay rather than against those unwilling to pay.' 'Social historians have only recently begun to realize the importance of studying private litigation': T. Stretton, *Women Waging Law in Elizabethan England* (Cambridge: Cambridge University Press 1998), 4.

6 See variously T.L. Snyder, 'Legal History of the Colonial South: Assess-

ment and Suggestions,' *William and Mary Quarterly* 50 (1993): 18–29; C.H. Dayton, 'Turning Points and the Relevance of Colonial Legal History,' *William and Mary Quarterly* 50 (January, 1993): 13; M.B. Norton, 'Gender and Defamation in Seventeenth-Century Maryland,' *William and Mary Quarterly* 44 (1987): 3–39; M. Salmon, *Women and the Law of Property in Early America* (Chapel Hill: University of North Carolina Press 1986). Salmon studied Massachusetts, Connecticut, New York, Pennsylvania, Maryland, Virginia, and South Carolina. L. Briggs Biemer, *Women and Property in Colonial New York: The Transition from Dutch to English Law, 1643–1727* (Ann Arbor: UMI Research Press 1983).

7 Newer research is by T. Johnson, 'Matrimonial Property Law in Newfoundland to the End of the Nineteenth Century' (PhD thesis, Memorial University of Newfoundland, 1998), and her 'Women and Inheritance in Nineteenth-Century Newfoundland,' *Journal of the Canadian Historical Society*, New Series 13 (2002): 1–22; C. Backhouse, *Petticoats and Prejudice: Women and Law in Nineteenth-Century Canada* (Toronto: Osgoode Society for Canadian Legal History and Women's Press 1991), which mentions Nova Scotians in matters of prostitution, infanticide, and wife battery. See as well J. Phillips, '"Securing Obedience to Necessary Laws": The Criminal Law in Eighteenth-Century Nova Scotia,' *Nova Scotia Historical Review* 12 (December 1992): 87–124, and his 'Women, Crime and Criminal Justice.'

8 J.A. Dickinson, *Justice et justiciables: la procédure civile à la prévoté de Québec, 1667–1759* (Quebec: Les Presses de l'Université de Laval 1982); E. Kolish, 'Some Aspects of Civil Litigation in Lower Canada, 1785–1825: Towards the Use of Court Records for Canadian Social History,' *Canadian Historical Review* 70 (1988): 337–65; B. Bradbury et al., 'Property and Marriage: The Law and the Practice in Early Nineteenth-Century Montreal,' *Histoire sociale-Social History* 26 (1993): 9–39; L. Chambers, *Married Women and Property Law in Victorian Ontario* (Toronto: Osgoode Society for Canadian Legal History and University of Toronto Press 1997).

9 As examples, see R. Baehre, 'From Bridewell to Federal Penitentiary: Prisons and Punishment in Nova Scotia before 1880,' in Girard and Phillips, *Essays*; B.J. Price, '"Raised in Rockhead. Died in the Poor House": Female Petty Criminals in Halifax, 1864–1890,' in ibid.; J. Fingard, *The Dark Side of Life in Victorian Halifax* (Porter's Lake, NS: Pottersfield Press 1989).

10 P. Girard, 'Married Women's Property, Chancery Abolition, and Insolvency Law: Law Reform in Nova Scotia, 1820–1867,' in Girard and Phillips, *Essays*; P. Girard and R. Veinott, 'Married Women's Property Law In Nova Scotia, 1850–1910' in J. Guildford and S. Morton, eds., *Separate Spheres: Women's Worlds in the 19th Century Maritimes* (Fredericton: Acadiensis Press 1994).

11 Examples are J. Snell, 'Marital Cruelty: Women and the Nova Scotia Divorce Court, 1900–1939,' *Acadiensis* 13 (1988): 3–32; K. Smith Maynard, 'Divorce in Nova Scotia, 1750–1910,' in Girard and Phillips, *Essays*; R. Veinott, 'Child Custody and Divorce: A Nova Scotia Study, 1868–1910,' in ibid.; J. Fingard, 'The Prevention of Cruelty, Marriage Breakdown and the Rights of Wives in Nova Scotia, 1880–1900,' in Guildford and Morton, eds., *Separate Spheres*.

12 Salmon, *Women*, 185. She believed that since 'chancery administered trust estates, the vehicle under which wives owned property separately from their husbands, the presence or absence of an equity court virtually determined a colony's position on female separate estates,' 11. For Chancery in Nova Scotia see Cahill and Phillips, this volume. Chancery courts existed in New York, Maryland, Virginia, and South Carolina before 1776: Salmon, *Women*, 11. Established in Upper Canada only in 1837, the court was given jurisdiction in specified equity matters: fraud, trusts, executors and administrators, mortgages, dower, infants, 'idiots and lunatics' and their estates, and specific performance of contracts.

13 J. Gwyn, 'Female Litigants before the Civil Courts of Nova Scotia, 1749–1801,' *Histoire sociale-Social History* 37 (2003): 311–46.

14 A study for 1830–2, by way of comparison, found that debt cases constituted some 80–90 per cent of all Supreme Court litigation. See D. Darling, 'Nova Scotia Supreme Court Records, Halifax County, 1830–1832' (unpublished MS, Dalhousie Law School, 1993).

15 E. Mancke, 'At the Counter of the General Store: Women and the Economy in Eighteenth-Century Horton, Nova Scotia,' in M. Conrad, ed., *Intimate Relations: Family and Community in Planter Nova Scotia 1759–1800* (Fredericton: Acadiensis Press 1995).

16 Debts of less than H£5 were sued before the Inferior Court of Common Pleas; for sums between H£5 and H£10 the plaintiff could sue either in that court or in the Supreme Court, where they could be tried in summary fashion, that is, without a jury: P.V. Girard, 'Patriot Jurist: Beamish Murdoch of Halifax, 1800–1876' (PhD thesis, Dalhousie University 1998), 161.

17 *Woodmass v. Webb*, an appeal: NSARM, Supreme Court Records, RG 39, Series C, vol. 3; *Tyson v. Tyler, ibid.*, vol. 45; *Utterson v. Tyler and Tyson*, ibid.; *Black et al. v. Henry*, ibid., vol. 125.

18 As plaintiff in that court she recovered H£189. See *Moody v. Hamilton*, NSARM, Inferior Court of Common Pleas Records, RG 37, Hfx, 25/2/186; *Moody v. Archibald*, ibid., 23/3/26; *Moody v. Hynes*, ibid., 23/3/62; and *Moody v. Brewer* , ibid., 23/3/93. As co-administrator of her husband's estate, she sued for a further H£6.48: see *Moody & Lyon v. Keys*, ibid., 25/2/195, and *Moody & Lyon v. Bill*, ibid., 25/2/196.

19 'A general assortment of groceries and dry goods' in *Valentine* (Capt. Critchell), 9 Apr. 1801; 'A general assortment of British merchandize' in *Tyger* (Capt. Hughes), 23 July 1801. Other advertisements appeared in 1802 and 1805 offering for sale wine, port, sherry, ladies' and gentlemen's shoes. 'A large and excellent assortment of the most fashionable merchandize, suitable for the season' in *Acorn* and *Elizabeth*, 12 June 1806. Information from Professor Phillips, for which I am grateful.

20 Summons 21 Dec. 1805; arrested and imprisoned 16 Jan. 1806: *Moody v. Grant*, RG 39, Series C, vol. 89.

21 Her successive clerks were Theophilus M. Chamberlain and John Brown. In 1805 she sued Chamberlain and his father, a Preston Esq., for the balance of an 1804 demand loan of which H£20.54 remained unpaid two years later, when the jury rendered its verdict: *Moody v. Chamberlain*, ibid.

22 Evidence at the 20 July 1808 trial indicated that she and her husband had in the 1790s carried on trade both with Boston and New York: *Lyon v. Moody*, ibid., vol. 92.

23 *Lyon & Butler v. Moody*, ibid., vols. 92 and 98.

24 J.N. Grant, 'Black Immigrants into Nova Scotia, 1776–1815,' *Journal of Negro History* 58 (1973): 253–70.

25 J.B. Cahill, '*Habeas Corpus* and Slavery in Nova Scotia: *R. v. Hecht ex parte Rachel*, 1798,' *University of New Brunswick Law Journal* 44 (1995): 195.

26 Ibid., 196.

27 *Hecht v. Moody*, RG 39, Series C, vol. 81.

28 *Woodin v. Watson*, RG 37, Hfx, 22/45. Woodin, a joiner, came to Halifax from England in 1749 accompanied by his family and a male servant: E.C. Wright, *Planters and Pioneers: Nova Scotia, 1749 to 1775*, rev. ed. (Wolfville: privately printed 1982), 328.

29 Elias Marshall (1737–1806); apprenticed to the ship's carpenter of *Grafton*, 1752; carpenter's mate, 1759; carpenter, 1761; foreman of Halifax naval yard, 1763–82, appointed by Commodore Spry; Commodore Colvill thought him 'very well qualified as a foreman'; Jacob Hurd described him as 'an active, stirring man'; deeply implicated in the then master shipwright's frauds at the yard, 1775; Commissioner Arbuthnot thought him 'really valuable & does more real duty than any person' and asked Navy Board 'to overlook past errors'; acting master shipwright, 1776; acting joint-master shipwright with Thomas Johnson, 1782–3; superseded by Provo Wallis, 1783; master shipwright when Wallis retired, 1793; dismissed by Commissioner Coffin for peculation and fraud, 1800; defended himself in England; Navy Board thought his misdemeanours minor; master shipwright, 1793–1805; 'greatly afflicted with the gout and asthma and other-

wise very infirm,' superannuated, 1805; m. Mary (1737–1813) in England; d. Halifax, aged sixty-eight; son John Houlton made career in navy and retired as commander; son Elias Jr, a simpleton, tried to set fire to naval yard buildings; son Samuel a naval yard shipwright, was dismissed for embezzlement.

30 Which Phillips is uncertain, as there were three – George, John, and William: A.E. Marble, *Surgeons, Smallpox and the Poor: A History of Medicine and Social Conditions in Nova Scotia, 1749–1799* (Montreal: McGill-Queen's University Press 1993), 86 and 170.

31 Two surgeons were named Fletcher: Richard and William: ibid., 107 and 170.

32 *Watson v. Proud*, RG 39, Series C, vol. 21, no. 33.

33 *Proud v. Watson*, RG 37, Hfx, 22/45.

34 20 Oct. 1779: RG 39, Series C, vol. 21, no. 33, and Series J, vol. 2, 365.

35 Haines was a Windsor victualler. The attached goods included six horses, saddles and harness, a cask of West Indies rum, and '1 Negro wench named Sillah': *McMonogle v. Haines*, RG 39, Series C, vol. 21. Priscilla Ball died in Halifax 10 May 1791 and was buried in St Paul's graveyard: A.E. Marble, *Deaths, Burials, and Probate of Nova Scotians, 1749–1799, from Primary Sources* (Halifax: Nova Scotia Genealogical Society 1994), vol. 1, 25.

36 J.B. Cahill, 'Slavery and the Judges of Loyalist Nova Scotia,' *University of New Brunswick Law Journal* 43 (1994): 81.

37 *Winston v. Grant*, RG 39, Series C, vol. 2, no. 172.

38 His was a military career, with service at Louisbourg 1746–9 and then at Halifax, where he was a lieutenant colonel of the 45th Regiment in 1755. At the 1758 siege of Louisbourg he commanded a brigade, and later in 1762, the 80th Foot Regiment at Quebec. He became lieutenant governor of Nova Scotia in 1763: P.R. Blakeley, 'Montagu Wilmot,' *DCB*, 3: 663–4.

39 *Tracey v. O'Brien*, writ of summons 27 Apr. 1773, RG 39, Series C, vol. 14.

40 *O'Brien v. Quin, (alias Tracey), Sherlock and Sherlock*, filed 12 Nov. 1770, NSARM, Chancery Records, RG 36, A/27.

41 J.B. Cahill, 'Richard Gibbons's "Review" of the Administration of Justice in Nova Scotia, 1774,' *University of New Brunswick Law Journal* 37 (1988): 51.

42 *Ryan v. Sullivan*, RG 39, Series C, vol. 85.

43 Summons 18 July 1812; verdict 14 Apr. 1813: ibid., vol. 102.

44 *Hurd v. Newman*, plea filed 27 Nov. 1815: ibid., vol. 108.

45 *Embley v. Baisley*, summons 11 May 1816, ibid., vol. 115. See also similar cases involving Catherine Warren where the outcomes are unknown: *Warren v. Murphy*, summons 8 Apr. 1816, and *Warren v. Wainwright and Bell*, summons 8 Apr. 1816, ibid., vol. 123; and widow Susannah Green of

Lawrencetown, *Green v. Mungervin and Mungervin*, ibid., vol. 129. Susannah's plea, filed 17 Mar. 1818, is found in ibid., vol. 142; and *Green v. Crooks*, ibid., vol. 163, plea filed 4 Aug. 1821; and Mary and Edward Bowers with the Ketch Harbour fisherman, Jordan Flemming, who had illegally felled trees on their property, *Bowers and Bowers v. Flemming*. Plea filed 21 Mar. 1820, ibid., vol. 157.

46 Outcome unknown, *Baisley v. Embley*, ibid., vol. 124.

47 Jury's verdict against Embley, 22 Jan. 1818: *Baisley and Baisley v. Embley*, ibid., vol. 139; see their plea in vol. 141.

48 Plea filed 31 Aug. 1821: *Letson and Letson v. Thompson and Parker*, ibid., vol. 160.

49 S.N.S. 1768, c. 8; 1771, c. 6.

50 Costs of H£2.75 were awarded her against each of the three defendants: *Gerrish v. Walker, Jacobs, and Breynton*, RG 39, Series C, vol. 13.

51 Outcome unknown, *Dunn v. Lawlor*, ibid., vol. 170.

52 24 Oct. 1794: *Thomas and Bateman v. Jennings*, ibid., vol. 70.

53 *Clyne v. Horton*, ibid., vol. 83.

54 *Cantley v. Allardice*, ibid., vol. 85.

55 *Ward v. Lindop*, ibid., vol. 97.

56 *Smith and Hackett v. Crabb, ibid.*, vol. 122. In 1817 Crabb was sued by fisherwoman Elizabeth Crabb, also of Duncan's Cove, for trespass for having 'possessed himself of divers goods and chattels' belonging to Elizabeth which she valued at H£20. It included ten tons of grass. Summons 21 Oct. 1817: *Crabb v. Crabb*, ibid., vol. 127, outcome unknown.

57 Outcome unknown, *Jones v. Polette*, ibid., vols. 108 and 117.

58 There is a rapidly expanding literature on defamation, gossip, and honour. Examples include S.M. Waddams, *Sexual Slander in Nineteenth-Century England* (Toronto: University of Toronto Press 2000); M.L. Kaplan, *The Culture of Slander in Early Modern England* (New York: Cambridge University Press 1997); L. Gowing, 'Language, Power and the Law: Women's Slander Litigation in Early Modern London,' in J. Kermode and G. Walker, eds., *Women, Crime and the Courts in Early Modern England* (London: UCL Press 1994); Norton, 'Gender and Defamation'; P.N. Moogk, '"Thieving Buggers" and "Stupid Sluts": Insults and Popular Culture in New France,' *William and Mary Quarterly* 36 (1979): 524–47.

59 As an example, in 1783 Attorney General Richard Gibbons, Jr, seeking H£10,000 in damages, sued a man who had cried out at a meeting of freeholders gathered to elect a member of the House of Assembly, 'Who will vote for him but Hell? He is a damned rascal, a damned scoundrel, a dia-

bolical villain ... and shall never be in the House. He shall never be elected!' Gibbons lost both the election and his suit. Writ of summons 20 Mar. 1783, *Gibbons v. Avery*, RG39, Series C, vol. 25, cited in J. Gwyn, 'Capitalists, Merchants and Manufacturers in Early Nova Scotia, 1769–1791: The Tangled Affairs of John Avery, James Creighton, John Albro and Joseph Fairbanks,' in Conrad, ed., *Intimate Relations*, 191.

60 Outcome unknown, *Thorogood v. Wolfe*, RG 39, Series C, vol. 67.

61 *Moody and Moody v. Johnston*, ibid., vol. 75.

62 *Moody v. Brown and Brown*, ibid., vol. 81.

63 *Moody v. Schoedde*, ibid., vol. 89.

64 *Moschell v. Spindler*, ibid., vol. 74.

65 *Beckett v. Waddington*, ibid., vol. 35.

66 *Ann Mason v. Dauphine*, ibid., vol. 104. Their lawyer was Lewis M. Wilkins. *John Mason v. Dauphine*, ibid., vol. 104. In 1815 Mary Cowper claimed that the Halifax merchant, John Stanfield, had on three occasions made a promise of marriage – on 18 and 25 June and 5 November 1814 – but had failed to act and so in October 1815 she sought damages of H£5,000: *Cowper v. Stanfield*, ibid., vol. 106.

67 Costs came to H£15.85: *Smith v. Feener*, RG 37, Lun, 26/36.

68 Costs amounted to H£14.85 and, with the damages, remained unpaid: *Arenburg v. Wile*, ibid., 30/84.

69 *Randall v. Wile*, ibid., 32/7 and 32/76. There was another such case in 1840, but it was heard by the Inferior Court of Common Pleas for Shelburne County. On 1 Oct. 1839 David Snow and Mary Ann Snow had exchanged promises of marriage at Port LaTour, but three months later, on New Year's Day 1840, David instead married Phoebe Snow. The jury awarded her H£20 in damages. The costs, if taxed, were not stated: *Snow v. Snow*, RG37, Shel. 14/18.7.

70 There is some supporting evidence for my estimate that about 9 per cent of all Supreme Court cases involved women. Professor Girard, for instance, found that some 10–12 per cent of Beamish Murdoch's clients were women, and 'virtually all of them widows' needing assistance with debt collection and dealing with tenants: Girard, 'Patriot Jurist,' 175 and 196.

71 Of the numerous examples I will cite only three: Chambers, *Married Women in Victorian Ontario*; J. Perkin, *Women and Marriage in Nineteenth-Century England* (London: Routledge 1989); B. Hill, ed., *Eighteenth-Century Women: An Anthology* (London: Allen and Unwin 1984).

72 Examples include Johnson, 'Women and Inheritance in Nineteenth-Century Newfoundland'; J. Gwyn, 'Disposal of Property in Female Wills: Nova

Scotia, 1750–1830,' in M. Conrad and B. Moody, eds., *Planter Links: Community and Culture in Colonial Nova Scotia* (Fredericton: Acadiensis Press 2001); M. Berg, 'Women's Property and the Industrial Revolution,' *Journal of Interdisciplinary History* 24 (1993): 233–50; and Salmon, *Women*.

73 By contrast, widows were almost never involved in trespass, assault, or in a miscellaneous group of suits from breach of promise to defamation.

10

Her Majesty's Yankees: American Authority in the Supreme Court of Victorian Nova Scotia, 1837–1901

BERNARD J. HIBBITTS

Introduction: The Fourteenth Colony

Over the course of its history, Nova Scotia has been by turns French, British, and Canadian. Less obviously, it has also been American – not by allegiance, but rather by virtue of its close demographic, cultural, economic, and even legal ties with various American colonies and states.[1] Nova Scotia's legal ties to America date back to the early eighteenth century, when Colonel Richard Philipps, the English captain general and governor of Nova Scotia, was ordered to conduct himself according to the 'instructions given by his majesty to the governor of Virginia.'[2] After the founding of Halifax in 1749, the laws of Virginia and later Massachusetts provided models for new Nova Scotian legislation and guidelines for the operation of the redesigned Nova Scotian courts.[3] The Massachusetts influence on Nova Scotian judicial procedure quickly proved controversial, but into the mid-nineteenth century, Nova Scotian lawmakers continued to copy or at least derive some of their most important civil statutes from American precedents.[4]

To what extent, in what manner, and with what result was this clear American influence on early Nova Scotian statute law complemented, grounded, and even furthered by the use of American case law and legal literature in Nova Scotia's courts? The answers to these questions may ultimately reveal much about the dynamics of Nova Scotian legal culture, the shifting loyalties and mentalités of the Nova Scotian bench and bar, and the historical place of Nova Scotia in the constellation of other colonial and post-colonial Canadian jurisdictions.

At this juncture, a comprehensive investigation of the historical use of American authority in the Nova Scotian courts would be impractical, if not impossible. In this paper I have therefore set myself the more manageable task of investigating the use of American authority in the decisions of the Nova Scotia Supreme Court during the Victorian era, 1837–1901. Focusing on these cases has several advantages: first, the task is institutionally and chronologically limited; second, the Victorian era is the one in which judgments of that court were first officially reported and printed; and third, the era embraces the chronological fault line (c. 1890) identified in at least one other provincial jurisdiction as marking a critical decline in the Canadian use of American case law and legal literature.[5]

The body of this paper is divided into two parts, covering the years 1837–75 and 1875–1901 respectively. I will break my discussion at 1875 because I believe – for reasons I will articulate later – that American case law and legal literature played a more significant role in the legal culture of the Nova Scotia Supreme Court before that time, and a less significant role afterward. Within each of my two time periods I shall consider how and why NSSC judges made recourse to American law, and the general impact that American authority had on Nova Scotian legal culture. In the conclusion of the paper I will offer some observations on how the Nova Scotia Supreme Court's experience with American authority in the Victorian era is both comparable to and can be contrasted with the experiences of courts elsewhere in Canada.

But first, a few caveats and disclaimers. This is not the first investigation of the use of American authority in the Nova Scotian courts. In 1935, while attending Dalhousie Law School, Alan Sprague wrote a prize-winning essay (finally published in 1992) examining references to American authorities in reported Supreme Court cases decided prior to 1853[6] as part of a much broader analysis of American influence on early Nova Scotian law. Sprague's pioneering effort did not, however, have the benefit of recent scholarship on general trends in Canadian legal history, on the dynamics of Nova Scotian legal history, and on the use of American authority in other Canadian contexts and jurisdictions.[7]

Second, the present exercise is not based on the counting of cited American cases or other American references. Citation counting has occasionally been used as a means of assessing American influence on Canadian courts, but it is a very blunt and very limited measure.[8] Such a count can easily be distorted by a few cases in which American authority was heavily employed, or by the presence on a court of one or two judges who use American authority much more than their colleagues. It overlooks important factors such as whether American cases were approved or disapproved, and whether they were seriously discussed, quoted, or simply cited. It ignores the extent to which American law and legal literature may have influenced the overall flavour of Canadian legal debate or the general context of Canadian legal development. Here, then, I will eschew citation counts in favour of other, ostensibly more subjective but ultimately more substantive, indicia of influence.

Third and finally, I should emphasize that this study is far from definitive. Much work remains to be done on the subject of overall American influence on Nova Scotian jurisprudence during, before, and after the Victorian period, and I would encourage further research by other historians who may be literally closer to the sources than I am in Pittsburgh.[9]

The Law of 'Our Neighbors,'[10] 1837–1875

Although eighteenth-century case records from the Nova Scotia Supreme Court are very limited, we know that at least some American authority leavened the English precedents which were routinely used by the Court years immediately prior to Victoria's ascension. Select cases from the early to mid-1830s, subsequently collected and published in the 1850s, show Supreme Court judges occasionally considering both American case law and treatise literature. In 1835, for instance, Chief Justice Brenton Halliburton declared in the case of *Tarratt v. Sawyer*, 'I have not overlooked the American cases which have been cited, for although we are not bound to defer to them as we might to the decisions at Westminster, we derive great satisfaction and advantage from the views taken by the able lawyers who sit on many of the Benches in that country, of transactions so similar to those which frequently occur in this.'[11] Even (or perhaps especially) at this stage, however, Nova Scotian reliance on American authority was complicated by the local absence, or at least a shortage, of all but the most basic American law books.[12] This problem of access was arguably underneath a complaint of Bliss J. in the 1836 case of *Ralston v. Barss*: 'We have been referred to the work of an eminent lawyer of the United States [James Kent] from which it would appear that this question has been fully settled in that country by a judge of great reputation [Joseph Story] ... But even if we recognize the authority of that decision, we ought first to have the case submitted to us at large (and I am not aware of its being within reach) ...[13]

This direct, if limited, evidence that American authority figured in the judgments of the pre-Victorian Supreme Court of Nova Scotia is supported by the recurring references to American law contained in Beamish Murdoch's *Epitome of the Laws of Nova Scotia* (1832–3).[14] The *Epitome*, of course, was a summary of Nova Scotian law, not a record of judicial proceedings. The fact that Murdoch was comfortable citing Kent's *Commentaries* in such a work, combined with the fact that he at one point recommended an American text (David Hoffman's *Course of Legal Study*) as an appropriate manual for Nova Scotian law students, nonetheless reinforces the impression given by the few published case records that citations from American legal works and writings were welcomed by members of the pre-Victorian Nova Scotian bench.[15]

The extent to which Nova Scotian judges used American authority certainly did not change overnight in 1837, but my reading of the official reports (which were highly selective through the late 1850s) suggests that it gradually increased over the 1840s, 1850s, and early 1860s. In these years, as compared to the pre-Victorian period, Supreme Court judges referred to American law and legal literature more frequently, noted American precedents more precisely, discussed them at greater length, and praised their American counterparts more often. Observers of the Nova Scotian legal scene were conscious of the impact American law was having: writing in 1853, Alexander James, the Supreme Court reporter, noted that 'American decisions are ... frequently employed with effect to influence the decisions of our Provincial Courts.'[16] In the mid-1860s through the early 1870s the rate and extent of Nova Scotian references to American authorities seems to have increased still further.[17] Although English law was never in any danger of being overtaken by its American equivalent, American law had clearly become a strong secondary influence on Nova Scotian jurisprudence.

But exactly what sorts of 'American law' were the Nova Scotia Supreme Court judges citing in the early Victorian era? Where did their American cases come from? Which American treatises did they rely on? Most of the case law came from Massachusetts and (after 1850) New York. United States Supreme Court decisions were also occasionally cited.[18] Citations to the decisions of other American state or federal courts were very rare; when such citations were made, the Nova Scotian judges usually acknowledged that they were derived, second-hand, from American texts (although multistate American collections such as

American Leading Cases and *Abbott's Digest of the Law of Corporations* were occasionally mentioned, and presumably employed).[19] As regards the texts themselves, early Nova Scotian references to James Kent's *Commentaries*, Nathan Dane's *Abridgement*, and the various works of Joseph Story were supplemented in the 1850s and 1860s by citations to newer works, such as those of Angell (on limitations and insurance), Greenleaf (on evidence), Duer (on insurance), Morris (on replevin), Parsons (on contracts and mercantile law), Washburn (on real property), Hilliard (on real property, torts and sales), and Sedgewick (on damages).[20] In 1853, Desbarres J. cited to a by-then defunct American legal periodical – the *American Jurist*, published out of Boston.[21] From the 1860s, Nova Scotian judges also drew increasingly on American editions of English legal works: either collections of English cases with American notes (such as the *Exchequer Reports, Law and Equity Reports*, Cruise's *Digest*, the *English Common Law Reports*, or White and Tudor's *Equity Cases*), or American-annotated editions of English treatises (e.g. *Chitty on Bills, Hill on Trustees, Stephen's Nisi Prius, Williams on Personal Property, Smith's Mercantile Law*).[22] At this stage, such Americanized English books served as a kind of jurisprudential Trojan horse, bringing American case law and analysis to Nova Scotia under the cover of English precepts and precedents.

In the early Victorian period, the NSSC judges offered many overlapping reasons for their recourse to these various forms of American legal authority. First, Nova Scotian jurists clearly perceived the American courts and treatise writers as working within the same English cultural and legal tradition as they themselves did; the Americans were, if you like, partners in elaborating a truly 'common' law, a perspective encouraged by a certain open-textured approach in ante-bellum American jurisprudence itself which tolerated and even encouraged borrowing from other jurisdictions.[23] In this context, the Nova Scotian judges did not hesitate to use American cases and commentaries to bolster and confirm English ones. In 1858, for instance, Wilkins J. adopted an oft-repeated formula in *Levatte & Salter v. Twining*: 'in this case I have not perceived any discrepancy between the English and United States decisions; and on the combined authority of both I think the plaintiff is entitled ...'.[24] By virtue of the same perceived American commitment to the common law, Nova Scotia judges were very willing to cite American cases and commentators when no English precedents were available. Thus, in an 1863 case, Chief Justice Young seemed relieved to report, 'I have not found any late English authority upon the point, but the American cases are clear.'[25]

Second, Nova Scotian judges perceived American judges and legal writers to be especially knowledgeable and competent in certain doctrinal and practical matters with which English jurists were notably less familiar. The developing law of insurance – largely pioneered by American jurists – was one such matter. As early as 1840 Bliss J. acknowledged, 'we may with great propriety, and perhaps with advantage too, inquire how such a case would probably be viewed in a great commercial country, where the law of marine insurance is so continually, and under such varied circumstances, discussed and decided.'[26] For similar reasons, Nova Scotian judges were also drawn to American jurisprudence on the general law of business corporations. As Chief Justice Young noted in an 1871 case, 'Corporations of this class are so much more abundant on this side of the Atlantic than in the mother country, that we must look mainly to American authorities, and especially to those of the United States.'[27]

Third, members of the Nova Scotia Supreme Court appreciated that Nova Scotia and the various American jurisdictions often had, as developing societies (albeit, perhaps, at somewhat different stages of development), more in common than did Nova Scotia and England. General common law had always permitted colonial judges to reject English doctrines which they considered inappropriate for colonial conditions;[28] the existence of American precedents, however, meant that in circumstances of dissimilarity, Nova Scotians had an alternative model to which they could turn. In 1851, Chief Justice Halliburton incidentally identified both the problem and the solution in *Lessees of Lawson v. Whitman*: 'the situation of lands in this Province resembles that of those in the United States so much more than of those old and long cultivated lands in the mother country, that we may frequently consider with advantage the view which their courts have taken of questions of this nature.'[29]

A fourth reason why Nova Scotian jurists used American authority in the early Victorian period has to do with the fact that a number of the Nova Scotian statutes they were interpreting (such as those on probate and divorce)[30] had been based on, or were at least similar to, American models. The decisions of the American courts interpreting those models or their American successors were therefore directly relevant to the construction of similar statutes in Nova Scotia. In 1841, Chief Justice Halliburton made passing reference to this common statutory history in *Ells v. Ells*: 'I am supported in [my] opinion [of the Probate Act] by the decisions of the courts of Massachusetts, from which

State, when it was a Colony, we borrowed our law upon this subject.'[31] Young C.J. repeated the general point in 1871: '[o]ur own statute [on partition of lands] was borrowed almost word for word from chapter 103 of the Revised Statutes of Massachusetts, published in 1836, and founded upon acts passed in 1783 and 1785. The clauses which affect this question ... are literally the same in both. It is of importance, therefore, to trace the decisions of the Courts of Massachusetts ...'[32]

Fifth, Nova Scotian lawyers and judges appear to have been drawn towards American case law and legal literature by the considerable intellectual reputations of their American authors.[33] In 1864, for instance, Johnston E.J. noted that 'American decisions have not the weight of absolute authority here, [but] they are uniformly considered with the attention due to the learning and ability conspicuous in them.'[34] At one point or another, Nova Scotian jurists singled out James Kent, Theophilus Parsons, and Joseph Story for special praise. In 1861, Chief Justice Young called Kent and Parsons 'two of the ablest lawyers who have ever adorned the judicature of our neighbouring states.'[35] In 1848, Bliss J. actually dignified Story with a Latin phrase, *clarum et honorabile nomen*, making him the only American (or, for that matter, English) judge ever to be so distinguished in the Nova Scotia Reports.[36]

Closely related, but technically separate from this fifth reason for citing American authority was a sixth: the perceived general 'good sense' and 'justice' of American judgments. For instance, in an 1859 decision, Wilkins J. commented that a Massachusetts ruling was of course not binding, but 'it has good sense to recommend it, and ... it will, if it be law for us, promote justice – of which, otherwise, there might be, in this case, a failure ... [W]hen I find a [Massachusetts] judgment precisely in point, promoting ... real and substantial justice, the opposing British authority must be very decisive, much more so than any that I have discovered in my present researches, that would preclude my mind from availing itself of the aids and illustrations thus afforded to it.'[37]

In addition to these six judicially articulated reasons for Nova Scotian citation of American authority in the early Victorian period, there were others – just as, if not more, important – which by accident or design remained unarticulated (at least by the judges themselves). The first of these pertains to the range and availability of contemporary American legal resources. Relatively little American treatise literature in particular was produced prior to 1830 (which may be one reason why, before 1837, Nova Scotian courts did not cite that much American authority in general), but for a variety of domestic reasons the number of American legal texts multiplied rapidly afterwards, creating a legal literature which rivalled and in some respects exceeded the quality of existing English legal commentary.[38] Nova Scotian judges were naturally drawn to good texts, and found them easier to get hold of from the 1840s, when trade and transport links with New York improved.[39] American law books moreover tended to be cheaper for Nova Scotians than were their English equivalents, as the former were not burdened by the cost of transatlantic shipment.[40]

The second unarticulated reason for Nova Scotian citation of American authority in the early Victorian era relates to the English judiciary's attitude towards using American case law and legal literature in its own proceedings. From at least the 1830s, it appears that American authorities enjoyed a certain currency and recognition in the English courts.[41] English 'tolerance' of American law was not lost on some Nova Scotian observers: in the preface to his first volume of Nova Scotia reports, Alexander James seemed anxious to mention that the American decisions which the Nova Scotian courts were citing were also 'cited with approval at Westminster Hall.'[42]

The third unarticulated reason for Nova Scotian citation of American legal authority between 1837 and 1875 leads us outside the realm of the law altogether. In the early Victorian period, Nova Scotian judges were probably attracted to American law because they did not draw a sharp cultural distinction between themselves and their American confreres.[43] Just before and immediately after the American Revolution Nova Scotia had been largely settled by Americans, most of whom had come from New England.[44] Down to the 1870s, the American migrations to Nova Scotia were the stuff of living memory. Many Nova Scotian lawyers and judges were the sons and grandsons of New Englanders; others retained close family ties with relatives in Massachusetts and New York. In such an environment, American law – especially law from New England and New York – was not completely foreign, and in fact provided a 'natural' reference point for Nova Scotian jurists needing legal guidance.

Fourth and finally, between the late 1830s and the mid-1870s Nova Scotian jurists were drawn to American authority as a result of the broad economic and trade connections which Nova Scotia enjoyed throughout this period with the northeastern states. Of course, Nova Scotia, Massachusetts, and New York had always been partners in North Atlantic commerce. Regional trade links nonetheless improved through the 1840s and 1850s and were given an additional boost by the

Reciprocity Treaty of 1855.[45] Increased economic connection with the United States inevitably induced a new degree of familiarity and interdependence that may well have encouraged Nova Scotian judges to tolerate and even favour the use of American case law and legal literature in the provincial Supreme Court.

Even at its peak of influence, however, American authority played only a limited and secondary judicial role in Nova Scotian jurisprudence. Its further impact was compromised by several factors, some obvious, others not. In the first place, American case law was at times seen to conflict directly with English law, and when that happened the Nova Scotian judges saw their duty clear. In 1858, for instance, Chief Justice Halliburton concluded: 'Much as I respect in general the authority of the American Judges they are not as binding upon us as the decisions of the courts at Westminster.'[46] In 1870, Wilkins J. was painfully forthright: 'The opinion I am called upon to give in this case must be in accordance with our own law and it must be governed by English decisions. Authorities derived from the Courts of the United States of America are entitled to our highest respect, but they cannot be regarded as ruling precedents ... As a judge of a British Colony I must look to the English rule as it existed and was judicially reconsidered in Westminster Hall ...'[47]

A second reason the Supreme Court judges had for not following American authority was the presence of contrary Nova Scotian statute law, or at least the absence of similar Nova Scotian legislative provisions (in which case certain Nova Scotian judges felt themselves compelled to conform to the unaltered English common law). Although American legislation often served as a model for Nova Scotian lawmakers, it sometimes added, changed, or left out certain terms, prompting Nova Scotian judges to part company with their American colleagues. In an 1840 case, for instance, Chief Justice Halliburton felt he had no choice but to reject the American cases cited to him. '[W]e can,' he said, 'derive little aid from them, for their act is differently worded than ours.'[48] In an 1870 case, Desbarres J. faced no such direct statutory conflict, but even while proclaiming his preference for an American rule, felt compelled to conclude that 'as the Legislature of this Province has not spoken on [this subject] as has the Legislature of the State of Massachusetts, we are necessarily thrown back upon, and are bound to decide the case upon the [contrary] principle of the common law.'[49]

Nova Scotian judges were additionally troubled by inconsistencies in the American law itself. Unlike England, the United States was made up of a large and increasing number of separate state jurisdictions which frequently took different stands on particular legal questions. In this context, looking to the States for legal guidance often became a complicated exercise. Dodd J. first articulated the problem (and one Nova Scotian 'solution') in an 1859 case: 'The cases in the Courts of the United States referred to in the arguments ... are conflicting with other decisions of the same Courts, so that they cannot be relied upon as authorities in this case for the plaintiffs.'[50] On occasion, conflicting American case law drove the Nova Scotian judges directly into the arms of more uniform English precedent. In 1869, Chief Justice Young observed that certain English cases 'deserve our attention far more than the American cases, not only as a binding authority, but also on account of the utter inconsistency of the American decisions, which as their judges and text writers confess, it is ultimately impossible to reconcile with each other.'[51]

American law was also distinguished or dismissed when it seemed implausible or inconsistent with general principle. When this happened Nova Scotian judges took pains to proclaim their overall respect for members of the American judiciary (perhaps because of the criticism implicit in this sort of rejection). In 1843, for instance, Chief Justice Halliburton baulked at a Massachusetts precedent which made no sense to him: 'I entertain a high respect for the opinions of the learned judges ... but I should like to know on what ground they understood this, before I bow to their authority.'[52] In 1867, Chief Justice Young likewise refused the lead of a Massachusetts decision, commenting that 'the respectable name of Chief Justice Shaw scarcely reconciles us with so strange a doctrine ...'[53]

Finally, despite increases in the supply of American law books to Nova Scotian lawyers and judges throughout the early Victorian period, Supreme Court judges occasionally rejected American authority – in the form of case law and statute in particular – because it was unavailable for direct judicial perusal.[54] Even the Nova Scotian collections of the much-cited Massachusetts and New York reports had significant gaps, which the Nova Scotian judges publicly lamented on several occasions.[55] In these circumstances, the judges were often left to rely on the word of American treatises,[56] a predicament they complained about loudly. Chief Justice Young was among the most vociferous complainers. In 1861, he observed that 'Of the course pursued in the United States, the books within our reach afford but a vague and imperfect notion. The two passages from Dane's Abr[idgement] ... and the note to Waterman's Archbold ... convey no reliable information. We have no reason of knowing whether the privilege [of a jury *de medietate linguae*][57] ever existed in Massachusetts: we are only told that it does not exist now. We know that it has been abolished by the Revised Statutes of New York, but have no access to the earlier Acts referred to in the case [from Johnson's NY reports] which was so much referred to in argument.'[58] By 1869, access to American legal literature was still somewhat problematic, leading Wilkins J. to sputter: 'Positions and inferences found in American treatises are unsatisfactory, as we have in most cases no means of examining the authorities referred to.'[59]

The fact that there were both good reasons for using American authority and good reasons for not using (or at least not following) it, inevitably encouraged individual judges on the Nova Scotian bench to employ American authority in different ways and to different extents. The first Nova Scotian chief justice of our period, Brenton Halliburton, was rather appreciative of American assistance, a point not lost on his modern biographer.[60] Halliburton's appreciation of American law may have had at least something to do with his own heritage and upbringing: born in Rhode Island, he was the son of Loyalists,[61] and perhaps preserved a lingering affection for his former homeland. Halliburton may also have shared the conservative political sympathies of Kent, Story, and other senior members of the contemporary American bench.[62] Halliburton's successor as chief justice, William Young, worked with more American material than Halliburton ever did, but comes across in retrospect as having been relatively less enthusiastic about it.[63] A Scottish emigrant, Young worked in New York as a young man. In 1852, while speaker of the Nova Scotia House of Assembly, he had solicited copies of the statutes of Massachusetts and New York from their respective secretaries of state;[64] as attorney general he had later considered American legislation while leading an initiative to reform Nova Scotia's Count of Chancery. As chief justice, despite regular travels to the United States, he nonetheless seemed more inclined than his predecessor to turn towards English law and legal literature as an antidote to American authorities.[65] He seemed particularly impressed (not to mention *au courant*)[66] with recent changes in English law which, as he saw it, promised to modernize English jurisprudence and bring it up to the best American procedural and intellectual standards. In 1869, for instance, he somewhat obsequiously praised the First Report of the Judicature Committee on reforming the English judicial structure (which he erroneously referred to as the 'report of the Judicial Committee') for 'its breadth of view, its emancipation from the subtleties which so often sacrificed substance to form, and from the fetters of the olden time, its tone of rational and bold philosophy ... significant of a new era.'[67] Somewhat more substantively, Young hoped that what he construed as a contemporary English tendency to draw more civil law principles into the common law would ultimately 'produce a race of English lawyers who may cope on equal terms with the [civil law] learning and genius of Kent and Story.'[68] Young seems to have realized, however, that his relative Anglophilia set him apart from some of his colleagues.[69] He highlighted the difference of views on the Nova Scotian bench in an 1865 decision: 'On ... the extent to which the common law as it has been declared in the House of Lords ... is to be accounted the common law prevailing in this province ... or whether we have the power of limiting its operation as has been done by the Courts of New York, Pennsylvania, and others of the United States – is a very large and important question[ ], on which differences of opinion exist among ourselves ...[70]

Given, however, that between 1837 and 1875 all the judges of the Nova Scotia Supreme Court used American authority (albeit with greater or lesser degrees of enthusiasm), what difference did that make? Did the importation of American case law and treatise literature have any fundamental or discernable effect on Nova Scotian law and legal culture? Did it matter, in other words, that the Nova Scotia Supreme Court drew a significant portion of their law from the United States, or was the American jurisprudence really so much 'common law'? This is a – perhaps the – critical question for this paper, but it is very difficult to answer beyond the level of impression.

At this point, I think that the importation of American law had at least two effects. To begin, it made Nova Scotian law more flexible and practicable, freeing it from some of the formal strictures which burdened contemporary law in England and which might have been unmanageable, unreasonable or at least inconvenient in Nova Scotia's colonial environment. In the 1841 case of *Lessees of Lawson v. Whitman*, for example, Nova Scotian adherence to the English law of adverse possession would have imposed on adverse possessors having colour of title the onerous obligation of clearing and actively occupying all the land they were claiming; the Supreme Court's decision to follow American law, however, allowed them to claim adverse possession of wilderness land adjacent to property they had already brought under cultivation.[71] Along similar lines, Halliburton C.J. ruled in the 1853 case of *Cunard v. Irvine* that in Nova Scotia, American law was preferred to English insofar as it permitted conveyances of wild lands to be validly made without requiring the grantor having colour of title to show actual possession or, failing that, derivation of title from the Crown. Halliburton commented: 'A large portion of land in this province still remains uncultivated, of which no actual possession has ever been taken, and I think [a contrary holding] would hamper the transfer of such property very inconveniently ...'[72] Somewhat more speculatively, the Supreme Court's tendency to follow the lead of American jurisprudence (especially in the areas of insurance and corporations law) may also have made Nova Scotian law more friendly to commerce, and perhaps contributed in an amorphous way to the province's pre-Confederation prosperity. To this extent, early to mid-nineteenth-century American law may indirectly have favoured the same economic growth in early Victorian Nova Scotia that it is said to have favoured directly in the United States itself.[73]

The Law of a Foreign Power, 1875–1901

The year 1875 hardly marks a radical break in the use of American case law and legal literature in the Nova Scotian courts, but my reading of the cases nonetheless suggests that in the last quarter of the nineteenth century American authority generally played a less significant role in the jurisprudence of the Nova Scotia Supreme Court than it had previously. I can point to several symptoms of American authority's declining significance. First, after 1875 the Supreme Court tended to give shorter shrift to American decisions when they conflicted with (and even when they supported) English cases.[74] Second, the Supreme Court judges put more stress on the English basis of those American decisions they cited, especially where there were few, if any, English cases directly on point.[75] Third, the judges frequently ignored the numerous American authorities which Nova Scotian lawyers routinely cited to them in argument, preferring to rest their judgments on other grounds.[76] Fourth, the judges were in this period less overtly deferential to American case law and commentary in specific doctrinal areas (such as insurance and commercial law) where, formerly, American jurisprudence had commanded great respect.[77] Fifth, acknowledged similarities of condition or practice in Nova Scotia and the United States no longer guaranteed the Supreme Court's adoption of American (as opposed to English) law.[78] Sixth, the NSSC judges offered substantially fewer personal encomiums to their American colleagues.[79] Seventh, from the mid-1870s the judges referred to the United States itself in somewhat less familiar terms; rather than 'our neighbors,' they were (at best) a 'great kindred nation.'[80]

What happened? Why in this second period of our survey did the Nova Scotian judges pay noticeably less attention to – and draw notably fewer lessons from – American law? These are not easy questions to answer, if only because the Nova Scotian judges were generally not inclined to articulate their reasons for turning away from American authority in the same way that they had articulated their reasons for turning towards it years before. We can, however, posit a few probable rationales for their behaviour.

First of all, in the last quarter of the nineteenth century the judges of the Nova Scotia Supreme Court clearly felt an increased attraction to English law and precedent, which consequently took up at least some of the space formerly allotted to American legal materials. This heightened devotion to English law had many roots of its own. Most obviously, perhaps, the Supreme Court judges – like many other Nova Scotians – were dazzled by the power and the glory of the late Victorian Empire. Applying English law with renewed vigour enabled Nova Scotian jurists to share that power and glory in ways which gave their decisions renewed authority and legitimacy.[81] The looming presence of a revitalized and revamped Judicial Committee of the Privy Council which would (and did) hear an increasing number of Nova Scotian appeals[82] only encouraged the Supreme Court's anglicization. In the late nineteenth century, NSSC judges were additionally attracted to English law as a symbol of political and scientific progress. In the wake of the Judicature Acts of 1873–5 and the helpful reconceptualizations of a new generation of liberal English legal academics,[83] that law was seen to rest on a new, rational, modern foundation which must have impressed Nova Scotian judges living in a liberal and scientific age. From a somewhat more parochial perspective, the broader application of English law was seen as a welcome mark of Nova Scotia's own economic and social maturity;[84] having supposedly succeeded in creating a society very much like England, Nova Scotians were (it was generally thought) finally ready to be ruled as Englishmen. English law also became more attractive to Nova Scotian jurists in the late Victorian era because it was physically more accessible to them. Technological improvements in the printing process, reduced transatlantic shipping charges, and relatively favourable trading arrangements with England combined to bring more English law reports and treatises into Nova Scotia at lower cost than before. Dalhousie's Benjamin Russell, later named to the Nova Scotia Supreme Court, even edited three English law texts (*Fry on Specific Performance, Odgers on Evidence,* and *Leake on Contracts*). All of made reliance on American materials less necessary.

Nova Scotia's late nineteenth-century legal turn to England made the Supreme Court judges particularly vulnerable to suggestion when, in the late 1880s, the English courts reversed their earlier tolerance for American case law,[85] and began to criticize its use in their own proceedings. In *Re: Missouri Steamship* (1889), Lord Halsbury censured counsel advancing American cases by saying: 'We should treat with great respect the opinion of eminent American lawyers on points which arise before us, but the practice, which seems to be increasing, of quoting American authorities in the same way as if they were decisions in our own courts, is wrong.'[86] Fry L.J. added, 'I also have been struck by the waste of time occasioned by the growing practice of citing American authorities.' These words were widely reported by the legal press in both the United States and Canada,[87] and it is hard to believe that Nova Scotian judges did not at some level feel their impact (although they never admitted as much).

Nova Scotian judges also lost interest in American authority in the later Victorian period because their jurisdiction had become part of a new nation: Canada. Prior to 1867, the judges of the Nova Scotia Supreme Court had rarely cited to the law of other British North American colonies.[88] English law had generally been deemed better authority than colonial precedent, but after Confederation, the courts of Nova Scotia, Ontario, and New Brunswick all became collateral tribunals in the bosom of a single federal state; after 1875, all were subordinate to the new Supreme Court of Canada, even if that body was slow to assert dominance and itself operated in the shadow of the Judicial Committee of the Privy Council. In this context (especially after 1875), it made sense for Nova Scotian judges to take greater account of broader Canadian jurisprudence. This inevitably resulted in the relative marginalization or rejection of American authority which might otherwise have applied as being more in keeping with Nova Scotian practice and circumstance than were English rules and cases.[89]

A fourth general reason for Nova Scotian judges' decreased reliance on American authority in the last quarter of the nineteenth century arguably has to do with an increased sense of disconnection from American culture in general. By 1875, the eighteenth-century American migrations to Nova Scotia had receded from living memory. Among third and fourth generation Nova Scotians, Massachusetts and New York were no longer thought of, even romantically, as 'home.' In the 1870s and 1880s, many Nova Scotians relocated to the northeastern United States to avoid a deteriorating domestic economy,[90] but most regarded this movement as 'leaving' rather than 'returning.' As fewer

Nova Scotian judges and lawyers retained substantive family or psychological ties with 'Americans' (as opposed to expatriate 'Nova Scotians'), the tug of American legal authority declined. At the same time, Nova Scotians were coming to terms with new economic arrangements which mirrored their new political realities. In the wake of Prime Minister Macdonald's National Policy, Nova Scotian trade was no longer oriented along an North-South axis. Economic interchanges with Massachusetts and the other northeastern States decreased in relative importance,[91] and American legal authority no longer provided a convenient framework for Nova Scotian commercial activity.

Finally, the reduced popularity of American authority in the Nova Scotia Supreme Court after 1875 is at least partially attributable to factors endemic to American law and legal culture. In the first place, the last quarter of the late nineteenth century witnessed a huge increase in the published volume of American case reports and treatises. By their own admission, the Americans could not keep up with it all; inevitably, neither could the Nova Scotians, who doubtless turned with some relief to the more limited legal literatures of England and Canada. Second and more fundamentally, American law towards the end of the 1800s was becoming more distinctly 'American.' Despite the efforts of legal scholars such as Harvard's Christopher Columbus Langdell and James Bar Ames to anglicize American law as it was taught to law students,[92] the number of English cases cited and discussed in the American courts steadily decreased as the corpus of home-grown American law increased. The decline in American citations to English law was both a cause and a symptom of the positivism infecting the late nineteenth-century American legal environment: notwithstanding its inherent logic or reasonableness, American judges increasingly began to doubt the technical applicability of English or other varieties of 'foreign' law in the United States.[93] In this context, the American courts had less to offer Nova Scotian jurists that was obviously relevant to the jurisprudence which the latter interpreted and applied. Third and finally, although this is hard to document, the American Civil War and, in the legal context, the struggles of the American courts with slavery and other sensitive issues might have given pause to Nova Scotian jurists who had previously shown great respect and even enthusiasm for American legal authority – the reputation of the American bench and even the nation may have been subtly sullied by these events, prompting Nova Scotian judges to look elsewhere for legal inspiration.

Nova Scotian lawyers and jurists did not lose all interest in the rulings of American courts and the writings of American commentators after 1875. On the contrary, a significant number of American cases and sources continued to be cited, albeit usually to lesser effect.[94] Again, most of the cited American case law came from Massachusetts and New York. United States Supreme Court cases became more popular, perhaps reflecting, on one level, a subtle attenuation of Nova Scotian ties with specific American regions and, on another, a felt need to cite the highest American authority available in order to forestall worsening problems of jurisdictional inconsistency.[95] Multistate collections like the *American Decisions* and the *American Reports* figured in Nova Scotian decisions from the 1880s, and Nova Scotian judicial references to various reporters produced by the West Publishing Company (Northeastern, Northwestern, Pacific) appeared in the 1890s.[96]

The range of American treatise literature cited by the Nova Scotian courts in the late nineteenth century remained considerable, and even increased slightly, reflecting the growing number of titles being published south of the border. References to the works of Kent, Story, Angell, Duer, Greenleaf, Parsons, and Washburn were joined by citations to Redfield (on railways), May (on insurance and on fraudulent conveyances), Bigelow (on estoppel and on fraud), Perry (on trusts), Bump (on fraudulent conveyances and on bankruptcy), Schouler (on husband and wife), Cooley (on constitutional limitations, taxation, and torts), Bishop (on criminal law and criminal procedure), Dillon (on municipal corporations), Shearman & Redfield (on negligence), Keener (on quasi-contract), and Gray (on perpetuities).[97] *Bouvier's Law Dictionary, Wharton's Law Lexicon, Abbott's Law Dictionary,* and (in the 1890s) the new *American and English Encyclopedia of Law* were occasionally referenced; in 1881 Weatherbe J. even made mention of the *American Law Review*.[98]

Finally, the Supreme Court judges employed numerous American editions of English legal works, which in this period (unlike the earlier one) seem to have been plumbed more for their English content than for their American notes or addenda. At one time or another the judges cited to American editions of *Chitty and Hulme on Bills, Stephen on Pleading, Adams on Ejectment, Benjamin on Sales,* and *Taylor on Evidence*.[99] They also continued to employ American editions of such English reports and case collections as White and Tudor's *Leading Cases*, Smith's *Leading Cases*, and the *English Common Law Reports*.[100]

Despite the changing times, NSSC judges had their reasons for continuing to cite these various American authorities. At least ostensibly, Nova Scotian judges still considered the Americans as partners in the development and application of a 'common' law; consequently, American cases were still considered plausible supplements and even substitutes for English authority. In an 1882 case, for instance, McDonald C.J. noted that 'the general principles governing the execution of deeds are the same in England and the United States, and the authority of the cases from the latter country ... must be received as of great weight.'[101] In certain (if perhaps diminishing) circumstances, American and Nova Scotian conditions were also still seen as being sufficiently proximate to warrant the Nova Scotian courts following the lead of their American counterparts. In 1876, for instance, Young C.J. noted in a case regarding dower in wild lands that for 'the law upon a point like this ... we must look for chiefly in the American cases; wild lands, as they are called, being very rare or unknown on the other side of the Atlantic, though abundant on this.'[102] 'The common heritage of much Nova Scotian and American statute law was similarly still recognized by judges of the Supreme Court, notwithstanding the tendency of late nineteenth century Nova Scotian legislators to turn towards imperial models.[103] The American roots of Nova Scotia's probate laws received particular attention in the late Victorian era. In 1878, for instance, James J. noted: "The [provincial Probate] Act 32 Geo. 2, c.ll ... was founded, as it appears by the note of the editor, on the laws of the other colonies, and especially of Massachusetts Bay ..."'[104]

The Supreme Court judges also acknowledged the American roots of Nova Scotian municipal law. In 1890, for instance, Joseph N. Ritchie observed that: 'The United States statutes in relation to highways, statute labour, etc., more particularly those of Massachusetts, are in principle similar [to] those in force in this province, and the decisions of their courts in relation to such matters would probably be better guides to us than those under the English statutes which differ materially in many respects.'[105]

Those Nova Scotian judges who after 1875 chose (for whichever reason) to cite American authority ran into many of the same problems that their predecessors (and in some cases, they themselves) had encountered in the early Victorian era. Young C.J. acknowledged one unresolved (and worsening) difficulty in 1878, observing that he had been confronted with 'strange and inconsistent decisions from all parts of the Union.'[106] Three years later, James J. noted: 'the [American] decisions vary in different States, and the law cannot be regarded as at all settled.'[107] Some judges also continued to complain about the relative unavailability of American sources. In 1878, Young C.J. observed that he was 'shut out from the reasoning of almost all the [American] cases referred to' in a section of *May on Insurance;* he therefore had no choice but to 'adhere to the English decisions.'[108] In 1896, Graham J. pointedly referred to the 'few American reports at my disposal.'[109] The fact that more judges did not make such complaints was ultimately less indicative of American holdings in the Legislative Library than it was of decreasing judicial interest in the American cases themselves.[110]

That diminished judicial interest, however, patently did not mean that all the Nova Scotia Supreme Court judges had the same opinion of the virtue and value of citing American authority in the late Victorian period. As before, some judges were relatively comfortable with American law, while others were less comfortable with it, even if, this time, the judge who were less comfortable predominated. Between 1875 and his retirement in 1881, Chief Justice Young, who in the early Victorian era had been critical of American law despite an obvious inclination to use it, ironically stood out from his fellows as its strongest and ablest advocate (or, at least, expositor).[111] In the 1880s and 1890s, American law was effectively championed by Weatherbe and Graham JJ.,[112] who repeatedly used American law to resolve or at least aid in the analysis of many knotty legal points, although it could hardly be said that either was willing to adhere to American authority in the face of what they regarded as clear English precedent to the contrary.[113] It turns out that Weatherbe had numerous relatives in the United States; his family moved to Kansas at one point, and his siblings had died in the Civil War.[114] Perhaps these personal connections predisposed him to take a greater interest in American affairs and American law – at one point, we know that he went so far as to write an article on codification for a major American law journal.[115] Graham, too had family connections with the United States – most of his siblings had emigrated there.[116] In addition, he was a partner in Weatherbe's law firm and there is even evidence to suggest that he thought his specific identity as a Canadian depended on an American association.[117]

In the late Victorian era, however, most judges of the Nova Scotia Supreme Court were less inclined than were Young, Weatherbe, and Graham to cite American cases or American commentators in their decisions.[118] American authority figured occasionally in the judgments of James, Thompson, Townshend, Joseph N. Ritchie, Meagher, and Henry JJ., but appeared only rarely (and often only to be rejected) in the rulings of John W. Ritchie, Hugh McDonald, Henry Smith, and Samuel Rigby.[119] The fact that John W. Ritchie, McDonald, and Smith in particular came onto the Nova Scotian bench in fairly short order in the early to mid-1870s as the powers of Chief Justice Young faded and other older judges retired (Dodd and Johnston),[120] or declined (Wilkins, who eventually retired in 1878) helps to explain, from a prosopographical perspective this time, why 1875 is a plausible marker of a Nova Scotian judicial turn from American case law and legal literature.

But what did it matter that after 1875 the Nova Scotian bench and bar began to turn away from American case law and legal literature? It is just as difficult to answer this question as it is to assess the impact American authority had on Nova Scotia's courts and legal culture in the early Victorian period. We might hypothesize, however, that turning away from American towards English authority in particular had, at the very least, a formalizing impact on Nova Scotian law.[121] Such an impact can be seen in the 1886 case of *Grindley v. Blaikie*, where the majority of the Supreme Court ruled that the failure of a party to properly record a deed prior to one of his creditors registering judgment against the same land precluded a successful action of ejectment against someone purporting to take title from the judgment creditor. Weatherbe J. argued in dissent that American law (on which, due largely to proximate physical conditions in America and Nova Scotia, most Nova Scotian land law had been based) would allow ejectment to succeed on the basis that the party taking the land from the judgment creditor had actual or at least constructive notice of the prior deed, even if the deed had not been formally recorded. Weatherbe's colleagues disagreed: in a noteworthy turn of phrase, McDonald J. observed that there were 'a number of American cases which go far in support of [Weatherbe's] view, but no English authority was cited to sustain it.'[122] What ultimately mattered was not what the ultimate buyer knew in practice, but what had been formally set down in writing.[123] In this and other cases in the late Victorian era, formerly Americanized Nova Scotian law was consciously reshaped in an English image, with little consideration being spared for the question of which law best suited Nova Scotia's own circumstances.

Conclusion: 'Goin' Down the Road'

Given my suggestion that the Nova Scotia Supreme Court placed relatively less emphasis on American authority in the years after 1875, one might consider how the history of American authority in the Supreme Court of Victorian Nova Scotia compares with the history of American authority in other 'Canadian' jurisdictions between 1837 and 1901. Unfortunately, most such comparisons are problematic. Despite suggestive beginnings,[124] we need much more specific information on the nature and extent of American influences on the courts of nineteenth-century Lower Canada and Quebec. Preliminary secondary analysis[125] and my own reading of the case reports suggests that the judges of the New Brunswick Supreme Court used a good deal of American case law in the mid- to late nineteenth century, but this impression needs to be confirmed by further work. It seems that British Columbian judges repeatedly appealed to American authority when making decisions on the ethnic Chinese in the 1870s and 1880s, but as yet we know little about their use of American case law and legal literature outside that context.[126]

We do, however, know a considerable amount about the fortunes and fate of American authority in Upper Canada/Ontario, thanks largely to Blaine Baker.[127] In a nutshell, his work suggests that down to roughly 1890, American case law and legal literature enjoyed a significant presence and even a certain prominence in an eclectic provincial legal culture, but that afterward Ontario jurisprudentially degenerated from 'nation to colony,' rejecting both its native legal legacy and its erstwhile legal continentalism in favour of increased recourse to English authority.[128]

The late nineteenth-century Ontarian transition as Baker describes it certainly bears a strong, perhaps even an encouraging resemblance to what I see as having happened in the Nova Scotia Supreme Court after 1875. But the resemblance between the two phenomena is not complete. In the first place, the two jurisdictions started from different points in dealing with American case law and treatise literature. Certainly a number of Ontarian lawyers actively promoted that law and literature in the 1850s and 1860s, and certainly American legal materials were conscientiously stocked by Ontarian law libraries and cited by Ontarian judges both before and after Confederation, but for a variety of social, economic, and even political reasons American authority never figured as prominently in the legal culture of Ontario as it did in the Supreme Court of Victorian Nova Scotia.[129] In the second place, the two jurisdictions 'ended up' in different situations. Ontarian attention to American authority fell off dramatically in the decades after 1890. Judging from the Supreme Court Reports, Nova Scotian attention to American authority declined substantially after 1875, although Nova Scotian jurists persisted in citing some American legal materials through the 1920s.[130]

In the third place, the direction (and by implication, the motivation) of Ontario's legal re-orientation after 1890 was not exactly the same as the direction (and motivation) of the Nova Scotia Supreme Court's reorientation after 1875. While both Ontarian legal culture and the Nova Scotia Supreme Court turned towards England and away from the United States, the Nova Scotian court made (as I have already indicated) a simultaneous and complementary judicial turn towards Canada, and in particular Ontario. In the process of this turn, Ontario largely replaced the United States (in particular Massachusetts) as the court's secondary legal metropolis.[131] Of course, Confederation and its attendant economic and psychological realignments provided the stimulus for this shift, and in a small jurisdiction Nova Scotian jurists had to look somewhere for authority that could fill in the gaps in their own local legal tradition. In light, however, of Baker's provocative characterization of Ontario's late nineteenth-century turn towards England as a degeneration from 'nation to colony,' one might argue, on the basis of the Supreme Court's behaviour, that after 1875 Nova Scotia experienced not a single, but a double jurisprudential colonization – by England and by Ontario itself.[132]

Although the second of these jurisprudential 'colonizations' of Nova Scotia has received scant historiographical attention to this point (perhaps because it took place within the context of Canadian nation building, and perhaps because we have tended to follow a central Canadian intellectual agenda focusing on broader international tensions between 'continentalism' and 'imperialism'), it was arguably more dramatic than the first. The extent of Nova Scotia's legal dependence upon England admittedly increased after 1875, but that dependence itself was nothing new. By contrast, before 1875 Nova Scotia had never been significantly dependent on law drawn from another Canadian jurisdiction. It was therefore in turning away from American law to the law of Ontario that the Nova Scotia Supreme Court of the late Victorian era was more obviously turning away from its own cultural and legal heritage. After all, American statutes, case law, and/or treatise literature had been part and parcel of the Nova Scotian legal identity since the colony's English foundation, a foundation itself largely – if not initially – accomplished by settlers coming from the American colonies.[133] Clearly, times were changing. In the last quarter of the nineteenth century, Nova Scotian jurists who could once have been counted in the ranks of Her Majesty's Yankees began to establish a new national affiliation in the midst (and perhaps in the guise)[134] of re-affirming an old imperial one. Even as they looked to England, they were gleefully 'goin' down the road' to Toronto, in search of Canadian law.[135]

NOTES

This essay is dedicated to the memory of my great-aunt, M. Grace Wamboldt, QC, the fifth woman to graduate from Dalhousie Law School and the first to be honoured for fifty years of service at the Bar of Nova Scotia.

1 Note, however, that after Sir William Phips's capture of Port Royal in 1690, Nova Scotia (as part of Acadia) was briefly considered a dependency of Massachusetts Bay by conquest; this understanding was later (if temporarily) affirmed by royal charter. J.B. Cahill, '"How Far English Laws are in Force Here": Nova Scotia's First Century of Reception Jurisprudence,' *University of New Brunswick Law Journal* 42 (1993): 133. On various connections between Nova Scotia and the New England colonies, and later states, see generally J.B. Brebner, *The Neutral Yankees of Nova Scotia* (New York: Columbia University Press 1937); G. Rawlyk, *Nova Scotia's Massachusetts* (Montreal: McGill-Queen's University Press 1973).

2 Instructions, Article 10, quoted in T.G. Barnes, '"The Dayly Cry for Justice": The Juridical Failure of the Annapolis Royal Regime, 1713–1729,' in Girard and Phillips, *Essays*, 14. See also 'Virginia and Nova Scotia: An Historical Note,' *Virginia Law Register* 6 (1921): 744–51.

3 See Cahill and Phillips, this volume; Barnes, '"The Dayly Cry for Justice,"' at 16; J.B. Brebner, *New England's Outpost: Acadia Before the Conquest of Canada* (New York: Columbia University Press 1927), 239–41; A.B. Sprague, 'Some American Influences on the Law and Law Courts of Nova Scotia, 1749–1853,' *Nova Scotia Historical Review* 12 (1992): 5–7.

4 On controversies, see Cahill and Phillips, this volume; also Brebner, *New England's Outpost*, 244–7; S. Oxner, 'The Evolution of the Lower Court in Nova Scotia,' *Dalhousie Law Journal* 8 (1984): at, 62–3; Sprague, 'Some American Influences,' 15–16. On statutory influences, see generally ibid., 19–22; P.V. Girard, 'Married Women's Property Law, Chancery Abolition, and Insolvency Law: Law Reform in Nova Scotia, 1820-1867,' in Girard and Phillips, *Essays*, 80, 87–9, 97, 108–1. On possible Massachusetts influences on early Nova Scotiancriminal statutes (especially those defining capital crimes) see T.G. Barnes, 'As Near as May be Agreeable to the Laws of this Kingdom: Legal Birthright and Baggage at Chebucto, 1749,' *Dalhousie Law Journal* 8 (1984): 17.

5 See G.B. Baker, 'The Reconstitution of Upper Canadian Legal Thought in the Late-Victorian Empire,' *Law and History Review* 3 (1985): 219–92.

6 See Sprague, 'Some American Influences.'

7 On Nova Scotia legal history, see, e.g., Girard and Phillips, *Essays*; P.B.

Waite et al., eds., *Law in a Colonial Society: The Nova Scotia Experience* (Toronto: Carswell 1984). On U.S. authority in other Canadian jurisdictions see, e.g., Baker, 'Reconstitution'; S.I. Bushnell, 'The Use of American Cases,' *University of New Brunswick Law Journal* 35 (1986): 157–81; D. Casswell, 'Doctrine and Foreign Law in the Supreme Court of Canada: A Quantitative Analysis,' *Supreme Court Law Review* 2 (1981): 435–50; Donald V. Macdougall, 'Canadian Legal Identity and American Influences,' *Legal Studies Forum* 15 (1991): 15–35; J.P.S. McLaren, 'The Early British Columbia Judges, the Rule of Law and the "Chinese Question": The California and Oregon Connection,' in McLaren et al., eds., *Law for the Elephant, Law for the Beaver: Essays in the Legal History of the North American West* (Regina: Canadian Plains Research Center 1992), 237–73; J.M. MacIntyre, 'The Use of American Cases in Canadian Courts,' *University of British Columbia Law Review* 2 (1966): 479–90.

8 For instances of citation counting, see Bushnell, 'Use of American Cases,' and Casswell, 'Doctrine and Foreign Law.' On its limitations see generally Baker, 'Reconstitution,' 260–1.

9 The fact that in Pittsburgh I can say anything at all about Nova Scotian legal history is a testament to what Blaine Baker has termed the early twentieth-century 'migration' of Canadian law libraries and law books to the United States: see Baker, 'Reconstitution.' The set of Nova Scotia Reports held by the Library of the University of Pittsburgh School of Law is complete to 1908. Volume 2 of the Reports (1853) contains the signature of one 'S.E. Gourley, Truro N.S,' a barrister [my thanks to Barry Cahill for the identification]. It also contains stickers suggesting that sometime after publication of the 1908 volume of Reports, the volumes were rebound in a lot by Carswell in Toronto, leading one to wonder whether Carswell had acquired them from their Nova Scotian owners by sale or swap, as was common in that period. Between April and October 1909 (judging from ink stamps on the title pages of the Reports), the volumes were received (probably from Carswell) by the Library of the United States Court of Appeals, Ninth Circuit (San Francisco, California). At some unknown point later in the century, they were sold or discarded by the Ninth Circuit's Library and fell into the hands of Joseph M. Mitchell, a law book seller in Philadelphia, who apparently sold them to the University of Pittsburgh Law Library, where they gathered dust until very recently.

10 This felicitous reference to the Americans, complete with its 'American' spelling, is taken from the judgment of Halliburton C.J. in *Koch v. Dauphinee* (1853), 2 N.S.R. 159 at 160, 161, 163, where Halliburton in fact used it three different times.

11 *Tarratt v. Sawyer* (1835), 1 N.S.R. 46 at 52.
12 See P.V. Girard, 'Themes and Variations in Early Canadian Legal Culture,' *Law and History Review* 11 (1993): 133.
13 *Ralston v. Barss* (1836), l N.S.R. 75 at 82.
14 On Murdoch's use of American authorities, see Sprague, 'Some American Influences'; on Murdoch and the *Epitome* generally, see Girard, 'Themes and Variations.'
15 For Murdoch's recommendation of Hoffman, see B. Murdoch, *Epitome of the Laws of Nova Scotia* (1832; Homes Beach: W.W. Gaunt 1971), vol. 1, 10. I do not know whether any Nova Scotian law students took Murdoch's advice. In an 1847 letter to James Kent, however, the Nova Scotian Master of the Rolls, Alexander Stewart, indicated that the former's *Commentaries* enjoyed wide usage as a textbook in the province: see J. Horton, *James Kent: A Study in Conservatism, 1763–1847* (New York: D. Appleton-Century Company 1939), 299. In the context of these observations about American influence on the Nova Scotian courts in the early to mid-1830s, it may be relevant that about 1834 Nova Scotian judges abandoned their wigs and scarlet robes, following the habit of the American courts in effect if not necessarily by design: see Sprague, 'American Influences,' 10–11.
16 Alexander James, 'Preface,' (1853), 2 N.S.R. vi.
17 In 1864, for instance, Johnston E.J. acknowledged that 'many important causes have been determined in this Court by the light thrown on the law in American decisions': *Brush v. Aetna Insurance Company* (1864), 5 N.S.R. 458 at 482. The increasing influence of American materials in the Nova Scotia Supreme Court and (one presumes) in Nova Scotian legal culture in general around this time may have been stimulated by certain Nova Scotian law students entering American law schools, which they increasingly did in the 1860s and' 70s. See P.V. Girard, 'The Roots of a Professional Renaissance: Lawyers in Nova Scotia, 1850–1919,' in D. Gibson and W. W. Pue, eds., *Glimpses of Canadian Legal History* (Winnipeg: Legal Research Institute 1991), 173.
18 *Cunard v. Irvine* (1853), 2 N.S.R. 31 at 32; *Campbell v. Aetna Insurance Co.* (1859), 4 N.S.R. 21 at 25; *Smyth v. McDonald* (1863), 5 N.S.R. 274 at 280; *Brush v. Aetna Insurance Company* (1864), 5 N.S.R. 458 at 463; *McKenzie v. Gordon* (1867), 7 N.S.R. 153 at 157; *Wheelock v. Chesley* (1870), 8 N.S.R. 49 at 52; *Duvar v. Burkner* (1871), 8 N.S.R. 460 at 462; *Inglefield v. Merkel* (1873), 9 N.S.R. 188 at 194. Some of these citations were clearly lifted from treatises. In 1867, however, Johnstone E.J. reported that he had direct access to a case in 9 *Wheaton*: *McKenzie v. Gordon*, 157.
19 For instances of rare citations to the decisions of other American state or

federal courts, see *Ripley v. Baker* (1860), 5 N.S.R. 23 at 30 (citing to American cases from Maine, New Hampshire, Ohio, and Pennsylvania); *Smyth v. McDonald* (1863), 5 N.S.R. 274 at 285–6 (citing to American cases from Pennsylvania, Tennessee, and South Carolina); *Nova Scotia Telegraph Company v. American Telegraph Company* (1864), 5 N.S.R. 426 at 443 (citing to a Virginia case); *Conlon v. City Railroad Co.* (1871), 8 N.S.R. 209 at 213 (citing to cases from Missouri and Indiana); *Inglefield v. Merkel* (1873), 9 N.S.R. 188 at 194 (citing a Pennsylvanian case). For instances of citations of U.S. authority from American texts, see *Cunard v. Irvine* (1853), 2 N.S.R. 31 at 38 (citing a Pennsylvanian decision from *Angell on Limitations*); *Smyth v. McDonald* (1863), 5 N.S.R. 274 at 277 (citing a Pennsylvanian decision from *Angell on Limitations*); *Brush v. Aetna Insurance Company* (1864), 459 at 466 (citing a Maine decision from *Angell on Fire and Life Insurance*); *Foster v. Fowler* (1865), 5 N.S.R. 752 at 764 (citing a Vermont case from Kent's *Commentaries*); *Pope v. Pictou Steamship Company* (1865), 6 N.S.R. 18 at 61 (citing a Pennsylvanian case from *Hilliard on Sales*); *Boyd v. Millett* (1873), 9 N.S.R. 292 at 296 (citing a Maine case from *Washburne on Real Property*). For an instance of Nova Scotian citation of *American Leading Cases*, see *Conlon v. City Railroad Co.* (1871), 8 N.S.R. 209 at 217. Wilkins J. (at 231) called this a 'very useful work.'

20 For citations to Dane's *Abridgment*, see *Ralston v. Barss* (1836), 1 N.S.R. 75 at 78; *Re: Estate of McKay* (1861), 5 N.S.R. 131 at 138; *McGregor v. Patterson* (1862), 5 N.S.R. 211 at 243; *LeCain v. Hosterman* (1871), 8 N.S.R. 413 at 416; *Bank of Nova Scotia v. Forman* (1873), 9 N.S.R. 141 at 159. For citations to Story, see *Hardy v. Fairbanks* (1847), 2 N.S.R. 432 at 440; *Brazen v. Graham* (1848), 3 N.S.R. 271 at 274; *Morton v. Campbell* (1859), 4 N.S.R. 1 at 9; *McAgy v. Gray* (1860), 4 N.S.R. 52 at 57, 61. For citations to Angell, see *Cunard v. Irvine* (1853), 2 N.S.R. 31 at 32; *Moody v. Aetna Insurance Company* (1857), 3 N.S.R. 173 at 177; *Brazen v. Graham* (1848), 3 N.S.R. 271 at 274; *Smyth v. McDonald* (1863), 5 N.S.R. 274 at 277; *McPherson v. Cameron* (1868), 7 N.S.R. 208 at 213. For citations to Greenleaf, see *Freeman v. Harrington* (1863), 5 N.S.R. 352 at 355; *Inglefield v. Merkel* (1873), 9 N.S.R. 188 at 196; *McDonald v. Blois* (1873), 9 N.S.R. 283 at 285. For citation to Duer, see *Hennessey v. N.Y. Mutual Marine Insurance Co.* (1863), 5 N.S.R. 259 at 261, 272. For citation to Morris, see *Freeman v. Harrington* (1863), 5 N.S.R. 352 at 356; *Lane v. Dorsay* (1865), 5 N.S.R. 575 at 578. For citations to Parsons, see *Orange v. McKay* (1864), 5 N.S.R. 444 at 446; *Pope v. Pictou Steamboat Company* (1865), 6 N.S.R. 18 at 28, 53; *Campbell v. McCaskell* (1867), 7 N.S.R. 36 at 41; *Gordon v. Gordon* (1867), 7 N.S.R. 80 at 81; *Wheelock v. Chesley* (1870), 8 N.S.R. 49 at 52; *LeCain v. Hosterman* (1871), 8 N.S.R. 413 at 419. For citations to Washburn, see *Hali-*

burton v. Haliburton (1866), 6 N.S.R. 312 at 317; *Desbarres v. Shey* (1871), 8 N.S.R. 327 at 346; *Dunn v. Miller* (1873), 9 N.S.R. 347 at 348. For citations to Hilliard, see *Re: Estate of Simpson* (1863) 5 N.S.R. 317 at 325; *Lane v. Dorsay* (1865), 5 N.S.R. 575 at 578; *Pope v. Pictou Steamship Company* (1865), 6 N.S.R. 18 at 60; *Smith v. Smith* (1866), 6 N.S.R. 303 at 310; *Desbarres v. Shey* (1871), 8 N.S.R. 327 at 345. For citation to Sedgewick, see *Bannerman v. Fullerton* (1862), 5 N.S.R. 200 at 203.

21 *Ring v. Brenan* (1853), 2 N.S.R. 20 at 30.

22 For citations to an American-annotated version of *Exchequer Reports*, see *Bannerman v. Fullerton* (1862), 5 N.S.R. 200 at 202; *Desbarres v. Shey* (1871), 8 N.S.R. 327 at 346. For citations to an American-annotated version of *Law and Equity Reports*, see *Thibedeau v. Ryerson* (1873), 9 N.S.R. 221 at 223. For citations to an American-annotated version of Cruise's *Digest*, see *Re: Estate of Simpson* (1863), 5 N.S.R. 317 at 323; *Slayter v. Johnstoa* (1864), 5 N.S.R. 502 at 506. For citation to an American-annotated version of *English Common Law Reports*, see *Pitts v. Taylor* (1871), 8 N.S.R. 378 at 380. For citations to an American-annotated version of White and Tudor's Equity Cases, see *Vass v. Letson* (1868), 7 N.S.R. 375 at 378; *Hornsby v. Johnstone* (1872), 9 N.S.R. 1 at 13 16. For citations to an American-annotated citation of Chitty, see *Lawson v. Salter* (1861), 5 N.S.R. 731 at 734; *Wylde v. Wetmore* (1869), 7 N.S.R. 504 at 507; *Bank of Nova Scotia v. Chipman* (1871), 8 N.S.R. 438 at 445. For citation to an American-annotated version of Hill, see *McLeod v. Gillies* (1868), 7 N.S.R. 257 at 260. For citation to an American-annotated edition of Stephen, see *Mackenzie v. Brodie* (1868), 7 N.S.R. 243 at 249. For citation to an American-annotated edition of Williams, see *McKenzie v. Gordon* (1867), 7 N.S.R. 153 at 157. For citation to an American-annotated edition of Smith, see *Fraser v. Salter* (1869), 7 N.S.R. 424 at 444.

23 In some instances, nineteenth-century Nova Scotian lawyers described American independence as having represented little more than a change in sovereignty. See for instance B. Murdoch, 'An Essay on the Origins and Sources of the Law of Nova Scotia,' reprinted in Waite et al., eds., *Law in a Colonial Society*, 191. On American attitudes to foreign jurisprudence, see P. Glenn, 'Persuasive Authority,' *McGill Law Journal* 32 (1987): 261–98.

24 *Levatte & Salter v. Twining* (1858), 3 N.S.R. 387 at 399.

25 *Martin v. Barnes* (1863), 5 N.S.R. 291 at 293.

26 *Kenny v. Halifax Marine Insurance Co.* (1840), 1 N.S.R. 141 at 154.

27 *Duvar v. Burkner* (1871), 8 N.S.R. 460 at 462.

28 Sprague, 'Some American Influences,' 12–13.

29 (1851), 1 N.S.R. 208. See also *Cunard v. Irvine* (1853), 2 N.S.R. 32 at 39 per Dodd J.: 'In a country like England, where lands are of great value, and

where they are seldom or never allowed to remain unoccupied ... it is extremely difficult to find cases and decisions in the books of reports applicable to the case under consideration. We may therefore be excused if we turn to the decisions of the Courts of law of the United States.' Of this latter decision, Wilkins J. said some years later, 'To have looked to Westminster Hall for an authority applicable to the forest land of America would have been hopeless': *Taylor v. Archibald* (1873), 9 N.S.R. 233 at 239.

30 On probate, see Sprague, 'Some American Influences,' 21–2. On divorce, see K. Smith-Maynard, 'Divorce in Nova Scotia, 1750–1890,' in Girard and Phillips, *Essays*, 232 and 238–9.

31 *Ells v. Ells* (1841), 1 N.S.R. 173.

32 *LeCain v. Hosterman* (1871), 8 N.S.R. 413 at 415–16.

33 See Murdoch, 'Essay on the Origins,' 191.

34 *Brush v. Aetna Insurance Co.* (1864), 5 N.S.R. 958 at 482.

35 *Re: Estate of Mckay* (1861), 5 N.S.R. 131 at 140. In 1835, Young's predecessor, Sir Brenton Halliburton, had opined that Kent's *Commentaries* 'are probably destined to carry his name down to posterity as an ornament to the profession': *Tarratt v. Sawyer* (1835), 1 N.S.R. 46 at 52.

36 *Brazen v. Graham* (1848), 3 N.S.R. 271 at 274. One must wonder whether the obvious affection shown by the Nova Scotian judges for these American jurists was not also born of a certain political sympathy with the latter; at the very least, such sympathy would have been broadly in line with the apparent bias of prominent Nova Scotian lawyers towards American Federalist politicians in the pre-Victorian era: see B. Cuthbertson, *The Old Attorney-General: A Biography of Richard John Uniacke* (Halifax: Nimbus Publishing 1980), 111.

37 *Morton v. Campbell* (1859), 4 N.S.R. 1 at 13.

38 On American treatise literature prior to 1830, see generally J. Parrish, 'Law Books and Legal Publishing in America, 1760–1840,' *Law Library Journal* 72 (1979): 355–76; E.C. Surrency, *A History of American Law Publishing* (New York: Oceana Publications 1990), 141–92. On its growth afterwards see, e.g., Baker, 'Reconstitution,' 253. On comparisons with contemporary English legal literature see Baker also, noting that nineteenth-century American treatises were exported to England itself.

39 At least one case decided prior to 1875 contains a suggestion that in certain circumstances, Nova Scotian judges clearly preferred American treatises to English ones: see *Pope v. Pictou Steamship Company* (1865), 6 N.S.R. 18 at 33, per Young C.J. On improvements in access to American law books, see Girard, 'Themes and Variations,' 134; also Alexander James, 'Preface,' in (1853) 2 N.S.R. vi.

40 A Halifax bookseller actually advertised in 1848 that he could 'furnish Books at as low a rate as can be purchased in New York or Boston, including freight and exchanges, and in many instances, much lower: quoted in Girard, 'Themes and Variations,' 134.

41 B. Laskin, *The British Tradition in Canadian Law* (London: Hamlyn Trust 1969), 100. See, e.g., *Beverley v. Lincoln Gas Light and Coke Co.* (1837), 111 E.R. 318 at 321 (where Patteson J. acknowledged that American decisions could not be cited as direct authority in the English courts, but at the same time declared that those decisions were 'intrinsically entitled to the highest respect'). See also 'American Law in England,' *American Jurist* 8 (1832): 225.

42 Alexander James, 'Preface,' in 2 N.S.R. vi.

43 See, e.g., Murdoch, 'Essay on Origins,' 191.

44 See generally M.L. Hansen, *The Mingling of the Canadian and American Peoples* (New Haven: Yale University Press 1940), 32–9, 51–4.

45 On improved regional trade in the 1840s and 1850s, see, e.g., Girard, 'Themes and Variations,' 134. On the impact of the 1855 Reciprocity Treaty see generally S.A. Saunders, 'The Maritime Provinces and the Reciprocity Treaty,' in G.A. Rawlyk, ed., *Historical Essays on the Atlantic Provinces* (Toronto: McClelland & Stewart 1967).

46 *Chisolm v. McDonald* (1858), 3 N.S.R. 367 at 374.

47 *Wheelock v. Chesley* (1870), 8 N.S.R. 49 at 53.

48 *Murison v. Murison* (1840), 1 N.S.R. 131 at 133.

49 *Hunter v. Ronne* (1870), 8 N.S.R. 113 at 115.

50 *Morton v. Campbell* (1859), 4 N.S.R. 1 at 8; see also *Brush v. Aetna Insurance Company* (1864), 459, 463.

51 *Fraser v. Salter* (1869), 7 N.S.R. 424 at 441–2.

52 *Scott v. Henderson* (1843), 3 N.S.R. 115 at 122.

53 *Haliburton v. DeWolfe* (1867), 7 N.S.R. 12 at 17.

54 See, e.g., *Scott v. Henderson* (1843), 3 N.S.R. 115 at 122; *Brush v. Aetna Insurance Co.* (1864), 5 N.S.R. 458 at 463; *Conlon v. City Railroad Co.* (1871), 8 N.S.R. 209 at 223.

55 In *LeCain v. Hosterman* (1871), 8 N.S.R. 413 at 416, Young C.J. observed that it was important to trace the decisions of the Massachusetts courts 'as far as we have access to them – and there is a blank in them which we are unable to fill up.' Because of this gap, he concluded in frustration, 'we have no means of ascertaining the modern practice of Massachusetts.' In *Baker v. Brown* (1872), 9 N.S.R. 100 at 108, Young actually said that 'we have none of the Massachusetts reports since those of 1840.' See also *Fraser v. Salter* (1869), 7 N.S.R. 424 at 432, 438.

56 See above, note 20.

57 Literally, 'of the half tongue,' accorded in the common law when one party was an alien who (at least as the privilege was originally conceived) did not speak English. Under these circumstances, a jury was supposed to be half composed of Englishmen and half composed of the alien's countrymen. In this criminal case, the defendants were American citizens (albeit, it seemed, English-speaking).

58 *The Queen v. Burdell* (1861), 5 N.S.R. 126 at 128.

59 *Fraser v. Salter* (1869), 7 N.S.R. 424 at 423. See also *Humphrey v. London & Lancashire Ins. Co.* (1870), 8 N.S.R. 39 and 43.

60 For instances of Halliburton's appreciation, see *Jackson v. Campbell* (1855), 1 N.S.R. 18 at 28 (holding that a provincial statute had to be interpreted counter to the English rule: 'It has been satisfactory for me to learn that the Supreme Court in Massachusetts have [sic] decided that an action for taking insufficient bail will lie against the Sheriff there, although they admit it will not in England'); *Tarratt v. Sawyer* (1835), 1 N.S.R. 46 at 53; *Gilmore v. Dewar* (1838), 1 N.S.R. 101 at 103; *Ells v. Ells* (1841), 1 N.S.R. 173 at 177; *Murison v. Murison* (1840), 1 N.S.R. 131 at 132. See generally P.R. Blakeley, 'Halliburton, Sir Brenton,' in *DCB*, 8: 354–6.

61 Ibid., 354.

62 At least in the pre-Victorian era, a number of leading Nova Scotian lawyers and jurists had likewise been sympathetic with the American Federalist cause: see Cuthbertson, *The Old Attorney-General*, 111.

63 See, e.g., *Fraser v. Salter* (1869), 7 N.S.R. 424 at 440–1.

64 Girard, 'Married Women's Property,' 116.

65 See, e.g., *Baker v. Brown* (1872), 9 N.S.R. 100 at 108.

66 For example, in *Gardner v. Home & Colonial Insurance* (January, 1871), 8 N.S.R. 204 at 207–8 Young mentioned that he had just received a copy of the *London Law Times* (21 December 1870) by the last mail, commenting: 'this periodical is conducted with so much of legal ability and knowledge that its opinions are always worth the studying.'

67 *Fraser v. Salter* (1869), 7 N.S.R. 425 at 444. On reform of the English judicial structure, see generally R. Stevens, *Law and Politics: The House of Lords as a Judicial Body 1800–1976* (Chapel Hill: University of North Carolina Press 1978), 47–48.

68 *Fraser v. Salter* (1869), 7 N.S.R. 425 at 444–5. See also *Roper v. Shannon* (1871), 8 N.S.R. 146 at 153, where Young praised recent developments in British equity and statute law regarding married women.

69 Particularly Wilkins J. and Johnston E.J. For cases in which the former made significant use of American authority, see *Morton v. Campbell* (1859), 4 N.S.R. 1 at 12–13; *Brush v. Aetna Insurance Company* (1864), 5 N.S.R. 458 at

483; *Athole Lodge v. Williamson* (1868), 7 N.S.R. 170 at 172; *Taylor v. Archibald* (1873), 9 N.S.R. 233 at 239. Desbarres and Dodd, on the other hand, seem to have been more sympathetic with Young, at least judging from their comparative disinterest in applying or following American jurisprudence, and their concomitant deference to English law.

70 *The Queen v. Allan* (1867), 7 N.S.R. 5 at 10. See also *Hennessy v. N.Y. Mutual Marine Insurance Co.* (1863), 5 N.S.R. 259 at 263, in which Young indicated that certain principles derived from American insurance law 'have found, I confess, a more ready acceptance with my learned brethren than with myself.'

71 *Lessee of Lawson v. Whitman* (1851), 1 N.S.R. 208 at 209.

72 (1853), 2 N.S.R. 31 at 33–4.

73 See generally M. J. Horwitz, *The Transformation of American Law, 1780–1860* (Cambridge: Harvard University Press 1977).

74 A comment of Weatherbe J. from 1880 is typical: 'We think the [English] case of Tweddle v. Atkinson settles the question, and notwithstanding the decisions in the United States as to whether a man can sue on a contract made for his benefit, but to which he is not directly a party, we know of no authority and none was cited in support of such a right in England.' See also *Cann v. International Trust Co.* (1907, reprinting case from 1894), 40 N.S.R. 65 at 67, per Graham J.: 'I have read a number of United States decisions, but I only cite two English cases'; *Wurzburg v. Andrews* (1896), 28 N.S.R. 387 at 402, per Graham J.: 'I cite two American cases [from Maine and New York] merely because they are like this one.'

75 See, e.g., *Foster v. Walker* (1899), 32 N.S.R. at 156, where Weatherbe J. endorsed a Massachusetts decision of Shaw C.J., noting that it was 'decided upon English authority,' and Graham J. noted that a decision of the United States Supreme Court (which he went on to quote extensively) was 'founded, I think, on English precedents.'

76 Perhaps in response to this inclination, lawyers citing American cases before the Supreme Court became more inclined to bury the cases in 'string cites' instead of making them a prime focus of argument.

77 English and even Canadian courts and commentators were deemed increasingly competent in these areas. See, for instance, the English and Canadian authorities cited in *O'Connor v. Commercial Insurance Co.* (1878), 12 N.S.R. 119 at 123. In *McLeod v. Citizens Insurance Co.* (1878), 12 N.S.R. 156 at 163, James J. countered American authorities on an insurance point with an Upper Canadian case.

78 See, for instance, *The Queen ex rel. Laurence v. Patterson* (1900), 33 N.S.R. 425 at 460, per Meagher J.: 'Our municipal corporations are, I presume, of much

the same character and endowed with powers somewhat, if not to a large extent, the same as those of the United States, and it seems to me the [point of municipal law contained in *Dillon on Municipal Corporations*] could with propriety and advantage be made applicable to Nova Scotia. But I do not feel myself at liberty, merely because of a difference in character or constitution between our municipal corporations, and those [English municipal corporations] whose powers came in question in the cases cited to us ... to depart from the principle recognized and acted upon in the mother country for so many years.'

79 The encomiums which the Nova Scotian judges did offer American judges and jurists in the late Victorian era stand out by virtue of their scarcity. See, for instance, *The Queen v. Holmes and Brecken* (1884), 17 N.S.R. 498 at 500, where Thompson J. praised Chancellor Kent as an 'eminent' jurist and said that the decisions of any court he presided over were entitled to 'great weight,' and *Fitzrandolph v. Shanley* (1881), 14 N.S.R. 199 at 223, where James J. spoke with undisguised adoration of 'my friend Mr. Bigelow.'

80 James J. in *Berry v. Berry* (1882), 16 N.S.R. 66 at 79. In the context of the various observations in this paragraph it is worth recalling that 'in its etiquette and terminology, the [Nova Scotian] bar and judiciary gravitated to English [and away from American] models in the post-Confederation period: "your Lordship" replaced "your Honour" as a form of address, the old title "assistant judge" yielded to the English "puisne judge," the title "attorney" with one and a half centuries' standing in the province, was replaced by "solicitor" in the 1899 legislation governing the profession ... and so on': Girard, 'Roots of a Professional Renaissance,' 166, n.31.

81 See generally P.V. Girard, 'The Supreme Court of Nova Scotia, Responsible Government, and the Quest for Legitimacy, 1850–1920,' *Dalhousie Law Journal* 17 (1994): 430–57.

82 According to Blaine Baker, the average number of Nova Scotia appeals to the JCPC between 1807 and 1888 was four per decade; between 1889 and 1913, the number increased to six per decade, representing a 50 per cent increase in the frequency of Imperial appeal: Baker, 'Reconstitution,' 251, n.105, and 269, n.156. As early as 1876, Wilkins J. was prompted to bow to the JCPC in these terms: '[N]obody can entertain a higher sense than I do of the dignity, the impartiality, the learning and the wisdom of the Judicial Committee of Her Majesty's Privy Council. We hear a good deal of "autonomy" just now, in relation to the absorbing question of the day. I trust the day is far distant when Nova Scotia will have an "autonomy" that will make its highest court independent of the control of the high tribunal referred to.' *Woodworth v. Troop* (1876), 11 N.S.R. 84 at 120–1.

83 The amended English Judicature Act was (with some adjustments) eventually imported to Nova Scotia itself by the Judicature Act of 1884, 47 Vict., c. 25, most immediately modelled on the Ontario Judicature Act of 1881: see J.M. Beck, *The Government of Nova Scotia* (Toronto: University of Toronto Press 1957), 288, and the chapter by Girard, this volume. On English legal liberalism see generally D. Sugarman, 'Legal Theory, the Common Law Mind, and the Making of Textbook Tradition,' in W. Twining, ed., *Legal Theory and Common Law* (Oxford: B. Blackwell 1986).

84 It was also, in some instances, regarded as an active agent of maturation. In *The Queen v. Townsend v. Whiting* (1896), 28 N.S.R. 468 at 489, Meagher J. wished to import a stricter English rule into Nova Scotian practice in order to prevent the usual procedural irregularities or informalities which the American law would have recognized and, in practice, endorsed.

85 For one of the last English endorsements of American law, see the remarks of Lord Justice Cockburn in *Scaramanga v. Stamp* (1880), 49 Law J. Rep. C.P. 674: 'Although the decisions of the American courts are, of course, not binding on us, yet the sound and enlightened views of American lawyers in the administration and development of the law – a law, except so far as altered by statutory enactment, derived from a common source with our own – entitle their decisions to the utmost respect and confidence on our part.' In Nova Scotia, Thompson J. quoted these words with approval in *The Queen v. Holmes and Brecken* (1884), 17 N.S.R. 498 at 500.

86 *Re: Missouri Steamship Co.* (1889), 42 Ch.D. 321, 330. Perhaps partially as a result of this and other negative comments, the number of citations made to American cases in English courts between 1876 and 1914 was quite low: of the approximately 11,000 decisions recorded in the English Law Reports in these years there were a mere 251 judicial references to American cases and 106 references to American texts: A.M. Munson, 'The Influence of American Law on the English Reports,' *American Law Review* 48 (1914): 558–69.

87 See 'Citation of American Decisions in the English Courts,' *American Law Review* 23 (1889): 816–17; 'Citation of American Decisions in the English Law Courts,' *Canada Law Journal* 25 (1889): 561–2.

88 The few Nova Scotian citations to British North American jurisprudence in the pre-Confederation era were mostly to decisions in the courts of neighbouring New Brunswick. See, e.g., *Uniacke v. Dickson* (1848), 2 N.S.R. 287; *Lessee of Shey v. Chisolm* (1853), 2 N.S.R. 52 at 54; *Allison v. Desbrisay* (1859), 4 N.S.R. 19 at 21. See generally Murdoch, 'Essay on the Origins,' 191. The earliest Nova Scotian reference to an Upper Canadian case or statute in the published Supreme Court Reports appears to be *The Queen v. Dowsey, Douglas et al.* (1866), 6 N.S.R. 93 at 108.

89 In *Berry v. Berry* (1882), 16 N.S.R. 66 at 71, James J. considered American and Canadian (Ontarian and New Brunswick) cases as collateral authorities, noting that all used the same form of 'mongrel' deed (a variant on the English norm); see also *Halifax Pilot Commissioners v. Farquhar*, (1893), 26 N.S.R. 323 at 329,where Meagher J. considered in the same breath a United States Supreme Court case and a case from the Upper Canadian Court of Queen's Bench. In *Coombs v. Fairbanks* (1893), 25 N.S.R. 525 at 531, Townshend J. countered a Massachusetts decision on mortgages with one from Ontario.

90 See Hansen, *Mingling of the Canadian and American Peoples*, 161 and 209–10.

91 See Baker, 'Reconstitution,' 281.

92 See R. Cosgrove, *Our Lady the Common Law: An Anglo-American Legal Community, 1870–1930* (New York: New York University Press 1987), 25–58.

93 See Baker, 'Reconstitution,' 265.

94 The continuing attraction of Nova Scotian jurists to American notions, cases, and commentaries was not lost on observers in the United States. In 1885, an editorial note in the prestigious *American Law Review* opined that '[t]here is more sympathy with American ideas in Nova Scotia, and less in Ontario, than in any other portion of the Dominion ... American law books seem to be studied more, and cited oftener in that country [sic] than in other portions of Canada. Much of the American spirit underlies the foundation of the promising law school [Dalhousie] which has lately been established in Halifax': 'The Dalhousie University Law School,' *American Law Review* 19 (1885): 108.

95 As an instance of attenuation, see *Hart v. Maguire* (1896), 29 N.S.R. 181 at 183, where Graham J., in a very odd turn of phrase, 'explained' (as if he had forgotten the real historical reasons) that Nova Scotian courts had followed the Massachusetts law of assignments '[f]or some reason or other.' For an instance of citing high-level American authority, see *Phinney v. Clark* (1895), 27 N.S.R. 384 at 394, where, in a break from tradition, Townshend J. turned to decisions of the United States Supreme Court instead of Massachusetts on a question of Nova Scotia probate law.

96 For citations to the *American Decisions* series, see *McDonnell v. McMaster* (1882), 15 N.S.R. 372 at 375; *Municipality of Shelburne v. Marshall* (1886), 19 N.S.R. 171 at 176; *Kieley v. Morrison* (1892), 24 N.S.R. 327 at 331; *Munro v. McDonald* (1894), 26 N.S.R. 349 at 353; *McNeil v. McDougall* (1896), 28 N.S.R. 296 at 300; *O'Brien v. Christie* (1897), 30 N.S.R. 145 at 149. *Pudsey v. Dominion Atlantic Railway* (1895), 27 N.S.R. 498 at 507. For citations to the *American Reports*, see *Blair v. The Sovereign Fire Ins. Co.* (1886), 19 N.S.R. at 372, 373, 381; *White v. Flemming* (1888), 70 N.S.R. 335 at 339; *Geldert v. The Municipal-*

ity of Pictou (1891), 23 N.S.R. 483 at 519; *Nixon v. The Queen Ins. Co.* (1893), 25 N.S.R. 317 at 335; *Travis v. Way* (1901), 33 N.S.R. 551 at 557. For citations to West's *Northeastern Reporter*, see *Creelman v. Tupper* (1893), 25 N.S.R. 334 at 339; *Jost v. McNutt* (1907, reprinting case from 1893), 40 N.S.R. 41 at 46. For a citation to the *Northwestern Reporter*, see *York v. The Canada Atlantic Steamship Co.* (1892), 24 N.S.R. 436 at 459. For a citation to the *Pacific Reporter*, see *Pudsey v. Dominion Atlantic Railway* (1895), 27 N.S.R. 498 at 507.

97 In 1894, Henry J. notably quoted from the *English* edition of Story's *Equity Jurisprudence*, suggesting a subtle anglicization of the American books the Nova Scotian jurists used in the later Victorian period. *Munro v. McDonald* (1894), 26 N.S.R. 349 at 356. For citation to Redfield, see *Harris v. Sheffield* (1875), 10 N.S.R. 1 at 11. For citation to May, see *O'Conner v. Commercial Union Insurance Co.* (1878), 12 N.S.R. 119 at 123; *Cox v. Worrall* (1894), 26 N.S.R. 366 at 377. For citation to Bigelow, see *McKay v. Bonnett* (1878), 12 N.S.R. 137 at 140; *Fitzrandolph v. Shanly* (1881), 14 N.S.R. 199 at 216; *Munro v. McDonald* (1894), 26 N.S.R. 349 at 353. For citation to Perry, see *Trustees Public Property v. Kerr* (1878), 12 N.S.R. 317 at 323; *Munro v. McDonald* (1894), 26 N.S.R. 349 at 353. For citation to Bump, see *Re: A. Mooney* (1877), 11 N.S.R. 563 at 564. For citations to Schouler, see *Kieley v. Morrison* (1892), 24 N.S.R. 327 at 331; *Redden v. Tannel* (1896), 29 N.S.R. 40 at 45. For citations to Cooley, see *Windsor and Annapolis Railway Company v. Western Counties Railway Company* (1878), 12 N.S.R. 376 at 381; *Geldert v. The Municipality of Pictou* (1891), 23 N.S.R. 483 at 520; *Vantassel v. Trask* (1894), 27 N.S.R. 329 at 337; *Fielding v. Church* (1895), 28 N.S.R. 136 at 143; *City of Halifax v. Jones* (1896), 28 N.S.R. 452 at 459; *The Queen v. Gibson* (1896), 29 N.S.R. 3 at 10; *Williams v. Woodworth* (1899), 32 N.S.R. 271 at 277; *Meisner v. Meisner* (1899), 32 N.S.R. 320 at 330. For citations to Bishop, see *The Queen v. Townsend v. Whiting* (1896), 28 N.S.R. 468 at 484; *The Queen v. Gibson* (1896), 29 N.S.R. 3 at 7. For citations to Dillon, see *Oakes v. City of Halifax* (1879), 13 N.S.R. 98 at 114; *Gillis v. Town of Pictou* (1886), 19 N.S.R. 128 at 131; *Meisner v. Meisner* (1899), 32 N.S.R. 320 at 330; *The Queen ex rel. Laurence v. Patterson* (1900), 33 N.S.R. 425 at 459. For citations to Shearman & Redfield, see *Conlon v. Connolly* (1875), 10 N.S.R. 95 at 99; *Gilbert v. Municipality of Yarmouth* (1890), 23 N.S.R. 93 at 120; *Drake v. The Town of Dartmouth* (1893), 25 N.S.R. 177 at 189. For citation to Keener, see *Lindberg v. City of Halifax* (1898), 31 N.S.R. 154 at 159. See citation to Gray, see *McDonald v. Jones* (1907, reprinting case from 1898), 40 N.S.R. 232 at 234.

98 For citation to Bouvier, see *The Queen v. Carter* (1880), 13 N.S.R. 307 at 310; *Grant v. Booth* (1893), 25 N.S.R. 266 at 270. For citation to Wharton, see *King v. Gardner* (1892), 25 N.S.R. 48 at 51. For citation to Abbott, see *Naas v.*

Backman (1896), 28 N.S.R. 504 at 512. For citation to the *American and English Encyclopedia*, see *Weeks v. The Town of North Sydney* (1894), 26 N.S.R. 396 at 401; *Naas v. Backman* (1896), 28 N.S.R. 504 at 512; *The Queen v. Dixon* (1897), 29 N.S.R. 462 at 480; *Kenny v. Harrington* (1898), 31 N.S.R. 290 at 296; *Harrington v. Peters* (1900), 32 N.S.R. 464. For Weatherbe's citation to the *American Law Review*, see *McKay v. Bonnett* (1881), 14 N.S.R. 96 at 116.

99 For citation to Chitty and Hulme, see *Merchants' Bank v. Spinney* (1879), 13 N.S.R. 87 at 93. For citation to Stephen, see *McKeen v. Nass* (1878), 12 N.S.R. 225 at 259; *Anderson v. Taylor* (1879), 12 N.S.R. 526 at 535. For citation to Adams, see *Jost v. Church-Wardens of St. George's* (1880), 13 N.S.R. 451 at 455. For citations to Benjamin, see *Whitman v. Parker* (1885), 18 N.S.R. 155 at 160; *Snow v. Fraser* (1897), 30 N.S.R. 80 at 89. For citations to Taylor, see *The Queen v. Troop* (1898), 30 N.S.R. 339 at 343; *Miller v. Green* (1899), 32 N.S.R. 129 at 137.

100 For citations to White and Tudor, see *Power v. Meagher* (1888), 21 N.S.R. 184 at 197. For citations to Smith, see *Hawes v. Hart* (1885), 18 N.S.R. 42 at 59; *Cowling v. Gates* (1888), 21 N.S.R. 78 at 81. For citations to the *English Common Law Reports*, see *McKay v. Bonnett* (1881), 14 N.S.R. 96 at 110; *Wright v. Morning Herald Co.* (1881), 14 N.S.R. 399 at 407.

101 *McDonnell v. McMaster* (1882), 15 N.S.R. 372 at 378. See also *Wallace v. Creelman* (1884), 17 N.S.R. 418 at 428, per Weatherbe J.: 'The Massachusetts decisions are valuable on this question because they were able judges and they adopted the English law.'

102 *Titus v. Haines* (1876), 11 N.S.R. 542 at 546.

103 See generally P.V. Girard and R. Veinott, 'Married Women's Property Law in Nova Scotia, 1850–1910,' in J. Guildford and S. Morton, eds., *Separate Spheres: Women's Worlds in the Nineteenth Century Maritimes* (Fredericton: Acadiensis Press 1994).

104 *Re: Estate of John Simpson* (1878), 12 N.S.R. 357 at 361.

105 *Gilbert v. Municipality of Yarmouth* (1890), 23 N.S.R. 93 at 113. See also *McDonnell v. McMaster* (1882), 15 N.S.R. 372 at 378.

106 *O'Connor v. Commercial Union Insurance Co.* (1878), 12 N.S.R. 119 at 127.

107 *McLean v. Garnier* (1881), 14 N.S.R. 432 at 437.

108 *O'Connor v. Commercial Union Insurance Co.* (1878), 12 N.S.R. 119 at 124. See also *The Queen v. Carter* (1880), 13 N.S.R. 307 at 312.

109 *Hart v. Maguire* (1896), 29 N.S.R. 181 at 195.

110 In *O'Donnell v. Confederation Life Insurance Co.* (1877), 11 N.S.R. 570 at 576 Wilkins J. crowed that a statute of Massachusetts he had cited 'will be found in the volume of the General Statutes of Massachusetts, page 673,

sec. 14, which book will be found in the Legislative Library.' Consistent with the proposition in the text, however, increased Nova Scotian interest in other Canadian cases in the late Victorian period was reflected in a *rising* number of complaints (at least early on) regarding their inaccessibility: see, for instance, *Oakes v. City of Halifax* (1879), 13 N.S.R. 98 at 114.

111 *Titus v. Haines* (1876), 11 N.S.R. 542 at 546; *O'Conner v. Commercial Union Ins. Co.* (1878), 12 N.S.R. 119 at 123; *Merchants' Bank v. Spinney* (1879), 13 N.S.R. 87 at 93.

112 Weatherbe cited American authority in *McKay v. Bonnett* (1881), 14 N.S.R. 96 at 110; *Town of Windsor v. Commercial Bank* (1882), 15 N.S.R. 420 at 427; *Wallace v. Creelman* (1884), 17 N.S.R. 418 at 428; *Whitman v. Parker* (1885), 18 N.S.R. 155 at 160; *The Queen v. Lantz* (1886), 19 N.S.R. 1 at 6; *Grindley v. Blaikie* (1886), 19 N.S.R. 27 at 44; *Geldert v. The Municipality of Pictou* (1891), 23 N.S.R. 483 at 517; *Cahoon v. Parks* (1892), 25 N.S.R. 1 at 7; *Vantassel v. Trask* (1894), 27 N.S.R. 329 at 337; *The Queen v. Townsend v. Whiting* (1896), 28 N.S.R. 468 at 478; *Taylor v. McKinnon* (1896), 29 N.S.R. 162 at 170; *Hart v. Maguire* (1896), 29 N.S.R. 181 at 183; *The Queen v. Corby* (1897), 30 N.S.R. 330 at 332; *McLeod v. Insurance Co. of North America* (1901), 33 N.S.R. 88 at 106.

113 Re Weatherbe, see above, note 74. See also note 75, where Weatherbe and Graham JJ. both made a point of saying that the American decisions they referred to were firmly based on English law. In this context it is worth noting that both Weatherbe and Graham have been identified as prominent actors in the 'imperialization' of Nova Scotian legal culture in the late nineteenth century: Girard, 'The Supreme Court,' *passim.*

114 Girard, 'The Supreme Court,' 451–2.

115 *American Law Review* 20 (1885): 322.

116 Girard, 'The Supreme Court,' 453.

117 For cases in which Graham offered multiple American authorities to the Supreme Court in his capacity as counsel, see *The Queen v. Fraser* (1876), 11 N.S.R. 431 at 432. At one point, while travelling in England, Graham wrote to John Thompson: 'we are a different race altogether. I think the US has affected us': quoted in Girard, 'Supreme Court,' 453.

118 This does not mean, however, that American ideas did not prevail in particular (albeit unusual) cases. For instance, in *The Queen v. Townsend v. Whiting* (1896), 28 N.S.R. 468, Weatherbe, Graham, and Henry JJ. constituted a majority (Townshend and Meagher dissenting) holding that under the 1892 Canadian Criminal Code (as in American, if not English law) the words 'true bill' did not have to appear on the back of an indictment signed by the foreman of the jury.

119 Thompson cited American authority in *Fielding v. Mott* (1885), 18 N.S.R. 339 at 354; *Robertson v. Williams* (1885), 18 N.S.R. 393 at 400. Townshend cited American authority in *Pitcher v. Bingay* (1888), 21 N.S.R. 31 at 38; *Re: Estate of Murray* (1889), 22 N.S.R. 125, 131; *Gilbert v. Municipality of Yarmouth* (1890), 23 N.S.R. 93, at 120; *Northrup v. Cunningham* (1892), 24 N.S.R. 188 at 196; *Cox v. Worrall* (1894), 26 N.S.R. 366 at 375; *Fulton v. The Kingston Vehicle Co., Ltd.* (1897), 30 N.S.R. 455 at 465. Joseph N. Ritchie cited American authority in *Gilbert v. Municipality of Yarmouth* (1890), 23 N.S.R. 93 at 108; *Cox v. Worrall* (1894), 26 N.S.R. 366 at 373; *The Queen v. Major* (1897), 29 N.S.R. 373 at 375. Meagher cited American authority in *Gilbert v. Municipality of Yarmouth* (1890), 23 N.S.R. 93 at 131; *Casey v. Smith* (1894), 26 N.S.R. 177 at 192; *The Queen v. Gibson* (1896), 29 N.S.R. 3 at 7; *Barrowman v. Fader* (1898), 31 N.S.R. 20 at 27; *The Queen ex rel. Laurence v. Patterson* (1900), 33 N.S.R. 425 at 459. Henry cited American authority in *Munro v. McDonald* (1894), 26 N.S.R. 349 at 353; *Miller v. Green* (1899), 32 N.S.R. 129 at 137. Hugh McDonald cited American authority in *North American Life Ass. Co. v. Craigen* (1885), 18 N.S.R. 440 at 446; *Kieley v. Morrison* (1892), 24 N.S.R. 327 at 331. Henry Smith cited American authority in *Robertson v. Williams* (1885), 18 N.S.R. 393 at 406 (where he cited Massachusetts cases, only to reject them in favour of English cases to the contrary). Samuel Rigby cited American authority in *Kenny v. Chisolm* (1886), 19 N.S.R. 497 at 500.

120 A comment in the Halifax *Morning Chronicle* from 1870 captures the sorry state of the judges which eventually encouraged the new appointments: 'The Chief Justice has long since passed the period fixed in Holy Writ for the life of man, and is now verging on eighty years of age [*sic*: Young was born in 1799, making him 71 in 1870] ... In consequence of the age and infirmity of the Judge in Equity, the Island of Cape Breton ... has been deprived of the administration of justice for a whole year ... Mr. Justice Dodd is very old and infirm. Over and over again he has pronounced himself unfit to endure the enormous responsibility and fatigue of a judgeship of the Supreme Court': quoted in Beck, *Government of Nova Scotia*, 288.

121 In the context of this point, however, it is important to recall that in the late nineteenth century American law was itself becoming more formalistic. See generally, M. Horwitz, *The Transformation of American Law, 1870–1960* (New York: Oxford University Press 1993). The formalistic effect of Nova Scotian adoption of English law therefore lay in its replacement of American rules from the early nineteenth century; continuing to apply American law might ironically have led to similar effects. From a some-

what different perspective, it might also be suggested that lesser Nova Scotian recourse to American authority in the last quarter of the nineteenth century contributed at least indirectly to the substantial post-1880 decline in the number of Nova Scotian law students seeking their legal education in the United States: see Girard, 'Roots of a Professional Renaissance,' 173.

122 *Grindley v. Blaikie* (1886), 19 N.S.R. 27 at 34.

123 For another instance when English law favoured a more formalistic, literal approach to a rule than did American law would have, see *Robertson v. Williams* (1885), 18 N.S.R. 393.

124 See, e.g., Baker, 'Reconstitution,' 242–3; D. Howes, 'From Polyjurality to Monojurality: The Transformation of Quebec Law, 1875–1929,' *McGill Law Journal* 32 (1987): 523.

125 See McIntyre, 'The Use of American Cases,' 480.

126 On recourse to American authority in the ethnic Chinese cases, see McLaren, 'The Early British Columbia Judges.' For what we do know about B.C. judges' use of American case law otherwise, see McIntyre, 'The Use of American Cases,' 483–6.

127 But see also McIntyre, 'The Use of American Cases,' 482–3.

128 Baker, 'Reconstitution,' 274.

129 For instances of Ontario lawyers promoting American materials in the 1850s, see, e.g., 'American Law Publications,' *Upper Canada Law Journal* 2 (1856): 94; Oliver Mowat, 'Observations on the Use and Value of American Reports in Reference to Canadian Jurisprudence,' *Upper Canada Law Journal* 3 (1857): 3–7. On American holdings policies of Ontario law libraries, see generally Baker, 'Reconstitution,' 243–9. On Ontarian use of U.S. authority generally, see R.C.B. Risk, 'The Law and the Economy in Mid-Nineteenth Century Ontario,' in D.H. Flaherty, ed., *Essays in the History of Canadian Law: Volume One* (Toronto: Osgoode Society for Canadian Legal History and University of Toronto Press 1981), 88 and 108.

130 McIntyre, 'The Use of American Cases,' 482. This divergent result may indirectly reflect a lesser 'imperialization' of late nineteenth-century Nova Scotian law (suggested by, inter alia, the fact that while Nova Scotian appeals to the JCPC increased 50 per cent in the years between 1888 and 1913, those from Ontario increased 1000 per cent): see Baker, 'Reconstitution,' 269; also, C. Berger, *The Sense of Power: Studies in the Ideas of Canadian Imperialism 1867–1914* (Toronto: University of Toronto Press 1970), 155. In this context a comment of Philip Girard's seems particularly apt: especially when dealing with the legal history of the Maritimes, 'we should not think in terms of exclusive loyalty to a particular cultural metropolis, but

rather of shifting and overlapping patterns of cultural influence from various sources': Girard, 'Roots of a Professional Renaissance,' 167.

131 On the concept of 'legal metropolis,' see generally E. Kolish, 'The Impact of the Change in Legal Metropolis on the Development of Lower Canada's Legal System: Judicial Chaos and Legislative Paralysis in the Civil Law, 1791–1838,' *Canadian Journal of Law and Society* 3 (1988): 1–25.

132 See generally Girard, 'Themes and Variations,' 143: 'we must be sensitive to regional variations in Canadian legal culture and not presuppose some undifferentiated "national" experience of the law.'

133 Of course, this latter 'turning away' also involved a rejection of law and legal literature completely indigenous to Nova Scotia (such as Murdoch's *Epitome*). See generally Girard, 'Themes and Variation.'

134 Especially after 1890, English and Canadian jurisprudence probably reinforced each other's impact in Nova Scotia. The more Nova Scotian judges turned towards England, the more attractive the increasingly anglicized law of Ontario must have become to them. At the same time, their importation of anglicized Ontarian law would only have supported their bias in favour of English precedent and practice. In a technical context, Philip Girard has wondered whether the English legal terms increasingly accepted in Nova Scotia in the late nineteenth century 'filtered into Nova Scotia from Ontario.' See Girard, 'Roots of a Professional Renaissance.'

135 This expression, familiar to all Atlantic Canadians as descriptive of leaving home and moving to Ontario, is probably best known to central and western Canadians from the award-winning Don Shebib film, *Goin' Down the Road* (1970).

11

Instrumentalism and the Law of Injuries in Nineteenth-Century Nova Scotia

JAMES MUIR

The industrial revolution came to Nova Scotia in the mid-nineteenth century. Trains crossed the province, large-scale industrial mining opened, manufacturers and factories began the displacement of local craft production.[1] Law played a key role in the industrial revolution by apportioning the costs and benefits for those affected by the changes. The Nova Scotia Supreme Court was often forced to interpret statutes and precedents and even make law to govern these changes. Those decisions merit investigation so as to understand the way in which the law and the economy interacted, and the place of the Supreme Court in defining the path of development taken in the province.

In *The Transformation of American Law, 1780–1860*, Morton Horwitz argues that between Independence and the Civil War the common law in the United States was fundamentally changed to promote a particular type of capitalist development that 'enabled emergent entrepreneurial and commercial groups to win a disproportionate share of wealth and power in American society.'[2] The changes in the common law, Horwitz claims, were made possible by the development of an instrumental conception of the law that allowed judges to break from established British and American precedents and make decisions on new policy grounds. Horwitz traces this development in a number of areas of law, particularly property, tort, commercial, and contract law. His most important conclusions are as follows. First, the common law aided in the development of a particular capitalist economy in the antebellum United States through decisions that favoured the interests of industry over others in the community. Second, the judiciary was conscious of what it was doing and made instrumental decisions to this effect *when necessary*. This last qualification is very important: not every jurisdiction had to invent new rules; once a rule existed in one jurisdiction, subsequent judges could adopt it while employing the more conservative rhetoric of stare decisis or analogy.

While inspiring to some historians of law, there have been many attacks on Horwitz's interpretation. Most recently it has come under searching review in two books by Peter Karsten: *Heart versus Head* and *Between Law and Custom*.[3] Karsten is particularly concerned with contesting Horwitz's innovation and instrumentalism theses. In the first book, Karsten argues that nineteenth-century judges made decisions based on precedent (a jurisprudence of the head) or, if they acted instrumentally, it was not to support the new capitalist class but those less fortunate who were unjustly treated by the law (a jurisprudence of the heart). In several areas of law he questions whether the rules Horwitz highlights were actually nineteenth-century innovations and, regardless of innovation, whether they were as broadly accepted across the United States as Horwitz suggests. In the second book Karsten expands his purview, comparing the law in the United States to that of England's other 'white settler societies': Canada, Australia, and New Zealand. Building on the heart and head dichotomy, Karsten notes that colonial courts 'did not formally have available to them an option chosen by some high courts of the United States – that of creating a "principled exception" to the English Rule ... [and] were not empowered to make new Common Law for themselves.' Nonetheless, he argues that this condition 'did not totally prevent some [colonial jurists] from finding other ways around unappealing English precedents.'[4] Where he finds judges attempting to evade English precedent or complaining about the state of the law they were enforcing, it is to support the less fortunate who were harmed by the strict application of English rules.

Both Horwitz and Karsten focused on the reported decisions of appellate judges, and their contrasting analyses and explanations of judicial decision making in the nineteenth century have ramifications beyond the history of judicial interpretation. Horwitz asserted that the legal decisions he found served the development of industrial capitalism in the United States; Karsten forces historians to reconsider whether a strong relationship existed between judicial decision making and economic development in the nineteenth century. Both, moreover, cover a great many areas of law. Negligence and liability for injuries to property and people touch on tort, contract, employment, and property law. Industrial accidents were inevitable. Strict liability for accidents could increase the cost of doing business, and in particularly dangerous or large enterprises those costs could become prohibitive. Yet liability also encouraged caution, and an absence of liability could lead to recklessness. Determining one person or corporation's liability to other people was thus central to understanding the opportunity for judicial innovation and the attitudes of judges towards economic development. Horwitz and Karsten both recognise this, and devote much of their works to discussing negligence.[5]

For Horwitz, 'the rise of the negligence principle in America overthrew basic eighteenth century private law categories and led to a radical transformation not only in the theory of legal liability but in the underlying conception of property on which it was based.' Before 1800 injuries were treated by 'a standard of strict liability that tended to ignore the specific character of the defendant's act.' Sixty years later, 'many types of injuries had been reclassified under a "negligence" heading, which had the effect of substantially reducing entrepreneurial liability.'[6] Karsten allows that 'injured plaintiffs did not have an easy time of it in collecting damages in the nineteenth century' but also argues that they faced no *new* "roadblocks and hurdles. Since the medieval period plaintiffs had to prove the defendant acted negligently to collect; 'there was no shift *from* "strict liability" to negligence.' Defences like 'contributory negligence' and 'fellow servant' existed before the nineteenth century, and jurists in the nineteenth century developed ways to circumvent them.[7]

Canadian historians of law and the economy have shied away from describing nineteenth-century legal development as judicial instrumentalism supplementing capitalist development. In his examination of the economy and law in Canada West in the mid-nineteenth century, R.C.B. Risk argues that Canadian judges were more conservative in their reliance upon precedent and less willing to make instrumental decisions than the judges Horwitz studied.[8] Jennifer Nedelsky, in two analyses of civil law in the late nineteenth and early twentieth centuries, likewise concluded that Canadian judges were generally conservative. In describing the Nova Scotian judiciary's treatment of water rights Nedelsky asserts, 'there is no clear pattern of the courts' trying to encourage or facilitate one use [of water] over another. In the decisions one finds no articulation of a policy of water allocation, or of which uses were most important or desirable.'[9] Nedelsky and Jamie Benidickson, in an essay covering water rights over roughly the same time period for Ontario,[10] find legislatures and the expanding state responsible for legal innovation, not the courts. In his study of industrial accident law in the nineteenth and early twentieth centuries, Eric Tucker finds some grounds for an instrumental explanation but feels the theory insufficient on its own to explain developments in the law.[11] Constance Backhouse has presented the most sustained instrumental analysis of law in the nineteenth century, in relation to rape and child custody law, but this work, while suggestive, is not necessarily connected to industrial development.[12]

The present article examines the nineteenth-century Nova Scotia Supreme Court's attitude towards questions of injury and negligence. Like Horwitz and Karsten I rely on reported decisions, the earliest of which date from 1834. The court had set the basic law on injury and accidents by 1880, five years after the establishment of the Supreme Court of Canada and a turning point in the judicial make-up of the Nova Scotia court.[13] Three areas of law will be considered: the ability of common carriers to contract out of liability for damage to goods they shipped; the liability of employers and corporations for injuries to third parties; and the liability of employers for injuries to their own workers. The cases studied here are drawn from a review of all reported Supreme Court cases to 1880, and are representative of the developing law of liability for accidents in the province. Nova Scotia's judges demonstrated a willingness to think instrumentally about the law and in favour of private industrial interests, but they were seldom explicitly required to act instrumentally, and at many times several of the judges expressed concern with the decisions they made.

Contracting Out of Liability

The transformative economic effect of railways and steam ships is well known: by shortening the length of time it took to ship goods and allowing for a large volume of trade over greater distances, both were important to economic growth in nineteenth-century Canada.[14] But while shipping times may have decreased, traders could not be certain that the goods they shipped or had shipped to them would arrive in the condition they expected. The Nova Scotia Supreme Court heard a great many cases about the liability of common carriers for the goods they moved.

At common law, common carriers had a strict liability for the goods in their care, meaning that they were responsible for any damage to goods they carried. Damage to shipped goods was not infrequent, and common carriers tried to limit their liability by contracting out of it. Horwitz argues that before 1830 'there were intimations by [United States'] courts that common carriers were free to contract out of legal liability.' More importantly, 'after 1830 ... American courts fell into line in allowing carriers to limit their strict liability by contract and, in many cases, even to immunize themselves from liability for negligence.' This was, to Horwitz, one of many examples of the nineteenth-century legal tendency to 'redefine all economic relationships in terms of contract.'[15] By accepting such limitations in shipping contracts, courts could help limit the risks of common carriers. The courts created an opening for carriers to protect their profits by allowing carriers to shift the costs of damaged goods to the consignors, or to demand premiums from consignors for insurance. This, in turn, could promote reinvestment and expansion of the carrier networks and lower shipping costs to those consignors willing to absolve the carrier of liability.

English law dealt with this situation somewhat differently, permitting carriers to contract out of the strict liability, but not under the common law. A number of regulatory statutes were passed by Parliament beginning in 1830 and culminating in the Railway and Canal Traffic Act of 1854. In decisions such as *Peek v. North Staffordshire Railway Co.* the statutes were interpreted by the courts to allow carriers to contract out of liability by printed notice. Carriers were, however, required to offer alternative rates whereby they would not contract out.[16]

The Nova Scotia Supreme Court dealt with the question of carrier liability for damages in shipment a number of times in the 1870s. In *Dodson v. The Grand Trunk Railway Co.*,[17] the court was asked to determine if the railway could contract out of liability for damage to one hundred dressed hogs caused not by 'wilful wrong ... or wanton abuse,' but by 'mis-management, carelessness and neglect.' At trial the jury 'found ... that the injury was caused by the negligence of the defendants' servants, and gave verdict for [the] plaintiff subject to the opinion of the Court on all legal objections.' The contract for shipping contained a clause noting that dressed hogs, along with other perishables, were 'to be carried only at the owner's risk.' Thus, in writing the decision, Chief Justice William Young asserted the only question to be determined was whether the Grand Trunk could contract out of all liability for damage to the meat.

Young asserted that the English statutes did not apply and there were no local statutes, so 'it is to be decided according to the principles of the Common Law.' He referred to a number of English precedents, particularly *Peek*, as well as United States Supreme Court justice Joseph Story's treatise on bailments. Young concluded that at common law 'there is no law to restrain the Grand Trunk Railway Company from exacting such terms and imposing such conditions as they think fit in their printed papers, which the public using the railway must accede to,' but he was troubled by his ruling. He wrote that this power would allow the railway even to contract out of damage caused by fraud or other wilful conduct by its employees and cautioned the railroad, 'We are far from thinking that the Grand Trunk Railway Company would push its advantages, or avail itself of the law to such extremes.' Although Young thought that in this case the railway was in the right, the rule he made could lead to injustice. He felt 'constrained by the authorities' to make his decision for the railway: 'It may be that with a view to their protection Parliament may deem it advisable to enact a law for the whole *Dominion*.'[18]

As will be seen below, Young remained sceptical about allowing carriers to contract out of liability even nine years later. Yet he may have misread the British case law. Young cited Lord Ellenborough in *Nicholson v. Willan*: 'there is no case ... in which the right of a carrier to limit by special contract his own responsibility has ever been by express decision denied.' Legal historian Patrick Atiyah suggests that in cases of negligent liability, there was no English precedent to *allow* such special contracts prior to the permissive legislation of the mid-nineteenth century. Perhaps Young erred, and felt compelled to apply the law as he understood it.

Despite Young's concerns, his fellows on the bench routinely sided with the carriers. In January 1872 the Windsor and Annapolis railway appealed a lower court ruling that found it liable for the complete cost of a roll of oilcloth damaged in shipping through the negligent acts of its employees.[19] The plaintiff Dodge ordered the $26.50 oilcloth shipped from Halifax to him in Bridgetown. Upon delivery he noticed that it was cracked and peeling. He asked the conductor whether it was like that when loaded onto the train. The conductor told him 'it had been placed on some barrels of flour in place of putting it on the floor of the car ... and they took the barrels from under the end of the oilcloth, and the package dropped at one end ... and that caused the damage.' Dodge refused to accept the oilcloth and sued the railway for its total cost. The railway accepted responsibility for damaging the oilcloth but was only willing to pay the difference in value between the cloth as received and as it was when delivery was attempted. The railway paid $3 into court prior to trial in an effort to settle. At trial they produced six witnesses who assessed the damage between 25 cents and $2.50, three of whom separately valued the damage and cost of repair at 50 cents. Dodge's witness valued the damage at $10. The jury returned a verdict for Dodge with damages of $23.50 (the total cost, less the $3 already paid into the court).

This case did not deal directly with contracting out of strict liability, but it did return the NSSC to the question of the cost of liability to be borne by common carriers. The appeal turned on whether the jury had proper direction at trial as to whether the plaintiff could recover the complete cost of the damaged goods. McCully J. wrote the majority decision. He noted, as had Young five months before, the absence of 'statutes qualifying the Common Law in reference to the responsibilities and rights of common carriers or railway companies.' McCully could find no cases on point to guide him, asserting that 'the plaintiff is attempting to establish a new principle': 'I have searched in vain to find a single case to show that negligence, carelessness, or misconduct of any kind on the part of a common carrier does more than entitle the contractor to recover damages for the non-fulfilment of his contract to the extent of the depreciation produced by the carrier's default.' Failing to find decisions directly on point that would allow him to limit the railway's liability to only the damage done did not deter McCully or incline him to find for the plaintiff. Instead, he looked to an analogy: 'in ... cases where carriers are in fault as to delay of delivery, the amount of damage and the principle as to measure and computation are well settled.' McCully found liability could only be for the value the railway had paid into court: any difference in value between that expected and that finally received had to be proven by the plaintiff, and the plaintiff would be limited to collecting only the difference and not the complete costs.

The limit placed on the railway's liability here is clear, but cast in sharper relief when the dissent by Wilkins J. is considered. Wilkins asked a question that went unanswered: 'why, if this chattel had been rendered by the defendants' want of due care ... useless to the plaintiff in relation to the purpose for which alone he required it, the company should not be required to pay the full value of it[?]'[20] McCully's analogy to goods delivered late was of little value in this case, according to Wilkins, because Dodge's intention was to use the oilcloth, not resell it. Having, through their employees' negligence, rendered this impossible, Dodge should not have been expected to take delivery of it, and should receive complete compensation. The key here is that Dodge did not take delivery: by compensating him completely the railway paid for and owned the oilcloth; it was up to them to repair or resell it to recoup some of their loss.

Young's reticence in *Dodson v. The Grand Trunk Railway* was not matched by the majority, represented by McCully, in *Dodge v. Windsor and Annapolis Railway*. With no precedent on point, the majority was free to decide the railway's liability, and they chose to limit it. As Wilkins's dissent makes clear, McCully's analogy to goods depreciated by late delivery was weak: Dodge lost the use of the oilcloth, not expected earnings. By limiting the liability of the railway in this case, the court reduced the railway's potential costs for negligent damage of goods to only the demonstrable value of the loss. If Wilkins had carried the majority, railways would have been required to fully compensate the receiver for goods damaged through negligence – a potentially significant added burden.

In an 1880 decision, *Wood v. Allan*,[21] Young found himself not merely bemoaning the state of the law but in the minority as the court overturned his trial ruling and preserved a common carrier's right to contract out of liability. In this case a trunk owned by a Miss Wood was damaged by sea water in a voyage from Liverpool to Halifax when a 'dummy' covering a porthole broke open. Smith, the ship's carpenter, was responsible for checking the hatches. He testified: 'I had seen that dummy about ten o'clock on the morning of the same day, (*i.e.*, the day the leak was discovered). It was perfectly good then and no sign of any water about it – no sign of any water then between decks. I had examined it every day before that. It was customary to examine them every morning during the voyage.' None of the ship's officers testified or made depositions. Zachariah Wood, Miss Wood's travelling companion, did testify that after the damage had been discovered, 'I heard the captain and officers of the vessel repeatedly state that the damage to the said luggage had been caused, not by the perils of the sea, but by the omission of the officer whose duty it was to visit and inspect the luggage room for several days after leaving port, but had not done so, whereby the open port hole had not been discovered.' As one of the conditions of the passengers' tickets, the Allan Line contracted out of its liability for damage to any goods caused by 'perils of the sea.' The issue at trial was whether the broken hatch was as a result of the carpenter's negligence or a peril of sea travel.

Chief Justice Young tried the action at first instance without a jury. He accepted, despite plaintiff arguments to the contrary, that the company's contracting out of liability for accidents at sea was valid. He was more troubled by the testimony of Smith and Wood regarding Smith's actions. In his dissent on appeal he stated his concerns: 'The defendant was liable for any negligence of his servants, and, if the carpenter was to be believed, there was no negligence. He had a direct and powerful inducement to exempt himself, but if he was free from blame it was surely most unlikely that the captain and his officers ... in the presence ... of young Wood, would repeatedly state that the damage to the luggage had not been caused by the perils of the seas, but by the omission of the officer for several days to visit and inspect the luggage as was his duty ... If this was said by the captain and was true, as I believe it was, the plaintiff was entitled to a verdict for damage done to her own clothing, and which any jury, I think, would have given her.' This was for Young, although he does not repeat his words from *Dodson*, an example of a company attempting to contract out of liability for wilful misconduct and fraud by its employees.

Young's willingness to take Wood's hearsay evidence over Smith's testimony of his own behaviour was of some concern to his fellows at the appeal hearing. All three other judges wrote decisions and all three began by restating that the defendants could contract out of their strict liability. The judges then turned to Smith's and Wood's testimony. Judge Smith clarified the issue: 'we have only to contrast the value of [the captain's] admission, not made under oath, and almost certainly outside of any personal knowledge, with the *sworn* statement of Smith.' Having determined that Smith's testimony was of greater veracity at law than the reports about what the captain said, the judges each concluded that the carpenter was not negligent and there was no evidence to show a defect in construction or negligence in not supplying the vessel with appropriate fixtures. Judge Smith concluded, 'I regret to differ from the learned Chief Justice, who probably may be right.' The other judges made their decision on the same grounds. In the context of both his own decision and those of his fellows, Judge Smith's comment as to the correctness of Young's position probably reflects deference to the chief justice rather than any concurrence with his opinion on the law.

Dodson v. The Grand Trunk Railway Co., *Dodge v. Windsor & Annapolis Railway Co.*, and *Wood v. Allan* are consistent in conceding limits on the liability of common carriers for the goods they carried. Although

Young expressed his dislike for the rule in 1871, by 1880 it was accepted by and acceptable to the court. Young, writing for the whole court in 1871, could express dissatisfaction with the rule; although he remained unsatisfied nine years later, the other judges no longer expressed any similar distaste for it. Smith's suggestion that Young might be correct, if taken at face value, would only concede ground on the carpenter's honesty as a witness, as opposed to the rule itself. Therefore, there are signs of a transformation of judicial thinking from questioning a rule to general acceptance. This change might not have marked a change in the minds of particular judges, but in the judiciary itself: four of the seven judges on the bench for *Dodson* were gone when *Wood* was heard. As judicial opinion changed to support these nineteenth-century innovations, judges became less willing to find ways of distinguishing cases and more willing to allow an expansive application of the rule.

Injuring Strangers: Collisions

The legal theory of negligence developed over the nineteenth century in both the United States and Britain and its colonies.[22] Under legal theories established centuries earlier, defendants could be held responsible for damages either in the case of an implied contract or contractual term (the source of the common carrier's original strict liability) or through a positive act by the defendant that injured a passive plaintiff (as in assault cases). At the core of negligence is the idea that individuals at law owe a duty of care to others, absent either a contractual relationship or intent to do harm. Now a defendant could be held liable for people injured or things damaged so long as the individual failed to act as a reasonable person or business would in the same circumstance. Although this development would seem to have expanded liability, the reasonableness standard actually *limited* it. In defining reasonable duties of care, and in allowing for a variety of defences that absolved individuals and businesses of any liability, common law courts restricted the scope of negligence. The language of negligence in turn affected the older sources of defendant liability, over time serving to limit them as well. The Nova Scotia Supreme Court's application of negligence in the nineteenth century can be seen clearly in the way it dealt with accidents, both those caused to strangers (people not employed by or otherwise in some contractual relationship with the injuring party) and employees.

Collision cases were important in the early development of both negligence and the defences against it. Unlike assaults and similar trespasses, in collision cases both parties were active, and the courts had to determine fault. In the process of making this determination, the courts allowed defendants to argue that the plaintiff shared fault for the accident.[23] Fault could be proven by demonstrating that the defendant acted unreasonably for the rules of the road or the conditions at the time. Defendants could, in turn, attempt to demonstrate the plaintiff's contributory negligence. If the plaintiff's own actions played some role in the accident or injury, then the defendant could not be held liable. Contributory negligence in the nineteenth century was considered a complete defence, meaning that any contributory negligence would absolve the defendant of liability, even if he or she was more responsible. The Nova Scotia Supreme Court dealt with several collision cases that show the application of contributory negligence and a second key doctrine in tort law: *respondeat superior*. Under *respondeat superior*, masters or employers were held liable for injuries caused by their servants or employees in the conduct of the business.

In *Martin v. Taylor* (1872)[24] Taylor's servant, driving his master's carriage at seven or as much as twelve miles an hour, on the right hand side of Spring Garden Road in Halifax, collided with Martin's milkman, horse, and wagon as they were crossing at the intersection with Dresden Row. At this time the statutes governing roadways for Nova Scotia declared that someone 'being to the right of the centre of the street was on the wrong side of the road.' The jury found for Martin and awarded him ten dollars in damages.

At trial and on appeal Taylor attempted to assert contributory negligence on the part of Martin's milkman who, it was claimed, failed to exercise due caution by crossing Spring Garden Road without properly checking to see if it was clear. McCully J. paraphrased the English jurist Pollock in *Williams v. Richards*: 'the injury to plaintiff must have been caused by defendant's negligence only, without the negligence of plaintiff contributing in any way to the accident.'[25] McCully found that contributory negligence had been properly explained to the jury and by awarding damages to the plaintiff they had clearly 'negatived it.' Both the jury at the original trial and McCully were sympathetic to the injured milkman and his employer. Neither the Halifax jury nor the Supreme Court judge was prepared to assume that not noticing someone racing down the wrong side of the street as one prepared to cross it was sufficient to count as contributory negligence.

Three years later the Supreme Court heard another action in which the defendant's servant collided with the plaintiff's servant on Spring Garden Road; this time in sleighs at night. Once again the defendant pleaded contributory negligence and appealed on the grounds that the evidence of contributory negligence was so great 'as to leave nothing to be submitted to the jury, and that they should have been directed to find a verdict for the defendant.'[26]

In January 1874 a heavy layer of snow covered Halifax, narrowing Spring Garden Road near The Rink. On the night of 11 January, the plaintiff's servant, driving a three-seated sleigh, tried to pass two sleighs going in the opposite direction, the defendant's being the second. Both of the sleighs he attempted to pass may have been on the wrong side of the street due to the snow. Having successfully passed the first, one of the plaintiff's horses ran into the shaft of the defendant's sleigh. The plaintiff maintained that by being on the wrong side of the street, failing to move aside, and not having lights the defendant was negligent. The trial jury accepted this argument and awarded the plaintiff thirty dollars in damages.

But the defendant and the plaintiff's two witnesses (his servant and the driver of the third sleigh) gave evidence to suggest some contributory negligence. During the appeal hearing, McCully J., the trial judge as well, commented, 'I think that perhaps I did not put the matter of contributory negligence clearly enough to the jury.' The plaintiff's driver admitted to not having lights on his sleigh either and that 'I was not coming *extra fast – pretty fast*.' He also admitted, 'I saw [the defendant's sleigh] was on the wrong side. I still kept on. I was depending on him hauling off before we met. If I had known he was not going to haul off, *I could have passed him on the other side*. I saw that if he kept on, as he was, and I kept on, we would have a collision.'

In a lengthy decision Smith J. outlined the premises of negligence. First, he referred to both English treatises and cases to establish that negligence exists where one party injures another, but that injury must not have been caused by a mere accident. On this ground alone, he found no evidence of defendant negligence, except that the defendant may have been at least in part on the wrong side of the road. Citing treatises again, Smith asserted that taking the wrong side of the road was not inherently a negligent act, so long as a 'sufficiency of room' was left for those coming the opposite way. To define contributory negligence, Smith quoted the English judge Wightman J. to the effect that if the 'plaintiff himself so far contributed to the misfortune by his own negligence, or want of ordinary and common care and caution that, but for such negligence, or want of ordinary care and caution on his part, the misfortune would not have happened,' then the plaintiff would not be entitled to recover his losses.[27] Smith concluded: 'the fact of negligence on the part of the defendant has not been satisfactorily established, and ... the evidence is so much against the plaintiff, on the ground of contributory negligence that [the verdict must be] set aside.' In the court's opinion the evidence was so great it was unnecessary to order a new trial with a better definition of contributory negligence.

These two cases reveal the basic rules of negligence in Nova Scotia in the late nineteenth century: masters were liable for the actions of their servants, individuals injured by the unreasonable (and not simply accidental) actions of someone else could sue for damages, and defendants could plead contributory negligence and completely avoid liability. They indicate the general acceptance of negligence doctrine in Nova Scotia and the balance between fault and contributory negligence. When defendants were corporations, however, both legislatures and the courts tended to further limit the liability of the defendant through the determination of reasonableness and the expansion of the breadth of the defences.

Corporations and Injured Strangers

Karsten opens *Between Law and Custom* with three 1870s cases from Upper Canada concerning the liability of municipal corporations for injuries caused on their streets and sidewalks. Later in the book he returns to the general question of whether courts in Canada and other British settler colonies would find civic corporations liable for injuries people received walking on sidewalks or using the streets. Karsten finds that 'throughout most of the nineteenth century English jurists held that individual plaintiffs had *no* rights to sue either turnpike or municipal authorities for their neglect "to perform a public duty" unless a statute sanctioned such suits.'[28] A similar rule existed in the state of Massachusetts and other parts of New England, but in other states, such as New York or Pennsylvania, U.S. courts began finding municipal corporations liable without specific statutory provisions. Karsten shows that while Quebec and New Brunswick moved towards adopting similar rules, most settler colony judges, including Nova Scotia's, adopted the English rule: 'All things being equal – that is, where the facts and legal principles in the case appeared to be "four-square" consistent with an English precedent – colonial, provincial, and Dominion courts generally followed the English precedent even though the trial court judge's views may have been "fortified with strong authority from the American courts."'[29]

Karsten describes one Nova Scotia case from before 1880 as exemplary of this trend: *Evens v. City of Halifax* (1861).[30] Here, the plaintiff was injured on a June 1859 evening when his carriage ran over a pile of soil left on Argyle Street by a private homeowner named Veith. Evens contended that the city was liable because Veith had received permission to pile the soil from Mr Pollock, superintendent of the streets. Pollock had told Veith he could pile in the street so long as any debris was removed by 10:00 p.m., as per a city ordinance. The accident happened around 9:30. Among the duties prescribed by statute to the superintendent was to keep the streets clean. The plaintiff maintained the city was liable for Pollock's failure to keep the street clear of obstructions on the principle of *respondeat superior*.

Dodd J. rejected the plaintiff's reasoning from a number of positions, often with reference to British precedents. Yet the decision is striking as an example of Dodd's instrumentalism and sloppiness. Dodd accepted that the 1853 statute that created the office of the superintendents charged the city with keeping the streets clean. But, he asserted, this responsibility only existed when the city commissioners were aware of obstructions. He noted: 'Neither can they be charged with negligence for not doing that which they were empowered to do, for although the streets of the city are to be kept free from encumbrances by the superintendent acting under their authority, yet before they can be charged with negligence in this particular case, it must appear that they were aware of the encumbrance, and allowed it to remain without sufficient guards to protect the citizens from injury. Now, on the contrary, as I have already said, they were totally unacquainted with the earth having been placed in the street, until after the accident, when it was immediately moved.' Pollock, not the city commissioners, gave Veith permission to pile soil in the streets, thus, the commissioners did not know of the pile of soil. If they did not know about the pile, they had no responsibility to clean it up. Of course, Pollock knew about the pile, and as Dodd acknowledged, the statute that allowed the commissioners to appoint superintendents vested all of the commissioners' duties on the superintendent. But according to Dodd, the principle of *respondeat superior* held masters liable for the damage done by their servants because masters profited from the work of their servants. He argued, 'the city could not be made liable for in no manner could they derive advantage from the act of the superintendent who gave Veith permission to put earth in the street.' Certainly the commissioners derived some benefit from hiring Pollock: if nothing else, they avoided doing his work themselves. By narrowly defining 'advantage' Dodd was able to carve out a special place protecting certain corporation masters from one of the core premises of liability. In deciding this, Dodd relied on no direct precedents and made his decision on policy grounds. As Karsten points out, Dodd expressed concern that were he to find the city liable in this case, there would be no end to actions against the city.

Underscoring Dodd's instrumental decision was his sloppiness in discussing the facts of the case. At two different points Dodd also asserted that responsibility for the accident rested with Veith because he had 'exceeded the permission given to him ... [in that he] allowed the earth to remain in the street during the night.' But, in reciting the facts, Dodd stated that Veith had been given permission to pile the soil until 10:00 and 'the accident occurred half an hour before that time.' This error in the facts served to emphasize Veith's fault and further deny the liability of either Pollock or the city.

Two decisions from the 1870s concerning people injured by falling into open drains along streets demonstrate the judges were willing to allow some suits against the city corporation, but only in limited circumstances. The decision in the first of these cases, *Ward et ux. v. City of Halifax* (1873),[31] relied on English precedents to find the city liable. John Ward and his wife were walking along Hanover Street when Mrs Ward fell into an open drain and injured herself. At first instance the jury found for the plaintiffs and awarded them damages. On appeal, Young, writing for the court, distinguished *Ward* from *Evens*, which 'was decided upon exceptional facts,' and asserted, 'The liability of the City, therefore, is now for the first time to be determined, and it is a pretty large, and a very difficult question.' Young laid out the central issues in determining if the city could be liable. First, 'In the Act of 1864 ... the objects to be provided for by assessment are strictly defined, and to pay such damages and costs, the City Council must misappropriate money raised for other purposes.' On the other hand, 'it is more accordant with natural justice, that the loss should fall on the whole community, than on the individual, who has been injured without any fault of his own.'

Young traced the two streams of decisions in the United States, noting they remained 'in conflict,' and offered no clear analogy. The English cases 'are infinitely more at variance.' Nonetheless, Young fastened onto the rule affirmed in a House of Lords decision, *The Mersey Board v. Gibbs*[32] that the statute that creates the city (or like corporation) sets any liability that may exist. This was similar to the Massachusetts rule and the rule Karsten suggests applied in most colonial courts. Young applied it to decide that the City of Halifax *was* liable despite the absence of a specific clause to that effect in the statute.

Young recognized two limitations on the city's liability: there must be proof of negligence by the city and there must be no contributory negligence by the injured parties. On the former, Young asked if the drain was properly constructed and kept up. He found that it was properly constructed, but the evidence suggested it may have deteriorated over the subsequent dozen years due to a lack of maintenance. On the latter limitation, Young acknowledged that in their declaration the plaintiffs were careful to demonstrate the care they took on the street. At trial, however, they did not prove the absence of contributory negligence. Thus, Young ruled a new trial was necessary where the city could be held liable providing the plaintiffs demonstrated no contributory negligence.

Ward v. City of Halifax opened up the possibility of liability for the city. It was a remarkable decision that ran completely contrary to the logic of Dodd's decision in *Evens*: Young did not even question the city's liability for the acts of its agents or employees. Unlike Dodd, Young de-emphasized the differences between public and private corporations. Considering both *Ward* and the common carrier decisions, Young appears to have been more willing than his fellow judges to find corporations liable when they injured clients and third parties.

The opening for liability Young created in *Ward* was subsequently closed in 1877 in *MacKinlay v. City of Halifax*.[33] MacKinlay lost a horse after it fell into an open drain along Quinpool Road. He argued that the drain should have been covered or better constructed to prevent such an accident. The city maintained that the drain, being on the side of the road, was properly constructed and safe. Had MacKinlay's horse not been spooked by oncoming traffic and bolted to the side of the road, there would have been no injury.

Smith J. turned to the city's charter to determine if the municipality could be held liable. He found 'nothing in the revised charter under which the plaintiff seeks to fasten liability on the defendants, prescribing any particular mode of constructing such drains, or any duty imposed upon them to cover them.' Having decided the statute did not limit the city to construct only closed or covered drains, Smith asserted 'such drains should be constructed, when contiguous to a public road or thoroughfare, on the best practicable plan under the circumstances, in view of their necessity and danger to travellers.' Reviewing the evidence of the city engineer, Smith was convinced that the drain was proper and safe, and thus the city was not negligent. He overturned the jury's verdict for MacKinlay, noting that he did this without even raising the plaintiff's contributory negligence, 'upon which much may be said.'

Running through these decisions are two themes. First, city corporations could be held liable, but only in instances where there was clear evidence from the statutes that suggests they should be liable. Even Young, asserting the 'natural justice' of holding the whole community and not merely the injured party responsible for a loss, relied on a reading of the appropriate statute to find the city's liability. Second, contributory negligence, although not always used to absolve the city, remained a potent defence in situations where the city may have been liable. The court's decisions in these cases displayed varying degrees of instrumentalism and interest in protecting the civic corporation from liability. Even Young, although finding the city potentially liable, wrote a decision that may have protected it in the end: instead of accepting the original jury's verdict for the plaintiff he ordered a retrial on the question of contributory negligence. The Wards had to decide whether it was worth their time and investment to go to trial again. This may have saved the city in the short term, yet it could offer little protection from subsequent suits; Dodd and Smith, in making decisions that explicitly placed limits on the city's liability, protected the city both in the specific actions on appeal and from some future actions.

Simultaneous with their decisions regarding the negligence liability of the City of Halifax, the NSSC dealt with the liability of private corporations. Although the restrictions on corporate liability in the Halifax city cases rested in large part on the peculiarities of the city being a public corporation, the tendency to limit liability revealed in those actions extended to private corporations as well. *Spence v. Windsor & Annapolis Railway*[34] concerned fire damage caused by a grass fire ignited by a passing locomotive. Ritchie J. acknowledged that the evidence was 'sufficient to justify the jury in [concluding] ... that the fire ... arose from sparks from the defendant's engine.' But 'whether there was, or was not, sufficient evidence of negligence or carelessness on the part of the defendants to render them liable for the damage ... is not so clear.' As in *MacKinlay v. City of Halifax*, the question came down to whether the corporation had acted with due care.

The plaintiff asserted that the locomotive 'was not properly constructed so as to prevent the escape of sparks.' This assertion was essential, because the statutory regulations for the railroad freed it from liability if the 'engine was properly constructed and in good order, and had the usual appliances for preventing the escape of sparks.' To prove his case at trial, the plaintiff proffered two witnesses, a one-time railway fireman and engineer and a locomotive superintendent of the defendant railway. The fireman described how engines should have smoke stacks constructed with deflectors and sieves to prevent the emission of sparks. The engine responsible for the fire was not so equipped.

The plaintiff's second witness, however, suggested that the defendant's engines 'were supplied with all modern appliances for preventing the escape of sparks.' Although a 'spark arrester' was found in engines that burn wood, it was not used in coal-powered engines as it suppressed the drafts required to keep the fires burning. In addition to this plaintiff's witness who argued against the plaintiff's case, the defendants supplied several witnesses who likewise argued that the engine had all the spark suppression equipment that would be reasonable. A new trial was ordered, overturning the original jury verdict for the plaintiff. Ritchie advised the plaintiff, 'if the appliances of the defendants' engines were not such as are usual and necessary to prevent the escape of sparks, the plaintiff will have no difficulty in obtaining witnesses who are disinterested, and, from their skill and knowledge, thoroughly capable of speaking on the subject.'

Cases such as these were not uncommon in nineteenth-century Canada. In Canada West in 1856 John Beverley Robinson summed up the rights and responsibilities for landowners and railways thus: 'The plaintiff had a right to use his barn and barnyard as farmers generally use them, and ... if he chose to allow it to remain near the track he must submit to the risk which would exist as a consequence of the Legislature having entrusted the defendants with an agent of a dangerous character, provided they used all the appliances and precautions which could be expected reasonably from them.'[35] Whether in Nova Scotia or Ontario, accidental fires caused by railway sparks were expected. But instead of seeing these as a regular cost of doing business for the railways, the burden had to be borne by the victim. Statute law made clear that only in cases where the railways failed to properly equip their trains could they be held liable. As *Spence v. Windsor & Annapolis Railway* shows, this could be difficult to prove. Most of the potential expert witnesses were themselves railway employees, as Spence found when one of his two witnesses testified that the railway was actually in the right.[36]

In the City of Halifax cases and *Spence v. Windsor and Annapolis Railway* the courts limited the liability of corporations. Legislatures laid the ground for the law of corporate liability through acts that created and regulated public and private corporations and set some limits for liability. The judges followed the elected assemblies' lead and further supplemented the corporation by interpreting those statutes through the application of common law notions of reasonable care and contributory negligence. Thus, the plaintiff's contributory negligence could absolve a defendant from liability. In some cases, like Dodd's discussion of *respondeat superior* in *Evens*, the judges clearly acted instrumentally. In other cases such explicit instrumentalism was not required.

Corporations and Injured Employees

The liability of employers, particularly corporations, for injuries caused to their employees was a combination of the two streams of law discussed so far. As servants, employees had a contractual relationship with their employer or master. But, in cases where they were injured or killed on the job, negligence principles would shape the judicial response. The doctrine of *respondeat superior* had long held that employers could be held liable to injuries done to strangers. The nineteenth century saw the first clearly enunciated exception to this principle for employees.[37]

Many historians have traced a line in the development of the Anglo-American law of industrial accidents through three cases in England and Massachusetts: *Priestly v. Fowler*, *Farwell v. Boston and Worchester R.R.*, and *Bartonshill Coal Co. v. Reid*.[38] Horwitz focuses his discussion on *Farwell v. Boston and Worchester R.R.*, an 1842 case from Massachusetts, asserting that Chief Justice Lemuel Shaw's decision 'more than any other nineteenth century case reveals the triumph of' contract ideology where 'all pre-existing legal duties were inevitably subordinated to the contract relation.'[39] In arguing the case, the injured worker's counsel conceded that the doctrine of *respondeat superior* did not apply, and that the railroad's liability lay in the implied terms of the contract. Shaw decided, on the contrary, that 'he who engages in the employment of another ... for compensation, takes upon himself the natural and ordinary risks, and in legal presumption, the compensation is adjusted accordingly.'[40] If there were implied terms relating to liability for accidents, most seem to have been the servant's responsibility. Shaw believed the voluntary assumption of risk implied by a servant's willingness to work even included an assumption of the risk of injuries caused by other servants of the master, although this was often referred to separately as the 'fellow servant rule.'

Shaw's formulation that wages were commensurate with risk was cited by Lord Cranworth in the House of Lords decision in *Bartonshill Coal Co.* as he concluded: 'if men engage for certain wages in a work of great risk, it is to be supposed that the risk forms an element in their contemplation in agreeing to accept the stipulated remuneration.'[41] In this 1858 decision, the House of Lords made a precise statement of the common law for all of Great Britain and the rest of the Empire, including Nova Scotia. The voluntary assumption of risk, the fellow servant rule, and the doctrine of contributory negligence (applied to these cases as well) formed a trinity of employer defences that in Britain and at least parts of the United States meant servants were almost never able to collect for injuries on the job.

Karsten, however, offers an alternative history of the fellow servant rule and like defences. In urging that a jurisprudence of the heart often shaped its application, Karsten notes that in several of the United States, like Wisconsin and Missouri, the judiciary 'adopted the rule ... very reluctantly.' In some states, exceptions to the rule were adopted. For instance, in 1854 the Ohio Supreme Court found that a train conductor was superior to the other employees on the train, and thus an agent of the employer. His negligence was the employer's negligence and thus the fellow servant rule did not apply.[42] In Great Britain, by contrast, superiors of all sorts were included within the definition of 'fellow servant.'[43]

The Nova Scotia Supreme Court first clearly applied the fellow servant rule and related doctrines in *Campbell v. General Mining Association* in December 1868.[44] Chief Justice Young wrote the decision for the entire court. An explosion in a colliery at Sydney Mines injured three men, including the plaintiff. The explosion seemed to have resulted from foul gas coming into contact with the open flame of a miner's lamp, and the plaintiff tried to assert that the foreman was responsible. After the plaintiff presented his evidence, the defendants moved to nonsuit. The trial judge referred the case to the Supreme Court, where either the nonsuit would be granted or judgment would be made for the plaintiff and referees would be asked to determine damages.

In making his findings on the facts, however, Young concluded that 'no personal negligence was attributed to the defendants – the negligence, if any, was that of their *employees*. There was no neglect in providing suitable appliances and materials for working the mines, and their principal agent and his overseer underground were persons of undoubted competency and skill' (emphasis in original). The defendant was injured in part at least because either he or one of the others brought an open flame into the shaft. Turning from this, Young quoted at length from the ruling in *Bartonshill Coal Co*. He concluded by applying the fellow servant and voluntary assumption of risk rules and finding for the company.

Young and his fellow justices did not simply apply precedent. In making his ruling, Young explained, 'in this Court we are bound by the decisions of the Courts at *Westminster*, and which, I must add, in this instance are also in conformity with our own judgment.' If the court had a heart, it was with the mine owners. The decision seemed to the judges to be a foregone conclusion. Young added: 'We were all of opinion, therefore, at the argument in the present term, this action could not be maintained, but thought it better to deliver a written judgment, as our people are now so extensively employed in mineral enterprises, and it is proper for their guidance in case of accident, as well as for their personal safety, in observing due caution in their work, that the rule of law should be defined and well known.' Young was well aware of the industrializing economy of Nova Scotia: it was that, in fact, that compelled him to write as long a decision as he did. The decision was no reticent application of a cruel rule – on the contrary, the court was applying the rule fully believing it was the best for the province. The rule would encourage every worker to be safe at work and watch that their co-workers were being safe as well. This marrying of the safe worker and the industrial workplace came together in the conclusion of the decision: the case 'afforded an excellent occasion of impressing upon engineers, overseers, and labourers in our numerous mines, the obligation of attending to each other's safety, and the necessity of adopting the precautions which a long experience and the resources of modern science have supplied and recommended.' Safety was thus an obligation to be shared by all; but in the process liability was vested in the servant and not his master.

Campbell v. General Mining Association was not truly an instrumental decision. Yet it is clear that Young accepted the contract ideology at the root of the rule, and believed in the rule's justice. There was no need for the court to invent new rules for employer liability, but there was also no need for the judges to expressly agree with the policy behind the precedent. Young's willingness to do so cannot be ignored.

Young's decision in this case seems to contrast rather sharply with his decisions in the common carrier and city corporation cases discussed above, in which he was reticent about limiting corporate liability. This underscores the difference in judicial opinion between employees and either customers or strangers. Employees, probably most susceptible to injury in the day-to-day business of their employer, also had the least right to claim damages from their employer for the injury. Any restrictions on the rights of third parties to collect damages were only more stringent when employees tried to collect.

Nine years later the court dealt once again with a mining explosion that injured an employee. The employee, Smith, was injured in a gas explosion in a new pit dug too close to an older pit. One important exception to the fellow servant rule available to injured workers was to prove that their employer had knowingly hired incompetent servants. The arguments made to the court in *Smith v. The Intercontinental Coal Mining Co.*[45] by the company's lawyers stressed that both the manager and the underground foreman were competent men. The problem with this defence was that the company lawyers then had to explain why the two pits were so close.

The plaintiffs argued that the men directing the digging of the new pit were not actually fellow servants. But, accepting that they were, the company was not absolved. On the contrary, the men digging the new pit were guided by a plan apparently provided to the manager by the company vice-president. One of the plaintiff's counsel argued, 'There is nothing to show that any steps were taken to ascertain whether the plan was correct or not. The Company has two duties to perform: to provide suitable outfit and machinery, and also, to provide suitable workmen. The plan, which is a part of the outfit of the mine, is proved to be absolutely incorrect.'

According to the defendant company's counsel, 'the jury [found] that the negligence is that of Mr. Simpson [the manager], and this is the only question [at the appeal]. The fact of a plan being handed to Simpson by Mr. Budden [the vice-president] has nothing strictly to do with the matter according to the verdict. The sole question under the verdict is whether Simpson is competent, of which there is abundant proof.' In any case, the company argued that the plan was made up by the former manager, Dunn, who himself had died in an explosion at the mine, and not the vice-president.

For the court, Wilkins J. opened by writing, 'I regret and commiserate' with the plaintiff's injuries. He noted that the plaintiff was a fine worker, not guilty of any contributory negligence in the accident. Wilkins continued, 'He worked, however, under no special contract with the defendant company, and not otherwise than as a servant retained and employed by managers of the company, who, although superior to himself and he subordinate to them, were in the eye of the law his fellow servants ... *Wilson v. Merry*, 1 H.L.Sc. 326, decided by the highest tribunal in England, furnishes the rule of law to govern such a case as this ... As the Company is not proved to have selected for the management of its affairs any person under whom [the] plaintiff worked who was incompetent for what he assumed to perform ... the verdict [at the lower court for the plaintiff] must be set aside.' This was a clear statement of the fellow servant rule.

Young, author of the decision in *Campbell*, was not pleased with this result, and the report records he 'expressed a strong opinion that Companies in such cases should be held liable.' Unlike in *Wood v. Allan*, however, Young was not so concerned as to make a formal dissenting judgment. None of the other judges are reported to have publicly shared this view, though Wilkins's ruling does not contain the sort of rhetorical support for the fellow servant doctrine that Young included in his decision in *Campbell*.

Earlier Supreme Court decisions may seem to have taken the court in a different direction. In the 1836 decision of *Ralston v. Barss et al.*[46] a sailor was left at Port Medway, Nova Scotia, in care of his vessel's owner after breaking his leg while loading the ship. Upon his recovery the sailor demanded, as per Maritime custom, his full wages. The owner baulked, and tried to pay him only for the time he actually served and to deduct the cost of medical care from the wages the sailor would have earned in the course of his voyage prior to being sent ashore. This case, and others like it, turned in part on the exceptional status of sailors in Nova Scotia and the common law.[47]

Both Hill and Bliss JJ. wrote decisions, and both found for the sailor Ralston. Both decisions deal with the two issues: whether Ralston was to be paid for the whole voyage (New York to Liverpool, U.K.) and whether or not the doctor's fees could be charged against him. Hill's decision is the longer of the two. In dealing with the first question Hill referred to a variety of sources, including Malynes's *Lex Mercatoria* and Chancellor Kent's commentaries, all to the conclusion that injured sailors were to receive their full pay. In concluding this section of his decision, Hill wrote: 'This unfortunate plaintiff, who is occupied in a service calculated to induce injuries of the description he received, has his leg broken. Is it good policy? [*sic*] is it for the maritime interest that he shall be turned on shore in a foreign country, and lose his wages for the rest of the voyage?' He then turned to whether Ralston's medical expenses could be offset against his wages owed. Hill opined, 'I confess I entertain a strong leaning and inclination in favour of the risk of the seaman to such maintenance and medical aid.' He discussed the Laws of Oleron, early treatises, and the Imperial statutes that established Greenwich Hospital to establish masters' responsibility for the care and wages of injured sailors. But, he concluded, none of this was very relevant, because 'the defendants have voluntarily provided the medical aid and attendance on shore,' and so 'shall not now be permitted to deduct the expenses thereof from the wages due to the plaintiff.'

Bliss's reasoning was similar, finding for the plaintiff both in regards to the full wages and the attempt to charge him for medical care. On the latter, his language parallels Hill, but has a stronger contractarian tinge: 'There was no contract between the parties that the plaintiff should pay for them, nor is there anything stated in the case from which, when there was a moral obligation on the part of the defendant to provide them, I can say that the law will raise an implied promise on the part of the plaintiff to pay for them.'

Karsten argued that the decisions here ran contrary to 'the views of certain economic-oriented scholars that jurists were particularly concerned with the well-being of commercial entrepreneurs in the nineteenth century.'[48] For instance, Hill justified finding for the sailor in part by writing: 'In upholding and protecting the interests of seamen we best subserve the interest of the mercantile world who employ them; for what can be a greater inducement to a sailor to enter the merchant service than if he should be disabled in the performance of his duty in the course of a voyage, he is still entitled to his full wages.' Hill's reasoning here is of a piece with a long tradition in common law and admiralty jurisdictions that recognized sailors were essential to commerce in the Empire and deserved to be treated differently from other working people.[49]

Karsten discusses *Ralston v. Barss et al.* in a section relating to contracts of employment, not workplace injury, yet it serves as a comment on both. Although it predates any legal enunciation of the voluntary assumption of risk, the case suggests some willingness by an earlier bench than that which decided *Campbell* and *Smith* to conceive that employees deserve some protection. Nonetheless, the basis of this protection is not some implied contractual term but the *absence* of a contract that made the sailor liable for medical costs willingly paid by his master or that allowed the master to reduce wage payments for a failure to complete the journey. This understanding of the employment relationship was dead when the court addressed the mine accidents of the 1860s and 1870s.

Conclusion

The judges of the Supreme Court of Nova Scotia were caught between a belief in stare decisis on the one hand and the desire to do justice, as they saw it, on the other. Young, on behalf of the whole court, applied the fellow servant rule in *Campbell v. General Mining Association* because it was the applicable precedent. He was conscious of its effect on both the miners and mine owners and spoke directly to both in his decision, noting the importance of the decision to their respective interests and practices. Dodd's decision in *Evens v. The City of Halifax* referred to some precedents, but he more obviously wrote a decision to suit what he imagined was the best policy result, to the point of contradicting himself on the facts. Young reluctantly applied precedent in *Dodson v. The Grand Trunk Railway*, and the rest of the court followed his lead in *Wood v. Allan*. The Nova Scotian judges, perhaps like other colonial judges, while demonstrating great fealty for English precedent, thus used it in a number of ways, sometimes accurately and sometimes not. Facts could be distinguished to avoid precedents. And even when applying the precedents the judges were often willing to comment on the efficacy of the rules. Young found applying what he believed to be the law relating to carrier liability distasteful, and wholeheartedly supported the introduction of the fellow servant rule to the province (even though he might have moderated his views on this rule over time). Young, Dodd, Smith, and McCully may not have been instrumentalists in the mould of Lemuel Shaw or Joseph Story, but they showed some of that spirit.

Karsten's theses about heart and head or the effect of Westminster's precedents ultimately prove to be insufficient in explaining the Supreme Court's approach to tort law. The Nova Scotian judges tried to apply the relevant precedent when they knew it. Such application of precedent is not in and of itself an argument against instrumentalism. When McCully decided that damages for Dodge's oilcloth should be determined in the same way as damages for goods delayed in shipping he applied an analogous precedent. Choosing the precedents he did, however, shifted liability onto the consignor and off of the railway. The common law may be thought of as building blocks: in building decisions, judges have some leeway in deciding what blocks fit where, or whether new blocks need to be made. The instrumental judge in nineteenth-century Nova Scotia chose already existing blocks whenever he could, but in deciding cases about liability for accidents he chose blocks only of a certain mould, and when those blocks were unavailable he made his own. That so many of the judges acted in this way and towards the same end lends credence to Horwitz's thesis about judicial response to industrialization.

The judges at mid-century were not all of the same cast. Young is the most complex; he restricted liability in the 1860s and early 1870s but by the late 1870s appears to have grown concerned with protecting at least some people from corporations. In some ways, however, his steps forward and back show him caught between the older Wilkins and the younger judges who followed. Young served on the court from 1860 to 1881, slightly later than Wilkins (1856–78) and only somewhat later than Dodd (1848–73). McCully was appointed ten years after Young in 1870 (although he died in 1877), while Smith was appointed even later, in 1875 (and served until 1890). Wilkins and Young's successors seem to have been less willing to reverse the trend and more willing to restrict liability for defendants even further. The 1870s may, then, reflect one more part of Horwitz's thesis: Horwitz argued that after the instrumental decisions in the first half of the nineteenth century, a stricter notion of formalism was applied by the judiciary in the United States to shore up the transformation of the law. Although Young's successors were themselves intrumentalists, they refused to turn back, but continued down the line set by Young and the earlier judges of the court, in turn shoring up the changes made.

The NSSC demonstrated a predilection towards supporting the interests of new industries and corporations over the interests of those injured by these entities. Its judges were often able to make such decisions based on precedent and without explicitly making new law or deciding cases on policy grounds alone. They were aware of the policy implications, however, and by the 1860s and 1870s were on the whole willing to make decisions that in law and dicta supported corporate interests. Nova Scotia may have been a colony and province on the edge of Empire and Dominion, with courts subject to the precedents of England, and slow to industrialize. Even here, however, judges made decisions with the intent to effect the development of industrial capitalism in the colony.

NOTES

Earlier versions of this paper were presented to the Courts and Communities Conference, in Halifax in October 2003, and the Osgoode Hall Law School Law and Markets reading group. I would like to thank the participants for their questions and suggestions. The editors of this volume, Paul Craven, Chris Frank, Eric Tucker, and David Yarrow all made helpful comments on drafts of the paper. Research assistance was provided by Petra Fisher.

1 See, generally, J. Gwyn, *Excessive Expectations: Maritime Commerce & the Economic Development of Nova Scotia, 1740–1870* (Montreal and Kingston: McGill-Queen's University Press 1998), 78–84, 96–101, 188–201; E. Sager with G. E. Panting, *Maritime Capital: The Shipbuilding Industry in Atlantic Canada, 1820–1914* (Montreal and Kingston: McGill-Queen's University Press 1998), 172–202; C. Heron, *Working in Steel: The Early Years in Canada, 1883–1935* (Toronto: McClelland and Stewart 1988), 16–18.

2 M. Horwitz, *The Transformation of American Law 1780–1860* (Cambridge: Harvard University Press 1977), xvi.

3 P. Karsten, *Heart versus Head: Judge Made Law in Nineteenth Century America* (Chapel Hill: University of North Carolina Press 1997) and Karsten, *Between Law and Custom: 'High' and 'Low' Legal Cultures in the Lands of the British Diaspora – The United States, Canada, Australia, and New Zealand, 1600–1900* (Cambridge: Cambridge University Press 2002).

4 Karsten, *Between Law and Custom*, 8.

5 Horwitz and Karsten both devote a great deal of their histories to negligence, as will be seen in the discussion below. Many other historians of nineteenth-century law have also looked at negligence in Canada and elsewhere. See, for instance, P. Craven, 'The meaning of Misadventure: The Baptiste Creek Railway Disaster of 1854 and Its Aftermath,' in R. Hall et al., eds., *Patterns of the Past: Interpreting Ontario's History* (Toronto: Dundurn Press for the Ontario Historical Society 1988); E. Tucker, *Administering Danger in the Workplace* (Toronto: University of Toronto Press 1990); R.W.

Kostal, *Law and English Railway Capitalism, 1825–1875* (Oxford: Clarendon Press 1994).

6 Horwitz, *Transformation*, 85, but see 85–99 *passim*.

7 Karsten, *Heart versus Head*, 80, 85, but see 79–127, *passim*.

8 R.C.B. Risk, 'The Nineteenth-Century Foundations of the Business Corporation in Ontario,' *University of Toronto Law Journal* 23 (1973): 270–306; 'The Golden Age: The Law about the Market in Nineteenth-Century Ontario,' *University of Toronto Law Journal* 26 (1976): 307–46; 'The Last Golden Age: Property and the Allocation of Losses in Ontario in the Nineteenth Century,' *University of Toronto Law Journal* 27 (1977): 199–239; 'The Law and the Economy in Mid-Nineteenth-Century Ontario: A Perspective,' 27 (1977): 403–38. Only the last two of these appeared after *The Transformation of American Law* was published. See, in particular, 'The Law and the Economy,' 434–6.

9 J. Nedelsky, 'From Private Property to Public Resource: The Emergence of Administrative Control of Water in Nova Scotia,' in Girard and Phillips, *Essays*, 328, and 327–31 generally. See also Nedelsky, 'Judicial Conservatism in an Age of Innovation: Comparative Perspectives on Canadian Nuisance Law 1880–1930,' in D. Flaherty, ed., *Essays in the History of Canadian Law, Volume 1* (Toronto: Osgoode Society for Canadian Legal History and University of Toronto Press 1981).

10 J. Benidickson, 'Private Rights and Public Purposes in the Lakes, Rivers, and Streams of Ontario 1870–1930,' in D. Flaherty, ed., *Essays in the History of Canadian Law, Volume II* (Toronto: Osgoode Society for Canadian Legal History and University of Toronto Press 1983).

11 E. Tucker, 'The Law of Employers' Liability in Ontario 1861–1900: The Search for a Theory,' *Osgoode Hall Law Journal* 22 (1984): 258–9; *Administering Danger*, 53–66. See also R.C.B. Risk, 'This Nuisance of Litigation: The Origins of Workers' Compensation in Ontario,' in Flaherty, ed., *Essays, Volume II*, 462.

12 C.B. Backhouse, 'Shifting Patterns in Nineteenth-Century Canadian Custody Law,' in Flaherty, ed., *Essays, Volume 1*; 'Nineteenth-Century Canadian Rape Law 1800–92,' in Flaherty, ed., *Essays, Volume II*.

13 Of the seven Supreme Court judges sitting in 1877, only two remained on the bench by 1883: see C. Greco, 'The Superior Court Judiciary of Nova Scotia, 1754–1900: A Collective Biography,' in Girard and Phillips, *Essays*, 67–8.

14 K. Norrie and D. Owram, *A History of the Canadian Economy* (Toronto: Harcourt Brace Canada 1991), 224–42.

15 Horwitz, *Transformation*, 204, 207.

16 P.S. Atiyah, *The Rise and Fall of Freedom of Contract* (Oxford: Clarendon Press 1979), 556–9; *Peek v. North Staffordshire Rly. Co.* (1862–3), 10 H.L.C. 473, 11 E.R. 1109.
17 (1871), 8 N.S.R. 405; quotations at 405, 411, 412; emphasis in original.
18 It is unclear to whom the pronoun 'their' refers in this passage. Read in context, it seems to refer to either Parliament or the railways, although Young may have been referring to the consignors.
19 *Dodge v. Windsor & Annapolis Railway Co.* (1872), 8 N.S.R. 537; quotations at 538, 540–1, 544.
20 Ibid., 544.
21 (1880), 13 N.S.R. 477; quotations at 481, 482.
22 Horwitz, *Transformation*, 85–99; Atiyah, *Rise and Fall*, 501–5.
23 Horwitz, *Transformation*, 95.
24 (1872), 9 N.S.R. 94; quotation at 95.
25 3 C. & K., 82, as cited in (1872), 9 N.S.R. 95.
26 *Conlon v. Connolly* (1875), 10 N.S.R. 95; quotations at 97, 98, 101, 104.
27 *Tuff v. Warman*, 5 C.B., N.S., 573, as quoted in ibid., at 103.
28 Karsten, *Between Law and Custom*, 378; emphasis in original. Quoted passage in quotation from *Russell v. Men of Devon* (1788), 2 Term R. 667, 100 E.R. 359 (K.B.).
29 Karsten, *Between Law and Custom*, 388, but see 368–88 and 5–8 *passim*. Quoted passage in quotation from *Lockhart v. City of St. John* (1891), 30 New Br. 445.
30 (1861), 5 N.S.R. 111; quotations at 113, 116, 117. Karsten's discussion is in *Between Law and Custom*, 378, n 41.
31 (1873), 9 N.S.R. 264; quotation at 265.
32 L.R. 1 H.L. 93; 14 L.T. Rep., N.S. 677.
33 (1877), 11 N.S.R. 305; quotations at 307, 308, 309.
34 (1875), 10 N.S.R. 106; quotations at 109, 112.
35 *Hill v. The Ontario, Simcoe and Huron Railroad Union Company* (1856), 13 U.C.Q.B. 503, 504, as quoted in P. Brode, *Sir John Beverley Robinson: Bone and Sinew of the Compact* (Toronto: Osgoode Society for Canadian Legal History and University of Toronto Press 1984), 253. See also Risk, 'The Last Golden Age,' 230. In the United States, railways attempted to escape liability for similar accidents through the doctrine of proximate cause, but see Karsten, *Between Heart and Head*, 101–8, for both a critique and a brief discussion of negligence and sufficient attempts to prevent accidents.
36 On railway labour relations and the structure of inducements that may have limited the willingness of employees to testify, see P. Craven, 'Labour and Management on the Great Western Railway,' in P. Craven, ed., *Labour-*

ing Lives: Work & Workers in Nineteenth-Century Ontario (Toronto: University of Toronto Press 1995).

37 Karsten argues that the fellow servant rule was not an innovation of the mid-nineteenth century; in the eighteenth century Lord Mansfield in the Court of King's Bench, and in the early nineteenth century, the English Court of Common Pleas, both absolved masters of responsibility for the medical costs accrued by servants injured in the course of their work. Thus, the later fellow servant decisions 'were *not* innovations, but were based on "general principles."' In both cases Karsten cites, however, the rulings relied on the existence of the poor laws that created a positive duty for poor law administrators to cover these costs. Where a legislated responsibility for care of the injured fell on the poor law administrators, the common law courts would not find another party liable. But, by the time the fellow servant cases were decided in the nineteenth century, the poor law had changed in Britain, limiting the option of assigning the costs to the county, and similar institutions to care for the destitute by statutory order did not exist in places like Massachusetts or Nova Scotia: Karsten, *Heart versus Head*, 117–20.

38 See, e.g., Kostal, *Law and English Railway Capitalism*, 259–74; Tucker, *Administering Danger*, 42–6; W.R. Cornish and G. de N. Clark, *Law and Society in England 1750–1950* (London: Sweet and Maxwell 1989), 496–9; Risk, 'This Nuisance of Litigation,' 419–21. This history has been recently challenged by a detailed re-reading of *Priestly v. Fowler*: M.A. Stein, '*Priestly v. Fowler* (1837) and the Emerging Tort of Negligence,' *Boston College Law Review* 44 (2003): 689–732.

39 Horwitz, *Transformation*, 209–10.

40 45 Mass. (4 Met.) at 56–7, as quoted in Horwitz, *Transformation*, 210.

41 3 Macqu. 265 at 275, as quoted in Cornish and Clark, *Law and Society in England*, 498. Rande Kostal notes that the inclusion of fellow servants within the voluntary assumption of risk was first clearly enunciated in English law in *Hutchinson v. York, Newcastle and Berwick Ry.* (1850), 5 Ex. 343: Kostal, *Law and English Railway Capitalism*, 271.

42 Karsten, *Heart versus Head*, 120–4.

43 Karsten, *Between Law and Custom*, 435.

44 (1868), 7 N.S.R. 415.

45 (1877), 11 N.S.R. 556; quotations at 559, 560–1.

46 (1836), 1 N.S.R. [1836] 75; quotations at 78, 79, 81, and 87. See Karsten, *Between Law and Custom*, 301–2.

47 A similar case is *Welsh v. MacDonald* (1867), 7 N.S.R. 87, decided on the agent-status of a ship's master. In another 1867 case the court underlined

the exceptional status of sailors among labourers by approving the use of corporal punishment on board ship: *Gordon v. Gordon* (1867), 7 N.S.R. 80.

48 Karsten, *Between Law and Custom*, 302.

49 Eighty years before, Chief Justice Jonathan Belcher addressed the law for sailor's contracts, and the policy behind it, in an unreported action at the Nova Scotia Court of Chancery for an injunction against a Vice-Admiralty action for wages. After citing a number of authorities to refuse the injunction, Belcher concluded, in part, 'Halifax is a Country where the Fishery & the Seamen ought to be indulg'd & protected': *The King in Proh. v. Ryan*, Edward Belcher Family Papers, University of British Columbia Special Collections, file 1-45. See also J. Muir, 'Law and Economy in Colonial Halifax' (unpublished PhD dissertation, York University 2004), chap. 5.

12

Confederation, Adjudicative Culture, and the Law of the Constitution: The Late Nineteenth-Century Persistence of Local Autonomy in the Nova Scotia Supreme Court

WILLIAM LAHEY

This essay is about how the Nova Scotia Supreme Court decided constitutional cases between 1867 and 1900. It is not, however, primarily about the outcomes reached by the court in particular cases, or about the court's constitutional doctrine; instead, it focuses on what the constitutional cases can tell us about the court's adjustment to the changes that came with or through confederation. These changes included the transfer of powers of judicial appointment from provincial governments to the new federal government, and the power to rule upon the constitutionality of legislation. But most important for the purposes of this paper was the new subordinate position of Canadian provincial courts in a multilayered and far flung judicial hierarchy.

Decisions of the Nova Scotia Supreme Court were subject to appeal before Confederation. With leave, decisions could be taken to the Judicial Committee of the Privy Council. Few decisions were, however, making the court en banc into a de facto court of final appeal. A few years before Confederation appeal as of right to the Privy Council became available, but the Privy Council continued to be a remote institution and the Nova Scotia Supreme Court remained largely autonomous.

After Confederation, this situation changed. In 1875, the Supreme Court of Canada was established; more importantly, the work of the Privy Council as Canada's true court of final appeal greatly increased, especially through its engagement with the new field of Canadian constitutional law. Although Nova Scotian litigants continued to go to London less frequently than the litigants of some other provinces, the decisions of the Nova Scotia Supreme Court, like those of all other provincial courts, were increasingly subject to leading cases decided either by the Supreme Court of Canada or, more usually, by the Privy Council.[1] This more pervasive jurisprudential influence was more profound in constitutional law than in any other area of law. There, the Privy Council's decisions most obviously and consistently had pan-Canadian implications, regardless of their province of origin; they created doctrine and guidance where none otherwise existed; and they helped to give shape to the new nation itself.

My objective in looking into the constitutional decisions of the Nova Scotia Supreme court is to understand the court's adjustment to this new set of institutional relationships and jurisprudential influences. The court's constitutional decisions are my data, but my subject is the court's transition from a largely autonomous to a truly subordinate tribunal. This aspect of Nova Scotia's integration into Confederation has received little attention, despite the long-standing interest of historians of the province with the themes of resistance and integration in the post-Confederation period.

My conclusions are multifaceted. They relate to the personalities of the judges and of the lawyers who appeared before them, the capacity and qualities of the judges as constitutional jurists, and the role of relationships, both among the judges and between the judges and others, in the court's adjudicative processes. They deal with the understandings of Canadian federalism and the experiences of prior careers in politics and law that the judges brought to bear on the adjudication of constitutional cases. My conclusions also concern the apparent responsiveness of Nova Scotia judges to Nova Scotia's post-Confederation political scene and, in particular, to the persistence of opposition to Confederation and the terms on which it had been applied to the province. I also offer conclusions on the court's abandoning in the space of a decade, a functional style of adjudication that emphasized the objectives of Confederation for one that was much more formalistic in its emphasis on the meaning of particular words and the *ratio* of precedential cases. Finally, my conclusions profile the stability of fundamental elements of the court's interpretation of the British North America Act (BNA Act) from the 1870s, when no guidance was yet available from the Privy Council, to the 1890s, when cases were increasingly argued and decided under Privy Council authority.

On each of these points, my conclusions and observations contribute to a more general argument: that until the end of the nineteenth century at least, the Supreme Court remained surprisingly responsive to local influences, even as it came increasingly within the orbit of the Privy Council. The evidence does not permit precise quantification of the importance of these local influences relative to those that unquestionably were emanating with increasing power from London or, to a lesser degree, from Ottawa and the Supreme Court of Canada. It is, however, strong enough to support the conclusion that it is not entirely accurate to say of the Nova Scotia Supreme Court, as it has been said of Canadian courts more broadly, that it had been captured as early as 1881 by the Privy Council and its versions of Canadian federalism and constitutional adjudication.[2] The court continued to exercise considerable adjudicative autonomy well into the 1890s, albeit within steadily narrowing parameters. I will argue that it fashioned an amalgam of its own early decisions on the BNA Act and the later decisions of the Privy Council that reflected Nova Scotia's broader political experience through the first three decades of confederation as much as it did Privy Council doctrine. On the one hand, the court's jurisprudence can be seen responding to provincial frustrations with Confederation by giving large scope to provincial legislative powers. On the other hand, it can be seen to have responded to the same frustrations by refusing to accept provincial claims that implied provincial autonomy. The explanation I suggest is that the court was particularly attuned to the need for federal supervision of the provinces, located as it was in the founding provinces where opposition to confederation extended to flirtation with secession as late as the 1880s.

To make this argument, I have found it helpful to depart from a strictly chronological discussion. I have instead organized my discussion of the cases around three themes that I see cutting across the court's encounters with the BNA Act through the late nineteenth century. The most apparent of these was the dramatic change that took place in the court's adjudicative methodology between the 1870s, when the court's approach was highly functional, explicitly constitutional, and broadly pre-classical, and the late 1880s and early 1890s, by which time the court's approach had become imbued with legal formalism. Like other studies of early Canadian constitutional law, this one reveals judicial arguments about the purposes of confederation, the nature of constitutional law, the similarities and differences of the Canadian and American constitutions and the lessons to be learned from colonial, imperial, and British history being largely displaced by more narrow arguments about the meaning of cases and their *ratios*. But it also suggests that influences that emerged from within the Nova Scotian legal community, as well as the adjudicative example of the Privy Council, lay behind these changes.

The other two themes relate to substantive constitutional law. The first of these was the tendency of the court to uphold provincial legislation in division of powers cases, primarily on the basis of a broad reading of the provincial power over 'property and civil rights in the province.' Here, the influence of the Privy Council obviously played a significant role, but the point is that its influence was significantly one of reinforcement of indigenous ways of thinking about the structure and logic of sections 91 and 92 of the BNA Act. Thus, the court's benevolent reading of the all-important provincial power to deal with the liquor trade will be seen to rest ultimately in the 1890s as much on the wisdom of a Nova Scotia ruling from 1876 as on the major Privy Council rulings of the 1880s.

The third theme is the seemingly contradictory refusal of the court to recognize the provinces as a co-equal order of government with (for example) executive powers derived directly from the Crown and a legislature that was equal to the House of Commons at Ottawa in its possession of the powers and privileges of the British House of Commons. In this, the court's adjudicative independence was strong enough to prevent the court from following the reasonably clear logic of major Privy Council decisions on questions of doctrine that were fundamental to the constitutional character of Confederation. My interpretation of this resistence – which lies at the heart of my argument – is that it is a crack in the court's growing formalism through which the court can be seen reaching the limits of its capacity to integrate Privy Council direction with its own 'local knowledge.' The court was confronted with a choice between local imperatives and doctrinal compliance. The fact that it opted for the former, albeit largely by default, suggests the need for a reappraisal of our ideas about how and when Canadian courts, or at least one of them, became captive to the Privy Council and its vision of Canada's constitution.

The Shift to Formalism

The emergence of legal formalism as judicial technique, of the underlying philosophy of legal liberalism as judicial ideology, and the relationship of both to Canadian constitutional law have become significant themes in Canadian legal history. In his seminal article on the nineteenth-century transformation of Upper Canada's legal culture, Blaine Baker suggested that one of the agents of that cultural change was the Privy Council's growing dominance after 1867 over Canadian law, and especially over Canadian constitutional law.[3] It increased the exposure of Canadian lawyers and courts to legal formalism and thereby reinforced the many other influences that underpinned a broad shift away from the more eclectic and more explicitly normative legal culture of Upper Canada of the early to mid-nineteenth century. In his detailed study of cases decided under the BNA Act on the division of legislative power over liquor legislation, as well as in other writings, R.C.B. Risk has stressed a fundamental change in how Canadian courts interpreted the BNA Act in the 1870s and early 1880s and how they came to interpret it in the 1890s, under the Privy Council guidance that was by then available.[4] In the early period, many Canadian judges interpreted the Act purposively and functionally by reference to understandings of the objects of Confederation as much as by reference to the words of the BNA Act. In contrast, by the later period, Canadian courts had in large measure abandoned their "judicial statesmanship" and instead adopted the methodology of the Privy Council by restricting themselves to conventional techniques of statutory interpretation, concentrated overwhelming on discovering the ordinary meaning of words and on the parsing and rationalization of prior judicial pronouncements.[5] More recently, John Saywell has observed the transition to formalism playing itself out across a more comprehensive study of late nineteenth-century constitutional adjudication, while doubting the extent of its influence relative to other factors in determining ultimate outcomes. He has characterized the period from the 1880s to the eventual abolition of appeals to the Privy Council more broadly as one of intellectual captivity for Canadian courts as regards constitutional law.[6]

The transition to formalism is evident in the constitutional jurisprudence of the Nova Scotia Supreme Court. In the 1870s and the early 1880s, the judges gave meaning to the words of the BNA Act by ranging broadly over the history of confederation and their understandings of the objectives of union. They went further afield into their own colonial history and into the history of England and the United States. They used an eclectic body of secondary materials to glean relevant insight and interpretative principles, including English textbooks on statutory interpretation and American constitutional cases and treatises, especially Cooley's book on constitutional limitations.[7] In modern parlance, their interpretive approach was functional and purposive. They accepted responsibility for producing outcomes that were consistent with broader understandings of what the constitution was meant to achieve or with even broader notions of constitutionalism and of statesmanship. By the later 1880s, much of this approach had disappeared. It was replaced almost entirely by the parsing of the phrases used in the judgments of the Privy Council to differentiate federal from provincial powers. Not only the general structure but also the words of the BNA Act came to be hardly mentioned. Little was said about the nation-building intentions that had informed the drafting of the Act, and almost all reference to other constitutions, or even to the broader constitutional context of the Act itself, was gone.

One of the best examples of the earlier methodology can be found in the dissenting judgment of Alexander James J. in a 1878 case, *Windsor & Annapolis Railway v. Western Railways Company.*[8] The case arose from a dispute over a branch line of the Windsor to Annapolis Railway between the company (Windsor & Annapolis) that had been put into possession by the province before Confederation and by the different company (Western Counties) that had been put into possession after confederation by the Dominion government,[9] acting under federal legislation passed in 1874. Windsor & Annapolis had sued and won at trial before the highly regarded judge in equity, Justice John William Ritchie,[10] and again on appeal, where Chief Justice William Young gave the majority opinion.[11] Like Ritchie (who, according to the conventions of the time, also sat on the appeal), Young thought the case only called for the application of the standard rule of statutory interpretation under which legislation did not displace property rights unless it did so expressly. The provision of the BNA Act under which ownership of the line had been transferred to the federal government at Confederation did not displace the possessory rights that Windsor & Annapolis had held from the province. This meant that the federal government's title was subject to the rights of possession of Windsor & Annapolis. The federal legislation of 1874 was subject to the same limitation. It did not expressly rescind the rights of Windsor & Annapolis, and therefore it did not legally justify the putting out of Windsor & Annapolis and the putting in of Western Counties. If the legislation had purported to rescind the rights of Windsor & Annapolis, it would have been unconstitutional. Implicitly, this ruling connected the protection of the vested rights of Windsor & Annapolis to the protection of the province's authority to deal with 'property and civil rights in the province.'

As will be seen, the idea that Dominion legislation could not interfere with property and civil rights, at least not if adopted under Parliament's more general powers, would become the abiding core of the court's division of powers jurisprudence. But first, its application in *Windsor & Annapolis* provoked a lengthy dissent from Alexander James J. He could not accept that the imperial Parliament had set out to create such a 'jumble of title and jurisdiction' over railways, which demanded a 'unity of management.'[12] It was wrong to construe the BNA Act as giving the Dominion 'several millions worth of railways, without giving the Parliament, directly and as a matter of course, a controlling power over all this valuable property.'[13] Ritchie and Young had also misinterpreted and misunderstood the legislation of 1874 by seeing it as legislation about merely private interests. It no doubt affected private rights, but it did so for reasons of 'wise and liberal public policy.' Railways were built 'not at all for the benefit of any individuals, nor only for the benefit of the whole public of Nova Scotia, but for the benefit of every traveller from Europe, or the United States, or the adjoining colonies, who wished to traverse our country on business or pleasure.' They 'were constructed to bind us to, and make us part of the great world; not only to develop our own local resources, but that we might become partakers in a much larger degree than we could otherwise have been, of the commerce, of the intelligence, of the civilization of other lands.' Opposite principles of interpretation to those invoked by Ritchie and Young were required. Instead of demanding express interference with the rights of Windsor and Annapolis, James was ready to infer the termination of its rights from the legislative creation of the rights of Western.[14]

More fundamentally, James charged Ritchie and Young with failing to live up to the court's important and unique obligation in constitutional cases. To make the point, he grandly declared,

> That act [the BNA Act] ought, I think, to be constructed with extreme liberality. Its scope and effect are to transform three great provinces, each with a separate and independent Legislature possessing almost national powers, into one great Dominion, with a central Legislature; to re-settle the provincial governments and legislatures with limited powers and upon a new basis; and to vest in the Central Government and Legislature all the public property of the separate provinces and all the powers withdrawn from the provincial governments and legislatures ... It is rather in the nature of a treaty between nations such as that recently accomplished

> at Berlin, than an ordinary act of Parliament. Its provisions are expressed with extreme brevity and in the most general and comprehensive terms; and, if the principles of construction applied to ordinary acts of Parliament are applied to it, instead of giving it the very liberal construction which its nature and circumstances demand, in my opinion, the most mischievous consequences must necessarily result.[15]

Accordingly, the scope of Parliament's jurisdiction over railways was 'a question in the consideration of which, in any view we may take of it, we will get very little assistance from our law books, because the circumstances are very peculiar – so much so as to have seldom come into discussion in courts of Justice.' Indeed, James had 'never met with any decision to throw light on such a question; and I have consulted the treatises on constitutional and international law within my reach in vain for some guidance in the consideration of it. In truth questions of this sort are usually settled by treaties between nations, or by the legislation of a supreme parliament as in the case of the British North America Act. It seems to me that this is not a question which can be argued solely on abstract principles of public policy; but it is to a large extent a question of the construction of that act. In what manner and to what extent did the British North America Act transfer this railway to Canada?'[16]

On a petite scale, this was a call to the kind of grand judicial statesmanship that is most often associated with Chief Justice John Marshall of the United States Supreme Court, and which earlier scholarship has detected in the constitutional jurisprudence of other Canadian courts of the 1870s.[17] At bottom, James was arguing that judges must interpret the constitution not as an ordinary statute but as an instrument of state concerned with nation building. This demanded 'extreme liberality' in constitutional interpretation.

Clearly, James was no John Marshall.[18] He was seen by some, including the highly regarded Wallace Graham, the court's future chief justice, as possibly the weakest member of a very weak court.[19] The lecture he gave to his colleagues on adjudicative methodology, particularly the much-admired Ritchie, must therefore be approached with some caution. It nevertheless captured some of the defining characteristics of the pre-classical or grand style of adjudication that was best exemplified by Marshall's constitutional jurisprudence. Nor was James an outlier among his colleagues in what he thought constitutional adjudication to involve. He was different only in attempting to put a common understanding into words. Despite his scolding of Young and Ritchie, their judgments in *Windsor & Annapolis* also had functional elements, particularly in the sheltering role that they assigned to the provincial jurisdiction over property and civil rights. So also were most of the judgments they rendered in other cases.[20]

By the 1890s, the court's constitutional decisions had a very different look. This was most strongly evident in the series of liquor licensing cases that started with *R. v. McDougall* in 1889 and culminated with *R. v. Ronan* in 1891.[21] In both of these, and in the other cases in the series, debate and analysis revolved around the efforts of lawyers and judges alike to find a single coherent thread through the Privy Council's prior decisions in *Russell v. The Queen* (upholding federal temperance), *Hodge v. The Queen* (upholding provincial regulation of taverns), and the *McCarthy Act Reference* (striking down federal licensing).[22] The shift was neatly captured in the opening statement of Attorney General James Wilberforce Longley in *R. v. McDougall*. Directing the attention of the judges to the table before him, Longley grandly declared, 'I have here before me three volumes of Cartwright's cases, and I regard them as the very essence of the constitution of the Dominion.'[23] A better and more succinct counterpoint to the older vision of constitutional adjudication that James had articulated is difficult to imagine. James had found the 'law books' to be useless as guides to the interpretation of the constitution. For Longley, the 'law books', especially the law reports, had become the constitution.

Despite Longley's confidence in the cases, the outcome in *McDougall* was a hopeless jumble of rulings that demonstrates the confusion that existed among Canadian judges and lawyers about the meaning of the various rulings of the Privy Council. Two judges (Chief Justice James McDonald and J. Norman Ritchie) ruled that the essential distinction between federal and provincial jurisdiction was that between wholesaid and retail and found Nova Scotia's Act unconstitutional to the extent that it dealt with wholesaling. The three others (Robert Weatherbe, Charles Townshend, and Henry Smith) all thought that the key distinction was instead between a provincial power to regulate both retail and wholesale and a federal power to prohibit that also applied to both branches of the trade. But they then divided on the application of this distinction, with Weatherbe, unlike the others, finding the Nova Scotia Act to be prohibitory and therefore invalid.

This was the beginning of the able Weatherbe's quixotic battle against Nova Scotia's Liquor Licensing Act of 1886 that would lead him into increasing isolation in subsequent cases.[24] But even in its isolation, Weatherbe's judgment was the best example of the penetration of formalist technique into the court's constitutional jurisprudence. His premise was that *Russell v. The Queen* and *Hodge v. The Queen* could each be reduced to a key phrase that captured their respective ratios. On this approach, *Russell* meant that laws on intoxicating liquors were federal if they placed 'restrictions on their sale, custody or removal, on the ground that the free sale or use of them is dangerous to public safety.' Conversely, *Hodge* meant that liquor laws were provincial if they interfered with 'liberty of action to the extent that was necessary to prevent disorder and the abuses of liquor licenses.' With these 'essences' derived, Weatherbe could conclude, with little analysis (the words themselves were the analysis), that the 'detached words' of *Russell* applied better to Nova Scotia's liquor licensing legislation than the 'detached words' of *Hodge*. The reason was that the legislation contained a plebiscite provision that could prevent all licences from being issued in particular localities. Somehow, this was more about placing restriction on the selling of liquor for public safety (and therefore within *Russell*) than it was about the prevention of disorders and abuses of liquor licences (the 'essence' of *Hodge*).

Weatherbe's 'cut and paste' formalism was extreme. But all the other *McDougall* judges also operated largely within the parameters set by the Privy Council case law, despite their deep disagreement about its meaning. What most obviously accounts for this rapid and dramatic narrowing in the adjudicative frame of reference was the simple availability of binding authorities from the highest court of the land. The context for constitutional adjudication had changed significantly from the days when James had looked in vain for guidance from the 'law books.' Like any other provincial court, the Nova Scotia Supreme Court had no choice but to try to make sense of the higher rulings and to frame their analysis in the new terms. And clearly, the Privy Council rulings did more than delimit federal and provincial legislative powers; they also modelled a methodology of interpretation that was very different from the methodology of the early Nova Scotia decisions. The appeal to the Privy Council in *Windsor & Annapolis* became an example of how appeals on constitutional cases might have encouraged the transition of Canadian courts to the narrower and more technical methodology. The Nova Scotia Supreme Court was upheld, essentially on the grounds applied by Ritchie and Young.[25] The judgment then closed with a typical Privy Council caution against deciding cases on unnecessarily wide grounds. James was not mentioned, but his advocacy for 'extreme liberality,' and perhaps Young's obiter explanation of how confederation had changed the constitutional foundations of Canadian legislatures, may well have prompted the observation.[26] Thus, *Windsor & Annapolis* became one of the cases used by the Privy Council to instruct Canadian judges to limit the adjudication of each case to the narrowest ground on which it could be determined.[27] Later cases, including *McDougall*, suggest that Nova Scotia judges took these instructions to heart. Their rapid adoption of the Privy Council's constitutional formalism suggests that, by 1889, they had become as captive to the methodology of the imperial tribunal as had Canadian courts more generally.[28] It suggests that the window of opportunity for independent and indigenous thinking about how constitutional adjudication might be framed closed as quickly in Nova Scotia as it did elsewhere in Canada.

This interpretation is, however, in need of qualification. First of all, the shift to formalism was not all embracing. After *Windsor & Annapolis*, the judges continued to allow broader considerations into their analysis. In particular, they continued to be sensitive to their immediate context and to the implications of interpretive outcomes to the functioning of the federation. For example, in *McDougall* itself, Chief Justice James McDonald, hardly a bold thinker, held to the view that the court had to maintain the distinction between retail and wholesale because it was still bound by *Severn v. The Queen*, the 1878 decision of the Supreme Court of Canada that had created that distinction. He did so (and J. Norman Ritchie did the same), even though the distinction was contrary to what had been decided by the Privy Council in the *McCarthy Act Reference*.[29] Their refusal to accept the demise of *Severn* rested on the technicality that *McCarthy*, as a reference case, had been decided without reasons, meaning that it did not explicitly overrule *Severn*. But for McDonald especially it also reflected resistance to the truncation of the trade and commerce power that was implicit in *McCarthy* and explicit in other Privy Council cases.[30] Ever so carefully, McDonald went beyond the boundary of the cases to quote business definitions of 'wholesale' and 'retail' from McCullogh's Dictionary of Commerce that he found sensible and practicable.[31] The problem, said McDonald, came in the translation of these business concepts into 'statutable' language, but such problems were problems of implementation only. Contrary to what the English lawyers who had argued *McCarthy* had said, they did not justify abandonment of the concepts, or of the founding intentions that they embodied. Clearly McDonald, former though not very successful attorney general in the Cabinet of John A. MacDonald, adhered to *Severn* because he supported its centralist vision of Canada and of the Dominion's economic power and leadership.[32] One further hint of this is that McDonald not only used *Severn* for the distinction between wholesale and retail but also in place of *Hodge* as his authority for the scope of the provincial police power.[33]

Weatherbe, who applied almost a caricature of formalism with his 'detached words' as the templates for constitutional analysis, was at the same time even more sensitive to local context. He bolstered his conclusion that the Licensing Act of 1886 was disguised temperance legislation by invoking the political reality that the legislation was supported by the 'large class, who, with a laudable desire to abate the evils of intemperance, hope, if they cannot altogether prohibit the traffic in every part of the country, [that] they may in some "electoral" districts prohibit it entirely, and greatly restrict its sale everywhere.'[34] Indeed, it was legislation that had been 'drafted in the interest of the Total Abstinence Organization.'[35] Judges were not only allowed but required to take this into account. As Weatherbe put it, 'knowing what we could not in a general way help knowing, we cannot too scrupulously and jealously be on our guard, in considering the rules and principles applicable to the construction of the British North America Act, in arriving at a judicial determination.' Thus, although he purported to base his judgment on a sifting of the phraseology found in *Hodge* and in *Russell*, it clearly also rested on policy grounds and on a highly contextualized and pragmatic understanding of the purposes and effect of Nova Scotia's licensing legislation. Like McDonald, his concern was probably the broader one of protecting the federal government's capacity to create and maintain a national economy.[36] To get there, he could play the formalist but there was much in his reasoning that looks more like the earlier functionalism, to say nothing of the later realism of the twentieth century.[37]

Second, deferential submission to Privy Council methodology does not fit easily with the irreverence that both lawyers and judges directed towards their judicial superiors. Throughout the argument in *McDougall*, there was puzzlement and disapproval expressed at what the Privy Council had said and why. There was explicit disapproval of its methodology.[38] Benjamin Russell, co-counsel with Longley, thought that the Privy Council had said that prohibition was federal and regulation provincial, but that otherwise he did not 'know of any way of reconciling the judgments given.'[39] Weatherbe, in one of his more than 120 interjections into oral argument, tried to sum up the argument of

Longley on the federal power over 'trade and commerce' by saying that there were actually two distinct powers over trade and commerce, one federal and one provincial, and that the Privy Council had called the latter the municipal or police power to distinguish the two.[40] In this, he wondered if they had not made a mistake.[41] Bell, co-counsel with former attorney general Otto Weeks for McDougall, regretted the Privy Council's resistance to the use of American constitutional cases. That was 'throwing away one of the most valuable sources of information we have,' since '[t]he reasoning of the American judges is as applicable to Canada as it is to the United States.'[42]

However, it was Longley, who had with one breath celebrated the cases as constitutional 'essence,' went farthest with the next breath in doubting the correctness and even the capacity of the Privy Council. His fundamental point was that *Hodge v. The Queen* not only had significance for liquor but sent a larger message – that the provinces were better protected under the BNA Act than the Dominion.[43] He portrayed provincial powers as being 'carved out' of federal powers and as sheltered from federal encroachment by a protective circle of exclusive jurisdictional control. In contrast, the provinces had the right to interfere with the federal power over trade and commerce. In the specific case of liquor licensing, this meant trade and commerce legislation could not interfere with provincial 'restrictions for the good of the public.' Longley presented his argument as an attempt 'to work out the theory of the BNA Act as applied to the liquor traffic' so as to challenge the court to draw the line between legislation that regulated (and was provincial) and legislation that prohibited (and was federal).[44] He portrayed provincial powers as being misleadingly described (both in the BNA Act and in the cases) as 'local,' as if to mean small, when the reality was that provincial responsibilities were 'enormously big.' He declared the results coming from the Privy Council, and especially from *Hodge v. The Queen*, more important than the reasons, because the reasons used misleading words like 'local' and 'police' that did not appropriately convey the enormous powers given to the provinces to protect 'peace and good order.' A disdainful interjection from Weatherbe, that the Privy Council did not understand the federal order, drew the rejoinder from Longley that 'They are getting it into their heads now.' On this basis, he confidently ventured to say that *Russell v. The Queen* would 'not survive long.'

Third, the methodological influence of the Privy Council needs broader context. Part of that context was the transformation in the membership of the court that took place during the 1880s. The court that decided *Windsor & Annapolis* was not the same court that decided *McDougall*. Chief Justice Young, pre-Confederation premier, was replaced in 1881 by James McDonald, post-Confederation attorney general for Canada. More importantly, by the time of *McDougall*, the court included J. Norman Ritchie and Charles Townshend.[45] Soon afterwards, Wallace Graham was appointed.[46] Each had been a leader at the bar, as few of the judges that they replaced had been. More significantly, as Philip Girard has pointed out, each was a representative of the new professionalism that revitalized the legal profession in late nineteenth-century Nova Scotia.[47] This revitalization included the foundation of Dalhousie Law School in 1883 and the remaking of the Nova Scotia Barristers' Society into a modern regulatory body in the early 1880s. Both developments owed much to the leadership of a younger generation of lawyers that included Ritchie, Graham, and Townshend. Each represented a shift in professional identity from the law as a gentlemanly pursuit to law as a technocratic profession that rested on specialized knowledge and skills. The same wave of professional revitalization would also contribute to the rehabilitation of the reputation of the court, primarily through the tenures of the younger Ritchie, Townshend, and Graham (all of whom played significant parts in the Court's constitutional jurisprudence), as well as by the shorter tenures of John S.D. Thompson and Samuel Rigby and the appointment of Hugh Henry in 1893.[48]

The professional ethos of this new generation of Nova Scotia judges was broadly consistent with the late nineteenth-century rise of legal formalism across the Anglo-American world. This view aligns with the understanding of legal formalism, and of the underlying ideology of legal liberalism, that has been so richly reconstructed in recent years, particularly in the writing of R.C.B. Risk.[49] This literature portrays the shift to formalism as the methodological manifestation of a transformation in legal culture that was too large and diffuse to have been caused simply by the Privy Council or by any other single institutional change or influence. It views the formalism of the Privy Council as itself a reflection of a broader transatlantic shift in legal thinking and practice that affected Canadian constitutional law, and Canadian law in general, through many portals. In England and in North America, especially in leading universities, law came to be regarded as an autonomous way of thinking and acting and, above all, of deciding and justifying, that was distinct from politics and from the more explicit functionalism of an earlier era. Law became scientific, a suitable subject for scholarly study and for a university education that emphasized rigorous and systematized learning of generally applicable rules and principles and their rational elaboration through cases. Like other areas of law, statutory interpretation came increasingly to depend on the application of general rules, and less on the general (and distinct) purpose of each statute. The definition and protection of individual autonomy became the common rationale for doctrine in areas of law that had previously been thought discrete and distinct.[50]

For Risk and others, this leads to the conclusion that the formalism of the Privy Council in constitutional law was the consequence of influences that were a pervasive part of the intellectual and ideological context for all law, as much in North America as in England. This broader context can be seen at work in the new professionalism that was in the process of transforming the Nova Scotian legal profession long before the Privy Council decided its first case under the BNA Act. The appointment to the Nova Scotia Supreme Court of leading representatives of that professionalism almost certainly brought understandings of law and adjudication to the court that were informed by the web of ideas, values, and attitudes coalescing into legal formalism on both sides of the Atlantic. The point is not that the court's changing membership was the sole cause of its shift to formalism; rather, the shift to formalism was almost surely the product of both imperial and local influences. This is not to suggest that Nova Scotians such as Townshend, Graham, and the younger Ritchie had somehow imbibed all of what was being said and thought about law in distant universities and in broader metropolitan legal circles. Rather, it is only to suggest that they were probably as much men of their time as were the generation of judges they replaced.

The court's transition to formalism was thus not as comprehensive by the late 1880s as first impressions might suggest, nor was the transition that did occur attributable solely or perhaps even primarily to captivity at the hands of the Privy Council. Imperial influences were unquestionably important, but their importance was in some measure due to their resonance with influences of more diverse origin that operated from within Nova Scotia as well as from beyond. At the same time, Privy Council influences were being mediated and qualified to some extent by local dynamics. This sets the stage for my consideration of the substance of the Supreme Court's constitutional jurisprudence and my argument that the court's lingering methodological autonomy reflected the continuing importance of understandings of the BNA Act that the abstract formalism of the Privy Council could not accommodate.

The Division of Powers Cases

Between confederation and the end of the nineteenth century, the Nova Scotia Supreme Court decided seventeen cases that were primarily division of powers cases, with thirteen dealing with challenges to provincial legislation and four involving the constitutionality of federal statutes.[51] A simple calculation of wins and losses suggests an understanding of sections 91 and 92 that gave ample scope for provincial lawmaking. Only twice did the court strike down a provincial law. It struck down the same number of federal laws, but of course this meant that it struck down half of the federal laws that came forward for review.

The fact that legislation was only struck down in four of seventeen cases may, however, be of equal significance. Given the time and place, it comes as no surprise that the judges of Nova Scotia sometimes explicitly articulated and more frequently implicitly applied a presumption of constitutionality validity. Constitutional adjudication that maximized legislative supremacy and minimized judicial encroachment is what might be expected from judges anywhere in post-confederation Canada. Such generic judicial deference to legislative authority, rather than a nascent commitment to provincial rights, might seem to be the more plausible explanation for the court's benevolence to provincial jurisdictional claims.

But this does not give adequate attention to the reasoning the court used to uphold provincial legislation in the more significant division of powers cases. The first of these was *Keefe v. McLennan*, decided in 1876 by Justice John W. Ritchie as one of the very first constitutional cases to come before the court and as the court's first engagement with what would become the tangled constitutional aspects of the plethora of liquor legislation that Canadian legislatures enacted in the late nineteenth century. It arose from the conviction of a Cape Breton tavern keeper for selling without a licence after the Court of Sessions for the County of Cape Breton declined all licence applications, relying on the provisions of provincial licensing legislation that permitted local-option temperance.[52] Keefe's lawyer was Wallace Graham, the rising star of the Halifax bar and the future chief justice of the court, who would play a leading role in later constitutional cases. In *Keefe* his argument was based on *Justices of Kings County*,[53] in which the New Brunswick Supreme Court had in 1873 found comparable New Brunswick legislation to be an unconstitutional interference with the federal power over trade and commerce. The judgment had been written by

New Brunswick's Chief Justice, William Johnstone Ritchie, the younger brother of John William Ritchie, the presiding judge in *Keefe*.[54]

In rejecting Graham's argument, the Nova Scotian Ritchie followed some of the same reasoning that had recommended itself to his brother. He also saw in section 92 a 'police power' that embraced legislation for the 'protection of the health and morals of the people, and the preservation of the peace and good order of the community'.[55] It rested for Ritchie primarily on provincial control under section 92(13) over 'property and civil rights.' Also like his brother, Ritchie used American constitutional cases as his authority for the existence and the importance of this power.[56] But unlike the New Brunswick Ritchie, who had seen the provincial power of police as being subordinate to the federal power to regulate trade and commerce, the Nova Scotian Ritchie saw matters coming within property and civil rights as being for that reason outside federal legislative competence. The provincial powers were 'very comprehensive' and it was 'evident that the framers of the Act did not intend that they should receive a very restricted interpretation.' Even in their most restricted interpretation, said Ritchie, 'they embrace the subjects I have referred to, for life, health and personal safety are the rights of the people of every free country and to preserve them is the duty of the Legislature, and any such laws which have for their object the prevention of intemperance directly affects these subjects for not only does drunkenness destroy the health and reputation, waste the property and ruin the happiness and comfort of those addicted to it, but it is the cause of most of the crimes committed in the land.' Powers that existed to protect and guarantee such important objectives had to be interpreted broadly and protected by the courts because they were important to the 'lives, health, morals, of the community – whether it be intoxicating liquors, poisons or unwholesome provisions' that demanded regulation. For Ritchie, general temperance was of a piece with prohibitions against the selling of liquor to minors or on Sundays. It restricted trade and yet was clearly within provincial power.

Unlike his brother, who had opposed Confederation from afar, John W. Ritchie had been an active supporter of union.[57] He had been government leader in the Legislative Council during the debate on Tupper's resolution in favour of union in 1866, one of the conduits of Tupper's government to Lieutenant Governor Fenwick Williams during the manoeuvring for Nova Scotia's entry into Confederation on the basis of the 'Quebec scheme,' a spokesperson for union in the broader community, and a delegate to the London Conference. When he spoke as a judge of what had been intended by the all-important provincial power over property and civil rights, he spoke with some authority. But equally important, Ritchie was probably the most highly regarded of the judges who sat on the court during the first decade of confederation. It seems probable that his understanding of the scope and exclusivity of provincial legislative authority was accepted in 1876 and followed later because it was regarded as highly authoritative. Thus it can be suggested that in the years before the Privy Council had started its decentralization of Canadian federalism, the Nova Scotia Supreme Court brought to the process of constitutional adjudication an understanding of Confederation and of the BNA Act that anticipated more than the ultimate success of the provinces on the battle for jurisdiction over liquor. It also anticipated the broader recognition of continuing provincial sovereignty over communal life – what we might today be called 'social issues.'[58]

These conclusions are large ones to rest on the decision of a single judge consisting of barely six pages. *Keefe v. McLennan* has been viewed by others as fitting within a pattern of provincial court jurisprudence that was balanced and did no particular harm to the wider and higher legislative powers of Parliament.[59] This may discount the importance of the core of Ritchie's short judgment – the connection it made between the duty of the provincial legislature to protect life, health and personal safety and a judicial mandate to broadly interpret and vigilantly protect the legislative powers that the provinces had been given to discharge the duty. The same connection was made in 1878 by the judges of the New Brunswick Supreme Court, particularly by Charles Fisher, Ritchie's fellow Father of Confederation.[60] Thus, it is possible to see *Keefe v. McLennan* as representative of a broader pattern of judicial thinking in the Maritimes that conceived of provincial legislative control over local affairs, and particularly over the regulation of property and civil rights, as being as central to the general shape of the division of powers as it was eventually to become through Privy Council rulings. One aspect of this was a tendency to read the broader powers of Parliament as being subject to the more specific powers of the provinces. The decision of the court in *Windsor & Annapolis*, where Ritchie again played a leading role, provides another example of this tendency. In both cases, but particularly in *Windsor & Annapolis*, the power of the provinces to deal with property and civil rights was applied as a kind of shelter for the protection of such rights from federal encroachment. The conclusion that the court was broadly provincialist on jurisdictional questions in the early years of constitutional adjudication is reinforced by several other cases from the early 1880's.[61]

After *Keefe v. McLennan* and *Windsor & Annapolis*, the division of powers cases that stand out are the five licensing cases the court decided in the late 1880s and early 1890's. All arose from challenges to Nova Scotia's Liquor Licensing Act of 1886. Each called on the court to make sense of the confusing body of rulings that had, by 1889, come down from the Supreme Court of Canada and the Privy Council on legislative jurisdiction over liquor.[62] The most important of these were the rulings of the Privy Council in *Russell v. The Queen* (1882) and *Hodge v. The Queen* (1884). Like Ritchie in *Keefe v. McLennan*, both associated legislation on liquor with the health and morals of the people and with the preservation of peace and good order in the community. The problem was that the Privy Council seemed to accord the responsibility for what Ritchie had called the 'lives, health, and morals of the community' to both the federal and to the provincial governments. It did so by ruling first in *Russell* that the Canada Temperance Act was valid, not as a regulation of trade and commerce, but because it advanced these social and communal objectives and was therefore legislation on peace, order, and good government.[63] It then ruled in *Hodge* that an Ontario licensing law that regulated the playing of billiards in taverns was valid because it advanced the same, or at least very similar, objectives, making it a valid provincial regulation of 'municipal police.'[64] The view that *Hodge* therefore modified *Russell* in some unspecified way was reinforced by the conclusion reached by the Privy Council in the *McCarthy Act Reference*, given without reasons, that federal licensing of the selling of liquor was unconstitutional whether the selling was wholesale or retail.[65]

Finally, there was the uncertain status of the earlier decisions of the Supreme Court of Canada in *Severn*, which had said that wholesaling was trade and commerce, and *City of Fredericton*, where the Canada Temperance Act had also been upheld primarily under trade and commerce.[66] The *Severn* ruling seemed at odds with the *McCarthy Act Reference*, *Fredericton* with *Russell*, and both with *Citizen's Insurance v. Parsons*, where the Privy Council had removed the regulation of specific categories of trade from the general federal authority over trade and commerce. But neither *Severn* or *Fredericton* had been expressly overruled.[67]

This was the jurisprudential context for the court's various rulings on the constitutionality of Nova Scotia's Liquor Licence Act of 1886. The

Act was modelled on the earlier Ontario statute and passed by the same session of the Legislature that had adopted Premier Fielding's resolutions for Nova Scotia's secession.[68] It was challenged for the first time in 1889 in *R. v. McDougall*, where the issue was the constitutionality of the Act's wholesale licensing requirements. Clearly, the case was regarded as an important one. Unusually, a full record of the oral argument was kept and printed in the Journals of the House of Assembly.[69] It was also a case enmeshed in the political relationships of the day and in Nova Scotia's smallness. As noted above, Attorney General Longley made the lead argument for the constitutionality of the legislation. Although he was assisted by the well-respected (and ubiquitous) practitioner-scholar Benjamin Russell, the case unquestionably belonged to Longley, a politician who had distinguished himself as a member of Fielding's Liberal administration primarily as a forceful advocate for provincial rights and for a North American commercial union.[70] He could be described even by a political ally as 'conceited, unlovable and unbearable.'[71] On the other side was Otto Weeks, who had been attorney general before Longley in the 1870s in the Liberal administration of P.C. Hill until being extraordinarily removed from office by the Lieutenant-Governor for inattention to his duties caused by insobriety.[72] In the provincial election of 1886, he had run as an independent liberal committed to Nova Scotia's secession from confederation against Fielding's candidates in Guysborough, causing the defeat of two of them.[73]

The proceedings were dominated however, not by Longley or by Weeks, but by Judge Robert Weatherbe. He interrupted Weeks an amazing ninety-three times, first when Weeks was barely out of his chair. Many of the exchanges that Weatherbe initiated, with Weeks as well as with Longley, were caustic, dismissive, and sarcastic, the lawyers giving as good as they took. Even so, it was Weatherbe and not the lawyers who set the pace and the parameters of debate, since the lawyers spent most of their time responding to his questions, with the other judges (Chief Justice McDonald and Justices Ritchie, Townshend, and Smith) watching and listening. The point of Weatherbe's activism was not obvious – playing devil's advocate was the main sport. One point did seem important, that the constitution created two distinct powers over trade and commerce, one provincial and the other federal, and that the Privy Council had caused much unnecessary confusion by calling the provincial one a municipal police power.

Whatever the source of the confusion, it was apparent in the result. The court divided 3–2 on what distinguished federal from provincial authority. Weatherbe, Townshend, and Smith all said the distinction was between provincial regulation and federal prohibition, with Weatherbe alone concluding that the 1886 Act prohibited. Chief Justice McDonald and the younger Justice Ritchie thought the distinction was between retailing and wholesaling, with the provinces having no power either over the regulating or the prohibiting of the latter. This rendered the wholesale licensing provisions of the 1886 Act invalid. In the end, the quashing of McDougall's conviction was the only sure outcome, without any consensus on the grounds.

In such confusion, further challenges were inevitable. The next came in *R. v. McKenzie*,[74] where the validity of the retail licensing sections of the 1886 Act were challenged on the grounds that they authorized local-option temperance. Again the court, sitting in a panel of four, splintered badly. Townshend appeared to shift to the retail-wholesale distinction and found the provisions to be valid because related to retailing, but also because (in his view) they regulated and did not prohibit. He interpreted the Supreme Court of Canada as having reached the same conclusion, in a case decided after *McDougall*, on the New Brunswick Liquor Licence Act of 1887 which had been modelled closely on the Nova Scotia legislation and on their common source, the Ontario statute.[75] Graham agreed that the constitutional question was governed by the recent Supreme Court of Canada ruling, but without clearly accepting that provincial authority ended at the boundary between retail and wholesale or the boundary between regulating and prohibiting. He also agreed with Justice J. Norman Ritchie, who did not address the division of powers question, that the convictions before the Court were invalid because of procedural irregularities. This again isolated Weatherbe, who again argued for the root and branch invalidity of Nova Scotia's not so surreptitious prohibition statute.

McKenzie set the stage for a climax of sorts, and it came in *R. v. Ronan*, a further challenge to the Act's local-option retail temperance machinery.[76] In effect, the case was Nova Scotia's version of the *Local Prohibition Reference*, in which the Privy Council would conclude in 1896 that the provinces also could prohibit in addition to regulating.[77] In large measure it was a rehearing of *McKenzie*, made necessary by the increasingly pointed disagreements between the judges. Again, Weatherbe gave a long and detailed argument against the 1886 Act, being careful to disavow any suggestion that the legislature had acted to fraudulently usurp federal power. Instead, with the younger Ritchie's concurrence, he limited himself to explaining the prohibitory effect that the Act would unavoidably have if enforced as written.

Much of his time was spent trying to distinguish the Nova Scotian legislation from the New Brunswick version that had been recently upheld by the Supreme Court of Canada, where even the arch-centralist John Wellington Gwynne had accepted provincial prohibition.[78] But Weatherbe also spent time showing that the essence of *Russell v. The Queen*, which he had previously tried to capture in a phrase from that case, really came down to the single word 'temperance.'[79] This essence was the core of the 1886 Act not only because it could be used to withhold all licences, but also because the word 'temperance' appeared among the stated legislative purposes.

This brought a curt and even condescending instruction from Wallace Graham, the recently appointed judge in equity and Weatherbe's old law partner. Bluntly, he told Weatherbe that 'Hardly anything was to be gained in this discussion by calling a thing a name.'[80] Graham wrote the leading opinion of the majority that upheld the Act and isolated Weatherbe, ending his insurgency on behalf of adjudicative realism, supported only by his increasingly untenable reading of *Russell*. Two further cases would be argued on the 1886 legislation, but they were disposed of in a way that suggested that they were straightforward, raising narrow issues that were governed by authority, particularly *Ronan*.[81] Neither produced any dissenting opinions, although this probably reflected Weatherbe's non-participation as much as it did universal consensus.

For the rest of the court, *Ronan* did represent a new consensus with Graham's opinion being the important one. In it, he undertook his own careful parsing of the cases to show that *Russell v. The Queen* did not 'support the proposition that all acts which are in effect temperance acts, must be enacted by the Parliament of Canada.' As Attorney General Longley had in the argument in *McDougall*, he anticipated the Privy Council coming to this conclusion itself, as it would in *Local Prohibition Reference*. But in addition and more significantly, Graham reminded Weatherbe and everyone else that Nova Scotia's own eminent Mr Justice John W. Ritchie had decided the question before the court in *Keefe v. McLennan*, long before all the complications and fine distinctions had been layered on by the Privy Council. As Graham put it, Ritchie seemed 'in advance of other courts, to have discovered the true solution of the difficulties in connection with such legislation and justified it as a matter of police regulation, as was done long afterwards in *Hodge v. The Queen* by the Court of Appeal in Ontario and the Privy Council.'

Graham had sat in *McKenzie* but had waited until *Ronan* to take such strong exception to Weatherbe's approach. Perhaps by then he had become concerned that the court's credibility, something he cared about deeply, was being undermined by its inability to be definitive on an important constitutional question. If so, it is interesting that he attacked Weatherbe's formalism as well as his conclusions. Graham was of the younger generation that was more likely to be in tune with the changing understandings of legal method that included the shift towards formalism. Yet it was Graham who objected to Weatherbe's insistence on the clear and self-sufficient meaning of words, rather than the other way around. It was also Graham rather than Weatherbe who reached back to the court's pre-formalist past for guidance. This fits neatly with one of the 'strategies of legitimation' that Philip Girard has argued contributed to the court's rehabilitation in the 1890s and early 1900s.[82] One of these was to celebrate the history of the court and the contribution of its great judges. It is possible that Graham's reclaiming of the indigenous wisdom of *Keefe v. McLennan* was a small application of this strategy. Certainly, his point was more than the technical correctness of *Keefe v. McLennan*; rather, Ritchie had been a great judge who could be depended upon, even in sorting out the Privy Council.

In effect, Graham cut through the confusion that was being created by the uncertainty in the Privy Council rulings by setting those rulings aside and recovering an indigenous interpretation of the rationale and scope of provincial authority over liquor and its social consequences. As with the court's transition to formalism, *R. v. Ronan* shows the court evolving in response to local influences and dynamics in ways that can be overlooked if we look simply to the fact that it ended up in the same place as the Privy Council. It shows the Privy Council outcomes being followed, and to some degree anticipated, because they were determined in a local light to be, in some sense, the right outcomes.

The consistency of Graham's analysis with the argument that Longley had made in *McDougall* is noteworthy. Like Longley, Graham anticipated the Privy Council coming to the conclusion that provinces could prohibit as well as regulate. Accordingly, he implicitly shared Longley's view that the Privy Council sometimes got the reasons wrong even when they got the outcomes right. Given that Graham was a Conservative and a close confidant of John S.D. Thompson, and that *Russell v. The Queen* represented the high point of Dominion jurisdictional dominance, his more natural position might have been with Weatherbe against Longley, who had argued *McDougall* from within classic provincial rights orthodoxy. But perhaps the important point is that *Ronan* not only restored consensus within the court. It also achieved consensus on the scope of provincial legislative powers in an important jurisdictional domain between the court and a provincial government that was, at best, tentatively and only conditionally committed to Canada and dominated by 'temperance men.' Thus, Graham's objective may have been to defuse a potential justification for increased or perpetuated resistance to confederation while enhancing the image of the court in provincial political circles. One aspect of his motivation may have been the provincial legislation passed in 1890 that gave the Executive Council the authority to refer constitutional questions to the court.[83] *Ronan* may have been Graham's attempt to respond positively to that legislative expression of confidence in the court.

Whatever his motives, Graham's *Ronan* judgment assigned a broad swath of social life exclusively to the province. Like the senior Ritchie in *Keefe v. McLennan*, Graham implicitly endorsed the belief that confederation had preserved the provinces as autonomous communities governed by legislatures that had vitally important responsibilities and commensurate powers. It is too much to say that the Nova Scotia Supreme Court was a 'provincial rights' court. For one thing, the court was never challenged to reconcile the broad reading it gave to property and civil rights with federal legislation that depended on an equally robust reading of the trade and commerce power. For another, it will be seen that the basic precepts of provincial rights seemed to have played no part in how the court handled the constitutional status cases. Even so, at least on the liquor question, *Ronan* placed the court close to where the Privy Council would be after *Local Prohibition Reference*, the case that would set Canadian constitutional law on a decentralizing path that would last for half a century.

Here though, it must be noted that Graham followed in the tradition of Ritchie in more than his generous reading of provincial legislative jurisdiction. He would also follow him in being simultaneously resistant to claims of provincial equality with the Dominion. This is suggested by his decision in an 1894 case, *Fielding v. Thomas*, in which the question was whether provincial legislatures were equal heirs with the Dominion Parliament to the powers, rights, and privileges of the British House of Commons. Again, Graham and Weatherbe would be at odds. But it would be Weatherbe arguing on the side of provincial rights and Graham arguing to the contrary.

The Constitutional Status Cases

Aside from the court's work on the division of powers, it decided a smaller number of cases that raised – or might have raised – a basic question: were the provinces sovereign governments exercising plenary authority, or simply statutory bodies wielding perhaps large but only delegated and therefore subordinate authority?[84] The answer depended largely on whether the provinces were the creations of the BNA Act or, instead, the self-governing communities that had come together to establish the Dominion and to allocate certain of their rights of self-government to the Dominion Parliament while retaining the balance of those rights. Given that sovereignty flowed from the Crown under British constitutional principles, a key issue was whether the Crown, through the office of the lieutenant governor, was still part of the constitution of the provinces. Judicial recognition of the vice-regal status of lieutenant governors became a crucial objective for Oliver Mowat, Ontario's great champion of provincial rights. It would ultimately be achieved in the Privy Council in 1892.[85] But the issue was already a live one in Nova Scotia in 1876 when one of the first cases to raise these questions in any court came before the Nova Scotia Supreme Court.[86]

The case was *In re Precedence of Ritchie, Q.C.*, better known (as it will be here) as *Lenoir v. Ritchie*, the name it took on appeal in the Supreme Court of Canada.[87] It involved Joseph Norman Ritchie, the half-brother of John W. Ritchie, a leading Halifax lawyer, a future judge of the court, and a Tory. In 1872, he had been appointed Queen's Counsel (QC) under letters patent from the governor general. In 1874, the Nova Scotia legislature passed one statute that authorized appointments of Queen's Counsel by the lieutenant governor in council and another authorizing the lieutenant governor in council to specify the relative precedence of QCs before the courts.[88] Ritchie soon found himself behind a raft of provincial appointees that included Peter Lenoir (and Peter Carteret Hill, who became Liberal premier in 1875). He sued on various grounds, including that the lieutenant governor did not have and could not be given the constitutional authority to exercise a prerogative power through ordinary provincial legislation.[89]

Here then, was an opportunity for Nova Scotia's judges to pronounce, one way or the other, on a question that could be fundamental to the shape of the new nation, and to the place of Nova Scotia within it. It was an opportunity that came to the court in the same year as *Keefe v. McLennan*, which had so strongly interpreted provincial legislative rights. It was an opportunity that a majority of the Supreme Court of Canada would pounce upon when *Lenoir v. Ritchie* made it there on appeal in 1879. In that court, Ritchie's claim about the status of the lieutenant governor, carrying with it the implication that the provinces were a lower order of government, would be embraced by a majority with enthusiasm. Justices Gwynne and Taschereau, as well as Nova Scotia's Justice William Henry, all agreed that only the governor general represented the Crown. It followed that only the federal executive possessed the prerogative powers. For Henry, another of Nova Scotia's Fathers of Confederation, this meant that provincial legislation authorizing QC appointments was as invalid as a municipal by-law giving the same power to a mayor or municipal reeve.[90] Ontario's Gwynne used *Lenoir v. Ritchie* more grandly to declare the Dominion government to be a 'quasi-imperial power,' with the provinces having been 'carved out of, and subordinated to' this power.[91] As Paul Romney would have it, in *Lenoir v. Ritchie,* the judges of the Supreme Court 'declared war on provincial rights.'[92]

In the Nova Scotia Supreme Court Ritchie had also been successful, but on more narrow grounds.[93] It was a 3–2 decision, with Chief Justice William Young writing for the majority that included Justices William Desbarres and Hugh McDonald. He gave two grounds for concluding that Ritchie's precedence at the bar remained unaffected. The first was that Nova Scotia's legislation did not operate retroactively. It was therefore incapable of authorizing any retroactive reordering of Ritchie's place.[94] This meant Ritchie won his case but also that he lost his constitutional arguments, for Young's premise was that the provincial reordering of precedence had been statutorily and not constitutionally invalid. Yet Young appeared to agree that lieutenant governors were not vice-regal and that, therefore, they did not possess the prerogative power to create Queen's Counsel. He appeared to take this to be obvious, not bothering to be explicit on the point. He referred to the governor general as 'the Queen's representative in Canada' in a way that strongly implied exclusivity. But at the same time, he accepted that provincial legislatures could give lieutenant governors the power that they did not otherwise possess. He gave two reasons for this conclusion. One was the despatch that the colonial secretary, Lord Kimberley, had sent to Ottawa confirming the validity of provincial legislation such as that which had been passed by Nova Scotia. The other was that Nova Scotia's legislation had gone 'into operation,' meaning it had been assented to by the lieutenant governor (the very officer whose constitutional status was at issue) and not disallowed by the governor general. These points made the argument that the legislation was not only limited in effect but ultra vires 'quite untenable.'

Young's other ground for ruling for Ritchie was uniquely Nova

Scotian. The province, he said, had wrongly affixed the pre-Confederation seal of Nova Scotia to its appointments instead of the new seal that had been sent to Halifax via Ottawa from London in 1869. This issue arose unexpectedly during argument, causing a flurry of excitement. Proceedings had to be adjourned, documents collected, and new affidavits filed. An element of high drama was added by the personalities involved, as the new seal had been transmitted to Nova Scotia by Joseph Howe, acting briefly as MacDonald's secretary of state for the provinces, and rejected by Premier William Annand, Howe's old ally, then estranged over the Confederation controversy.[95] For the pro-Confederation Young, who had gone to London as a kind of unofficial Father of Confederation to help with the work of making Confederation happen, the opportunity that this presented to judicially repudiate such provincial recalcitrance must have been irresistible. Thus the seal question came to occupy much of the court's attention in *Lenoir v. Ritchie*, while the much larger issue of the source and scope of executive power was addressed almost summarily.

This issue, unlike the rest of the case, would not go beyond the Nova Scotia Supreme Court; the question would be resolved (in favour of Nova Scotia keeping its old seal) by legislation at both the provincial and federal levels before *Lenoir v. Ritchie* reached the Supreme Court of Canada.[96] Yet it is of some historical interest. As a legal matter, the seal question was the fussy one of determining what formalities applied to the replacement of one seal by another. At this level, the debate was between Young and Alexander James. Young began, a bit self-consciously perhaps, by denying that the question was only one of 'peculiar or superstitious reverence.' Rather, it was one pertaining to 'a symbol of the supremacy of the great Empire to which we owe so much, and of the royal power which claims our affection as well as our obedience.'[97] On it depended not only the validity of the challenged QC appointments but also that of many official acts taken since 1869. To resolve it, Young indulged himself in pages of examination of the 'mysterious efficacy' of the Great Seal of the British monarch through the triumphant march of English history. Based on its 'ancient and modern uses and vicissitudes,' Young concluded that the coming into force of the new seal had depended entirely on the decision made in London that there should be a new seal, not on its adoption in Nova Scotia or on compliance with any further formalities. This rendered the QC appointments challenged by Ritchie (and every other action taken under the old seal since 1869) invalid. In contrast, James (Young's one-time law student) read the English authorities, especially Hale on Crown Pleas, as establishing that a new seal could only come into force after a date certain had been set and publicly announced. Since neither had happened to bring the seal of 1869 into force in Nova Scotia, the pre-Confederation seal was still the seal in force. His dissent was a technical one.

At another level, the questions raised by the seal débâcle were clearly more political than legal. Would Nova Scotia be allowed to keep the seal it wanted and which it had brought with it into Confederation, perhaps as an abiding symbol of a more independent past? Who was going to make that decision, authorities in London and Ottawa or the anti-confederate government in Halifax? Or would the court decide? At this level, the debate was between Young and the florid Lewis Wilkins, who put the seal controversy into the context of provincial autonomy and independence, if only on a symbolic and miniature scale. Wilkins declared his 'unqualified admiration of the patriotic cabinet, who appear to have clung with enthusiasm, – constitutionally or not, I am not called on to determine – to the old seal – the time honoured symbol of country, associated with the hallowed memory of that glory which had just departed from the '*haud inamabile regnum*' that once owned the Vice-regal sway *Cornwallis*.'[98] Young's answer was to concentrate on the Great Seal as 'a symbol of the supremacy of the great Empire to which we owe so much, and of the royal power which claims our affection as well as our obedience.' These words suggest that Young's real concerns were ones of political hierarchy and obedience, not the formalities by which one seal was validly replaced by another. From this vantage point, the arcane debate about ancient and modern seals between Young and Wilkins takes on more significance than might initially appear warranted. It shows Young articulating a vision of Confederation (and of the place of Nova Scotia and of other provinces within it) that is only implicit in his handling of the issue that looks like the more important one, that is, the question of the regal status and powers of the lieutenant-governor. It was a vision in which the provinces and provincial institutions, including symbolic ones, were subordinate to Ottawa and through Ottawa to London. The conclusion that provincial legislation was valid because the colonial secretary concluded it would be was of a piece with this vision, even though it resulted in *Lenoir v. Ritchie* being sustained in provincial legislation. Colonial office opinion, not independent judicial interpretation of the constitutional document, was determinative in constitutional adjudication. Similarly, the view that legislation could not be challenged once it had gone 'into operation' – meaning that it had not been disallowed – suggests Young saw provincial authority as being essentially dependent on the political management of federalism at higher and central levels of government. All this fits rather neatly with his comments in *Windsor & Annapolis* to the effect that the federal government was the 'larger and controlling power' as between two fundamentally subordinate powers.

When the pieces of Young's thinking from across the cases are reconstructed in this way, it seem plausible to conclude that he thought Ritchie's fundamental argument in *Lenoir v. Ritchie* – that provincial executives had no inherent Crown powers – was so obviously correct that it did not even have to be judicially decided. Desbarres and Hugh McDonald presumably agreed. So too, apparently, did James, who did not disagree with Young on the status of the lieutenant governor but only on the technicalities of Crown law as they pertained to the seal. An interesting possibility is that even Wilkins accepted that the subordinate position of the province within the post-Confederation constitution was beyond dispute. Despite his obvious support for Nova Scotia's continuing independence and autonomy, he invested all his energy in preserving the province's pre-Confederation seal and none in preserving the province's pre-Confederation executive powers.[99] Young and Wilkins were also more similar than dissimilar in one other fundamental respect: they thought of constitutional law as having political dimensions that were beyond their role as judges but that also took precedence to what they did as judges. Young's reliance on colonial office despatches and on the decision of the federal government not to disallow legislation are very substantial evidence of this belief. It can also be seen, however, in Wilkins's holding that the constitutionality of the decision of the Nova Scotia Cabinet to hold to the old seal was not for him to decide. To put the point in the language used earlier, Young, Wilkins and, by extension, the other judges in *Lenoir v. Ritchie*, were very pre-formalist. Of course, given their generation, this seems unsurprising. But their formalism reinforces the speculations offered above about the importance of generational change to the court's evolution through the late nineteenth century.

Judicial acceptance of the subordinate position of the provinces is also apparent in another decision from the relatively busy year of 1876, *Woodworth v. Troop*.[100] Woodworth was the obstreperous Tory member from Kentville who went too far in 1874 when he rose in his place to accuse the provincial secretary of corruption. He then refused to read a prescribed apology from the Bar of the House, 'with the doors open,' after the charges were shown to be unfounded. By resolution, he was found in contempt and ordered ejected by the sergeant-at-arms.[101] Woodworth sued for trespass, complaining in the language required by the pleading conventions of the day that he had been assaulted and beaten 'and with force and violence illegally ejected and expelled.' The presiding judge at trial was Justice Hugh McDonald, who instructed the jury to hold for Woodward if they found that he had not been obstructing the proceedings of the House when ejected.[102] With these instructions they did just that, awarding Woodward five hundred dollars in damages.

McDonald's instructions had been based on two pre-Confederation Privy Council rulings, one from Newfoundland and the other from Dominica.[103] Their gist was that colonial legislatures did not inherently possess the powers of the British House of Commons to sit as a court and to hold members or others in contempt and to impose punishments.[104] They were instead limited to the essentially administrative power of removing members where necessary to prevent an actual obstruction of proceedings. This power they held under the ordinary common law. The broader power to deal with contempt was part of the *'lex et consuetudo Parliamenti,'* a law that was 'peculiar' to the British Parliament. In contradiction of older rulings, the Privy Council thereby confirmed a fundamental distinction in authority and status between colonial legislatures and their English model.[105]

The Liberal members of the House of Assembly appealed Woodworth's verdict to the full court. According to their counsel, including the soon-to-be Justice Robert Weatherbe, the appeal raised the fundamental question of whether a provincial legislature had the same powers as the British Parliament to regulate its internal affairs, specifically by holding members in contempt. This was understood to have implications for the place of the provinces within Confederation: a negative answer would be consistent with the constitutional theories of the centralists that provincial legislatures were akin to municipal councils, while a positive answer would be consistent with the expectations for the provinces of advocates of provincial rights.[106]

The appeal was dismissed by a majority of 3–1. Justice John W. Ritchie, the author of *Keefe v. McLennan*, wrote the majority opinion, with Justices William Desbarres and (not surprisingly) Hugh McDonald concurring. Ritchie found both the argument that the House of Assembly was beyond the jurisdiction of the court in the regulation of its internal affairs and the more specific claim that the House could adjudicate and punish contempt 'wholly untenable.'[107] The decisions of the Privy Council meant that 'no inherent right to such powers can, with any reason, be claimed for a Provincial Legislature.' The same absolute principle prevailed on the unsuccessful appeal of the Liberals to the Supreme Court of Canada.[108] At both levels, the rationale for forceful application of the Privy Council authorities was manifestly reinforced by the view that Woodworth had not only not done anything wrong, but had actually done what he was obligated to do as a representative of the people.[109] Here, party political allegiances probably played a role. For example, Ritchie had been a Tory, like Woodworth. But perhaps more importantly, he had been a member of the Conservative government of Charles Tupper that had brought Nova Scotia into Confederation. He no doubt shared Woodworth's antipathy to his legislative tormentors, the Anti-confederate Liberals. But independently of the politics, the unequivocal vindication of Woodworth looks understandable. He had recent Privy Council authorities on his side that were not in any obvious way overtaken by Confederation. In addition, an 1875 amendment to the BNA Act had clarified the authority of the Dominion Parliament to pass legislation giving itself the powers and privileges of the British Parliament while being silent as to the provinces.[110] This strongly undermined any argument that the provinces had the same authority inherently or through the general language of either the BNA Act or, the Colonial Laws Validity Act.[111]

And yet, it is surprising that the judges who ruled for Woodworth did so largely without expressing any concern about the inescapable implication that the provincial legislatures were inferior bodies. In the Nova Scotia Supreme Court, Wilkins alone raised such concerns. In another dissent full of the Latin for which he was infamous, he argued that no matter how limited the inherent powers of a colonial legislature might be, it was a 'necessary incident to its status, and essential to the performance of its functions, that it may exact from a member an apology for that which the House had resolved to have been a breach of the privileges of the House.'[112] Protection against majority abuse lay not with the courts but in the accountability of each member and of members collectively to their constituents. It was a maxim of practical government and a principle of law, drawn by Wilkins from an American case on the inherent powers of the House of Representatives, that 'public functionaries must be left at liberty to exercise the power which the people have entrusted to them.'[113] This was 'indispensable to the attainment of the ends of their creation.' The Nova Scotia House of Assembly, like the House of Commons at Ottawa, was composed of 'British subjects, proudly conscious that they are such, possessing, relatively to its number, as large an amount of common sense, intellectual capacity, reverence for law and liberty, and knowledge for the broad leading principles of law, as can be predicated of any other Legislative Assembly under the British Crown, the House of Commons of Great Britain alone excepted.'[114]

There is no doubt that the implications Wilkins saw in the majority decision were there to be drawn, or at least recognized, by the other judges. Two judges of the Supreme Court of Canada saw them, albeit from very different angles, with Nova Scotia's own William Henry again being emphatically opposed to provincial pretensions and Ontario's William Buell Richards being surprisingly concerned about equality between and across Canadian legislative bodies.[115] The important point, however, is that the other judges of the Nova Scotia Supreme Court did not even see it as necessary to respond to Wilkins and his concerns. It may be that they took his long tirade, especially the digression into American law, to be simply beside the point. The case before them was governed by binding authority and that was that. Still, especially in light of the background of *Lenoir v. Ritchie*, it seems likely that the Nova Scotia judges approved of the law that they were mandated to apply by the Privy Council. Apart from this being convenient politics for most of them, it may well have been that the law resonated with their general understandings of the basically hierarchal relationship between Ottawa and the provinces.

The powers and privileges of the House of Assembly came back before the court in 1893, two years after it had decided *R. v. Ronan*. The case was *Thomas v. Haliburton*, eventually decided on appeal in the Privy Council as *Fielding v. Thomas* in 1895.[116] It was an appeal by Premier W.S. Fielding and his Liberal caucus from a jury verdict ordering that they pay two hundred dollars in damages to Thomas, the conservative Mayor of Truro, for having had him arrested and imprisoned.[117] It all arose from the petition that Thomas had circulated accusing Lawrence, the recorder of the town and a Liberal member of the House of Assembly, of using his position as a member to increase his salary as recorder. By resolution passed by the Liberal majority, the House judged this to be a libel that, under provincial legislation passed in 1876, constituted a breach of House privileges.[118] The same resolution summoned Thomas to attend, which he did, after which he was asked to withdraw while the

House deliberated. Upon being recalled to be reprimanded, he refused. The House then ordered him arrested for his contempt and jailed for forty-eight hours, which indeed he was, until released under habeas corpus. Like Woodworth before him, Thomas then successfully sued, with the jury being instructed by Justice Charles Townshend that the provincial legislature had exercised powers that provincial legislatures did not possess and could not give to themselves.

The case was different from Woodworth's in important ways. The House was now claiming jurisdiction over the actions of a non-member which had occurred beyond the walls of Province House. It had presumed the power to imprison, making untenable any argument that it was not punishing but merely protecting legislative processes from ongoing obstruction. The House had acted on provincial legislation that had not existed in 1876, but the validity of this legislation was questionable. It purported to give the House the powers and privileges of the Dominion House of Commons which, under federal legislation, were those of the British House of Commons. But whereas the federal legislation was expressly authorized by the BNA Act, the provincial legislation was not.[119] Further, even if the provincial legislation was valid in some aspects, it was arguably invalid on division of powers grounds to the extent that it dealt with libel and contempt as criminal matters, for section 91(27) of the BNA Act gave jurisdiction over the criminal law to Parliament.

On the other hand, the general constitutional environment had changed significantly since 1876. When Woodworth's case had been decided, the status of the provincial governments had been very much an open question. But in 1884, it had been held by the Privy Council in *Hodge* that the principle that a statutory (and therefore inferior) body could not sub-delegate its powers had no application to provincial legislatures because they were not, as Hodge had argued, inferior statutory bodies. Instead, they were declared to have an authority as plenary within the limits of section 92, as was the legislative authority of the imperial Parliament itself. Unmistakably, this represented the emergence of the provinces as an equal and autonomous order of government, on a foundation of inherent authority and status that had survived the transfer of legislative jurisdictions to the Dominion. This understanding of Confederation was confirmed and extended in 1892 by the ruling in *Receiver-General for New Brunswick v. Maritime Bank*, where the Privy Council confirmed that lieutenant governors did indeed directly represent the Crown.

Accordingly, there were good reasons for thinking that in *Fielding v. Thomas*, a different approach from that taken in *Woodworth* was available and even mandated by broader constitutional developments. These developments and their significance were the foundations of Attorney General Longley's arguments for the validity of the provincial legislation. In particular, he relied on *Maritime Bank* to claim that the Nova Scotia House of Assembly had come into Confederation as an independent legislature, enjoying all the powers and privileges of a legislative body under British constitutional principles, on terms that preserved and guaranteed that independence. Accepting this argument involved little more than adding to the already established equality between provincial and federal institutions. Accepting it two years after *R. v. Ronan*, where the court had partly based an expansive reading of provincial legislative powers on the centrality of those powers to the whole Confederation scheme, might have seemed particularly compelling and perhaps even straightforward.

Instead, the court deadlocked, sending the case to the Privy Council on appeal essentially from the jury verdict based on Townshend's instruction that the provincial legislation was invalid. One of the judges who held for the province was Weatherbe. For the most part, his reasoning consisted of showing why the provincial legislation was not invalid on division of powers grounds as criminal law. The details of this argument are less important than its premise, that the province had exclusive jurisdiction to deal with the constitution and powers of the provincial legislature, including the adoption of the powers and privileges of the British House of Commons, so long as it did not use this jurisdiction in ways that crossed the line between civil and criminal law. The power of the provinces to otherwise adopt and to apply the powers and privileges of the British and Canadian parliaments was virtually taken for granted. He was joined by J. Norman Ritchie, the same Ritchie who had fought for his precedence at the bar in 1876 by denying the continuing connection of the province to the Crown, and who, by implication, now seemed to embrace at least aspects of the provincial constitutional continuity that he had, as litigant, denied.

On the other side was Graham, who was joined by James McDonald, the chief justice. Like Weatherbe, Graham decided the case on the division of powers issue but with a contrary result. The libel with which Thomas had been charged, if it was a libel, was a criminal one and therefore beyond the scope of provincial legislation. But again, as with Weatherbe's contrary view, the underlying premises are more important than where they led Graham on the criminal law question. The principle one was that although the provincial legislatures could legislate on their privileges, they had no authority to adopt legislation giving themselves the privileges, powers, or immunities of either the Canadian or British House of Commons. Specifically, the legislatures had no inherent authority to make laws giving to themselves the power to imprison for contempt, and there was nothing in either the BNA Act or the Colonial Laws Validity Act that gave them this power implicitly. The authority for these conclusions was the Privy Council rulings from before confederation that denied parity between colonial legislatures and the Parliament of the United Kingdom as a court of record. But it was also the opinion of three federal ministers of justice and two imperial law officers of the Crown. Graham's reasoning thus had parallels to the deference that Chief Justice Young had shown to official and political opinion in *Lenoir v. Ritchie.* It also had parallels to his disagreement with Weatherbe in *R. v. Ronan*. There, Graham had scolded Weatherbe for his formalism, saying that 'Hardly anything was to be gained ... by calling a thing a name.' Two years later, in *Thomas v. Haliburton,* he linked judicial interpretation of the constitution to ministerial interpretation and, in particular, to federal ministerial interpretation. In both respects, it was the younger Graham who exhibited the greater continuing reliance on the older, pre-formalist methodologies.

Unlike the Liberal Assemblymen of 1876, who had appealed *Woodworth v. Troop* to the Supreme Court of Canada, Fielding and the Liberal Assemblymen of 1893 took their appeal directly to the Privy Council. There, Fielding and Weatherbe were vindicated in a judgment that, in typical Privy Council fashion, implied that the case was an easy and straightforward one. The provincial legislation was valid either under section 92 (1) of the BNA Act (under which each legislature was given authority to make laws on the constitution of the province), or under section 5 of the Colonial Laws Validity Act (under which colonial representative assemblies were given a comparable authority). These legislative rights extended to conduct that was a criminal offence as long as the legislation dealt with the offence for the protection of members in House of Assembly proceedings. No conflict or even tension between the pre-Confederation cases that portrayed all colonial legislatures as inferior legislatures and the post-Confederation cases that portrayed the legislatures and executive branches of the Canadian provinces in such different terms was discussed or even acknowledged. Indeed, *Woodworth v. Troop* was not even mentioned.

Viewed against the backdrop of *Woodworth v. Troop* and *Lenoir v. Ritchie, Fielding v. Thomas* suggests an enduring and intriguing tension between the decisions of the Nova Scotia Supreme Court in division of powers cases and its decisions in these three status cases. This tension is captured neatly in the disagreements between Weatherbe and Graham, not only in *Fielding v. Thomas,* but also in *R. v. Ronan.* In *Ronan,* as well as in *McDougall* and *McKenzie,* Weatherbe argued strenuously for limits on provincial legislative authority that he correctly perceived as a threat to the efficacy of the federal power over trade and commerce. In that context, he argued the letter of the Privy Council rulings and ignored their underlying spirit, which was running strongly in favour of broad rather than narrow construction of provincial legislative powers. But in *Fielding v. Thomas,* he was most prepared to see and to follow the implications of another underlying theme in Privy Council jurisprudence, that the provinces were not subordinate but coordinate governments within Canadian federalism. In contrast, Graham resisted these underlying themes of coordinate federalism in *Fielding v. Thomas* but seemed to follow the letter and the spirit of Privy Council jurisprudence in *R. v. Ronan.* In the latter, he had argued for a broad reading of provincial legislative powers, in fidelity to what he had portrayed as the great legacy of *Keefe v. McLennan,* but also because he was prepared to anticipate where the underlying premises of the Privy Council's decisions would take it in the future.

In effect, Weatherbe and Graham traded adjudicative approaches. Unquestionably, this could have happened for reasons that had little to do with general theories of Confederation or of the BNA Act. It is hard, for example, to believe that they were not respectively influenced by the obvious political overtones of *Fielding v. Thomas.* Weatherbe's political allegiances had been Liberal. These were neatly served by his ruling in favour of Fielding and the other Liberal members of the Assembly. He had the additional satisfaction of vindicating the arguments he had made as losing counsel in *Woodworth,* where of course, he had represented the Liberal majority of an earlier era. Similarly, Graham's strong ties to the Conservative Party, including his personal friendship with John S.D. Thompson, were served by his finding that the verdict against Fielding was valid.

It is also possible that the Nova Scotia judges were simply unable, in what might be called their window of opportunity during the early years of Confederation, to achieve an understanding of the constitution that was large enough to address both jurisdictional and status questions in a way that achieved an overarching coherence in one direction or the other. The combination of a decentralist reading of the division of powers with a centralist understanding of the BNA Act on the question of sovereignty, may not have been exceptional in the 1870s, when the relationship between provincial jurisdictional claims and the provincial claim to sovereignty may have been recognized by few and understood by even fewer. But it was an unusual combination by 1893. By then, whether provincialist or centralist, understandings of the BNA Act tended to align the jurisdictional and the status questions in consistent directions. But not in Nova Scotia. There, a majority of the judges involved in *Fielding v. Thomas*, including the most able, appeared to hold to the dichotomy after it had been overtaken by Privy Council jurisprudence.

Nova Scotia's distinctiveness in this regard is supported by comparing the deadlock that occurred in *Fielding v. Thomas* with the decision of the Ontario Court of Appeal, a decade earlier, in *Hodge v. The Queen*, as well as with the decision of the New Brunswick Supreme Court in 1888 in *Maritime Bank*.[120] In the former, a provincial high court anticipated the Privy Council view by declaring provincial legislative powers to be of plenary quality. In the latter, another provincial high court anticipated the Privy Council by extending the same basic theory of Confederation to conclude that provincial governments included the Crown, thereby confirming that they were sovereign governments within their delimited spheres. In contrast, in 1893, after the Privy Council had upheld both of these rulings, Nova Scotia's high court was unable to cleanly apply the underlying principles to the question of powers and privileges. The context was different of course, in that *Fielding* was, unlike *Hodge* and *Maritime Bank*, governed by pre-confederation Privy Council rulings that were adverse to the provinces. It was also different because there was a direct consequence in *Fielding v. Thomas* to federal legislative jurisdiction that was not present in the other two cases. Nevertheless, reaching the conclusion that the pre-Confederation precedents on colonial legislative status had been overtaken by jurisprudential developments after and within confederation should not have required much of a leap, at least not for any court that was understanding and accepting the central premises of the Privy Council jurisprudence.

One alternative explanation for this resistance is that the Nova Scotia cases were political in a more fundamental sense. The political context for constitutional adjudication in Nova Scotia was unique. Agitation for 'provincial rights' was heard in all provinces with increasing volume through the 1880s and 1890s, but only in Nova Scotia did this agitation extend to the promotion of repeal as government policy.[121] It does not seem implausible to suggest that public men such as Ritchie, Young, and Graham, all of whom were deeply committed to Confederation, responded to that political context in their adjudication of constitutional cases. This did not necessarily present any obstacle to the adoption of a generous interpretation of provincial legislative powers. Indeed, it may have provided a pragmatic rationale for such interpretative generosity. Judicial restraint maximized Nova Scotia's 'home rule' and thereby weakened the case for continuing resistance based on the jurisdictional restrictiveness of confederation. Local conditions had a different connotation, however, in cases that suggested equality of sovereignty and independence for the provinces. Such cases threatened the Dominion's capacity for ultimate control over provincial governments, including the government that was prepared at least to flirt with secession. In such a context, full acceptance of the equality and independence of the provinces may have seemed particularly at odds with nation building when viewed through a Nova Scotian lens.

Concluding Thoughts

In both the division of powers and the status cases, the experience of the Nova Scotia Supreme Court was one of continuity despite significant changes in the court's membership, and despite the growing presence of definitive adjudicative pronouncements from London. This continuity stands in significant contrast to the transformation that took place in the court's adjudication methodology. But this difference masks an underlying consistency. In both its change and its continuity, the court responded to a set of local influences as much as it did to the influence of the Privy Council.[122] This was most apparent in the status cases, where the court can be said to have ultimately baulked at the Privy Council's doctrinal lead. The status cases therefore suggest that the court's responsiveness to local influences was sometimes stronger than its responsiveness to the influence of the Privy Council. But the court's responsiveness to local context can also be seen at work in the division of powers cases, where it reinforced and anticipated the direction of Privy Council influence. In those cases, the court's best judge lifted the court from the doctrinal confusion that the Privy Council had created by taking his colleagues back to the court's own pre-Privy

Council jurisprudence. More elliptically, local influences can also be seen in operation in the transformation of the court's adjudicative approach. In that dimension, the undoubted influence of the Privy Council rulings as models of modern constitutional adjudication competed for influence with changes in court membership that transformed the court's ideological composition. Specifically, those changes brought to the fore a new generation of Nova Scotian judges who represented the new professionalism that was in the process of transforming the Nova Scotian legal landscape before the Privy Council had decided its first case under the BNA Act.

Thus, the Nova Scotia Supreme Court cannot be said to have become fully captive to the Privy Council by the early 1880s, or even by 1893. This is demonstrated most clearly in the persistence with which the court melded a broad reading of provincial legislative powers with a restrictive approach to provincial constitutional stature. In this chapter I have offered some possible explanations for the court's persistence in taking different directions in the division of powers and the status cases. I have considered the contributing influence of the political affiliations of particular judges, and the influence of interpersonal dynamics among them, as well as the possibility that the judges were simply not up to the task of crafting a constitutional jurisprudence that embraced both jurisdictional and status questions. But more importantly, I have suggested that the dichotomy between the two branches of the court's constitutional jurisprudence reflects the fundamentally political nature of that jurisprudence. Political considerations endured into the 1890s, despite the growing acceptance by the court of a legal formalism that sought to emphasize the separation between law and politics.

My interpretation suggests a parallel between the constitutional jurisprudence of the Nova Scotia Supreme Court and Nova Scotia's accommodation to Confederation in the political realm. By the 1880s, the complexity and ambiguity of the Nova Scotian reaction to Confederation in politics expressed itself through the popularity of a local Liberal government that advocated repeal (or at least a substantial reworking) of Confederation with virtually simultaneous majority support in federal elections for the Conservative Party, the federal party that was most unequivocally committed to centralism, to integration, and to the pre-eminence of national identities and priorities over local ones. It may be that in the realm of constitutional adjudication, the reflection of this complexity and ambiguity can be seen in the fashioning of a jurisprudence that was provincialist on the scope of provincial legislative powers but centralist on questions about the constitutional status of the provincial institutions that held those powers. Such a jurisprudence gave ample scope for provincial legislative initiative within the jurisdictional boundaries of the new Confederation while keeping the provinces, and perhaps one province in particular, under the supervising authority of the new Dominion.

On this view, Nova Scotia's continuing flirtation with secession made judicial benevolence in the construction of provincial legislative powers as sensible in a Nova Scotian context as it made judicial acceptance of the autonomy and independence of the provinces difficult. If so, what the constitutional jurisprudence of the Nova Scotia Supreme Court in the late nineteenth century may show above all else is that Nova Scotia's judges in this period, like Nova Scotians in general, were still uncertain about what being Canadian was going to mean for being Nova Scotian. One result was the persistence into the 1890s of at least some of the elements of the local adjudicative autonomy that had, on the surface of things, quietly disappeared in the late 1870s.

NOTES

I would like to express my thanks to Scott Nesbitt for his dedicated, insightful and otherwise exceptional research assistance in the preparation of this chapter, and to Aubrey Hilliard, who assisted with preliminary research. I have also benefited greatly from the comments of the editors on an earlier draft, and from comments and encouragement from Richard Devlin, William Laurence, and Blake Brown, all of whom also graciously agreed to read that earlier draft. I owe a particular debt to the scholarship of Philip Girard on Nova Scotia's nineteenth-century legal culture, as well as to our conversations during the preparation of this chapter.

1 J.G. Snell, 'Relations Between the Maritimes and the Supreme Court of Canada: The Pattern of the Early Years,' in P.B. Waite et al., *Law in a Colonial Society: The Nova Scotia Experience* (Toronto: Carswell 1984), 145–7 and 160–3.

2 J.T. Saywell, *The Lawmakers: Judicial Power and the Shaping of Canadian Federalism* (Toronto: Osgoode Society for Canadian Legal History and University of Toronto Press 2002); see, e.g., 56.

3 G.B. Baker, 'The Reconstitution of Upper Canadian Legal Thought in the Late-Victorian Empire,' *Law and History Review* 3 (1985): 219–292.

4 R.C.B. Risk, 'Canadian Courts Under the Influence,' *University of Toronto Law Journal* 40 (1990): 687–737; Saywell, *The Lawmakers*, 69–72.

5 See R.C.B. Risk, 'Constitutional Scholarship in the Late Nineteenth Century: Making Federalism Work,' *University of Toronto Law Journal* 46 (1996): 427–57, where the same transition is traced through the emergence and early development of the new field of Canadian constitutional law scholarship.

6 Saywell, *The Lawmakers*, 68–77, 56.

7 Thomas Cooley, *A Treatise on the Constitutional Limitations Which Rest Upon the Legislative Power of the States of the American Union*, 5th ed. (Boston: Little Brown 1874). It was a standard authority in Canadian courts in the early years of Confederation, and very important to the constitutional theories of the advocates of provincial right; see R.C. Vipond, *Liberty & Community: Canadian Federalism and the Failure of the Constitution* (Albany: State University of New York Press 1991), 39–41, 134, 175, and178. In Nova Scotia, perhaps the most exceptional reliance on American constitutional case law occurred in *Woodworth v. Troop* (1876–7), 11 N.S.R. 84, where Justice Lewis M. Wilkins, writing in dissent, relied on the decision of the United States Supreme Court in *Anderson v. Dunn*, 6 Wheaton 204; 19 U.S. Rep. 204 (1821), as authority for the power of the Nova Scotia House of Assembly (and other colonial legislatures) to deal with contempt.

8 *Windsor & Annapolis Railway Company v. Western Counties Railway Co.*, in B. Russell, ed., *The Equity Decisions of The Hon. John W. Ritchie, Judge in Equity of the Province of Nova Scotia, 1873–1882* (Halifax: A. & W. Mackinley 1883), 287.

9 Section 108 of the BNA Act said simply that 'The Public Works and Property of Each Province, enumerated in the Third Schedule to this Act, shall be the Property of Canada'; (U.K.), 30 & 31, c. 3. Item 6 of the Third Schedule was 'Railways and Railway Stocks, Mortgages, and other Debts due by Railway Companies.' The history of the development of railways through the Annapolis Valley is included in the broader history by G.M. Haliburton, 'The Development of Railways in Nova Scotia' (MA thesis, Dalhousie University 1955). The development of provincial railways was perennially a major concern and a source of considerable controversy in Nova Scotian politics through the 1870s, 1880s and 1890'. It was a major element of the persistent gap between provincial legislative and governmental activity and provincial fiscal capacity, which contributed to or justified continuing provincial unhappiness with Confederation and particularly its financial terms; see J.M. Beck, *Politics of Nova Scotia: Volume One: 1710–1896* (Halifax: Four East Publications 1985), 163, 174, 181, 192-212, 216–19, and 227–8. For the pre-Confederation background to these post-Confederation challenges

see Rosemarie Langhout, 'Developing Nova Scotia: Railways and Public Accounts, 1849–1867,' *Acadiensis* 14(2) (1984–85): 3.

10 N.J. MacKinnon, 'Ritchie, John William,' *DCB*, 11: 754–5. As leader of the government in the Legislative Council in 1866, Ritchie would have been closely associated with the government that had given Annapolis & Windsor the twenty-one-year possession that the Dominion government had terminated.

11 *Windsor & Annapolis Railway Co. v. Western Counties Railway Co.* (1877–9), 12 N.S.R. 376. On Young, see J.M. Beck, 'Young, Sir William,' *DCB*, 11: 943–9. For an interesting perspective on Young's intellectual formation as a lawyer, see W. H. Laurence, 'Acquiring the Law: The Personal Library of William Young, Halifax, 1835,' *Dalhousie Law Journal* 21 (1998); 490–515. Laurence questions the view, accepted by Beck, that Young was not very learned in the law. The view owes much to Benjamin Russell, 'Reminiscences of the Nova Scotia Judiciary,' *Dalhousie Review* 5 (1925–6): 504.

12 *Windsor & Annapolis*. This summary of James's judgment, including the quotations within this and the immediately following paragraphs, is from 409, 413, 415–16, 421, and 423.

13 Here, James noted that the federal legislation that had created the Intercolonial had not declared the previously distinct pieces of railway to be for the general advantage of Canada but had instead simply proceeded to knit them together as a single system on the assumption that they already were, under the BNA Act, within the legislative authority of Parliament. Apart from the fact that the Windsor line was connected to the Inter-colonial, it was good enough for James that it was a line like those that Parliament had already included in the Inter-colonial. In his view, only 'private railways' were intended to have been left with the provinces.

14 James went so far (at 423) as to say that he read the Act as referring to 'Windsor and Annapolis' when it spoke of a railway company generically. He also expressed confidence (at 424) that Windsor and Annapolis would receive compensation for its loss, 'because the people of all parties have too much pride in their country and its institutions to permit private parties to be sufferers from the acts of their rulers.'

15 Ibid., 407 and 412.

16 Ibid., 412.

17 Marshall's constitutional jurisprudence is reviewed in detail, with particular attention to its role in nation building, in J. E. Smith, *John Marshall: Definer of a Nation* (New York: Henry Holt 1996). As described by Alexander James and as practised (or attempted) in constitutional cases by James and other Canadian judges of the 1870s and 1880s, judicial states-

manship in constitutional law exhibited elements of a legal consciousness that has been described as 'pre-classical' to differentiate it from the legal formalism or positivism that became dominant in the last decades of the 1800s. On pre-classical legal consciousness, see E. Mensch, 'The History of Mainstream Legal Thought,' in D. Kairys, ed., *The Politics of Law: A Progressive Critique* (New York: Pantheon Books 1982), 19–23. For a careful reconstruction of the broadly pre-classical legal culture that was displaced by formalism in one Canadian jurisdiction, see G.B. Baker, 'So Elegant a Web: Providential Order and the Rule of Secular Law in Early Nineteenth-Century Upper Canada,' *University of Toronto Law Journal* 38 (1988); 184. For the affinity between the call of James for judicial statesmanship and the approach taken to constitutional adjudication by many Canadian judges in the 1870s and early 1880s, see Risk, 'Canadian Courts Under the Influence.'

18 James was appointed in 1877 by the Liberal administration of Alexander MacKenzie. He studied law with and was later a partner with Young. He was the first reporter of the Nova Scotia Reports (see Cahill and Phillips, this volume) and, as pointed out by Bernard Hibbitts in this volume, wrote in his preface to the series about the influence of American law on the decisions of the Nova Scotia Supreme Court: (1853), 2 N.S.R. v–vi. He died in 1889, while still on the bench, having been not very productive for a number of years due to illness. See generally, C. Greco, 'The Superior Court Judiciary of Nova Scotia, 1754–1900: A Collective Biography,' in Girard and Phillips, *Essays*, and also, *The Supreme Court of Nova Scotia and Its Judges: 1754–1978* (Halifax: Nova Scotia Barristers' Society 1978).

19 P. Girard, 'The Supreme Court of Nova Scotia, Responsible Government, and the Quest for Legitimacy, 1850–1920,' *Dalhousie Law Journal* 17 (1994): 436 and 432–40. See also as to the general quality of the court in the 1870s, P.B. Waite, *The Man From Halifax: Sir John Thompson, Prime Minister* (Toronto: University of Toronto Press 1985), 6, 52–3, 84–90, and 117–18, and J.M. Beck, *The Government of Nova Scotia* (Toronto: University of Toronto Press 1957), 287–8.

20 These cases were *In Re Precedence of Ritchie, Q.C.* (1876), 11 N.S.R. 450 (*sub non Lenoir v. Ritchie* [hereafter *Lenoir v. Ritchie*], which concerned the provincial power to create QCs; *Woodward v. Troop* (1876), 11 N.S.R. 84, which concerned the powers and privileges of the House of Assembly; and *Keefe v. McLennan* (1876), 11 N.S.R. 5, another ruling by Ritchie that would be celebrated in the court in the 1890s as having correctly defined federal and provincial powers over the liquor trade well before other and higher tribunals.

21 *R. v. McDougall* (1889), 22 N.S.R. 462; *R. v. Ronan* (1891), 23 N.S.R. 421.

22 The *Canada Temperance Act*, S.C. 1878, c. 16, was upheld by the Supreme

Court of Canada in *The Queen v. City of Fredericton* (1879), 3 S.C.R. 505, primarily as a regulation of trade and commerce. It was then also upheld by the Privy Council in *Russell v. The Queen* (1882), 7 A.C. 829, as legislation for the peace, order, and good government of Canada. The Privy Council reached this conclusion by emphasizing the objects of the Act in characterizing it as legislation 'designed for the promotion of public order, safety, or morals.' In contrast, a majority of the judges of the Supreme Court of Canada had emphasized the means (the regulation of the liquor traffic) in characterizing the Act as being on trade and commerce. In *Hodge v. The Queen* (1883), 9 A.C. 117, Ontario regulations that limited the hours during which billiards could be played in taverns were held by the Privy Council to be within provincial jurisdiction. They were regulations 'in the nature of police or municipal regulations of a merely local character for the good government of taverns & C., licensed for the sale of liquors by retail, and such as are calculated to preserve, in the municipality, peace and public decency, and repress drunkenness and disorderly and riotous conduct'; 131. In 1885 in the *McCarthy Act Reference*, the Privy Council struck down the so-called McCarthy Act, a federal liquor licensing statute that made the selling of liquor by retail and wholesale illegal unless authorized under a federal licence; An Act respecting the Sale of Intoxicating Liquors, and the Issue of Licenses Therefore, S.C. 1883, c. 30. Because the case was heard as a reference, no reasons were given for this conclusion, in accordance with the procedure on references in the period.

23 Nova Scotia, *Journals of the House of Assembly* 1889, Appendix 11. [hereafter, Appendix 11] Longley's reference to 'Cartwright's Cases' was a reference to J.R. Cartwright, *Cases Decided on the British North America Act, 1867, in the Privy Council, The Supreme Court of Canada, and the Provincial Courts* (Toronto, 1882–97). By 1889, volumes I, II, and III had been published, with the first two volumes being published in 1882 and volume III appearing in 1887. Volume IV followed in 1892 and volume V in 1897. The 1886 Act was called An Act respecting the Sale of Intoxicating Liquors, S.N.S. 1886, c. 3.

24 P. Girard, 'Weatherbe, Robert,' *DCB*, 14: 1044–6.

25 First, that 'statutory transfer' of the Windsor Branch under section 108 'had not the effect of vesting in Canada any other or larger interests in these railways than that which belonged to the province,' and second, on the basis of the principle that statutes 'must not be deemed to take away or extinguish the right of the respondent company, unless it appear, by express words, or by plain implication, that it was the intention of the Legislature to do so.' The conclusion about section 108 was an assertion of opinion without any supporting reasoning and the point of statutory interpretation was pre-

sented as straightforward; *Western Counties Railway Co. v. Windsor and Annapolis Railway Co.* (1881–2), App. Cas. 178, 188. The original decision in the Nova Scotia Supreme Court had been based on a demurrer and had sent the matter back for trial before Ritchie. His predictable ruling for Windsor & Annapolis was appealed, again with predictable lack of success, to the full court: (1881), 14 N.S.R. 280. Again, James dissented. The appeal to the Privy Council was from this later ruling of the Nova Scotia Supreme Court.

26 Young had stated that the BNA Act had established 'new sets of legislatures, deriving their authority from it, and plainly distinguishable from the legislatures it had superseded.' He had held that although both levels of 'new' legislatures were subordinate, 'the Dominion Legislature has the controlling and the largest power, but a power far inferior to that of the Imperial Parliament, because limited and restrained in its exercise, and expressly excluded from whole classes of subjects assigned to the local legislatures'; *Windsor & Annapolis*, 404–5. It seems clear that these remarks were meant to repudiate the notion that the provinces were a continuing order of government that had retained all powers and sovereign status not expressly taken from them. This is important background to Young's role in *Lenoir v. Ritchie*, where the issue was (or might have been) the continuity of Nova Scotia's direct connection to the British Crown, with the independent sovereignty this implied. It also shows that although Young seemed to share Ritchie's idea that provincial jurisdiction over property and civil rights was a kind of shelter for those rights from federal encroachment, he did not equate this idea with provincial autonomy. Indeed, in *Windsor & Annapolis*, he blithely contemplated disallowance by Ottawa of any provincial law on property and civil rights that interfered with federal management of railways.

27 Ibid., 191. A much more famous example of a similar admonition is found in *Citizens' Insurance v. Parsons* (1881), 7 A.C. 96, 109. Saywell makes the point that it was not an admonition that the Privy Council itself consistently followed by describing its construction of the trade and commerce power in the same case as a 'momentous voyage of discovery' that went well beyond the question at hand, that is, could the provinces regulate contracts of insurance: Saywell, *The Lawmakers*, 84–6.

28 Baker, 'Reconstitution'; Risk, 'Canadian Courts Under the Influence.'

29 On McDonald, see P.B. Waite, 'McDonald, James,' *DCB*, 14: 686–7. See also P. Girard, 'The Supreme Court of Nova Scotia,' 435. In *Severn v. The Queen* (1878), 2 S.C.R. 70, the Supreme Court of Canada ruled that the provinces had no authority over the licensing of breweries as brewing was held to be

within trade and commerce and thus federal jurisdiction. Beyond brewing, the decision appeared to place manufacturing and wholesale trade under federal control. The argument that the Privy Council had de facto overruled *Severn* with its decision in the *McCarthy Act Reference* was based on the fact that whereas the Privy Council struck down both retail and wholesale provisions of the federal McCarthy Act, the Supreme Court of Canada had struck down only its retail provisions. The implication was that the Privy Council could not have shared the distinction between retail and wholesale that the Supreme Court decision relied upon. In addition, those who argued that *Severn* had been overruled relied on the fact that counsel for both sides during the argument of *McCarthy* in the Privy Council had been dismissive of the distinction between retail and wholesale. See Risk, 'Canadian Courts Under the Influence,' 715–1 and Saywell, *The Lawmakers*, 100–7.

30 Especially *Citizen's Insurance v. Parsons*, where the 'regulation of trade and commerce' was held to encompass political arrangements in regard to trade requiring the sanction of Parliament, interprovincial trade, and the general regulation of trade affecting the whole Dominion, but not the regulation of the contracts of a particular business or trade.

31 *R. v. McDougall* (1889), 22 N.S.R. 462, 472.

32 Waite, *The Man From Halifax*, 102. Waite writes that McDonald was 'no political lion' and that, on the retirement of Chief Justice Young, McDonald was appointed because 'The Dominion government now had the opportunity to unload him, one that they could not pass over.'

33 *McDougall*, 473. McDonald also showed his 'functionalism' in stating that once brewers were held to be still outside provincial jurisdiction because of the continuing applicability of *Severn* (which on the facts only dealt with brewers and not wholesalers), it had to follow that wholesalers had also to be outside provincial jurisdiction because it would 'tend to serious commercial results' to have importers and brewers and distillers subject to different tax and regulatory regimes.

34 Ibid., 480.

35 Weatherbe's understanding of the politics behind the 1886 legislation corresponds to the views of Beck, *The Politics of Nova Scotia*, 229. See also J. Fingard, '"A Great Big Rum Shop": The Drink Trade in Victorian Halifax,' in J.H. Morrison and J. Moreira, *Tempered by Rum: Rum in the History of the Maritime Provinces* (Porters Lake, NS: Pottersfield Press 1988), 96–100. Fingard describes the legislature that passed the 1886 legislation as one 'dominated by temperance men.'

36 This interpretation of Weatherbe fits with *Re: Windsor and Annapolis Railway Co.* (1883), 16 N.S.R. 312, where he alone dissented from the view of the

court that provincial legislation called An Act to Facilitate Arrangements between Railway Companies and their Creditors, S.N.S. 1874, c. 104, was valid under the provincial jurisdiction over property and civil rights in the province. Weatherbe instead concluded that the Act was within the federal power over insolvency and bankruptcy.

37 For Canadian legal realism, particularly in the context of constitutional law, see R.C.B. Risk, 'The Scholars and the Constitution: P.O.G.G. and the Privy Council,' (1996) 23 *Manitoba Law Journal* 23 (1996): 496–523. More broadly on Canadian legal realism, see R.C.B. Risk, 'Volume 1 of the Journal: A Tribute and Belated Review,' *University of Toronto Law Journal* 37 (1987): 193–211. On the American legal realism that significantly influenced the Canadian realists, see M.J. Horwitz, *The Transformation of American Law, 1870–1960: The Crisis of Legal Orthodoxy* (New York: Oxford University Press 1992), 169–212.

38 This tone of irreverence towards the Judicial Committee of the Privy Council was not unique to the judges of the Nova Scotia Supreme Court. It was also much on display, for example, from both counsel and judges during the argument in the Supreme Court of Canada in the *McCarthy Act Reference*, which took place in 1884; see Canada, *Sessional Papers*, 1885, vol. 18, no. 12, 59.

39 Appendix 11, 67.

40 Ibid., 50.

41 The notes of argument did not make it perfectly clear whether Weatherbe thought the mistake lay in the recognition of a de facto provincial trade and commerce power or instead only in calling it the police power.

42 Ibid., 74.

43 Ibid. Longley's argument is at 41–53, with the key portions at 50–2, inclusive. Throughout, his language was recognizably that of the provincial rights understanding of Confederation and, more particularly, of the provincial rights understanding of the relationship between sections 91 and 92; see, e.g., Vipond, *Liberty and Community*, 113–43 and 151–90. See also the descriptions of the arguments by or on behalf of Oliver Mowat in various constitutional cases found in Saywell, *The Lawmakers*, 37–8, 82–3, 95–8, 100–6.

44 Longley was confident that the distinction could not be supported and that it would have to be abandoned just as the attempt to distinguish between retail and wholesale had been abandoned in the *McCarthy Act Reference*.

45 For biographical information on J. Norman Ritchie and Charles Townshend, see Greco, 'The Superior Court Judiciary'; Girard, 'The Supreme Court of Nova Scotia' ; and *The Supreme Court of Nova Scotia and Its Judges 1754–*

1978. The information provided by Girard on Townshend is much more extensive than that provided for Ritchie, as Townshend was eventually to become chief justice and a court historian and therefore warrants greater attention.

46 P. Girard, 'Graham, Wallace,' *DCB*, 14: 431–432.

47 Girard, 'The Supreme Court of Nova Scotia.' See also more broadly P. Girard, 'The Roots of a Professional Renaissance: Lawyers in Nova Scotia, 1850–1910,' *Manitoba Law Journal* 20 (1991): 148–80 and 'The Maritime Provinces, 1850–1939: Lawyers and Legal Institutions,' *Manitoba Law Journal* 23 (1996): 379–405.

48 For dates of appointment on these judges, see Girard, 'The Supreme Court of Nova Scotia.' The short judicial career of John S.D. Thompson (1882–5) is discussed in Waite, *The Man From Halifax*, 116–33. Thompson as judge had only three opportunities to deal with the constitution. The one noted by Waite is *Re Steele Company of Canada* (1884), 17 N.S.R. 49, where the issue was the applicability of the Dominion Winding Up Act to a foreign company. Thompson wrote that the Dominion Parliament had 'in dealing with the subjects assigned to it ... powers as great as that of the United Kingdom where there is no controlling Imperial legislation on the same matter, and where the exclusive powers of the Provincial Parliament are not transgressed.' He rejected the argument that because Canada was a colony that had received its powers from the imperial Parliament, it could only use its powers in relation to persons and rights within her own territory. Thus, he rejected the underlying premise that Dominion legislative power was not sovereign legislative power. While Waite may be right that this shows Thompson's clear-headedness on constitutional matters, such an argument had little chance of succeeding by 1884 and that perhaps explains why only Thompson dealt with it at any length. In *Re: Windsor and Annapolis Railway Co.* (1883), 16 N.S.R. 312 (Weatherbe dissenting), Thompson agreed with Chief Justice McDonald and Justice Rigby that a provincial law for the facilitation of arrangements between railways and their creditors was valid because related to property and civil rights in the province rather than to insolvency. In *Halifax (City) v. The Western Assurance Co.* (1885), 18 N.S.R. 387, he joined a unanimous decision (written by Weatherbe) upholding provincial licensing of federally incorporated insurance companies. Thus Thompson the judge was not particularly centralist.

49 These writings include 'Canadian Courts Under the Influence'; 'Constitutional Scholarship in the Late Nineteenth-Century: Making Federalism Work'; and 'The Scholars and the Constitution: P.O.G.G. and the Privy Council.' See also R.C.B. Risk, 'A.H.F. Lefroy: Common Law Thought in

Late Nineteenth-Century Canada: On Burying One's Grandfather,' *University of Toronto Law Journal* 41 (1991): 307–31 and 'Constitutional Thought in the Late Nineteenth Century,' *Manitoba Law Journal* 20 (1991): 196–203. See also Baker, 'Reconstitution,' for a broader view of the rise of legal formalism within Canadian legal culture. On the rise of legal formalism in the United States, see M.J. Horwitz, 'The Rise of Legal Formalism,' *American Journal of Legal History* 19 (1975): 251–4, and T.C. Grey, 'Langdell's Orthodoxy,' *University of Pittsburgh Law Review* 45 (1983): 1–53.

50 On legal liberalism more generally, see R.M. Gordon, 'Legal Thought and Legal Practice in the Age of American Enterprise,' in G.L. Geison, ed., *Professions and Professional Ideologies in America* (Chapel Hill: University of North Carolina Press 1983) and D. Sugarman, 'The Legal Boundaries of Liberty: Dicey, Liberalism, and Legal Science,' *Modern Law Review* 46 (1983): 102–11.

51 These numbers do not include the court's decisions in *Lenoir v. Ritchie* and *Thomas v. Haliburton* (1893–4), 26 N.S.R. 55. Although both of these cases had division of powers dimensions, they were more fundamentally about the status of the provinces and are discussed later in the text from that perspective. The numbers in the text also do not include *Re: Steel Company of Canada* where the applicability of the federal Winding Up Act to an English company was challenged. The reason is that the majority of the court decided the case (in favour of the Act's applicability) without really addressing the constitutional issue. In addition, the case involved not division of powers between the Dominion and the provinces but rather between the Canadian and the British Parliament.

52 *Keefe v. McLennan* (1876), 11 N.S.R. 5.

53 *Justices of Kings County, ex parte McManus* (1873–5), 15 N.B.R. 535.

54 G. Bale and E.B. Mellett, 'Ritchie, Sir William Johnston,' *DCB*, 12: 895–900; G. Bale, *Chief Justice William Johnstone Ritchie: Responsible Government and Judicial Review* (Ottawa: Carleton University Press 1991).

55 *Keefe v. McLennan*, 11. The other quotations from Ritchie's judgment are from 11–13.

56 Both Ritchies relied on *The License Cases* 5 Howard 504, 46 U.S. Rep. 504 (1847), where licensing laws of Massachusetts, Rhode Island, and New Hampshire that de facto authorized local-option temperance were upheld on federalism grounds; see *McLennan*, 12–13.

57 William Johnston Ritchie's opposition to Confederation is mentioned in Bale, *Chief Justice Ritchie*, 91–5. Little appears to be known of the basis of his opposition, as unlike others on the bench at the time of the Confederation debate who managed to make their views of Confederation known, such as

New Brunswick's Lemuel Wilmot and Nova Scotia's William Young, Ritchie apparently did not explain his opposition publicly. For John W. Ritchie's role in Nova Scotia's participation in Confederation, see MacKinnon, 'Ritchie.'

58 A classic articulation of the argument that the division of powers in section 91 and 92 was designed to give jurisdiction over the economy to the federal government and over 'social issues' or communal life to the provinces is found in A.S. Abel, 'The Neglected Logic of 91 and 92,' *University of Toronto Law Journal* 19 (1969): 487–521. It is itself now neglected.

59 Saywell, *The Lawmakers*, 79.

60 Fisher made the connection in *The Queen v. City of Fredericton* (1879–80), 16 N.B.R. 139, where the New Brunswick court found the Canada Temperance Act to be unconstitutional as an interference with various heads of provincial power, including property and civil rights; see W. Lahey, 'Constitutional Adjudication, Provincial Rights and the Structure of Legal Thought in Late 19th Century New Brunswick,' *University of New Brunswick Law Journal* 39 (1990–1): 185.

61 The other cases were *Re: Windsor and Annapolis Railway Co.* (1883), 16 N.S.R. 312, in which provincial legislation on arrangements between railways and creditors was upheld, and *Halifax (City) v. The Western Assurance Co.* (1885), 18 N.S.R. 387, in which provincial legislation that authorized municipalities to charge licence fees to federally incorporated insurance companies was upheld. Both cases had implications for the difficult financial situation of post-Confederation Nova Scotia.

62 For a thorough discussion of these and other 'liquor cases' as a discrete series of constitutional cases, see Risk, 'Canadian Courts Under the Influence.'

63 Therefore, whereas *Fredericton* (and most cases decided in Canada) had juxtaposed a federal power over trade and commerce to a provincial responsibility for safety, health, order, and morals, *Russell v. The Queen* suggested that the latter set of responsibilities were also federal.

64 Again, these were words and concepts that *Keefe v. McLennan* had used in 1876. The Privy Council applied them under the provincial powers over municipal institutions and local matters, rather than under the provincial jurisdiction over property and civil rights. But this did not change the fact that *Hodge* vindicated the basic point of *Keefe*, and various other provincial court rulings, that the provinces had an authority over the liquor trade that was rooted in a broader provincial authority over public life in the local community.

65 See note 26, above.

66 *Severn v. The Queen*, and *The Queen v City of Fredericton*.

67 *Citizen's Insurance v. Parsons* (1881), 7 App. Cas. 96.

68 The 1886 Act, like the Ontario Act, was part of a general push by the provinces to both drive home the jurisdictional advantage represented by *Hodge* and *McCarthy* and to remove the lingering uncertainties represented by *Russell, Severn* and *Fredericton*. New Brunswick also adopted very similar legislation; see *Danaher v. Peters* (1890), 17 S.C.R. 44, and S.N.B. 1887, c. 4. The Nova Scotian version required licences of both retailers and wholesalers and it made local-option temperance a possibility, through ratepayer plebiscite, for both classes of licences. As to retailing, the principle change made was to reduce the categories of permissible retail licences. Prior to 1886, provincial legislation provided for tavern licences, which permitted the licencee to sell by the glass; shop licences, which permitted sales by the bottle for off-premises consumption; and general licences, which permitted the licencee to sell other goods with liquor for on-premises consumption. Under the 1886 Act, only hotel and shop licences were permitted. Fingard, 'The Drink Trade in Victorian Halifax,' 98–100, describes the legislation as 'a blatant form of class legislation' in two respects. First, because it aimed to protect the access of the upper and middle classes to liquor in their homes and in hotels, while denying the lower and working classes the taverns which were the centre of their social lives. Second, because the restrictions on wholesaling were never as vigilantly enforced as the restrictions on retailing, with the result that the legislation applied more heavily to small than to large proprietors.

69 Appendix 11.

70 Beck, *Politics of Nova Scotia*, 224–37, 240–5 and J.B. Cahill and P. Girard, 'Longley, James Wilberforce' 15, *DCB*, forthcoming.

71 Ibid., 216. The ally was James A. Fraser of Guysborough, writing in 1883, who would be one of the two Fielding Liberals done in by Weeks three years later.

72 *R. v. McDougall*, 92–193.

73 Beck, *Politics of Nova Scotia*, 247. The contrasting positions of Longley and of Weeks on the confederation question are documented in C.D. Howell, 'W.S. Fielding and the Repeal Elections of 1886 and 1887 in Nova Scotia,' Acadiensis 8(2) (1979): 28–46. Despite his opposition to Fielding, Weeks supported the more or less official Liberal party repeal platform whereas Longley, although a member of Fielding's government, represented the part of Fielding's coalition that favoured stronger provincial rights within Confederation, the position that became Fielding's after 1887.

74 *R. v. McKenzie* (1890), 23 N.S.R. 6.

75 *Danaher v. Peters* (1890), 17 S.C.R. 44.

76 *R. v. Ronan* (1891), 23 N.S.R. 421.
77 *A.G. Ontario v. A.G. Canada*, [1896] A.C. 348.
78 *Danaher v. Peters.*
79 *R. v. Ronan*, 431, 433, and 439.
80 Ibid. The most important pages in Graham's judgment were 450–3. The quotations in the following paragraphs are from those pages.
81 The cases were *R. v. McDonald* (1891), 24 N.S.R. 35 and *King v. Gardner* (1892), 25 N.S.R. 48.
82 Girard, 'The Supreme Court of Nova Scotia,' 440–4.
83 An Act for expediting the decision of Constitutional and other Provincial Questions, S.N.S. 1890, c. 9. I am grateful to Philip Girard for suggesting this possibility to me.
84 P. Romney, *Mr. Attorney: The Attorney General for Ontario in Court, Cabinet and Legislature, 1791–1899* (Toronto: Osgoode Society for Canadian Legal History and University of Toronto Press 1986), 242–59; Vipond, *Liberty & Community*, 47–82; Saywell, *The Lawmakers*, 22–3, 49–56, and 124–8.
85 *Liquidators of the Maritime Bank v. Receiver-General for New Brunswick*, [1892] A.C. 437.
86 Beck, *The Government of Nova Scotia* , 172–4.
87 (1879), 3 S.C.R. 575.
88 An Act respecting the Appointment of Queen's Counsel, S.N.S. 1874, c. 20, and An Act to regulate the Precedence of the Bar in Nova Scotia, S.N.S. 1874, c. 21. The power to appoint QCs was one of the prerogative powers that the Crown held independently of the legislature under British constitutional principles. Nova Scotia's legislation therefore raised (or might have raised) the fundamental question of whether the Crown was or was not part of provincial constitutions after 1867.
89 The argument was put forward on Ritchie's behalf by John S.D. Thompson, for whom it must have come naturally enough. Thompson would, of course, become MacDonald's minister of justice and briefly his successor for one, after his own short tenure on the Nova Scotia Supreme Court: see Waite, *The Man From Halifax*, 116–33 and note 54.
90 *Lenoir v. Ritchie* (1879) 3 S.C.R. 575 at 613. On Henry, see P.R. Blakeley, 'Henry, William Alexander,' *DCB*, 11: 378–9.
91 *Lenoir v. Ritchie* (1879), 3 S.C.R. 575 at 634.
92 Romney, *Mr. Attorney*, 250.
93 *Lenior v. Ritchie*, 450.
94 Ibid. The quotations from Young's judgment are at 466–9.
95 Annand was the 'anti-confederate' premier from 1867 to 1875; see Beck, *Politics of Nova Scotia*, 291.

96 Ibid., 193. In respect of the furor that the Great Seal issue caused in the legislature, Beck notes that in the end, it was 'much ado about nothing,' presumably because the problem was fixed with simple federal and provincial legislation that validated actions taken under the old seal and confirmed its continued use. The provincial legislation is at S.N.S. 1877, c. 1, An Act to empower the Lieutenant-governor of the Province in Council to alter and change the Great Seal of the Province, and S.N.S. 1877, c. 2, An Act to ratify and confirm certain Acts and proceedings heretofor had and done under the Great Seal of the Province. The Dominion legislation is at S.C. 1877, c. 3, An Act respecting the Great Seal of the Provinces of Canada, other than Ontario and Quebec.

97 *Lenoir v. Ritchie*. The parts of Wilkins's judgment summarized here, including the quotations, are from 474–7 and 483–4.

98 Wilkins's treatment of the issue included a detailed description of the appearance of the pre-confederation seal. His grand and sweeping account of the hallowed significance of the Great Seal in English and Nova Scotia climaxed with a detailed description of the old seal and of its heraldic allusions that explained why 'the old device challenges our admiration' and questioned the adequacy of any possible substitute. That Wilkins asked (at 485) whether the replacement seal featured, '*Or*, on a *Fesse wavy-azure* between three thistles *proper*, a salmon *naiant argent*?,' indicates the style and level of the analysis.

99 For the prevalence of the view among the 'Confederation generation' that only one sovereign level of government could exist within a state, see Vipond, *Liberty & Community*, 20–7, 30–6 and P.J. Smith, 'The Dream of Political Union: Loyalism, Toryism and The Federal Idea in Pre-Confederation Canada,' in G. Martin, ed., *The Causes of Canadian Confederation* (Fredericton: Acadiensis Press 1990). For the operation of these ideas in Halifax, see P.B. Waite, 'Halifax Newspapers and the Federal Principle,' in J.M. Bumstead, ed., *Canadian History Before Confederation*, 2nd ed.(Georgetown: Irwin-Dorsey 1979).

100 *Woodworth v. Troop* (1876–7), 11 N.S.R. 84.

101 J.M. Beck, 'Privileges and Powers of the Nova Scotia House of Assembly,' *Dalhousie Review* 35 (1956): 351. See also Beck, *The Government of Nova Scotia*, 266–73.

102 Waite, 'McDonald, James.' MacDonald was appointed in 1873.

103 The Newfoundland case was *Kielley v. Carson* (1842), 13 E.R. 225, while the case from Dominica was *Doyle v. Falconer* (1866), L.R. 1 P.C. App. 328.

104 The minutes that McDonald had kept of his address to the jury were published in the law reports with the case on the application of the House of

Assembly to have the verdict set aside, largely on the basis of errors contained in the address. In keeping with the conventions of the time and the court's constitution, McDonald sat on what amounted to an appeal from his own instructions to the jury and interjected from time to time during counsel's argument; see *Woodworth v. Troop*, 93–7.

105 *Beaumont v. Barrett* (1836), 12 E.R. 733.

106 Vipond, *Liberty & Community*, 36–7, citing W. E. Hodgins, *Correspondence, Reports of the Ministers of Justice, and Orders in Council Upon the Subject of Dominion and Provincial Legislation, 1867–1895* (Ottawa, 1896), 83, 87, 88, and 256. The discussion relates to the federal disallowance of Ontario and Quebec legislation that conferred powers, privileges, and immunities of the British House of Commons on the legislature of each province respectively. Vipond characterizes the issues at stake in the dispute between Ottawa and Ontario in relation to the legislation of that province as follows: 'What Ontario affirmed, and what the federal government apparently denied, was that the provincial legislatures were full-fledged parliaments, not municipal councils or local corporations: independent, sovereign, and as deserving of respect as any other parliament, the one in Ottawa included.' This places the issues raised in *Woodworth v. Troop*, and those raised in the later case of *Thomas v. Haliburton*, also on powers and privileges, clearly into the context of federalism and the broader provincial quest for constitutional equality with the Dominion government. In contrast, J. Murray Beck paid little attention to this context in his analysis, instead emphasizing what I would call the parliamentary law aspects of the two cases. He did not, for example, give any consideration to the possibility of relationships between these two cases and other BNA cases, whether at the level of the Nova Scotia Supreme Court or more broadly: see Beck, 'Powers and Privileges.' My attempt to put both cases into that broader adjudicative context is part of what differentiates my interpretation from that offered by Beck.

107 *Woodworth v. Troop*, 100–1, 112.

108 (1877–9), 2 S.C.R. 158. In the Supreme Court of Canada, the case was argued as *Landers v. Woodworth*.

109 See in particular the judgment of William Johnston Ritchie in the Supreme Court of Canada at 201–5. In this connection, the ancillary argument of Weatherbe may have hurt more than it helped. It was that if Woodworth's conduct on this occasion did not warrant expulsion, his 'repeated and persistent efforts to annoy members' on previous occasions surely did.

110 An Act to remove certain doubts with respect to the powers of the Parliament of Canada under section 18 of the British North America Act, 1867,

38 & 39 Vict. c. 38. The gist of the amendment was to replace words that stipulated that the privileges, immunities, and powers of the Houses of the Canadian Parliament were never to exceed those possessed by the British House of Commons in 1867 with words that allowed the authority of the Canadian Parliament to define its privileges, immunities, and powers to evolve with the privileges, immunities, and powers of the British House of Commons.

111 28 & 29 Vict. (U.K.), c. 63. The most relevant provision of the Colonial Laws Validity Act was section 5, by which representative colonial legislatures were given the power to make laws respecting their own constitutions.

112 *Woodworth v. Troop*. The points taken from Wilkins's judgment are at 120–1, 122–4, 128, and 129.

113 The American case cited by Wilkins was *Anderson v. Dunn*, 6 Wheaton 204; 19 U.S. Rep. 204 (1821), in which the Supreme Court of the United States had recognized that the United States House of Representatives had the inherent power under the common law to punish and commit for contempt that went beyond the more limited power provided for in the Constitution of the United States. The use made of it by Wilkins reinforces the point made in the earlier discussion of *Lenoir v. Ritchie*, that he was guided in his judicial interpretation of the BNA Act by a general concern for provincial status and autonomy as well as by a quite traditional understanding of the limited role of the courts in the realm of constitutional law under the British system.

114 Wilkins concluded that the Privy Council had to be interpreted as permitting colonial legislatures to act not only in the face of physical obstruction of proceedings, but also in the face of conduct that so interfered with the dignity and stature of the legislative body as to make further proceedings intolerable without the behaviour being addressed. This covered Woodworth's behaviour and the decision to have him evicted.

115 *Landers v. Woodworth*, 213. Perhaps surprisingly, these sentiments were reiterated in the Supreme Court of Canada by the chief justice, William Buell Richards, who held for Woodworth despite finding that outcome to be contrary to 'All my reading, historical, political and legal.' In contrast, Nova Scotia's Henry again weighed in with what seemed like particular belligerence, to point out that the British House of Commons was a body 'numbering hundreds, drawn from the first-class men of the kingdom actuated by the highest aspiration and supported, resting on and reflecting, day by day, the highest toned public opinion.' It was not to be compared with a provincial Assembly, 'drawn, as a rule, not from the ranks of

first-class public men,' and consisting of numbers so small in comparison as to be much more likely to become "bitterly excited by political squabbles" that would not be modified, as they were in England and presumably in Ottawa, by 'a suitable controlling public opinion.'

116 *Thomas v. Haliburton* (1893–4), 26 N.S.R. 55 and *Fielding v. Thomas*, [1896] A.C. 600.

117 Beck, 'Privileges and Powers,' and *The Government of Nova Scotia*, 269–73.

118 An Act respecting the Legislature of Nova Scotia, S.N.S. 1876, c. 22.

119 An Act to define the privileges, immunities, and powers of the Senate and House of Commons, and to give summary protection to persons employed in the publication of Parliamentary papers, S.C. 1868, c. 23.

120 *R. v. Frawley; R. v. Hodge* (1882), 7 O.A.R. 246; *Province of New Brunswick v. Liquidators of the Maritime Bank* (1888), 27 N.B.R. 379.

121 The literature on post-Confederation Nova Scotian politics that deals most specifically either with the continuing opposition to Confederation in the 1860s and 1870s or with the agitation for repeal in the 1880s includes K.G. Pryke, *Nova Scotia and Confederation, 1864–74* (Toronto: University of Toronto Press 1979); C.D. Howell, 'Nova Scotia's Protest Tradition and the Search for a Meaningful Federalism,' in D.J. Bercuson, ed., *Canada and the Burden of Unity* (Toronto: MacMillan 1977); and, also by C.D. Howell, 'W.S. Fielding and the Repeal Elections of 1886 and 1887 in Nova Scotia,' The more general works dealing with Nova Scotia's reaction to Confederation include D.A. Muise, 'The 1860s: Forging the Bonds of Union,' in E.R. Forbes and D.A. Muise, eds., *The Atlantic Provinces in Confederation* (Toronto and Fredericton: University of Toronto Press and Acadiensis Press 1993), and, in the same volume, J. Fingard, 'The 1880s: Paradoxes of Progress,' 98–9. See also J.G. Reid, *Six Crucial Decades: Times of Change in the History of the Maritimes* (Halifax: Nimbus Publishing 1987), 108–18 and 136–8, as well as Beck, *Politics of Nova Scotia*, 157–86 and 215–37. In attempting to build on this literature, I am not intending to enter into the debate as to whether the persistence of opposition in the 1870s or the threat of secession in the 1880s were serious attempts to undo Confederation or simply strategies for obtaining better terms within it. My argument – that the court's jurisprudence can be understood as a reaction to the persistence of opposition in the 1870s and to the threat of secession in the 1880s – is one that I would be prepared to make on either understanding of the seriousness and objectives of the provincial government. Likewise, I do not see the argument as in necessary conflict with the view of political historians that the policy of secession had, by the early 1890s, been largely replaced by a more conventional policy of support for provincial rights

within Canada. The latter policy would easily have provided its own rationale for the courts persistence in an essentially asymmetrical reading of the BNA Act, precisely because it was adopted in Nova Scotia, unlike in other provinces, as an alternative to the more ambitious policy of opposition and repeal that had been followed for most of the first two decades of Confederation, albeit fitfully.

122 I am indebted to Richard Devlin for suggesting the relevance of the work of Clifford Geertz to my conclusions on the importance of local influences: see C. Geertz, *Local Knowledge: Further Essays in Interpretive Anthropology* (New York: Basic Books 1983). Geertz's exploration of the ways in which people use law to construct an understanding of the world around them and to embody a 'vision of community' might well enrich my analysis, but that will have to wait for a future paper. There is an impressive precedence for this in Robert Vipond's use of Geertz's work in his study of the provincial rights movement: see Vipond, *Liberty & Community*, 9–11.

13

'To Err Is Human, to Forgive Divine': The Labour Relations Board and the Supreme Court of Nova Scotia, 1947–1965

R. BLAKE BROWN

Introduction

Legal scholars examining the judicial review of labour board decisions after the Second World War often claim that Canadian courts skirted legislàtive privative clauses[1] and were highly intrusive in the determinations of labour boards. Legal commentators typically perceive these actions as efforts by a hostile judiciary to destroy the powers of tribunals. The judiciary is often portrayed as politically reactionary and conservative, out of step with modern times, and wedded to late nineteenth-century ideas concerning the rule of law, the value and importance of the common law, and freedoms of contract and property.[2] Social historians also critique the judiciary in the period after 1945, especially for its role in buttressing inequalities in class relations. Wealthy, middle-aged judges, it is generally said, could not or would not relate to the plights of workers seeking recognition for unions and a fair piece of the capitalist pie. While many social historians are less predisposed to discuss the evolution of legal doctrine and judicial biography, they have tended to assert that judges enforced a legal regime that disadvantaged workers.[3]

This article evaluates these perceptions of the post-war judiciary's response to the labour regime by examining the Nova Scotia Supreme Court's interaction with the province's Labour Relations Board (LRB) from the board's establishment in 1947 until 1965.[4] During this period the court decided a series of 'certification' disputes, in which the provincial judiciary was asked to decide whether the LRB had properly determined if a union represented a majority of eligible employees. An analysis of these cases fails to demonstrate a consistent anti-unionism among the court's judges; rather, in several high-profile cases the Nova Scotia judiciary defended the rights of labour, though one can detect a tendency to favour large, 'responsible' unions rather than small radical ones. It also shows two distinct periods in the NSSC's willingness to intervene in the work of the LRB. In the first period, ending in about 1953, the court gave little deference to the board and de-emphasized the legislative privative clause, which was to protect the board from judicial review. The subsequent period saw the judiciary extend more deference to the LRB, though standards of judicial review remained rather fluid and uncertain. The relative willingness of the court to extend deference to the board reflected the court's particular membership and the approach of Horace Read, who simultaneously acted as chair of the LRB and dean of Dalhousie Law School, and often employed rather 'legalistic' methods in running the board.[5]

This article first provides context to the judicial review of the LRB by very briefly sketching the history of labour relations in Nova Scotia before the Second World War, and by summarizing the growing acceptance of administrative agencies by some members of the legal profession. Attention then turns to the establishment of the LRB, and the NSSC's review of the board's certification decisions. The LRB rarely provided reasons for its decisions, usually issuing a short order that might, or might not, provide some indication of its rationale. However, transcripts of the oral arguments at certification hearings exist for many of the cases taken to the Supreme Court. These transcripts provide an excellent opportunity to infer the reasoning of the board and compare it with the judgments of the NSSC.

Labour and Law in Nova Scotia Prior to the Second World War

Nova Scotia's history of labour relations is marred by conflict, though the province was also a leader in establishing a system of industrial legality. From a relatively early date, provincial legislation sought to smooth out labour relations. The 1864 Act Relating to the Combination of Workmen prevented prosecutions against union members for meeting to discuss hours of work or wages, but also placed important limitations on employees. For example, employees were unable to enforce rates or hours through collective agreements.[6] In 1888, Nova Scotia became the first province to pass compulsory arbitration legislation.[7]

Despite occasional legislative attempts to provide some security to workers, the Nova Scotian government was also notorious for its willingness to employ state coercion against unions. Much of the labour strife occurred in industrial Cape Breton, where rich coal deposits led to large mining and steel industries. Nova Scotian coal miners organized a union as early as 1879, and throughout the first half of the twentieth century had a record of militant strikes and political radicalism.[8] One of the best-known examples of state coercion began in July 1909 when the coal workers walked out; their strike lasted for twenty-two months, but the workers gained little. Troops arrived and essentially occupied the coalfields to keep production moving.[9] Another serious conflict in the mines of Nova Scotia was averted by the appointment in 1917 of a royal commission chaired by Judge Joseph Chisholm. In the early 1920s the British Empire Steel Corporation (BESCO) reduced wages. The union went to court to prevent this, but the judges, Humphrey Mellish (a former coal company solicitor), Joseph Chisholm, and James J. Ritchie, upheld BESCO's unilateral reductions.[10] A new wave of labour militancy broke out in Nova Scotia in 1937; the government of Premier Angus L. Macdonald responded, and Nova Scotia became the first province to enact a version of Franklin Roosevelt's Wagner Act. The new legislation required employers to recognize and bargain with unions that had won the support of a majority of employees. It also permitted the check-off of dues to support labour unions, though it did not create a labour relations board.[11]

Although the province passed important labour legislation before the Second World War, the precursor to the Nova Scotia LRB was the Wartime Labour Relations Board established by the federal government in 1944. In peacetime, labour relations generally fell within provincial jurisdiction under the British North America Act. Increased labour activity, however, encouraged the recognition of trade unions as important players in the war effort. The order-in-council establishing the Wartime Labour Relations Board, PC 1003, came into effect in 1944 with much fanfare. PC 1003 dominated the labour relations field, compelling employers to bargain with unions, forcing conciliation of labour disputes, and requiring arbitration for labour grievances.[12]

Under the regime established by PC 1003, provincial labour relations boards heard and determined applications for the certification of unions and resolved claims of unfair labour practices. These boards were composed of representatives of labour, business, and an impartial chair. PC 1003 had an immediate effect on Canadian labour relations. Unions initially reacted positively, for the order-in-council promised legal recognition of much for which they had fought. Unions could achieve formal recognition and thereby compel employers to negotiate with them. In return, unions lost their ability to strike during the life of a collective agreement.[13] PC 1003 remained in place until 1947. As this date approached, provincial governments attempted to ease the transition over control of labour relations from Ottawa to the provinces. Nova Scotia responded by passing the Trade Union Act in May 1947.[14]

The Canadian Legal Profession and the 'New Despotism'

While the histories of labour conflict and legislative intervention are important contextual factors in understanding the relationship between the NSSC and the LRB, another significant trend was the Canadian legal community's evolving perception of the value and role of government boards and their correlative discretionary powers. The 1947 Nova Scotia Trade Union Act was not simply an outgrowth of the Canadian Wartime Labour Relations Board. Provincial labour boards, the Wartime Labour Relations Board, and other bureaucratic agencies were institutions that an intensive academic lobbying effort during the 1930s and 1940s had validated to many Canadian legal professionals and policy makers. Many Canadians asked for increased government intervention in the economy during the Depression through regulatory agencies and boards, but, in doing so, they had to combat traditional attitudes about the perceived dangers of an administrative state.

These traditional attitudes stemmed from a particular understanding of the role of courts, and ideas regarding how legal decisions should be made. Dominant in the late nineteenth and early twentieth centuries, this legal ideology, typically referred to as 'legal formalism,' was marked by several propositions. It was believed that legal rules could be formulated and legal problems solved by value-free analytical deduction from general premises.[15] 'Law,' it was thought, could be divorced from public policy and morals. Law was logical and right, while public policy was political and determined by self-interest. Formalists also generally applied a method of statutory interpretation whereby judges could interpret the meaning of legal documents by looking only for the 'plain meaning' of words, and not through a consideration of context or subjective intentions.[16]

Administrative boards troubled formalist lawyers for several reasons. Tribunals were thought free to disregard precedents and to interpret statutes by explicitly considering policy ramifications. They reduced the primacy of courts, and threatened individual rights by employing procedures different than those used in the courts. With the expansion of the administrative state, formalist-trained lawyers in England and the United States lashed out at the increasingly important government departments vested with authority to make administrative decisions. Lord Hewart, the lord chief justice of England, provided the most famous reaction to the growing bureaucratic state in his 1929 book, *The New Despotism*.[17]

Many Canadians in the 1930s and 1940s echoed these critiques of administrative bodies. Canadian lawyers compared the increasing use of administrative agencies in Britain and Canada to the rise of Fascist states in Europe; they expressed concerns about the discretion given to boards and the efforts of governments to ensure, by the inclusion of privative clauses, that the courts did not review the decisions of these new agencies. Lawyers charged that a failure in the administrative context to apply traditional procedures and common law principles, including an adherence to precedent and a reluctance to consider policy implications, would decrease the liberties of citizens, and risked throwing Canada into tyranny. Walter Johnson, a Montreal lawyer, offered a typical critique in 1943: 'The administrative Board whose decision is subject to no review by the Courts, before whom a lawyer cannot even represent his client, is by way of being or becoming a *Star Chamber* of dangerous tendencies.'[18]

With the onset of the Great Depression the widely held assumptions about the dangers of administrative law came into question, and many Canadians began to argue for increased use of tribunals and boards. In doing so, they criticized judges who struck down new regulatory initiatives aimed at alleviating the effects of the Depression.[19] Among the most prominent participants in the defence of administrative law was a group of law professors that included John Willis of Dalhousie University, the University of Toronto's Jacob Finkelman, and J.A. Corry of the University of Saskatchewan. Willis applied his knowledge of academic debates about the value of administrative agencies in England to the Canadian context, critiquing formalist assumptions and advocating a 'functional approach' to administrative law that would take advantage of the expertise of administrative boards and tribunals. Corry criticized the judiciary's tendency to emphasize individual rights over collective needs. He explained that the shift in political philosophy from laissez-faire to a more interventionist state required modern administrative agencies. Jacob Finkelman focused on issues relating to the judicial review of administrative decisions, arguing that judicial preferences, not doctrine, determined when judges overturned the decisions of administrative boards.[20] Many of these academics continued to argue for the acceptance of administrative machinery during and after the Second World War, and, as will be shown, some members of the Nova Scotian judiciary shared these new assumptions.

Nova Scotia Labour Relations Board

The Nova Scotian government created the province's LRB in May 1947.[21] The legislation provided that every employee had a right to be in a trade union, stipulated that employers were not to interfere in the creation of trade unions or to discriminate against unions, and, to ensure labour peace, provided for conciliation services. The Act dictated that trade unions representing a majority of the employees of a bargaining unit could act as bargaining agent. This required a certification process, in which the union had to present a certification application to the LRB. If the certification application succeeded, the union became the exclusive bargaining agent for the employees. The government appointed the members of the LRB, and selected the chair.[22] The province gave considerable discretion to the board to establish procedures and rules that would allow it to operate smoothly and efficiently. For example, the Act stated that the 'Board may receive and accept such evidence and information on oath, affidavit, or otherwise, as in its discretion it may deem fit and proper, whether admissible as evidence in a Court of law, or not.' The board was also to shape its own procedure, though it had to 'give an opportunity to all interested parties to present evidence and make representation.'[23] Importantly, the province attempted, through a privative clause, to protect the decisions of the board from judicial review. When the LRB made a decision concerning a number of questions – including whether someone was an employee within the meaning of the Act, whether an organization qualified as a trade union, or if a collective agreement has been entered into – 'the decision or order of the Board shall be final and conclusive and not open to question, or review, but the Board may, if it considers it advisable so do so, reconsider any decision or order made by it under this Act, and may vary or revoke any decision or order made by it under this Act.'[24] As will be shown, however, this privative clause initially provided little protection to the decisions of the LRB.

The Nova Scotia Supreme Court

Between 1947 and 1965, just five NSSC judges wrote substantial decisions in cases in which the court reviewed the LRB's certification decisions: John Doull, Vincent MacDonald, James Lorimer Ilsley, Frederick William Bissett, and Frank Harris Patterson. Collectively, these judges considered nine cases from the LRB in this period. Doull wrote the most judgments (six), while MacDonald wrote in four cases, Ilsley in two, and Bissett and Patterson in one each. Two general periods are apparent in the cases. The first period, from roughly 1947 to 1953, is marked by considerable intervention in the decisions of the Labour Board. The second period, however, witnessed increased deference on the part of the NSSC to the board. Both periods saw the court make decisions defending the rights of labour.

In the first period, the NSSC heard four cases, and in all four John Doull and/or Vincent MacDonald wrote the decisions, sometimes for themselves, sometimes for the court. Doull (1878–1969) acted as the general bookkeeper for the Dominion Coal Company in Glace Bay from 1903 to 1907. After receiving a BA and an LL.B from Dalhousie in 1909 and 1910, respectively, Doull articled in Glace Bay and became a member of the Nova Scotia legislature in 1925. He acted as the province's attorney general from 1931 to 1933, and, after his 1933 election defeat, received an appointment to the NSSC, a position he held until 1961. The oldest judge to write a decision in these cases, Doull was an amateur historian who wrote on such topics as the attorney generals of Nova Scotia and the provincial Bible Society. His personal papers demonstrate little concern with more philosophical questions concerning the law, or with the implications of judicial decisions for society, and he seems to have held a rather romantic notion of the role of judges and the historic development of the common law.[25]

Vincent MacDonald (1897–1964) had impressive credentials in the field of labour relations. After receiving a BA and an LL.B from Dalhousie, MacDonald practised in Halifax, acted as a law clerk to the Nova Scotia legislature, worked as secretary to Prime Minister King in 1927, and practised law in Toronto from 1928 to 1930. Having lectured in law at Dalhousie and Osgoode Hall law schools, MacDonald returned to Dalhousie as a full-time professor in 1930, replacing Angus

L. Macdonald. Just four years later he became dean of the law school, a position he held until his 1950 appointment as a justice of the NSSC. A 'clever, quick-witted, and articulate man,'[26] MacDonald's knowledge of labour law issues first derived from government. From 1942 to 1944, he served as the federal assistant deputy minister of labour. He was also an arbitrator between Halifax shipping companies and longshoremen, and acted as the controller for the port of Halifax. After the passage of PC 1003, he became the chair of the Nova Scotia Wartime Labour Relations Board, and from 1947 to 1950 he chaired the LRB established pursuant to the 1947 Nova Scotia Trade Union Act.[27]

MacDonald's judgments are of particular interest because he was the first of the 1930s Canadian legal scholars to be elevated to the bench. Bora Laskin is perhaps the best known of these academics who entered the judiciary, but Laskin did not join the bench until his appointment to the Ontario Court of Appeal in 1965, fifteen years after the older MacDonald received his judicial call. MacDonald wrote and spoke often on the need to ensure that the law fit new social realities. His opinions in these labour cases thus offer a unique opportunity to determine whether the 1930s radical criticisms were put into action during the 1950s and early 1960s.

The Interventionist Court, 1947–1953

The first of the four cases decided during the court's initial interventionist stage, *Re Lunenburg Sea Products,* was not a test of the Supreme Court's view of the Nova Scotia LRB, as it resulted from a decision of the Wartime Labour Relations Board. Nevertheless, the case is important in that it set the tone for the interventionist period and cast a shadow over future litigation. The case arose when representatives of the crews of several fishing vessels sought certification. The Wartime Labour Relations Board had granted certification; the owners responded with an application for a writ of certiorari on the ground that the regulations did not apply to the form of employment in question.[28] Given the court's lack of experience in such cases, Doull surveyed English and Canadian case law in providing a general discussion of whether it could inspect, and possibly overturn, a decision of the board. He believed that these cases held that the writ could be issued 'for the purpose of quashing the determinations of persons or bodies who are by statute or otherwise entrusted with judicial functions.' Doull indicated that a distinction had to be made between judicial bodies and administrative tribunals. If the purpose and operation of the body was strictly 'administrative,' the court could not issue the writ of certiorari. However, if 'it is a body which is deciding rights between parties and has a duty to act according to principles of law or pre-determined rules' then 'its acts are of a character which may be reviewed.'[29]

Doull understood that 'a great many bodies have both judicial and administrative functions,' and it 'is only when such a body is acting judicially that its orders are subject to review on *certiorari*.' He believed the Wartime Labour board fell into this category, and he thus turned to whether the board had acted judicially in this instance. He concluded that the board had acted judicially in deciding whether fishers were employees. For Doull this issue was a 'preliminary' legal one that had to be determined by the common law. 'If no such general relationship exists as a matter of law,' he asserted, 'the provisions of P.C. 1003 do not apply and the Board cannot by a wrong decision on a matter of law arrogate to itself a jurisdiction which it does not possess.'[30]

Doull then turned to the intricacies of the fishing business. Ship owners provided the ship with all necessary tackle and provisions of salt. The fishers, as 'sharesmen,' provided certain 'minor equipment' such as dory sails, compasses, and bait tubs. Under this arrangement, the owner or agent was authorized to sell the fish caught for the benefit of the captain, ship owner, and all fishers who took part in the undertaking. Doull concluded that this did not constitute an employee-employer relationship -- the fishers were not engaged in procuring fish for the owners or for the captain, but for all aboard the vessel. The relationship between the fishers and the owners of the vessels was that of a 'partnership in the limited sense which is sometimes described as a "joint adventure"' and thus the fishers could not be employees within the scope of PC 1003.[31] Doull thus quashed the finding of the Wartime Labour Relations Board.

Doull's decision received a negative academic response from University of Toronto law professor Bora Laskin. Laskin concluded that the judgment of the court exhibited 'a dreary conceptualism the persistence in which is the more remarkable when one considers that the Regulations expressly stipulate that the board shall decide whether a person is an employee if such a question arises under them.' After noting Doull's claim that this was a preliminary issue, Laskin asserted that this was 'so unreal that it carries its own refutation,' for 'if the court can instruct the board on who is an employee, it should equally feel able to say what is an appropriate bargaining unit and what constitutes bargaining in good faith. Why have a board?'[32]

The court's *Lunenburg* decision clearly affected the operation of the

LRB; this was apparent in how the board considered an application by the Canadian Association of Policemen for certification as bargaining agent for the Dartmouth police. When Vincent MacDonald became a member of the Supreme Court in 1950, he vacated his positions as dean of Dalhousie Law School and chair of the LRB. Horace Read succeeded MacDonald in both roles. Read had received an LL.M and an SJD from Harvard Law School, and he had taught at Dalhousie from 1925 to 1933 before taking up a position at Minnesota Law School, where he specialized in legislation. When he accepted the law deanship at Dalhousie, Premier Angus L. MacDonald made up for the lower salary offered by Dalhousie by making Read chair of the LRB, a position he held for more than two decades. Like many other Canadian legal scholars of his era, Read urged judges to shape the law to fit new social realities. His broadly progressive leaning, however, was tempered; unlike scholars such as Bora Laskin and John Willis, his work lacked biting criticism or rebellious tendencies. Rather than seeing courts as standing in the way of the smooth operation of the law in a modern society, he had faith in the good intentions of judges, and believed that courts and legislatures could work cooperatively.[33]

In the hearing to determine the certification application of the Canadian Association of Policemen Read expressed his extreme reluctance to determine whether police officers were employees under the Act, since he felt that the Supreme Court could quash any determination that the board made. 'The point as I see it is entirely a question of law,' he said, 'that turns entirely on whether a policeman, the nature of work, and his relations with the Corporation of the Town of Dartmouth are such as to bring him within the meaning of "employee" as that term "employee" is used in the statutes, not as the term is used popularly, because we have to decide according to law.'[34]

Read, who dominated the proceedings, was thus reluctant to make a determination. He instead expressed hope that the legislature would pass a statute to settle the question. This frustrated the union's lawyer, Ian MacKeigan, who urged the board to grasp the discretionary scope granted to it by the legislature. 'We have an Act here, [an] extremely good Act, which is wide in scope, which has been considered in many respects by both employer and employee [as] the charter of labour in this Province today,' argued MacKeigan, such that '[m]atters are placed not in the hands of the Court ... but in the hands of a tribunal.' This had been done because it was 'a specialized type of matter that can be dealt with by persons who have a specialized knowledge of the field of labour.' The board was meant to avoid the technicalities of the common law, MacKeigan implored. It should 'get away from some of the forms and technical pleading that historically has been found necessary for the type of matter coming before a Court.' MacKeigan discouraged the board from closely following the Supreme Court's ruling, for '[o]ne of the advantages of an administrative board is that it is not hidebound by precedent.'[35]

Read, however, would have none of this. 'I generally agree that is the purpose of having an administrative board in a specialized field,' he told MacKeigan, but 'the question before us was purely and simply a question of law, which the Court had already in the Lunenburg fisherman case held they should be the ones to decide,' and thus 'we cannot make the final decision.' If the government refused to pass legislation, then Read wanted a reference case to the court to decide the issue. If no reference came, it 'would then follow that whatever way we decided the case that the party against whom we decided certainly would be inclined to take certiorari to the Supreme Court.' Despite his reluctance to make a decision, Read ultimately found that the common law failed to support a claim that police work was a type of employer-employee relationship. He announced that courts had 'been uniform in holding that the common law relationship of employer and employee does not exist between a city, a corporation, and police.'[36]

The Canadian Association of Policemen applied for a writ of certiorari after the LRB rejected certification. The union argued that the question of whether the police were employees was a preliminary issue going to the jurisdiction of the board; that the privative clause of the Act did not exclude review as to the board's jurisdiction; and that, as a matter of law, the police were employees who could be certified. The NSSC, however, refused to quash the board's determination. Doull and MacDonald wrote decisions for the five-member court. Doull again claimed broad powers for the court to supervise the Board. He looked at the Trade Union Act's privative clause and all but dismissed it, asserting, 'I doubt whether *certiorari* has been taken away. Words of this character have been held not to take away the right of *certiorari* unless they are express negative words.' Nevertheless, in this particular case, Doull concluded that the board members did not arrogate to themselves 'an authority which they did not possess.'[37]

MacDonald also refused to overturn the board. On the one hand, this was unsurprising. Like other progressive legal scholars in Canada writing in the 1930s, he advocated the use of administrative agencies to oversee the growing welfare state. For example, in an address to the Nova Scotia Mining Society before his appointment to the bench, MacDonald discussed the broad shift that had occurred in the responsibility of government to citizens. He told his audience that a 'century ago the prevailing philosophy was that there should be as little government as possible.' With the industrial revolution, however, came a recognition that government had a positive duty to provide for the welfare and security of its citizens through the enactment of laws for the provision of public services 'and for the modernization of the ordinary law.' This trend produced a significant development in the techniques of government: 'This is the great use which is now being made of the device of creating administrative and regulative bodies, and delegating to them the capacity to make rules having the force of law, and to make decisions as to the application of laws to particular cases.' MacDonald acknowledged that many people were alarmed by the creation of an administrative state 'without the safeguards afforded to individuals by the rules, the traditions and the independent personnel of the established Courts of Justice,' but he concluded that boards were necessary, and that any potential problems with administrative bodies could be overcome. He told his audience that it was 'simply a *technique of government*, and one which flourishes in direct proportion to the people's demand on government for more paternalistic legislation; and that to a great degree it will be part of the price we will pay for our desired New Social Order, for a Planned Economy or for Cradle to the Grave Security.'[38]

In a convocation address at St Mary's College in May 1946 MacDonald gave a similar speech, but he also discussed the particular problems of labour that necessitated increased government intervention. According to MacDonald, the Canadian government was profoundly concerned with

> the great numerical increase in Labour organizations and their constant – and often concerted – efforts to secure concrete improvements in the workers' standard of living. What attitude is the State to take when the rival interest and philosophies of Industry and Labour collide? How to break down the barriers which the years have raised between these great classes? How are we to secure to each of these classes its rights, and hold each of them to its own responsibilities to other classes and to the State at large? These are problems which make it of supreme urgency that we

develop better techniques for the prevention, the conciliation and the ultimate settlement of disputes between Industry and labour, which far outrange in their effects the parties immediately concerned.[39]

As the chair of the Nova Scotia LRB from 1947 to 1950, MacDonald himself experimented with one of these new techniques of government, and he pleaded for all concerned to respect the board's decisions. Just after the board's establishment, he asked that management and labour should 'accept the decisions of the Board in the same way as litigants accept the decisions of the courts of law,' and asserted that '[s]urely it is time for the parties to labour controversies to abide by decisions made by the agencies set up by the State to deal with them in an orderly way.'[40]

MacDonald's judgments, beginning with his decision in the *Dartmouth Police* case, however, do not reflect this goal of consistent deference. In considering the application for certiorari by the Canadian Association of Policemen, MacDonald relied on *Lunenburg Fisheries* in asserting that the jurisdiction of the LRB depended upon the existence of an employer-employee relationship under the "general law." Since the definition of an 'employee' was again at issue, it followed that the question whether such a relationship existed between the Town of Dartmouth and its police was 'one going to the jurisdiction of the Board, whose decision thereon is reviewable on *certiorari*.' The Act's privative clause did not prevent judicial inspection of the LRB's decision, since 'very precise language is required to do so.' MacDonald concluded that under the common law constables were 'holders of offices of trust under the Crown'; they were, therefore, 'officers appointed (and sworn) *to perform public duties* of an executive character in the general administration of justice,'[41] and thus there was no employee-employer relationship.

Although Doull and MacDonald did not overturn the LRB, they demonstrated little deference to its expertise or respect for the Trade Union Act's privative clause. The board was clearly exposed to future judicial intervention, a point not lost on chair Horace Read. In a 1951 address to the Nova Scotia Barristers' Society Read made clear the impact of *Lunenburg* and *Dartmouth*. He said that these cases held that the Trade Union Act only conferred jurisdiction 'over persons between whom the relationship of employer and employee exists at common law.' Read also expressed some frustration about the apparent weakness of the Act's privative clause, pointing out that '[n]ot only does the

Act fail to provide for appeal from the Board's decisions,' but it also 'contains a so-called privative clause.' Like other courts across the country, however, the NSSC had held that it could quash an order of the board whenever the order was made without jurisdiction. This, he complained to Nova Scotia's lawyers, constituted a 'judicial gloss of the Act.'[42]

In noting Read's complaints, it is important to recognize that his chairmanship of the LRB also reflected his somewhat conservative legal philosophy, including his faith in the common law and its courts. He indicated his belief that the board should operate using a mixture of traditional legal principles and procedures, along with more policy-oriented goals. For example, he claimed that the board's procedures were 'simple and relatively informal,' but also said that '[p]roceedings at hearings before the Board follow in general those before a court.' On the one hand, he expressed his belief in the value of administrative agencies, saying that the LRB was created because some issues 'have been shown by experience not to be effectively amenable to resolution solely by judicial procedures.' On the other hand, Read encouraged lawyers to become involved in LRB cases, since there was 'no doubt that a lawyer can be very helpful to all concerned in proceedings before the Board.'[43] Further, transcripts of certification proceedings show Read running the proceedings like a courtroom, and generally asserting that the board must take a narrow approach to statutory interpretation.[44] As a long-time law professor, his occasional emphasis on the value of legal procedures and rules is perhaps unsurprising, but it was significant because Read dominated the board during this period, and his emphasis on precedent, the common law, and rather formal procedures could frustrate the goal of creating a flexible, policy-oriented institution, despite his claim that it was 'imperative that controversies be decided by it as "rightly" as possible, independently, if necessary, of the formal record the parties themselves produce.'[45]

In making this last claim, Read presciently, if accidentally, foreshadowed a key issue in the next Supreme Court case concerning a certification decision. In September 1951, the Industrial Union of Marine and Shipbuilding Workers of Canada, Local No. 18 applied for certification as the bargaining agent for the workers of six shipyards spread across the province, including the employees of Smith & Rhuland Ltd, a Lunenburg shipbuilding company. The application made clear that the union represented a majority of the eligible employees. However, after the deadline to challenge the certification application had passed,

Smith & Rhuland submitted a declaration to the effect that J.K. Bell, a union organizer who had signed the application for certification, was a communist. As proof, the company showed that Bell was a contributor to the *Daily Tribune*, a communist newspaper, and submitted articles from the *Ottawa Journal* and the *Financial Post* on the subject of communism that mentioned Bell. Smith & Rhuland's lawyer, C.B. Smith, told the board at the certification hearing that his case was 'based very flatly on the question of public policy.' The shipyard might some day build ships for the navy, warned Smith, yet communists 'are much more concerned with the welfare of the Soviet Union than they are with the welfare of Canada and the people in Canada.' R.A. Kanigsberg responded for the union by describing to the board the potential policy implications for labour. The danger was clear, said Kanigsberg, for 'to be consistent the Board would have to decertify the entire union as soon as they found a single member to belong to the Communist organization,' since the company's argument was 'that one apple will spoil the whole barrel.'[46]

The board refused to certify on the public policy ground that to certify the union would allow the leadership to pursue the goals of the Communist Party, not those of the employees, and it did not camouflage its reasons. It called the Communist Party a highly disciplined organization, whose members were rigidly controlled by leaders 'who require the policies and aims laid down by them to be slavishly followed by party members.' It differed from mainstream Canadian political parties in that it used positions of trade union leadership 'as a means of furthering policies and aims dictated by a foreign government.' 'Consequently,' the board continued, 'to certify as bargaining agent a union while its dominant leadership and direction is provided by a member of the Communist party would be incompatible with promotion of good-faith collective bargaining and would confer legal powers to affect vital interests of employees and employer upon persons who would inevitably use those powers primarily to advance Communist aims and policies rather than for the benefit of the employees.'[47]

In the context of the Korean War and the Red Scare, the LRB's decision created an immediate uproar. It was front-page news for the Halifax *Chronicle Herald*, the editors of which declared that the board had 'performed useful service to the orderly process of collective bargaining, to industry and to the public at large.'[48] In a public statement, Bell said the decision exposed the board 'as an employer influenced agency' interested in preventing poorly paid employees 'from exercising their legal right to organize and bargain collectively for decent wages and working conditions.'[49] Other Nova Scotian unionists also expressed displeasure. The Cape Breton Labour Council, six locals of District 26 of the United Mine Workers, and the Antigonish Garage Workers' Union critiqued the decision.[50]

The Marine and Shipbuilding Workers' Union went to the NSSC in banco to have the decision quashed. MacDonald wrote for the six-member court in overturning the board and finding for the union. The Trade Union Act stipulated that the board 'may' certify, and Read had believed the board could refuse to certify even when the application was technically complete. MacDonald, however, found this to be an error of law, reasoning that the Act gave the board discretion to determine only if the unit applied for was technically appropriate, not if it was socially beneficial.[51] He therefore quashed the board's decision. The judgment was a victory for labour,[52] and it continued to attract media and scholarly attention.[53] The Supreme Court of Canada subsequently heard its appeal. In a closely divided decision, Canada's highest court found in favour of the union, though a plurality did so on different grounds from MacDonald.[54]

MacDonald's motivation for defending the right of unions to have 'communist' members can be carefully discerned from his views on communism and individual and collective rights. He was no friend of communism, a point he made clear in his *Smith & Rhuland* judgment. The threats and methods of communism were 'well known to all the Governments of the English-speaking world,' he wrote, but 'no legislation of the Canadian Parliament was called to our attention which makes it unlawful for a man to be a member of the Communist Party or the Labour Progressive Party.'[55]

Rather than supporting communism, MacDonald was motivated by a desire to protect individual rights and collective goals, and by a belief that repression would only encourage communism. His emphasis on rights was apparent in a May 1939 convocation address. 'If we are to have government by opinion each citizen must have the right to express his own opinions, to discuss those of others, to organize with others for the propagation of those opinions he believes to be right, whether they accord with the views commonly held or not,' urged MacDonald. Interestingly, he also recognized that formal equality was not enough; the 'submerged classes' had to 'be emancipated from economic inequality if they are to be as essentially free as their fellow citizens.'[56] In a December 1950 speech to the Harvard Legal Aid Branch in

Boston, MacDonald drew out one of the implications of this idea. Instead of a coercive response, the communist threat required a firm affirmation of traditional rights and liberties, and a renewed effort by government to alleviate social inequality. '*Fear of Communism* has led to the realization that the denial of justice to a man because he cannot afford necessary legal assistance provides fertile ground for the spread of subversive thought and activity.' It was thus necessary for a democracy to 'demonstrate its ability to provide a respectable degree of *practical equality before the law* by such means as organized Legal Aid to needy persons.'[57] In *Smith & Rhuland* he made similar comments – he juxtaposed the oppressive treatment of communists in the United States with countries that relied 'on the inherent virtues of democracy, and on enlightened social service policies designed to remove the conditions in which subversive Communism thrives.'[58]

Though an advocate of administrative agencies, MacDonald's belief in individual rights led him to conclude that courts must vigilantly ensure that the administrative state did not trample the rights of citizens. The establishment of a social welfare state and planned economy led to the creation of boards that adjudicated questions, many of which affected the 'rights of citizens involved.' He noted that such decisions were 'expressed to be final and not open to review in the Courts,' but told the Canadian Association of Administrators of Labour Legislation that since 'all these enactments and decisions affect human rights, it is not surprising that an increasing resort has been had to the Courts to determine their validity.'[59] While in 1947, as the chair of the LRB, MacDonald had encouraged parties to accept the board's decisions, five years later, as a member of the NSSC, he suggested that 'courts accept – as they must – this new technique of government as an established feature of modern life,' but that it was 'their proper concern' to see that 'executive decisions are such as the deciding body had jurisdiction to make, and that they were arrived at by a procedure consistent with the elementary observances of justice.'[60] In a private letter to Cecil Wright, dean of the University of Toronto law school, he explained his view that legislatures, in fact, had this role in mind for courts. 'As to privative clauses I can only say that they are enacted in full knowledge of the rules laid down in the certiorari cases as to review of jurisdiction,' wrote MacDonald, who refused to 'believe that the English language is so impoverished that words cannot be found so strong as effectively to bar judicial review to whatever degree is desired. At all events it is notable that in jurisdictions where review has been had and the results have been criticized the Legislatures thereafter have seemed – by inertia at least – to acquiesce in the results – probably because statesmen are content to be able to refer to their inability to oust the courts whilst secretly glad to be able to escape the criticism which stronger clauses would arouse.'[61] MacDonald's judgment in *Smith & Rhuland* and his public and private comments thus reflect a firmly held belief in liberal concepts of individual rights and equality, but also a sense that these liberal goals must be tempered by more collectivist social and economic policies. His decision in *Smith & Rhuland* thus seems quite principled, and cannot be glossed over by the simple criticism that the post-war judiciary was jurisprudentially conservative in its intervention in labour board decisions.

The court soon became involved in another well-publicized labour dispute. The Canadian Gypsum Company, a wholly-owned subsidiary of the Chicago-based U.S. Gypsum Company, was the largest employer in Windsor, Nova Scotia, and controlled 65 per cent of all Nova Scotian gypsum production. The Canadian Gypsum Company, like its American parent, was 'unequivocally anti-union,'[62] and attempted to prevent any union successes. For many years, the Nova Scotia Quarry Workers' Union, a relatively ineffective company union, represented many of the employees at the Windsor plant, but with the election of Tom Shiers as president of the union in 1952, it developed a more independent agenda. Part of this new agenda was an attempt to have the Nova Scotia Quarry Workers' Union certified as the employees' bargaining agent. In June 1952 the LRB certified the union for the Windsor plant, but in the following year the union decided its position would be stronger if it was associated with the Canadian Congress of Labour, and it thus applied for re-certification as the Nova Scotia Quarry Workers Union Local 294 CCL. When the union applied for re-certification, the board contacted the company to inquire if it would challenge the application. The company responded by the deadline, but its submission simply consisted of a request for a hearing before the board in which it could present evidence against certification. The chief executive officer of the LRB did not respond to this request, and in August 1953 the board, without a written submission from the company or a hearing with the company present, certified the union.[63]

The company applied to the NSSC for a writ of certiorari. Hearing the case was John Doull, who for the third time in six years wrote a judgment favouring an employer in a certiorari proceeding concerning a union certification. The key issue became whether the LRB should have made some provision to hear the arguments of the Canadian Gypsum Company. The LRB's regulations indicated that the company could only respond after the deadline with the board's approval, and that the board had discretion to permit verbal evidence. Doull thought it was 'quite clear that the Board is not required to hold a hearing in the sense that a Court holds a hearing,' but that it had to 'give an opportunity to the employer to present evidence and make its representations some other way – presumably in writing,' and that the board did 'not give an opportunity when it simply ignores the request for a sitting.'[64] Doull thus quashed the board's decision, though when the board re-heard the application after a new union vote, it again certified the union in January 1954. The relationship between the Canadian Gypsum Company and Nova Scotia Quarry Workers' Union continued to deteriorate, however, ultimately leading to one of longest and most bitter strikes in Nova Scotia history.

The More Deferential Court, 1954–1965

Beginning in 1954, the NSSC began to demonstrate increased deference to the provincial LRB. Whereas in the 1947-53 period it overturned three of four certification decisions, between 1954 and 1965 the court refused to overturn the board in four of five instances. Perhaps even more telling, the judges adopted more deferential language in considering certiorari applications.

In 1954 the NSSC heard a case between a union representing construction workers and a construction company complaining that the board, in certifying the union, had failed to consider the company's seasonally fluctuating workforce. Writing for the court for the first time in a certification dispute was James Lorimer Ilsley (1894–1967). Ilsley, like Doull, had a background in politics. Born in King's County, he graduated from Acadia University in 1914, and from Dalhousie Law School 1916. After practising law in Halifax and Kentville, Ilsley became a Liberal member of the House of Commons in 1926, served as finance minister between 1940 and 1946, and from 1946 to 1948 acted as the minister of justice. He then briefly re-entered private practice, but soon accepted an appointment to the court in May 1949, and became chief justice in 1950, a position he held until 1967.[65] One of his fellow judges, Lauchlin Currie, recalled how Ilsley's 'wide experience in public life was of much advantage to him in sorting out the shades of legal controversy and then of digging into the heart of the matter.'[66]

Ilsley's decision in this case supports Currie's portrait of a justice affected by his experience in government. The International Union of Operating Engineers (Local 721) requested that the LRB certify it as the bargaining agent for all the workers (excluding supervisors and office staff) of Municipal Spraying & Contracting Ltd. Located near Bedford, the company quarried, sold gravel, had a machine shop, and built and repaired roads across Nova Scotia. The union submitted its application to be certified for the company's employees in March 1954, typically a seasonally low period in the size of Municipal Spraying's workforce. There were then fifty-one employees, forty to forty-three of whom were not supervisors or office staff. Of these, twenty-eight were members in good standing with the union. The board certified the International Union of Operating Engineers. In doing so, it re-defined the bargaining unit to encompass a smaller number of employees than the union had applied to represent.[67] The timing of the certification proceedings was relevant in the subsequent litigation. If the union had applied for certification at a time when there were more employees at the company, their success might have been in doubt. As Ilsley concluded, the union deliberately selected 'a time when there was what may be called a skeleton staff employed because a majority of that skeleton staff were members of the Union.'[68] The facts seemed perfect for a judicial pronouncement disfavouring labour.

At the NSSC, Municipal Spraying made several arguments, including that the board had exceeded its jurisdiction by including in the bargaining unit employees who were ineligible to belong to the union under the provisions of the union's constitution. The company argued that the board should not have certified during a period of low employment, and said that it had not appeared before the LRB, nor had it received notice of evidence being considered by the board other than original submissions.

Ilsley dismissed each of these claims. On the issue of the certification of a skeleton staff, he suggested that he personally disagreed with the LRB's finding on this issue, but that the court must defer to the board. 'In view of the permissive character of the Board's power to certify, they could, I think, have dismissed the application on the ground that there was an abnormally small number of persons employed,' he wrote, and '[p]erhaps they should have done so. But their decision not to do so was a matter within their discretion which cannot be interfered with on a *certiorari* application.' He also made apparent his willingness to defer in his discussion of the company's claim that the board included in the bargaining unit employees ineligible to be members of the union. Ilsley believed that, although '[i]t may be a very bad thing to do,' it was 'not beyond the jurisdiction of the Board to do it.'[69]

Ilsley then considered the board's creation of a different bargaining unit from the one described in the certification application. Again, he rejected the company's argument: 'I do not see how a Court in the exercise of its supervisory jurisdiction can say to the Board, "you excluded too many employees or the wrong employees and thereby lost jurisdiction. If you had excluded half as many or different employees you would have been within your jurisdiction."' He also concluded that the board could determine its own procedure and evidentiary requirements, and that he could not conclude 'that it is an abuse of jurisdiction for a Board to make exclusions, even very important ones, without giving the employer an opportunity to make representations against them, where ... substantially all the relevant evidence is in.'[70] Ilsley thus upheld the board's decision.

Ilsley's *Municipal Spraying* judgment turned away from the earlier, more interventionist decisions of Doull and MacDonald. His more deferential approach may have resulted from his extensive experience as a federal Cabinet minister during the Second World War, a golden period for respect of the civil service and a time when government boards and tribunals carried a large burden. In a telling indication of the policy behind his decision, Ilsley asserted that the LRB was designed to handle these types of cases, and thus '[s]ome latitude must be given such tribunals. They have to deal with very practical questions in a common sense and often in an expeditious way. There is a danger that lawyers and Judges with their professional preconceptions may seek to impose upon them technical requirements never contemplated by the legislation setting up the tribunals. I feel that to quash the Board's order in this case would be to disregard that danger.'[71]

Municipal Spraying, however, did not accept Ilsley's new line of reasoning and appealed. Since Nova Scotia did not create a separate Court of Appeal until 1966, the appeal of Ilsley's decision went to a panel composed of all the judges of the Nova Scotia Supreme Court.[72] Justice William Hall wrote a brief dissenting opinion in which he advocated overturning Ilsley, but Doull wrote for a four-judge majority in dismissing the appeal. Interestingly, Doull avoided some his own previous decisions and employed a more deferential tone. He rejected claims that the bargaining unit was inappropriate for collective bargaining since the board had 'jurisdiction over the question' and it was 'a question of fact.' Doull concluded that the 'objection that there was only a small staff on duty at the time of application is a question to be dealt with by the Board.' The judgment suggests that he had changed his views on reviewing the LRB. Although he did not explicitly refer to his previous decisions in *Lunenburg* and *Dartmouth*, Doull obliquely acknowledged their existence but suggested that they should not be carried too far: 'This Court has on several occasions upheld its own power to quash orders of Boards of the kind now before us,' he wrote, 'but on the other hand, this Court is not a Court of Appeal from the Labour Board and if that Board acts legally within its jurisdiction and gives parties an opportunity of stating their case, the decision of the Board must stand.'[73]

One can only speculate on the reason for Doull's more deferential approach. Perhaps he had sufficiently limited the discretion of the board. Or, perhaps he was influenced by some of his fellow judges. Ilsley clearly showed more deference to the LRB, and one of the concurring judges in Doull's opinion was Lauchlin Currie. From North Sydney, Currie (1893–1969) attended Dalhousie Law School, then worked as the solicitor for the town of Glace Bay and for the United Mine Workers of America, District 26. First elected to the Nova Scotia legislature in 1933, Currie held several portfolios, including minister of mines and labour and attorney general, before his 1949 elevation to the NSSC. He briefly served as the chair of the Nova Scotia Wartime Labour Relations Board before Vincent MacDonald replaced him, and, as minister of labour, he oversaw the passage of the 1947 Trade Union Act. These experiences seem to have led him to take a moderate approach to labour issues and judicial review, and he publicly called for the cooperation of labour, management, and government.[74]

Whatever the cause, Doull again displayed deference to the board in a case concerning Sobey's. Employees at a Truro Sobey's store joined the Retail, Wholesale and Department Stores Union Local 1015 and sought certification. Sobey's contested the application and successfully put pressure on all but one of the employees to revoke their union memberships prior to the board's certification decision. The board held a hearing, at which some of the employees were witnesses. To ensure that the employees would openly discuss the company's actions, the board excluded all representatives of the company except its lawyer.[75] The LRB granted certification after an impassioned plea by the union's representative that he was 'reluctant and scared to organize' at a Sobey's establishment 'because if I leave for a minute and get my back turned something happens' and 'all of the sudden the employees don't want the union.'[76]

In dismissing the Sobey's application for a writ of certiorari, Doull began by asserting the important role of the LRB. While the court had the power to issue writs of certiorari, the board had been set up by the legislature 'for the express purpose of dealing with applications such as the one which was before the Board in the present case, and if the Board acted within its jurisdiction and proceeded according to law, its decision should not be interfered with.' He pointed out that a majority of employees were clearly members of the union in good standing at the time of the certification application, and that it was for the board to consider the mass union revocation. Doull disposed of several complaints of the company, none of which were enough to quash the board's order. For example, he excused the Board's decision to exclude all representatives of the company since 'the board now being considered is not a Court.'[77]

The court's increased deference to the Labour Board was even more fully expressed in the *Central Auxiliary Workers' Union* cases of 1960. These two cases were the culmination of an extensive legal battle between the United Mine Workers (UMW) and two Glace Bay unions, the Central Auxiliary Workers' Union and the International Brotherhood of Electrical Workers, Local 2025. The Dominion Steel and Coal Corporation (DOSCO) had long recognized the UMW as bargaining agent for its workers, but the UMW had never applied for certification. The two smaller unions sought certification for specific groups of employees working for DOSCO. DOSCO and the UMW, however, successfully resisted this certification application.[78]

The Central Auxiliary Workers' Union then applied for a writ of certiorari to quash the LRB's decision. Hearing the case was Frank Harris Patterson (1891–1976), a member of a prominent legal family appointed to the NSSC in 1958. Born in Tatamagouche and a graduate of Pictou Academy and Dalhousie Law School, Patterson practised in Yarmouth until he moved to Truro in 1927. Active in civil and criminal litigation, Patterson was a former solicitor for the municipality of Colchester County and Truro, and, like Doull, an amateur historian.[79] The Auxiliary Workers' Union submitted that the board erred in law in holding that the Trade Union Act did not require it to be certified as the bargaining agent for the employees, and that the UMW did not fulfil the definition of a union as stipulated by the Trade Union Act. Patterson, however, found no grounds for the writ of certiorari, and he asserted that the board's decision deserved respect: 'Rightly or wrongly the Legislature has put into the hands of the Board a jurisdiction over certain subject matter that is not open to question or review.' The power of the courts was thus 'confined to ascertaining whether or not the Board acted contrary to some principles of law as appears from the face of the record.'[80] Patterson decided that the Auxiliary Workers' Union was unable to show anything in the record establishing an error in law by the board.

To help fend off further incursions by other unions, the UMW applied for certification, an application that the Central Auxiliary Workers' Union and the Electrical Workers contested.[81] The board granted certification to the UMW, and the Auxiliary Workers' Union applied for a writ of certiorari. The NSSC sat in banco, and three judges wrote decisions – Doull, MacDonald, and Ilsley – and all upheld the board's decision. A key issue on appeal became whether District 26 was a 'trade union,' as defined by the Act, which required a union to be an organization formed for the purposes of regulating employee and employer relations; to have a constitution; and to define the conditions under which people could be admitted to the union. While the UMW had long represented the workers at DOSCO, the Auxiliary Workers' Union argued that the UMW had not formally fulfilled these statutory conditions. It charged that the board, in deciding that the UMW was a union, had lost jurisdiction because it made an erroneous finding on a preliminary issue in the same way the Wartime Labour Board lost jurisdiction when it 'wrongly' decided the preliminary question of whether fishers were 'employees' in the *Lunenburg* case.

MacDonald (with Currie concurring) emphasized the board's considerable expertise and asserted that the court must refrain from imposing 'technical requirements uncontemplated by the Legislature.' Was there a mistake on a preliminary fact, as there had been in *Lunenburg Fisheries*, which meant that the board lost jurisdiction? This question led MacDonald to re-examine, and distance himself from, the *Lunenburg* and *Dartmouth* cases, though he was reluctant to overturn them. He also placed increased emphasis on the Trade Union Act's privative clause. Thus, the board had decided whether the UMW was a trade union, and it 'seems clear that the decision of the Board was on a matter within its jurisdiction to determine and unreviewable even if wrong.'[82]

Ilsley (with Eugene Troop Parker concurring) also dismissed the application. After briefly considering the union's constitution and the definition of trade union in the Act, he decided that the board was right in saying that the UMW fell sufficiently within the definition of a 'trade union.' Like MacDonald, Ilsley mentioned the *Lunenburg* and *Dartmouth* cases, but avoided analysing them, simply saying that he did not want to be understood 'as intimating any doubt' of their correctness.[83] Doull too refused to grant the application for certiorari. In doing so, he tried desperately to sort out the principles developed in *Dartmouth* and *Lunenburg*. Thus, the 'question of whether any particular person is or is not an employee is a question in regard to which the Board's decision is final.' 'The question of whether the general relationship of the parties is that of an employer and employee,' however, was 'one upon which the right to enter upon the inquiry depends.'[84]

The trend towards increased deference to the LRB was not without limits, however. In April 1961, the board certified the International Brotherhood of Boilermakers, Iron Ship Builders, Blacksmiths, Forgers & Helpers, Local 271 as the bargaining agent for Ocean Steel & Construction Ltd. The union had applied to represent the workers at Ocean's construction project at Port Hawkesbury. The company had responded that its only permanent plant operated out of Saint John, New Brunswick, and that its only business in Nova Scotia was the erection of materials fabricated in Saint John. Moreover, Ocean Construction pointed out that between the certification application in February 1961 and the hearing in April much of the company's workforce had changed because some employees had left and new employees had been hired.[85] Rather than certify the unit applied for by the union (that is, the Port Hawkesbury construction site), the board granted a provincewide certification. The board, it appears, intended to craft a more permanent bargaining unit that would alleviate the special problem of unionizing in the construction industry in which a fluctuating body of employees made it difficult to establish a unit that did not automatically cease to exist upon completion of a building project.[86]

The facts of the case were thus similar to *Municipal Spraying* – a certification application for the workforce of a construction company with a seasonally fluctuating workforce, although here the board had expanded, not limited, the bargaining unit. MacDonald, on behalf of the court, granted the certiorari application. He noted that at the certification hearing no reference had been made to the possibility of certifying a different unit. In *Municipal Spraying*, the court had said that the board could add or exclude 'certain classes of employees,' and thus the court had approved an alteration 'which reduced the unit from all the employees in a plant to employees engaged in the maintenance or operation of specialist equipment.' The present case was not analogous, however. 'What the Board did herein was vastly different,' for 'it created a unit entirely unlike that desired by the applicant union' and this unit 'could not be determined to be appropriate,' especially for 'all future employees of the Company who may be engaged in unknown projects in other and unrelated parts Nova Scotia.'[87]

Eighteen years of the NSSC's shifting jurisprudence left a mark on the LRB. Horace Read and the board were forced to consider each court decision, and to shape their subsequent rulings accordingly. The effect of the jurisprudence could be seen in how the board evaluated an application by the Teamsters, Chauffeurs, Warehousemen and Helpers, Local 927 to become the bargaining agent for several Nova Scotian dairies. In 1954, the Teamsters began a large-scale organizing drive throughout Canada, and in October 1963 the board considered a certification application by the Teamsters for Woodlawn Dairy Ltd.[88] The dairy did not contest the certification, but the Canadian Union of Chauffeurs, Dairy Workers, Warehousemen, Helpers and General Workers (the 'Canadian Union') did, since it had been certified as the employees' agent since 1955. In effect, the Teamsters sought to replace the Canadian Union. The board was unsure if the Teamsters represented a majority of the employees, and ordered an election so that the workers could choose between the two unions. Of sixty-four potential voters, sixty cast ballots: thirty favoured the teamsters, twenty-nine the Canadian Union, while one ballot was spoiled. At the hearing to evaluate the election, the board accepted the Canadian Union's argument that sixty votes had been cast, and that thirty votes were not a majority; the board thus refused to certify the Teamsters. The Teamsters then asked for a rehearing on the ground that the board had erred because the spoiled ballot should have been discounted – that is, that the board should have evaluated the results as if thirty of fifty-nine votes had been cast for the Teamsters. The board granted a rehearing, and discussed the spoiled ballot.

In the rehearing in November 1963, Read demonstrated his frustration at parties who, he believed, had unnecessarily applied for judicial review; at the same time, he hinted that his view of the Labour Board was not that different from the one imposed by the judges of the NSSC. The Canadian Union's lawyer, D.M. Nunn, strenuously argued that the board could not reconsider its earlier decision. Read responded by telling counsel that the law was murky when it came to the board's right to decide issues of law. 'We are looking for light, if we can find it,' said Read, for 'this question as to how far a Board or any other can decide a question of law is certainly a twilight zone at the present time, even if it is not complete darkness.'[89] The Teamsters' lawyer, Matheson, argued it was better to keep this at the board: 'We are here because the alternative is to go to the Supreme Court for certiorari and this is not desirable.' Matheson, however, did not have principled objections to taking the matter to the court; rather, he was concerned that the previous order by the board made no mention of the spoiled ballot, and that this might prevent the Teamsters' success in a future certiorari application. Read debated whether the board should decide the ballot issue, and concluded that it should. 'The question,' said Read, was the 'best way to proceed to accomplish the function of the Board.' 'The Board is bound to make mistakes occasionally,' he admitted, but '[t]o err is human, to forgive divine. Now, if we err, we would like to be forgiven, and to be given an opportunity, if we made a mistake, to correct the mistake ourselves.'[90]

Read expressed his annoyance at some of the instances in which the board's decisions had been taken to the court on certiorari. He questioned why the parties did not simply apply for a rehearing, 'come in, be given the opportunity to say if we had made a mistake; if we had, just correct it and save the litigation and delay. Because after all, the reason this Board is set up, is to expedite certain cases, when certification is established as being justified under the *Act*.' If the purpose of the board was not to expedite certification proceedings, then the legislature 'would never have set up an administrative Board, they would have left it to the Courts,' and unions would receive certifications 'about 2 years after the application.' 'So, surely we should have an opportunity to ... correct a mistake,' asserted Read, 'whether a mistake of fact or law, I would think.' While avoiding harsh criticism of the court, he suggested that the judges had been duped by litigants on more than one occasion and chafed at the court's insistence that any error of law automatically meant that the board lost jurisdiction. 'The Board welcomes being corrected on a question of law in the Court as long as we are corrected on the mistake we have made,' but 'once or twice we have been corrected on a mistake we didn't make because what we did was not accurately represented to the Court, in my opinion.'[91]

The board decided to confirm its earlier order. After examining the spoiled ballot, it held that the employee who cast the ballot had intended to vote for the Canadian Union, and thus there was a 30–30 tie.[92] The

Teamsters brought an application for writs of certiorari and mandamus to the court. Writing for the court in banco was Frederick William Bissett (1902–1978). After receiving his legal education at Dalhousie, Bissett entered private practice in Halifax, where he operated a sole practice and became a noted trial lawyer. He gained notoriety for (unsuccessfully) defending Viola Desmond, an African-Canadian woman who was forcibly removed from a theatre after sitting in the 'white's only' section. After running unsuccessfully for the Conservatives in the 1949 and 1953 federal elections, Prime Minister Diefenbaker appointed Bissett to the Nova Scotia bench in 1961.[93] Bissett upheld the decision of the board by first disposing of the Teamsters' claim that the spoiled ballot should not have been counted, saying that the difficulty with their objection was that 'the determination of the intention of a voter is a question of fact and not of law and therefore not subject to *certiorari*.' Though the board possessed the jurisdiction to evaluate the questioned ballot, he nevertheless went on to discuss the ballot and concluded that the board had, in fact, correctly interpreted the intention of the voter. Finally, Bissett declared that there was no breach of natural justice: 'The hearing was long, the argument complete,' and the Teamsters' lawyer 'did not ask for time to call further evidence or make additional submissions and he was given every opportunity to be heard and was dealt with most fairly by the Chairman of the Board.'[94]

Conclusion

This review of the relationship between the LRB and the NSSC establishes two trends. First, *Smith & Rhuland*, and the pro-union decisions in *Municipal Spraying* and *Sobey's*, suggest that the judges of Nova Scotia were far from averse to defending the rights of labour. Though counter intuitive to the received view of the post-war relationship between courts and labour boards, it is obvious that judicial disapproval of the board sometimes entailed support for labour. The best example of this was the 1952 *Smith & Rhuland* decision. In overturning the board's decision to refuse certification because of a possible communist among the union's organizers, MacDonald's judgment illustrates that in evaluating the post-war labour regime, we must avoid assuming that it was always the courts that were socially conservative. In *Smith & Rhuland*, MacDonald applied a jurisprudentially conservative approach to the review of the LRB to achieve a pro-union decision.

Second, this article has demonstrated the existence of two periods in the court's approach to the judicial review of the LRB. The court freely intervened in the first period, from the passage of the Trade Union Act in 1947 to the *Canadian Gypsum* case of 1953. Doull and MacDonald wrote decisions that stymied the legislature's attempt to create a board protected from judicial review. Doull seemed generally annoyed by the broad powers granted to the board, felt secure that the court could liberally grant certiorari, and all but dismissed the Trade Union Act's privative clause. MacDonald gave the issue of judicial supervision of boards more thoughtful attention. He knew that boards were an important tool of government, but viewed the court as an important protector of individual rights that had to be vigilant of bureaucratic excess.

A less interventionist period began with the *Municipal Spraying* decision in 1954 and lasted until at least the mid-1960s.[95] Ilsley led this trend, writing deferential judgments in *Municipal Spraying* and the *Auxiliary Workers' Union* cases. Doull also apparently had a change of heart, deferring to the board in three cases in the second period. MacDonald still took his role as judicial overseer seriously, overturning the board in the *Ocean Steel* case, but supporting it in *Central Auxiliary Workers' Union*. Newer members of the court – Frederick Bissett and Frank Patterson – also refused to grant certiorari in the latter period.[96]

In evaluating the court's intervention in LRB decisions, it is also useful to discuss the propensity of the court to hear applications for certiorari, and to weigh the impact of its decisions. Allan Hutchinson has argued that the doctrine of judicial review of administrative action was 'quantitatively insignificant and qualitatively indeterminate.'[97] Hutchinson's claim is partly correct in the context of Nova Scotia between 1947 and 1965. The NSSC's judgments were 'qualitatively indeterminate' to the extent that one can look in vain for clear, consistent, incisive doctrine. That the Nova Scotian judiciary never developed a coherent jurisprudence of judicial review is not surprising. After decades of extensive judicial and academic writing on the topic, Harry Arthurs declared in 1983 that 'the present vocabulary and conceptual structure of judicial review is largely incoherent' because of 'the inevitable tendency of good judges to want to do the right thing, to shield citizens against perceived injustices, to vindicate legal values.'[98] Arthurs's assertions ring true for the Nova Scotia cases. Even during the latter period, strong assertions that the court should act deferentially were accompanied by an acknowledgment that the court would always reserve its discretion to intervene and examine the merits of each case.

Whether the NSSC's decisions were 'quantitatively insignificant' is a more difficult issue. The LRB annually heard (and most often granted) dozens of applications for certification.[99] Horace Read reported in July 1964 that since the board's establishment it had decided 866 cases. Of these, just seven had been challenged in the courts – three judicial decisions had favoured the board, three were against the board, and one was pending.[100] In Nova Scotia, at least, the traditional view of a highly interventionist court is thus somewhat misleading. The board determined hundreds of certification applications, and in only a tiny fraction did the court directly overturn the board's decision.

From Read's discussions with counsel during proceedings, however, it is clear that the court shaped the procedure and rulings of the LRB. The board, led by Read, was prone to fall into legal forms, and the court encouraged this tendency by complaining of procedural abuses and questioning the board's ability to adequately determine questions of law. In this respect, Hutchinson's claim seems off the mark. The doctrine of judicial review of administrative action was 'quantitatively insignificant' only to the extent that a small percentage of the board's decisions went to the court; the court's findings, however, had a great impact, as the board incorporated the judiciary's concerns in its procedures and determinations.

In offering these claims, it is still important to note that while the NSSC sometimes looked unfavourably on the LRB, it issued no judgments equivalent to some of the immensely hostile decisions written in other provinces. For example, in a 1948 challenge to the very existence of the Saskatchewan Labour Board, the province's Court of Appeal ruled that the legislature had granted the board powers equivalent to those of Superior, District, or County Courts. Under the federal division of powers, only the Dominion government could create such courts, and thus the statute that created Saskatchewan's labour board was unconstitutional.[101] The Ontario Court of Appeal failed to even mention the legislative privative clause in one of its early judgments concerning the Ontario Labour Board,[102] and in 1963, the same court virulently attacked the Ontario Labour Board by questioning its right to decide any question of jurisdiction or law.[103]

There are several explanations for the relative deference of the NSSC to the LRB. First, Read often ran many aspects of the board like a court – he insisted on common law rules, precedent, and narrow judgments. Read's Labour Board, though not bound by stare decisis, seems to have generally sought consistency at the expense of policy, a trend that may have pleased Nova Scotia's judges. This conservatism was probably furthered by the power of the provincial government to appoint the membership of the board. Though this issue requires further study, it seems that the province did not appoint radical elements of the labour movement to the board.[104] Second, the court had several judges with extensive labour backgrounds. This experience perhaps led them to conclude that labour boards were necessary in an industrialized society, and thus the courts owed them some respect. Finally, the small legal community in Halifax probably meant close professional and personal ties between judges, lawyers, and board members.[105]

That the NSSC exhibited deference to the LRB is significant because it contradicts the assumption of most academic commentators that all courts across Canada were extremely hostile to administrative boards. Roger Carter claims that '[f]rom about the early 1960s on ... Canadian courts have become more and more sensitive to the needs of a properly functioning administrative machine, while at the same time being mindful to protect the individual against arbitrary action.'[106] This assertion may be true for the country as a whole, but in the context of Nova Scotia it is a decade off the mark. By 1954, Nova Scotia's judges expressed a belief in the importance of the LRB, and a willingness to grant certiorari only in cases of gross procedural or substantive unfairness. That only one scholar has briefly noted this suggests a failure on the part of many Canadian scholars to investigate seriously the views of a judiciary tucked away on the Atlantic coast.

NOTES

The author gratefully acknowledges the financial support of the Social Science and Humanities Research Council of Canada and the Izaak Walton Killam Trust. For their insightful comments, thanks are owed to the editors of this volume and Bruce Archibald, Innis Christie, Robert Gordon, Bill Lahey, Jennifer Llewellyn, and Dianne Pothier. Earlier versions of this paper were presented at the Canadian Law and Society Association meetings, Dalhousie University, 4 June 2003, and at the J. Willard Hurst Summer Institute in Legal History, University of Wisconsin, 17 June 2003.

1 A privative clause is a statutory enactment limiting the ability of courts to review the decision of another body.
2 See, e.g., F.R. Scott, 'Administrative Law: 1923–1947,' *Canadian Bar Review*

26 (1948): 268–85; J. Willis, 'Administrative Law in Canada,' *Canadian Bar Review* 39 (1961): 251–65; P.J. Millward, 'Judicial Review of Administrative Authorities in Canada,' *Canadian Bar Review* 39 (1961): 351–95; B. Laskin, 'Certiorari to Labour Boards: The Apparent Futility of Privative Clauses,' *Canadian Bar Review* 30 (1952): 986–1003; R.C.B. Risk, 'Lawyers, Courts, and the Rise of the Regulatory State,' *Dalhousie Law Journal* 9 (1984): 31–54; J. Fudge and E. Tucker, *Labour Before the Law: The Regulation of Workers' Collective Action in Canada, 1900–1948* (Don Mills, ON: Oxford University Press 2001), 306–7.

3 See, e.g., L. Panitch and D. Swartz, *The Assault on Trade Union Freedoms: From Consent to Coercion Revisited* (Toronto: Garland Press 1988), 22.

4 From 1947 to 1965 a small number of judges decided the relevant cases. This study also ends in 1965 because in that year the chair of the Labour Board offered some insightful comments on the first eighteen years of the relationship between the board and the NSSC.

5 By 'legalistic,' I mean that Read drew from court procedures, common law principles, and traditional modes of legal reasoning.

6 S.N.S. 1864, c. 11.

7 M.E. McCallum, 'The Mines Arbitration Act, 1888: Compulsory Arbitration in Context,' in Girard and Phillips, eds., *Essays*.

8 M. Earle and I. McKay, 'Introduction: Industrial Legality in Nova Scotia,' in M. Earle, ed., *Workers and the State in Twentieth Century Nova Scotia* (Fredericton, NB: Acadiensis 1989), 12.

9 Fudge and Tucker, *Labour Before the Law*, 72–3.

10 *District No. 26 United Mine Workers of America v. Dominion Coal Co.* (1922), 63 D.L.R. 274.

11 An Act Respecting the Right of Employees to Organize, S.N.S. 1937, c. 6.

12 '*Wartime Labour Relations Order*, P.C. 1003,' *Labour Gazette* 44 (1944): 136; The Nova Scotia Wartime Labour Regulations Act, S.N.S. 1944, c 8; L.S. MacDowell, 'The Formation of the Canadian Industrial Relations System During World War II,' in L.S. MacDowell and I. Radforth, eds., *Canadian Working Class History: Selected Readings* (Toronto: Canadian Scholars' Press 1992); B.D. Palmer, *Working-Class Experience: Rethinking the History of Canadian Labour, 1800–1991* (Toronto: McClelland & Stewart 1992), 278–81.

13 See J. Fudge and H. Glasbeek, 'The Legacy of PC 1003,' *Canadian Labour and Employment Law Journal* 3 (1995): 357–99; A. McCrorie, 'PC 1003: Labour, Capital, and the State,' in C. Gonick, P. Phillips, and J. Vorst, eds., *Labour Gains, Labour Pains: Fifty Years of PC 1003* (Halifax: Fernwood Publishing 1995).

14 *Trade Union Act*, S.N.S. 1947, c. 3.

15 T.A. Grey, 'Langdell's Orthodoxy,' *University of Pittsburgh Law Review* 45 (1983): 11. For general discussions of legal formalism see, e.g., W.M. Wiecek, *The Lost World of Classical Legal Thought: Law and Ideology in America, 1886–1937* (New York: Oxford University Press 1998); M.J. Horwitz, *The Transformation of American Law, 1870–1960: The Crisis of Legal Orthodoxy* (New York: Oxford University Press 1992); N. Duxbury, *Patterns of American Jurisprudence* (New York: Oxford University Press 1995).

16 R.C.B. Risk, 'Here Be Cold and Tygers: A Map of Statutory Interpretation in Canada in the 1920s and 1930s,' *Saskatchewan Law Review* 63 (2000): 195–213; R.B. Brown, 'Realism, Federalism, and Statutory Interpretation during the 1930s: The Significance of *Home Oil Distributors* v. *A.G. (B.C.),*' *University of Toronto Faculty of Law Review* 59 (2001): 1–23.

17 Lord Hewart, *The New Despotism* (London: Ernest Benn 1929).

18 W.S. Johnson, 'The Lawyer and Administrative Boards,' *R. du B.* 3 (1943): 239. See also, e.g., W.S. Johnson, 'The Reign of Law Under an Expanding Bureaucracy,' *Canadian Bar Review* 22 (1944): 380–90; W. Mulock, 'Address of the Chief Justice of Ontario,' *Canadian Bar Review* 12 (1934): 35–41; J.W. de B. Farris, 'Justice of the Courts,' *Canadian Bar Review* 16 (1938): 509–523.

19 Most famous are the New Deal cases of 1936 and 1937. See W.H. McConnell, 'The Judicial Review of Prime Minister Bennett's New Deal,' *Osgoode Hall Law Journal* 6 (1968): 39–86.

20 For a detailed discussion of the work of these scholars see R.B. Brown, 'The Canadian Legal Realists and Administrative Law Scholarship, 1930–1941,' *Dalhousie Journal of Legal Studies* 9 (2000): 36–72.

21 Trade Union Act, S.N.S. 1947, c. 3.

22 Ibid., ss. 3, 4, 7, 9, 10, 55(1), 55(2).

23 Ibid., ss. 55(7), 55(8).

24 Ibid., s. 58.

25 *The Supreme Court of Nova Scotia and Its Judges, 1754–1978* (Halifax: Nova Scotia Barristers' Society 1978), 84; NSARM, MG 1, 263–71; J. Doull, *A number of short lectures on legal matters delivered to the students of Pine Hill Divinity Hall in the Session of 1961–62* (n.p. 1963); J. Doull, *Sketches of Attorney Generals of Nova Scotia, 1750–1926* (Halifax: Pine Hall Divinity School 1964); J. Doull, *A History of the Bible Society in Nova Scotia, 1813–1963* (Halifax: Nova Scotia District, Canadian Bible Society 1964).

26 J. Willis, *A History of Dalhousie Law School* (Toronto: University of Toronto Press 1979), 104.

27 *The Supreme Court of Nova Scotia and Its Judges*, 89; Willis, *A History of Dalhousie Law School*, 127–8, 134.

28 *Re Lunenburg Sea Products*, [1947] 3 D.L.R. 195 at 197 [hereinafter, *Lunenburg*

Sea Products]. A writ of certiorari is a writ issuing out of a superior court, to call up the records of an inferior court in order that the party may have more sure and speedy justice, or that errors and irregularities may be corrected. It is obtained upon complaint of a party that he or she has not received justice, or cannot have an impartial trial in the inferior court. Some of the litigants in the certification cases in Nova Scotia also brought writs of mandamus. This writ could issue from a higher court; it ordered lower courts or administrative officers to act in a specified way.

29 *Ibid.*, 198. In making this 'jurisdiction' distinction, Doull drew from contemporary ideas concerning the judicial review of administrative decisions. In the judicial review of administrative decisions in Canada after the Second World War 'the concept of "jurisdiction" soon became the battleground.' H.W. Arthurs, 'Protection against Judicial Review,' *R. du B.* 43 (1983): 279.

30 Ibid., 201, 202.

31 Ibid., 206. Chief Justice Joseph Chisholm wrote a very brief concurring judgment, concluding that the NS Wartime Labour Labour Relations Board 'were acting in a judicial and not in a merely administrative capacity,' and 'that the fishermen who manned the vessels of the applicants were not employees of the shipowners.' Ibid., 196.

32 B. Laskin, 'Labour Law: 1923–1947,' *Canadian Bar Review* 26 (1948): 304.

33 Willis, *A History of Dalhousie Law School*, 121, 203–4; 'A Distinguished Life of Service' *Halifax Chronicle Herald*, 1 Mar. 1975, 6; H.E. Read, *Cases and Other Materials on Legislation* (Brooklyn: Foundation Press 1948); Letter from Angus L. MacDonald to Horace Read (17 Feb. 1950), NSARM, Angus L. MacDonald Papers, MG 2, vol. 952, File 24-3. Thanks to Stephen Henderson for referring me to this last citation. For an example of Read's tendency to mix progressive and conservative ideas see H.E. Read, 'The Judicial Process in Common Law Canada,' *Canadian Bar Review* 37 (1959): 265–93.

34 NSLRB, B 97, File: Can. Assoc. Policemen (Dartmouth): NSARM, Accession 2002-024, Hearing (19 Jan. 1951), Re Canadian Association of Policemen (Dartmouth Branch), Dartmouth, N.S., Applicant and Corporation of the Town of Dartmouth, Dartmouth, N.S., Respondent, 5 [hereinafter, Dartmouth Police transcript].

35 Dartmouth Police transcript, 9, 10.

36 Ibid., 10, 11, 23. In 1957 the Nova Scotia legislature amended the Act to permit the board to state a case in writing for the opinion of the Supreme Court in banco on a question that, in the view of the board, was a question of law. An Act to Amend Chapter 295 of the Revised Statutes, 1954, the Trade Union Act, S.N.S. 1957, c. 53. *In banco* refers to a session when the entire membership of the court participates in the decision.

37 *The King v. The Labour Relations Board (Nova Scotia)* (1951), 1 C.L.L.C. 51 at 55, 56 [hereinafter, *Dartmouth Police*].
38 DUA, Vincent MacDonald Papers, MS-2-171, B23, Speeches – Address to the Mining Society of Nova Scotia (emphasis in original).
39 DUA, MS-2-171, B-5, Speeches – Address to Graduates – Convocation – St Mary's College, 3–4.
40 DUA, MS-2-171, B-7: Speeches – Nova Scotia Labour Relations Board, 11–12.
41 *Dartmouth Police*, 53, 54 (emphasis in original).
42 H.E. Read, *Some Aspects of the Jurisdiction and Procedure of the Nova Scotia Labour Relations Board in Certification Proceedings* (Halifax: Nova Scotia Barristers' Society 1952), 4, 16.
43 Ibid., 8, 12, 13, 16. Also see Read address on CJCH (June 1951), DUA, H.E. Read Papers, MS-1-13, G-21, File: Broadcast Lectures.
44 See, e.g., Dartmouth Police transcript.
45 Read, *Jurisdiction and Procedure*, 13.
46 NSLRB, A 172, File: I.U.M. S.W.C. Local 18: NSARM, Accession 2002-024, Hearing in the matter of the application for certification of the Industrial Union of Marine & Shipbuilding Workers of Canada, Local No. 18, Lunenburg, N.S., Applicant and Smith & Rhuland, Respondent, 3, 9, 15.
47 Ibid. A copy of the board's order can be found in NSLRB, A 172, File: I.U.M. S.W.C. Local 18: NSARM, Accession 2002-024.
48 'A Decision in the Public Interest,' *Halifax Chronicle Herald*, 11 Dec. 1951, 4. See also 'On All Fours With Labour Policy,' *Halifax Chronicle Herald*, 12 Dec. 1951, 4.
49 '"Red"' Leadership Charge Blocks Union's Bid for Certification,' *Halifax Chronicle Herald*, 11 Dec. 1951, 6.
50 'Some Unions Disapprove N.S. Labour Board's Act,' *Labour Gazette* 52 (1952): 547; 'Disagrees with Board Order,' *Halifax Chronicle Herald*, 12 Dec. 1952, 3. Disgust at the board's decision was not unanimous. Two of the five members of the board, Sydney Owram and Jimmy Dwyer, had been representatives of labour. Halifax Local 83, United Brotherhood of Carpenters and Joiners of America approved the decision after hearing a presentation by board member Jimmy Dwyer, who was a member of their union. '1 Union Approves Ruling by N.S. Labour Board,' *Labour Gazette* 52 (1952): 260. The Halifax Postal Employees, Halifax Branch, sent a letter to Premier MacDonald 'heartily approving' the board's decision. Letter from the Canadian Postal Employees, Halifax Branch (signed by the secretary, J.R. Glazebrook) to Premier Angus L. MacDonald (21 Jan. 1952). NSLRB, A 172, File: I.U.M. S.W.C. Local 18: NSARM, Accession 2002-024.

51 *Re Labour Relations Board (Nova Scotia)* (1952), 1 C.L.L.C. 83 at 86–90 [hereinafter, *Smith & Rhuland*].

52 However, the board's initial decision stunted the growth of the union. S. Calhoun, *'Ole Boy': Memoirs of a Canadian Labour Leader – J.K. Bell* (Halifax: Nimbus 1992), 63; Earle and McKay, 'Introduction: Industrial Legality in Nova Scotia,' 20.

53 The *Financial Post* said that the quashing of the ruling 'was something to write to Moscow about.' R. Williams, 'Quashing of N.S. Anti-Red Union Ruling Has Bearing in Internal CCL Struggle,' *Financial Post*, 17 May 1952, 14. Also see M. Cohen, 'Communists – Labour Law – Public Policy – Certification and Decertification – Certiorari – Interpretation of Statutes,' *Canadian Bar Review* 30 (1952): 412–13.

54 *Smith & Rhuland Ltd. v. Nova Scotia*, [1953] 2 S.C.R. 95. The court split 4–3. Kerwin, Rand, Estey, and Kellock dismissed the appeal. Rand, in his plurality judgment (Estey and Kerwin concurring), held that 'may' was to be interpreted as permissive and indicated an area of discretion for the board to refuse certification; however, the board did not act within its discretion. Kellock thought the board had no discretion if the application was technically complete. The dissenting justices (Taschereau, Cartwright, and Fauteux) said that the board possessed discretion to refuse certification on any grounds. For a discussion, especially of Rand's judgment, see T.R. Berger, *Fragile Freedoms: Human Rights and Dissent in Canada* (Toronto: Clarke, Irwin & Company 1981), 151–5.

55 *Smith & Rhuland*, 92.

56 DUA, MS-2-171, B-2, Speeches – Address to Graduates – Commencement Day – St. Frances University – 10 May 1939, 9, 12.

57 DUA, MS-2-171, B-9, Address to Harvard Legal Aid Branch (emphasis in original).

58 *Smith & Rhuland*, 92.

59 DUA, MS-2-171, B-12, Speeches – Government and the Law, 10. See also 'Administrators of Labour Legislation Hold 11th Annual Conference in Halifax,' *Labour Gazette* 52 (1952): 1494–5.

60 DUA, MS-2-171, B-12, Government and the Law, 10–11.

61 Letter from Vincent MacDonald to Cecil Wright (26 Feb. 1953), University of Toronto Archives, Cecil A. Wright Papers, B82-0028/003. Thanks to Philip Girard for referring me to this letter. In asserting the judiciary's role in overseeing boards, however, MacDonald generally expressed concern about the out-of-date and unwieldy tools available to the courts: mandamus and certiorari. See DUA, MS-2-171, B-12, Speeches – Government and the Law, at 12; Letter from Vincent MacDonald to Cecil Wright (26 Feb.

1953), University of Toronto Archives, Cecil A. Wright Papers, B82-0028/003.

62 C.H.J. Gilson and A.M. Wadden, 'The Windsor Gypsum Strike and the Formation of the Joint Labour/Management Study Committee: Conflict and Accommodation in the Nova Scotia Labour Movement, 1957–1979,' in Earle, ed., *Workers and the State in Twentieth Century Nova Scotia*, 194; *Canadian Gypsum Co. Ltd. and Nova Scotia Quarry Workers Union, Local 294* (1959), 20 D.L.R. 319.

63 *In re Labour Relations Board (Nova Scotia) and Canadian Gypsum Company Limited* (1953), 1 C.L.L.C. 234 at 235–6 [hereinafter *Canadian Gypsum*]; C.H.J. Gilson, ed., *Strikes: Industrial Relations in Nova Scotia, 1957–1987* (Hantsport, NS: Lancelot Press 1987), 21–7.

64 *Canadian Gypsum*, 236.

65 L.J. Hayes, 'Final Tribute Paid: Chief Justice J.L. Ilsley,' *Canadian Bar Journal* 10 (1967). 141.

66 John Doull Papers, MG 1, 267, File 6(f): Miscellaneous: 'Service Held in Memory of Right Honourable J.L. Ilsley, Chief Justice of Nova Scotia by the Nova Scotia Barristers' Society' (17 Jan. 1967), 2.

67 For example, the board excluded 'labourers' from the bargaining unit. It was mostly 'labourers' who swelled the ranks of the company during periods of high employment.

68 *Re Labour Relations Board (Nova Scotia), International Union of Operating Engineers, Local No. 721 v. Municipal Spraying & Contracting Ltd.*, [1955] 1 D.L.R. 353 at 356 [hereinafter, *Municipal Spraying*].

69 Ibid., 361, 362.

70 Ibid., 364, 369.

71 Ibid., 370.

72 Nova Scotia Court Structure Task Force, *Report of the Nova Scotia Court Structure Task Force* (Halifax 1991) appendix 1, xvii. The earlier trial judge did not sit on the appeal, however.

73 *The Queen* v. *Labour Relations Board et al.*, [1955] 2 D.L.R. 681 at 687, 688, 688–9.

74 L.D. Currie, 'Basic Principles of Labour Legislation,' *Public Affairs* 11 (1947): 40–3; Nova Scotia, Department of Social Services, *Social Welfare Pioneers in Nova Scotia*, 2nd ed. (Halifax: Minister of Social Services 1979); 'Industrial Executives Hold Conference at Dalhousie University,' *Labour Gazette* 47 (1947): 20; 'Industrial Relations Conference at Dalhousie,' *Labour Gazette* 47 (1947): 1779.

75 The actions of the board may have been motivated by a similar mass revocation of union memberships by Sobey's employees in Stellarton in 1958. See NSLRB, A 548: File: Retail, Wholesale Local 1015: NSARM, Accession

2002-024. On Sobey's anti-unionism see H. Bruce, *Frank Sobey: The Man and the Empire* (Toronto: Macmillan 1985), 367–9.

76 NSLRB, A 559: File: Retail, Wholesale Local 1015: NSARM, Accession 2002-024.

77 *Re Labour Relations Board, and Sobey's Stores and Retail, Wholesale and Department Stores Union* (1959), 1 C.L.L.C. 963 at 964, 966; 'Supreme Court Upholds Certification,' *Halifax Chronicle Herald*, 17 Mar. 1959, 28.

78 NSLRB, A 408, File: Auxiliary Workers: NSARM, Accession 2002-024; *District No. 26, United Mine Workers of America* v. *Harold McKinnon et al.* (1944–1959), 1 C.L.L.C. 826.

79 A.E. Marble, *Nova Scotians at Home and Abroad: Biographical Sketches of Over Six Hundred Native Born Nova Scotians*, rev. ed. (Windsor, NS: Lancelot Press 1986), 325; F.H. Patterson, *Acadian Tatamagouche and Fort Franklin* (Truro, NS: Truro Printing & Publishing 1947).

80 *In the Matter of the Application for a Writ of Certiorari on behalf of Central Auxiliary Workers Union with respect to the Pattern Makers of the Dominion Coal Company Limited at Glace Bay, Nova Scotia* (21 Mar. 1960), S.C. No. 4874 (SCNS) at 4.

81 See NSLRB, A 561, File: UMWA: NSARM, Accession 2002-024; and NSLRB, A 549, File: Central Auxiliary Workers: NSARM, Accession 2002-024; 'UMW Will Seek Appointment as Miners "Agent,"' *Halifax Chronicle Herald*, 23 Mar. 1959, 13; 'UMW District 26 is Certified as Bargaining Agent,' *Halifax Chronicle Herald*, 28 Mar. 1960, 13.

82 *Re: Certification of District No. 26, United Mine Workers of America* (1960), 44 M.P.R. 270 at 276, 283, 284 (emphasis in original) [hereinafter, *UMW*].

83 Ibid., 285.

84 Ibid., 286.

85 NSLRB, A 684, File: I.B.B.I.S.B.B.F.: NSARM, Accession 2002-024.

86 In doing so, the board foreshadowed the implementation of 'sector bargaining' in 1971 that attempted to solve this issue. See Construction Projects Labour-Management Relations Act, S.N.S. 1971, c. 1.

87 *R. v. Labour Relations Board (Nova Scotia) and International Brotherhood of Boilermakers, et al. ex rel. Ocean Steel & Construction Limited* (1961), 2 C.L.L.C. 358 at 362.

88 'Teamsters Launch Drive for Canadian Members,' *Labour Gazette* 54 (1954): 1237; 'Lucien Tremblay Heads Teamsters in East,' *Labour Gazette* 54 (1954): 1682.

89 NSLRB, A 799, 805, 816, 819, File: Teamsters: NSARM, Accession 2002-024. The quotation comes from Case 816: Re Woodland Dairy, Hearing (29 Nov. 1963), 9.

90 NSLRB, A 816, File: Re Woodland Dairy: NSARM, Accession 2002-024: Hearing (29 Nov. 1963), 12, 15, 21.

91 NSLRB, A 816, File: Woodland Dairy, 21, 22.

92 *In the Matter of the Trade Union Act of Nova Scotia, and In the Matter of the Teamsters, Chauffeurs, Warehousemen and Helpers, Local 927, Applicant, and Woodlawn Dairy Ltd., Respondent, and Canadian Union of Chauffeurs, Dairy Workers, Warehousemen, Helpers and General Workers, Local Union No. 1.* Labour Relations Board (Nova Scotia), LRB No. 819. A copy of the order can be found in NSLRB, A 799, 805, 816, 819, File: Teamsters: NSARM, Accession 2002-024.

93 'Bissett, Frederick William, B.A., LL.B.,' *Maritime Reference Book: Biographical and Pictorial Record of Prominent Men and Women of the Maritime Provinces* (Halifax: Royal Print 1931), 34; C. Backhouse, *Colour-Coded: A Legal History of Racism in Canada, 1900–1950* (Toronto: Osgoode Society for Canadian Legal History and University of Toronto Press 1999), 252; 'Mr. Justice Bissett, 76, Dies in Halifax,' *Halifax Mail Star*, 10 Nov. 1978, 1–2.

94 *Teamsters, Chauffeurs, Warehousemen and Helpers, Local 927* v. *Woodlawn Dairy Ltd. et al.* (1965), 3 C.L.L.C. 168 at 170, 171.

95 The timing of this transition cannot, I think, be attributed to the Supreme Court of Canada's first decision concerning the judicial review of a certification decision by a labour board. *Toronto Newspaper Guild v. Globe Printing Co.*, [1953] 2 S.C.R. 18. In this case the Supreme Court of Canada was 'even more prone to regard judicial review as an appeal in everything but name than its contemporary English counterparts.' I. Holloway, '"A Sacred Right": Judicial Review of Administrative Action as a Cultural Phenomenon,' *Manitoba Law Journal* 22 (1993): 52.

96 Whether this deference ultimately stemmed from the relatively progressive attitude of Nova Scotia's judges, or whether it came from the conservative nature of the Board under Read, is difficult to demonstrate with certainty. The relative deference of the court could be evaluated by examining the court's intervention into other administrative regimes in this period. For example, there are at least two cases in which the court refused to overturn decisions of arbitration boards. See *Canadian Gypsum Co. Ltd. and Nova Scotia Quarry Workers Union, Local 294* (1959), 20 D.L.R. 319; *R. v. O'Connell et al. ex parte Cumberland Railway Company* (1967), 4 C.L.L.C. 392.

97 A.C. Hutchinson, 'The Rise and Ruse of Administrative Law and Scholarship,' *Modern Law Review* 48 (1985): 293.

98 Arthurs, 'Protection against Judicial Review,' 284.

99 For example, in 1948 the board received fifty applications for certification. Of these, it granted forty-two certifications and rejected eight. Nova Scotia,

Department of Labour, *Annual Report of the Department of Labour* (Halifax: King's Printer 1949), 33.

100 Letter from Horace Read to E. Etchen (9 July 1964), DUA, H.E. Read Papers, MS-1-13, G-366, File: Nova Scotia Labour Relations Board.

101 *John East Iron Works Ltd.* v. *United Steel Workers of America, Local 3493*, [1948] 1 D.L.R. 652 (Sask. CA). The Judicial Committee of the Privy Council subsequently overturned the Court of Appeal. See *Labour Relations Board of Saskatchewan* v. *John East Iron Works Ltd.*, [1948] 4 D.L.R. 673 (J.C.P.C.).

102 *Re Ontario Labour Relations Board, Re Toronto Newspaper Guild, Local 87 and American Newspaper Guild (C.I.O.) and Globe Printing*, [1952] 2 D.L.R. 302.

103 *Ontario Food Terminal Board and International Brotherhood of Teamsters, et al.* (1963), 38 D.L.R. 530. For an indication of the limitations the courts placed on the Ontario Labour Board peruse J. Finkelman, *The Ontario Labour Relations Board and Natural Justice* (Kingston: Industrial Relations Centre, Queen's University 1965).

104 The Labour Relations Board consisted of three, then five, members, with an equal division between industry and labour representatives, plus Read. In the period under study, only six men sat on the Labour Board. David Burchell was president of Bras D'or Coal. H.V.D. Laing had practised law in Nova Scotia before becoming vice-president of National Sea Products Limited. A.R. Harrington was an executive with Nova Scotia Light and Power. Sidney Oram served as president of the Nova Scotia Federation of Labour, while Jim Dwyer was a politically conservative leader of the Nova Scotia Carpenter's Union. 'Burchell, David G.,' in K. Simpson, ed., *Canadian Who's Who*, vol. 15 (Toronto: University of Toronto Press 1980), 134; Calhoun, *'Ole Boy,'* 62–3; 'Laing, Brig. Horace Vivian Darrell,' in *Canadian Who's Who*, vol. 7 (Toronto: Trans-Canada Press 1957), 604; 'Laing, Horace Vivian Darrell,' in *Maritime Reference Book: Biographical and Pictorial Record of Prominent Men and Women of the Maritime Provinces* (Halifax: Royal Print & Litho 1931), 34; 'Brig. Laing Dies at 59 in Halifax,' *Halifax Chronicle Herald*, 2 Sept. 1958, 1; I. McKay, *The Craft Transformed: An Essay on the Carpenters of Halifax, 1885–1985* (Halifax: Holdfast Press 1985), 111–13.

105 I have not made a systematic effort to track down these connections, though they are often apparent. For example, Doull and H.V.D. Laing were both members of the Dalhousie Board of Governors, and Doull paid tribute to Laing after his 1958 death. 'Brig. Laing Dies at 59 in Halifax,' *Halifax Chronicle Herald*, 2 Sept. 1958, 2. Read sent Ilsley copies of some of

his academic writing, and Ilsley discussed this writing in correspondence to Read. Letter from J.L. Ilsley to Horace Read (16 July 1959), DUA, MS-1-13, G-111, File: Correspondence, G-J.

106 R. Carter, 'The Privative Clause in Canadian Administrative Law, 1944–1985: A Doctrinal Examination,' *Canadian Bar Review* 64 (1986): 282.

Appendix: The Records of the Nova Scotia Supreme Court

JIM PHILLIPS AND JOHN MACLEOD

Introduction

The records of the Nova Scotia Supreme Court are an extensive and immensely rich source for the study not only of the court itself but also of many aspects of the province's social, economic, and political history. While they are not complete – fires in the later eighteenth century destroyed some of the early records and custodial practices were not always as rigorous as they might have been – they are voluminous, comprising some three hundred metres of shelving at the Nova Scotia Archives and Records Management in Halifax.[1] The records are better for the court sitting in Halifax than for the various circuits, but there are nonetheless substantial collections for at least some of the circuits.

What follows is a brief general description of the extent and nature of the records available to historians. Not included in this description are the papers of the judges, which may be located in the various Manuscript Group series of NSARM, and in other repositories. We have, however, noted a few collections of NSSC records in repositories other than NSARM. What follows is by no means a comprehensive description of the records; researchers who want a fuller description should consult the various finding aids available at NSARM.

A note on the reference system is in order here. For many years NSARM and its predecessor, the Public Archives of Nova Scotia, catalogued the NSSC records, for both internal purposes and for the purposes of retrieval by researchers, as Record Group 39 (RG 39). Within

RG 39 the records were further divided – first by county and then, within each county, by series, such as Series C (Case Files) or Series J (Judgement Books). This system is still employed in the public reading room of the archives, so that researchers still use it to access the records and cite them, as indicated by many of the papers in this volume. However, the archives administration no longer uses the RG system for internal purposes, and instead simply designates the records as the Supreme Court of Nova Scotia Fonds, divided into three principal sous fonds (discussed below). This arrangement is also the one used on NSARM's website. Because the RG system is cited in all published work using the NSSC records, and because it is the one that archives users will find on the public shelves, we have referred to it at various points in this description.

The Principal Records Series

As indicated above, NSARM now divides the Supreme Court of Nova Scotia fonds initially into three general categories: Supreme Court at Halifax; Supreme Court on Circuit; and Supreme Court as a Court of Appeal. These sous fonds are discussed below.

The Supreme Court at Halifax

This sous fonds is further divided into two series: *Case Files* and *Official Record Books*. Both series are subdivided into subseries. For more detailed information consult NSARM's Inventory No. 704, also available through the official NSARM website.

Series – Case Files. There are six subseries:
i) Bankruptcy Case Files. Formerly RG 39, Halifax, Series B, this subseries consist of forty-nine boxes of material covering the years 1870–3 and 1921–63. The case files may contain applications for relief from debt, inventories of assets and liabilities, statements of income and expenses, decisions of the bankruptcy court or registrar, and other related documents. A complete file listing is available. Note that the Commissioner of Public Records collection contains record books related to the proceedings of the Executive Council in relation to insolvent estates covering the periods 1761–81 and 1826–43. In addition, the General Case Files subseries, discussed immediately below, contains additional case files relating to bankruptcy for the period 1873–1921.

ii) General Case Files. This is the largest subseries of the Case Files series, covering the period 1750–1990 and consisting of 1,110 boxes. It was formerly known as RG 39, Halifax, Series C. As the 1750 date indicates, it includes files of cases prosecuted in the General Court, predecessor to the NSSC. While the vast majority of the files are for civil cases, there are criminal case files scattered through the boxes for the early decades. Files prior to 1960 are as they have been received by NSARM and generally represent all extant files of the court. Subsequent file transfers have been limited by records schedules which permit the destruction of some types of files by the court. Remaining case files transferred are subject to an approved selection process which has further reduced the number of files retained. The vast majority of case files destroyed are from routine debt claims or suits discontinued by the parties. There is a complete case file listing for this subseries covering the period 1750–1860. Case file numbering commenced in 1861, and as a result the indexes to civil causes associated with the cause books subseries of the Official Record Books series (discussed below) can be used as indexes for the period up to 1927.

iii) Criminal Case Files. This subseries contains sixty-eight boxes of files for the period 1906–49. The files may contain charges, statements from witnesses, transcripts of testimony, evidence, verdicts from judge or jury, and sentencing details. This subseries was previously classified as Series C of the Halifax Supreme Court records.

iv) Bar Admission Case Files. These cover the period 1830–1987, although most fall before 1902. The files contain documents presented to demonstrate qualification to practise law in Nova Scotia, including articles of clerkship, certificates of good character, and certificates of legal knowledge. Most files also contain a brief biography used to introduce the applicant at the Bar Admission ceremony.[2]

v) Court for Divorce and Matrimonial Causes Case Files. These cover the years 1750–1963. The content of the files varies over time, and they may include petitions outlining the cause of action, affidavits, transcripts of evidence, and decrees, as well as documents concerning spousal or child support. The case files can be cross-referenced with the Divorce Cause books subseries of the official record books series, discussed below.

vi) Fire Investigation Case Files. From 1858 legislation required that the papers relating to fire investigations in the city of Halifax be filed with the Supreme Court. This subseries has thirty-three files covering the period 1873–1911.

Series – Official Record Books. There are two hundred volumes of these, divided into twenty-one subseries. Many of the volumes were previously part of RG 39, Halifax, Series J. Twelve of the subseries are very small, consisting of only one to three volumes and covering short periods. They are briefly listed together at the end of this section, under '(x) Other Subseries.' The nine larger subseries are discussed here in more detail:

i) Criminal Proceedings Books. There are thirteen volumes in this subseries, covering the years 1749–1804 and 1843–1972. They provide brief summaries of criminal cases, recording the defendant, charge, plea, verdict, and sentence, but little else.

ii) Judgment Books. These 130 volumes provide brief summaries of the parties, cause of action, disposition, and damages in civil cases from 1766 to 1980. Most volumes contain an index.

iii) County Judgment Books. Containing the same kind of information as the previous subseries, these fourteen volumes list cases decided in Halifax but for which the award related to another county. The books record the parties involved in the case, the date judgment was awarded, and the amount of damages or costs awarded, as well as the cost to transmit the judgment to the recipient county where it would be entered in the local judgment books.

iv) Cause Books. Covering the period 1767–1980, this subseries consists of books used to record the issuance of documents initiating a lawsuit. Some books, particularly the early ones, are titled 'original entry books' and record the residence and occupations of parties to a case. Generally, the books record the parties, plaintiff's attorney, the date the originating document was issued, and the amount of damages or judgment sought. Beginning in 1884 the books record, although not consistently, the issuance and filing of all documents related to a case.

v) Case File Registers. The eleven volumes in this subseries comprise indexes of cases listed in the cause books, above. One volume dates from the early nineteenth century, but the registers predominantly cover the 1875–1927 period.

vi) Civil Proceedings Books – 1817–1973. This subseries comprises minute books in which civil proceedings were recorded by the prothonotary. The books record the day-by-day business of the court noting cases, barristers, witnesses, actions and outcomes and some volumes also record discontinued cases at the end of each term. The 22 volumes cover the period from 1817 to 1973.

vii) Chambers Books. These fifty-seven volumes cover the period 1872–1993, and comprise minute books of chambers proceedings. They record the case, usually the case number, the plaintiff's attorney, and the outcome. See also below under 'other subseries,' the chambers summons books.

viii) Rules of the Supreme Court. Six bound volumes comprise rules of both the General and the Supreme Courts, from 1750 to 1903. The first volume also contains records of the admission of barristers.

ix) Divorce Cause Books. This subseries consists of eighteen volumes of registers used to record the filing of petitions for divorce and the ensuing proceedings. A recent (2000) acquisition, they cover the period 1840–1962.

x) Other Subseries. There are twelve additional subseries, each comprising no more than three volumes:
- a one-volume appearance book for 1767–70, noting the parties to each case and appearances made.
- three volumes of docket books, 1774–8 and 1875–1920, recording the parties, the plaintiff's attorney, and the disposition of each case.
- a one-volume 'Record of Executions, Returns and Appearances,' for the period 1768–74. It contains documents related to the collection of judgments, including executions and attachments.
- a one-volume record of writs of mesne process issued in 1815 and 1816.
- a one-volume 'Citizenship and Estates Tail Proceeding Book,' recording the proceedings in cases involving fee tail estates, 1815–49. It also records oaths of allegiance by three people.
- two volumes of chambers summons books for 1884–1909, registers of summons issued for chambers proceedings.

- two volumes of docket books, 1875–1920, which record the docket of the court, including case numbers, docket numbers, parties, and the plaintiff's attorney.
- three volumes of equity chambers docket books, 1872–84, which list cases heard before the equity judge in chambers. Records case numbers, parties, type of action, and the plaintiff's attorney.
- one volume of proceedings in controverted election cases, 1875–92.
- a one-volume register of warrants of attorney, 1871–78. By these warrants defendants authorized attorneys to enter a confession of indebtedness.
- a one-volume bankruptcy proceedings book, recording in some detail bankruptcy cases for the years 1921–28 and 1952–60.
- one-volume of minutes of meetings of the judges dealing with court administration, 1899–1933. Previously part of RG 39, Series M (miscellaneous).

The Supreme Court on Circuit

Records for the court sitting outside of Halifax comprise the second of three sous fonds of the NSSC's records. The NSSC went on circuit from 1774, with the circuit being expanded over time until it was completed for all the extant mainland counties in 1816. Circuits to Cape Breton were added after its re-annexation in 1820, and as new mainland counties were created by dividing existing ones new circuit locations were added.[3] Records are available from most, although not all, of the circuits. The records are organized by county, with each county being a series, and by subseries within each county; the subseries represent the various different kinds of documents which have survived for each county. Not all counties have all the subseries. In the previous system the records were designated as RG 39, County, followed by a series (C for case files, J for judgment books, etc.).

The periods for which records are available vary substantially among the counties, although one consistent feature is that there are no records prior to the early nineteenth century. Some county collections have records which pre-date the establishment of the county, because the circuit location that later became a county was initially a district of another county. The summary that follows is organized by county and provides a brief indication of what subseries are available within each series.

Annapolis County. NSARM Inventory No. 144. Annapolis was one of the four counties on the circuit when it was first established in 1774, the court always sitting at Annapolis Royal. A total of twenty-five volumes and twelve boxes cover the period 1802–1972, although most records fall within the years between 1882 and 1913. Five subseries are available: docket books; judgment books; cause books; proceedings books; and case files.

Antigonish County. NSARM Inventory No. 145. These circuit records are from what was initially known as Sydney County, with the court sitting at Antigonish and Guysborough, and from Antigonish after it was renamed. Only case files are available, 22 cm, for the years 1819 through 1889.

Cape Breton – Island and County. NSARM Inventory No. 704. This substantial subseries has records from 1767 to 1949. Those prior to 1820, when the island ceased to be a separate colony and was re-annexed to Nova Scotia, are records of the Cape Breton Supreme Court, which sat in Sydney. Later records are of the NSSC on circuit for Cape Breton County, also meeting at Sydney. Eight subseries are available, totalling 1.35m: case files; civil proceedings books; criminal proceedings books; Exchequer proceedings books; cause books; judgment books; rules (Cape Breton Supreme Court); and an index to inquests.

Colchester District and County. NSARM Inventory No. 147. Circuit records for Colchester date from 1805, three years after the circuit first went to the region. It was Colchester District of Halifax County until 1835, when it became a county; the court met at Truro from 1804. The series consists of four subseries: case files; proceedings books; cause book; and judgment books. There are over seventy volumes covering the years between 1805 and 1957. The Colchester Historical Museum also has some record books from 1892 onwards.

Cumberland County. NSARM Inventory No. 148. Cumberland was one of the four counties on the original 1774 circuit, with the court meeting at Amherst for most of the time. This series has only case files, totalling 4.4m, from 1774 until 1962.

Digby County. NSARM Inventory No. 149. The circuit went to Digby, meeting at Digby Township, after the county was created in 1837. There are three subseries: case files, judgment books; and docket books. The records begin in 1860 and run to 1975. There are also two volumes of judgment books for Digby in the Colchester County

Museum, covering the years 1838–40 and 1843–66; for further information on these see NSARM Inventory No. 153.

Guysborough County. NSARM Inventory No. 150. Supreme Court sittings at Guysborough began in 1834, when Guysborough was a district of Sydney (later Antigonish) County. Guysborough County was created two years later, in 1836. There are three subseries: case files; court dockets; and cause book. The collection is small – respectively one box, one volume, and eighteen files, covering the period 1836–1977.

Hants County. See NSARM Inventory No. 152. Hants was placed on the circuit in 1781, when it was created out of Kings County; the court met at Windsor. The sixteen volumes and twenty-eight boxes divided into five subseries: case files; criminal cause book; cause books; judgment books; and proceedings books. Most of the records date from after 1897, although there are a few case files from before that date.

Inverness County. NSARM Inventory No. 704. The circuit first went to Port Hood in 1834, with Inverness County being established the following year. This series has just six boxes of case files from the circuit sitting at Port Hood, covering the years 1842–1967.

King's County. NSARM Inventory No. 154. King's was one of the original counties put on the circuit in 1774, the court meeting at Horton (Wolfville) until 1841, when it was relocated to Kentville. There are four subseries – case files; judgment books; cause books; and proceedings book – comprising a total of twenty-five volumes and thirty-four boxes. Although there are a few early case files, most records are from after 1849, when fire destroyed the Kentville courthouse.

Lunenburg County. NSARM Inventory No. 154. Lunenburg County joined the circuit in 1805, the court sitting at Lunenburg. This is a large collection, covering the period from 1806–1969; the case file boxes alone cover 21m of shelf space. The collection is divided into four subseries: docket books; registers; judgment books; and case files.

Pictou County. NSARM Inventory No. 156. The town of Pictou was added to the circuit in 1805, when the area it served was a district of Halifax County. It became a county in 1835. A large collection, covering the period 1807–1949, which consists of seven subseries: case files;

judgment books; cause books; docket books; criminal proceedings book; register of warrants; and proceedings book. The majority of the more than 51m of records are the case files (50.5m), but there are also thirty-seven volumes making up the other sub-series.

Queen's County. NSARM Inventory No. 157. The circuit first went to Queen's (Liverpool) in 1816. There is a substantial collection of case files, sixty-four boxes, down to 1949. Three volumes of judgment books for the period 1837–1967 are available at the Thomas Raddall Archives in the Queen's County Museum in Liverpool.

Richmond County. NSARM Inventory No. 158. The circuit went to Arichat from the early 1820s, more than a decade prior to the formation of Richmond County in 1835. This series has records from sittings at Arichat from 1829, when the area was part of Cape Breton County, to 1975. There are four subseries, totalling ten volumes and two boxes: case files; cause books; judgment books; and proceedings books.

Shelburne County. NSARM Inventory No. 159. The Shelburne circuit was established in 1816, the court sitting at Shelburne and, later, at Yarmouth as well. This collection has four subseries covering the years from then until 1971: case files; judgment books; cause books; and docket books. There are fifteen boxes, five volumes, and some microfilm.

Victoria County. NARSM Inventory No. 160. The circuit went to Baddeck from 1851, when Victoria County was created out of Cape Breton County. There is a small collection of case files, two boxes covering the years 1852–88, as well as one microfilm containing copies of cause books and a judgment book, the originals of which are held at the Beaton Institute, University College of Cape Breton, Sydney.

Yarmouth County. NSARM Inventory No. 161. Yarmouth town was added to the circuit in 1834, while still in Shelburne County, and two years later Yarmouth County was established. This collection has twenty-two boxes of case files from the period 1838–1966.

The Supreme Court as a Court of Appeal

This sous fonds is further divided into two series: *Case Files* and *Official Record Books*. Both series are subdivided into subseries. For more detailed information consult NSARM's Inventory No. 704.

Series: Case Files. There is only one subseries, a large collection of *Appeal Case Books* for the years between 1890 and 1947. The Judicature Act of 1884 required that copies of the appeal case record be printed and filed with the prothonotary. The printed case record was to contain the appeal papers, rules, minutes of evidence, statements of case, affidavits, report of trial, exhibits and all other matters on which argument could be made. The cases in these volumes were collected by the Nova Scotia Barristers' Library and bound in annual volumes. This subseries was previously classified as Series A of the Supreme Court records.

Series: Official Record Books. There are four subseries:
i) Appeals Proceedings Books. There are eleven volumes covering the period 1902–93. The books record the names of judges on the bench, the presiding judge, the parties, counsel, remedy sought, and disposition. Many volumes have an internal index to the names of parties.

ii) Appeal Cause Books. These two volumes record the case number, names of parties, appellants' counsel, and the dates actions were commenced and documents filed, for civil and criminal cases, 1977–81.

iii) Appeal Chambers Books. This subseries comprises four volumes which record Appeal Division chambers proceedings, 1974–90. They document the parties, the presiding judge, counsel, the nature of the application, and the disposition.

iv) Supreme Court Appeals Docket Book – 1878–86. – This single volume contains court dockets, arranged by session, for the 1878–86 period. Cases, case numbers, plaintiffs' attorney, and dispositions are noted.

NOTES

1 On the loss by fire see Chief Justice Brenton Halliburton's lament in 1836 that '[t]he records of the Supreme Court have twice been exposed to the ravages of fire. In the last instance, which took place about 40 years ago ... it was with great difficulty that any of them was preserved': Halliburton to James, 23 Mar. 1836, RG 1, vol. 278, No. 47. On the poor condition of some of the records when they were organized by J.T. Bulmer in the late nineteenth century see Bulmer's 'Trials for Treason in 1776–1777,' *Collections of the Nova Scotia Historical Society* 1 (1878): 111.

2 For the transition from court regulation of admission to practice to regulation by the profession, see the chapters by Cahill and Phillips, and Girard, this volume. For the period prior to 1830 see RG 39, Halifax, Series M, Vol. 24A, which contains an alphabetical and chronological listing of names found on the Barristers' rolls, 1768–1903, and Attorneys' rolls, 1827–76.
3 For the origins and evolution of the circuits see Cahill and Phillips, this volume.

Illustration Credits

Argyle Township Court House Archives: Argyle Township Courthouse in Tusket (Gordon S. Hatfield, *Election Day in Tusket*, c.1901, photograph from glass plate negative courtesy of Argyle Township Court House Archives, P1992:222)

Art Gallery of Nova Scotia: The First Courthouse, 1754–1789 (Richard Short, Dominic Serres, and James Mason, *The Town and Harbour of Halifax looking down George Street*, 1777, engraving, 33.0 ×53.8 cm, purchased with funds provided by the Government of Canada through the Cultural Property Export Review Board and by Shirley Locke and Gerald Shortt, Art Gallery of Nova Scotia 2003.1) and William Moorsom and J. Clarke, *Province House, Hollis Street, Halifax*, 1830, etching and aquatint, 11.4 ×18.9 cm, gift of John and Norma Oyler, AGNS 1998.420; The Second Courthouse, 1790–*c*. 1819 (John Elliott Woolford, *A View of Halifax from Fort George*, 1817, oil on paper laid down on canvas, 43.0 ×128.5 cm, purchased with funds from the Government of Canada under the terms of the Cultural Property Export and Import Act, the Art Gallery of Nova Scotia Gallery Shop, and Marguerite Zwicker, Art Gallery of Nova Scotia 1986.51); The Court at Province House, 1819–61 (Robert D. Wilkie and George DuBois, *Nova Scotian Industrial Exhibition Building*, 1854, tint stone lithograph, 52.3 ×77.5 cm, gift of John and Norma Oyler, AGNS 1995.102)

Beaverbrook Art Gallery: Portrait of Jonathan Belcher, 1756 (John Singleton Copley [1738–1815]. 121.28 × 101.92 cm. Gift of the Canadian International Paper Co., The Beaverbrook Art Gallery, Fredericton, NB)

Canadian Inventory of Historic Buildings: Interior, Spring Garden Road Courthouse (Supreme Court Room, Spring Garden Road Courthouse, Canadian Inventory of Historic Buildings)

Castle, Gary: Interior Court House IV (Court Room No 3, Spring Garden Road Courthhouse. Gary Castle Photo) and (*Lady Justice*, stained glass window at Spring Garden Courthhouse designed by Thomas Bladon of Robert McCausland Limited, Castle Photo.); The Law Courts, 1971– (Gary Castle, The Law Courts, 2004, photograph, The Law Courts)

Chronicle Herald Limited, The: The Nova Scotia Justice System, *Chronicle Herald*, 30 January 1990 (Bruce MacKinnon, *The Nova Scotia Justice System*, 30 January 1990, 'Republished with permission from The Chronicle Herald Limited'); Anything on the Hook? (Bruce MacKinnon, *Anything on the Hook?*, 2 February 1990, 'Republished with permission from The Chronicle Herald Limited')

Communications Nova Scotia: Lorne Otis Clarke, puisne judge 1981–5, chief justice of Nova Scotia 1985–98 (Communications Nova Scotia/Shirley Robb, *Portrait of Lorne Clarke*, 1996); Constance Rachelle Glube, puisne judge 1977–82, chief justice of the Trial Division, 1982–98, chief justice of Nova Scotia 1998– (Communications Nova Scotia/Shirley Robb, *Portrait of Constance Glube*, 2003)

Karsh, Yousuf: Vincent-Joseph Pottier (1897–1980), puisne judge 1965–70 (Yousuf Karsh, *Portrait of Vincent-Joseph Pottier*, 1965, photograph, Nova Scotia Barristers' Society, with permission from the Estate of Yousuf Karsh)

Law, Jane Shaw: Spring Garden Road Courthouse in oils (Anthony Law, *The Old Court House (based on the Joseph S Rogers photograph of c.1871)*, oil on canvas, The Law Courts, courtesy of Jane Shaw Law); The Law Courts in oils (Anthony Law, *The New Law Courts*, oil on canvas, The Law Courts, courtesy of Jane Shaw Law.)

Library and Archives Canada: Nova Scotia Five Donald Marshall, June 1990 (Denny Pritchard, *Nova Scotia 5 Donald Marshall*, June 1990, Library and Archives Canada, 1992-257-64, with permission from the Estate of Denny Pritchard)

Owen, Phoebe: Cover photo (Entrance to Spring Garden Road Courthouse, Halifax, N.S.)

Nova Scotia Archives and Records Management: Spring Garden Road Courthouse, 1860–1971 (Joseph S. Rogers, *The New Courthouse*, c.1871, photograph in the Rogers Album, NSARM, N-441); General Trollope's Arch (Wellington Chase, in honour of the visit of the Prince of Wales, designed by Col. Nelson, RE, 1860, photograph, NSARM N-1253); *The Joe Howe Victory, Daily Star* (Halifax), 4 March 1935 (Robert Chambers, *The Joe Howe Victory*, in *The Daily Star* for 4 March 1935, NSARM N-10,337, with permission of the Estate of Robert Chambers); Warrant for the execution of Walter Lee, 1812 (Warrant for the execution of Walter Lee, 1812, NSARM MG100, Vol. 174, #28); Gallows, Halifax, 1935 (Halifax Gallows, 1935, NSARM N-10,331); Sampson Salter Blowers (1742-1842), chief justice of Nova Scotia 1797–1833 (Gauvin & Gentzel, photograph of *Portrait of Sampson Salter Blowers* by John Poad Drake, NSARM N-10,332); Sir Brenton Halliburton (1775–1860), assistant justice, 1807–33, chief justice of Nova Scotia, 1833–60 (Notman Studio, photograph of *Portrait of Brenton Halliburton* by Albert Gallatin Hoit, NSARM N-10,333); Thomas Chandler Haliburton (1796–1865), a justice of the Nova Scotia Supreme Court 1841–56 (1838 drawing by E.H. Eddis, lithograph by M. Gauci, published in London by M.M. Holloway, 7 January 1839, printed by P. Gauci, N-0345); Sir William Young (1799–1887), chief justice of Nova Scotia 1860–1881 (Notman Studio, *Portrait of Sir William Young*, c.1870, NSARM N-1334); Sir Charles Townshend (1844-1924), puisne judge 1887–1907, chief justice of Nova Scotia 1907–15 (Gauvin & Gentzel, photograph of *Portrait of Sir Charles J. Townshend* by Sir E. Wyly Grier, NSARM N-9710); James Lorimer Ilsley (1894–1967), puisne judge 1949–50, chief justice of Nova Scotia 1950–67 (Jack Dodge, *Portrait of James Lorimer Ilsley*, photograph, NSARM N-10,336)

Nova Scotia Museum, History Collection: Liverpool Court House (*Court House, Liverpool, N.S.*, 1901, postcard, courtesy of the Nova Scotia Museum, History Collection 88.78.14); Annapolis Court House (*Court House, Annapolis Royal, N.S.*, 1910, postcard, courtesy of the Nova Scotia Museum, History Collection 75.113.13)

Province House: Bas-relief of Joseph Howe's trial for libel, 1835 (Louis-Philippe Hébert, *Joseph Howe Addressing the Supreme Court*, bronze bas-relief on pedestal of Joseph Howe statue, Province House)

Index

PUBLICATIONS OF THE OSGOODE SOCIETY FOR CANADIAN LEGAL HISTORY

1981 David H. Flaherty, ed., *Essays in the History of Canadian Law: Volume I*

1982 Marion MacRae and Anthony Adamson, *Cornerstones of Order: Courthouses and Town Halls of Ontario, 1784–1914*

1983 David H. Flaherty, ed., *Essays in the History of Canadian Law: Volume II*

1984 Patrick Brode, *Sir John Beverley Robinson: Bone and Sinew of the Compact*
David Williams, *Duff: A Life in the Law*

1985 James Snell and Frederick Vaughan, *The Supreme Court of Canada: History of the Institution*

1986 Paul Romney, *Mr Attorney: The Attorney General for Ontario in Court, Cabinet, and Legislature, 1791–1899*
Martin Friedland, *The Case of Valentine Shortis: A True Story of Crime and Politics in Canada*

1987 C. Ian Kyer and Jerome Bickenbach, *The Fiercest Debate: Cecil A. Wright, the Benchers, and Legal Education in Ontario, 1923–1957*

1988 Robert Sharpe, *The Last Day, the Last Hour: The Currie Libel Trial*
John D. Arnup, *Middleton: The Beloved Judge*

1989 Desmond Brown, *The Genesis of the Canadian Criminal Code of 1892*
Patrick Brode, *The Odyssey of John Anderson*

1990 Philip Girard and Jim Phillips, eds., *Essays in the History of Canadian Law: Volume III – Nova Scotia*
Carol Wilton, ed., *Essays in the History of Canadian Law: Volume IV – Beyond the Law: Lawyers and Business in Canada, 1830–1930*

1991 Constance Backhouse, *Petticoats and Prejudice: Women and Law in Nineteenth-Century Canada*

1992 Brendan O'Brien, *Speedy Justice: The Tragic Last Voyage of His Majesty's Vessel* Speedy
Robert Fraser, ed., *Provincial Justice: Upper Canadian Legal Portraits from the Dictionary of Canadian Biography*

1993 Greg Marquis, *Policing Canada's Century: A History of the Canadian Association of Chiefs of Police*
F. Murray Greenwood, *Legacies of Fear: Law and Politics in Quebec in the Era of the French Revolution*

1994 Patrick Boyer, *A Passion for Justice: The Legacy of James Chalmers McRuer*
Charles Pullen, *The Life and Times of Arthur Maloney: The Last of the Tribunes*
Jim Phillips, Tina Loo, and Susan Lewthwaite, eds., *Essays in the History of Canadian Law: Volume V – Crime and Criminal Justice*
Brian Young, *The Politics of Codification: The Lower Canadian Civil Code of 1866*

1995 David Williams, *Just Lawyers: Seven Portraits*
Hamar Foster and John McLaren, eds., *Essays in the History of Canadian Law: Volume VI – British Columbia and the Yukon*
W.H. Morrow, ed., *Northern Justice: The Memoirs of Mr Justice William G. Morrow*
Beverley Boissery, *A Deep Sense of Wrong: The Treason Trials and Transportation to New South Wales of Lower Canadian Rebels after the 1838 Rebellion*

1996 Carol Wilton, ed., *Essays in the History of Canadian Law: Volume VII – Inside the Law: Canadian Law Firms in Historical Perspective*
William Kaplan, *Bad Judgment: The Case of Mr Justice Leo A. Landreville*
F. Murray Greenwood and Barry Wright, eds., *Canadian State Trials: Volume I – Law, Politics, and Security Measures, 1608–1837*

1997 James W. St.G. Walker, *'Race,' Rights, and the Law in the Supreme Court of Canada: Historical Case Studies*
Lori Chambers, *Married Women and Property Law in Victorian Ontario*
Patrick Brode, *Casual Slaughters and Accidental Judgments: Canadian War Crimes and Prosecutions, 1944–1948*
Ian Bushnell, *A History of the Federal Court of Canada, 1875–1992*

1998 Sidney Harring, *White Man's Law: Native People in Nineteenth-Century Canadian Jurisprudence*
Peter Oliver, *'Terror to Evil-Doers': Prisons and Punishments in Nineteenth-Century Ontario*

1999 Constance Backhouse, *Colour-Coded: A Legal History of Racism in Canada, 1900–1950*
G. Blaine Baker and Jim Phillips, eds., *Essays in the History of Canadian Law: Volume VIII – In Honour of R.C.B. Risk*
Richard W. Pound, *Chief Justice W.R. Jackett: By the Law of the Land*
David Vanek, *Fulfilment: Memoirs of a Criminal Court Judge*

2000 Barry Cahill, *The Thousandth Man: A Biography of James McGregor Stewart*
A.B. McKillop, *The Spinster and the Prophet: Florence Deeks, H.G. Wells, and the Mystery of the Purloined Past*
Beverley Boissery and F. Murray Greenwood, *Uncertain Justice: Canadian Women and Capital Punishment*
Bruce Ziff, *Unforeseen Legacies: Reuben Wells Leonard and the Leonard Foundation Trust*

2001 Ellen Anderson, *Judging Bertha Wilson: Law as Large as Life*
Judy Fudge and Eric Tucker, *Labour before the Law: The Regulation of Workers' Collective Action in Canada, 1900–1948*
Laurel Sefton MacDowell, *Renegade Lawyer: The Life of J.L. Cohen*

2002 John T. Saywell, *The Lawmakers: Judicial Power and the Shaping of Canadian Federalism*

Patrick Brode, *Courted and Abandoned: Seduction in Canadian Law*
David Murray, *Colonial Justice: Justice, Morality, and Crime in the Niagara District, 1791–1849*
F. Murray Greenwood and Barry Wright, *Canadian State Trials, Volume II: Rebellion and Invasion in the Canadas, 1837–1839*

2003 Robert Sharpe and Kent Roach, *Brian Dickson: A Judge's Journey*
Jerry Bannister, *The Rule of the Admirals: Law, Custom, and Naval Government in Newfoundland, 1699–1832*
George Finlayson, *John J. Robinette, Peerless Mentor: An Appreciation*
Peter Oliver, *The Conventional Man: The Diaries of Ontario Chief Justice Robert A. Harrison, 1856–1878*

2004 Philip Girard, Jim Phillips, and Barry Cahill, *The Supreme Court of Nova Scotia, 1754–2004: From Imperial Bastion to Provincial Oracle*
Frederick Vaughan, *Aggresive in Pursuit: The Life of Justice Emmett Hall*

www.ingramcontent.com/pod-product-compliance
Lightning Source LLC
LaVergne TN
LVHW090756070826
844660LV00022B/1004

* 9 7 8 1 4 4 2 6 2 3 7 7 4 *